토익 Reading 목표 달성기와 함께
목표 점수를 달성해 보세요.

나의 토익 Reading 목표 달성기

나의 목표 점수	나의 학습 플랜
________ 점	□ [400점 이상] 2주 완성 학습 플랜 □ [300~395점] 3주 완성 학습 플랜 □ [295점 이하] 4주 완성 학습 플랜

* 일 단위의 상세 학습 플랜은 p.22에 있습니다.

각 Test를 마친 후, 해당 Test의 점수를 • 으로 표시하여 자신의 점수 변화를 확인하세요.

495
450
400
350
300
토익의 고수!
고득점은 이제 시간 문제!
토익 감 잡았어!
토익 초보예요!

	TEST 01	TEST 02	TEST 03	TEST 04	TEST 05	TEST 06	TEST 07	TEST 08	TEST 09	TEST 10
학습일	/	/	/	/	/	/	/	/	/	/
맞은 개수	개	개	개	개	개	개	개	개	개	개
환산점수	점	점	점	점	점	점	점	점	점	점

* 리딩 점수 환산표는 p.329에 있습니다.

해커스 토익 RC

실전 1000제 1

READING

해커스 어학연구소

최신 토익 경향을 완벽하게 반영한

해커스 토익 실전 1000제 1 READING 문제집을 내면서

해커스 토익이 항상 독보적인 베스트셀러의 자리를 지킬 수 있는 것은 늘 **처음과 같은 마음으로** 더 좋은 책을 만들기 위해 고민하고, **최신 경향을 반영하기 위해 끊임없이 노력**하기 때문입니다.

그리고 이러한 노력 끝에 **최신 토익 경향을 반영한 《해커스 토익 실전 1000제 1 Reading 문제집》(최신개정판)**을 출간하게 되었습니다.

최신 출제 경향 완벽 반영!

최신 토익 출제 경향을 철저히 분석하여 실전과 가장 유사한 지문과 문제 10회분을 수록하였습니다. 수록한 모든 문제는 실전과 동일한 환경에서 풀 수 있도록 실제 토익 문제지와 동일하게 구성하였으며, Answer Sheet를 수록하여 시간 관리 연습과 더불어 실전 감각을 보다 높일 수 있도록 하였습니다.

점수를 올려주는 학습 구성과 학습 자료로 토익 고득점 달성!

모든 문제의 정답과 함께 정확한 해석을 수록하였으며, 해커스토익(Hackers.co.kr)에서 'Part 5&6 해설'을 무료로 제공합니다. 지문과 문제의 정확한 이해를 통해 토익 리딩 점수를 향상할 수 있으며, 토익 고득점 달성이 가능합니다.

《해커스 토익 실전 1000제 1 Reading 문제집》은 별매되는 해설집과 함께 학습할 때 보다 효과적으로 학습할 수 있습니다. 또한, 해커스인강(HackersIngang.com)에서 '온라인 실전모의고사 1회분'과 '단어암기 PDF&MP3'를 무료로 제공하며, 토익 스타 강사의 파트별 해설강의를 수강할 수 있습니다.

《해커스 토익 실전 1000제 1 Reading 문제집》이 여러분의 토익 목표 점수 달성에 확실한 해결책이 되고 영어 실력 향상, 나아가 여러분의 꿈을 향한 길에 믿음직한 동반자가 되기를 소망합니다.

해커스 어학연구소

CONTENTS

Part 5&6 무료 해설 바로 보기

토익, 이렇게 공부하면

확실하게 고득점 잡는다!

토익에 완벽하게 대비한다!

READING TEST

In this section, you must demonstrate your ability to read and comprehend English. You will be given a variety of texts and asked to answer questions about these texts. This section is divided into three parts and will take 75 minutes to complete.

Do not mark the answers in your test book. Use the answer sheet that is separately provided.

PART 5

Directions: In each question, you will be asked to review a statement that is missing a word or phrase. Four answer choices will be provided for each statement. Select the best answer and mark the corresponding letter (A), (B), (C), or (D) on the answer sheet.

PART 5 권장 풀이 시간 11분

101. The CEO will ------- meet with clients during his visit to Berlin.
(A) brief
(B) briefing
(C) briefest
(D) briefly

102. The Lee Valley Fire Department launched

105. Charles Hayes is ------- the top chess players in England, having defeated many former champions.
(A) around
(B) between
(C) among
(D) inside

최신 토익 출제 경향을 반영한 실전 10회분 수록

시험 경향에 맞지 않는 문제들만 풀면, 실전에서는 연습했던 문제와 달라 당황할 수 있습니다. 《해커스 토익 실전 1000제 1 Reading 문제집》에 수록된 모든 문제는 **최신 출제 경향과 난이도를 반영하여 실전에 철저하게 대비**할 수 있도록 하였습니다.

Answer Sheet

TEST 01

READING (Part V~VII)

101	Ⓐ Ⓑ Ⓒ Ⓓ	121	Ⓐ Ⓑ Ⓒ Ⓓ	141	Ⓐ Ⓑ Ⓒ Ⓓ	161	Ⓐ Ⓑ Ⓒ Ⓓ	181	Ⓐ Ⓑ Ⓒ Ⓓ
102	Ⓐ Ⓑ Ⓒ Ⓓ	122	Ⓐ Ⓑ Ⓒ Ⓓ	142	Ⓐ Ⓑ Ⓒ Ⓓ	162	Ⓐ Ⓑ Ⓒ Ⓓ	182	Ⓐ Ⓑ Ⓒ Ⓓ
103	Ⓐ Ⓑ Ⓒ Ⓓ	123	Ⓐ Ⓑ Ⓒ Ⓓ	143	Ⓐ Ⓑ Ⓒ Ⓓ	163	Ⓐ Ⓑ Ⓒ Ⓓ	183	Ⓐ Ⓑ Ⓒ Ⓓ
104	Ⓐ Ⓑ Ⓒ Ⓓ	124	Ⓐ Ⓑ Ⓒ Ⓓ	144	Ⓐ Ⓑ Ⓒ Ⓓ	164	Ⓐ Ⓑ Ⓒ Ⓓ	184	Ⓐ Ⓑ Ⓒ Ⓓ
105	Ⓐ Ⓑ Ⓒ Ⓓ	125	Ⓐ Ⓑ Ⓒ Ⓓ	145	Ⓐ Ⓑ Ⓒ Ⓓ	165	Ⓐ Ⓑ Ⓒ Ⓓ	185	Ⓐ Ⓑ Ⓒ Ⓓ
106	Ⓐ Ⓑ Ⓒ Ⓓ	126	Ⓐ Ⓑ Ⓒ Ⓓ	146	Ⓐ Ⓑ Ⓒ Ⓓ	166	Ⓐ Ⓑ Ⓒ Ⓓ	186	Ⓐ Ⓑ Ⓒ Ⓓ
107	Ⓐ Ⓑ Ⓒ Ⓓ	127	Ⓐ Ⓑ Ⓒ Ⓓ	147	Ⓐ Ⓑ Ⓒ Ⓓ	167	Ⓐ Ⓑ Ⓒ Ⓓ	187	Ⓐ Ⓑ Ⓒ Ⓓ
108	Ⓐ Ⓑ Ⓒ Ⓓ	128	Ⓐ Ⓑ Ⓒ Ⓓ	148	Ⓐ Ⓑ Ⓒ Ⓓ	168	Ⓐ Ⓑ Ⓒ Ⓓ	188	Ⓐ Ⓑ Ⓒ Ⓓ

실전과 동일한 구성!

《해커스 토익 실전 1000제 1 Reading 문제집》에 수록된 모든 문제는 **실전 문제지와 동일하게 구성**되었습니다. 또한, **교재 뒤에 수록된 Answer Sheet**를 통해 답안 마킹까지 실제 시험처럼 연습해볼 수 있도록 함으로써 시간 관리 방법을 익히고, 실전 감각을 보다 극대화할 수 있도록 하였습니다.

02 한 문제를 풀어도, 정확하게 이해하고 푼다!

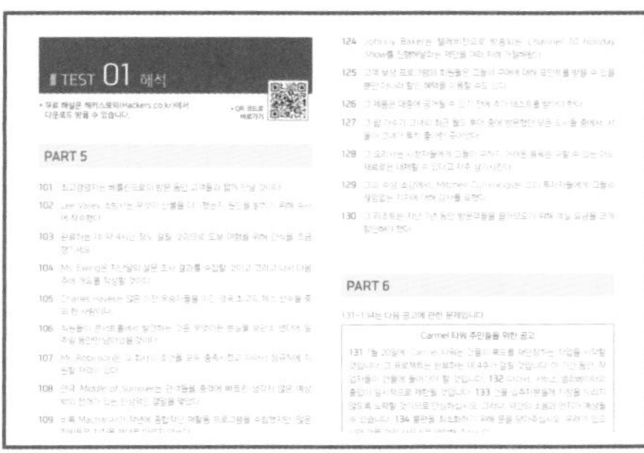

정확한 지문/문제 해석

수록된 모든 지문 및 문제에 대한 정확한 해석을 수록하였습니다. 테스트를 마친 후, 교재 뒤에 수록된 해석을 참고하여 **자신의 해석과 맞는지 비교하고, 지문과 문제를 정확하게 이해**할 수 있습니다.

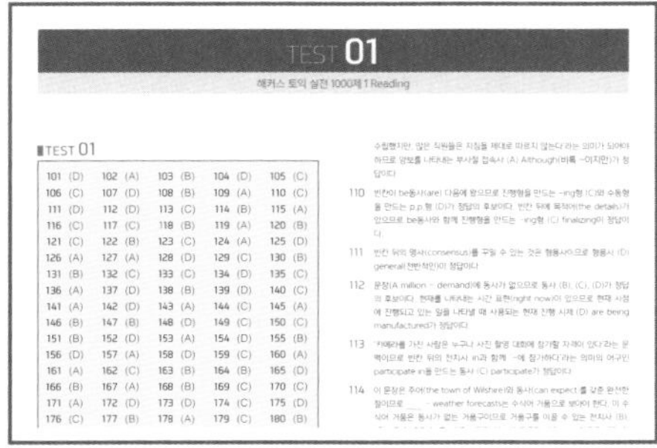

무료 해설 PDF

Part 5, 6 문제에 대한 해설을 **해커스토익(Hackers.co.kr) 사이트에서 무료로 제공**합니다. 이를 통해 테스트를 마친 후, 해석을 봐도 잘 이해가 되지 않는 문제를 보다 확실하게 이해하고, **몰랐던 문법 사항이나 어휘의 의미와 쓰임까지 학습**할 수 있도록 하였습니다.

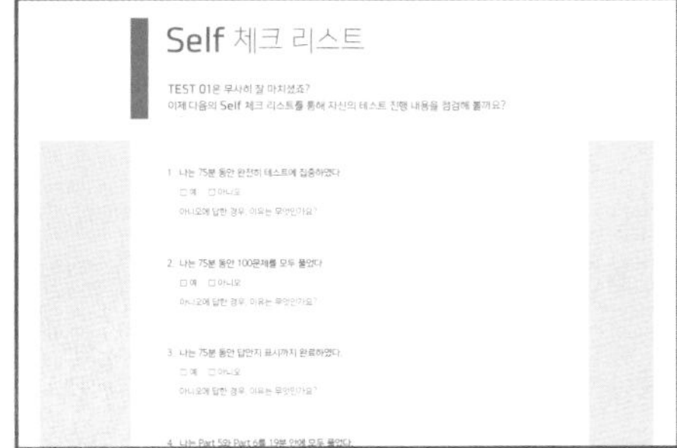

Self 체크 리스트

각 테스트 마지막 페이지에는 Self 체크 리스트를 수록하여 **테스트를 마친 후 자신의 문제 풀이 방식과 태도를 스스로 점검**할 수 있도록 하였습니다. 이를 통해 효과적인 복습과 더불어 목표 점수를 달성하기 위해 개선해야 할 습관 및 부족한 점을 찾아 보완해나갈 수 있습니다.

03 내 실력을 확실하게 파악한다!

점수 환산표

해커스 토익 실전 1000제 1 READING

• 아래 점수 환산표로 자신의 토익 리딩 점수를 예상해봅니다.

정답 수	리딩 점수	정답 수	리딩 점수	정답 수	리딩 점수
100	495	66	305	32	125
99	495	65	300	31	120
98	495	64	295	30	115
97	485	63	290	29	110
96	480	62	280	28	105
95	475	61	275	27	100
94	470	60	270	26	95
93	465	59	265	25	90
92	460	58	260	24	85
91	450	57	255	23	80
90	445	56	250	22	75
89	440	55	245	21	70
88	435	54	240	20	70
87	430	53	235	19	65

점수 환산표

교재 부록으로 점수 환산표를 수록하여, 학습자들이 테스트를 마치고 채점을 한 후 바로 점수를 확인하여 **자신의 실력을 정확하게 파악**할 수 있도록 하였습니다. 환산 점수를 교재 첫 장의 목표 달성 그래프에 표시하여 실력의 변화를 확인하고, 학습 계획을 세울 수 있습니다.

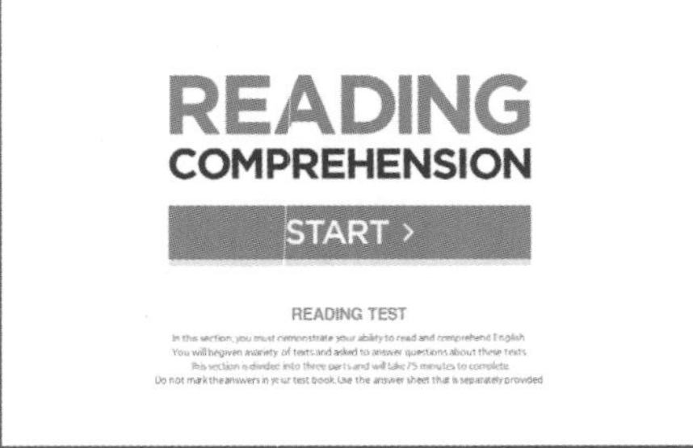

무료 온라인 실전모의고사

교재에 수록된 테스트 외에 **해커스인강(HackersIngang.com) 사이트에서 온라인 실전모의고사 1회분을 추가로 무료 제공**합니다. 이를 통해 토익 시험 전, 학습자들이 자신의 실력을 마지막으로 점검해볼 수 있도록 하였습니다.

인공지능 1:1 토익어플 '빅플'

교재의 문제를 풀고 답안을 입력하기만 하면, 인공지능 어플 '해커스토익 빅플'이 **자동 채점은 물론 성적분석표와 취약 유형 심층 분석까지 제공**합니다. 이를 통해, 자신이 가장 많이 틀리는 취약 유형이 무엇인지 확인하고, 관련 문제들을 추가로 학습하며 취약 유형을 집중 공략하여 약점을 보완할 수 있습니다.

04 다양한 학습 자료를 활용한다!

해커스 토익 실전 1000제 1 READING 단어암기장 TEST 01-A

단어_RC_Test01-A.mp3 해커스인강(www.HackersIngang.com)에서 무료로 다운 받으세요.
각 어휘는 캐나다식/영국식 두 가지 발음으로 한 번씩 들려줍니다.

1	client	n. 고객	26	master's	n. 석사 학위
2	briefing	n. 브리핑, 요약 보고	27	due	adj. 마감인, ~하기로 되어 있는
3	investigatory	adj. 조사의, 연구의	28	shift	v. 바뀌다, 달라지다
4	summary	n. 요약	29	radicalize	v. 급진적으로 하다
5	defeat	v. 이기다, 물리치다	30	radical	n. 급진주의자; adj. 급진적인
6	former	adj. 이전의	31	prestigious	adj. 명성 높은, 일류의
7	lost and found	phr. 분실물 보관소	32	press	n. (신문·잡지) 기자, 언론계
8	requirement	n. 조건	33	badge	n. 신분증
9	unexpected	adj. 생각지 않은, 뜻밖의	34	venue	n. 장소
10	twist	n. (이야기·사건 등의) 예상 밖의 전개, 비틀기	35	apologetic	adj. 미안해하는
11	guideline	n. 지침	36	succinct	adj. 간단명료한, 간결한
12	outline	v. 윤곽을 그리다	37	for free	phr. 무료로
13	organizer	n. 주최자, 조직자	38	stem cell	phr. 줄기세포

단어암기 PDF&MP3 / 정답녹음 MP3

해커스인강(HackersIngang.com) 사이트에서 **단어암기 PDF와 MP3를 무료로 제공**하여, 교재에 수록된 테스트의 중요 단어를 복습하고 암기할 수 있도록 하였습니다. 또한 **정답녹음 MP3 파일을 제공**하여 학습자들이 보다 편리하게 채점할 수 있도록 하였습니다.

방대한 무료 학습자료(Hackers.co.kr) / 동영상강의(HackersIngang.com)

해커스토익(Hackers.co.kr) 사이트에서는 토익 적중 예상특강을 비롯한 **방대하고 유용한 토익 학습자료를 무료로 이용**할 수 있습니다. 또한 온라인 교육 포털 사이트인 **해커스인강(HackersIngang.com) 사이트에서 교재 동영상강의**를 수강하면, 보다 깊이 있는 학습이 가능합니다.

해커스 토익 실전 1000제 1 READING

해설집 미리보기

<해설집 별매>

01 정답과 오답의 이유를 확인하여 Part 5&6 완벽 정복!

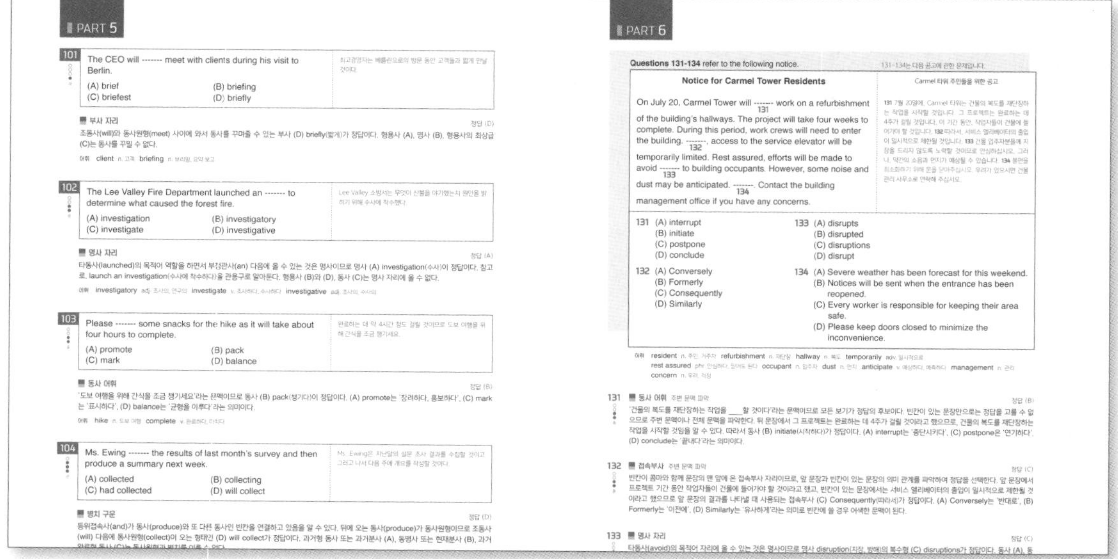

PART 5

101 The CEO will ------- meet with clients during his visit to Berlin.
(A) brief (B) briefing
(C) briefest (D) briefly

최고경영자는 베를린으로의 방문 동안 고객들과 짧게 만날 것이다.

부사 자리 정답 (D)
조동사(will)와 동사원형(meet) 사이에 와서 동사를 꾸며줄 수 있는 부사 (D) briefly(짧게)가 정답이다. 형용사 (A), 명사 (B), 형용사의 최상급 (C)는 동사를 꾸밀 수 없다.
어휘 client n. 고객 briefing n. 브리핑, 요약 보고

102 The Lee Valley Fire Department launched an ------- to determine what caused the forest fire.
(A) investigation (B) investigatory
(C) investigate (D) investigative

Lee Valley 소방서는 무엇이 산불을 야기했는지 원인을 밝히기 위해 수사에 착수했다.

명사 자리 정답 (A)
타동사(launched)의 목적어 역할을 하면서 부정관사(an) 다음에 올 수 있는 것은 명사이므로 명사 (A) investigation(수사)이 정답이다. 참고로, launch an investigation(수사에 착수하다)을 관용구로 알아둔다. 형용사 (B)와 (D), 동사 (C)는 명사 자리에 올 수 없다.
어휘 investigatory adj. 조사의, 연구의 investigate v. 조사하다, 수사하다 investigative adj. 조사의, 수사의

103 Please ------- some snacks for the hike as it will take about four hours to complete.
(A) promote (B) pack
(C) mark (D) balance

완료하는 데 약 4시간 정도 걸릴 것이므로 도보 여행을 위해 간식을 조금 챙기세요.

동사 어휘 정답 (B)
'도보 여행을 위해 간식을 조금 챙기세요'라는 문맥이므로 동사 (B) pack(챙기다)이 정답이다. (A) promote는 '장려하다, 홍보하다', (C) mark는 '표시하다', (D) balance는 '균형을 이루다'라는 의미이다.
어휘 hike n. 도보 여행 complete v. 완료하다, 마치다

104 Ms. Ewing ------- the results of last month's survey and then produce a summary next week.
(A) collected (B) collecting
(C) had collected (D) will collect

Ms. Ewing은 지난달의 설문 조사 결과를 수집할 것이고 그러고 나서 다음 주에 개요를 작성할 것이다.

병치 구문 정답 (D)
등위접속사(and)가 동사(produce)와 또 다른 동사인 빈칸을 연결하고 있음을 알 수 있다. 뒤에 오는 동사(produce)가 동사원형이므로 조동사(will) 다음에 동사원형(collect)이 오는 형태인 (D) will collect가 정답이다. 과거형 동사 또는 과거분사 (A), 동명사 또는 현재분사 (B), 과거완료형 동사 (C)는 동사원형과 병치를 이룰 수 없다.

PART 6

Questions 131-134 refer to the following notice.

131-134는 다음 공고에 관한 문제입니다.

Notice for Carmel Tower Residents

On July 20, Carmel Tower will ---131--- work on a refurbishment of the building's hallways. The project will take four weeks to complete. During this period, work crews will need to enter the building. ---132---, access to the service elevator will be temporarily limited. Rest assured, efforts will be made to avoid ---133--- to building occupants. However, some noise and dust may be anticipated. ---134---. Contact the building management office if you have any concerns.

Carmel 타워 주민들을 위한 공고

131 7월 20일에, Carmel 타워는 건물의 복도를 재단장하는 작업을 시작할 것입니다. 그 프로젝트는 완료하는 데 4주가 걸릴 것입니다. 이 기간 동안, 작업자들이 건물에 들어가야 할 것입니다. 132 따라서, 서비스 엘리베이터의 출입이 일시적으로 제한될 것입니다. 133 건물 입주자분들께 지장을 드리지 않도록 노력할 것이므로 안심하십시오. 그러나, 약간의 소음과 먼지가 예상될 수 있습니다. 134 불편을 최소화하기 위해 문을 닫아주십시오. 우려가 있으시면 건물 관리 사무소로 연락해 주십시오.

131 (A) interrupt
(B) initiate
(C) postpone
(D) conclude

132 (A) Conversely
(B) Formerly
(C) Consequently
(D) Similarly

133 (A) disrupts
(B) disrupted
(C) disruptions
(D) disrupt

134 (A) Severe weather has been forecast for this weekend.
(B) Notices will be sent when the entrance has been reopened.
(C) Every worker is responsible for keeping their area safe.
(D) Please keep doors closed to minimize the inconvenience.

어휘 resident n. 주민, 거주자 refurbishment n. 재단장 hallway n. 복도 temporarily adv. 일시적으로 rest assured phr. 안심하다, 믿어도 된다 occupant n. 입주자 dust n. 먼지 anticipate v. 예상하다, 예측하다 management n. 관리 concern n. 우려, 걱정

131 동사 어휘 주변 문맥 파악 정답 (B)
'건물의 복도를 재단장하는 작업을 ___할 것이다'라는 문맥이므로 모든 보기가 정답의 후보이다. 빈칸이 있는 문장만으로는 정답을 고를 수 없으므로 주변 문맥이나 전체 문맥을 파악한다. 뒤 문장에서 그 프로젝트는 완료하는 데 4주가 걸릴 것이라고 했으므로, 건물의 복도를 재단장하는 작업을 시작할 것임을 알 수 있다. 따라서 동사 (B) initiate(시작하다)가 정답이다. (A) interrupt는 '중단시키다', (C) postpone은 '연기하다', (D) conclude는 '끝내다'라는 의미이다.

132 접속부사 주변 문맥 파악 정답 (C)
빈칸이 콤마와 함께 문장의 맨 앞에 온 접속부사 자리이므로, 앞 문장과 빈칸이 있는 문장의 의미 관계를 파악하여 정답을 선택한다. 앞 문장에서 프로젝트 기간 동안 작업자들이 건물에 들어가야 할 것이라고 했고, 빈칸이 있는 문장에서는 서비스 엘리베이터의 출입이 일시적으로 제한될 것이라고 했으므로 앞 문장의 결과를 나타낼 때 사용되는 접속부사 (C) Consequently(따라서)가 정답이다. (A) Conversely는 '반대로', (B) Formerly는 '이전에', (D) Similarly는 '유사하게'라는 의미로 빈칸에 쓸 경우 어색한 문맥이 된다.

133 명사 자리 정답 (C)
타동사(avoid)의 목적어 자리에 올 수 있는 것은 명사이므로 명사 disruption(지장, 방해)의 복수형 (C) disruptions가 정답이다. 동사 (A), 동

1 **문제 및 문제 해석**

최신 토익 출제 경향이 반영된 문제를 해설집에도 그대로 수록해, 해설을 보기 전 문제를 다시 한번 풀어보며 자신이 어떤 과정으로 정답을 선택했는지 되짚어 볼 수 있습니다. 함께 수록된 정확한 해석을 보며 문장 구조를 꼼꼼하게 파악하여 문제를 완벽하게 이해할 수 있습니다.

2 **문제 유형 및 난이도**

모든 문제마다 문제 유형을 제시하여 자주 틀리는 문제 유형을 쉽게 파악할 수 있고, 사전 테스트를 거쳐 검증된 문제별 난이도를 확인하여 자신의 실력과 학습 목표에 따라 학습할 수 있습니다. 문제 유형은 모두 《해커스 토익 Reading》의 목차 목록과 동일하여, 보완 학습이 필요할 경우 쉽게 참고할 수 있습니다.

3 **상세한 해설 및 어휘**

문제 유형별로 가장 효과적인 해결 방법을 제시하며, 오답 보기가 오답이 되는 이유까지 상세하게 설명하여 틀린 문제의 원인을 파악하고 보완할 수 있습니다. 또한 지문 및 문제에서 사용된 단어나 어구의 뜻을 품사 표시와 함께 수록하여, 중요 문법・어휘를 함께 학습할 수 있습니다.

02 효율적인 Part 7 문제 풀이를 통해 고득점 달성!

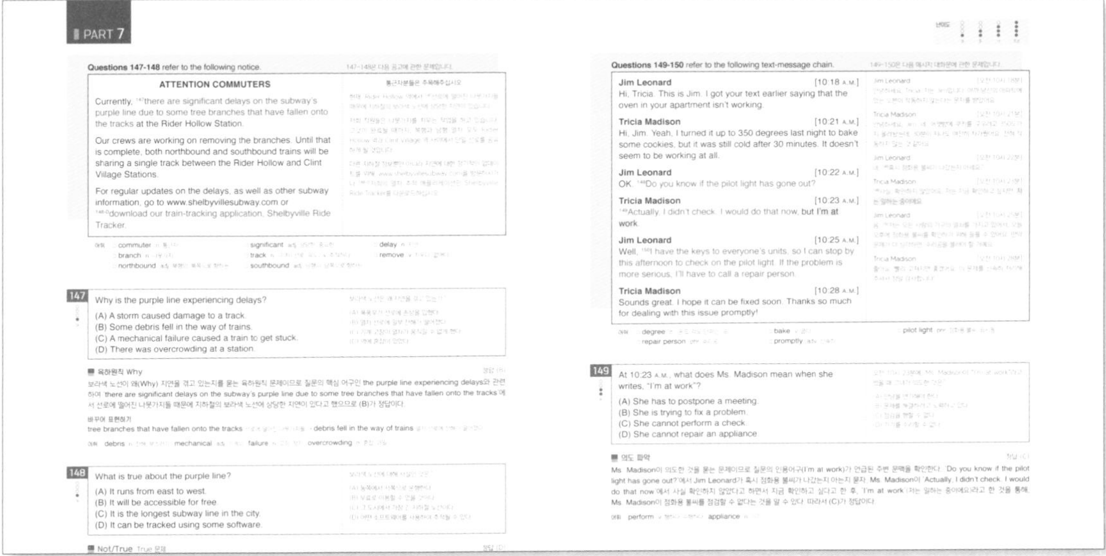

PART 7

Questions 147-148 refer to the following notice.

ATTENTION COMMUTERS

Currently, [147]there are significant delays on the subway's purple line due to some tree branches that have fallen onto the tracks at the Rider Hollow Station.

Our crews are working on removing the branches. Until that is complete, both northbound and southbound trains will be sharing a single track between the Rider Hollow and Clint Village Stations.

For regular updates on the delays, as well as other subway information, go to www.shelbyvillesubway.com or [148-D]download our train-tracking application, Shelbyville Ride Tracker.

어휘 commuter / significant / delay / branch / track / remove / northbound / southbound

147 Why is the purple line experiencing delays?
(A) A storm caused damage to a track.
(B) Some debris fell in the way of trains.
(C) A mechanical failure caused a train to get stuck.
(D) There was overcrowding at a station.

■ 육하원칙 Why

보라색 노선이 왜(Why) 지연을 겪고 있는지를 묻는 육하원칙 문제이므로 질문의 핵심 어구인 the purple line experiencing delays와 관련하여 'there are significant delays on the subway's purple line due to some tree branches that have fallen onto the tracks'에서 선로에 떨어진 나뭇가지들 때문에 지하철의 보라색 노선에 상당한 지연이 있다고 했으므로 (B)가 정답이다.

바꾸어 표현하기
tree branches that have fallen onto the tracks → debris fell in the way of trains

어휘 debris / mechanical / failure / overcrowding

148 What is true about the purple line?
(A) It runs from east to west.
(B) It will be accessible for free.
(C) It is the longest subway line in the city.
(D) It can be tracked using some software.

■ Not/True True 문제

Questions 149-150 refer to the following text-message chain.

Jim Leonard [10:18 A.M.]
Hi, Tricia. This is Jim. I got your text earlier saying that the oven in your apartment isn't working.

Tricia Madison [10:21 A.M.]
Hi, Jim. Yeah, I turned it up to 350 degrees last night to bake some cookies, but it was still cold after 30 minutes. It doesn't seem to be working at all.

Jim Leonard [10:22 A.M.]
OK. [149]Do you know if the pilot light has gone out?

Tricia Madison [10:23 A.M.]
[149]Actually, I didn't check. I would do that now, **but I'm at work.**

Jim Leonard [10:25 A.M.]
Well, [150]I have the keys to everyone's units, so I can stop by this afternoon to check on the pilot light. If the problem is more serious, I'll have to call a repair person.

Tricia Madison [10:28 A.M.]
Sounds great. I hope it can be fixed soon. Thanks so much for dealing with this issue promptly!

어휘 degree / bake / pilot light / repair person / promptly

149 At 10:23 A.M., what does Ms. Madison mean when she writes, "I'm at work"?
(A) She has to postpone a meeting.
(B) She is trying to fix a problem.
(C) She cannot perform a check.
(D) She cannot repair an appliance.

■ 의도 파악

Ms. Madison이 의도한 것을 묻는 문제이므로 질문의 인용어구(I'm at work)가 언급된 주변 문맥을 확인한다. 'Do you know if the pilot light has gone out?'에서 Jim Leonard가 혹시 점화용 불씨가 나갔는지 아는지 묻자, Ms. Madison이 'Actually, I didn't check. I would do that now'에서 사실 확인하지 않았다고 하면서 지금 확인하고 싶다고 한 후, 'I'm at work'(저는 일하는 중이에요)라고 한 것을 통해, Ms. Madison이 점화용 불씨를 점검할 수 없다는 것을 알 수 있다. 따라서 (C)가 정답이다.

어휘 perform / appliance

1 지문, 문제, 해석, 정답의 단서

최신 토익 출제 경향이 반영된 지문 및 문제와, 함께 수록된 정확한 해석을 보며 지문 및 문제의 내용을 완벽하게 이해할 수 있습니다. 또한, 각 문제별로 표시된 정답의 단서를 확인하여, 모든 문제에 대한 정답의 근거를 정확하게 파악하는 연습을 할 수 있습니다.

2 문제 유형별 상세한 해설 및 문제 풀이 방법

문제 유형별로 가장 효율적인 해결 방법이 적용된 문제 풀이 방법을 제시하였습니다. 질문의 핵심 어구를 파악하고, 이를 지문에서 찾아 보기와 연결하고 정답을 선택하는 과정을 읽는 것만으로도 자연스럽게 Part 7의 유형별 문제 풀이 전략을 익힐 수 있습니다.

3 바꾸어 표현하기

지문의 내용이 질문이나 보기에서 바꾸어 표현된 경우, 이를 [지문의 표현 → 보기의 표현] 또는 [질문의 표현 → 지문의 표현]으로 정리하여 한눈에 확인할 수 있도록 하였습니다. 이를 통해 Part 7 풀이 전략을 익히고 나아가 고득점 달성이 가능하도록 하였습니다.

토익 소개 및 시험장 Tips

토익이란 무엇인가?

TOEIC은 **Test Of English for International Communication**의 약자로 영어가 모국어가 아닌 사람들을 대상으로 언어 본래의 기능인 '커뮤니케이션' 능력에 중점을 두고 일상생활 또는 국제 업무 등에 필요한 실용영어 능력을 평가하는 시험입니다. 토익은 일상생활 및 비즈니스 현장에서 필요로 하는 내용을 평가하기 위해 개발되었고 다음과 같은 실용적인 주제들을 주로 다룹니다.

- 협력 개발: 연구, 제품 개발
- 재무 회계: 대출, 투자, 세금, 회계, 은행 업무
- 일반 업무: 계약, 협상, 마케팅, 판매
- 기술 영역: 전기, 공업 기술, 컴퓨터, 실험실
- 사무 영역: 회의, 서류 업무
- 물품 구입: 쇼핑, 물건 주문, 대금 지불
- 식사: 레스토랑, 회식, 만찬
- 문화: 극장, 스포츠, 피크닉
- 건강: 의료 보험, 병원 진료, 치과
- 제조: 생산 조립 라인, 공장 경영
- 직원: 채용, 은퇴, 급여, 진급, 고용 기회
- 주택: 부동산, 이사, 기업 부지

토익의 파트별 구성

구성	내용		문항 수	시간	배점
Listening Test	Part 1	사진 묘사	6문항 (1번~6번)	45분	495점
	Part 2	질의 응답	25문항 (7번~31번)		
	Part 3	짧은 대화	39문항, 13지문 (32번~70번)		
	Part 4	짧은 담화	30문항, 10지문 (71번~100번)		
Reading Test	Part 5	단문 빈칸 채우기 (문법/어휘)	30문항 (101번~130번)	75분	495점
	Part 6	장문 빈칸 채우기 (문법/어휘/문장 고르기)	16문항, 4지문 (131번~146번)		
	Part 7	지문 읽고 문제 풀기(독해) - 단일 지문(Single Passage) - 이중 지문(Double Passages) - 삼중 지문(Triple Passages)	54문항, 15지문 (147번~200번) - 29문항, 10지문 (147번~175번) - 10문항, 2지문 (176번~185번) - 15문항, 3지문 (186번~200번)		
Total		7 Parts	200문항	120분	990점

토익 접수 방법 및 성적 확인

1. 접수 방법
   - 접수 기간을 TOEIC위원회 인터넷 사이트(www.toeic.co.kr) 혹은 공식 애플리케이션에서 확인하고 접수합니다.
   - 접수 시 jpg형식의 사진 파일이 필요하므로 미리 준비합니다.

2. 성적 확인
   - 시험일로부터 약 10일 이후 TOEIC위원회 인터넷 사이트(www.toeic.co.kr) 혹은 공식 애플리케이션에서 확인합니다. (성적 발표 기간은 회차마다 상이함)
   - 시험 접수 시, 우편 수령과 온라인 출력 중 성적 수령 방법을 선택할 수 있습니다.
     *온라인 출력은 성적 발표 즉시 발급 가능하나, 우편 수령은 약 7일가량의 발송 기간이 소요될 수 있습니다.

시험 당일 준비물

신분증 / 연필&지우개 / 시계 / 수험번호를 적어둔 메모 / 오답노트&단어암기장

* 시험 당일 신분증이 없으면 시험에 응시할 수 없으므로, 반드시 ETS에서 요구하는 신분증(주민등록증, 운전면허증, 공무원증 등)을 지참해야 합니다. ETS에서 인정하는 신분증 종류는 TOEIC위원회 인터넷 사이트(www.toeic.co.kr)에서 확인 가능합니다.

시험 진행 순서

정기시험/추가시험(오전)	추가시험(오후)	진행내용	유의사항
AM 9:30 - 9:45	PM 2:30 - 2:45	답안지 작성 오리엔테이션	10분 전에 고사장에 도착하여, 이름과 수험번호로 고사실을 확인합니다.
AM 9:45 - 9:50	PM 2:45 - 2:50	쉬는 시간	준비해간 오답노트나 단어암기장으로 최종 정리를 합니다. 시험 중간에는 쉬는 시간이 없으므로 화장실에 꼭 다녀오도록 합니다.
AM 9:50 - 10:10	PM 2:50 - 3:10	신분 확인 및 문제지 배부	
AM 10:10 - 10:55	PM 3:10 - 3:55	Listening Test	Part 1과 Part 2는 문제를 풀면서 정답을 바로 답안지에 마킹합니다. Part 3와 Part 4는 문제의 정답 보기 옆에 살짝 표시해두고, Listening Test가 끝난 후 한꺼번에 마킹합니다.
AM 10:55 - 12:10	PM 3:55 - 5:10	Reading Test	각 문제를 풀 때 바로 정답을 마킹합니다.

* 추가시험은 토요일 오전 또는 오후에 시행되므로 이 사항도 꼼꼼히 확인합니다.
* 당일 진행 순서에 대한 더 자세한 내용은 해커스토익(Hackers.co.kr) 사이트에서 확인할 수 있습니다.

파트별 형태 및 전략

Part 5 단문 빈칸 채우기 (30문제)

· 한 문장의 빈칸에 알맞은 문법 사항이나 어휘를 4개의 보기 중에서 고르는 유형
· 권장 소요 시간: 11분 (문제당 풀이 시간: 20초~22초)

문제 형태

1 문법

101. Mr. Monroe announced his ------- to retire from the firm at a meeting last week.
(A) decides
(B) decisively
(C) decision
(D) decisive

해설 101. 빈칸 앞에 형용사 역할을 하는 소유격 인칭대명사(his)가 왔으므로 형용사의 꾸밈을 받을 수 있는 명사 (C)가 정답이다.

2 어휘

102. Effective on Monday, employees must start ------- a new procedure for ordering office supplies.
(A) causing
(B) following
(C) excluding
(D) informing

해설 102. '직원들은 새로운 절차를 ____하기 시작해야 한다'라는 문맥에 가장 잘 어울리는 단어는 동사 follow의 동명사 (B)이다.

문제 풀이 전략

1. 보기를 보고 문법 문제인지, 어휘 문제인지 유형을 파악합니다.
네 개의 보기를 보고 문법 사항을 묻는 문제인지, 어휘의 의미를 묻는 문제인지를 파악합니다. 보기가 첫 번째 예제의 decides, decisively, decision, decisive처럼 품사가 다른 단어들로 구성되어 있으면 문법 문제이고, 두 번째 예제의 causing, following, excluding, informing처럼 품사는 같지만 의미가 다른 단어들로 구성되어 있으면 어휘 문제입니다.

2. 문제 유형에 따라 빈칸 주변이나 문장 구조 또는 문맥을 통해 정답을 선택합니다.
문법 문제는 빈칸 주변이나 문장 구조를 통해 빈칸에 적합한 문법적 요소를 정답으로 선택합니다. 어휘 문제의 경우 문맥을 확인하여 문맥에 가장 적합한 단어를 정답으로 선택합니다.

* 실제 시험을 볼 때, Part 1과 Part 2의 디렉션이 나오는 동안 Part 5 문제를 최대한 많이 풀면 전체 시험 시간 조절에 도움이 됩니다.

Part 6 장문 빈칸 채우기 (16문제)

· 한 지문 내의 4개의 빈칸에 알맞은 문법 사항이나 어휘, 문장을 고르는 유형. 총 4개의 지문 출제.
· 권장 소요 시간: 8분 (문제당 풀이 시간: 25초~30초)

문제 형태

Questions 131-134 refer to the following e-mail.

Dear Ms. Swerter,

It was a treat to see your group ------- **131.** its music at the community event in Morristown. Do you think you could do the same for us at a private gathering next month? My company ------- **132.** a welcoming celebration for some clients. ------- **133.**. We are planning a special dinner and are hoping your group can provide the accompanying entertainment. We'd also like to book the dancers who were with you at the concert. Their performance was quite ------- **134.** to watch. Our guests would surely enjoy seeing both acts together. Please let me know.

Shannon Lemmick

어휘 **131.** (A) act
(B) explain
(C) perform
(D) observe

문법 **132.** (A) will be hosting
(B) hosted
(C) hosts
(D) to host

문장 고르기 **133.** (A) I'd like to buy tickets for the afternoon show.
(B) You may request their services for an additional charge.
(C) It will be their first time meeting with my company's staff.
(D) We approve of the schedule you have proposed.

어휘 **134.** (A) tough
(B) thrilling
(C) content
(D) punctual

해설 131. '당신의 그룹이 지역 사회 행사에서 곡을 연주하는 것을 보게 되어 좋았다'라는 문맥이므로 동사 (C)가 정답이다.
132. 앞 문장에서 다음 달에 같은 공연을 해줄 수 있는지 물었으므로 행사가 미래에 열린다는 것을 알 수 있다. 따라서 미래 시제 (A)가 정답이다.
133. 앞 문장에서 '회사는 몇몇 고객들을 위한 환영 행사를 개최할 것이다'라고 했으므로 빈칸에는 고객들과의 만남에 대한 추가적인 내용이 들어가야 함을 알 수 있다. 따라서 (C)가 정답이다.
134. '그들의 공연은 관람하기에 꽤 황홀했다'라는 문맥이므로 형용사 (B)가 정답이다.

문제 풀이 전략

1. 보기를 보고 문제 유형을 파악합니다.

보기를 먼저 보고 문법 문제, 어휘 문제, 문장 고르기 문제 가운데 어떤 유형의 문제인지를 파악합니다.

2. 문제 유형에 따라 빈칸이 포함된 문장이나, 앞뒤 문장, 또는 전체 지문의 문맥을 통해 정답을 선택합니다.

Part 6에서는 빈칸이 포함된 문장뿐만 아니라 앞뒤 문장, 전체 지문의 문맥을 통해 정답을 파악해야 하는 문제도 출제됩니다. 그러므로 빈칸이 포함된 문장의 구조 및 문맥만으로 정답 선택이 어려울 경우 앞뒤 문맥이나 전체 문맥을 통해 정답을 선택합니다.

Part 7 지문 읽고 문제 풀기 (54문제)

· 지문을 읽고 지문과 관련된 질문들에 대해 가장 적절한 보기를 정답으로 고르는 유형
· 구성: Single Passage에서 29문제, Double Passages에서 10문제, Triple Passages에서 15문제 출제
· 권장 소요 시간: 54분 (문제당 풀이 시간: 1분)

문제 형태

1 단일 지문 (Single Passage)

Questions 164-167 refer to the following advertisement.

AVALON WINDOWS
The window professionals

For over 30 years, homeowners have trusted Avalon Windows for expert window installation and repair. We offer quick and efficient service no matter what the job is. — [1] —. We ensure total customer satisfaction for a reasonable price. — [2] —. We provide accurate measurements, a complete project estimate with no hidden fees, and a 10-year warranty on all installations. We also offer a selection of window styles and sizes for you to choose from. — [3] —. Simply call us at 555-2092 to receive a free catalog in the mail or to schedule a consultation. Mention this advertisement when you call and receive 15 percent off your next window installation. — [4] —.

164. For whom is the advertisement intended?
(A) Real estate consultants
(B) Proprietors of residences
(C) Construction contractors
(D) Building supply retailers

165. What is true about Avalon Windows?
(A) It offers guarantees on installations.
(B) It also offers construction services.
(C) It plans to expand style selections.
(D) It charges a small fee for job estimates.

166. How can customers obtain discounts on a service?
(A) By ordering a specific number of windows
(B) By signing up on a Web site
(C) By mailing in a special coupon
(D) By mentioning an advertisement

167. In which of the positions marked [1], [2], [3], and [4] does the following sentence best belong?
"In fact, if you aren't pleased with our work, you'll get your money back."
(A) [1]
(B) [2]
(C) [3]
(D) [4]

해설 164. 주택 소유자들이 Avalon Windows사에 전문적인 창문 설치와 수리를 믿고 맡겨왔다고 했으므로 (B)가 정답이다.
165. Avalon Windows사가 모든 설치에 대해 10년의 보증을 제공한다고 했으므로 (A)가 정답이다.
166. 전화해서 이 광고를 언급하면 다음 창문 설치 시 15퍼센트 할인을 받는다고 했으므로 (D)가 정답이다.
167. 제시된 문장이 실제로 작업에 만족하지 않을 시에는 돈을 돌려받을 것이라고 했으므로, [2]에 제시된 문장이 들어가면 Avalon Windows사는 전면적인 고객 만족을 보장하므로 실제로 작업에 만족하지 않을 시에는 돈을 돌려받을 것이라는 자연스러운 문맥이 된다는 것을 알 수 있다. 따라서 (B)가 정답이다.

2 이중 지문 (Double Passages)

Questions 176-180 refer to the following e-mails.

To: Natalie Mercer <n.mercer@silverfield.com>
From: Robert Altieri <r.altieri@silverfield.com>
Subject: Digital Creators Conference (DCC)
Date: October 9
Attachment: DCC passes

Natalie,

I have attached four passes for you and your team to the upcoming DCC in San Francisco and would now like to go ahead and book your accommodations there. I know you stayed at the Gordon Suites and the Grand Burgess Hotel in previous years, but I think I have found some better options. Please indicate which of the following hotels you wish to stay at in response to this e-mail.

The Bismarck Hotel is close to the convention center but unfortunately does not offer access to Wi-Fi. Those who need to work from the hotel may thus be interested in the Newburg Plaza, which provides free Internet use. However, staying at this location would require the reservation of a car service, as it is a 20-minute drive from the conference venue.

Let me know which one you prefer when you have a moment. Also, please note that the passes I have attached allow entry to the event halls on all four days. Meals are not included, but there are places to purchase food at nearby restaurants. Thank you.

Robert

To: Robert Altieri <r.altieri@silverfield.com>
From: Natalie Mercer <n.mercer@silverfield.com>
Subject: Re: Digital Creators Conference (DCC)
Date: October 9

Robert,

I think it's best for us to have access to the Internet at the hotel. Some of my team members will be convening on evenings following the conference events and may want to reference information online. As for the car service, I believe we can have expenses reimbursed for that. Everyone agrees that a 20-minute ride doesn't sound like a major inconvenience.

But before you make the reservation, could you check what the rates are for parking at the hotel? Francine will be taking her own vehicle to San Francisco and will need to leave it in a lot for the duration of the conference. Thanks in advance.

Natalie

176. Why did Mr. Altieri write the e-mail?
(A) To invite a guest to speak at a conference
(B) To ask about a preference for a trip
(C) To explain a travel expense policy
(D) To ask for airline recommendations

177. What is NOT mentioned about the Digital Creators Conference?
(A) It lasts for four days.
(B) It is a short drive from the airport.
(C) It is close to dining establishments.
(D) It is being held in San Francisco.

178. In the second e-mail, the word "reference" in paragraph 1, line 2, is closest in meaning to
(A) mention
(B) supply
(C) search
(D) adapt

179. Which hotel will Mr. Altieri most likely book?
(A) The Gordon Suites
(B) The Grand Burgess Hotel
(C) The Bismarck Hotel
(D) The Newburg Plaza

180. What is indicated about Ms. Mercer?
(A) She has a team member who will bring her own car.
(B) She might change her mind about attending the DCC.
(C) She has an issue with Mr. Altieri's proposals.
(D) She is busy preparing for a series of presentations.

해설 176. 선택할 수 있는 2가지 숙박 시설 중 어느 것을 더 선호하는지 알려달라고 했으므로 (B)가 정답이다.

177. 공항에서 차로 가까운 거리에 있다는 내용은 지문에 언급되지 않았으므로 (B)가 정답이다.

178. reference를 포함하고 있는 구절 'will be convening ~ and may want to reference information online'에서 reference가 '찾아보다, 참고하다'라는 뜻으로 사용되었다. 따라서 '찾다'라는 의미의 (C)가 정답이다.

179. 두 번째 이메일에서 호텔에 인터넷 이용이 가능한 것이 좋을 것 같다고 했고, 첫 번째 이메일에서 Newburg Plaza가 무료 인터넷 이용을 제공한다고 했으므로 (D)가 정답이다.

180. 같이 회의에 가는 Francine이 자신의 차량을 샌프란시스코에 가져올 것이라고 했으므로 (A)가 정답이다.

3 삼중 지문 (Triple Passages)

Questions 186-190 refer to the following e-mail, schedule, and article.

TO: Ben Finch <ben.finch@mymail.com>
FROM: Taylor Gray <t.gray@streetmag.com>
SUBJECT: Welcome to *Street Magazine*
DATE: June 12

Hi Ben,

Congratulations on being selected as an intern for *Street Magazine*. For 25 years, the citizens of Seattle have looked to us weekly for the latest fashion, art, and music news.

Your internship will be from July 1 to December 31. You will report to me five days a week from 9:00 A.M. to 6:00 P.M. As an intern, you will not be a salaried employee, but we will provide an allowance for some expenses. If you do well, there may be a place for you here after your internship ends.

Please note that although you will have to do office work for various departments as the need arises, your responsibilities will be to research, take notes, and fact check content for me.

Taylor Gray

Personal Work Schedule: Taylor Gray
Thursday, August 7

Time	Activities	To do
09:30	Discuss budget with Mr. Robinson	
11:30	Leave for lunch appointment with photographer Stacy Larson	
13:00	Review photo submissions for "People" section	
14:30	Proofread articles for print version of lifestyle section	Send final list to Ms. McKee
16:00	Cover photo shoot at West Town Music Club	Assign to Ryan Oakley
16:30	Fact check music section for Web site	
17:30	Pick up laundry at Van's Cleaners	
18:00	Interview owner of Contempo Art Space	

Street Magazine

"Fusion In Fusion"
Opening Reception, Contempo Art Space
Thursday, August 7, 6:00 P.M. – 8:00 P.M.

This exhibit of artwork expresses an appreciation for all creative art forms, such as visual art, music, dance, film, and more. Works are representational or abstract, in 2D or 3D. All pieces exhibited in the main gallery will be for sale. This exhibit will be on display until November 6. For details, please contact gallery owner Mischa Michaels at 555-3941.

186. What is NOT true about the internship position at *Street Magazine*?

(A) It does not pay a regular salary.
(B) It involves working with different departments.
(C) It can lead to offers of a permanent job.
(D) It is available only during the summer.

187. What is suggested about *Street Magazine* in the e-mail?

(A) It is planning to relocate its office.
(B) It is published on a weekly basis.
(C) It is mainly devoted to fashion news.
(D) It has subscribers in many cities.

188. What task will Mr. Finch most likely be assigned on August 7?

(A) Proofreading lifestyle section material
(B) Collecting items from a laundry facility
(C) Reviewing photographic submissions
(D) Fact checking music section content

189. What can be inferred about Ms. Gray?

(A) She will be interviewing Ms. Michaels.
(B) She is unable to make her lunch appointment.
(C) She will be supervising a photo shoot.
(D) She is responsible for approving a budget.

190. What is mentioned about the exhibit at Contempo Art Space?

(A) It is a collection of past works by a group.
(B) Some of the artworks may be purchased on-site.
(C) It will run in conjunction with another event.
(D) Most of the participants are known artists.

해설 186. 이메일에서 *Street*지에서의 인턴직이 7월 1일부터 12월 31일까지라고 했으므로 (D)가 정답이다.

187. 지역 독자들이 *Street*지가 주간 단위로 최신 사건들을 알려줄 것이라고 기대해왔다고 했으므로 (B)가 정답이다.

188. 이메일에서 Ms. Finch가 맡을 일 중 Ms. Gray를 위해 온라인 기사의 사실 확인을 하는 것이 있다고 했고, 일정표에서 Ms. Gray의 8월 7일 일정에 웹사이트의 음악 부문에 대한 사실 확인이 포함되어 있으므로 (D)가 정답이다.

189. 일정표에서 Ms. Gray의 일정에 Contempo Art Space의 소유주와의 인터뷰가 있고, 기사에서 Contempo Art Space의 소유주가 Mischa Michaels라고 했으므로 (A)가 정답이다.

190. 기사에서 Contempo Art Space의 주요 갤러리에 전시된 모든 작품들은 판매될 것이라고 했으므로 (B)가 정답이다.

문제 풀이 전략

아래 전략 선택 TIP을 참고하여 <문제 먼저 읽고 지문 읽기> 또는 <지문 먼저 읽고 문제 읽기> 중 자신에게 맞는 전략을 택하여 빠르고 정확하게 문제를 풀 수 있도록 합니다.

전략 선택 TIP

1) 다음 주어진 글의 내용을 이해하며 읽는 데 몇 초가 걸리는지 기록해 둡니다.

Come join the annual office party on Friday, December 20th! Be sure to stop by Mr. Maschino's desk to inform him of your participation as well as the attendance of any accompanying family members. We hope to see you all there!

2) 아래 문제를 풀어봅니다.

What should employees tell Mr. Maschino about?

(A) Bringing family members to a party
(B) Planning for a celebration
(C) Catering for company events
(D) Giving cash to a charity

정답: (A)

글을 읽는 데 10초 이상이 걸렸거나 문제를 풀면서 다시 글의 내용을 확인했다면 → **전략 1**

글을 읽는 데 10초 미만이 걸렸고, 문제를 한번에 풀었다면 → **전략 2**

전략 1 문제 먼저 읽고 지문 읽기

1. 질문들을 빠르게 읽고 지문에서 확인할 내용을 파악합니다.

지문을 읽기 전 먼저 질문들을 빠르게 읽어서, 어떤 내용을 지문에서 중점적으로 읽어야 하는지 확인합니다.

2. 지문을 읽으며, 미리 읽어 두었던 질문과 관련된 내용이 언급된 부분에서 정답의 단서를 확인합니다.

미리 읽어 두었던 질문의 핵심 어구와 관련된 내용이 언급된 부분을 지문에서 찾아 정답의 단서를 확인합니다.

3. 정답의 단서를 그대로 언급했거나, 다른 말로 바꾸어 표현한 보기를 정답으로 선택합니다.

전략 2 지문 먼저 읽고 문제 읽기

1. 지문의 종류나 글의 제목을 확인하여 지문의 전반적인 내용을 추측합니다.

2. 지문을 읽으며 문제로 나올 것 같은 부분을 특히 꼼꼼히 확인합니다.

중심 내용, 특정 인물 및 사건, 예외 및 변동 등의 사항은 문제로 나올 가능성이 크므로 이러한 부분들을 집중적으로 확인하며 지문을 읽습니다.

3. 정답의 단서를 그대로 언급했거나, 다른 말로 바꾸어 표현한 보기를 정답으로 선택합니다.

수준별 맞춤 학습 플랜

TEST 01을 마친 후 자신의 환산 점수에 맞는 학습 플랜을 선택하고 매일매일 박스에 체크하며 공부합니다. 각 TEST를 마친 후, 다양한 자료를 활용하여 각 테스트를 꼼꼼하게 리뷰합니다.

* 각 테스트를 마친 후, 해당 테스트의 점수를 교재 앞쪽에 있는 [토익 Reading 목표 달성기]에 기록하여 자신의 점수 변화를 확인할 수 있습니다.

400점 이상

2주 완성 학습 플랜

- 2주 동안 매일 테스트 1회분을 교재 뒤쪽의 Answer Sheet(p.411)를 활용하여 실전처럼 풀어본 후 꼼꼼하게 리뷰합니다.
- 리뷰 시, 틀린 문제를 다시 풀어본 후 교재 뒤의 **해석**을 활용하여 해석이 잘 되지 않았던 부분까지 완벽하게 이해합니다.
- 해커스토익(Hackers.co.kr)에서 무료로 제공되는 **Part 5&6 무료 해설**로 틀린 Part 5&6 문제를 확실하게 이해합니다.
- 해커스인강(HackersIngang.com)에서 무료로 제공되는 **단어암기장 및 단어암기 MP3**로 각 TEST의 핵심 어휘 중 모르는 어휘만 체크하여 암기합니다.

	Day 1	Day 2	Day 3	Day 4	Day 5
Week 1	☐ Test 01 풀기 및 리뷰	☐ Test 02 풀기 및 리뷰	☐ Test 03 풀기 및 리뷰	☐ Test 04 풀기 및 리뷰	☐ Test 05 풀기 및 리뷰
Week 2	☐ Test 06 풀기 및 리뷰	☐ Test 07 풀기 및 리뷰	☐ Test 08 풀기 및 리뷰	☐ Test 09 풀기 및 리뷰	☐ Test 10 풀기 및 리뷰

※ **≪해커스 토익 실전 1000제 1 Reading 해설집≫**(별매)**으로 리뷰하기**

- 틀린 문제와 난이도 최상 문제를 다시 한번 풀어보며 완벽하게 이해합니다.
- 틀린 문제는 정답 및 오답 해설을 보며 오답이 왜 오답인지 그 이유까지 확실하게 파악합니다.

300~395점

3주 완성 학습 플랜

- 3주 동안 첫째 날, 둘째 날에 테스트 1회분씩을 풀어본 후 꼼꼼하게 리뷰하고, 셋째 날에는 2회분에 대한 심화 학습을 합니다.
- 리뷰 시, 틀린 문제를 다시 한번 풀어본 후 교재 뒤의 **해석**을 활용하여 해석이 잘 되지 않았던 부분까지 완벽하게 이해합니다.
- 해커스토익(Hackers.co.kr)에서 무료로 제공되는 **Part 5&6 무료 해설**로 틀린 Part 5&6 문제를 확실하게 이해합니다.
- 해커스인강(HackersIngang.com)에서 무료로 제공되는 **단어암기장 및 단어암기 MP3**로 각 TEST의 핵심 어휘를 암기합니다.

	Day 1	Day 2	Day 3	Day 4	Day 5
Week 1	☐ Test 01 풀기 및 리뷰	☐ Test 02 풀기 및 리뷰	☐ Test 01&02 심화 학습	☐ Test 03 풀기 및 리뷰	☐ Test 04 풀기 및 리뷰
Week 2	☐ Test 03&04 심화 학습	☐ Test 05 풀기 및 리뷰	☐ Test 06 풀기 및 리뷰	☐ Test 05&06 심화 학습	☐ Test 07 풀기 및 리뷰
Week 3	☐ Test 08 풀기 및 리뷰	☐ Test 07&08 심화 학습	☐ Test 09 풀기 및 리뷰	☐ Test 10 풀기 및 리뷰	☐ Test 09&10 심화 학습

※ **≪해커스 토익 실전 1000제 1 Reading 해설집≫**(별매)**으로 리뷰하기**

- 틀린 문제와 난이도 상 이상의 문제를 다시 한번 풀어보며 완벽하게 이해합니다.
- 틀린 문제는 정답 및 오답 해설을 보며 오답이 왜 오답인지 그 이유까지 확실하게 파악합니다.
- 모든 문제마다 표시된 문제 유형을 보며 자신이 자주 틀리는 문제 유형이 무엇인지 파악하고 보완합니다.
- 지문에 파란색으로 표시된 정답의 단서를 보고 정답을 선택해보며 문제 풀이 노하우를 파악합니다.

295점 이하

4주 완성 학습 플랜

· 4주 동안 이틀에 걸쳐 테스트 1회분을 풀고 꼼꼼하게 리뷰합니다.
· 리뷰 시, 틀린 문제를 다시 풀어본 후 교재 뒤의 **해석**을 활용하여 해석이 잘 되지 않았던 부분까지 완벽하게 이해합니다.
· 해커스토익(Hackers.co.kr)에서 무료로 제공되는 **Part 5&6 무료 해설**로 틀린 Part 5&6 문제를 확실하게 이해합니다.
· 해커스인강(HackersIngang.com)에서 무료로 제공되는 **단어암기장 및 단어암기 MP3**로 각 TEST의 핵심 어휘 중 모르는 어휘만 체크하여 암기합니다.

	Day 1	Day 2	Day 3	Day 4	Day 5
Week 1	□ Test 01 풀기	□ Test 01 리뷰	□ Test 02 풀기	□ Test 02 리뷰	□ Test 03 풀기
Week 2	□ Test 03 리뷰	□ Test 04 풀기	□ Test 04 리뷰	□ Test 05 풀기	□ Test 05 리뷰
Week 3	□ Test 06 풀기	□ Test 06 리뷰	□ Test 07 풀기	□ Test 07 리뷰	□ Test 08 풀기
Week 4	□ Test 08 리뷰	□ Test 09 풀기	□ Test 09 리뷰	□ Test 10 풀기	□ Test 10 리뷰

※ **≪해커스 토익 실전 1000제 1 Reading 해설집≫**(별매)**으로 리뷰하기**
· 틀린 문제와 난이도 중 이상의 문제를 다시 한번 풀어보며 완벽하게 이해합니다.
· 틀린 문제는 정답 및 오답 해설을 보며 오답이 왜 오답인지 그 이유까지 확실하게 파악합니다.
· 모든 문제마다 표시된 문제 유형을 보며 자신이 자주 틀리는 문제 유형이 무엇인지 파악하고 보완합니다.
· 지문에 파란색으로 표시된 정답의 단서를 보고 정답을 선택해보며 문제 풀이 노하우를 파악합니다.
· Part 7의 중요한 바꾸어 표현하기를 정리하고 암기합니다.

해커스와 함께라면 여러분의 목표를 더 빠르게 달성할 수 있습니다!

자신의 점수에 맞춰 아래 해커스 교재로 함께 학습하시면 더욱 빠르게 여러분이 목표한 바를 달성할 수 있습니다.

400점 이상	300~395점	295점 이하
≪해커스 토익 Reading≫	≪해커스 토익 750+ RC≫	≪해커스 토익 스타트 Reading≫

TEST 01

PART 5

PART 6

PART 7

Self 체크 리스트

잠깐! 테스트 전 확인사항

1. 휴대 전화의 전원을 끄셨나요? □ 예
2. Answer Sheet, 연필, 지우개를 준비하셨나요? □ 예
3. 시계를 준비하셨나요? □ 예

모든 준비가 완료되었으면 목표 점수를 떠올린 후 테스트를 시작합니다.
TEST 01을 통해 본인의 실력을 평가해 본 후, 본인에게 맞는 학습 플랜(p.22~23)으로 본 교재를 효율적으로 학습해 보세요.

문제 풀이를 마치는 시간은 지금부터 75분 후인 ___시 ___분입니다.
테스트 시간은 총 75분이며, 시험 종료 전 2~3분은 정답 검토 및 답안지 마킹을 위해 사용합니다.

READING TEST

In this section, you must demonstrate your ability to read and comprehend English. You will be given a variety of texts and asked to answer questions about these texts. This section is divided into three parts and will take 75 minutes to complete.

Do not mark the answers in your test book. Use the answer sheet that is separately provided.

PART 5

Directions: In each question, you will be asked to review a statement that is missing a word or phrase. Four answer choices will be provided for each statement. Select the best answer and mark the corresponding letter (A), (B), (C), or (D) on the answer sheet.

PART 5 권장 풀이 시간 11분

101. The CEO will ------- meet with clients during his visit to Berlin.

(A) brief
(B) briefing
(C) briefest
(D) briefly

102. The Lee Valley Fire Department launched an ------- to determine what caused the forest fire.

(A) investigation
(B) investigatory
(C) investigate
(D) investigative

103. Please ------- some snacks for the hike as it will take about four hours to complete.

(A) promote
(B) pack
(C) mark
(D) balance

104. Ms. Ewing ------- the results of last month's survey and then produce a summary next week.

(A) collected
(B) collecting
(C) had collected
(D) will collect

105. Charles Hayes is ------- the top chess players in England, having defeated many former champions.

(A) around
(B) between
(C) among
(D) inside

106. ------- workers find in the concert hall will remain in the lost and found center for only one week.

(A) Few
(B) Several
(C) Anything
(D) Most

107. Mr. Robinson fulfilled all of the company's requirements and is therefore ------- to apply for a permanent position.

(A) qualify
(B) qualifying
(C) qualifies
(D) qualified

108. The play *Middle of Summer* had a ------- ending, with an unexpected twist that left audiences in shock.

(A) conventional
(B) memorable
(C) marginal
(D) prosperous

109. ------- Mactran Corporation established a comprehensive recycling program last year, many staff members don't follow the guidelines properly.

(A) Although
(B) Until
(C) If
(D) Before

110. The route for the New Year's Day Parade has been outlined, but organizers are still ------- the details.

(A) finalize
(B) finalizes
(C) finalizing
(D) finalized

111. At the Wilkinsburg city council meeting, there was a ------- consensus that property taxes should be raised.

(A) generalization
(B) generally
(C) generalize
(D) general

112. A million new units of the video game console ------- at CX's factories right now to meet customer demand.

(A) to manufacture
(B) would have manufactured
(C) had been manufactured
(D) are being manufactured

113. Anyone with a camera is eligible to ------- in the Sydney 48-Hour Photography Competition.

(A) result
(B) obtain
(C) participate
(D) choose

114. ------- weather forecasts, the town of Wilshire can expect up to eight inches of snow tomorrow.

(A) Provided that
(B) According to
(C) Other than
(D) Along with

115. Staff members will ------- Harmon Inc.'s latest kitchen appliances on stage at this weekend's Food Expo.

(A) demonstrate
(B) implement
(C) conceive
(D) express

116. Because of his extensive experience, board members consider Mr. Peters the ------- candidate for the CEO position.

(A) inferior
(B) factual
(C) ideal
(D) polite

117. All applications to Florian University's Master's in Business Administration Program are due ------- January 1.

(A) through
(B) with
(C) by
(D) into

118. The company shifted ------- from its old business model to a fully digital one.

(A) radicalizing
(B) radically
(C) radicalize
(D) radical

119. Priyanka Reddy is the youngest ------- ever to receive the prestigious Clinton Film Award.

(A) director
(B) directly
(C) directed
(D) direction

120. Reporters ------- don't carry an official press badge will not be allowed into the venue.

(A) what
(B) who
(C) which
(D) they

GO ON TO THE NEXT PAGE

121. The waiter was very ------- since the food wasn't being served in a timely manner.

(A) appropriate
(B) succinct
(C) apologetic
(D) competent

122. ------- the product warranty has expired, Jassen Manufacturing will not repair the customer's item for free.

(A) As though
(B) Given that
(C) Besides
(D) Nevertheless

123. Over the past decade, much ------- has been made in stem cell research, leading to many medical breakthroughs.

(A) approval
(B) efficiency
(C) progress
(D) preference

124. Johnny Baker has ------- declined the offer to host the televised *Channel 10 Holiday Show*.

(A) repeatedly
(B) repeats
(C) repetition
(D) repeated

125. Members of the loyalty program may take advantage of discount offers ------- earn points for their purchases.

(A) in case
(B) so that
(C) regarding
(D) as well as

126. The product must ------- further testing before it can be released to the public.

(A) undergo
(B) perceive
(C) discover
(D) examine

127. ------- all the cities that the pop singer visited during her recent world tour, Seoul was her favorite.

(A) Of
(B) About
(C) To
(D) Upon

128. The chef often reminds viewers that they can replace hard-to-find items with ------- ingredients they have available.

(A) either
(B) both
(C) another
(D) whichever

129. During his award acceptance speech, Mitchell Cummings thanked his investors for their ------- support.

(A) continuously
(B) continuity
(C) continuous
(D) continue

130. The resort has had to ------- discount its room rates to attract visitors over the past year.

(A) neatly
(B) heavily
(C) densely
(D) evenly

PART 6

Directions: In this part, you will be asked to read four English texts. Each text is missing a word, phrase, or sentence. Select the answer choice that correctly completes the text and mark the corresponding letter (A), (B), (C), or (D) on the answer sheet.

PART 6 권장 풀이 시간 8분

Questions 131-134 refer to the following notice.

Notice for Carmel Tower Residents

On July 20, Carmel Tower will ------- (131.) work on a refurbishment of the building's hallways. The project will take four weeks to complete. During this period, work crews will need to enter the building. ------- (132.), access to the service elevator will be temporarily limited. Rest assured, efforts will be made to avoid ------- (133.) to building occupants. However, some noise and dust may be anticipated. ------- (134.). Contact the building management office if you have any concerns.

131. (A) interrupt
(B) initiate
(C) postpone
(D) conclude

132. (A) Conversely
(B) Formerly
(C) Consequently
(D) Similarly

133. (A) disrupts
(B) disrupted
(C) disruptions
(D) disrupt

134. (A) Severe weather has been forecast for this weekend.
(B) Notices will be sent when the entrance has been reopened.
(C) Every worker is responsible for keeping their area safe.
(D) Please keep doors closed to minimize the inconvenience.

GO ON TO THE NEXT PAGE

Questions 135-138 refer to the following information.

Setting up the Audipro SL-2

Congratulations on your purchase of the Audipro SL-2 speaker system. The SL-2 ------- (**135.**) to deliver powerful home audio in a package that is easy to install.

To begin the setup process, download the Audipro app and register your speaker. ------- (**136.**). Then, while still on the app, connect the speaker to your Wi-Fi network. The speaker will ------- (**137.**) detect compatible media players or televisions on your network. Follow the instructions on the app to connect to each ------- (**138.**). The SL-2 can also be connected manually by using the cables enclosed within the box.

135. (A) has designed
(B) designed
(C) is designed
(D) will design

136. (A) This can be done by entering the product number on the box.
(B) Hold down the button on the side to reset your speaker.
(C) Some older brands will need additional modifications.
(D) Speaker stands for each component are sold separately.

137. (A) hardly
(B) randomly
(C) occasionally
(D) automatically

138. (A) outlet
(B) device
(C) video
(D) account

Questions 139-142 refer to the following e-mail.

TO: Beth Carlin <bcarlin@eduswiftsystems.org>
FROM: John Statler <statler@agpfoundation.org>
DATE: October 22
SUBJECT: AGP Nonprofit Awards

Dear Ms. Carlin,

------- (**139.**) AGP, it is my honor to inform you that EduSwift Systems has been shortlisted for the AGP Nonprofit of the Year Award. An invitation to the year-end awards banquet will be forthcoming. Your ------- (**140.**) would be greatly appreciated. The event will provide an opportunity to network with members of similar organizations. Also, prominent publications such as *The National Herald* ------- (**141.**) representatives from each finalist every year. So, the event will be good for increasing publicity.

To confirm, please reply to this e-mail. ------- (**142.**). We can reserve up to eight seats for you at the event.

Congratulations again,
John Statler
AGP Foundation

139. (A) Including
(B) Without
(C) As for
(D) On behalf of

140. (A) support
(B) insight
(C) attendance
(D) investment

141. (A) interview
(B) interviewing
(C) interviews
(D) is interviewing

142. (A) Let us know where you would like it delivered.
(B) The menu will feature food from a range of cuisines.
(C) You will receive a call from a magazine representative.
(D) Please indicate the number of people in your party.

GO ON TO THE NEXT PAGE

Questions 143-146 refer to the following article.

(BRANSON)—Local children's charity Riley's Kids ------- **143.** a donation of $1 million. Riley's Kids CEO Amber Thomas expressed gratitude for the donation that was made early last month. Evidently, it came from a single ------- **144.** donor. "We've had donations come from undisclosed sources before," Thomas said, "but never one of this size." Thomas said that the donation will allow Riley's Kids to continue expanding its downtown Branson Youth Center. ------- **145.** will soon have a new library and basketball court. -------. **146.** Now the center may open as early as April of next year.

143. (A) has received
(B) will receive
(C) receiving
(D) to receive

144. (A) well-known
(B) frequent
(C) anonymous
(D) influential

145. (A) It
(B) They
(C) We
(D) She

146. (A) The donated books will need to be sorted first.
(B) The work was halted last year due to a budget shortfall.
(C) Visitors to the center must sign in at the reception desk.
(D) Businesses have agreed to sponsor the annual event.

PART 7

Directions: In this part, you will be asked to read several texts, such as advertisements, articles, instant messages, or examples of business correspondence. Each text is followed by several questions. Select the best answer and mark the corresponding letter (A), (B), (C), or (D) on your answer sheet.

PART 7 권장 풀이 시간 **54분**

Questions 147-148 refer to the following notice.

ATTENTION COMMUTERS

Currently, there are significant delays on the subway's purple line due to some tree branches that have fallen onto the tracks at the Rider Hollow Station.

Our crews are working on removing the branches. Until that is complete, both northbound and southbound trains will be sharing a single track between the Rider Hollow and Clint Village Stations.

For regular updates on the delays, as well as other subway information, go to www.shelbyvillesubway.com or download our train-tracking application, Shelbyville Ride Tracker.

147. Why is the purple line experiencing delays?

(A) A storm caused damage to a track.
(B) Some debris fell in the way of trains.
(C) A mechanical failure caused a train to get stuck.
(D) There was overcrowding at a station.

148. What is true about the purple line?

(A) It runs from east to west.
(B) It will be accessible for free.
(C) It is the longest subway line in the city.
(D) It can be tracked using some software.

GO ON TO THE NEXT PAGE

Questions 149-150 refer to the following text-message chain.

Jim Leonard [10:18 A.M.]
Hi, Tricia. This is Jim. I got your text earlier saying that the oven in your apartment isn't working.

Tricia Madison [10:21 A.M.]
Hi, Jim. Yeah, I turned it up to 350 degrees last night to bake some cookies, but it was still cold after 30 minutes. It doesn't seem to be working at all.

Jim Leonard [10:22 A.M.]
OK. Do you know if the pilot light has gone out?

Tricia Madison [10:23 A.M.]
Actually, I didn't check. I would do that now, but I'm at work.

Jim Leonard [10:25 A.M.]
Well, I have the keys to everyone's units, so I can stop by this afternoon to check on the pilot light. If the problem is more serious, I'll have to call a repair person.

Tricia Madison [10:28 A.M.]
Sounds great. I hope it can be fixed soon. Thanks so much for dealing with this issue promptly!

149. At 10:23 A.M., what does Ms. Madison mean when she writes, "I'm at work"?

(A) She has to postpone a meeting.
(B) She is trying to fix a problem.
(C) She cannot perform a check.
(D) She cannot repair an appliance.

150. Who most likely is Mr. Leonard?

(A) An apartment resident
(B) A repair person
(C) A building manager
(D) A prospective tenant

Questions 151-152 refer to the following survey.

Snappeshop

Name: *Gabe Edwards*

Would you recommend our company to others? Y / N

For the questions below, please select an option from 1 to 5 with 5 being the highest.

How satisfied are you with our service?

1 ☐ 2 ☐ 3 ☐ 4 ☒ 5 ☐

How efficient is our delivery service?

1 ☐ 2 ☐ 3 ☐ 4 ☐ 5 ☒

How would you rank our customer service?

1 ☐ 2 ☒ 3 ☐ 4 ☐ 5 ☐

What do you think about our catalog?

Compared to other online outlets, you don't have a wide range of items.

What do you think about our customer service?

When I called customer service, they kept passing me around to different departments.

Which aspect of our service do you like the most?

I like the low shipping fees and the speed of delivery.

151. What is indicated about Mr. Edwards?

(A) He is a longtime user of Snappeshop.
(B) He uses several online shopping sites.
(C) He has asked for a refund before.
(D) He recently changed his address.

152. Which aspect of Snappeshop does Mr. Edwards like?

(A) The variety of items being offered
(B) The special deals during holidays
(C) The fast customer service
(D) The cheap price of shipping

GO ON TO THE NEXT PAGE

Questions 153-155 refer to the following job advertisement.

HISTORIC LONDON TOURS: GUIDES WANTED

Do you consider yourself a local history expert? Are you an engaging public speaker? Are you passionate about the city? If so, consider applying to be a guide at Historic London Tours. We are the oldest and most popular tour agency in the city. We organise bus, boat, and walking tours for thousands of visitors a year. Right now, we are looking for five individuals to help us conduct our walking tours.

Applicants must:

- Show a thorough knowledge of the city's history by taking a 30-minute exam
- Deliver a 10-minute presentation on a neighbourhood of the city of their choosing
- Pass a background check

The successful candidates will work 25 to 30 hours per week including weekends, with extra hours added during the summer. The standard pay is £14 per hour, and we pay £21 per hour on holidays. Full employment benefits are provided.

To apply, go to www.historiclondon.co.uk/jobs and submit a résumé and cover letter explaining why you would be the ideal candidate. The deadline for applications is March 31.

153. What is stated about Historic London Tours?

(A) It provides multiple types of tours.
(B) It is expanding its service into other cities.
(C) It is cheaper than other tour agencies.
(D) It trains its employees for months.

154. What must job applicants do?

(A) Submit a copy of a certificate
(B) Provide a recommendation letter
(C) Prepare a tour schedule
(D) Complete a history test

155. What is indicated about the guide job?

(A) It requires a special uniform.
(B) It is busier during the summer.
(C) It pays more for people with experience.
(D) It often leads to an upper-management job.

Questions 156-157 refer to the following text message.

FROM: Swift Link (555-4278)
SENT: May 18, 12:10 P.M.

This is a notification that your International Travel Plan has been activated. Between May 18 and May 25, you will receive cellular service within Poland. The cost of this coverage is $10 per day. Note that you will be charged extra if you exceed five gigabytes of data, so we suggest turning off applications that use lots of data. To switch to a plan with more data, please use the Swift Link mobile application. Thank you.

156. Why was the text message sent?

(A) To report that a data limit has been exceeded
(B) To remind the recipient about an unpaid bill
(C) To promote a new international travel plan
(D) To announce that the recipient is receiving service

157. What does the message recommend that the recipient do?

(A) Limit data consumption
(B) Upgrade to a newer phone model
(C) Download a user manual
(D) Stay within certain areas

GO ON TO THE NEXT PAGE

Questions 158-160 refer to the following article.

Paisley Park Diner Changes Management

For decades, Paisley Park Diner has been one of the most iconic restaurants in Indianapolis. Its colorful interior filled with vintage items evokes an innocent, bygone era. According to *Indianapolis Now* magazine, it also boasts the city's friendliest servers and best apple pie.

Now, founder and longtime manager Guy Hubert has decided to step down. — [1] —. At 72, Mr. Hubert is ready to leave the stresses of running the restaurant behind and looks forward to enjoying his retirement. Succeeding him will be his 38-year-old son, Gavin. "Gavin has been working at the diner as head chef for over 15 years," says Mr. Hubert. — [2] —. "I have every confidence that he knows what it takes to keep the place running smoothly."

The younger Hubert says he plans to keep the core aspects of the diner fully intact. — [3] —. However, he wants to add international dishes to the menu that go beyond traditional American fare. — [4] —. He also aims to make selected menu items available for delivery.

158. What is NOT an attraction of Paisley Park Diner?

(A) A visually appealing interior
(B) Friendly service staff
(C) A popular dessert item
(D) Food discounts on some days

159. What does Gavin Hubert want to do once he becomes manager?

(A) Remodel the interior
(B) Extend the operating hours
(C) Add a delivery option
(D) Open up a second branch

160. In which of the positions marked [1], [2], [3], and [4] does the following sentence best belong?

"His last day will be on February 28."

(A) [1]
(B) [2]
(C) [3]
(D) [4]

Questions 161-164 refer to the following online chat discussion.

Fumiko Suzuki	[10:51 A.M.]	I would like your input on employee satisfaction. In our staff survey, several employees complained about having too much work. The stress this has caused has affected overall productivity. What could be some solutions?
Jintao Bang	[10:52 A.M.]	I think one good idea would be to stop sending work-related e-mails after the office has closed.
Hendrick Schulz	[10:54 A.M.]	That would be beneficial. Moreover, more breaks should be encouraged. Maybe even offer a team-building activity at the office. Engaging socially with colleagues has been proven to eliminate or reduce stress.
Fumiko Suzuki	[10:56 A.M.]	Those are great suggestions. I'll bring them up with the board of directors and push for reforms. I know other offices offer similar perks and amenities, too.
Hendrick Schulz	[10:58 A.M.]	Yes, but it's not about copying other companies. Those things actually help retain and attract highly skilled talent. These days, it's important to maintain a mutually beneficial relationship between employees and employers.
Fumiko Suzuki	[10:59 A.M.]	We also had a budget surplus last quarter. I recommend we invest in other improvements. For instance, we could update the cafeteria interior or add some new menu choices.
Jintao Bang	[11:01 A.M.]	I like the idea of changing the menu. That would bring about positive reactions from everyone. I can consult with an acquaintance, Stacy Hill. She used to run her own catering business. Now, she's writing a book of healthy recipes.
Fumiko Suzuki	[11:02 A.M.]	Let's all think about these ideas some more and meet tomorrow morning to discuss them further.

Send

161. What is mentioned about the survey?

(A) It revealed issues among employees.
(B) It has been delayed for a while.
(C) It suggests an overall lack of work.
(D) It is related to staff evaluations.

162. At 10:54 A.M., what does Mr. Schulz imply when he writes, "That would be beneficial"?

(A) He sees the value in purchasing new devices.
(B) He supports a contract renewal.
(C) He agrees with limiting work e-mails.
(D) He would like to request additional help.

163. What does Ms. Suzuki suggest?

(A) Applying for a government grant
(B) Using some available funds
(C) Moving an office to another building
(D) Hiring a marketing expert

164. What is true about Stacy Hill?

(A) She developed a cafeteria's menu.
(B) She no longer runs a business.
(C) She submitted a proposal.
(D) She helps businesses with work-life balance.

GO ON TO THE NEXT PAGE

Questions 165-168 refer to the following e-mail.

TO:	Harry Riley <h.riley@webmail.com>
FROM:	Brenda O'Connell <b.oconnell@secondcity.com>
SUBJECT:	Info
DATE:	June 18

Dear Mr. Riley,

Thank you for submitting your résumé to the Second City Temp Agency. I believe we have found a job that matches your skills. — [1] —.

The Ross and Donahue Law Firm is seeking an assistant to help with data entry. They posted the announcement a week ago. Essentially, you would be updating the firm's database of clients. According to your résumé, you worked with a variety of database programs, including HX2 and Organizer, throughout your time in college. — [2] —. By all indications, you have the right experience for the job.

With your permission, I will go ahead and submit your materials to the Ross and Donahue Law Firm. — [3] —. They are interviewing applicants now and will make a decision by June 28. If you are offered an interview, I would strongly suggest going on the firm's Web site and reading about their mission and what type of law they specialize in. — [4] —. Please let me know if you want me to send in your application.

Sincerely,

Brenda O'Connell

165. Why was the e-mail written?

(A) To request technical assistance
(B) To promote a new law firm
(C) To provide instructions on data entry
(D) To give notification of a potential job

166. What is stated about Mr. Riley?

(A) He has a law degree.
(B) He knows about database software.
(C) He has a large network of clients.
(D) He is currently a college student.

167. What does Ms. O'Connell recommend that Mr. Riley do?

(A) Read about a law firm online
(B) Review his knowledge of a program
(C) Practice a job interview with her
(D) Change some information in a database

168. In which of the positions marked [1], [2], [3], and [4] does the following sentence best belong?

"You also previously served as an intern at the Kelson Law Firm."

(A) [1]
(B) [2]
(C) [3]
(D) [4]

Questions 169-171 refer to the following e-mail.

To: Gelson Cable <customerservice@gelsoncable.com>
From: Candice Novak <c.novak@raymailer.com>
Date: February 13
Subject: Subscription

To Whom It May Concern,

I recently spent 50 minutes waiting on the phone to talk to one of your representatives about a problem with my cable subscription. This is not the first time this has happened, and I have had enough. I would like to cancel my subscription, effective immediately.

Over the years, I have regularly called about the quality of the signal in my building, but your representatives have ignored my complaints. Furthermore, they did not explain why some of my favorite cable channels were suddenly dropped from my subscription. When I called to find out about this, I was informed that they were only available in the Premium Package now.

After having been a loyal customer for more than a decade, I have no interest in paying for another month of service. I also strongly suggest that you start treating your subscribers differently.

Sincerely,
Candice Novak

169. What is Ms. Novak trying to do?

(A) Inquire about service upgrades
(B) Schedule a repair
(C) Cancel her cable plan
(D) Join a loyalty program

170. What can be inferred about Gelson Cable?

(A) It mailed a bill to the wrong address.
(B) It charges a fee for equipment repairs.
(C) It made changes to cable packages.
(D) It was bought by another company.

171. What advice does Ms. Novak provide?

(A) Improving customer service
(B) Offering some free merchandise
(C) Waiving an initiation fee
(D) Lengthening a contract

GO ON TO THE NEXT PAGE

Questions 172-175 refer to the following press release.

BookED CEO Opens New Chapter in Company's Story

August 26—BookED CEO Lisa Wang, who took over the role in January, has already introduced significant changes to the popular online application. The existing subscription-based model allows users to read a selection of essays, books, and other publications by authors who are not backed by large publishing houses. These independent releases are curated by BookED's team of literary experts and presented to customers as personalized recommendations.

Now, BookED is publishing its own original material. They have directly commissioned freelance journalists and novelists to create content to be released starting next month. This has been accompanied by the application's launch of a points system. BookED has engineered a system that allows customers to earn points by recommending the company's new content on social media platforms. The points may be used to access any other content provided on the application. BookED has said it will continuously develop new methods for its users to earn points.

Industry observers say the changes will grow the application's customer base. They also believe BookED may begin offering the public a chance to buy shares of stock in the company beginning next year.

172. What did Ms. Wang do in January?

(A) Signed with a literary agent
(B) Published a novel
(C) Created a business venture
(D) Assumed a new job

173. The word "backed" in paragraph 1, line 5, is closest in meaning to

(A) inspired
(B) reversed
(C) retired
(D) supported

174. What is mentioned about BookED?

(A) It has many followers on social media.
(B) It has partnered with news organizations.
(C) It produces its own content.
(D) It attracted more investors after its announcement.

175. What is suggested about the points system?

(A) It requires a preapproved bank account.
(B) It will be launched in the following year.
(C) It allows points to be shared between users.
(D) It could help generate new users.

GO ON TO THE NEXT PAGE

Questions 176-180 refer to the following e-mails.

To: Sally Hartley <sally.hartley@southgeorgiafinancial.com>
From: Raymond Moran <raymond@trebeldesigns.com>
Subject: Order #7190-1715
Date: April 1

Dear Ms. Hartley,

We are very happy that you chose Trebel Designs to create personalized marketing items for your company. Your order of 500 pens was shipped yesterday, and it should arrive within one to two business days. You may view the invoice on our Web site. As mentioned, you received a 10 percent discount for being a first-time customer.

With your order, I have also included a catalog of all the products we offer. Many of our customers have found that handing out T-shirts, hats, coffee mugs, pens, bags, or other items with a company logo on them is an effective way to market their businesses. Trebel Designs can use any logo design you send us, or we'd be happy to create a new one for you using one of our template designs. Please note that it will take us one week to create the design.

Thank you for your business, and we look forward to working with you again in the future.

Sincerely,
Raymond Moran

To: Raymond Moran <raymond@trebeldesigns.com>
From: Sally Hartley <sally.hartley@southgeorgiafinancial.com>
Subject: RE: Order #7190-1715
Date: April 2

Dear Mr. Moran,

I would like to thank you for the great customer service. We received our order this morning, and everything looks fantastic. In fact, some of us will be attending a career expo next month to recruit some new employees, so I would like to place an order for 300 more of the same item.

I'd also like you to design a logo for a training program we are planning for new staff. Could you start working on this immediately? I'd like to unveil it to our board at their next meeting. I've sent the details in a separate e-mail.

Thank you again.

Sally Hartley
Senior Marketing Director
South Georgia Financial

176. What is one purpose of the first e-mail?

(A) To announce a policy update
(B) To verify some specifications
(C) To confirm a shipment
(D) To set up a payment plan

177. What is indicated about Trebel Designs?

(A) It just opened a store.
(B) It offers discounts to new clients.
(C) It is planning to launch a Web site.
(D) It is looking to hire a graphic artist.

178. What will South Georgia Financial do in May?

(A) Participate in a job fair
(B) Transfer some employees
(C) Attend a marketing conference
(D) Hold a press conference

179. Which items does Ms. Hartley want to order more of?

(A) Hats
(B) Coffee mugs
(C) Pens
(D) Bags

180. What is true about Ms. Hartley's design?

(A) It is intended for a career expo.
(B) It will take a week to fulfill.
(C) It must be in black and white.
(D) It will include ideas from new employees.

GO ON TO THE NEXT PAGE

Questions 181-185 refer to the following information and form.

Bull Run Ski Resort Sports Shop
Equipment Rental Information

In addition to selling equipment by several manufacturers, the Bull Run Ski Resort's sports shop rents out a variety of equipment so you can enjoy your time on the ski slopes.

We have:

- Ski packages including skis, boots, and poles from $50 per day or $150 per week
- Ski jackets and pants from $30 per day or $90 per week
- Helmets for $15 per day or $45 per week*
- Goggles for $10 per day or $30 per week
- Gloves for $5 per day or $15 per week

We offer various sizes for children and adults. Sizing charts to help you determine the correct sizes based on height and weight are available at the counter. All rental bills must be settled immediately. A 15 percent discount is offered to guests staying at the Bull Run Ski Resort.

*For safety reasons, all skiers must wear a helmet while on the slopes.

Bull Run Ski Resort Sports Shop
Equipment Rental Form

Name: Marcus Carver
Address: 945 Elgin Avenue, Winnipeg, MB R3E 1B3, Canada
Phone Number: 555-9708
Date: February 15
Rental Period: 1 day

Credit Card Number: ****-****-****-3533
Billing Address: Same as above

Item	Quantity	Price per Item	Cost
Ski package	2	$50	$100
Helmet	2	$15	$30
Goggles	2	$10	$20
Gloves	2	$5	$10
Subtotal			$160
15% discount			-$24
Total due			$136

Please note: One-day rentals must be used on the day they are rented. There are no refunds for rentals.

181. What is stated about the Bull Run Ski Resort sports shop?

(A) It offers all of the top sportswear brands.
(B) It rents out compulsory safety gear.
(C) It is closed for several weeks during the year.
(D) It sells used equipment at low prices.

182. According to the information, how can people figure out what size they need?

(A) By calling an attendant
(B) By reading a pamphlet
(C) By visiting a Web site
(D) By looking at a chart

183. In the information, the word "settled" in paragraph 3, line 2, is closest in meaning to

(A) placed
(B) demanded
(C) paid
(D) established

184. What is implied about Mr. Carver's rental?

(A) The equipment is for more than one person.
(B) The total qualifies him for a membership rate.
(C) It may be extended at no extra cost.
(D) It may be refunded for a partial amount.

185. What is indicated about Mr. Carver?

(A) He will be taking classes as a beginner.
(B) He plans to practice winter sports for a week.
(C) He has recently purchased a ski jacket.
(D) He rented a room at the resort.

GO ON TO THE NEXT PAGE

Questions 186-190 refer to the following Web page, list, and e-mail.

ROSENSTEIN REAL ESTATE

Home | **About Us** | Agents | Contact

Rosenstein Real Estate is among the most trusted real estate agencies in the Chicago area. Though we can help you find properties anywhere in the city and its neighboring suburbs, we specialize in locating upscale housing in the city's north and northwestern areas.

When you use us to find a property, you not only get a thorough tour of the premises, but you also receive extensive information to help you make the best decision. We provide a complete rundown of a property's amenities and an overview of its history.

A list of all of the properties we represent is available here. Properties within Chicago are represented by real estate agents George Rosenstein and Mary Kowalski. Those in surrounding areas are represented by Karl Mitchell.

Properties represented by Rosenstein Real Estate as of January 1

Address	Price	Bedrooms	Bathrooms
980 Boston Street, Chicago, IL	$380,000	3	2
118 Michigan Street, Chicago, IL	$410,100	4	3
1001 Lipton Street, Evanston, IL	$360,500	2	2
280 Irving Street, Chicago, IL	$550,400	4	3
190 Sherman Road, Chicago, IL	$290,900	2	1

Call 555-3928 to schedule a tour. We are available from 9 A.M. to 6 P.M. on weekdays.

TO: Rosenstein Real Estate <inquiries@rosenstein.com>
FROM: Anne Dahlberg <anned98@mittermail.com>
SUBJECT: Apartment
DATE: January 3

To Whom It May Concern,

My husband and I recently accepted teaching positions at Northbrook University in Chicago. Along with our son, we plan on moving to the city next month. We've been browsing real estate listings for a while now. Ideally, we'd like an apartment that costs under $400,000, and has two bedrooms and two bathrooms. However, we're somewhat flexible with those requirements. The apartment at 190 Sherman Road is quite appealing. We like how close it is to our university. Is that apartment still available? If so, we'd love to arrange a tour of it, preferably this upcoming weekend, when my husband and I will be in the city. Please let me know.

Best,

Anne Dahlberg

186. What is true about Rosenstein Real Estate?

(A) It employs over a dozen real estate agents.
(B) It requires tenants to provide personal references.
(C) It concentrates on a particular area of Chicago.
(D) It has offices in three different cities.

187. What does Rosenstein Real Estate do to help its clients make decisions?

(A) It posts videos of properties online.
(B) It arranges meetings with owners.
(C) It provides comprehensive information.
(D) It offers professional estimates for repairs.

188. Which property is NOT represented by Mr. Rosenstein or Ms. Kowalski?

(A) 980 Boston Street
(B) 118 Michigan Street
(C) 1001 Lipton Street
(D) 280 Irving Street

189. What is indicated about Ms. Dahlberg?

(A) She just completed a university course.
(B) She is planning on moving on the weekend.
(C) She wants to sell an apartment.
(D) She currently lives outside of Chicago.

190. What can be inferred about Ms. Dahlberg's tour request?

(A) She has to rent a vehicle.
(B) The agent will be unavailable.
(C) She cannot go without the owner.
(D) The tour will take place virtually.

GO ON TO THE NEXT PAGE

Questions 191-195 refer to the following notice, letter, and report.

NOTICE

Crystal Condominiums will be inspecting all units from January 6 to 10. The facilities manager will accompany a technician from FailSafe Home Inspections as he tours the building. Each inspection will take approximately 60 minutes.

The inspection will include a check for the following:

- Insect infestation
- Plumbing problems
- Gas leaks

You will receive additional information in your mailbox to let you know when your inspection is scheduled. On the day of the inspection, you'll also receive text-message alerts notifying you when the technician enters and exits your unit.

Residents of Units 1 to 20 will receive their inspection report on January 11.
Residents of Units 21 to 40 will receive their inspection report on January 15.

Ms. Alyssa Matthews
Unit 38

Dear Ms. Matthews,

Your inspection is scheduled for January 10 at 10 A.M. The facilities manager will unlock your unit for the technician and relock the unit when the technician leaves.

We encourage you to leave your unit during the inspection to allow the technician to work freely. If it's necessary for you to be at home during your scheduled time, please notify the facilities manager as soon as possible.

Please also notify the facilities manager of any concerns you may have.

Sincerely,

The Management

Crystal Condominiums Inspection Report

Below are the results of your recent condominium unit inspection. Please review this report carefully.

Inspection date: January 10
Arrival time: 10:30 A.M.
Unit: 38
Technician: Allen Scott

Inspection Key:
A – No problems detected
B – Minor problems detected
C – Major problems detected

Items	Grade	Issue	Recommended Action
Windows	A		
Walls/Ceilings	B	Minor crack in dining room ceiling	No action needed
Alarm system	A		
Smoke detectors	B	Batteries in three devices replaced	No further action needed
Carbon monoxide detectors	A		
Plumbing	B	Minor leak in pipes beneath kitchen sink	Contact facilities manager to arrange repair
Gas	A		
Electricity	A		
Insects	B	Several ants in dining room	Contact facilities manager to arrange for exterminator

Comments: Unit 38 is in good shape overall. However, the resident should reach out to the facilities manager to arrange for repair of a leaking pipe in the kitchen. Unit 38 should also receive extermination services to prevent future insect problems.

191. For whom is the notice most likely intended?

(A) The FailSafe technician
(B) The Crystal Condominiums manager
(C) Crystal Condominiums residents
(D) Building maintenance workers

192. What information can be found in the letter?

(A) The date of an inspection
(B) The name of a technician
(C) The details of a problem
(D) The location of an office

193. When did Ms. Matthews most likely receive her inspection report?

(A) January 6
(B) January 10
(C) January 11
(D) January 15

194. What is suggested about Mr. Scott?

(A) He arrived late for his appointment.
(B) He performed simple plumbing repairs.
(C) He left the apartment before 11 A.M.
(D) He was informed about some problems in advance.

195. According to the report, which item requires further action?

(A) The windows
(B) The walls
(C) The alarm system
(D) The plumbing

GO ON TO THE NEXT PAGE

Questions 196-200 refer to the following flyer, schedule, and e-mail.

Writers' Workshops
November 17
Kilwin City Library

Have you always dreamed of publishing your own novel or poetry collection?
Are you curious to learn if you have what it takes to become a writer?
It's time to make this dream a reality!

Join us for our writers' workshop series,
sponsored by the Southern Ohio Writers' Guild.

Workshops are hosted at the Kilwin City Library. Light refreshments will be provided, courtesy of Blueberry Bakery and Café. All workshops presented by the Southern Ohio Writers' Guild are available at no cost to participants. However, space is limited, so sign up today!

Ask one of our librarians for more information or contact Lola Nicholson at the Southern Ohio Writers' Guild at lnicholson@sowg.org.

Kilwin City Library Writers' Workshop Schedule

Workshop Title	Dates	Times	Location
The Great American Novel	Dec 1 to Feb 13	Mondays, 6 to 8 P.M.	Conference Room A
Simplifying Sonnets	Dec 18 to Feb 13	Thursdays, 1 to 2 P.M.	Conference Room A
English Poetry	Dec 19 to Feb 14	Fridays, 3 to 4 P.M.	Main Lecture Hall
Teen Essay Writing	Dec 20 to Feb 15	Saturdays, 3 to 4 P.M.	Children's Room

Writers' workshops rely upon regular attendance. Attendees who miss more than two workshops without prior notice may be dropped from the register.

If you are interested in a more casual environment, the Southern Ohio Writers' Guild hosts a weekly coffee hour for writers on Wednesdays from 4 to 5 P.M. at the Blueberry Café and Bakery. No preregistration is required, and all walk-ins are welcome!

To: Barbara Espinoza <barbespin@capomail.com>
From: Lola Nicholson <lnicholson@sowg.org>
Date: November 27
Subject: Re: Workshop

Hi, Barbara! I have enrolled you in your requested workshop. The first session is scheduled for December 18 at 1 P.M. However, please arrive at least 10 minutes early to receive your workshop materials. Your workshop will be held in the same location at the Kilwin City Library as the literacy workshop you attended last summer.

Laptop computers are not needed for the workshop, but participants are welcome to bring one. If you are willing to have your work reviewed, we encourage you to bring some samples as well, but please limit these to a few short selections.

Please let me know if you have any other questions!

Sincerely,
Lola Nicholson
Outreach Coordinator
Southern Ohio Writers' Guild

196. According to the schedule, what is indicated about the Southern Ohio Writers' Guild weekly coffee hour?

(A) Individuals who want to attend must reserve seats in advance.
(B) Writers are not required to attend each session.
(C) Guests are not permitted to visit these meetings.
(D) Students can receive complimentary coffee or tea.

197. What is the purpose of the e-mail?

(A) To confirm an enrollment
(B) To announce new expenses
(C) To report a change of schedule
(D) To introduce a speaker

198. What is suggested about the Kilwin City Library?

(A) It rents out laptop computers.
(B) It was the former workplace of Ms. Nicholson.
(C) It owns a collection of works by local authors.
(D) It held a free event in the past.

199. What workshop has Ms. Espinoza enrolled in?

(A) The Great American Novel
(B) Simplifying Sonnets
(C) English Poetry
(D) Teen Essay Writing

200. According to the e-mail, what are workshop participants encouraged to do?

(A) Join a separate seminar
(B) Download some information
(C) Leave a detailed review
(D) Bring examples of personal work

This is the end of the test. You may review Parts 5, 6, and 7 if you finish the test early.

정답 p.326 / 점수 환산표 p.329 / 해석 p.330 / Part 5&6 무료 해설 바로 보기(정답 및 정답 음성 포함)

* 다음 페이지에 있는 Self 체크 리스트를 통해 자신의 문제 풀이 방식과 태도를 점검해 보세요.

Self 체크 리스트

TEST 01은 무사히 잘 마치셨죠?
이제 다음의 Self 체크 리스트를 통해 자신의 테스트 진행 내용을 점검해 볼까요?

1. 나는 75분 동안 완전히 테스트에 집중하였다.

   □ 예 □ 아니오

   아니오에 답한 경우, 이유는 무엇인가요?

2. 나는 75분 동안 100문제를 모두 풀었다.

   □ 예 □ 아니오

   아니오에 답한 경우, 이유는 무엇인가요?

3. 나는 75분 동안 답안지 표시까지 완료하였다.

   □ 예 □ 아니오

   아니오에 답한 경우, 이유는 무엇인가요?

4. 나는 Part 5와 Part 6를 19분 안에 모두 풀었다.

   □ 예 □ 아니오

   아니오에 답한 경우, 이유는 무엇인가요?

5. Part 7을 풀 때 5분 이상 걸린 지문이 없었다.

   □ 예 □ 아니오

6. 개선해야 할 점 또는 나를 위한 충고를 적어보세요.

* 교재의 첫 장으로 돌아가서 자신이 적은 목표 점수를 확인하면서 목표에 대한 의지를 다지기 바랍니다. 개선해야 할 점은 반드시 다음 테스트에 실천해야 합니다. 그것이 가장 중요하며, 그래야만 발전할 수 있습니다.

TEST 02

PART 5

PART 6

PART 7

Self 체크 리스트

잠깐! 테스트 전 확인사항

1. 휴대 전화의 전원을 끄셨나요? □ 예
2. Answer Sheet, 연필, 지우개를 준비하셨나요? □ 예
3. 시계를 준비하셨나요? □ 예

모든 준비가 완료되었으면 목표 점수를 떠올린 후 테스트를 시작합니다.

문제 풀이를 마치는 시간은 지금부터 75분 후인 __시 __분입니다.

테스트 시간은 총 75분이며, 시험 종료 전 2~3분은 정답 검토 및 답안지 마킹을 위해 사용합니다.

READING TEST

In this section, you must demonstrate your ability to read and comprehend English. You will be given a variety of texts and asked to answer questions about these texts. This section is divided into three parts and will take 75 minutes to complete.

Do not mark the answers in your test book. Use the answer sheet that is separately provided.

PART 5

Directions: In each question, you will be asked to review a statement that is missing a word or phrase. Four answer choices will be provided for each statement. Select the best answer and mark the corresponding letter (A), (B), (C), or (D) on the answer sheet.

PART 5 권장 풀이 시간 11분

101. The interns will work ------- the direction of the research department manager.

(A) beyond
(B) among
(C) under
(D) beside

102. The historic house on Ambrose Road has changed ------- since it was built 150 years ago.

(A) considered
(B) considerably
(C) considerable
(D) considering

103. The directors of PenTex are meeting with executives from DRW Corporation, which ------- have talked about merging with.

(A) them
(B) themselves
(C) their
(D) they

104. Tenants who wish to end their lease should ------- the proprietor a minimum of 30 days before moving out.

(A) notify
(B) notified
(C) notifying
(D) notifies

105. Sylvia Lyman graduated at the top of her class and was immediately hired by a ------- law firm.

(A) practical
(B) prestigious
(C) deliberate
(D) supplemental

106. Comparing samples can help customers ------- the perfect tiles for their bathroom walls and floors.

(A) select
(B) complete
(C) harm
(D) reveal

107. Hotel managers communicate ------- with their staff to ensure operations are running in a smooth manner.

(A) regular
(B) regularity
(C) regulars
(D) regularly

108. Arrow Publicity produced a campaign that is designed to ------- audiences between the ages of 18 and 25.

(A) appeal to
(B) approve of
(C) point out
(D) result from

109. The company will provide training to new recruits, so neither experience ------- a degree is required.

(A) and
(B) but
(C) nor
(D) or

110. Meta Rail passengers are entitled to full ticket refunds ------- their train is canceled or delayed.

(A) along with
(B) except for
(C) as though
(D) provided that

111. Analysts have predicted that the price of oil ------- by approximately 30 percent in the coming year.

(A) increase
(B) will increase
(C) were increased
(D) have increased

112. Employees will now be offered the ------- of working from home for up to half of their weekly hours.

(A) benefit
(B) benefited
(C) beneficial
(D) benefiting

113. Knoll Consulting tries to hire staff ------- personal values match the company's.

(A) whom
(B) which
(C) whose
(D) who

114. Unlike ------- mobile phones, Tektone's innovative TX-81 can be repaired with parts produced by other companies.

(A) habitual
(B) defective
(C) appropriate
(D) conventional

115. Colora house paints are 50 percent more ------- to weather damage than similar products on the market.

(A) resist
(B) resists
(C) resistant
(D) resistance

116. Some of the new office furniture is ------- sized and does not fit in the intended office space.

(A) silently
(B) awkwardly
(C) solidly
(D) sharply

117. Housing costs in New York are far higher than ------- in its neighboring state, New Jersey.

(A) anyone
(B) other
(C) that
(D) those

118. The Martinsburg Fine Arts Museum is ------- known for its collection of classical paintings.

(A) widely
(B) wide
(C) wider
(D) widen

119. Making surveys anonymous is a good way to get honest ------- from consumers.

(A) opinions
(B) clues
(C) chances
(D) decisions

120. Having made a reservation, Mr. Quinn and his colleagues were seated immediately ------- arriving at the restaurant.

(A) up
(B) in
(C) upon
(D) to

GO ON TO THE NEXT PAGE

121. The contract can be legally ------- if one party fails to satisfy the terms of the agreement.

(A) terminated
(B) recovered
(C) designated
(D) disconnected

122. During her first year as editor-in-chief, Ms. Reed expanded *The National Gazette*'s ------- to over 250,000.

(A) read
(B) readers
(C) reading
(D) readership

123. To conserve paper, Florence Media Productions has placed ------- on the number of photocopies employees can make each day.

(A) limit
(B) limitless
(C) limitations
(D) limited

124. People who are ------- to wear eyeglasses when driving can be penalized for not doing so.

(A) obligate
(B) obligation
(C) obligated
(D) obligating

125. The e-mail sent by Mr. Duchene at Laudner Holdings is ------- Ms. Coleman was waiting for.

(A) who
(B) what
(C) how
(D) when

126. Residents anticipate that the ------- construction project for a new city library will begin in a month.

(A) proposal
(B) proposed
(C) proposing
(D) propose

127. Dr. Andrea Griffin received the Scientific Achievements Award for her ------- of a new South American butterfly species.

(A) translation
(B) acceptance
(C) dedication
(D) identification

128. Ms. Kowalski's marketing staff ------- worked all night to prepare the presentation material.

(A) currently
(B) especially
(C) diligently
(D) entirely

129. ------- a workplace injury, Mr. Galvert was provided with three months of paid leave.

(A) On behalf of
(B) In compensation for
(C) To the extent of
(D) In preference to

130. Sales records for Forest Fleece Jackets showed an ------- after a harsh winter was forecast.

(A) improvement
(B) attraction
(C) occupation
(D) absence

PART 6

Directions: In this part, you will be asked to read four English texts. Each text is missing a word, phrase, or sentence. Select the answer choice that correctly completes the text and mark the corresponding letter (A), (B), (C), or (D) on the answer sheet.

PART 6 권장 풀이 시간 8분

Questions 131-134 refer to the following article.

A ribbon-cutting ceremony for the Palm Lane Youth Center took place in downtown Jalisco yesterday evening. The center is the ------- **131.** building of the city's four planned facilities for people aged 8 to 18. Three more will be built over the coming years, fulfilling the mayor's campaign promise to provide recreational and educational opportunities to the city's children and teenagers.

Overall, the ceremony went ------- **132.** well. Important members of the community came in large numbers to show their support. ------- **133.**. The mayor thanked everyone for their contributions to the center and ------- **134.** a group of local children onto the stage to help him when it came time to cut the ribbon.

131. (A) first
(B) tallest
(C) last
(D) finest

132. (A) enough
(B) rather
(C) so far
(D) right

133. (A) It is nearly impossible to get a ticket.
(B) Many shared happy memories of the center.
(C) More funds will need to be raised soon.
(D) Several celebrities were present, too.

134. (A) invites
(B) inviting
(C) invited
(D) will invite

GO ON TO THE NEXT PAGE

Questions 135-138 refer to the following letter.

Vince Johnson
4897 Buford Street
Atlanta, GA 30329

Dear Mr. Johnson,

Welcome to Skyspan Airlines' loyalty program, Skyspan Rewards. As a member, you will be ------- (**135.**) points every time you fly with us.

Once you have collected over 50,000 points, you will be entitled to a free round-trip domestic ticket on Skyspan Airlines. If you accumulate over 100,000 points, you will qualify for the ------- (**136.**) benefits of our platinum-level membership. These include the full use of our special luxury Platinum Lounge, which is only accessible to our highest-ranking card carriers.

Your membership card has been included with this letter, along with a temporary access code for your online account. ------- (**137.**). You can learn more about ------- (**138.**) points and how to keep track of them on the Web site.

Respectfully,

Karen Lawson
Membership Coordinator

135. (A) praised
(B) admired
(C) elevated
(D) awarded

136. (A) necessary
(B) residual
(C) exclusive
(D) mutual

137. (A) Your subscription will be renewed in a few weeks.
(B) Skyspan Airlines flies to many exciting destinations.
(C) The Internet makes booking hotels more convenient.
(D) Please use it to log in and then change your password.

138. (A) acquire
(B) acquisition
(C) acquiring
(D) to acquire

Questions 139-142 refer to the following announcement.

Valentine Fragrances is very happy to announce that our boutique in Verona is officially opening on March 2 at 10:00 A.M. We'd like to thank our loyal customers for keeping our online store ------- **139.** business for these last two years. -------. **140.** A grand opening event ------- **141.** at the boutique, which is located at 623 Main Street. All are welcome to stop by and try some samples, watch a demonstration on the process of making fragrances, and meet the founder, Ms. Carly Brown. Additionally, Valentine Fragrances requires three sales associates for various shifts. ------- **142.** will be accepted until February 22.

139. (A) below
(B) out of
(C) in
(D) over

140. (A) We have decided to extend our hours for the holidays.
(B) Moreover, new perfumes are being developed and tested.
(C) Your support has allowed us to finally have a physical store.
(D) A customer service training session will be organized shortly.

141. (A) will be held
(B) was held
(C) has been held
(D) to be held

142. (A) Proposals
(B) Coupons
(C) Applications
(D) Checks

GO ON TO THE NEXT PAGE

Questions 143-146 refer to the following Web page.

www.shanemcgovernaccounting.com

Struggling to create and maintain accurate records is more common among entrepreneurs than you might think. -------, hiring an experienced accountant like Shane McGovern can help **143.** you understand the basics of accounting and prevent costly mistakes from being made. Mr. McGovern has ------- countless business owners in filing tax forms, maintaining records, **144.** and managing finances. He ------- offers customized organization systems. This service in **145.** particular has been appreciated by many prominent business owners. Check out feedback from previous customers here: Testimonials.

Still not sure if Shane McGovern Accounting can help you with your business? -------. **146.**

143. (A) Specifically
(B) However
(C) In fact
(D) Otherwise

144. (A) assists
(B) assist
(C) assisting
(D) assisted

145. (A) barely
(B) also
(C) never
(D) only

146. (A) Thank you for submitting an inquiry.
(B) Your business is greatly appreciated.
(C) Call today to schedule a free consultation.
(D) Make sure to balance your account promptly.

PART 7

Directions: In this part, you will be asked to read several texts, such as advertisements, articles, instant messages, or examples of business correspondence. Each text is followed by several questions. Select the best answer and mark the corresponding letter (A), (B), (C), or (D) on your answer sheet.

PART 7 권장 풀이 시간 **54분**

Questions 147-148 refer to the following Web page.

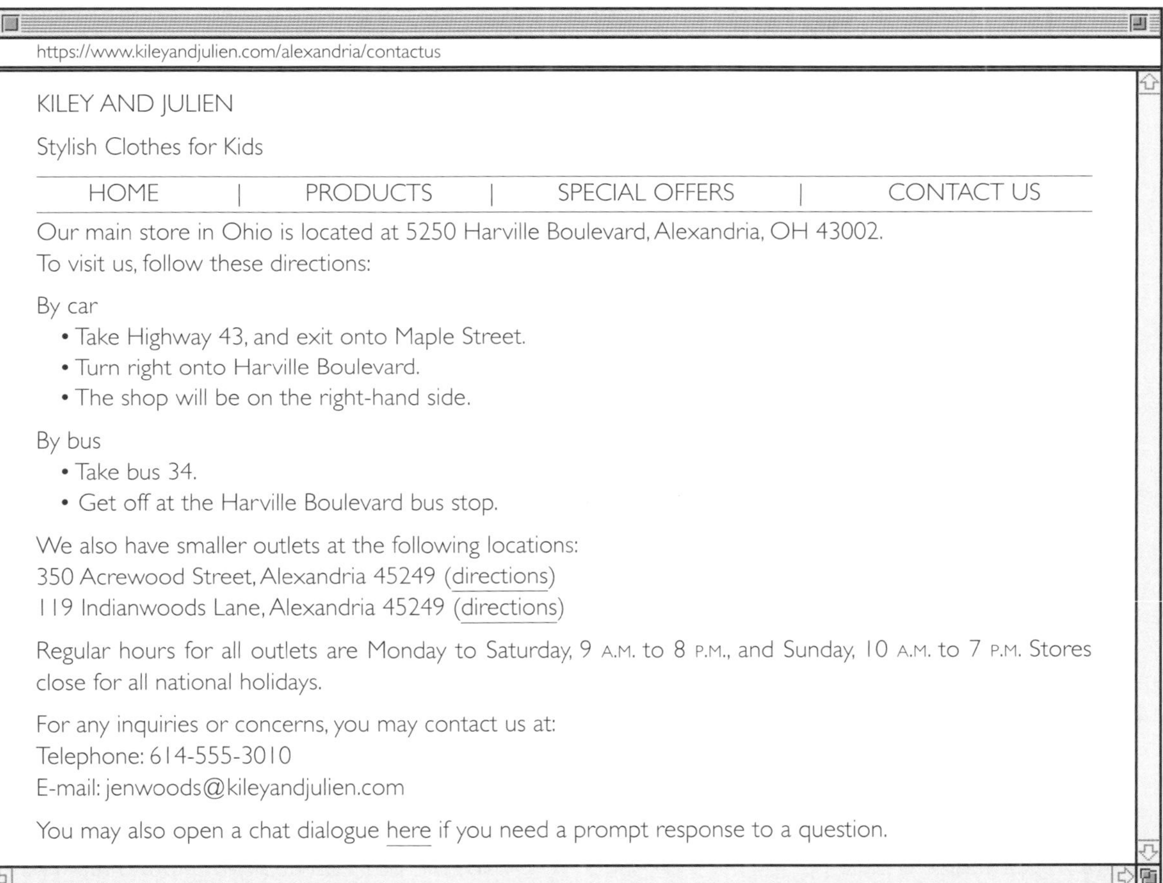

https://www.kileyandjulien.com/alexandria/contactus

KILEY AND JULIEN

Stylish Clothes for Kids

HOME | PRODUCTS | SPECIAL OFFERS | CONTACT US

Our main store in Ohio is located at 5250 Harville Boulevard, Alexandria, OH 43002.
To visit us, follow these directions:

By car
- Take Highway 43, and exit onto Maple Street.
- Turn right onto Harville Boulevard.
- The shop will be on the right-hand side.

By bus
- Take bus 34.
- Get off at the Harville Boulevard bus stop.

We also have smaller outlets at the following locations:
350 Acrewood Street, Alexandria 45249 (directions)
119 Indianwoods Lane, Alexandria 45249 (directions)

Regular hours for all outlets are Monday to Saturday, 9 A.M. to 8 P.M., and Sunday, 10 A.M. to 7 P.M. Stores close for all national holidays.

For any inquiries or concerns, you may contact us at:
Telephone: 614-555-3010
E-mail: jenwoods@kileyandjulien.com

You may also open a chat dialogue here if you need a prompt response to a question.

147. What is NOT true about Kiley and Julien?
(A) It has branches in Alexandria.
(B) Its main store is accessible by public transport.
(C) It closes earlier than usual on Sundays.
(D) It holds special sales on holidays.

148. What can a customer do to get a fast response?
(A) Write an e-mail
(B) Enter a code
(C) Start an online discussion
(D) Call a number

GO ON TO THE NEXT PAGE

Questions 149-150 refer to the following text-message chain.

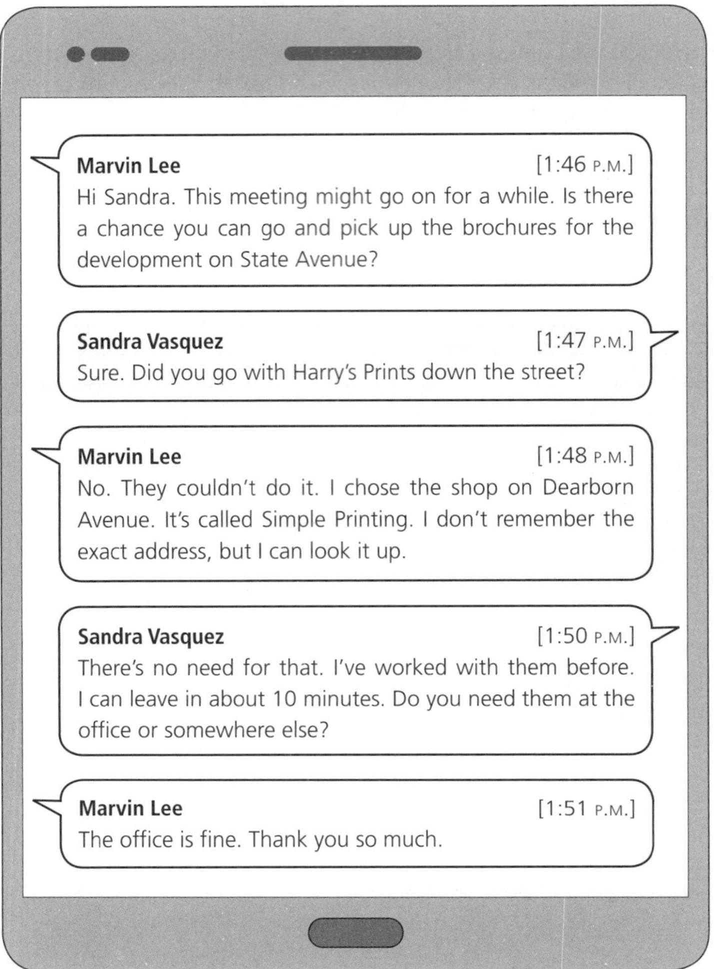

Marvin Lee [1:46 P.M.]
Hi Sandra. This meeting might go on for a while. Is there a chance you can go and pick up the brochures for the development on State Avenue?

Sandra Vasquez [1:47 P.M.]
Sure. Did you go with Harry's Prints down the street?

Marvin Lee [1:48 P.M.]
No. They couldn't do it. I chose the shop on Dearborn Avenue. It's called Simple Printing. I don't remember the exact address, but I can look it up.

Sandra Vasquez [1:50 P.M.]
There's no need for that. I've worked with them before. I can leave in about 10 minutes. Do you need them at the office or somewhere else?

Marvin Lee [1:51 P.M.]
The office is fine. Thank you so much.

149. Why does Mr. Lee contact Ms. Vasquez?

(A) To report a technical issue
(B) To give an update on a meeting
(C) To get a recommendation
(D) To organize a pickup

150. At 1:50 P.M., what does Ms. Vasquez mean when she writes, "There's no need for that"?

(A) Some prints can be left on a desk.
(B) Mr. Lee can easily postpone his next meeting.
(C) Some extra material does not have to be collected.
(D) Mr. Lee does not have to look up information.

Questions 151-152 refer to the following article.

Snow Tourism Skyrockets!

By Pete Jenkins

February 28—According to research conducted by the Boulder Tourism Bureau, more people visited the city and surrounding ski lodges this past December and January than in any winter in the past five decades. More tourists mean that the area's economy experienced an unexpected boost. Of course, local business owners could not have been happier about their additional profits.

Well-known local meteorologist Laura Nowak forecast that the area would have several weeks of light, powdery snow in zero degree weather. She referred to "perfect snow conditions" for skiers, and her prediction helped attract tourists to the Boulder area in record-breaking numbers this season. Nowak also expects similar conditions for next winter, and possibly for winters after that. This is welcome news for hotels and ski resorts in the region. Bookings are already filling up for next year, and most local businesses are hopeful that the tourism boom will continue.

151. What does the article indicate about local business owners?

(A) They are seeking ways to draw tourists year-round.
(B) Their profits have increased.
(C) They are pleased with Boulder's economic plan.
(D) They are expanding lodges and ski resorts.

152. What is stated about Ms. Nowak?

(A) She influenced people's travel plans.
(B) She works as a tourism agent.
(C) She engages in winter sports.
(D) She moved to Boulder in December.

GO ON TO THE NEXT PAGE

Questions 153-155 refer to the following announcement.

To all subscribers of Excellent Publications:

— [1] —. For over 50 years, readers subscribed to *The World Today*, our monthly print magazine, for articles about global events. However, it was discontinued and, instead, readers had access to the first online version of the magazine, which we renamed *The Thinker*, soon after the last print issue was released. — [2] —.

It has been one year since that change, and Excellent Publications has continued to offer subscribers the same outstanding articles as before, only exclusively on the Internet. — [3] —. Though the new electronic news magazine is continuing to grow in popularity, some readers are still requesting that the traditional printed version be brought back. So, we have decided to put out an annual print edition of *The Thinker*, beginning this year. The print issue will include our most popular articles from the previous 12 months. — [4] —. It will be delivered to all digital subscribers' homes as a bonus at the end of the year. For any questions regarding the annual print issue, please visit www.thethinker.com/bonusprint.

153. What is mentioned about Excellent Publications?

(A) It recently celebrated the anniversary of its founding.
(B) It will continue to sell old issues at a discount.
(C) It was sold to a new owner 50 years ago.
(D) It switched over to a new medium last year.

154. What is suggested about the print issue of *The Thinker*?

(A) It will feature content contributed by readers.
(B) It will be sold at newsstands across the country.
(C) It will include translations for overseas readers.
(D) It will contain articles that were published online.

155. In which of the positions marked [1], [2], [3], and [4] does the following sentence best belong?

"In this short time, *The Thinker*'s readership has more than doubled."

(A) [1]
(B) [2]
(C) [3]
(D) [4]

Questions 156-157 refer to the following e-mail.

To: All Staff
From: Carl Eklund
Subject: Conference
Date: July 1

Hello, everyone.

I just wanted to provide you all with an update on the 11th annual Bird Conservation Conference, which will take place this year from August 7 to 9 in Montreal. We usually choose one representative at random to attend the conference. However, this year I'm looking for a volunteer because the person who attends will have more responsibilities than usual. I'll be at the research center in Antarctica at the time, so I'm unable to volunteer myself.

The head of the conference, Georgia Proctor, reached out to me asking if someone from our institute could give a presentation this year. She was particularly interested in our findings about penguin migration patterns in Antarctica. So, the volunteer will have to present on this subject.

If you are interested in this opportunity, please let me know as soon as possible.

Sincerely,
Carl Eklund
Lead Researcher
Wildlife Research Institute

156. What is the purpose of the e-mail?
(A) To update scientists on some new discoveries
(B) To request a volunteer for a presentation
(C) To assign responsibilities to a new department
(D) To announce an upcoming charity event

157. What is suggested about the Wildlife Research Institute?
(A) It was originally established to research bird migration.
(B) It will send all its employees to an academic conference.
(C) It is waiting for permission to conduct a project in Antarctica.
(D) It has taken part in the Bird Conservation Conference before.

GO ON TO THE NEXT PAGE

Questions 158-160 refer to the following notice.

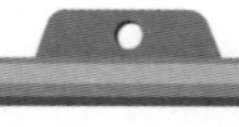

Notice

Thank you for coming today. We organised today's activity to choose 20 dancers for Hannah Levi's upcoming concert tour. Some adjustments have been made due to the overwhelming response to our advertisement.

We will no longer hold individual sessions with each dancer. Instead, we will see groups of six at a time. When you step into the audition room, please put your résumé and photograph on the judge's desk. All six dancers will then perform a dance to one of Ms. Levi's songs together.

You will be notified if you are chosen to advance to the next round. If selected, please stay in the vicinity. In the second round, dancers will work with our lead choreographer. Afterward, the remaining candidates will undergo one more round in the evening before the final announcement is made. Good luck!

158. What is the notice mainly about?

(A) The course of a selection process
(B) The requirements for renting a venue
(C) The details of a touring contract
(D) The reasons for a concert delay

159. The word "advance" in paragraph 3, line 1, is closest in meaning to

(A) bring
(B) promote
(C) introduce
(D) proceed

160. What is suggested about the final announcement?

(A) It will depend on a group's size.
(B) It will be posted on a Web site.
(C) It will be made by Hannah Levi.
(D) It will take place after a third round.

Questions 161-164 refer to the following advertisement.

Reliance 7 to Be Released!

Productivity on the go is essential in today's world. We made the Reliance 7 tablet so thin and light that you can take it anywhere!

Our tablet has a sleek design and all the tools you need at your fingertips. You'll love the rich colors and clear images on the high-resolution screen. Also, this new tablet comes with a uniquely designed stylus.

To stand out from the competition, Reliance has partnered with the bag designer Top Crafter. This brand has created a fashionable pouch for the Reliance 7 that will be sold for just $30. This is a limited edition item—only 1,000 pieces have been made, each one stamped with a serial number.

The Reliance 7 will be available at retail outlets starting January 12, but eager customers can preorder them on our Web site, www.reliance.com. Reserve yours on our site today!

161. What is mentioned about the Reliance 7?

(A) It is larger than previous models.
(B) It has a high level of visual quality.
(C) It has a unique shape.
(D) It is ideal for office tasks.

162. What is indicated about Top Crafter?

(A) It is experiencing increased competition.
(B) It lowered the prices of its products.
(C) It partnered with another business.
(D) It sells bags that are handmade.

163. What is NOT stated about the pouch?

(A) It will be stocked at various stores.
(B) It cannot be purchased after an initial set runs out.
(C) It was designed specifically to hold a mobile device.
(D) It was uniquely marked during manufacturing.

164. According to the advertisement, what are customers encouraged to do on the Web site?

(A) Provide some feedback
(B) Order some device accessories
(C) Reserve an item
(D) Download an application

GO ON TO THE NEXT PAGE

Questions 165-167 refer to the following letter.

January 6

Debonair Publishing
1800 Dundee Street
Toronto, ON
M6J 1X7

To Whom It May Concern:

I have been a big fan of Brian Warburton's work for a long time now, and his books have been a real inspiration to me over the years. I just finished writing a novel of my own, and I would very much like to quote two lines from *The Returning*, the third and final book of his Lost Sanctuary series. These lines have always had deep meaning for me. Because of that, I'd like the quotation to appear at the beginning of my novel, after the title and dedication pages.

I am not entirely sure how to get permission to use the quotation. I checked my copy of Mr. Warburton's book and saw that your company was the copyright owner the year it was printed. If you still own the rights, could you let me know if I may use the quotation? If so, please inform me of how to proceed and how much I can expect to pay. If your company no longer owns the rights, can you please provide me with the e-mail address or phone number of the person or company who does?

Thank you, and I look forward to your response.

Chester M. Gleason

165. What is implied about Mr. Warburton?

(A) He transferred his copyright to a family member.
(B) He will be acknowledged on a dedication page.
(C) He began writing three decades ago.
(D) He wrote a set of three books.

166. What does Mr. Gleason say he is uncertain about?

(A) Where a first edition was published
(B) Whether he will have to pay a penalty
(C) How to obtain approval for a request
(D) Who will be editing a novel

167. What information does Mr. Gleason ask Debonair Publishing to provide?

(A) The location of a bookstore
(B) A printing cost estimate
(C) A postal address
(D) The amount of a fee

Questions 168-171 refer to the following article.

Restoration Efforts Begin

By Mary Harding

Roughly 50 years ago, the city of Western Point constructed an elaborate memorial park to remember one of its early residents, Lester Muller. Mr. Muller was a wealthy industrialist who opened the first factories here. — [1] —. The park, with its famous clock tower, has become a popular destination for visitors, bringing in over 20,000 people annually.

Over the years, however, the park has suffered from maintenance issues. — [2] —. The clock in the tower no longer works, and the building's interior paint has faded. Consequently, the committee that oversees the park's operations has decided to close the tower for a two-month restoration. It has hired a team of experts from HC Architects. The team includes Sam Hunt, who has worked on similar restoration projects such as the Rosenberg Monument in Washington, DC. — [3] —. Over the next two months, he will supervise the necessary repairs.

During this time, the adjacent sculpture garden and other sections of the park will remain freely accessible to the public. — [4] —. Opening hours are from Tuesday to Sunday, 8 a.m. to 7 p.m. The clock tower's repairs should be completed by October 1.

168. According to the article, what did Mr. Muller do?

(A) Founded some plants
(B) Wrote a famous poem
(C) Served as a mayor
(D) Constructed a clock tower

169. What is mentioned about Mr. Hunt?

(A) He is the director of a memorial park.
(B) He helped repair other sites.
(C) He pioneered a new restoration technique.
(D) He is an employee at the Rosenberg Monument.

170. What is true about the sculpture garden?

(A) It is situated across from the park entrance.
(B) It will be closed for two months.
(C) It is only open for part of the year.
(D) It offers access to all visitors.

171. In which of the positions marked [1], [2], [3], and [4] does the following sentence best belong?

"He is among the top professionals in the field."

(A) [1]
(B) [2]
(C) [3]
(D) [4]

GO ON TO THE NEXT PAGE

Questions 172-175 refer to the following online chat session.

Andrew Marks	[5:09 P.M.]	So, following up on our meeting, I think Ms. Foster from GDE Motors is ready to conclude negotiations. She wants to meet with Mr. Mueller next week to work out the terms of a contract.
Robert Crane	[5:11 P.M.]	Won't Mr. Mueller be on a business trip to New Zealand next week?
Allison West	[5:12 P.M.]	Right. He won't be here next week. Why don't we schedule an appointment for Ms. Foster with Deanna Lane?
Andrew Marks	[5:13 P.M.]	She already has a very heavy workload. I don't think she has time for the appointment.
Robert Crane	[5:15 P.M.]	Could we ask Mr. Mueller to do a videoconference from New Zealand?
Allison West	[5:16 P.M.]	That could work. And I don't think the client would mind doing that.
Andrew Marks	[5:18 P.M.]	I'll go talk with Mr. Mueller right now and find out if he'd be willing to do that. If so, you can arrange a date and time with Ms. Foster, Allison.
Allison West	[5:19 P.M.]	No problem. I'll wait until I hear from you.

Send

172. What does Ms. Foster want to do?

(A) Reschedule an executive meeting
(B) Finalize an agreement
(C) Renew a contract
(D) Book a business trip

173. What does Ms. West recommend?

(A) Sending Mr. Mueller on a business trip
(B) Booking a facility for an appointment
(C) Buying some new equipment
(D) Having Ms. Lane meet with a client

174. At 5:16 P.M., what does Ms. West mean when she writes, "That could work"?

(A) She thinks a client will agree to contract terms.
(B) She believes a videoconference may solve a problem.
(C) She agrees that Ms. Lane can take some time off.
(D) She wants Mr. Mueller to postpone a trip.

175. What will Mr. Marks do next?

(A) Prepare a meeting agenda
(B) Send an e-mail to a client
(C) Speak with a colleague
(D) Change a reservation

GO ON TO THE NEXT PAGE

Questions 176-180 refer to the following product review and advertisement.

www.reviews.com/refrigerators00071

ColdPro 2000 by Kitchen-Max

Reviewed by Roger Ling on January 5

The ColdPro 2000 refrigerator is top-notch, like all of Kitchen-Max's appliances. In the second version of the ColdPro, the company has kept the same stainless steel, contemporary design that matches well with most kitchens. It has several extra functions, including a convenient water dispenser.

However, one major weakness of this model is the placement of the water filter. It is hidden behind a shelf, making it difficult to change. According to the user manual, the filter should be replaced every three months, which could become burdensome for owners.

Overall, this is a great refrigerator, though it is relatively expensive. But Kitchen-Max announced at a press conference in December that it will introduce the next model in its refrigerator line this coming February. I'd suggest holding off until then, as the price of the ColdPro 2000 is expected to be lowered at that time.

The Future of Appliances: Kitchen-Max's ColdPro 3000 Refrigerator!

Kitchen-Max is proud to introduce its newest state-of-the-art refrigerator, the ColdPro 3000. The appliance has all the useful functions of our previous model, the ColdPro 2000, and also includes an ice-making feature and temperature-controlled storage drawers for produce.

Find out more about this innovative appliance by visiting www.kitchenmax.com/refrigerators. The ColdPro 3000 will be available starting February 25 at a retailer near you! Find a list of locations where Kitchen-Max products are sold by visiting our Web site.

176. What is suggested about Kitchen-Max?

(A) It only sells refrigerators.
(B) It is merging with another manufacturer.
(C) It produces high quality appliances.
(D) It held a press conference in February.

177. According to the product review, what is a feature of the ColdPro 2000?

(A) It comes in various colors.
(B) It has a modern look.
(C) It is relatively lightweight.
(D) It has customizable settings.

178. What does Mr. Ling recommend?

(A) Attending a promotional event
(B) Looking at different brands
(C) Waiting until next month
(D) Contacting a manufacturer

179. What do the ColdPro 2000 and ColdPro 3000 have in common?

(A) They have permanent water filters.
(B) They contain a water dispenser.
(C) They include an ice-making function.
(D) They feature temperature-controlled drawers.

180. What will happen on February 25?

(A) A company will announce a new branch location.
(B) Some vouchers will be distributed by a retailer.
(C) A recall will be issued for a refrigerator model.
(D) Customers will be able to purchase a new appliance model.

GO ON TO THE NEXT PAGE

Questions 181-185 refer to the following letter and memo.

Allen Realty

www.allenrealty.com

March 5

Michelle Simon
Simon Digital Consulting
5883 Dunn Road
Mableton, GA 30126

Dear Ms. Simon,

Congratulations! The owner of the North Avenue office space—the only one in Atlanta that fully met your needs—has accepted your offer. Please review the proposed contract enclosed with this letter. It has been modified to include the new terms you requested. Rent has been lowered by $220 a month, conditional on your agreement to occupy the space for three years beginning April 1. Additionally, the owner will check the floor tiles and fix anything necessary before then. However, you will need to arrange the air cooling system on your own.

If you are satisfied, send a signed copy of the contract back to me. Otherwise, we can discuss matters further.

Sincerely,
Damien Horowitz
Property Consultant

Enclosure: Contract

Simon Digital Consulting
MEMO

To: All staff
From: Michelle Simon
Subject: Move
Date: March 7

I have good news. Mr. Horowitz, our realtor, has helped us rent the office in Atlanta that meets all our requirements. We will be moving into our new office next month. As I said before, this change will allow us to be closer to existing clients, pursue new business opportunities, and accommodate additional staff members. I am positive that all of you will be pleased. There is a train station just five minutes away on foot and several restaurants in the area.

Most things in the new office are being taken care of by the owner, but some essential appliances are not provided. So, before the sales team's equipment and office furniture are moved into the new space on April 2, we will have those appliances set up on April 1. The sales staff will begin working in the new space on April 3. The administration and accounting teams will begin doing so on April 15. The production team will be last since their editing equipment cannot be installed until May 1. So, their move will take place on May 2.

181. What is the main purpose of the letter?

(A) To request changes to a contract
(B) To confirm the date of an appointment
(C) To present a revised agreement
(D) To welcome a newly hired executive

182. What is suggested about the office on North Avenue?

(A) It is located near a transportation stop.
(B) It has restaurants on the ground floor.
(C) It was constructed in the past month.
(D) It has been fully furnished by the owner.

183. In the memo, the word "positive" in paragraph 1, line 4, is closest in meaning to

(A) more than willing
(B) at full strength
(C) without doubt
(D) on good terms

184. According to the memo, how will Ms. Simon's company benefit from a move?

(A) Its employees will have more break rooms.
(B) It will be more accessible to clients.
(C) Its tax obligations will be reduced.
(D) It will be able to participate in more industry events.

185. What will probably happen on April 1?

(A) Staff from the accounting team will be transferred.
(B) Air conditioning units will be installed.
(C) Sales staff will begin working in a new office space.
(D) Furniture and equipment will be relocated.

TEST 01 02 03 04 05 06 07 08 09 10 해커스 토익 실전 1000제 1 Reading

GO ON TO THE NEXT PAGE

Questions 186-190 refer to the following e-mail, schedule, and notice.

To	Elsie McDaniel <emd333@weblively.com>
From	Wayne Sward <wsward@bluescreen.au>
Subject	Trip to Adelaide
Date	August 14
Attachment	Buxton classes

Dear Elsie,

You mentioned last week that it would be great to take a cooking class together during our trip to Adelaide in September. I've followed up on this and found a culinary school that offers half-day sessions. It's called Buxton Cooking School, and it's just around the corner from our hotel.

They have four courses we could take, but given our schedule, we'll have to take a weekday class. I know you have Joel Denton's cookbook and are a big fan of his recipes. He's teaching one of the courses, so we could actually meet him in person.

I'm attaching a schedule for you from the Buxton Cooking School. Please check it and get back to me. I'll register for a class as soon as I hear back from you.

Best regards,

Wayne

Buxton Cooking School ⇨ Class Schedule for September

	8 A.M.-11 A.M.	1 P.M.-4 P.M.	4 P.M.-7 P.M.
Tuesday		Exploring Seafood (Sheila Ryer)	Using Vegetables (Martin Ames)
Wednesday	Baking Bread (Joel Denton)		Using Vegetables (Martin Ames)
Thursday		Exploring Seafood (Sheila Ryer)	
Friday			Making Sauces (Marie Pierre)
Saturday	Exploring Seafood (Sheila Ryer)	Baking Bread (Joel Denton)	Making Sauces (Marie Pierre)
Sunday	Using Vegetables (Martin Ames)		Baking Bread (Joel Denton)

Remarks:

□ No classes are held on Mondays.
□ The minimum class size is 5; the maximum class size is 20.
□ Morning classes include a visit to Pinkston Food Market, where a talk will be given.

Attention Group Visitors to Pinkston Food Market

While Pinkston Food Market welcomes everyone—shoppers and browsers alike—some stall owners have recently complained about groups of five or more people blocking the aisles and preventing regular customers from gaining access. Thus, stall owners have asked that tour group leaders and cooking class instructors keep their groups moving from one stall to the next. Guides wishing to give short talks to their groups are kindly asked to do so in our food court. There are lots of seats and it is equipped to deal with high numbers of visitors. Also, attendees can try free samples of local specialties at the food court.

186. Why did Mr. Sward contact Ms. McDaniel?

(A) To provide an update about an activity
(B) To offer some alternative travel routes
(C) To ask about her level of cooking experience
(D) To list the benefits of moving to another city

187. When will Mr. Sward probably attend a class at Buxton Cooking School?

(A) On Tuesday
(B) On Wednesday
(C) On Thursday
(D) On Friday

188. According to the schedule, what is true about Buxton Cooking School?

(A) It hosts a special session each month.
(B) It only offers sauce making classes on weekends.
(C) It is closed one day each week.
(D) Its class about vegetables is taught by multiple instructors.

189. According to the notice, what did some stall owners request?

(A) That market aisles be widened
(B) That more seating be installed in a dining area
(C) That groups not stay too long in one spot
(D) That customers avoid touching fresh products

190. What is suggested about students in Buxton Cooking School's morning classes?

(A) They will split up into groups of five during tours.
(B) They will be provided with complimentary meals.
(C) They will have to purchase their own ingredients.
(D) They will visit a food court in Pinkston Market.

GO ON TO THE NEXT PAGE

Questions 191-195 refer to the following article, advertisement, and e-mail.

Westburg Announces Water-Saving Initiative

By Augustus Brandt

The Westburg City Council has announced an initiative to lessen water usage. The plans include subsidizing businesses and residences that install water recycling systems. "One major way to reduce water consumption is by reusing water," said Mayor Arnell Lee. She explained that the city will offer a rebate to homeowners who install a water recycling system, though the system must be functioning by August at the latest.

Unusually low precipitation has led to serious water shortages in the city over the past decade. Due to that, water prices have soared, and the cost of keeping all of Westburg's public spaces green has forced the city to increase local property taxes. The city has budgeted about $8.9 million for addressing the water supply issues.

Save Money With a Home-Vert Water Recycling System!

Lower your bills and help conserve water by installing a Home-Vert Water Recycling System!

- We install systems in homes or businesses.
- We can help you cut down on utility bills.
- Depending on the location, we can complete the installation within 1-3 days.

Our staff will also show you how the system works and how to maintain it. Visit www.home-vert.com to complete a request form for installation. Everyone who submits a completed form will receive a voucher worth $50 from one of our many local business partners!

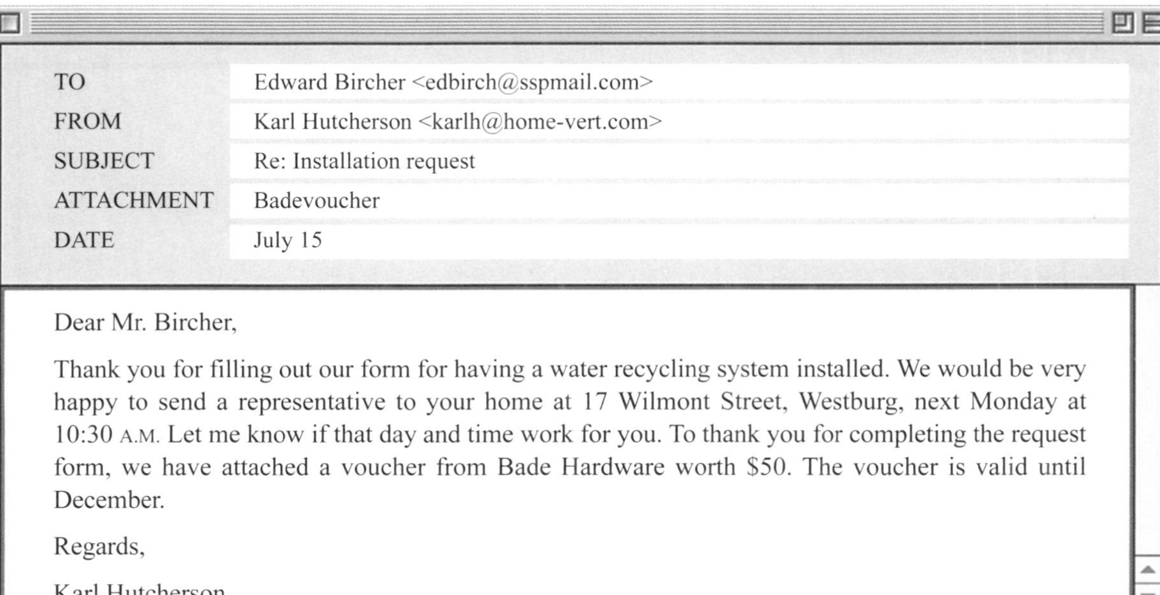

TO	Edward Bircher <edbirch@sspmail.com>
FROM	Karl Hutcherson <karlh@home-vert.com>
SUBJECT	Re: Installation request
ATTACHMENT	Badevoucher
DATE	July 15

Dear Mr. Bircher,

Thank you for filling out our form for having a water recycling system installed. We would be very happy to send a representative to your home at 17 Wilmont Street, Westburg, next Monday at 10:30 A.M. Let me know if that day and time work for you. To thank you for completing the request form, we have attached a voucher from Bade Hardware worth $50. The voucher is valid until December.

Regards,

Karl Hutcherson

191. Why was the article written?

(A) To announce a city plan regarding water
(B) To provide details on water system upgrades
(C) To introduce a new recycling center
(D) To offer information on a rise in utility prices

192. According to the article, what caused the price of water to increase?

(A) Water recycling costs
(B) Population growth
(C) Low rainfall
(D) City subsidy cuts

193. What will Home-Vert staff do for its customers?

(A) Schedule regular water tests
(B) Recommend installation technicians
(C) Print out billing statements
(D) Explain a system maintenance process

194. What is implied about Mr. Bircher?

(A) He will be partly reimbursed for installing a system.
(B) He serves on a municipal budget committee.
(C) He missed the payment deadline for a water bill.
(D) He learned about Home-Vert from Mr. Brandt.

195. What can be inferred about Bade Hardware?

(A) It supplies water filtration systems.
(B) It is affiliated with Home-Vert.
(C) It will accept vouchers starting from December.
(D) It is discounting some of its products.

GO ON TO THE NEXT PAGE

Questions 196-200 refer to the following form, e-mail, and Web page advertisement.

www.websitewizards.com/contact_us/

Web Site Wizards

Home | About Us | **Services** | Portfolio | FAQ | Jobs

First name	Brady	**E-mail address**	brady@ponderosaclothing.com
Surname	Grayson	**Phone number**	555-3786
Current Web site	www.ponderosaclothing.com	**Address**	31 North Pima Road, Scottsdale, AZ

Tell us about the work you would like us to do for you.

I run a store called Ponderosa Clothing that specializes in T-shirts. I have a Web site, but it only contains a brief description of my business, some information about our best-selling products, and a map. I would like to have the site upgraded so that customers can use it to order items.

How would you like us to contact you?

■ By e-mail ☐ By phone

Which of the following services are you seeking?

■ Site design
■ E-commerce setup
■ Web site traffic analytics
■ Internet advertising
☐ Logo design
☐ Web site security
☐ Promotional videos
☐ E-mail marketing
☐ Mobile application design

Select the services you need, and we will send you a price estimate.

To: Brady Grayson <brady@ponderosaclothing.com>
From: Anita Hernandez <customerservice@websitewizards.com>
Subject: Request for quote
Date: August 2
Attachment: Project estimate

Dear Mr. Grayson,

Thank you for contacting Web Site Wizards. One of our designers has reviewed your current Web site and compiled a project estimate, which I have attached. The total cost for designing www.ponderosaclothing.com and setting up e-commerce functions is expected to be $1,250.

If you are satisfied with our estimate, send us some links to Web sites you like. We will review these and try to use similar design elements in the new version of your Web site. Also, you will need to send a picture of your store as it will appear on the main page of the Web site.

If you change your mind and choose to add other services, such as the development of promotional videos or a mobile application, please e-mail our customer services department so that they can recalculate your quote.

Yours truly,
Anita Hernandez

Ponderosa Clothing: A Perfect Memory from Scottsdale!

Looking for an authentic, one-of-a-kind souvenir to remember your time in Scottsdale? Then why not check out some of Ponderosa Clothing's offerings? Many items feature artistic patterns found in the American Southwest, and only plant-based dyes are used in all our clothing. We do this in order to preserve a regional tradition from centuries ago.

Ponderosa Clothing products are available at our store in Scottsdale, on our newly redesigned Web site, and through our downloadable mobile application! Visit www.ponderosaclothing.com to check out our promotional videos, browse our most popular products, and use our new shopping cart function to make purchases. Domestic shipping is free for all online orders, but there are charges for international purchases.

196. In the form, what can be inferred about Ponderosa Clothing?

(A) It has several branches in the Southwest.
(B) It hired Web Site Wizards previously to create a logo.
(C) Its original Web site did not allow for the sale of merchandise.
(D) It sends most of its orders to overseas customers.

197. What is one purpose of the e-mail?

(A) To propose a strategy for raising sales
(B) To offer a catalog of available items
(C) To inquire about product prices
(D) To discuss redesigning a Web page

198. What is most likely shown on Ponderosa Clothing's new Web site?

(A) A diagram of a process for making dye
(B) A picture of a shop on North Pima Road
(C) A counter indicating the total number of shirts sold
(D) A photograph of Mr. Grayson

199. What did Mr. Grayson probably do?

(A) Rejected a project quote
(B) Added a number of new products to his store
(C) Removed a map from his Web site
(D) Contacted a customer service department

200. What is stated about Ponderosa Clothing's products?

(A) They were featured in a tourist brochure.
(B) They are made with a traditional process.
(C) They can be shipped free if purchased in bulk.
(D) They are designed by a local artist group.

This is the end of the test. You may review Parts 5, 6, and 7 if you finish the test early.

정답 p.326 / 점수 환산표 p.329 / 해석 p.338 / Part 5&6 무료 해설 바로 보기(정답 및 정답 음성 포함)

* 다음 페이지에 있는 Self 체크 리스트를 통해 자신의 문제 풀이 방식과 태도를 점검해 보세요.

Self 체크 리스트

TEST 02는 무사히 잘 마치셨죠?
이제 다음의 Self 체크 리스트를 통해 자신의 테스트 진행 내용을 점검해 볼까요?

1. 나는 75분 동안 완전히 테스트에 집중하였다.

   □ 예　□ 아니오

   아니오에 답한 경우, 이유는 무엇인가요?

2. 나는 75분 동안 100문제를 모두 풀었다.

   □ 예　□ 아니오

   아니오에 답한 경우, 이유는 무엇인가요?

3. 나는 75분 동안 답안지 표시까지 완료하였다.

   □ 예　□ 아니오

   아니오에 답한 경우, 이유는 무엇인가요?

4. 나는 Part 5와 Part 6를 19분 안에 모두 풀었다.

   □ 예　□ 아니오

   아니오에 답한 경우, 이유는 무엇인가요?

5. Part 7을 풀 때 5분 이상 걸린 지문이 없었다.

   □ 예　□ 아니오

6. 개선해야 할 점 또는 나를 위한 충고를 적어보세요.

* 교재의 첫 장으로 돌아가서 자신이 적은 목표 점수를 확인하면서 목표에 대한 의지를 다지기 바랍니다. 개선해야 할 점은 반드시 다음 테스트에 실천해야 합니다. 그것이 가장 중요하며, 그래야만 발전할 수 있습니다.

TEST 03

PART 5
PART 6
PART 7
Self 체크 리스트

잠깐! 테스트 전 확인사항

1. 휴대 전화의 전원을 끄셨나요? □ 예
2. Answer Sheet, 연필, 지우개를 준비하셨나요? □ 예
3. 시계를 준비하셨나요? □ 예

모든 준비가 완료되었으면 목표 점수를 떠올린 후 테스트를 시작합니다.

문제 풀이를 마치는 시간은 지금부터 75분 후인 __시 __분입니다.
테스트 시간은 총 75분이며, 시험 종료 전 2~3분은 정답 검토 및 답안지 마킹을 위해 사용합니다.

READING TEST

In this section, you must demonstrate your ability to read and comprehend English. You will be given a variety of texts and asked to answer questions about these texts. This section is divided into three parts and will take 75 minutes to complete.

Do not mark the answers in your test book. Use the answer sheet that is separately provided.

PART 5

Directions: In each question, you will be asked to review a statement that is missing a word or phrase. Four answer choices will be provided for each statement. Select the best answer and mark the corresponding letter (A), (B), (C), or (D) on the answer sheet.

PART 5 권장 풀이 시간 **11분**

101. Ms. Ortega ------- a financial advisor to seek help with her investment portfolio.

(A) consulting
(B) consultation
(C) consulted
(D) consulter

102. Minors are welcome to attend the concert ------- must be accompanied by a parent or guardian.

(A) so
(B) for
(C) with
(D) but

103. Ms. Conner did not win the Employee of the Year Award because a colleague's sales record was better than -------.

(A) hers
(B) herself
(C) her
(D) she

104. Everyone at yesterday's seminar ------- to put their electronic devices in silent mode.

(A) asking
(B) was asked
(C) is asked
(D) would ask

105. Ruby Cakes' staff handed out ------- samples of baked goods to celebrate the grand opening.

(A) proportional
(B) complimentary
(C) contradictory
(D) intensive

106. Ms. Koenig agreed to transfer to Norway for a year, believing it would be an excellent learning -------.

(A) compensation
(B) feature
(C) relationship
(D) opportunity

107. The script for the film adaptation of the best-selling novel *Vaunted* was taken ------- from the book.

(A) directly
(B) direction
(C) directing
(D) director

108. A photography exhibition entitled *The Awakening* is currently ------- in the Pulsen Gallery's main hall.

(A) expressed
(B) transformed
(C) displayed
(D) reflected

109. The municipal government has promised that it will take ------- to reduce downtown traffic.

(A) acting
(B) action
(C) activation
(D) activists

110. Soft drink manufacturer Fizz Life ------- a backlash from customers after changing its recipe for Ricochet Cola last year.

(A) was faced
(B) has been faced
(C) faced
(D) to face

111. As a branch manager, Mr. Finley finds resolving staff conflicts ------- of his duties.

(A) difficult
(B) more difficult
(C) the most difficult
(D) difficultly

112. The dinner plates and utensils manufactured by Tessio are suitable for any -------.

(A) leisure
(B) occasion
(C) performance
(D) effect

113. The Villier Resort struggles to attract visitors these days, but it was ------- a very popular vacation destination.

(A) about
(B) once
(C) last
(D) as

114. The bank's loan officer determined how much money Ms. Demers would be eligible to ------- for her new home.

(A) purchase
(B) borrow
(C) earn
(D) donate

115. The manager decided to provide the employees with additional training, ------- their weaknesses.

(A) addressing
(B) addressed
(C) address
(D) addresses

116. Contributing to discussions ------- meetings is a good way to show initiative.

(A) from
(B) along
(C) against
(D) during

117. Business owners in the town have been ------- to keep their shops open after 7 P.M.

(A) optimal
(B) reluctant
(C) elaborate
(D) preferable

118. Ms. Diaz will be able to attend the conference ------- her train arrives on time.

(A) as long as
(B) otherwise
(C) as a result of
(D) by means of

119. Although Mr. Miller had been given clear directions to the conference venue, he drove right ------- it.

(A) toward
(B) over
(C) past
(D) out

120. Participants at the swimming competition will be divided into four different age -------.

(A) categorizes
(B) categorical
(C) categorized
(D) categories

GO ON TO THE NEXT PAGE

121. New recruits are required to join a training course ------- they have relevant work experience.

(A) in spite of
(B) even if
(C) as though
(D) in case

122. All the team members will be traveling together aside from Ms. Bateman, who will be flying out ------- tomorrow.

(A) physically
(B) partially
(C) separately
(D) commonly

123. The office expansion will be approved if the suggested budget is ------- to investors.

(A) ready
(B) permanent
(C) definite
(D) acceptable

124. A company that adopts telecommuting practices allows its staff members to work ------- their location.

(A) regardless of
(B) rather than
(C) on behalf of
(D) in exchange for

125. The head chef of a restaurant takes care of a ------- of tasks, including menu planning.

(A) condition
(B) variety
(C) notification
(D) renewal

126. Ms. Turner downloaded a free trial version of the program ------- she could test its features.

(A) as if
(B) so that
(C) in order to
(D) because of

127. The job duties of an editor consist of checking for spelling and grammar errors and verifying that information is ------- accurate.

(A) factual
(B) fact
(C) factuality
(D) factually

128. For the next group project, students are free to team up with ------- they want.

(A) whomever
(B) which
(C) however
(D) whatever

129. If politicians fail to follow through on their promises, they lose credibility and their reputations -------.

(A) injure
(B) reject
(C) endure
(D) suffer

130. ------- at work frequently is unprofessional, and it also makes coworkers feel uncomfortable.

(A) Complained
(B) Complaint
(C) Complain
(D) Complaining

PART 6

Directions: In this part, you will be asked to read four English texts. Each text is missing a word, phrase, or sentence. Select the answer choice that correctly completes the text and mark the corresponding letter (A), (B), (C), or (D) on the answer sheet.

PART 6 권장 풀이 시간 **8분**

Questions 131-134 refer to the following letter.

December 8

Dear Ms. Ambrosio,

We are very selective about the products we provide our guests here at Dane County Resort. However, we were surprised with the toothpaste sample you sent us. ------- **131.** having a refreshing scent, it was gentler on the gums than many of the other brands we've tried. Therefore, we've ------- **132.** to include your toothpaste in our new hotel toiletries package. This decision means that it will be provided to all of our guests on a daily basis. ------- **133.**, we would like you to ship us 500 units for January. ------- **134.**. As we intend on repeating this order in the future, we would also like to know whether a discount can be applied.

Yours truly,

Teddy Lawrence
General Manager
Dane County Resort

131. (A) Less than
(B) In addition to
(C) Not only
(D) Notwithstanding

132. (A) chosen
(B) remembered
(C) attempted
(D) declined

133. (A) Meanwhile
(B) Likewise
(C) Initially
(D) Nonetheless

134. (A) Many of our competitors do not provide standard amenities.
(B) Do you happen to still have the receipt for your last shipment?
(C) Before placing an order, we need to inspect the product.
(D) Please send me a quote for this amount as soon as possible.

GO ON TO THE NEXT PAGE

Questions 135-138 refer to the following information.

Swansea Ferries

Advice for Passengers

When you arrive at Swansea Terminal, follow the signs to the ------- **135.** check-in booth. Here, an officer will check your booking number, and you will be provided with a boarding card indicating the section of the ferry you will be parking in. If you are traveling to an international destination, you will also need to ------- **136.** your passport at this time. If you are traveling domestically, however, you will be asked to show your driver's license instead. Before boarding time, there will be an announcement. -------. **137.** You should proceed to the boarding lane, where staff will help guide your car ------- **138.** the ferry.

135. (A) hotel
(B) luggage
(C) vehicle
(D) conference

136. (A) issue
(B) renew
(C) cancel
(D) present

137. (A) This should occur about half an hour prior to departure.
(B) It is advisable to remain seated while the ferry is docking.
(C) Please check our Web site for changes to travel schedules.
(D) Parking permits are available at Swansea Ferries' main office.

138. (A) aside
(B) between
(C) onto
(D) throughout

Questions 139-142 refer to the following article.

Young African Designer Wins Acclaim

Futuristic Furniture Magazine

By Rhonda Thiessen

In the weeks leading up to this year's Basel Decor Fair, veteran designers received most of the media attention. But once the event started, the ------- (139.) suddenly shifted to a little-known designer, Harry Mashaba. He was showing his creations at a space in the main hall. ------- (140.).

"Mr. Mashaba's work is very unique. He's managed to update traditional South African furniture so that it's attractive and convenient for people today," said Lara Dahn, a fair organizer. "His pieces fit perfectly in a ------- (141.) living room."

Owing to his ------- (142.) at the fair, Mr. Mashaba has been hired to design a dining set for Swiss furniture maker Rulesten. It will be released in Europe this fall.

139. (A) position
(B) trend
(C) focus
(D) criticism

140. (A) His course, which was intended for professionals, took place on the final day.
(B) So far, sales of the item have failed to live up to his high expectations.
(C) The admission fee has been raised by €5 due to the venue rental cost.
(D) Critics in attendance agreed that they were unlike anything else on display.

141. (A) modern
(B) spacious
(C) historic
(D) spotless

142. (A) succeeded
(B) success
(C) succeeds
(D) successful

GO ON TO THE NEXT PAGE

Questions 143-146 refer to the following advertisement.

Introducing Avenuu, the best streaming service out there. See hundreds of popular TV series, movies, kids' shows, and live concerts. Stream ------- (143.) in high quality on any device, including smartphones, tablets, and computers. Avenuu also gives you recommendations based on your ------- (144.). The more you use it, the more we learn what you like. So, stop scrolling through menus and ------- (145.) your time. Sign up today to watch high-quality content.

------- (146.). Try our ad-supported service for $5.99 a month, or go ad-free for $10.99 a month. Visit www.avenuu.com today!

143. (A) itself
(B) yours
(C) them
(D) theirs

144. (A) budget
(B) history
(C) location
(D) schedule

145. (A) waste
(B) wasted
(C) wasting
(D) to waste

146. (A) Any movies you buy will be charged to your account.
(B) You can even choose how you want to subscribe.
(C) Enjoy discounts by using this promotional code.
(D) Your concerns will be handled by one of our agents.

PART 7

Directions: In this part, you will be asked to read several texts, such as advertisements, articles, instant messages, or examples of business correspondence. Each text is followed by several questions. Select the best answer and mark the corresponding letter (A), (B), (C), or (D) on your answer sheet.

PART 7 권장 풀이 시간 **54분**

Questions 147-148 refer to the following notice.

The staff entrance of Wilson Mall was damaged by last week's storm and will be repaired on August 2. Mall employees may enter using the emergency exit on the south side of the building. Your identification badges will be automatically updated in the security system to give you access to this door. Swipe your badge at this entrance as you normally would. Note, though, that you will not be able to enter the mall at this location after August 2.

147. What is the reason for the notice?

(A) To report on the status of a construction project
(B) To remind employees of extended holiday hours
(C) To provide instructions for emergency situations
(D) To announce a temporary change for workers

148. What is suggested about Wilson Mall?

(A) It has an exit that is usually restricted.
(B) It requires that staff wear a badge at all times.
(C) It is hiring more security guards.
(D) It will be closed for renovations.

GO ON TO THE NEXT PAGE

Questions 149-150 refer to the following e-mail.

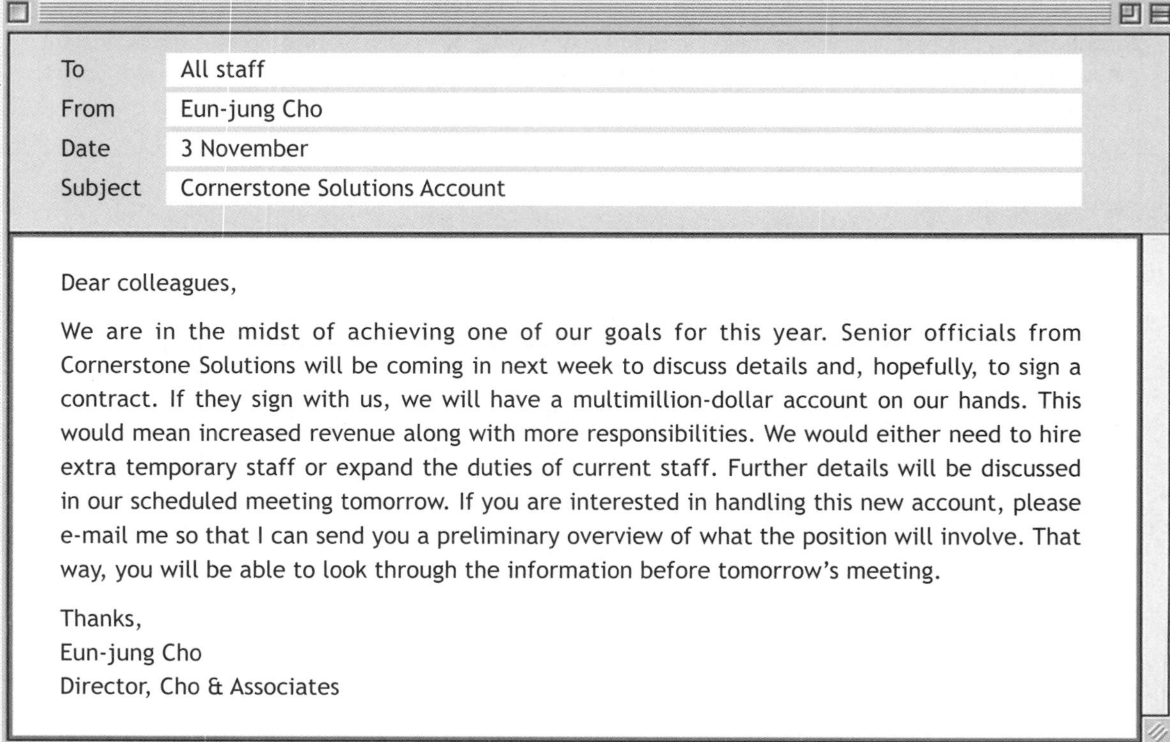

To	All staff
From	Eun-jung Cho
Date	3 November
Subject	Cornerstone Solutions Account

Dear colleagues,

We are in the midst of achieving one of our goals for this year. Senior officials from Cornerstone Solutions will be coming in next week to discuss details and, hopefully, to sign a contract. If they sign with us, we will have a multimillion-dollar account on our hands. This would mean increased revenue along with more responsibilities. We would either need to hire extra temporary staff or expand the duties of current staff. Further details will be discussed in our scheduled meeting tomorrow. If you are interested in handling this new account, please e-mail me so that I can send you a preliminary overview of what the position will involve. That way, you will be able to look through the information before tomorrow's meeting.

Thanks,
Eun-jung Cho
Director, Cho & Associates

149. What is stated about Cornerstone Solutions?

(A) It is expected to withdraw from some negotiations.
(B) It is trying to decide how to spend extra funds.
(C) It might agree to secure the services of Cho & Associates.
(D) It has made an offer to purchase another firm.

150. What does Ms. Cho ask her employees to do?

(A) Add some terms to a contract
(B) Contact her for job details
(C) Assess some coworkers
(D) Set up a room for a meeting

Questions 151-152 refer to the following text-message chain.

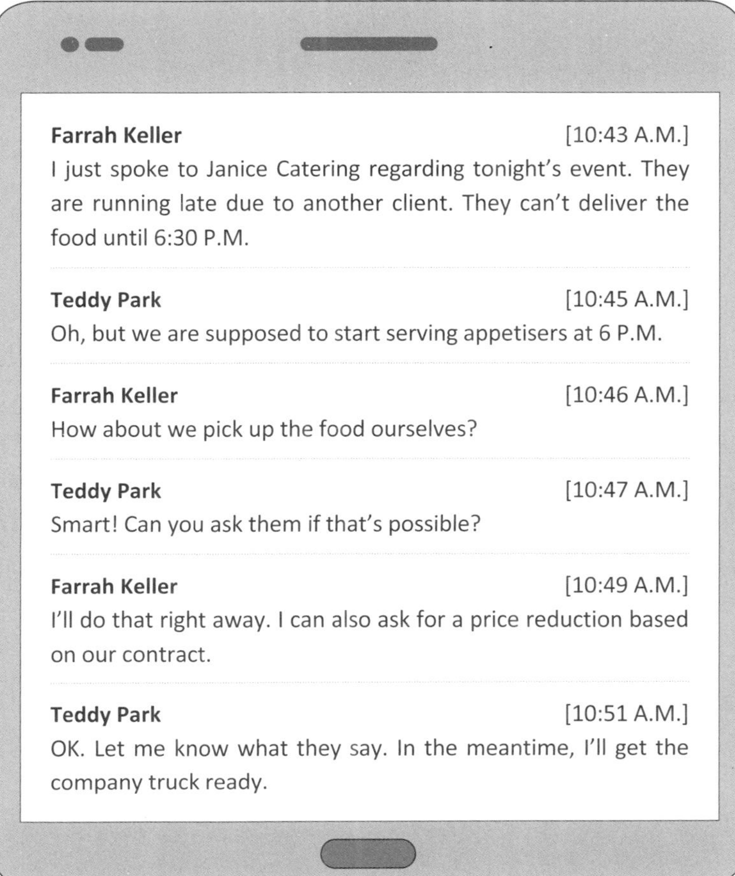

Farrah Keller [10:43 A.M.]
I just spoke to Janice Catering regarding tonight's event. They are running late due to another client. They can't deliver the food until 6:30 P.M.

Teddy Park [10:45 A.M.]
Oh, but we are supposed to start serving appetisers at 6 P.M.

Farrah Keller [10:46 A.M.]
How about we pick up the food ourselves?

Teddy Park [10:47 A.M.]
Smart! Can you ask them if that's possible?

Farrah Keller [10:49 A.M.]
I'll do that right away. I can also ask for a price reduction based on our contract.

Teddy Park [10:51 A.M.]
OK. Let me know what they say. In the meantime, I'll get the company truck ready.

151. At 10:47 A.M., what does Mr. Park most likely mean when he writes, "Smart"?

(A) He thinks it would be wise to notify a client.
(B) He is impressed by his colleague's idea.
(C) He believes the caterer can solve a problem.
(D) He is pleased that she hired an employee.

152. What is suggested about Janice Catering?

(A) It specializes in local food varieties.
(B) It has been hired by Mr. Park before.
(C) It mentions discounts in its contract.
(D) It only operates one food delivery truck.

GO ON TO THE NEXT PAGE

Questions 153-154 refer to the following announcement.

Athens College Event Listing

Artist Spotlight

While our last few Artist Spotlight events have featured accomplished painters, this month's guest will be a self-taught animator named Grant Marek. He will present his latest film, *Coloratura,* which was screened at the Global Animation Festival. The *Georgia Sentinel* calls Mr. Marek's newest movie "an uplifting and masterful interplay of sight and sound." The film screening will include a live narrator and sound effects, and a quartet of musicians led by professor Wallace Herbert. After the screening, audience members will have a chance to ask Mr. Marek questions about his film. He will also participate in a panel discussion a day after the screening on Friday, February 12, at 7 P.M. in the Watkins Auditorium.

Admission: Free and Open to the Public
Date and time: Thursday, February 11, at 6:30 P.M.
Venue: Charles Theater

153. What is suggested about Athens College's Artist Spotlight?

(A) It is a recurring event.
(B) It includes an art exhibit.
(C) It exclusively features musicians.
(D) It will be recorded for television.

154. What is NOT indicated about Mr. Marek?

(A) He will participate in more than one activity at Athens College.
(B) He has received no formal training in animation.
(C) He will hold a rehearsal in the Charles Theater.
(D) His work was shown at an international film festival.

Questions 155-157 refer to the following advertisement.

Palm Creek Tours

No visit to California is complete without a trip to one of its dozen national parks. Each year, millions of visitors from around the world come to enjoy the state's stunning natural vistas and wide range of outdoor activities. – [1] –.

Palm Creek Tours specializes in planning fully customizable tours of California's national parks. We offer everything from single-day packages to multiday trips to one or more locations. – [2] –. You can sleep in a tent, in a five-star resort, or anything in between. Should you require a guide for any activity, we can arrange one for you at an added cost. Our multilingual guides can help you and your companions feel comfortable and ensure that your trip goes smoothly. – [3] –.

Tour packages start at $150 per person for a single-day trip including meals and transportation. All packages require a minimum of four people. – [4] –. Call Palm Creek Tours today at 555-8012, or visit www.palmcreektours.com.

155. What is suggested about the tour packages?

(A) They are being offered for a limited time.
(B) They are not inclusive of tour guides.
(C) They must be reserved months in advance.
(D) They cannot be booked for fewer than six people.

156. What is true about Palm Creek Tours?

(A) It was recognized for its outstanding service.
(B) It handles foreign visitors exclusively.
(C) It offers a service in multiple languages.
(D) It operates resorts throughout California.

157. In which of the positions marked [1], [2], [3], and [4] does the following sentence best belong?

"We cannot make any exceptions to this policy."

(A) [1]
(B) [2]
(C) [3]
(D) [4]

GO ON TO THE NEXT PAGE

Questions 158-160 refer to the following brochure.

Biz-Equip Repair Services

The cost of replacing broken or malfunctioning office equipment can be high! Before you rush out to buy a new printer, photocopier, projector, computer, or other office device, call Biz-Equip Repair Services!

Equipment Repair

We have a team of experienced specialists who can visit to check your machine. If it's possible to fix your item on the spot, we will. If it requires major repairs, your equipment will be taken to our service center and returned to you in good working order. Most types of repairs are done within just 48 hours!

Equipment Maintenance

Biz-Equip also provides companies and other organizations with regular maintenance services. Our technicians can conduct weekly inspections of your equipment to ensure that everything is functioning properly.

Equipment Cartridge Supply

In addition, Biz-Equip has a selection of ink and toner cartridges that fit most office printers and photocopiers. Prices vary according to brand and type. For details, visit www.bizequiprepairservices.com/products.

To book an appointment with a technician, call our toll-free number at 1-800-555-9288. Provide the address of your office or business establishment, and we'll send someone as soon as possible.

158. What is NOT indicated about Biz-Equip?

(A) It provides clients with periodic services.
(B) It offers on-site equipment inspections.
(C) It sells a line of office machines.
(D) It operates a center for making repairs.

159. According to the brochure, what can customers do on Biz-Equip's Web site?

(A) Print out a billing statement
(B) Make a payment for printer cartridges
(C) Find cost information for some products
(D) Request an equipment upgrade

160. What information does Biz-Equip require to arrange a visit by a technician?

(A) A customer account number
(B) The location of an office
(C) Proof of purchase
(D) The date on a warranty card

Questions 161-164 refer to the following article.

Murals Bring Life and Color to Downtown Core

Charlotte, October 19—When the city of Charlotte launched a mural program last June in the downtown core, the idea was to revitalize and brighten up the area. The large, artistic images are being painted directly onto building walls and are nearing completion. — [1] —. Plans call for all the murals to be finished within two months. The project has transformed the city center into an outdoor art gallery, and it will be important to maintain all the artwork. The Axon Arts Group is in charge of the project and will also be under contract for the next five years to maintain the murals. — [2] —.

Axon Arts Group was chosen to carry out the project as it has been holding art workshops at local schools and community centers for the past 20 years. — [3] —. The group was eager to accept the offer when it was first proposed by Charlotte's planning committee last spring. "Many local artists are excited about this project," said Axon Arts Group cofounder Matthew Stewart. "It's a once-in-a-lifetime opportunity for many of them." The initial funding was a $50,000 grant supplied by the Community Initiative Foundation. — [4] —. The Charlotte Tourism Board matched that contribution shortly thereafter. "Now when people come to visit our city," said Tourism Board director Jill Myers, "they'll see it bursting with positivity and inspiration, and they'll want to come back."

161. Why did Charlotte implement the mural program?

(A) To promote local artists
(B) To attract more downtown shoppers
(C) To revitalize part of the city
(D) To teach painting to students

162. What is implied about Axon Arts Group?

(A) It will work for the city for five years.
(B) It manages a local gallery.
(C) It asked the public for mural ideas.
(D) It has an office at a community center.

163. What can be suggested about the Charlotte Tourism Board?

(A) It is hosting a public fund-raising event.
(B) It launched an information campaign about the arts.
(C) It requested funding from the Community Initiative Foundation.
(D) It provided about $50,000 for the project.

164. In which of the positions marked [1], [2], [3], and [4] does the following sentence best belong?

"This will involve cleaning them and touching them up as required."

(A) [1]
(B) [2]
(C) [3]
(D) [4]

GO ON TO THE NEXT PAGE

Questions 165-167 refer to the following e-mail.

TO	All employees <staff@portlandvalleyjournal.com>
FROM	Isaac Dyer <isdyer@portlandvalleyjournal.com>
SUBJECT	January edition
DATE	December 2

Hello, everyone.

Our January edition is always special because it sets the tone for our magazine for the rest of the year. I have already started working on the layout for our articles and features. The head reporters and I agreed that it would be good to have more interaction between our staff and readers next year. So, the January cover will be determined through a photography competition that both our readers and employees can take part in. I've already sent out a press release to the local paper about it. I will also put up the contest rules and guidelines on our Web site by the end of the day.

As I mentioned, the competition will be open to employees. Unfortunately, this does not apply to our photographers as they would have an unfair advantage. However, I talked with Brianna Griffin, our lead photographer, and we decided that they can serve as contest judges. There is no prize other than the winning photo being featured on the cover.

I hope everyone takes part if they can. Please e-mail your submission to me by December 10. The winner will be announced on December 20.

Good luck!
Isaac Dyer, Managing Editor
Portland Valley Journal

165. Why did Mr. Dyer send the e-mail?

(A) To announce some new publication guidelines
(B) To ask for a team member to write a press release
(C) To encourage employees to send in some photos
(D) To request feedback regarding some cover art

166. According to the e-mail, what has Mr. Dyer NOT done yet?

(A) Contacted a newspaper
(B) Posted some rules online
(C) Consulted some journalists
(D) Worked on a layout

167. What is suggested about Ms. Griffin?

(A) She was recently promoted.
(B) She will be helping to judge a contest.
(C) She sits near Mr. Dyer's office.
(D) She works for several magazines.

Questions 168-171 refer to the following online chat discussion.

Lenny Vogler	11:57 A.M.	Hi, everyone. I'm worried that our online marketing isn't working. Is there a way for us to improve our online visibility?
Dorothy Hughes	11:57 A.M.	What about expanding our social media page?
Lenny Vogler	11:58 A.M.	Our social media page hasn't been very successful in getting images of our products out there for consumers to see. Pictures really help in promoting our product lines.
Burl Seaver	11:58 A.M.	Perhaps we should start a Momento-Pic account. It's a photo-sharing application people use to share and comment on pictures. It would also allow us to post links to our social media page.
Anya Pearson	11:59 A.M.	I've heard of that. But businesses have to pay a fee.
Lenny Vogler	11:59 A.M.	If the monthly fee is reasonable, it should be within our marketing budget. Should we go ahead and set up an account?
Burl Seaver	12:00 P.M.	We may also want to check out other popular image-sharing applications before we do that.
Dorothy Hughes	12:01 P.M.	I agree. There are other image-sharing programs that have even more subscribers than Momento-Pic.
Lenny Vogler	12:02 P.M.	I see. Well, could I get one of you to come up with a list of applications that could be beneficial to join? Please also find out about their fees and functions.
Anya Pearson	12:03 P.M.	I can take care of that right now. I'll send you an e-mail with the information this afternoon.

Send

168. What is Mr. Vogler concerned about?

(A) Drawing potential consumers to a showroom
(B) Raising public awareness of products on the Internet
(C) Improving the efficiency of a computer program
(D) Launching an image sharing application

169. What is indicated about Momento-Pic?

(A) It can be used for free during a trial period.
(B) It charges businesses to sign up.
(C) It has more subscribers than its competitors do.
(D) It allows users to edit their photos.

170. In which department do the people most likely work?

(A) Marketing
(B) Product development
(C) Customer support
(D) Information technology

171. At 12:01 P.M., what does Ms. Hughes mean when she writes, "I agree"?

(A) She would like to contact current subscribers.
(B) She wants to expand a social network page.
(C) She thinks the team should check other programs.
(D) She wants to start an account with Momento-Pic.

GO ON TO THE NEXT PAGE

Questions 172-175 refer to the following information.

Looking to learn a new skill or start a new hobby? Check out what's coming to the Anderson Community Center starting from the week of May 11!

Baking Extravaganza

Mondays, 6-8 P.M., $35 per session
Discover how to make simple baked goods from one of the city's pastry chefs. Each week, we learn a new recipe with a different guest teacher. All ingredients are provided.

Piano for Adults

Tuesdays, 5-6 P.M., $15 per session
Learn the basics of playing the piano from classical pianist Susan Dickinson. No experience is necessary. No materials are required.

Short Story Writing

Wednesdays, 7-9 P.M., $25 per session
Develop your writing skills with published author William Davis. This engaging weekly seminar is intended for novice writers. Please bring a pen and paper or a laptop computer.

Introductory Knitting

Thursdays, 5:30-7 P.M., $30 per session
Make gloves, scarves, socks, and many other items in this crafting class taught by Paula Booker. Yarn and equipment are provided. However, if you prefer to knit with a specific color of yarn, you are welcome to bring your own.

172. What is the purpose of the information?

(A) To announce a center's new business hours
(B) To describe some handmade products
(C) To offer an early enrollment discount
(D) To give information on some new classes

173. Which class will have multiple instructors?

(A) Baking Extravaganza
(B) Piano for Adults
(C) Short Story Writing
(D) Introductory Knitting

174. What is mentioned about Mr. Davis?

(A) He will provide some tips for getting published.
(B) He will teach inexperienced writers.
(C) He will hold his sessions on Thursdays.
(D) He will supply writing materials.

175. What is indicated about the Anderson Community Center?

(A) It raises money by selling crafts.
(B) Its instructors serve on a volunteer basis.
(C) Each of its classes lasts for two hours.
(D) All its classes meet once every week.

GO ON TO THE NEXT PAGE

Questions 176-180 refer to the following article and memo.

Colfer Inc.'s Fruit Juice Sales Dry Up

Beverage manufacturer Colfer Inc. experienced a 12 percent decline in fruit juice sales between July and September this year. According to company representative Fred Hines, multiple factors contributed to the decline in sales of these products, which typically account for over $500,000 of the company's annual profits. "The summer was not as warm as normal, so fewer people bought our juices to cool down," he said. "Furthermore, some of Colfer's juice drinks rose in price due to an increase in the cost of ingredients. The price of grapes, for example, has gone up, so the manufacturing cost of our grape-flavored beverages has as well," Mr. Hines explained.

An increase in competition has also affected Colfer Inc.'s sales. Colfer Inc. and other large companies are losing ground to smaller brands that offer healthier alternatives. In fact, research data has indicated that natural juices with no added sugar have been continually increasing in popularity. In an attempt to address changing consumer preferences, Colfer Inc. has begun establishing affiliations with a large number of fast-growing companies that make healthy foods and beverages. It has also replaced the blue bottles its fruit juices have long been packaged in with redesigned red ones. The company believes that this will help to change its brand image.

To: Colfer Inc. board of directors
From: Carl Bryant, president, Colfer Inc.
Subject: Changes
Date: November 30

I know that the last few months have been difficult, but I'm confident that we're getting back on track. Our affiliation with Friendly Farm Foods and Natgreen Cereals has helped in this regard, but I think that Colfer Inc. will ultimately need to change with the times. Therefore, at our meeting this week, I'd like to discuss developing new flavors and expanding the price range of our products. Also, I think we need to reintroduce our original juice bottles as the new color and design have not been popular with consumers. Let's focus on offering unique, high-quality products. That's how we'll meet our goals for the coming year.

176. What is the main purpose of the article?

(A) To explain why consumer preferences are changing
(B) To introduce a new manufacturing business
(C) To announce the release of a new product line
(D) To report a decline in product sales

177. What problem is mentioned in the article?

(A) A lack of necessary ingredients
(B) A rise in distribution costs
(C) A cooler summer than normal
(D) A drop in competitors' prices

178. What is indicated about Colfer Inc.?

(A) It makes most of its products from grapes.
(B) It has partnered with healthy food businesses.
(C) It operates factories around the world.
(D) It has been steadily losing money for several years.

179. What does Mr. Bryant believe that Colfer Inc. should do?

(A) Use blue containers for some products
(B) Find a less expensive local supplier
(C) Introduce a quality-control process
(D) Collaborate more with other companies

180. In the memo, the word "meet" in paragraph 1, line 8, is closest in meaning to

(A) introduce
(B) encounter
(C) fulfill
(D) adjust

GO ON TO THE NEXT PAGE

Questions 181-185 refer to the following e-mail and form.

To: George Billings <g.billings@southernbakedgoods.com>
From: Lane Emerson <l.emerson@gourmetdessert.com>
Subject: RE: Gourmet Dessert Fair
Date: October 27

Dear Mr. Billings,

Thank you for your interest in selling cakes at the 16th Gourmet Dessert Fair, which has earned the distinction of being the largest and most successful event of its kind. To answer your question, a space costs $55 regardless of size unless you are a member of the Canadian Specialty Food Association (CSFA). For members, the price is $45. Also, all sellers can enjoy the free use of a computer and access to our Privileged Vendor program, through which sellers are introduced to potential buyers.

Please note that the prices above are for priority booking and only apply to applications and payments sent to us by November 30. In December, booth charges increase to $65 for members and $75 for nonmembers.

Sincerely,
Lane Emerson
Event Coordinator

16th Gourmet Dessert Fair

January 4 to 8 | Vancouver, Canada

Registration Details
Business: *Southern Baked Goods*
Representative Name: *George Billings*
Telephone: 555-5497
E-Mail: *g.billings@southernbakedgoods.com*

☒ Mark here if you are a CSFA member

Booth preference
☐ Standard ☐ Double ☒ Corner
- Note that only those with priority bookings are guaranteed their booth preferences. All booths include a table, chairs, and signage.

Optional Inclusions:
☐ Exhibitor lunch (January 8)
☒ Privileged Vendor program

Payment Enclosed: $45.00
Date of Registration: November 16
- All checks must be payable to the Gourmet Dessert Fair.

181. Why did Ms. Emerson write the e-mail?

(A) To invite a coworker to an event
(B) To respond to a vendor's inquiry
(C) To describe an ordering process
(D) To solicit payment for a service

182. In the e-mail, the word "distinction" in paragraph 1, line 2, is closest in meaning to

(A) contrast
(B) division
(C) satisfaction
(D) honor

183. According to the e-mail, what is true about booth prices?

(A) They are unaffected by the size of a space.
(B) They include the fee for joining an association.
(C) They vary depending on the number of participants.
(D) They have been raised since last year.

184. What can Southern Baked Goods do at the event?

(A) Request extra tables and chairs
(B) Hold product demonstrations
(C) Purchase goods from suppliers
(D) Meet potential customers

185. What is suggested about Mr. Billings?

(A) He wants to renew his CSFA membership.
(B) He will be guaranteed his choice of booth.
(C) He paid for a booking with a credit card.
(D) He will be at a venue one day early.

GO ON TO THE NEXT PAGE

Questions 186-190 refer to the following e-mails and article.

To: Fiona Bezark <fiona.bezark@wallacerealty.com>
From: Ronald Hasbun <rhasbun@myemail.com>
Subject: Rental Property
Date: October 12

Dear Ms. Bezark,

Thank you for taking the time to speak with me on the phone yesterday. As I mentioned, I am looking for an apartment in the Lakeview neighborhood with a lease starting December 1. My current apartment is approximately 1,200 square feet. I need a larger place with at least two bedrooms and two bathrooms. I would also prefer an apartment that is located on the first or second floor and has an assigned parking space.

I will be out of town on business for all of November, so I was hoping to see some apartments this month. My schedule is fairly flexible since I work from home as a freelance journalist. Please let me know what times and dates might work best for you.

Sincerely,
Ronald Hasbun

To: Ronald Hasbun <rhasbun@myemail.com>
From: Fiona Bezark <fiona.bezark@wallacerealty.com>
Subject: RE: Rental Property
Date: October 15

Mr. Hasbun,

Thank you for your recent inquiry regarding available apartments. I have four properties in mind that I think might work for you. Below is a list of basic information about each one. One meets all of your requirements, while the others have a few of the aspects you requested. All except one are in your desired neighborhood. I included it on the list because it is the only property to have undergone a full renovation recently. It is a beautiful, old building in the Edgewater district.

If you are interested in touring one or more of these apartments, I can show them to you sometime next week.

Location	Bed/Bath	Floor	Size (square feet)	Details
Georgian Apartments	3 bedrooms 2 bathrooms	1st	1,400	- Parking space included
Peterson Residences	3 bedrooms 1 bathroom	15th	1,600	- In-unit washer and dryer - Parking for a fee
Lawrence Tower	2 bedrooms 2 bathrooms	2nd	1,300	- Street parking only (city sticker required)
Sunnyside Apartments	2 bedrooms 2 bathrooms	2nd	1,700	- New appliances - Parking space included

Sincerely,
Fiona Bezark
Wallace Realty

Sunnyside Apartments Gets a New Look

By Leslie Reed

CHICAGO (October 10)—The renovation of Sunnyside Apartments, located at 123 Wilson Boulevard, was finally completed last week. The building had been undergoing improvements for over a year. Mr. Robert Kern, who has been running the apartment complex for the past two decades, wanted to completely renovate the building without displacing any of the tenants. As it turns out, some of them actually volunteered their time to help Mr. Kern with the renovation work, including painting, plumbing, and repairs. The building has been fully transformed, and several of the units are now available for rent. Interested parties should contact Ms. Fiona Bezark at Wallace Realty by calling 555-9888.

186. What is stated about Mr. Hasbun?
(A) He is currently living with a roommate.
(B) He will be unavailable in November.
(C) He met Ms. Bezark at her office.
(D) He was recently hired as a journalist.

187. Which feature of the Lawrence Tower unit does NOT meet Mr. Hasbun's requirements?
(A) Floor number
(B) Parking conditions
(C) Number of bedrooms
(D) Square footage

188. Which property is not in Lakeview?
(A) Georgian Apartments
(B) Peterson Residences
(C) Lawrence Tower
(D) Sunnyside Apartments

189. What did some of Mr. Kern's renters do?
(A) Asked to extend their lease
(B) Helped to refurbish a building
(C) Spoke to a newspaper reporter
(D) Volunteered at a community center

190. What is suggested about Sunnyside Apartments?
(A) Some of the units are currently vacant.
(B) It has not increased rents in decades.
(C) It is managed by a corporation.
(D) Some rentals are fully furnished.

GO ON TO THE NEXT PAGE

Questions 191-195 refer to the following online advertisement, Web page, and online review.

Come to the Winwright Gallery Reopening!

Don't miss the Winwright Gallery's opening celebration, which is scheduled for 5 P.M. to midnight on Saturday, March 1. Live music will be played in the city plaza outside the building, and anyone who has donated funds to the gallery will be invited to join a tour.

The Winwright Gallery will welcome the public for the first time since closing for renovations last July. In addition to significant upgrades to exhibition spaces and IT infrastructure, the Winwright Gallery has added a brand-new wing. While the wing is devoted to displaying the work of emerging artists, it is also home to the gallery's only dining facility, Column.

For more information about the event and the gallery's upcoming exhibitions, visit www.winwrightgallery.com.

www.winwrightgallery.com/membership

Annual Membership Plans

Members of the Winwright Gallery receive exclusive benefits.
Choose one of the options below and click "SELECT."

Type	Price	Benefits
▭ Individual	$100	- Free admission to all exhibit spaces - 20 percent discount on lectures
▭ Family	$200	- Free admission to all exhibit spaces for you and one guest - 20 percent discount on lectures and classes for children
▭ Enthusiast	$600	- Free admission to all exhibit spaces for you and two guests - 20 percent discount on lectures and museum store merchandise - Priority tickets to events and invitations to previews of special displays
▭ Connoisseur	$1,000	- Invitation to the Winwright Gallery's Annual Holiday Luncheon - Free admission to all exhibit spaces for you and up to four guests - 20 percent discount on lectures, museum store merchandise, and restaurant dishes - Free admission to more than 30 partner museums in North America

SELECT

www.triptips.com/attractions/reviews/winwrightgallery

Tania Swanson Reviewed on April 9

★★★★☆ **A great evening**

I was excited when a friend invited me to visit the Winwright Gallery with her today. It was fascinating to watch a presentation and be shown techniques for making abstract art. I just wish it hadn't been so crowded. We spent about two hours walking around and then dined at the restaurant in the new wing of the gallery. We sat on the patio, which has a view of the sculpture garden below. The food was excellent, and because my friend is a member, we even got a discount on our bill. Reservations are available but not necessary.

191. What is NOT true about the Winwright Gallery?

(A) It added a section for exhibiting the work of new artists.
(B) It is offering free tours to all visitors.
(C) It underwent some construction work.
(D) It is adjacent to a public square.

192. What does the Web page mention about the Enthusiast membership?

(A) It is recommended for emerging artists.
(B) It grants access to advance viewing of exhibits.
(C) It includes discounts at partner museums.
(D) It has to be paid for on a monthly basis.

193. What is indicated about Column?

(A) It requires reservations.
(B) It specializes in Italian food.
(C) It overlooks a garden.
(D) It hosts an annual luncheon.

194. What did Ms. Swanson do at the Winwright Gallery on April 9?

(A) Viewed a demonstration
(B) Created some artwork
(C) Redeemed a voucher
(D) Met a famous designer

195. How much did Ms. Swanson's friend pay for her gallery membership?

(A) $100
(B) $200
(C) $600
(D) $1,000

GO ON TO THE NEXT PAGE

Questions 196-200 refer to the following Web page, e-mail, and feedback.

www.nilsoncandy.com

 Keep Your Business Sweet 

The Nilson Candy Company provides bulk candy for hotels, transportation companies, business conventions, and more. Buy your favorite candies today!

Choose from hundreds of popular treats, including:
Mints
Caramels
Chocolates
Lollipops

Spend over $250 on your entire order, and your purchases can be personalized with your company name and logo on the packaging at no additional charge! Gift baskets and candy bouquets are also available. Give your clients and customers a sweet treat they won't forget!

Call our automated order hotline at 555-9635 or use our online chat to speak to a Nilson Candy representative. Don't forget to request a copy of our holiday catalog for access to special products and to sign up for our newsletter to learn about additional discounts!

Please note that chocolate items will be shipped in our patented GOOD-SEAL packs. These can prevent melting for up to four days. If you anticipate any problems receiving a delivery, please let us know so that we can adjust the delivery date.

To: Lisa Choi <lisachoi@starsoftware.com>
From: Nilson Candy <orders@nilsoncandy.com>
Date: June 16
Subject: Your order was received

Thank you for placing an order with Nilson Candy Company! Please review your order details below.

Order number: 34V8K **Ship to:** Star Software
Contact: Lisa Choi **Phone:** 555-3202

Item	Quantity	Price
Peppermints	10 kg – BULK	$99.00
Chocolates	5 kg – BULK	$79.00
Caramels	5 kg – BULK	$89.00
Small candy bouquets	50 items	$225.00
	Shipping fee	$50.00
	TOTAL COST	$542.00

Our standard shipping time for all orders is 2 days. However, if you have requested personalized labels, shipping may take up to 7 days.

www.nilsoncandy.com

Online Feedback Form

My name is Lisa Choi. Overall, I was satisfied with my order. The delivery was made on time and the items were complete. However, although most of the candy arrived intact, a few of the caramels were crushed during shipping. Still, I think the packaging did a great job of preserving the items even though it was left outside for almost two hours. And our customers very much enjoyed all of the candy! I was not able to try the personalization option because of a lack of time, but I would definitely like to try it in the future.

196. According to the Web page, what are Nilson Candy customers encouraged to do?

(A) Ask for a holiday catalog
(B) Visit a store location
(C) Read online reviews
(D) Taste some samples

197. What function does GOOD-SEAL serve?

(A) It certifies that a product is authentic.
(B) It maintains the condition of merchandise.
(C) It allows customers to track a delivery.
(D) It proves that a company meets high standards.

198. What is indicated about order number 34V8K?

(A) It qualifies for free personalization.
(B) It is eligible for a discount.
(C) It will be picked up in person.
(D) It includes items from overseas.

199. What problem did Ms. Choi experience with her order?

(A) A piece of candy tasted bad.
(B) A chocolate melted in the heat.
(C) Products were missing.
(D) Items were damaged.

200. What is true about Ms. Choi's order?

(A) It was sent to a residence.
(B) It was also ordered the year before.
(C) It was delivered within two days.
(D) It was labeled incorrectly.

This is the end of the test. You may review Parts 5, 6, and 7 if you finish the test early.

정답 p.326 / 점수 환산표 p.329 / 해석 p.346 / Part 5&6 무료 해설 바로 보기(정답 및 정답 음성 포함)

* 다음 페이지에 있는 Self 체크 리스트를 통해 자신의 문제 풀이 방식과 태도를 점검해 보세요.

Self 체크 리스트

TEST 03는 무사히 잘 마치셨죠?
이제 다음의 Self 체크 리스트를 통해 자신의 테스트 진행 내용을 점검해 볼까요?

1. 나는 75분 동안 완전히 테스트에 집중하였다.

   □ 예 □ 아니오

   아니오에 답한 경우, 이유는 무엇인가요?

2. 나는 75분 동안 100문제를 모두 풀었다.

   □ 예 □ 아니오

   아니오에 답한 경우, 이유는 무엇인가요?

3. 나는 75분 동안 답안지 표시까지 완료하였다.

   □ 예 □ 아니오

   아니오에 답한 경우, 이유는 무엇인가요?

4. 나는 Part 5와 Part 6를 19분 안에 모두 풀었다.

   □ 예 □ 아니오

   아니오에 답한 경우, 이유는 무엇인가요?

5. Part 7을 풀 때 5분 이상 걸린 지문이 없었다.

   □ 예 □ 아니오

6. 개선해야 할 점 또는 나를 위한 충고를 적어보세요.

* 교재의 첫 장으로 돌아가서 자신이 적은 목표 점수를 확인하면서 목표에 대한 의지를 다지기 바랍니다. 개선해야 할 점은 반드시 다음 테스트에 실천해야 합니다. 그것이 가장 중요하며, 그래야만 발전할 수 있습니다.

TEST 04

잠깐! 테스트 전 확인사항

1. 휴대 전화의 전원을 끄셨나요? □ 예
2. Answer Sheet, 연필, 지우개를 준비하셨나요? □ 예
3. 시계를 준비하셨나요? □ 예

모든 준비가 완료되었으면 목표 점수를 떠올린 후 테스트를 시작합니다.

문제 풀이를 마치는 시간은 지금부터 75분 후인 ___시 ___분입니다.

테스트 시간은 총 75분이며, 시험 종료 전 2~3분은 정답 검토 및 답안지 마킹을 위해 사용합니다.

READING TEST

In this section, you must demonstrate your ability to read and comprehend English. You will be given a variety of texts and asked to answer questions about these texts. This section is divided into three parts and will take 75 minutes to complete.

Do not mark the answers in your test book. Use the answer sheet that is separately provided.

PART 5

Directions: In each question, you will be asked to review a statement that is missing a word or phrase. Four answer choices will be provided for each statement. Select the best answer and mark the corresponding letter (A), (B), (C), or (D) on the answer sheet.

PART 5 권장 풀이 시간 11분

101. In the interview, Billy Zuckerman mentioned that he had learned to play guitar all by -------.

(A) he
(B) himself
(C) him
(D) his own

102. The installation instructions ------- describe what users should do.

(A) enormously
(B) precisely
(C) invisibly
(D) privately

103. The chief financial officer had a ------- with the department supervisors about the new benefits policy.

(A) converses
(B) conversed
(C) conversational
(D) conversation

104. Baron Inc. would prefer to promote an ------- candidate who is already familiar with its overseas operations.

(A) extensive
(B) apparent
(C) internal
(D) irrational

105. The building's elevators are all in good condition except for -------, which may have to be replaced.

(A) another
(B) other
(C) one
(D) any other

106. The mayor ------- to reduce traffic congestion by constructing high-occupancy vehicle lanes along Highway 62.

(A) planning
(B) to plan
(C) was planned
(D) is planning

107. The Medland hiring manager ------- that writing samples be submitted along with résumés.

(A) inquired
(B) requested
(C) persuaded
(D) predicted

108. A design proposal will be approved by city officials who ------- to redevelop Wilsonville's downtown area into a commercial hub.

(A) agreeing
(B) agreement
(C) has agreed
(D) have agreed

109. New customers of Palace Golf can choose one free set of golf balls from the store's vast -------.

(A) partition
(B) designation
(C) selection
(D) decision

110. An increase in global wheat prices could make flour production costs rise -------.

(A) mark
(B) marked
(C) markedly
(D) marking

111. Mr. Carver moved to the city ------- advance his career as a real estate agent.

(A) even if
(B) in regard to
(C) given that
(D) in order to

112. Before ------- her restaurant, chef Andrea Michaels trained in several award-winning kitchens.

(A) open
(B) opens
(C) opening
(D) openness

113. The company posted a ------- from its retreat on the front page of its Web site.

(A) photograph
(B) photographed
(C) photography
(D) photographing

114. The ------- brochures should answer any questions you might have.

(A) encloses
(B) enclose
(C) enclosing
(D) enclosed

115. The weather conditions were ------- for the 21st Emerald Bay Yacht Race last weekend.

(A) favor
(B) favorable
(C) favorably
(D) favorite

116. If serious building code violations are discovered, the city council has the ------- to halt the tower's construction.

(A) notice
(B) objection
(C) authority
(D) deliberation

117. Having no experience operating a retail store, Ms. Philips relied ------- her business partner's advice.

(A) upon
(B) beside
(C) toward
(D) with

118. Regardless of seniority, ------- employee is entitled to 15 days of paid vacation per year.

(A) each
(B) which
(C) some
(D) those

119. Mr. Alden has asked to be notified ------- the clients visiting from Japan arrive in the building lobby.

(A) whereas
(B) so that
(C) as soon as
(D) or else

120. ------- staff members dress is a reflection on the company, so please wear professional attire throughout the workweek.

(A) When
(B) What
(C) How
(D) Who

GO ON TO THE NEXT PAGE

121. The annual Independence Day fireworks show will ------- at 8 P.M. behind Stapleton Park.

(A) enter
(B) commence
(C) withstand
(D) originate

122. Jenkins Hospitality ------- Starlite Hotels if the negotiations had not broken down.

(A) will acquire
(B) could be acquired
(C) has been acquired
(D) would have acquired

123. Ms. Sutter left some portions of the registration form ------- because she did not know all of the information necessary to complete it.

(A) hollow
(B) flat
(C) blank
(D) pure

124. Dearden Inc. must comply with safety regulations by placing ------- visible emergency exit signs on every floor.

(A) clears
(B) clearance
(C) clearly
(D) cleared

125. Tomorrow's baseball game has been canceled ------- the storm that is expected to hit Houston.

(A) unlike
(B) up to
(C) on account of
(D) on behalf of

126. Most fitness professionals ------- a low-calorie, high-fiber diet to those who wish to lose weight.

(A) express
(B) recommend
(C) compliment
(D) examine

127. Ms. Simpson is meeting with the board of directors and should not be disturbed ------- there is an emergency.

(A) only if
(B) as long as
(C) unless
(D) thereafter

128. Ray's Sandwiches opened 10 years ago and has ------- become a popular lunch spot for office workers in Weyburn.

(A) yet
(B) since
(C) still
(D) while

129. ------- a few typos that can be easily fixed, the report looks ready to be submitted.

(A) Supposing
(B) In case
(C) As though
(D) Apart from

130. Astrophysicist Dr. Bryan Healy and aerospace engineer Dr. Marie Duns are experts in their ------- fields.

(A) plausible
(B) respective
(C) negligible
(D) intrusive

PART 6

Directions: In this part, you will be asked to read four English texts. Each text is missing a word, phrase, or sentence. Select the answer choice that correctly completes the text and mark the corresponding letter (A), (B), (C), or (D) on the answer sheet.

PART 6 권장 풀이 시간 8분

Questions 131-134 refer to the following instructions.

To replace a printer cartridge, start by opening the top of the printer. This will cause the ink cartridges to move to the center of the printing area and then stop. -------. (**131.**) It should slide out easily. ------- (**132.**) you have your new cartridge ready, shake it to move the ink around. This will ensure even color -------. (**133.**) Next, look for a piece of protective tape sealing the bottom. This must be peeled off prior to use. Otherwise, the ink will not be -------. (**134.**) Finally, close the top of the printer and print a few test pages to make sure that the colors match those on the monitor.

131. (A) Select the cartridge you wish to change and pull it toward you.
(B) Line up the paper stack to prevent it from getting jammed.
(C) Refilling cartridges is much more economical than replacing them.
(D) Refer to the user manual to identify the broken part.

132. (A) When
(B) Accordingly
(C) Unless
(D) As if

133. (A) customization
(B) reservation
(C) distribution
(D) explanation

134. (A) detected
(B) released
(C) restored
(D) evaporated

GO ON TO THE NEXT PAGE

Questions 135-138 refer to the following Web page.

http://www.weissert.com

HOME | **ABOUT** | ACCOUNT | HELP | CONTACT US

Weissert Antivirus safeguards computers and networks. Since it was launched five years ago, it has become one of the leading forms of protection against viruses and malware. Download a free ------- **135.** version today. You'll get full access to our services on any single device for 90 days. At the end of this period, you can easily ------- **136.** the service. Simply choose a subscription plan, and enter your payment information. -------. **137.** That's all there is to it. ------- **138.** 90 days, we won't charge you at all. To start your installation, click here.

135. (A) future
(B) mobile
(C) trial
(D) alternative

136. (A) extend
(B) cancel
(C) suspend
(D) return

137. (A) Protecting your children from harmful content is our number one concern.
(B) This is the one that most of our customers choose.
(C) We accept all major credit cards and can also do direct withdrawals.
(D) Follow the enclosed instructions to reinstall the software now.

138. (A) Past
(B) Under
(C) Without
(D) Except for

Questions 139-142 refer to the following e-mail.

To: Cynthia Ryerson <cynry@terratiles.com>
From: Alex Jones <jones@jonesinteriors.com>
Date: November 18
Subject: Purchase order

Dear Ms. Ryerson,

I appreciate your sending the tile ------- **139.** as requested. The actual products look better than they do on your Web site. I visited my client and showed them to her. Although she was impressed with the stone and ceramic tiles, she found neither of these options -------. **140.** On the other hand, the terra-cotta tiles are exactly what she is looking for. ------- **141.** will complement her Mediterranean-themed restaurant perfectly.

I've provided you with the measurements, so could you tell me what the total price will be for the materials and installation? -------. **142.** I believe my client is expecting her furniture and appliances to arrive in two weeks, so it would be best to do the installation before then.

Thanks again, and I hope to hear from you soon.

Alex Jones
Jones Interiors

139. (A) images
(B) costs
(C) samples
(D) specifications

140. (A) afford
(B) affording
(C) affordably
(D) affordable

141. (A) It
(B) Nothing
(C) They
(D) She

142. (A) She was very pleased with the results of the renovation.
(B) After that, when will you be able to settle your balance?
(C) I'd also like to know how soon you can carry out the work.
(D) Have you heard whether there were any issues with the installation?

GO ON TO THE NEXT PAGE

Questions 143-146 refer to the following article.

Jackson City is showing strong signs of an economic recovery, attracting a great influx of both residents and businesses. This growth is due to the sale of a 3.7-million-square-foot plot of land along Highway 34 that ------- (**143.**) accommodated Sibbet Manufacturing. The company went bankrupt after three years of operation and closed its doors over a decade ago, leaving the infrastructure on the property unused. The new proprietors plan ------- (**144.**) everything and build new office buildings. If this development is successful, it will provide more than 50,000 jobs over the next few years. ------- (**145.**). The demand for housing is already on the rise. ------- (**146.**), commercial properties that will ultimately cater to the future residents are being rented at an unprecedented rate.

143. (A) steadily
(B) conveniently
(C) previously
(D) momentarily

144. (A) to demolish
(B) demolishing
(C) will demolish
(D) demolished

145. (A) There are more manufacturing jobs than qualified applicants at the moment.
(B) Some residents are opposed to the idea of living so close to a factory.
(C) Such a major increase in sales is expected to boost the company's profits.
(D) People from neighboring areas have been moving to Jackson City as a result.

146. (A) Rather
(B) Likewise
(C) Instead
(D) However

PART 7

Directions: In this part, you will be asked to read several texts, such as advertisements, articles, instant messages, or examples of business correspondence. Each text is followed by several questions. Select the best answer and mark the corresponding letter (A), (B), (C), or (D) on your answer sheet.

PART 7 권장 풀이 시간 54분

Questions 147-148 refer to the following policy statement.

Cancellation Policy for Whitmore River Campground

If you need to cancel your reservation, we will return your full deposit provided that you call the park office at 555-7722 a minimum of 48 hours before your scheduled arrival. Please note that the park office is only open until 5 P.M. each day, and cancellation notifications sent by text message and e-mail are not accepted. If you cancel at short notice or fail to arrive, you will lose your deposit, and we will be entitled to accommodate another guest at your campsite.

147. What information is NOT mentioned in the policy statement?

(A) A deadline for making a cancellation
(B) A reason a regulation was changed
(C) The contact number of an office
(D) The closing time of a facility

148. What can Whitmore River Campground do when a customer does not show up?

(A) Restrict the individual from booking again
(B) Send a bill for a cancellation fee
(C) Charge the full rental fee
(D) Give a reserved space to another person

GO ON TO THE NEXT PAGE

Questions 149-150 refer to the following information sheet.

Volunteer Applications

Thank you for your interest in volunteering at Coral Rock Aquarium. We are no longer accepting applications for fall volunteer positions as that quarterly period is currently under way. If you wish to apply for another quarterly period, please see the chart below for relevant dates.

Quarterly period	Dates for volunteering commitment	Dates for accepting applications
Spring	March 1 to May 31	December 15 to February 15
Summer	June 1 to August 31	March 15 to May 15
Fall	September 1 to November 30	June 15 to August 15
Winter	December 1 to February 28	September 15 to November 15

The first part of the application process involves submitting a form and being interviewed by our volunteer director. If you meet our requirements, you will need to join a three-hour orientation session, which Coral Rock Aquarium is offering on February 24, May 23, August 22, and November 22.

149. When will Coral Rock Aquarium's current volunteering period end?

(A) On May 31
(B) On August 15
(C) On November 30
(D) On December 1

150. What is NOT a requirement for volunteers?

(A) Submit a list of professional references
(B) Take part in an interview
(C) Hand in a completed document
(D) Attend an informational meeting

Questions 151-152 refer to the following text-message chain.

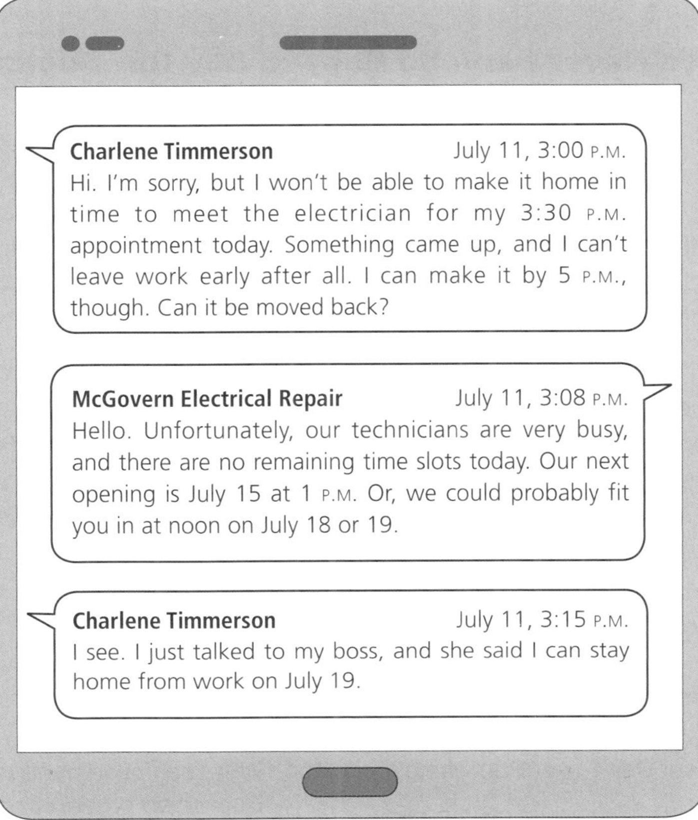

Charlene Timmerson July 11, 3:00 P.M.
Hi. I'm sorry, but I won't be able to make it home in time to meet the electrician for my 3:30 P.M. appointment today. Something came up, and I can't leave work early after all. I can make it by 5 P.M., though. Can it be moved back?
McGovern Electrical Repair July 11, 3:08 P.M.
Hello. Unfortunately, our technicians are very busy, and there are no remaining time slots today. Our next opening is July 15 at 1 P.M. Or, we could probably fit you in at noon on July 18 or 19.
Charlene Timmerson July 11, 3:15 P.M.
I see. I just talked to my boss, and she said I can stay home from work on July 19.

151. At 3:00 P.M., what does Ms. Timmerson mean when she writes, "Can it be moved back"?

(A) She is upset about a suddenly increased workload.
(B) She would like to reschedule an appointment.
(C) She hopes that some furniture can be repositioned.
(D) She wants to change a moving date.

152. When will Ms. Timmerson meet the electrician?

(A) At 12:00 P.M.
(B) At 1:00 P.M.
(C) At 3:30 P.M.
(D) At 5:00 P.M.

GO ON TO THE NEXT PAGE

Questions 153-154 refer to the following advertisement.

It's Never Been So Easy to Buy Our Books!

At Bell Tower Publishing, we have long been known for our wide selection of science textbooks, reasonable prices, and top-notch customer service. Until recently, our products could only be ordered on our Web site. But now there is a faster, more convenient way to shop with us: Bell Tower Helper, an application for mobile phones and tablets.

All you have to do is download Bell Tower Helper from an application store and create a user profile. Then log in, select some titles, and push the "Order" button. Having a profile allows you to save your payment details and check the status of your orders. As always, discounts are provided for bulk orders, though they vary depending on the books. Of course, you can still order at www.belltowerpublishing.com if you prefer.

153. What is true about Bell Tower Publishing?

(A) It sells both fiction and nonfiction books.
(B) It holds promotional events on school campuses.
(C) It has just begun to offer price reductions on large orders.
(D) It formerly sold its products only on a Web site.

154. What can customers of Bell Tower Publishing probably do if they have a user profile?

(A) Find out if purchases have been sent
(B) Chat with customer service representatives
(C) Preview the first few pages of a book
(D) Earn points by writing reviews

Questions 155-157 refer to the following information.

South Loop Yard Sale

Join our second annual neighborhood yard sale, organized by the South Loop Community Center. Last year's event topped all expectations and inspired the creation of an annual tradition. The event will take place on Saturday, September 2. Come and shop for bargains, listen to local music, and taste great food.

This year, we have moved to the Dearborn Center. It offers more room for participants than last year's location. Booth spaces are still available for sellers. To sign up, simply register for a spot at www.southloop.org/yardsale.

Unlike last year, we will require a participation fee of $50. This will go directly to funding the organization's gift-giving activities this Christmas. If you are interested in making a donation, go to www.southloop.org/donate.

155. The word "topped" in paragraph 1, line 2, is closest in meaning to

(A) competed
(B) ranked
(C) defeated
(D) exceeded

156. What is indicated about an event?

(A) It will accommodate more visitors than before.
(B) It is being advertised in local newspapers.
(C) It will feature entertainment for children.
(D) It is the first of its kind in the neighborhood.

157. What is true about a fee?

(A) It cannot be paid with a credit card.
(B) It was not required the previous year.
(C) It qualifies visitors to receive a free gift.
(D) It varies depending on a person's age.

GO ON TO THE NEXT PAGE

Questions 158-160 refer to the following press release.

Newberry Continues to Capture Market Share

March 1—Newberry Inc. has quickly gained ground on its competitors in the market for e-readers. Its latest product has attracted a strong following with features such as a full-colour display, multiple dictionaries, and a wide selection of computer voices that can read text aloud. Unlike any other device, Newberry's product can also connect to speaker systems wirelessly. This lets users hear books read aloud with greater audio clarity.

Because of these features and more, the Newberry E-Reader has experienced consistent growth in its market share. Each month since the product was released two years ago, the company has added more and more new users. It currently accounts for nearly 22 percent of e-reader sales, placing it third behind the much older and larger firms Vandaread and Speclight Reader. Analysts believe that Newberry's share is likely to increase further.

Newberry Inc. CEO Ross Franklin announced recently that the company has signed a contract with popular fantasy author Larry Hamlin to promote the Newberry E-reader in an upcoming advertising campaign. The campaign will include television advertisements and speaking engagements at select branches of the country's biggest bookstores. The company also plans to release a new version of the product next year that features increased memory capacity.

158. What is distinct about the Newberry E-reader?

(A) It has a long-lasting battery.
(B) It is cheaper than competing products.
(C) It comes in a variety of colors.
(D) It connects with audio systems wirelessly.

159. The word "consistent" in paragraph 2, line 2, is closest in meaning to

(A) harmonious
(B) expected
(C) steady
(D) durable

160. What is mentioned about the Newberry E-Reader advertisements?

(A) They will be released in print form.
(B) They will use a well-known writer.
(C) They will appeal to young readers.
(D) They will be created by a famous director.

Questions 161-164 refer to the following letter.

Gloria Schaeffer
1763 Stanton Road
Chandler, Arizona 85226

11 February

Dear Ms. Schaeffer,

My name is Maury Dekalb, and I have worked as a real estate agent in the Chandler area for over two decades. — [1] —. I noticed that you have been trying to sell your house independently by listing it in local property guides. I believe that I can find a buyer for your home. — [2] —.

Many properties are up for sale all over the city, but there are not a lot of buyers at the moment. There is no doubt in my mind that these conditions will make it challenging to sell your home. — [3] —. I guarantee that, if you hire me, you will no longer have to worry so much. I will generate interest in your property among potential buyers, set up appointments with them so they can see your home, and act as a mediator during negotiations. — [4] —.

If you would like to meet with me sometime, please let me know. Together, we can come up with a sales strategy that meets your needs. I am available day or night at 555-7411.

Best wishes,
Maury Dekalb
Dekalb Realty

161. What is indicated about Ms. Schaeffer?

(A) She subscribes to a Chandler newspaper.
(B) She has met with Mr. Dekalb to discuss a strategy.
(C) She received a real estate license this year.
(D) She is not currently working with a realtor.

162. What problem is Ms. Schaeffer most likely facing?

(A) A construction project is behind schedule.
(B) The housing market is in a downturn.
(C) She is unable to secure a bank loan.
(D) Her property is far from a public transport stop.

163. What does Mr. Dekalb NOT promise to do for Ms. Schaeffer?

(A) Get the attention of buyers
(B) Raise the value of her home
(C) Arrange viewing times
(D) Help bring about an agreement

164. In which of the positions marked [1], [2], [3], and [4] does the following sentence best belong?

"Finding a purchaser is certainly not impossible, though, when you've got the right sort of help."

(A) [1]
(B) [2]
(C) [3]
(D) [4]

GO ON TO THE NEXT PAGE

Questions 165-167 refer to the following job advertisement.

Tulsa College Seeks Research Assistant

The Tulsa College economics department is seeking a knowledgeable research assistant to help gather and analyze income data. The assistant must be willing to dedicate at least 40 hours a week to the job. Normal work hours are from Monday to Friday, from 8 A.M. to 5 P.M. The job will last six months and pays $18 per hour.

Job responsibilities include:
- Collecting income data from published research studies
- Creating spreadsheets and infographics based on data
- Writing reports on the progress of multiple ongoing projects

All applicants must:
- Have at least a bachelor's degree in economics
- Have earned at least a 3.5 GPA during college
- Demonstrate knowledge of their field during an interview

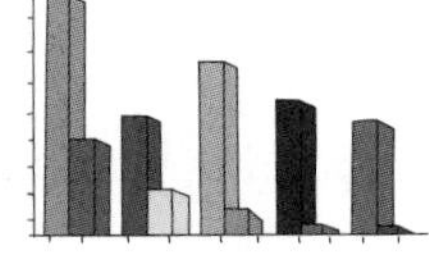

If you are interested, please submit a résumé and cover letter to the head of Tulsa College's economics department, Dr. William Ling, at w.ling@tulsacollege.edu. Successful applicants will be contacted by e-mail to arrange an interview date. All interviews will take place on-site with members of a hiring committee.

165. The word "dedicate" in paragraph 1, line 2, is closest in meaning to

(A) address
(B) promise
(C) devote
(D) appoint

166. What is mentioned about the research assistant job?

(A) It will require working six days a week.
(B) It will give participants college credits.
(C) It will only be a temporary job.
(D) It will pay more for overtime work.

167. What is a requirement for job candidates?

(A) Being graduates of Tulsa College
(B) Attending a panel interview
(C) Providing samples of previous work
(D) Having experience in a related firm

Questions 168-171 refer to the following notice.

Notice to North Portal Street Residents

Renwah Productions will be filming several scenes for an upcoming episode of QCC's television series *Farther Gone* on North Portal Street. – [1] –. Filming is set to take place from May 8 to May 12 at the following locations and times:

1. Monday, May 8, & Tuesday, May 9: Charbonneau Café, 1542 North Portal Street, from 8:30 A.M. until 7:00 P.M.
2. Wednesday, May 10, & Thursday, May 11: Outside of Azalea Apartments, 1294 North Portal Street, from 5:00 A.M. to 3:00 P.M.
3. Friday, May 12: Get-and-Grab Convenience, 1628 North Portal Street, from 10:00 A.M. to 9:00 P.M.

In order to accommodate the film crew's vehicles and equipment, "NO PARKING" signs will be set up near the filming locations on the relevant dates and times. – [2] –.

Renwah Productions has promised to keep traffic disruptions to a minimum. – [3] –. Please note that the first and third filming sites will be closed to the public while filming is under way. Access will be granted to the second location through its rear entrance only. – [4] –.

Thank you for your understanding and cooperation.

168. What is the purpose of the notice?

(A) To ask apartment tenants to report unauthorized visitors
(B) To provide details about a filming schedule
(C) To recommend some local businesses
(D) To state the requirements for attending a performance

169. What is indicated about Charbonneau Café?

(A) It will only be used as a filming site in the morning.
(B) It will have less nearby parking than normal on May 9.
(C) It was used to film a previous *Farther Gone* episode.
(D) It will only serve take out orders for a certain period.

170. What is true about residents of Azalea Apartments?

(A) They will receive a reminder next week.
(B) They will have to pass through a security check.
(C) They can use a rear entrance while filming is in progress.
(D) They are not allowed to drive on Portal Street for a week.

171. In which of the positions marked [1], [2], [3], and [4] does the following sentence best belong?

"However, some school bus routes may be adjusted slightly."

(A) [1]
(B) [2]
(C) [3]
(D) [4]

GO ON TO THE NEXT PAGE

Questions 172-175 refer to the following text-message chain.

Jeff Hervey	[10:35 A.M.]	Rosanne, are you in the office now? I have a favor to ask.
Rosanne Rutherford	[10:37 A.M.]	Hey. Aren't you supposed to be at the house on Vermont Street replacing roof tiles?
Jeff Hervey	[10:39 A.M.]	That's the problem. I'm here now, and there's more work to do than expected. I must have made a mistake with my measurements last time. I need several people to come and help me.
Rosanne Rutherford	[10:43 A.M.]	I'm not in the office right now, but I can help you. Todd might be available too. The fencing job he was scheduled to do on Grant Street was canceled.
Jeff Hervey	[10:45 A.M.]	That's a relief. Thanks!
Jeff Hervey	[10:46 A.M.]	Todd, do you have time to help out on a roofing job at 62 Vermont Street? I may need you to bring extra tools.
Todd Billings	[10:48 A.M.]	Hi, Jeff. Yes, I've got the time.
Jeff Hervey	[10:49 A.M.]	Thanks, Todd! Let me know how soon you can get here.
Rosanne Rutherford	[10:52 A.M.]	Jeff, I notified Ms. Richards, and she gave her approval for us to go over there. I'll be leaving shortly.
Todd Billings	[10:53 A.M.]	OK, Jeff. I can be there in about 45 minutes.

172. In which industry do the writers most likely work?

(A) Retail
(B) Manufacturing
(C) Construction
(D) Landscaping

173. At 10:45 A.M., what does Mr. Hervey mean when he writes, "That's a relief"?

(A) He is grateful that a deadline was extended.
(B) He is happy to learn that he will have help.
(C) He is thankful that his coworker is attending a meeting.
(D) He is glad that one of his jobs was canceled.

174. How many people will be working at Vermont Street?

(A) One
(B) Two
(C) Three
(D) Four

175. Who most likely is Ms. Richards?

(A) A new client
(B) A sales representative
(C) A company driver
(D) A work supervisor

GO ON TO THE NEXT PAGE

Questions 176-180 refer to the following e-mail and advertisement.

To: Jake Boyne <jake_boyne@renswoodinc.com>
From: Betty Herzfeld <betty_herzfeld@renswoodinc.com>
Subject: Broken projector
Date: August 5

Hi, Jake,

As I mentioned to you yesterday, the projector in the second floor conference room isn't working properly. I want to get a new device rather than have it fixed because the warranty expired last year. Apparently, the current one has a bulb that lasts 4,000 hours. I'd like to get a device that's better in this respect. If possible, I'd also like to upgrade to a projector with higher resolution.

I haven't been very pleased with the current projector, so let's get a GelwayCo device this time around. Anyway, please do some investigating together with the other interns and let me know when you find a suitable device. The maximum amount we can spend on this item is $600.

Thanks,

Betty Herzfeld
Purchasing Department

Want to improve your meetings?

A GelwayCo projector may be just what your office needs!

Model	Cost	Brightness	Resolution	Lamp hours
DR-7 Our classic projector, tailored for business use	$550	2,000 lumens	1024 x 768	5,000
DR-8 Our wireless option	$650	3,000 lumens	1280 x 800	5,000
BR-103X Our slim, lightweight model	$1,200	3,000 lumens	1280 x 800	4,000
F6-UR Our model for displaying images in tight spaces	$850	2,700 lumens	1024 x 768	5,000

We are committed to helping customers get the most out of their devices by providing easy access to software updates, manuals, and FAQ pages. Support is available online, in person at any of our stores nationwide, and over the phone at 1-800-555-9222.

176. What is the purpose of the e-mail?

(A) To provide advice about some equipment
(B) To respond to an inquiry
(C) To assign a research task
(D) To share the results of a conference

177. What is NOT true about the current projector?

(A) It is no longer covered under warranty.
(B) It failed to satisfy Ms. Herzfeld.
(C) It was made by GelwayCo.
(D) It is used in a meeting room.

178. What can be inferred about Ms. Herzfeld?

(A) She will approve a budget for office supplies.
(B) She was unable to give a presentation yesterday.
(C) She met with a technician to solve a problem.
(D) She will be told about an option from an intern.

179. Why will the purchasing department not buy the DR-8?

(A) Its maximum brightness is unsatisfactory.
(B) Its price exceeds an available budget.
(C) Its image quality is not good enough.
(D) Its bulbs need to be replaced too often.

180. What is mentioned about GelwayCo?

(A) It sells various types of office equipment.
(B) It has branches across the country.
(C) Its support hotline is open 24 hours a day.
(D) It makes equipment for both homes and offices.

GO ON TO THE NEXT PAGE

Questions 181-185 refer to the following article from a town newsletter and e-mail.

Concord Newsletter, September 30 edition

Seasonal Drinks Fuel Café Sales in Concord

Local cafés have been attracting more customers and boosting their sales by offering seasonally themed coffee beverages. At the Concord Food & Drink Convention on September 23, a group of café owners announced plans to add more seasonal drinks to their menus and carry out various promotions. They believe that, by doing so, they can turn Concord into a destination for coffee enthusiasts from neighboring areas. Their ultimate aim is to make the town the flavored-coffee capital of the U.S.

Already, unique coffee-based drinks can be found in Concord year-round. Olivia Lang, the owner of Bean Brewers, says that Pumpkin Spice is her café's most popular flavor during the fall. At Creative Cups, the staff members try to increase winter sales by inventing flavors with unique names. Last year, they served the winter-themed coffee drinks Xmas Espresso and Christmas Tree Cappuccino. This year, they plan to introduce the Santa Latte.

Meanwhile, the coffee shop Chill will bring back its refreshing Coconut Java, which debuted last March and was served until June, and 4th Street Coffee intends to make its popular Cherry Cappuccino available again in the summer.

To: Concord Newsletter advertising department <advertising@connews.com>
From: Kiana Lee <kianalee@entrepreneur.com>
Date: October 5
Subject: Advertisement
Attachment: advertisement_draft

Dear advertising department,

I was excited to see that my coffee shop, Creative Cups, was mentioned in an article in your September 30 edition. This week, a few customers have already asked when we will start selling our new flavor. I appreciate the publicity and wish to follow up by placing an advertisement in your newsletter.

The size I am interested in is one-eighth of a page. I have attached a draft of the advertisement. Your staff can recommend changes if needed. I reviewed the pricing on your Web site and saw that it costs $200 per month to advertise in your publication's Food and Dining section. As soon as you confirm that this is the correct amount, I will submit my payment.

I look forward to hearing back from you.

Thank you,

Kiana Lee

181. What happened on September 23?
(A) An interview for an article was conducted.
(B) An advertisement was printed in a publication.
(C) An industry event was held.
(D) Some investors were welcomed.

182. According to the article, why are coffee shops in Concord introducing more seasonal drinks?
(A) To attract patrons from other places
(B) To participate in a festival
(C) To make use of locally produced ingredients
(D) To take advantage of a nationwide trend

183. What is mentioned about Chill's Coconut Java?
(A) It will be available at a take-out window only.
(B) It can be purchased in a range of sizes.
(C) It is cheaper if ordered with a food item.
(D) It was offered for a limited time this year.

184. Which drink have some customers most likely asked Ms. Lee about this week?
(A) Pumpkin Spice
(B) Xmas Espresso
(C) Santa Latte
(D) Cherry Cappuccino

185. What does Ms. Lee ask the advertising department to do?
(A) Send a list of subscribers
(B) Confirm an advertising rate
(C) Suggest a beverage name
(D) Print a picture in color

GO ON TO THE NEXT PAGE

Questions 186-190 refer to the following announcement, list, and e-mail.

Hyde Park Job Fair
When: October 13
Where: Hyde Park Community Center, Main Hall

Are you a recent graduate with a bachelor's or master's degree? Come to the Hyde Park Job Fair and apply directly for positions in various fields from health care to software development and more. The fair is free for applicants as the City of Tampa has provided funding for the event.

Participating companies include local and international businesses with immediate openings for skilled applicants. These include part-time, full-time, and paid internship positions. We advise participants to do prior research on participating companies and to bring multiple copies of their résumés. The Hyde Park Community Center will also be providing professional résumé advice for students who require it.

Hyde Park Community Center
List of Attending Companies

Name	Industry	Details	Company Representative
Brentura Diagnostics	Science	Seeking laboratory consultants with a master's degree in chemistry or biology *prefer graduates from local universities	Sandra Parker
Gerber Inc.	Engineering	Seeking engineering majors for projects in the construction industries	Carter Lewis
Heston	Telecommunications	Seeking marketing graduates to fill various open positions	Eun-jung Bae
Jones Industries	Software Development	Seeking knowledgeable programmers for project-based work	Mario Lopez
Spitexx	Health Care	Seeking interns for positions in medical sales	Angela Mitchell
Verity Care	Services	Seeking individuals qualified to work with children	Belinda Hough

Many more companies will be added to the list once their job postings have been confirmed. Please check back for continuous updates.

To: Alex Conner <aconner@hydeparkcenter.org>
From: Eun-jung Bae <e.bae@heston.us>
Subject: Fair Attendance
Date: October 9

Dear Mr. Conner,

Thank you for confirming our booth reservation at the upcoming job fair. We are looking forward to meeting many qualified applicants and have heard that graduates from top schools will be attending.

Our plan is to hire several people as quickly as possible. Therefore, we will be screening applicants at the event. I would also like to conduct interviews on the same day. I'd like my colleagues in Singapore and Japan to participate in the process virtually. Is it possible to rent a small meeting room with Wi-Fi for this purpose? An hour should be sufficient. Please let me know.

Sincerely,

Eun-jung Bae
Human Resource Manager
Heston

186. For whom is the announcement most likely intended?

(A) Community center workers
(B) Faculty members
(C) Recent graduates
(D) Company executives

187. According to the list, what is a qualification to work at Verity Care?

(A) An understanding of software programs
(B) Some experience in sales
(C) Detailed knowledge of computers
(D) An ability to interact with children

188. What is indicated about Brentura Diagnostics?

(A) It will be represented by the company's CEO.
(B) It is seeking people with advanced degrees from the Tampa area.
(C) It requires that individuals have prior job experience.
(D) It will consider any applicant with a science degree.

189. What is implied about Ms. Bae?

(A) She is recruiting individuals for her department.
(B) She needs to leave early for a business trip.
(C) She will interview marketing graduates on-site.
(D) She participated in a job fair last year.

190. What is suggested about Ms. Bae's company?

(A) It has multiple overseas offices.
(B) It is looking for unpaid trainees.
(C) It wants to rent several meeting rooms.
(D) It requires an Internet connection at its booth.

GO ON TO THE NEXT PAGE

Questions 191-195 refer to the following article, memo, and e-mail.

Dorwing Air Continues to Adapt

By Aaron Sheffield

For any given flight, it is almost guaranteed that some passengers with reservations will not show up. Unsurprisingly, most airlines attempt to fill the empty seats by overbooking. This method is not without controversy, however, as it occasionally results in more passengers than seats and some ticket holders having to make alternative travel arrangements.

To ease some of the stress faced by passengers who are forced to miss a flight, the international airline Dorwing Air has recently changed its overbooking policy. Some affected passengers in economy class will be offered a business class seat on the next flight. If all else fails, Dorwing Air will also offer some ticket holders up to $1,000 in compensation. "We are confident that these measures will help us improve our customer satisfaction rate," said Dorwing Air CEO Valery Suarez.

To: All Dorwing Air passenger service agents
From: Dorwing Air administration
Subject: Overbooking policy reminders
Date: November 5

I'm sure you've all been briefed on the new policy by now, but here are some reminders just in case:

1. If a flight has been overbooked, offer SkySaver coupons to passengers who volunteer to take a later flight. They can use these to get reduced fares when booking future Dorwing Air flights.
2. If the flight remains overbooked within 30 minutes of the departure time, offer passengers a business class seat on the next available flight and access to our VIP lounge while they wait.
3. If the issue has still not been resolved by the time that passengers are about to start boarding, you may offer the maximum compensation amount available for that flight.

To: Joan Kreeger <joan_kreeger@wentleco.com>
From: Lewis Hopps <lew_hopps@wentleco.com>
Subject: Mr. Hunt's flight
Date: November 10
Attachment: Cost_estimates

Hi, Joan,

I just received a message from Mr. Hunt. He said the meeting he had yesterday with the Vorin Construction representative went well. He's at the airport in Roystonville now and said he'll arrive about an hour late. His 1:10 P.M. flight is overbooked, but Dorwing Air has secured him a business class seat on a plane that'll be leaving at 2:05 P.M. That'll give you more time to get to the airport. You can leave the office to pick him up at about 5:00 P.M. Until then, please check the accuracy of the file I'm sending you.

Best regards,
Lewis

191. Why was the article written?
(A) To propose a technological solution
(B) To criticize the handling of a situation
(C) To describe some policy changes
(D) To announce the hiring of an executive

192. What can Dorwing Air passenger service agents do if a flight is overbooked?
(A) Provide hotel accommodations
(B) Offer discount vouchers
(C) Contact partner airlines
(D) Cancel unconfirmed reservations

193. What are ticket holders who give up their seats just before boarding entitled to?
(A) A seat upgrade
(B) A sum of up to $1,000
(C) Entry to premium waiting space
(D) Extra mileage points

194. What is suggested about Mr. Hunt?
(A) He will go directly from an airport to an office.
(B) He was able to reach an agreement with a new client.
(C) He was in Roystonville for several days.
(D) He was given access to an exclusive waiting area.

195. What does Mr. Hopps ask Ms. Kreeger to do?
(A) Ensure that a file is correct
(B) Meet with representatives of a partner company
(C) Forward a flight itinerary
(D) Book an international flight

GO ON TO THE NEXT PAGE

Questions 196-200 refer to the following e-mail, announcement, and form.

To: Bennet Fraser <b.fraser@invercargill.com>
From: Clara Walker <c.walker@pos.co.nz>
Subject: 5th Annual POS Congress
Date: December 8

Dear Dr. Fraser,

Here at the Pacific Orthodontic Society (POS), we have begun making preparations for next year's congress, which will take place from April 23 to 24. Along with a special lecture and symposiums, we'd like to host a panel discussion. As you've led groundbreaking research at your workplace, I'd like to invite you to talk about your work on stage with Dr. Ellie Williams and Dr. Hannah Brown on the second day of the gathering.

Each speaker receives $2,000 in compensation. In addition, travel expenses are reimbursed and an all-access guest pass is provided for the activities, which include a private party in the ballroom of the conference venue. Rooms have been reserved for speakers at a local hotel, which is well equipped with various facilities. I'm sure you would appreciate the hotel's gym—all guests can use it for free. There's also a spa, which charges a reasonable entrance fee.

I look forward to hearing back from you.

Sincerely,

Clara Walker, Congress Organizer

Announcement of the 5th Annual POS Congress, scheduled for April 23 & 24

This year's gathering of the Pacific Orthodontic Society (POS) will be held in Auckland. Leading experts from the South Pacific region will present on the latest techniques and technologies for straightening teeth. The following events have already been confirmed:

Special Lecture	The Latest Advances in Braces	Dr. James Reid
Symposium	New Types of Dental Implants	Dr. Serena Singh
Symposium	Low-cost Tooth-Alignment Kits	Dr. Hazel Collins
Panel Discussion	Scanning Technology	Dr. Hannah Brown Dr. Bennet Fraser Dr. Ellie Williams

The fees are $540 for POS members and $600 for nonmembers, and the payment deadline is March 30. Payments can be made by credit card at www.pos.co.nz/congress5.

POS Travel Compensation Form

Thank you for contributing to the POS. To ensure that you are properly compensated, please complete this form and send a scanned copy of it and all receipts to Blake Henry at bh.accounting@pos.co.nz. Your stay at Eden Lake Hotel has already been paid for by the POS.

Name of Participant: Hannah Brown

Event Attended: 5th Annual POS Congress

Event Location: Centennial Hotel, Auckland

Expenditures

DATE	DESCRIPTION	COST	TOTAL
April 22	Te Anau Air, economy class	$547	$556
	Stationery supplies	$9	
April 24	Connection cord for laptop	$90.75	$90.75
April 25	Ether Airlines, business class	$612	$635
	Early morning taxi to airport	$23	
TOTAL			$1,281.75

196. Why did Ms. Walker contact Dr. Fraser?

(A) To invite him to become a member of a society
(B) To schedule a symposium at a university
(C) To request his participation in a conference
(D) To critique a newly developed system

197. What is suggested about the panel discussion on scanning technology?

(A) It was held on April 24.
(B) It featured a surprise guest.
(C) It was attended by a large audience.
(D) It included a technical demonstration.

198. According to the announcement, why should some people visit a Web site?

(A) To provide some feedback
(B) To upload some photographs
(C) To view a seating chart
(D) To complete a transaction

199. What did Dr. Brown probably receive for free from Eden Lake Hotel?

(A) A computer accessory
(B) Access to a fitness center
(C) Unlimited Internet usage
(D) A treatment at a spa

200. What is indicated about Dr. Brown?

(A) She traveled with some coworkers.
(B) She drove a rental car during her stay in Auckland.
(C) She booked flights with two different airlines.
(D) She spent $23 to reach Centennial Hotel.

This is the end of the test. You may review Parts 5, 6, and 7 if you finish the test early.

정답 p.326 / 점수 환산표 p.329 / 해석 p.354 / Part 5&6 무료 해설 바로 보기(정답 및 정답 음성 포함)

* 다음 페이지에 있는 Self 체크 리스트를 통해 자신의 문제 풀이 방식과 태도를 점검해 보세요.

Self 체크 리스트

TEST 04는 무사히 잘 마치셨죠?
이제 다음의 Self 체크 리스트를 통해 자신의 테스트 진행 내용을 점검해 볼까요?

1. 나는 75분 동안 완전히 테스트에 집중하였다.

   □ 예 □ 아니오

   아니오에 답한 경우, 이유는 무엇인가요?

2. 나는 75분 동안 100문제를 모두 풀었다.

   □ 예 □ 아니오

   아니오에 답한 경우, 이유는 무엇인가요?

3. 나는 75분 동안 답안지 표시까지 완료하였다.

   □ 예 □ 아니오

   아니오에 답한 경우, 이유는 무엇인가요?

4. 나는 Part 5와 Part 6를 19분 안에 모두 풀었다.

   □ 예 □ 아니오

   아니오에 답한 경우, 이유는 무엇인가요?

5. Part 7을 풀 때 5분 이상 걸린 지문이 없었다.

   □ 예 □ 아니오

6. 개선해야 할 점 또는 나를 위한 충고를 적어보세요.

* 교재의 첫 장으로 돌아가서 자신이 적은 목표 점수를 확인하면서 목표에 대한 의지를 다지기 바랍니다. 개선해야 할 점은 반드시 다음 테스트에 실천해야 합니다. 그것이 가장 중요하며, 그래야만 발전할 수 있습니다.

TEST 05

PART 5

PART 6

PART 7

Self 체크 리스트

잠깐! 테스트 전 확인사항

1. 휴대 전화의 전원을 끄셨나요? □ 예
2. Answer Sheet, 연필, 지우개를 준비하셨나요? □ 예
3. 시계를 준비하셨나요? □ 예

모든 준비가 완료되었으면 목표 점수를 떠올린 후 테스트를 시작합니다.

문제 풀이를 마치는 시간은 지금부터 75분 후인 ___시 ___분입니다.

테스트 시간은 총 75분이며, 시험 종료 전 2~3분은 정답 검토 및 답안지 마킹을 위해 사용합니다.

READING TEST

In this section, you must demonstrate your ability to read and comprehend English. You will be given a variety of texts and asked to answer questions about these texts. This section is divided into three parts and will take 75 minutes to complete.

Do not mark the answers in your test book. Use the answer sheet that is separately provided.

PART 5

Directions: In each question, you will be asked to review a statement that is missing a word or phrase. Four answer choices will be provided for each statement. Select the best answer and mark the corresponding letter (A), (B), (C), or (D) on the answer sheet.

PART 5 권장 풀이 시간 11분

101. Consumer surveys show that people would ------- spend up to $1,200 on a new computer.

(A) happy
(B) happily
(C) happiness
(D) happier

102. A well-organized résumé can boost ------- chances of obtaining a job interview.

(A) you
(B) your
(C) yours
(D) yourself

103. Alicia Doone's illustrations have been ------- in magazines around the city.

(A) publisher
(B) publish
(C) published
(D) publishing

104. The charity shop's 24-hour drop box allows people ------- used clothes whenever it is convenient for them.

(A) to donate
(B) donates
(C) donating
(D) donation

105. Chemie's Ice Cream offers an ------- of products that it changes every season.

(A) interest
(B) assortment
(C) advent
(D) influence

106. Travelers can earn reward points ------- than ever before with the new Perspectiva Plus credit card.

(A) quick
(B) quickly
(C) more quickly
(D) most quickly

107. According to ------- collected from diners, most customers are satisfied with the restaurant's new menu.

(A) content
(B) procedure
(C) feedback
(D) investigation

108. Sally's Candy Shop is the third building ------- the main square on Grant Street.

(A) from
(B) among
(C) under
(D) above

109. The winner of the photography competition will be ------- by a panel of five distinguished judges.

(A) contained
(B) determined
(C) implemented
(D) interpreted

110. Emblem Motor's new car lineup will be unveiled at the annual Chicago Auto Show ------- next year.

(A) previously
(B) typically
(C) early
(D) highly

111. The department head will assign a new project to Ms. Springs when she ------- to the office from her vacation.

(A) returns
(B) returning
(C) to return
(D) is returned

112. When companies prioritize their customers' needs ------- all else, they tend to generate repeat business.

(A) above
(B) where
(C) within
(D) toward

113. The engineers claimed that making a slight ------- to the existing solar panels would make them more effective.

(A) modify
(B) modified
(C) modifiable
(D) modification

114. Tenants who ------- in Waterford Apartments must pay their rent on the first of the month.

(A) occupy
(B) engage
(C) reside
(D) visit

115. Without ------- public funding, the Scott Foundation will need to raise more money from private sources.

(A) adequate
(B) incompetent
(C) receptive
(D) delightful

116. ------- he had only two years of experience, Mr. Black was named the regional sales director of TVD Incorporated.

(A) Even though
(B) As a result of
(C) In spite of
(D) So as to

117. A customer was ------- charged twice, so a refund was issued to her credit card.

(A) accidental
(B) accidentally
(C) accident
(D) accidents

118. Manuel Corporation workers will now receive life insurance coverage as one of their employment -------.

(A) skills
(B) benefits
(C) concerns
(D) deductions

119. Ms. Jung was displeased to learn that she was being transferred to the Houston office as she had ------- asked to move.

(A) before
(B) already
(C) often
(D) never

120. This weekend's Phoenix Marathon is going to take place as planned ------- the forecast of rainy weather.

(A) aside from
(B) notwithstanding
(C) regarding
(D) according to

GO ON TO THE NEXT PAGE

121. Visitors to the Shiller Children's Museum are more than ------- to interact with the items on display.

(A) pleasant
(B) welcome
(C) obvious
(D) brilliant

122. Paulson Electronics can ship the products by regular mail ------- express delivery, which involves an extra charge.

(A) so
(B) up
(C) at
(D) or

123. After its television commercial aired, Seaborn Cruises received a large ------- of inquiries from potential passengers.

(A) size
(B) result
(C) majority
(D) volume

124. The musicians practiced in the back room ------- the stage was being set up.

(A) in order to
(B) as
(C) during
(D) unless

125. By recycling batteries rather than discarding them, it is possible to ------- the amount of toxic materials entering landfills.

(A) seize
(B) reduce
(C) satisfy
(D) reserve

126. Waiters at Folza Bar and Grill are paid ------- two weeks at a rate of $9 per hour.

(A) most
(B) all
(C) every
(D) either

127. Novels ------- on actual events are often very popular with readers of all age groups.

(A) based
(B) are based
(C) base
(D) basing

128. All aspects of the job will be covered during the training course, which was designed to be as ------- as possible.

(A) decorative
(B) protective
(C) comprehensive
(D) tentative

129. The president met with several of the country's top ------- to discuss possible solutions to the supply shortage.

(A) manufacturer
(B) manufactured
(C) manufacture
(D) manufacturers

130. Failing to file your tax form ------- may lead to an amendment request from the National Tax Office.

(A) nearly
(B) moderately
(C) narrowly
(D) properly

PART 6

Directions: In this part, you will be asked to read four English texts. Each text is missing a word, phrase, or sentence. Select the answer choice that correctly completes the text and mark the corresponding letter (A), (B), (C), or (D) on the answer sheet.

PART 6 권장 풀이 시간 8분

Questions 131-134 refer to the following memo.

To: Department heads
From: Ronaldo Reyes
Subject: Next year's budgets
Date: May 15

Our monthly department head meeting will be held on Wednesday, May 30, at 7 P.M. As always, it will be in the conference room on the 16th floor.

The main topic of discussion will be our departmental budgets for next year. This is a subject of vital importance. -------. (**131.**) In preparation for the meeting, I'd like each of you to put together a report that summarizes your department's annual costs and highlights changes that may need to ------- (**132.**) to your budget. Specifically, look for unnecessary ------- (**133.**) to eliminate as this will save the company money overall.

Please ------- (**134.**) that you have received this memo. You may do this simply by confirming your attendance with my assistant Ms. Hertz. Thank you.

131. (A) The budget has already been decided.
(B) Our invited speakers are recognized experts.
(C) However, this is only a temporary setback.
(D) Therefore, the company's CEO will join us.

132. (A) make
(B) made
(C) be made
(D) be making

133. (A) expended
(B) expends
(C) expensive
(D) expenses

134. (A) explain
(B) confide
(C) remember
(D) acknowledge

GO ON TO THE NEXT PAGE

Questions 135-138 refer to the following review.

The first time I went to True Colors Paint Supply, I received ------- (135.) customer service. Unfortunately, my second experience with them was not nearly as good. Yesterday when I went in, there were no employees at the front of the store. After ten minutes of looking at color samples, an employee finally approached me. However, she excused herself almost immediately in order to go answer the phone. ------- (136.). If that weren't bad enough, someone else made a mistake on my order when I finally got some help. I ------- (137.) for Candy Apple Red but was given Scarlet Red instead. Next time, I will shop at another store that ------- (138.) more attention to its customers.

135. (A) questionable
(B) excellent
(C) deficient
(D) gradual

136. (A) Most importantly, I have been a loyal customer for many years.
(B) The managers who answer the phones are usually very friendly.
(C) Honestly, I was shocked to witness such unprofessional behavior.
(D) I've used their products for various home improvement projects.

137. (A) could ask
(B) am asking
(C) had asked
(D) will ask

138. (A) pays
(B) considers
(C) understands
(D) draws

Questions 139-142 refer to the following e-mail.

To: Julie Evans <julie@juliepaints.com>
From: David Whetzel <director@artunlimited.com>
Subject: Art class
Date: February 12

Dear Ms. Evans,

I recently saw your work at Wave Gallery and wanted to tell you that I was very impressed by your unique style. -------. (139.) I'm writing today as I run a small art studio ------- (140.) painting classes several times a week. We occasionally invite artists who can teach our students something other than basic oil or acrylic painting techniques, and I was wondering whether you would be interested in being our next guest instructor. You would have a lot of ------- (141.) in planning the class. As the teacher, you alone would decide on the materials to use and the concepts to teach.

I look forward to hearing from you. This e-mail address is the best way to contact me ------- (142.) you are interested.

Sincerely,

David Whetzel
Director of Art Unlimited

139. (A) Thank you for inviting me to the museum opening.
(B) The gallery will now be closing at 6 P.M. on weekdays.
(C) I am excited to begin working together at the studio.
(D) I've never seen paintings that look quite like yours.

140. (A) will hold
(B) that holds
(C) is holding
(D) being held

141. (A) flexibility
(B) assistance
(C) restrictions
(D) demonstrations

142. (A) before
(B) so that
(C) because
(D) in case

GO ON TO THE NEXT PAGE

Questions 143-146 refer to the following notice.

ATTENTION EMPLOYEES:

The Sebastian Hill Hotel is going to be closed ------- (**143.**) the month of June. The building is in need of some renovations that cannot be completed while guests are here.

Since June is the start of our busiest period, there are enough temporary job openings for everyone at our partner locations. Therefore, all Sebastian Hill staff members ------- (**144.**) their work at either the Daytona Hotel or the New Orleans resort after their final day here, on May 31.

Should you have a preference for which hotel you would like to work at, please tell Jim Stevens, the branch manager, before the end of this week. He cannot promise to fulfill any ------- (**145.**) but will consider them carefully. ------- (**146.**).

143. (A) except for
(B) as long as
(C) throughout
(D) following

144. (A) will begin
(B) have begun
(C) began
(D) were beginning

145. (A) contracts
(B) commitments
(C) requests
(D) offers

146. (A) Some of the guests might complain about the construction work.
(B) We hope this will be followed by many more overseas locations.
(C) We interviewed candidates for seasonal positions that start in June.
(D) All decisions about temporary work locations will be made by May 20.

PART 7

Directions: In this part, you will be asked to read several texts, such as advertisements, articles, instant messages, or examples of business correspondence. Each text is followed by several questions. Select the best answer and mark the corresponding letter (A), (B), (C), or (D) on your answer sheet.

PART 7 권장 풀이 시간 54분

Questions 147-148 refer to the following online form.

Global Engineering Monthly (GEM)

For over 30 years, we've been the publication of choice for professionals in the engineering field. Each issue of *Global Engineering Monthly* includes equipment reviews, articles on current trends, and profiles of successful engineers.

Subscription Packages

Six-month subscription	☐ $36.00 (amounts to $6/issue)
One-year subscription	■ $66.00 (amounts to $5.50/issue)
Two-year subscription	☐ $96.00 (amounts to $4/issue)

Would you like to subscribe to GEM's weekly newsletter, delivered conveniently by e-mail?

Yes ☐ No ■

Your Details

Name	Lorenza Cassar
Address	17 Triq Annetto Caruana
City	Qawra
Country	Malta
Postal Code	SPB 1215
E-mail Address	lorenza@rcengineering.com

*Customers who order a one-year subscription receive a free compact tool kit!

*Customers who order a two-year subscription receive a free pass to the Transnational Engineering Conference in New York City on May 9!

Go to Billing

147. What is indicated about *Global Engineering Monthly*?

(A) It sells individual issues at a discount.
(B) It sponsors engineering conferences.
(C) Its readership includes experts in their field.
(D) Its publisher prints other magazine titles as well.

148. What will Ms. Cassar receive with her subscription?

(A) A weekly newsletter
(B) A ticket to a conference
(C) A small tool kit
(D) A special edition

GO ON TO THE NEXT PAGE

Questions 149-151 refer to the following notice.

Attention:

If you frequently suffer from insomnia or suspect that you have a sleeping disorder, you may be qualified to participate in a new study taking place at the Carson Medical Institute. We are currently developing a drug that may help rid people of insomnia. During the study, all you have to do is take it at a regular time every night for two weeks. Then, you will be asked to complete a report about its effects on your sleep as well as any side effects.

If you are between the ages of 18 and 50, you are eligible to take part in this study. To sign up, please contact us at sleepstudy@cmi.org. In the e-mail, please specify any medical problems you have that may interfere with the drug. Please also list your work schedule and other obligations. The deadline to sign up is December 1. All participants will be paid $200 for their time.

149. What is the Carson Medical Institute planning to do?

(A) Open a research center
(B) Test a drug
(C) Hire new staff members
(D) Launch an advertisement

150. The word "regular" in paragraph 1, line 4, is closest in meaning to

(A) fixed
(B) orderly
(C) straight
(D) ordinary

151. What should people specify in the e-mail?

(A) Their familiarity with a drug
(B) Their preferred treatment method
(C) Their time commitments
(D) Their participation in previous studies

Questions 152-153 refer to the following text-message chain.

Kathleen Massee [6:18 P.M.]
Hi, Evan. I just noticed that the schedule for next week has already been posted, and it seems that I'm supposed to work Monday morning, which is strange. I don't usually get morning shifts.

Evan Rosenblatt [6:19 P.M.]
I guess Ms. Ross needs someone to replace Ms. Kovac while she's away on vacation.

Kathleen Massee [6:20 P.M.]
I see. Well, in any case, I was wondering if you'd be able to take that shift for me because I made a dentist appointment for that day.

Evan Rosenblatt [6:22 P.M.]
Not a problem at all. I don't have anything else to do at that time anyway. I'm sure Ms. Ross will be fine with the change, but you should let her know about it before the end of the day so that she can modify the schedule.

Kathleen Massee [6:23 P.M.]
Thanks so much. I owe you one.

152. What is suggested about Ms. Kovac?

(A) She will be requesting some vacation time.
(B) She does not want to contact her manager.
(C) She normally takes morning shifts.
(D) She will be transferred to another branch.

153. At 6:22 P.M., what does Mr. Rosenblatt mean when he writes, "Not a problem at all"?

(A) He is willing to take a colleague's work shift.
(B) An expense has already been covered by Ms. Ross.
(C) A dental procedure will not take long.
(D) He has not heard about any recent schedule conflicts.

GO ON TO THE NEXT PAGE

Questions 154-155 refer to the following advertisement.

Arts and Crafts Are Not Just for Kids!

This summer, local supply store Arts and Scraps will be holding a small after-hours class for adult learners every Tuesday and Thursday from 6:30 P.M. to 8:30 P.M. The class will provide instruction in a variety of techniques, including glass painting, linoleum block printing, and mixed media collage making. It will be taught by illustrator Maude Cumby, who worked in New York as an artist for 10 years and is a graduate of the Pulford Academy of Design.

The cost of the 12-session course is $100 if you book your spot before May 2, which is a month before classes start. After that date, our regular fee of $130 applies. All materials are provided. Visit www.artsandscraps.com/classes to sign up, or drop by our store and register during our normal hours of 10 A.M. through 6 P.M.

154. What is indicated about Arts and Scraps?

(A) It is located in New York.
(B) It is owned by Ms. Cumby.
(C) It closes at 6:30 P.M.
(D) It will hold two class sessions per week.

155. What is mentioned about the upcoming course?

(A) It will be taught by a recent design graduate.
(B) Its fees do not include class materials.
(C) It will take place in May.
(D) Its rates vary depending on the registration date.

Questions 156-158 refer to the following information.

Corogo Inc. Employee Transfer Policy

Corogo Inc. supports the professional development of its staff and recognizes that some employees may wish to pursue advancement opportunities within the company. Corogo Inc. employees may apply internally for open positions posted on the company Web site if they:

- have worked in their current position for at least 12 months*
- possess the minimum qualifications or requirements listed in one of our job postings
- have received a performance review level of at least "satisfactory" within the last six months
- have received no written warnings or notices within the last 12 months

Employees who are interested in applying for a different position are advised to notify their current managers as soon as possible. Regular full-time staff members are required to give their supervisors a minimum of two weeks' notice before submitting an application.

Should an employee be accepted for a position in a different department, previously approved plans for holidays will be subject to change.

*Only in rare circumstances will employees who do not meet the requirements above be considered for a transfer. In this situation, a Corogo Inc. human resources employee will meet with the staff member's current supervisor to determine whether a transfer is appropriate.

156. What is indicated about Corogo Inc.?

(A) It offers staff professional development classes.
(B) It is looking to hire a manager from within.
(C) It lists available positions on its Web site.
(D) It reviews staff members once a year.

157. What might change for transferred staff members?

(A) Their parking spots
(B) Their monthly salary
(C) Their vacation days
(D) Their working hours

158. According to the information, on what occasion might a supervisor and a human resources employee meet?

(A) When a disciplinary notice has been canceled
(B) When a candidate has held a current position for under a year
(C) When a performance review is inaccurate
(D) When a training period is coming to an end

GO ON TO THE NEXT PAGE

Questions 159-160 refer to the following information.

http://www.contestcraze.com/advertise

HOME	DAILY FEATURED CONTESTS	**ADVERTISE**	CONTACT	FORM

Advertising on Contest Craze:

Are you promoting a contest, draw, or giveaway for your business or organization? If you need help getting the word out, you've come to the right place. If you have a contest you think people should know about, send us a description, and we'll post it on our homepage for free for one day. If you'd like even more exposure, select one of our advertising options below to make your post a featured contest. This means that it will stay at the top of our homepage and be included in the daily e-mail newsletter sent to our members.

Prices for featuring a contest:

One day	$35
Two days	$65
Three days	$90
One week	$200

Please note that we do not post information about contests that require an entry fee.

159. What is the purpose of the information?

(A) To advertise products for businesses
(B) To share tips about winning prizes online
(C) To provide advice about managing a homepage
(D) To offer details on advertising services

160. What is true about the featured contests?

(A) They must be advertised for a week.
(B) They are described in mass e-mails.
(C) They are publicized on various Web sites.
(D) They require entrance fees from participants.

Questions 161-164 refer to the following article.

Environmental Awareness Day Giveaway

By Brenda Galway, staff reporter

To celebrate Environmental Awareness Day on May 1, Winstonville will be giving away 2,000 free young trees to members of the community on a first-come, first-served basis. This initiative is part of the municipal government's pledge to plant 10,000 trees in order to improve the sustainability of the city. According to urban planning manager Jane Stein, trees can be picked up at Mulligan's Nursery on Fennel Road and Central City Community Center from 8:00 A.M. to 11:30 A.M. A number of trees will also be available at the Home and Garden Shop on Clifton Avenue from 4:30 P.M. to 8:00 P.M. for those who can't make it in the morning.

"Just remember to follow the directions posted on the city's Web site for planting and caring for each tree you take," said Ms. Stein. "We're tracking the growth progress of the trees. I'm pleased to say that, according to the official list, we have already planted 800 new trees in the city so far." Residents who don't have their own property but still want to participate in the initiative can join special gardening events held by local nonprofit organization Planet Plant. Visit www.winstonvillegov.org/parksandrecdept for more details.

161. What is the purpose of the article?

(A) To explain the benefits of urban trees
(B) To describe a city project
(C) To announce a campaign promise
(D) To review a recently held event

162. What is mentioned about the free trees?

(A) They will be distributed only in the morning.
(B) They have been provided by a nonprofit organization.
(C) They will come with instructional brochures.
(D) They are available to residents in a limited quantity.

163. What does Ms. Stein remind people to do?

(A) Prepare an area in their gardens for trees
(B) Sign up to do volunteer work in the area
(C) Visit a Web site to find some instructions
(D) Get permission from the city for planting

164. The word "tracking" in paragraph 2, line 2, is closest in meaning to

(A) searching
(B) following
(C) maintaining
(D) pursuing

TEST 01 | 02 | 03 | 04 | 05 | 06 | 07 | 08 | 09 | 10 해커스 토익 실전 1000제 1 Reading

GO ON TO THE NEXT PAGE

Questions 165-168 refer to the following Web page.

www.dpqtransport.com/aboutus

About Us:

DPQ Transport is a charter bus rental company that provides service nationwide seven days a week, 24 hours a day. Whether you need to transport a group for a tour or a business retreat, we guarantee that traveling with us is the right choice.

Safety is our number one priority. Accordingly, our drivers are highly trained individuals with many years of experience behind the wheel. — [1] —. Furthermore, our vehicles are maintained regularly to ensure they are always functioning properly at the time of departure.

We also pride ourselves on comfort and convenience. — [2] —. Along with having plenty of legroom, each of the reclining seats in our vehicles is fitted with electrical sockets for your devices as well as adjustable air conditioning vents. Free wireless Internet is also available. You can also bring small meals or snacks with you or schedule a stop at a popular restaurant. — [3] —.

Finally, our buses can seat up to 56 people, meaning that using our service is a cost-effective way to travel as a group. — [4] —.

If DPQ Transport is the right choice for you, send the details of your trip to queries@dpqtransport.com. We'll respond with a competitive quote and a proposed itinerary within 24 hours.

165. What is true about DPQ Transport?

(A) It provides international transportation.
(B) It exclusively caters to tour groups.
(C) It has launched an express service.
(D) It operates at all hours of the day.

166. What is NOT mentioned about DPQ Transport vehicle seats?

(A) They are spacious.
(B) They have outlets for devices.
(C) They have built-in screens.
(D) They have a temperature control feature.

167. According to the Web page, what can people do through e-mail?

(A) Select a specific driver
(B) Receive a cost estimate
(C) Adjust the number of travelers
(D) Customize on-board meals

168. In which of the positions marked [1], [2], [3], and [4] does the following sentence best belong?

"They are thoroughly screened upon being hired and must pass annual evaluations."

(A) [1]
(B) [2]
(C) [3]
(D) [4]

Questions 169-171 refer to the following article.

Cell Phone Tower Construction to Begin Soon

The construction of a new cell phone tower in the seaside town of Farview is set to begin shortly, much to the dismay of some local residents. — [1] —. First proposed three years ago, the project was stalled when people began to raise concerns about its proposed location at a beachfront parking lot. Many said the tower would spoil the area's natural beauty. Others voiced fears that its presence might cause various health and safety issues for those who live near the site, not to mention lower property values. — [2] —.

In this regard, city officials reassured the public that the tower will not only be safe but will also generate substantial rental revenue in the amount of approximately $20,000 per year from each wireless carrier that rents space on it. — [3] —. Furthermore, the influx of tourists to Farview each summer means that the tower is becoming increasingly necessary for practical reasons. "The more visitors we have, the more phones there are," said city council member Fred White. — [4] —. As for concerns about the structure's appearance, local artist Katherine Tatum helped with its design so that the tower will blend in well with the natural surroundings.

169. What is NOT mentioned as a concern about the tower?

(A) It could damage local wildlife.
(B) It could pose various health problems.
(C) It could negatively affect the value of real estate.
(D) It could make the area appear unattractive.

170. What is indicated about Farview?

(A) It does not have any cell phone towers yet.
(B) It plans to develop a coastal area for tourism.
(C) It pays rental fees for land usage.
(D) It will earn money through a new structure.

171. In which of the positions marked [1], [2], [3], and [4] does the following sentence best belong?

"And that means there is a greater need for cellular service."

(A) [1]
(B) [2]
(C) [3]
(D) [4]

GO ON TO THE NEXT PAGE

Questions 172-175 refer to the following online chat.

Bryce Turner	[2:30 P.M.]	Did you hear that our company's shareholders want us to cut down on waste? I think it's important for us to respect their wishes, so I'd like to find some ways to reduce the amount of non-recyclable packaging materials we use here at Meerson.
Sophie Moore	[2:31 P.M.]	We recently lessened the amount of plastic foam we put inside boxes by 40 percent. Is there anything else we can do?
Bryce Turner	[2:34 P.M.]	Could we eliminate the foam completely and start using shredded newspaper instead?
Randy Poehler	[2:35 P.M.]	And only our fragile items need the extra padding. Our detergents, for instance, come in plastic bottles, so they don't need any special protection.
Randy Poehler	[2:36 P.M.]	Instead of focusing only on the shipping materials, what if we also changed some of our product containers?
Bryce Turner	[2:38 P.M.]	Are you proposing we use some other type of material for our containers? I don't see how that would be any better.
Randy Poehler	[2:39 P.M.]	No. I'm just saying that we could use plastic more efficiently. Some of our competitors sell detergents in pouches that can be used to refill empty bottles. They're using plastic but far less of it. We could do the same.
Bryce Turner	[2:41 P.M.]	That would actually save us money, too.
Sophie Moore	[2:42 P.M.]	I'll look into whether we can make that change.

Send

172. What does Mr. Turner want to reduce?

(A) The size of a distribution network
(B) The use of non-recyclable materials
(C) The amount of cleaning product in a bottle
(D) The number of fragile items for sale

173. What is indicated about Meerson?

(A) It plans to seek feedback from shareholders.
(B) Some of its bottles are made of recycled plastic.
(C) It is cutting staff in the warehouse department.
(D) Some of its products do not require padding.

174. What is suggested about the pouches?

(A) They are made of plastic.
(B) They take longer to produce than bottles.
(C) They come in a variety of sizes.
(D) They were patented by Meerson.

175. At 2:39 P.M., what does Mr. Poehler mean when he writes, "We could do the same"?

(A) He has an idea for eliminating all plastic packaging.
(B) He hopes to use a different type of container.
(C) He proposes that some detergents be improved.
(D) He wants to start cooperating with a competitor.

GO ON TO THE NEXT PAGE

Questions 176-180 refer to the following announcement and advertisement.

Bentota Beach Hotel Gains Strong Leadership

Gold Frond Resorts, one of India's most trusted accommodation chains, has chosen Gareth Sunderland as visitor services director at its newest property, Bentota Beach Hotel. Mr. Sunderland will assume his new role on June 14—three weeks before the resort begins operating. He has over 20 years of hospitality experience, with the last decade of his career having been spent with Gold Frond Resorts. Most recently, he has served as the front office manager at our island location. Due to his accomplishments there, he is expected to excel in the higher position of visitor services director.

At Bentota Beach Hotel, Mr. Sunderland will be supervising all staff members who deal directly with customers. He will be in charge of our reservation and check-in systems. Also, he will be responsible for staff training in order to help us maintain quality service. And last but not least, he will help coordinate a range of fun pursuits for guests, from water sports to cultural excursions.

Gold Frond Resorts has something for everyone!

With the opening of our luxurious Bentota Beach location, we now have a total of five resorts to choose from throughout India. Whatever your budget, whether you're looking for excitement or relaxation, we can provide your ideal experience.

Our resorts:

Komari Cove	Our original property; recently expanded to 315 rooms—more than any of our other locations
Matara Oceanside	Our most affordable option; a short walk from a popular public beach on the mainland
Tangalle Retreat	Named Best Resort by *Leisurist Magazine*; consists of 40 private villas on the mainland shore
Vergual Paradise	A 20-minute boat ride from Pondicherry Airport; occupies an entire island
Bentota Beach	Best suited for those who like to have an active vacation; located on a popular mainland surfing beach

You can find information on activities available at each resort at www.goldfrondresorts.com, and you can conveniently make an online reservation as well.

176. What is the main topic of the announcement?

(A) A delay with a building's opening
(B) A company event taking place
(C) An employee receiving a promotion
(D) A new staff training program

177. According to the announcement, what is NOT a responsibility of the visitor services director?

(A) Managing a booking system
(B) Organizing leisure activities
(C) Providing service training to staff
(D) Handling complaints about facilities

178. What is suggested about Mr. Sunderland?

(A) He began his career with Gold Frond Resorts.
(B) He developed a business expansion plan.
(C) He was employed at Vergual Paradise.
(D) He graduated with a degree in tourism.

179. What is true about Gold Frond Resorts?

(A) Its first location recently increased its capacity.
(B) It is preferred by visitors who intend to go shopping.
(C) It plans to establish a budget resort.
(D) Its resorts all have private beaches.

180. How can people get information on resort activities?

(A) By checking a Web site
(B) By calling a contact number
(C) By contacting a travel agent
(D) By sending a text message

GO ON TO THE NEXT PAGE

Questions 181-185 refer to the following e-mails.

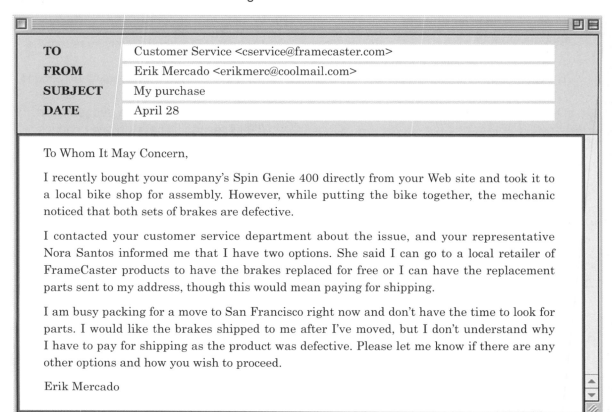

TO	Customer Service <cservice@framecaster.com>
FROM	Erik Mercado <erikmerc@coolmail.com>
SUBJECT	My purchase
DATE	April 28

To Whom It May Concern,

I recently bought your company's Spin Genie 400 directly from your Web site and took it to a local bike shop for assembly. However, while putting the bike together, the mechanic noticed that both sets of brakes are defective.

I contacted your customer service department about the issue, and your representative Nora Santos informed me that I have two options. She said I can go to a local retailer of FrameCaster products to have the brakes replaced for free or I can have the replacement parts sent to my address, though this would mean paying for shipping.

I am busy packing for a move to San Francisco right now and don't have the time to look for parts. I would like the brakes shipped to me after I've moved, but I don't understand why I have to pay for shipping as the product was defective. Please let me know if there are any other options and how you wish to proceed.

Erik Mercado

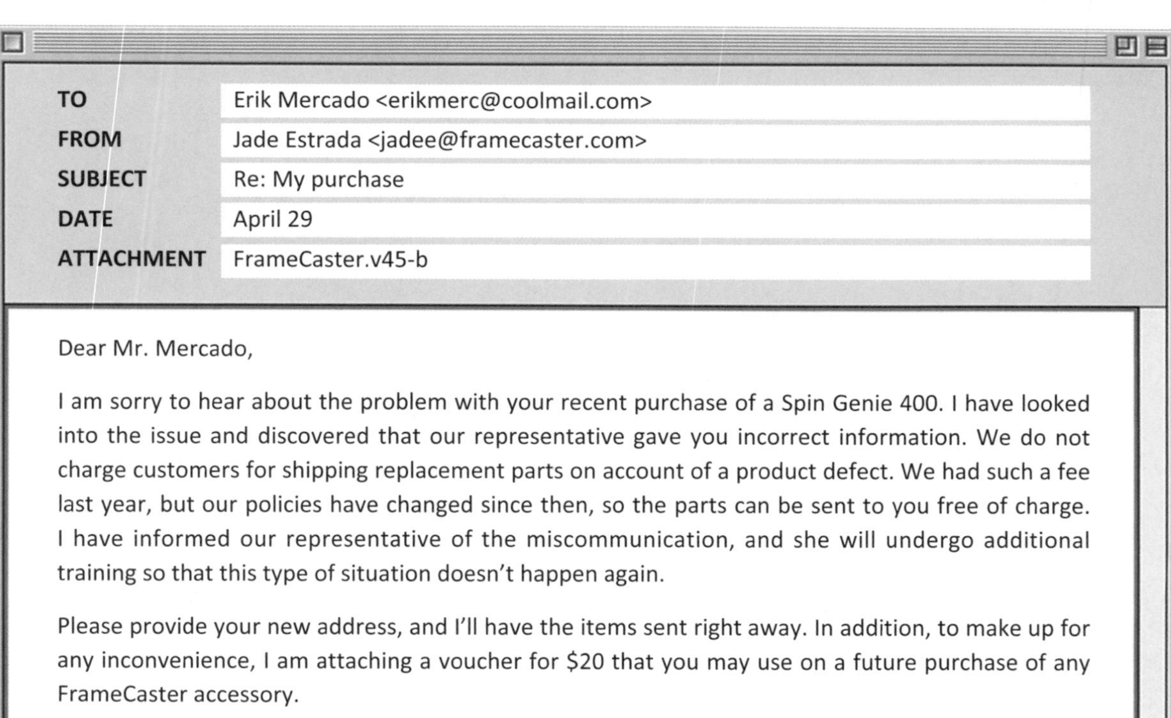

TO	Erik Mercado <erikmerc@coolmail.com>
FROM	Jade Estrada <jadee@framecaster.com>
SUBJECT	Re: My purchase
DATE	April 29
ATTACHMENT	FrameCaster.v45-b

Dear Mr. Mercado,

I am sorry to hear about the problem with your recent purchase of a Spin Genie 400. I have looked into the issue and discovered that our representative gave you incorrect information. We do not charge customers for shipping replacement parts on account of a product defect. We had such a fee last year, but our policies have changed since then, so the parts can be sent to you free of charge. I have informed our representative of the miscommunication, and she will undergo additional training so that this type of situation doesn't happen again.

Please provide your new address, and I'll have the items sent right away. In addition, to make up for any inconvenience, I am attaching a voucher for $20 that you may use on a future purchase of any FrameCaster accessory.

Thank you for your patience.

Sincerely yours,

Jade Estrada
Customer Service Chief
FrameCaster Cycles

181. What is suggested about the Spin Genie 400?

(A) It can be purchased unassembled.
(B) It is manufactured at a facility in San Francisco.
(C) It is made of lightweight materials.
(D) It was included in a special offer.

182. What is mentioned about Mr. Mercado?

(A) He purchased a bicycle from a local store.
(B) He paid an extra fee for express delivery.
(C) He has a couple of replacement options.
(D) He had an item assembled for free.

183. Why was the second e-mail written?

(A) To investigate the cause of an error
(B) To attempt to resolve a situation
(C) To question the validity of a rule
(D) To suggest imposing a penalty

184. What will Nora Santos do?

(A) Write an apology to a customer
(B) Get further training
(C) Send an item to an updated address
(D) Speak with a salesperson

185. According to the second e-mail, what has been provided to Mr. Mercado?

(A) A partial refund
(B) A store directory
(C) A bicycle accessory
(D) A product voucher

GO ON TO THE NEXT PAGE

Questions 186-190 refer to the following memo, e-mail, and article.

From: Dillon Zhou
To: All Staff
Subject: Office visit
Date: February 20

A writer from *The Sydney Sun* is scheduled to visit our new office on March 1. She is writing a short article about our office design and employee benefits. No photographs will be taken as we have already sent some images for the piece. As the reporter is directed through our halls, feel free to interact with her at your discretion. One of our senior executives will briefly introduce our latest software development plan to her. The reporter is welcome to use all the leisure and entertainment facilities.

From: Sela Singh <s.singh@thesydneysun.au>
To: Dillon Zhou <d.zhou@zazoosoftware.com>
Subject: Article
Date: February 27

Dear Mr. Zhou,

I apologize for the short notice, but I will not be able to return to Sydney on March 1 due to a travel emergency. If I can visit on another date, please contact my assistant, Dennis Worley, at d.worley@thesydneysun.au, and he will handle all the details. If not, please send a basic description of your new facilities in your reply to this e-mail.

Also, some of the photos you have sent are not very clear. Could you send me larger copies of each? That would be very helpful.

Thank you.

Sincerely,

Sela Singh
The Sydney Sun

Easing Office Stress at Zazoo
March 8
by Sela Singh

The computer giant Zazoo Software recently opened its newest office in Sydney and has attracted much speculation about the benefits it provides employees. Known for providing a nurturing work environment, Zazoo Software has plenty of places to relax in its new office building. I was able to see these for myself on March 4, when I was given a tour of the facilities. Free food is available for employees in every cafeteria, and there are plenty of healthy options.

In terms of exercise facilities, there is a basketball court, pool, and gym. In addition, plans call for the addition of a yoga and meditation studio by the end of the year. All these facilities help employees perform at high levels of efficiency, and I could see that this was true during my time at the office.

"We are currently in the final phase of designing our new software program," Cathy Sanchez said while showing me the plan for the project. "Everyone is working under immense pressure, but our environment should help ease that stress and make things more fun."

186. What does the memo indicate about the visitor?

(A) She will not speak with employees.
(B) She will start her visit at a leisure facility.
(C) She will not take any pictures.
(D) She will write about some sales strategies.

187. What is suggested about Mr. Zhou?

(A) He had his picture taken by a journalist.
(B) He met with Ms. Singh to make arrangements.
(C) He e-mailed Mr. Worley regarding a schedule.
(D) He is not based at Zazoo Software's headquarters.

188. Who most likely is Ms. Sanchez?

(A) A local newspaper reporter
(B) An architect of a new office building
(C) A building administrator
(D) An executive at a software company

189. According to the article, what is a benefit of Zazoo Software's work environment?

(A) It promotes cooperation among team members.
(B) It is designed to reduce workplace injuries.
(C) It improves the performance of staff.
(D) It offers large spaces for meeting with clients.

190. Which facility has NOT yet been opened at the Zazoo Software's newest office?

(A) A yoga studio
(B) A staff cafeteria
(C) An office gym
(D) A swimming pool

GO ON TO THE NEXT PAGE

Questions 191-195 refer to the following note, form, and bill.

From the desk of Rosa Mengistu

Hello, Mr. Fekade. I'm sorry you were unable to attend today's planning meeting. One thing we decided was that we require a photo of Dire Dawa Central Park. The photo needs to show people relaxing near the fountain during the daytime. It is up to you to find such an image, and keep in mind that it needs to be in high resolution. Please check our photo archive, as we may already have one that meets this description. Otherwise, you can search the collection of a photo agency such as Flash Photos or Baumgard Pics. If all else fails, you have the option of hiring a freelance photographer.

Baumgard Pics ★ Your source for photos from around the world

Customer:	**Image Details:**	**Our pricing is according to image size:**
Dawit Fekade	**Image Name:** Crowd Watching Musical Performance **Category:** Outdoor activities **Location:** Fountain at Dire Dawa Central Park **Image Code:** HEWZYXP **File Size:** 20 megabytes **Taken By:** Delores Ashburn	☐ Small (500x449) $3.99 ☐ Medium (1000x899) $4.99 ☐ Large (2000x1798) $5.99 ☐ Extra Large (3172x2851) $6.99

Buy Image Now!

Thank you for choosing Baumgard Pics!

770 Hickory Street
Omaha, Nebraska,
US 68124

(402) 555-2882
http://baumgardpics.org

Image Code	Billing address	Amount paid	
HEWZYXP	Dawit Fekade Aksum Services 4 Adwa Street Addis Ababa Ethiopia	Cost of photo	$5.99
		Taxes	$0.59
		Total	$6.58

To download your bill, log in at Baumgard Pics' Web site and click on the 'Purchase History' tab. Select the bills you would like to save, then click on the Download button.

You may use your current order starting on June 25. Please be aware that your right to use the photo expires after five years. Should you wish to extend your period of usage, you may do so at our Web site.

191. Why was the note written?

(A) To assign a task
(B) To express disappointment
(C) To recommend a device
(D) To seek advice

192. What information is NOT included on the form?

(A) The subject of a photo
(B) The location where an image was taken
(C) A client's contact information
(D) The name of a photographer

193. What can be inferred about Mr. Fekade?

(A) He has permission to negotiate contracts with agencies.
(B) He was unable to find a suitable image at his workplace.
(C) He is still undergoing training for recently hired personnel.
(D) He submitted some images taken at an incorrect location.

194. What size of image did Mr. Fekade purchase?

(A) Small
(B) Medium
(C) Large
(D) Extra large

195. According to the bill, what will happen after five years have passed?

(A) A photography supplier will update a user agreement.
(B) A company will replace its source of photos.
(C) A Web site membership will expire.
(D) A customer will no longer be entitled to use a picture.

GO ON TO THE NEXT PAGE

Questions 196-200 refer to the following announcement and e-mails.

Blue Ravine Medical School (BRMS)
ANNOUNCEMENT: *All students and faculty*

Please note that Dr. Janice Shen, from Kowloon University of Eastern Medicine (KUEM), will be presenting a lecture on September 4. Dr. Shen will describe successful treatments for spinal conditions. She is an expert in needle therapy and herbal medication, and she primarily treats back pain and spinal disease. For the past 12 years, she has been employed by KUEM, where she leads many different research projects.

Her lecture will take place on the BRMS campus in the Fasthead Auditorium at 3 P.M. Seats are limited, so please make a booking by visiting the school events office, dialing extension #364, or sending an e-mail to Jayne Marche in the events office at jaynemarche@brms.edu. The lecture is free for all instructional staff and students at BRMS, but guests must pay $16.

TO: Jayne Marche <jaynemarche@brms.edu>
FROM: Grayden Higgins <graydenhiggins@brms.edu>
SUBJECT: Request
DATE: August 19

Hello, Jayne.

I'm teaching an advanced course in alternative medicine here at BRMS, and nine students are currently enrolled. I'd like to make a reservation for all ten of us to attend Dr. Shen's upcoming lecture. Let me know if you require all the students' names or if the seats can be booked under my name.

Also, I was wondering if anyone will be making a video of the lecture. I would like to possibly share her talk with future students. Unfortunately, no one thought to record her previous visit, and I hope that will not be the case this time.

Thanks, and I hope to hear from you soon.

Dr. Grayden Higgins
BRMS, Department of Skeletal and Muscular Disorders

TO: Angelo Conti <angeloconti@brms.edu>
FROM: Jayne Marche <jaynemarche@brms.edu>
SUBJECT: Lecture event assignment
DATE: August 20

Hi, Angelo.

A BRMS instructor has requested that a video be recorded of the lecture taking place on September 4. Please add this filming assignment to your schedule. Based on Dr. Shen's previous presentation, I'm guessing the lecture will last for about an hour and a half, and it will be followed by a question-and-answer session that should take 30 minutes. I think we should film the latter as well, so the video's total time should be about two hours.

Try to finish editing the footage within three days and send me the video file. I will post it on the BRMS Web site, have it added to our multimedia library's collection, and forward it to the instructor who requested it. I'll make sure the auditorium is open an hour in advance so that you have time to set up.

Thanks!
Jayne

196. What type of work does Dr. Shen currently do?

(A) She develops medications for a company.
(B) She supervises projects at a university.
(C) She operates a physical therapy clinic.
(D) She writes health-care textbooks.

197. According to the announcement, what is NOT a booking method for the upcoming lecture?

(A) Visiting an office
(B) Calling a number
(C) Completing an online form
(D) Sending an e-mail

198. What is indicated about Dr. Higgins's students?

(A) They are in their final year of a medical program.
(B) They are exchange students from another university.
(C) They will be submitting reports following a talk.
(D) They will attend a lecture free of charge.

199. What will happen at the end of Dr. Shen's lecture?

(A) A video will be shown.
(B) Questions will be responded to.
(C) Assignments will be given.
(D) Certificates will be presented.

200. What will Ms. Marche most likely do after September 4?

(A) Share a video recording with Dr. Higgins
(B) Attend a special medical seminar at KUEM
(C) Extend another invitation to Dr. Shen
(D) Meet with a department head at BRMS

This is the end of the test. You may review Parts 5, 6, and 7 if you finish the test early.

정답 p.327 / 점수 환산표 p.329 / 해석 p.362 / Part 5&6 무료 해설 바로 보기(정답 및 정답 음성 포함)

* 다음 페이지에 있는 Self 체크 리스트를 통해 자신의 문제 풀이 방식과 태도를 점검해 보세요.

Self 체크 리스트

TEST 05는 무사히 잘 마치셨죠?
이제 다음의 Self 체크 리스트를 통해 자신의 테스트 진행 내용을 점검해 볼까요?

1. 나는 75분 동안 완전히 테스트에 집중하였다.

   □ 예 □ 아니오

   아니오에 답한 경우, 이유는 무엇인가요?

2. 나는 75분 동안 100문제를 모두 풀었다.

   □ 예 □ 아니오

   아니오에 답한 경우, 이유는 무엇인가요?

3. 나는 75분 동안 답안지 표시까지 완료하였다.

   □ 예 □ 아니오

   아니오에 답한 경우, 이유는 무엇인가요?

4. 나는 Part 5와 Part 6를 19분 안에 모두 풀었다.

   □ 예 □ 아니오

   아니오에 답한 경우, 이유는 무엇인가요?

5. Part 7을 풀 때 5분 이상 걸린 지문이 없었다.

   □ 예 □ 아니오

6. 개선해야 할 점 또는 나를 위한 충고를 적어보세요.

* 교재의 첫 장으로 돌아가서 자신이 적은 목표 점수를 확인하면서 목표에 대한 의지를 다지기 바랍니다. 개선해야 할 점은 반드시 다음 테스트에 실천해야 합니다. 그것이 가장 중요하며, 그래야만 발전할 수 있습니다.

TEST 06

PART 5

PART 6

PART 7

Self 체크 리스트

잠깐! 테스트 전 확인사항

1. 휴대 전화의 전원을 끄셨나요? □ 예
2. Answer Sheet, 연필, 지우개를 준비하셨나요? □ 예
3. 시계를 준비하셨나요? □ 예

모든 준비가 완료되었으면 목표 점수를 떠올린 후 테스트를 시작합니다.

문제 풀이를 마치는 시간은 지금부터 75분 후인 ___시 ___분입니다.

테스트 시간은 총 75분이며, 시험 종료 전 2~3분은 정답 검토 및 답안지 마킹을 위해 사용합니다.

READING TEST

In this section, you must demonstrate your ability to read and comprehend English. You will be given a variety of texts and asked to answer questions about these texts. This section is divided into three parts and will take 75 minutes to complete.

Do not mark the answers in your test book. Use the answer sheet that is separately provided.

PART 5

Directions: In each question, you will be asked to review a statement that is missing a word or phrase. Four answer choices will be provided for each statement. Select the best answer and mark the corresponding letter (A), (B), (C), or (D) on the answer sheet.

PART 5 권장 풀이 시간 11분

101. It is wise to prepare ------- for retirement by investing in a pension plan.

(A) whose
(B) whichever
(C) theirs
(D) oneself

102. No applicant for a position at Carver Financial will ------- without three years of related experience.

(A) have considered
(B) be considered
(C) being considered
(D) consider

103. Passengers of the LT Airlines flight to Barcelona were asked to ------- in a designated area.

(A) wait
(B) carry
(C) reserve
(D) accept

104. Organizing a new product launch requires ------- among departments.

(A) cooperate
(B) cooperation
(C) to cooperate
(D) cooperative

105. The foundation's usual charitable activities were ------- suspended while it focused on assisting victims of the hurricane.

(A) evenly
(B) temporarily
(C) relatively
(D) morally

106. Median Bank follows strict guidelines for the ------- of its customers' private information.

(A) profit
(B) advice
(C) connection
(D) protection

107. ------- 16 companies, the City of Orlando chose Flaremont Construction to build the new sports stadium.

(A) Out of
(B) In front of
(C) Nearby
(D) Through

108. The weather forecast for December 14 calls for a cold wave, so people should dress -------.

(A) accordingly
(B) eagerly
(C) invitingly
(D) ultimately

109. A trade show representative called each participant a month before the event ------- their attendance.

(A) confirm
(B) to confirm
(C) will confirm
(D) is confirming

110. According to a recent report, Keller Auto is one of the ------- manufacturers of car tires in Australia.

(A) led
(B) leaders
(C) leading
(D) leads

111. The art historian did copious research while trying to ------- the painting as an original.

(A) adapt
(B) generate
(C) authenticate
(D) commission

112. By lowering the price of its streaming service, Jolio Inc. aims to reach customers ------- its existing market.

(A) beyond
(B) aboard
(C) after
(D) between

113. Gymnast Anna Stamos will replace the ------- brand ambassador of Knobel breakfast cereal.

(A) gradual
(B) extreme
(C) current
(D) entire

114. Thanks to hours of practice, the sales team was able to ------- present its proposal to the client.

(A) confide
(B) confident
(C) confiding
(D) confidently

115. Shipping within the United States is free for Buyer's Club members, but international shipping will require paying an ------- fee.

(A) opportune
(B) intentional
(C) additional
(D) exchangeable

116. Charging machines for electric cars will be installed in gas stations ------- the country.

(A) across
(B) opposite
(C) toward
(D) onto

117. The escalators at Davidson Station are subject to ------- inspection to ensure they are working properly.

(A) routinely
(B) routine
(C) routines
(D) routinize

118. ------- resident of West Bay who earns less than $25,000 a year is eligible to apply for housing assistance.

(A) Most
(B) Those
(C) Any
(D) All

119. The advertisements for the new stove place an ------- on its appearance and ease of use.

(A) order
(B) emphasis
(C) investment
(D) observation

GO ON TO THE NEXT PAGE

120. The partnership between Farrco and Slansea, Inc. will ------- benefit the firms by making them more competitive.

(A) strategy
(B) strategize
(C) strategic
(D) strategically

121. The Mill Creek Community Center started a cleanup ------- to get rid of litter around town.

(A) status
(B) initiative
(C) declaration
(D) compliance

122. Due to ------- economic conditions, the company may decide to stop hiring employees.

(A) worst
(B) worsen
(C) worsens
(D) worsening

123. The valet attendant at the Six Stars Hotel was unsure ------- car belonged to Mr. Carlton.

(A) whom
(B) as
(C) both
(D) which

124. Mr. Grady is training the new staff members on how to handle ------- clients in a calm manner.

(A) demanding
(B) measured
(C) suitable
(D) sparse

125. Joseph Baker will accept the promotion ------- he gets the 20 percent raise he asked for.

(A) only if
(B) furthermore
(C) other than
(D) apart from

126. Each year, every employee at Corehouse Technics undergoes a performance -------.

(A) evaluator
(B) evaluating
(C) to evaluate
(D) evaluation

127. To minimize transportation costs, the company moved to an office ------- the port.

(A) per
(B) regarding
(C) near
(D) plus

128. Rob Marshall's *Smart Investor's Guide* offers a lot of ------- insights for understanding the stock market.

(A) helped
(B) helpful
(C) helpfully
(D) help

129. Attendees of the conference in October will receive more detailed information about the speakers -------.

(A) alongside
(B) either
(C) further
(D) beforehand

130. The storage facility uses a system that is capable of ------- small changes in indoor air temperature.

(A) acting
(B) sensing
(C) cooling
(D) experimenting

PART 6

Directions: In this part, you will be asked to read four English texts. Each text is missing a word, phrase, or sentence. Select the answer choice that correctly completes the text and mark the corresponding letter (A), (B), (C), or (D) on the answer sheet.

PART 6 권장 풀이 시간 8분

Questions 131-134 refer to the following advertisement.

Ride in Style

If you're a cycling enthusiast, then it's time to get on board with Bango. Not only are our helmets stylish, ------- **131.** they keep you safe. The helmets are made with three layers of tough and sturdy materials for excellent impact absorption. They meet National Safety Board requirements. They also offer ------- **132.** for regular riders. ------- **133.**, they fold neatly into a compact size for easy storage. There is simply no excuse not to try a Bango helmet today. ------- **134.**. If you buy one at full price, you will receive a second helmet at 50 percent off. Check out www.bangohelmets.com, and start your next cycling journey with Bango.

131. (A) why
(B) but
(C) than
(D) or

132. (A) speed
(B) assistance
(C) durability
(D) convenience

133. (A) For example
(B) Conversely
(C) If so
(D) Otherwise

134. (A) Don't forget to sign up for the safety workshop.
(B) Get one now and take advantage of a special promotion.
(C) Find the widest variety of brands by shopping online.
(D) Our repair shop is located right across from the mall.

GO ON TO THE NEXT PAGE

Questions 135-138 refer to the following e-mail.

From: Hampton Institute <accountmanage@hamptoninstitute.org>
To: Kate Whitman <k.whitman@braxton.ca>
Subject: Payment Plan
Date: May 25

Dear Ms. Whitman,

This message is to confirm your ------- (**135.**) for Hampton Institute's coding seminar from June 30 through August 31. Since you have signed up to pay in installments, you will be charged on a monthly basis. -------. (**136.**) At any time, you are free to ------- (**137.**) the payment plan. To do this, simply log in to your account and select "Change plan." You can also do this here. Please note that the longest plan we offer is for 18 months. E-mail me right away if you have any -------. (**138.**) I am always happy to help.

Best,
Hampton Institute Account Management Team

135. (A) enrolls
(B) enrollment
(C) enroll
(D) enrolled

136. (A) The system needs to be checked for errors immediately.
(B) The discount will be available for a limited time only.
(C) The first invoice will be sent by e-mail on July 1.
(D) Please check in at the reception desk for your student ID.

137. (A) modify
(B) begin
(C) approve
(D) request

138. (A) options
(B) difficulties
(C) symptoms
(D) referrals

Questions 139-142 refer to the following announcement.

Lake County Animal Society to Hold Fundraising Gala

The Lake County Animal Society appreciates the contributions that have been made over the years. They have ------- (139.) the organization to provide food and shelter for hundreds of animals.

Please join us for a fundraising gala on December 11 at the Morrissey Civic Center. It will be a night of fun for a good cause. ------- (140.). Admission tickets will be available for only $100 each. Proceeds will ------- (141.) be used to repair the group's Willoughby facility as the building's roof needs to be replaced. However, a portion will also go to expanding programs ------- (142.) people to volunteer at our shelters. These campaigns are essential to maintaining community awareness of our work.

139. (A) known
(B) asked
(C) enabled
(D) instructed

140. (A) Our largest donation of the evening was $1,500.
(B) Members receive a newsletter every month.
(C) They will be moved to a larger facility to better accommodate them.
(D) The attendees will be treated to dinner and live entertainment.

141. (A) chiefly
(B) sometimes
(C) exclusively
(D) seldom

142. (A) encourage
(B) encouraged
(C) that encourage
(D) it can encourage

GO ON TO THE NEXT PAGE

Questions 143-146 refer to the following notice.

Jefferson Sports Center Notice

------- (143.) April 8, the indoor pool will be closed for one week. The pool needs to be completely drained before being cleaned, repaired, and sanitized. This is an annual procedure that is necessary to provide a safe and healthy environment for everyone. ------- (144.), other indoor facilities will remain available for use. ------- (145.) include the sauna, gym, and wellness area. The outdoor pool may be used as well. We apologize for any inconvenience the work might cause. ------- (146.). For more news and updates, follow us on social media.

143. (A) Effect
(B) Effects
(C) Effectively
(D) Effective

144. (A) After all
(B) Likewise
(C) In the meantime
(D) For this reason

145. (A) Mine
(B) Our
(C) Theirs
(D) These

146. (A) Normal operations will resume once it is done.
(B) Our latest post received thousands of likes and views.
(C) We are in the process of investigating the problem.
(D) Please report missing items to our lost-and-found counter.

PART 7

Directions: In this part, you will be asked to read several texts, such as advertisements, articles, instant messages, or examples of business correspondence. Each text is followed by several questions. Select the best answer and mark the corresponding letter (A), (B), (C), or (D) on your answer sheet.

PART 7 권장 풀이 시간 54분

Questions 147-148 refer to the following advertisement.

Do most cosmetics products give you a rash or make your skin itch? Betteskin Cosmetics is seeking individuals to test a new line of products designed specifically for people with sensitive skin.

To sign up, go to www.betteskin.com. Answer a brief online survey before June 30 to help us identify your skin problems. We will mail product samples to your home along with detailed instructions. Each product must be tested for a week. In exchange, participants will receive a $25 coupon for our Web site.

147. How can people participate in a test?
(A) By promoting a product line on the Internet
(B) By completing a survey before a deadline
(C) By submitting a letter of request
(D) By attending an interview in person

148. What will participants receive?
(A) A free meal
(B) A membership card
(C) An online voucher
(D) An event invitation

GO ON TO THE NEXT PAGE

Questions 149-151 refer to the following information.

Notification to All Charlotte Grocer Shoppers

Charlotte Grocer has stopped the sale of Hero Coco Water in its stores. The item is currently unavailable due to a worldwide product recall, but it will be restocked as soon as the recall order is lifted.

For now, we recommend trying the Cocolait and Biba brands of coconut water. We carry both brands in our stores nationwide. As with all products sold in our stores, they are certified by organic certification agencies and meet all regulatory requirements for food safety.

We apologize for the inconvenience. For any concerns regarding this matter, please visit the customer service desk at the store nearest you. And remember to register your e-mail address at www.charlottegrocer.com to receive our weekly newsletter containing promotional offers.

149. What problem is Charlotte Grocer having?

(A) A food supplier went out of business.
(B) A cash register system does not work.
(C) A product cannot be acquired.
(D) A store will have to close early.

150. What can be inferred about Charlotte Grocer?

(A) It merged with a competitor.
(B) It released its own brand of water.
(C) It maintains locations worldwide.
(D) It follows specific product standards.

151. Why should customers register on a Web site?

(A) To provide product feedback
(B) To take part in a special event
(C) To arrange home deliveries
(D) To receive a newsletter by e-mail

Questions 152-153 refer to the following text-message chain.

Christina Sanchez [12:23 P.M.]
Kenichi, could you please postpone my afternoon meeting? I am at lunch with Ms. Kim, and she seems ready to make an offer on the Lakewood house. Therefore, I will be driving her to the property shortly, and we will hopefully sign a contract.

Kenichi Yamamoto [12:24 P.M.]
That's great news. Yes, I can move Mr. Zhou to tomorrow morning. You have an opening at 9 A.M.

Christina Sanchez [12:26 P.M.]
That works for me. Please call Mr. Zhou directly rather than e-mail him since this is a last-minute change.

Kenichi Yamamoto [12:27 P.M.]
Will do. I have his phone number in front of me.

Christina Sanchez [12:29 P.M.]
Thank you so much. Unless there is an urgent matter, please let any other callers know that I will be back in the office tomorrow.

152. Why did Ms. Sanchez contact Mr. Yamamoto?

(A) To invite him to a lunch meeting
(B) To request a copy of a contract
(C) To move an appointment
(D) To schedule a visit to a house

153. At 12:27 P.M., what does Mr. Yamamoto most likely mean when he writes, "Will do"?

(A) He will contact a client by phone.
(B) He will follow up on a contract.
(C) He accepts a proposed appointment.
(D) He can take Ms. Sanchez's place at a meeting.

GO ON TO THE NEXT PAGE

Questions 154-155 refer to the following e-mail.

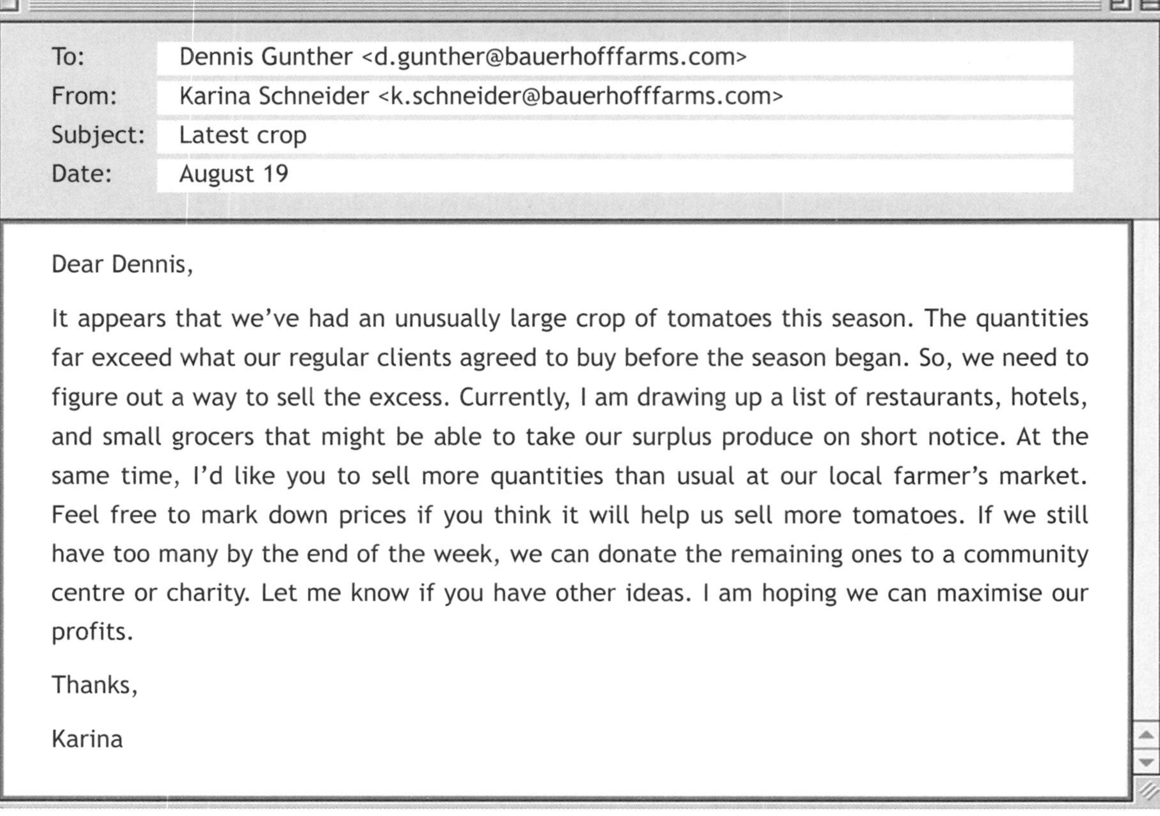

To: Dennis Gunther <d.gunther@bauerhofffarms.com>
From: Karina Schneider <k.schneider@bauerhofffarms.com>
Subject: Latest crop
Date: August 19

Dear Dennis,

It appears that we've had an unusually large crop of tomatoes this season. The quantities far exceed what our regular clients agreed to buy before the season began. So, we need to figure out a way to sell the excess. Currently, I am drawing up a list of restaurants, hotels, and small grocers that might be able to take our surplus produce on short notice. At the same time, I'd like you to sell more quantities than usual at our local farmer's market. Feel free to mark down prices if you think it will help us sell more tomatoes. If we still have too many by the end of the week, we can donate the remaining ones to a community centre or charity. Let me know if you have other ideas. I am hoping we can maximise our profits.

Thanks,

Karina

154. What is stated about Bauerhoff Farms' tomatoes?

(A) They are not ready to be harvested.
(B) Some of them need to be sold to new customers.
(C) They are of a lower quality than last season's.
(D) Some of them were rejected by regular clients.

155. What is Mr. Gunther asked to do?

(A) Pass on instructions to employees
(B) Contact some restaurant owners
(C) Make arrangements with a charity
(D) Increase sales at a local marketplace

Questions 156-157 refer to the following article.

Is the Sharing Economy Coming to an End?

April 23—Mumbai is taking steps to address issues with companies in the so-called sharing economy. Yesterday, it issued new regulations that target companies like the apartment-sharing application Househunt and the transportation service CallAuto. Both companies, and others like them, now have to meet more stringent requirements to operate in the city. For instance, Househunt will have to meet the same standards for hygiene and safety as the city's hotels and may be limited to certain neighborhoods. As for CallAuto, it will have to treat its drivers as regular employees and provide them with paid vacations and health insurance. The affected companies have argued that these measures will hurt profitability. However, officials counter that they are necessary to improve the public's safety and welfare.

156. What is the article mainly about?

(A) A demand for better treatment of employees
(B) A campaign to reduce the number of accidents
(C) A city's effort to regulate certain types of companies
(D) A plan to increase taxes on selected businesses

157. What is suggested about CallAuto?

(A) It has no competitors in an industry.
(B) It has plans to leave the city of Mumbai.
(C) It will have to give its drivers employment benefits.
(D) It took steps to improve its service quality.

GO ON TO THE NEXT PAGE

Questions 158-161 refer to the following advertisement.

Introducing Peacelid

Peacelid is an eco-friendly company selling reusable cups, straws, and utensils. Our products are made from 100 percent bamboo. Peacelid's products are also biodegradable, so they decompose safely and naturally after being discarded.

Furthermore, Peacelid advocates for environmentally friendly consumption practices and donates 3 percent of every purchase to organizations involved in preventing deforestation.

Check out www.peacelid.com to see our catalog. New customers can enjoy a 20 percent discount on their first order by entering the code "PEACE20" on the checkout page. Moreover, every order of $200 or more will include a free reusable straw.

158. What is NOT true about Peacelid?

(A) It makes products for eating and drinking.
(B) It supports other organizations.
(C) It uses a natural material.
(D) It operates a chain of stores.

159. What is an advantage of Peacelid's products?

(A) Durability
(B) Safe disposal
(C) Affordable price
(D) Wide availability

160. What is mentioned about the coupon code?

(A) It can be used multiple times.
(B) It only applies to some customers.
(C) It must be requested by e-mail.
(D) It expires after one month.

161. How can customers obtain a reusable straw?

(A) By buying over $200 worth of goods
(B) By donating to an environmental fund
(C) By exchanging some plastic items
(D) By volunteering for a cleanup effort

Questions 162-164 refer to the following announcement.

Attention Gymspan Customers

Beginning in August, users who have a subscription to the Gymspan app will no longer be able to take advantage of unlimited workouts at its network of affiliated fitness centers. We apologize for this change, but it is a necessary cost-cutting measure.

Customers who are presently enrolled in our unlimited membership plan may continue to use their benefits until the end of their current billing cycle. Afterward, they will be automatically moved to another plan. — [1] —. To make up for the change, Gymspan will award 500 loyalty points, which can be used to purchase other products and services. — [2] —.

In addition, Gymspan has introduced some improvements to the app. Each month, customers have the option to easily switch from one plan to another. You can also temporarily stop payments when you are out of the country. — [3] —. Lastly, you can enjoy more ways to earn points quickly. These improvements are intended to make your Gymspan membership truly flexible and responsive to your needs. — [4] —. For additional information, visit www.gymspan.com or download the app today.

162. What is mentioned about Gymspan?

(A) It is removing a subscription plan.
(B) It has cut ties with some affiliates.
(C) It is offering points for new members.
(D) It has merged with another firm.

163. According to the announcement, what are customers able to do?

(A) Sign up for a free trial membership
(B) Rate fitness studios on an application
(C) Adjust their plans on a monthly basis
(D) Inquire about franchise opportunities

164. In which of the positions marked [1], [2], [3], and [4] does the following sentence best belong?

"Accounts can now be paused for up to two months in a year."

(A) [1]
(B) [2]
(C) [3]
(D) [4]

GO ON TO THE NEXT PAGE

Questions 165-167 refer to the following letter.

November 20

Bernard Davidson
180 Whitfield Drive
Edmonton, AL T5A 0A2

Dear Mr. Davidson,

Congratulations! After reviewing your application materials, we have decided to award you a Clark Newman Scholarship for engineering students. This will allow you to pursue a degree in mechanical engineering at Alberta Technical College with your tuition entirely paid for.

As you know, this scholarship is only awarded to five applicants per year. The applicants are chosen based on their stellar academic record and their passion for engineering. All recipients were selected from a group of over 1,000 applicants.

During your first year at Alberta Technical College, you will be living in a small dormitory, Kensing House, with other engineering students. It is located just steps from the main engineering building, Mitchell Hall. Next week, we will send you your student card as well as more information about your housing situation. Once again, congratulations!

Sincerely,

Donald Neilson
Dean, College of Engineering
Alberta Technical College

165. What is the primary purpose of the letter?

(A) To inform Mr. Davidson about a scholarship
(B) To give details about a new program
(C) To recruit Mr. Davidson to a college
(D) To request follow-up application materials

166. What is indicated about Mr. Davidson?

(A) He wants to change his college major.
(B) He took part in a highly competitive process.
(C) He already made his first tuition payment.
(D) He lives near Alberta Technical College.

167. What will be sent to Mr. Davidson in the next week?

(A) An event brochure
(B) A housing application
(C) An identification card
(D) A financial aid form

Questions 168-171 refer to the following article.

Santa Monica (March 30)—Over the past few months, a new concept store offering custom fragrances has been drawing lots of attention. It occupies a busy spot for tourists along 3rd Street. Customers can create their own fragrances or buy one of dozens of premade ones with unique combinations of scents. All fragrances use natural oils.

Over the past four years, owner Sarah McKellen has developed a following on social media with her videos about fragrances. — [1] —. Last year, she began selling her creations online. The success of that venture convinced her to open the first Freesha store in January. To her surprise, she sold out her entire inventory within a week. — [2] —.

According to Ms. McKellen, most customers enjoy the idea of creating fragrances. — [3] —. That's why she has added a small room where up to four visitors at a time can watch how fragrances are made. In the future, Ms. McKellen plans to expand the room to accommodate hands-on workshops for larger groups. — [4] —.

168. What is the article mainly about?

(A) A recently established business
(B) A company's switch to natural ingredients
(C) A busy street in a growing neighborhood
(D) A newly reopened tourist attraction

169. The word "spot" in paragraph 1, line 2, is closest in meaning to

(A) post
(B) place
(C) stain
(D) situation

170. What is suggested about Freesha?

(A) It opened a week later than planned.
(B) It will soon have a second location.
(C) It is seeking a new supplier of ingredients.
(D) It will hold workshops for five or more people.

171. In which of the positions marked [1], [2], [3], and [4] does the following sentence best belong?

"Ms. McKellen had to hire more staff to help her meet the unexpected demand."

(A) [1]
(B) [2]
(C) [3]
(D) [4]

GO ON TO THE NEXT PAGE

Questions 172-175 refer to the following text-message chain.

Dwayne Jackson 9:22 A.M.
As you know, we have a major fundraiser tomorrow for our botanical gardens. If possible, I'd like you two to arrive by 6 P.M.

Sarah Chen 9:24 A.M.
Sure thing. I was actually going to be there early.

Frank Daniels 9:27 A.M.
I won't be able to show up until close to the starting time as I have to work at the Fry Factory until 6:30 P.M.

Dwayne Jackson 9:28 A.M.
OK, thanks for letting me know, Frank. Sarah, since you're coming early, I was wondering if you could help me set up the tables and chairs.

Sarah Chen 9:30 A.M.
I'd be happy to. Have we decided on a layout?

Dwayne Jackson 9:31 A.M.
Yes. I'll e-mail you pictures of how the room should look. Frank, since you're getting here around the start time, could you pass out programs at the entrance?

Frank Daniels 9:32 A.M.
Yeah, sure.

Dwayne Jackson 9:34 A.M.
Be ready to greet participants and help them with any questions they have about the event or about how to make a donation.

Frank Daniels 9:35 A.M.
Got it. I'll be there by 6:45 P.M., which is 15 minutes before the event starts.

172. Why is Mr. Daniels unavailable to come early?

(A) He has to work at another job.
(B) He must go to a medical appointment.
(C) He will be attending a class.
(D) He has to participate in a meeting.

173. What does Mr. Jackson ask Ms. Chen to do?

(A) Send him a layout
(B) Greet some attendees
(C) Arrange some furniture
(D) Clean up after the event

174. At 9:35 A.M., what does Mr. Daniels mean when he writes, "Got it"?

(A) He will provide assistance.
(B) He has received an item.
(C) He understands a layout.
(D) He will note down a meeting time.

175. When will the fundraiser officially start?

(A) At 6:00 P.M.
(B) At 6:30 P.M.
(C) At 6:45 P.M.
(D) At 7:00 P.M.

GO ON TO THE NEXT PAGE

Questions 176-180 refer to the following e-mails.

To: Olivia Brunelli <olivia@nathalieresort.fr>
From: Roger Keller <roger.keller@lowefinances.com>
Date: March 21
Subject: Inquiry

Dear Ms. Brunelli,

During a vacation last year, I stumbled upon your beautiful retreat in Rochemaure. I was able to book a massage and thoroughly enjoyed my experience. I am in charge of organizing a trip for my company this May, and I would like to make a reservation with you. We are welcoming a few investors from overseas and want to spend some relaxing time there as a group.

We will be staying at the resort from May 3 to 7. We would arrive late in the evening on May 3 and leave early on May 7. Can you reserve spa treatments for our investors for the afternoon of May 4? There are eight of them in total. This will be followed by dinner. If the weather permits, we would like to be seated outdoors and in a quiet area.

We will need 12 single rooms for the duration of the trip. We are also interested in wine tasting and visiting lavender farms.

Please let me know if all of this is possible by replying to this e-mail. I look forward to going over the reservation further with you.

Best regards,

Roger Keller
Lowe Finances

To: Roger Keller <roger.keller@lowefinances.com>
From: Olivia Brunelli <olivia@nathalieresort.fr>
Date: March 25
Subject: Your Inquiry

Dear Mr. Keller,

Thank you for your wonderful message. I am pleased you had a great time during your previous visit. We are happy to report that we can accommodate your party. We can reserve the whole outdoor area for your dinner. However, it would have to be moved to the next night if you are flexible. The proposed date is already booked. Of course, we also have a dining room indoors.

Furthermore, we can only accommodate six spa appointments at once. About the other activities, they can be booked once you are here.

Please let us know how you would like to proceed.

Best regards,

Olivia Brunelli
Resort Manager
Nathalie Resort & Spa

176. Why did Mr. Keller write the e-mail?

(A) To explain the reason for some changes
(B) To inquire about a business partnership
(C) To thank a colleague for her hospitality
(D) To make arrangements for a trip

177. What does Mr. Keller mention as a requirement?

(A) Renting a large meeting room
(B) Preparing special meals
(C) Booking single-occupancy rooms
(D) Staying in rooms with a view

178. In the first e-mail, the phrase "going over" in paragraph 4, line 1, is closest in meaning to

(A) discussing
(B) crossing
(C) acquiring
(D) responding

179. What does Ms. Brunelli mention about an outdoor area?

(A) It is decorated with exotic plants.
(B) It is located near a spa.
(C) It is already booked on May 4.
(D) It is closed for part of the year.

180. What can be inferred about the investors?

(A) They will not be staying overnight at a resort.
(B) They supported Lowe Finances from the start.
(C) They want to open several businesses in France.
(D) They will not receive spa treatments at the same time.

GO ON TO THE NEXT PAGE

Questions 181-185 refer to the following form and e-mail.

FORM

All arriving passengers must fill out the following form. If you are traveling with family members, fill out one form for the group. When you land, please present this form along with your passports to a customs official.

Family Name	Larson
First name	Harry
Middle name	Hughes
Number of Family Members With You	3
Address	88 Pingree Drive, Stamford, CT 06831
Passport Issued by	United States
Countries visited on this trip	Spain, Portugal

The primary purpose of this trip is
☐ Business ☐ Vacation ☑ Other

If other, please specify: My family and I flew to Spain to help my father move into his new home. Then we took a brief sightseeing trip to Portugal.

Are you bringing any fruits, meats, or animals with you?
☐ Yes ☑ No

If so, please list them here: N/A

Signature: *Harry Larson*

TO: Harry Larson <harrylarson@worldmail.com>
FROM: Customer Service <service@internationalairlines.com>
SUBJECT: Re: Request
DATE: July 28

Dear Mr. Larson,

Thank you for writing to us about your missing duffel bag. After an extensive search, we have finally located it, and we will ship it to your home address. We apologize for the inconvenience.

To compensate you for the missing bag, we will add 8,000 flyer points to your account. According to our records, that means you are now entitled to one round-trip domestic flight. You can take advantage of this offer at any time. To use it, visit our Web site and click "Redeem my flyer points" during the checkout process.

Best regards,

International Airlines Customer Service

181. Why did Mr. Larson fill up the form?

(A) To obtain permission to carry an item
(B) To comply with an arrival requirement
(C) To report a problem at an airport
(D) To get help with a travel document

182. What information is NOT provided on the form?

(A) The number of people in Mr. Larson's group
(B) The countries that Mr. Larson visited
(C) The airline Mr. Larson traveled with
(D) The country Mr. Larson obtained his passport from

183. Why did Mr. Larson go on a trip?

(A) To do some business
(B) To assist a family member
(C) To attend a ceremony
(D) To teach some classes

184. What does International Airlines promise to do?

(A) Look into some flight details
(B) Search for a missing package
(C) Ship an item to Stamford
(D) Correct some account information

185. How can Mr. Larson take advantage of a free domestic flight?

(A) By e-mailing an airline representative
(B) By calling a specific travel agency
(C) By downloading a mobile app
(D) By booking on a Web site

GO ON TO THE NEXT PAGE

Questions 186-190 refer to the following brochure, request form, and memo.

Mario's
Mediterranean cuisine catering service

Mario's has been in business for over 30 years. It is still owned by founder Mario Robledo but is currently managed by his younger brother, Sandro. The catering company serves a wide variety of dishes. Moreover, it owns an event space at 7738 Market Street with both indoor and outdoor seating. The outdoor patio is open from May 1 until September 30.

Mario's can also accommodate all dietary requirements and food sensitivities.

The following menu options are available:

Menu	Types of Dishes	Price per person
Menu A	2 appetizers, 2 main dishes, 1 dessert	$30
Menu B	Menu A + 1 appetizer	$35
Menu C	Menu B + 1 main dish	$40
Menu D	Menu C + 1 dessert * A 20 percent discount is applicable for groups of 40 or more.	$45

Unless otherwise indicated, all menus include a vegetarian option. For special requests or to complete a booking, please go to www.marios.com.

Mario's Catering Request Form

Name of contact: Marissa Thomas
Organization: Madison Private Bank
E-mail: m.thomas@madisonprivatebank.com
Date of event: August 28
Time of event: 7 p.m.
Number of guests: 45

Facility: ___ Mario's _X_ Other
If other, please specify here: Madison Private Bank office

Preferred Menu:
___ Menu A
___ Menu B
___ Menu C
_X_ Menu D

Comments:
I don't remember which dishes we had at last year's event, but they were absolutely delicious. It would be good to have something slightly different for this year's client appreciation dinner, but anything is fine. Please make sure to include at least one vegan appetizer and main dish.

To: Team
From: Marissa Thomas
Date: August 25
Subject: Upcoming Dinner

I would like to remind you that our annual client appreciation dinner takes place on Wednesday, September 3. Please note that the date has been changed. We look forward to having mostly new clients this time, and I am sure they will like what will be served. One client, Ms. Kim, is vegan, so I made sure that there is one main and one appetizer dish she can eat. Furthermore, apart from the regular desserts, I have added a fruit platter which I assume all of you will enjoy as well. Please make sure you wear formal attire as this is considered a business affair. Looking forward to seeing you there.

186. What is mentioned about Mario's?

(A) It earned an award for its food.
(B) It is testing out a new menu.
(C) It plans to add an event space.
(D) It is operated by the owner's brother.

187. What is true about Ms. Thomas?

(A) She heard about Mario's from a client.
(B) She has used Mario's services before.
(C) She has strict dietary requirements.
(D) She requested Mario's outdoor area.

188. What is indicated about Madison Private Bank?

(A) It is located on the same street as Mario's.
(B) It recently increased the size of its staff.
(C) It has a budget of $40 per person.
(D) It is entitled to a 20 percent discount.

189. What can be inferred about the client appreciation dinner?

(A) It was not registered on an online system.
(B) It includes mostly vegan dishes.
(C) It was postponed to the following month.
(D) It must be paid for before September.

190. What does Ms. Thomas instruct her coworkers to do?

(A) Show up at a restaurant early
(B) Follow a dress code
(C) Carpool to an event
(D) Pick up some clients

GO ON TO THE NEXT PAGE

Questions 191-195 refer to the following e-mail, online form, and Web page.

TO: All Staff <staff@craftmagazine.com>
FROM: Alicia Mendez <a.mendez@craftmagazine.com>
SUBJECT: Moving
DATE: April 23

Dear Staff,

After a lengthy search, we've finally decided on the new office space for our magazine. It's a fifth-floor office at 82 Grant Street in Allston. It's much more spacious than our current location, so it can accommodate the new writers and advertising staff we took on in the past few weeks. In addition, it is near a bus stop, has a pizza place downstairs, and has windows overlooking the beautiful Charles River.

We're going to start moving to the new office on May 1, when the lease begins. If you're free that Saturday and are able to assist, please let me know. I was going to rent two trucks, but if someone has a large van or pickup truck we can use, I'll only need to rent one. Please let me know immediately if you have one available.

Best regards,

Alicia Mendez
Editor-in-Chief, Craft Magazine

www.bostontruckhire.com

BOSTON TRUCK HIRE

Name	Alicia Mendez
Phone number	555-9182
Driver's license number	013403412
Rental date(s)	May 1, 2
Number of vehicles	1
Estimated distance to travel	10 miles
Pickup location	32 Cooper Street, Boston
Drop-off location	918 West Harding Street, Boston
Comments	Right now, I need the vehicle for 48 hours. I will notify the staff if I decide to use it for longer.

www.salepages.com

BOSTON > CLASSIFIEDS > FOR SALE

Craft Magazine is moving to a new location with new equipment, so we'll have some items for sale. These include a DX color printer, a XRM6 fax machine, a five-year-old Vista Plus laptop, a 20-inch computer monitor, and five keyboards. If you are interested in any of these items, please contact Alicia Mendez at a.mendez@craftmagazine.com. Prices are negotiable. We're even willing to give away some items for free. Please note that these items will not be available for pickup until the third and last day of our move on May 3. That is when we are putting the last items in a moving truck and shutting down our old office for good.

191. What did Craft Magazine do recently?

(A) Published its first issue
(B) Hired new employees
(C) Created a Web site
(D) Launched a campaign

192. What is a feature of the new office?

(A) A scenic view
(B) A conference room
(C) Access to a subway
(D) An on-site gym

193. What did one of Ms. Mendez's staff most likely do?

(A) Arrived early in the morning to pack items
(B) Asked to change a move-in date
(C) Sent in some complaints
(D) Lent a vehicle to use

194. What can be inferred about Craft Magazine?

(A) It is replacing some of its equipment.
(B) It is interested in buying secondhand furniture.
(C) It is trying to raise money to pay for a service.
(D) It is moving to be closer to clients.

195. What is indicated about Craft Magazine's move?

(A) It will cost less after a discount.
(B) It will take longer than initially planned.
(C) It will require traveling a longer distance than expected.
(D) It will be delayed on account of bad weather.

GO ON TO THE NEXT PAGE

Questions 196-200 refer to the following Web page, memo, and schedule.

http://www.rolandoesteban.com

About Rolando Esteban

Rolando Esteban is a visual artist who has earned praise for his clean brush lines, dynamic composition, and vivid colors.

Growing up in Manila, Mr. Esteban was exposed to various forms of American popular culture and became inspired by the noted comic-book illustrator Chad Grohl. Mr. Esteban taught himself to draw and, despite the lack of formal training, produced many iconic movie and travel posters. He left Manila in his 30s to pursue a painting scholarship in Madrid, where he eventually developed his signature painting style.

Now, Madrid's Vivi Gallery will hold an exhibit that covers Mr. Esteban's later work. The exhibit, titled *Brush and Line*, opens publicly on August 22, with a reception scheduled for August 21.

Vivi Gallery of Visual Arts
MEMO

To: Leon Aguilar
From: Esther Hernandez
Subject: *Brush and Line*
Date: July 20

We need to move *Brush and Line* because the exhibit hall needs to undergo some quick renovations. The only time we can schedule this work to begin is on the day of the reception. I've spoken to the artist and he has agreed to a new opening date of August 30. This means we'll have to reschedule the reception for August 28. The next scheduled exhibit will also need to be moved, so I would like you to communicate with the artist to find out which new dates are acceptable.

Vivi Gallery of Visual Arts
EXHIBITION SCHEDULE

Gallery hours are from Tuesday to Saturday, 10 A.M. to 6 P.M.
Receptions are held on Mondays from 6 P.M. to 8 P.M.

July 12 to July 29
- Delia Romano: *Of One Mind*
- Reception on July 10

August 2 to August 19
- Tom Moskowitz: *Ba Bi Bo Bu*
- Reception on July 31

August 30 to September 20
- Rolando Esteban: *Brush and Line*
- Reception on August 28

September 27 to October 14
- Remy Artaud: *Up is Down*
- Reception on September 25

196. Who was an early influence on Mr. Esteban?

(A) An arts professor
(B) A work colleague
(C) A famous illustrator
(D) A movie director

197. What is NOT true about Mr. Esteban?

(A) He grew up in the city of Manila.
(B) He used to produce movie posters.
(C) He attended art school in Manila.
(D) He is known for using sharp colors.

198. When will the gallery close for renovations?

(A) August 21
(B) August 22
(C) August 28
(D) August 30

199. According to the schedule, what is indicated about Vivi Gallery?

(A) It is closed on weekends.
(B) It holds a reception before an opening.
(C) It features only the work of local artists.
(D) It does not sell any exhibited work.

200. Who most likely did Mr. Aguilar contact?

(A) Delia Romano
(B) Tom Moskowitz
(C) Rolando Esteban
(D) Remy Artaud

This is the end of the test. You may review Parts 5, 6, and 7 if you finish the test early.

정답 p.327 / 점수 환산표 p.329 / 해석 p.370 / Part 5&6 무료 해설 바로 보기(정답 및 정답 음성 포함)

* 다음 페이지에 있는 Self 체크 리스트를 통해 자신의 문제 풀이 방식과 태도를 점검해 보세요.

Self 체크 리스트

TEST 06는 무사히 잘 마치셨죠?
이제 다음의 Self 체크 리스트를 통해 자신의 테스트 진행 내용을 점검해 볼까요?

1. 나는 75분 동안 완전히 테스트에 집중하였다.

   □ 예　□ 아니오

   아니오에 답한 경우, 이유는 무엇인가요?

2. 나는 75분 동안 100문제를 모두 풀었다.

   □ 예　□ 아니오

   아니오에 답한 경우, 이유는 무엇인가요?

3. 나는 75분 동안 답안지 표시까지 완료하였다.

   □ 예　□ 아니오

   아니오에 답한 경우, 이유는 무엇인가요?

4. 나는 Part 5와 Part 6를 19분 안에 모두 풀었다.

   □ 예　□ 아니오

   아니오에 답한 경우, 이유는 무엇인가요?

5. Part 7을 풀 때 5분 이상 걸린 지문이 없었다.

   □ 예　□ 아니오

6. 개선해야 할 점 또는 나를 위한 충고를 적어보세요.

* 교재의 첫 장으로 돌아가서 자신이 적은 목표 점수를 확인하면서 목표에 대한 의지를 다지기 바랍니다. 개선해야 할 점은 반드시 다음 테스트에 실천해야 합니다. 그것이 가장 중요하며, 그래야만 발전할 수 있습니다.

TEST 07

PART 5

PART 6

PART 7

Self 체크 리스트

잠깐! 테스트 전 확인사항

1. 휴대 전화의 전원을 끄셨나요? □ 예
2. Answer Sheet, 연필, 지우개를 준비하셨나요? □ 예
3. 시계를 준비하셨나요? □ 예

모든 준비가 완료되었으면 목표 점수를 떠올린 후 테스트를 시작합니다.

문제 풀이를 마치는 시간은 지금부터 75분 후인 __시 __분입니다.

테스트 시간은 총 75분이며, 시험 종료 전 2~3분은 정답 검토 및 답안지 마킹을 위해 사용합니다.

READING TEST

In this section, you must demonstrate your ability to read and comprehend English. You will be given a variety of texts and asked to answer questions about these texts. This section is divided into three parts and will take 75 minutes to complete.

Do not mark the answers in your test book. Use the answer sheet that is separately provided.

PART 5

Directions: In each question, you will be asked to review a statement that is missing a word or phrase. Four answer choices will be provided for each statement. Select the best answer and mark the corresponding letter (A), (B), (C), or (D) on the answer sheet.

PART 5 권장 풀이 시간 11분

101. Ms. Ament called to notify ------- that she would be late for the meeting.

(A) we
(B) ourselves
(C) our
(D) us

102. Everyone is cordially invited to the grand opening of Camellia Café, which is located ------- the City Hall subway station.

(A) throughout
(B) about
(C) into
(D) beside

103. A personal assistant ------- Ms. Petrovsky's daily schedule every morning after reviewing a list of her appointments.

(A) update
(B) updates
(C) is updated
(D) updating

104. The resort's watersports equipment may only be rented for ------- two hours at a time.

(A) up to
(B) versus
(C) despite
(D) as of

105. Ms. McCabe is a ------- employee who can work without direct supervision.

(A) capable
(B) capability
(C) capableness
(D) capably

106. Mr. Coulter is used to waking up early, so he wants to take the morning shift ------- the night shift.

(A) instead of
(B) aside
(C) due to
(D) regardless of

107. Investing in safe financial products can protect ------- from experiencing significant losses.

(A) retire
(B) retiree
(C) retirees
(D) retired

108. Bell Lake Inc. ------- became the largest company in the area when it hired 150 additional employees.

(A) continuously
(B) commonly
(C) recently
(D) occasionally

109. The flight attendant asked that all headphones ------- returned before landing.

(A) are
(B) be
(C) were
(D) to be

110. Solomo Industries will implement a new quality-control ------- at its main factory.

(A) process
(B) processing
(C) processed
(D) procession

111. Maintenance workers cannot ------- fix a machine while the power is still on.

(A) save
(B) safely
(C) safety
(D) safe

112. Residents are deeply divided on ------- to support during the next mayoral election.

(A) that
(B) whom
(C) which
(D) whose

113. Studies show that managers ------- in conflict resolution build stronger and more effective teams.

(A) signed
(B) submitted
(C) trained
(D) thanked

114. New employees of Hislop Industries must complete ------- training courses within their first month of employment.

(A) attentive
(B) intelligent
(C) permanent
(D) mandatory

115. Gamberetti is very busy ------- the only other Italian restaurant in Veraville has closed down.

(A) unless
(B) in order that
(C) owing to
(D) now that

116. Hundreds of vehicles had to be recalled, as they did not meet the government's emission -------.

(A) broadcasts
(B) standards
(C) reminders
(D) licenses

117. Ventera Inc. is ------- for a Chinese translator who can accompany executives on a business trip to Beijing.

(A) ordering
(B) dispatching
(C) referring
(D) searching

118. The CEO of Victory Holdings spoke ------- about his vision for the firm's future after its expansion into Europe.

(A) assure
(B) assured
(C) assuredly
(D) assurance

119. The customer made an inquiry ------- the order she had placed on October 13.

(A) along
(B) between
(C) regarding
(D) through

120. Meals at the downtown restaurant Chez Jacques are -------, so they are worth the wait.

(A) effective
(B) ready
(C) exceptional
(D) defective

GO ON TO THE NEXT PAGE

121. Customers who place bulk orders of Blossom Kitchen's items can ------- for a discount.

(A) diminish
(B) target
(C) consider
(D) negotiate

122. Although Mr. McIntyre felt nervous during his presentation, his discomfort was not ------- to anyone present.

(A) evidently
(B) evident
(C) evidence
(D) evidences

123. The product sample was analyzed ------- to identify every possible area in need of improvement.

(A) instinctively
(B) partially
(C) abstractly
(D) thoroughly

124. The performance last night featured graceful dancers showing ------- movements.

(A) effortless
(B) effort
(C) effortlessly
(D) efforts

125. The meeting room on the 10th floor is ------- used, so it might be converted to serve a more practical purpose.

(A) seldom
(B) almost
(C) always
(D) maybe

126. The director of operations aims to ------- the aquarium with a state-of-the-art filtration system.

(A) oblige
(B) equip
(C) certify
(D) revolve

127. Accepting merchandise returns more than 30 days after purchase is ------- to store policy.

(A) reverse
(B) dependent
(C) contrary
(D) negative

128. The inspector listed some ------- that still needed to be met before the bakery could open.

(A) require
(B) requirements
(C) requiring
(D) requires

129. ------- Mr. Jackson wants to eat an affordable lunch, he goes to the food court at Central Market.

(A) As though
(B) Rather than
(C) Until
(D) Whenever

130. Restaurants have been opening near the new apartment complex with increasing ------- to serve the residents.

(A) disagreement
(B) frequency
(C) knowledge
(D) limitation

PART 6

Directions: In this part, you will be asked to read four English texts. Each text is missing a word, phrase, or sentence. Select the answer choice that correctly completes the text and mark the corresponding letter (A), (B), (C), or (D) on the answer sheet.

PART 6 권장 풀이 시간 8분

Questions 131-134 refer to the following notice.

ATTENTION TRAVELERS

Beginning October 5, Barings Airport will begin constructing a new terminal to ------- (131.) international flights. -------, (132.) the addition of the terminal will increase our capacity by 40 percent. The new terminal, called Terminal 5, will be located in a separate building from the four that currently operate. Consequently, it will only be accessible by light rail train or shuttle bus. -------. (133.) Some sections of the airport may also experience temporary closures, ------- (134.) portions of Terminal 4. However, all terminals will fully open by next year.

131. (A) propose
(B) transmit
(C) reassure
(D) accommodate

132. (A) In all
(B) Then again
(C) Even so
(D) To repeat

133. (A) Reported delays will be reflected on flight message boards.
(B) Both options will be available from the other four terminals.
(C) Passengers are advised to stay seated throughout the flight.
(D) A valid ticket is required to enter the airline's lounge.

134. (A) later
(B) meanwhile
(C) according to
(D) including

GO ON TO THE NEXT PAGE

Questions 135-138 refer to the following announcement.

Duluth Grand Cinema is proud to announce that it ------- (135.) Elwood Barker's documentary, *Gideon's Revenge*, on Thursday, October 22, at 7:00 P.M. The event will last three hours in total, with the movie running for 115 minutes. Mr. Barker will then answer audience questions for the remaining time. ------- (136.).

Gideon's Revenge is based on Mr. Barker's ------- (137.) travels through Syria, Lebanon, and Iraq over the course of four years. If you are interested in viewing this first-hand account of life in the Middle East, act ------- (138.). Only a limited number of tickets are available.

135. (A) premiering
(B) was premiering
(C) premiered
(D) is premiering

136. (A) Mr. Barker attended the event with members of his family.
(B) Distributing copies of the film is strictly prohibited by law.
(C) This should give fans some insight into his creative process.
(D) We open at 4:00 P.M. on weekdays and 2:00 P.M. on weekends.

137. (A) temporary
(B) upcoming
(C) extensive
(D) concise

138. (A) professionally
(B) naturally
(C) responsibly
(D) quickly

Questions 139-142 refer to the following letter.

March 17

Clara Rodriguez
644 Lockley Street
Galt City, Ontario N1R 3Y8

Dear Ms. Rodriguez,

We are writing about your ------- (139.) to make your last Internet service payment. We attempted to reach you several times by telephone but were unsuccessful. Please note that your balance with Loft Net, in the amount of $63.97, was ------- (140.) on March 15. It is our policy to accept payments without applying additional fees for a week following the deadline. -------. (141.) As we value your business, we would appreciate your prompt attention to this matter. ------- (142.) the bill, contact 555-7843, and have your credit card handy.

Sincerely,

Albert Sanders
Loft Net Customer Service

139. (A) decision
(B) failure
(C) demand
(D) record

140. (A) changed
(B) received
(C) lost
(D) due

141. (A) After that, we are forced to charge interest.
(B) The credit card we have on file has expired.
(C) Alternatively, you could send a wire transfer.
(D) Please update your contact details immediately.

142. (A) Settles
(B) Having settled
(C) To settle
(D) Has settled

GO ON TO THE NEXT PAGE

Questions 143-146 refer to the following memo.

From: Mila Larson, Head of Marketing Communications
To: All employees
Subject: Liang Inc. campaign
Date: July 25

Dear Staff,

I'd like to thank everyone for contributing to the Liang Inc. promotional campaign proposal. The executives at Liang Inc. are ------- (143.) impressed with our designs and have decided to hire us. For the television commercial, we ------- (144.) everyone to participate. There is going to be a lot of work over the next few weeks, so your cooperation is vital. I have arranged for us all to meet with Liang Inc.'s CEO on July 27 so that we can figure out a detailed timeline. ------- (145.).

If you have any input or additional ideas, ------- (146.) to present them during the meeting.

Thank you,
Mila Larson

143. (A) high
(B) higher
(C) highly
(D) highest

144. (A) will need
(B) needed
(C) have needed
(D) needing

145. (A) I agree that their suggestions were better than ours.
(B) The advertisement will be airing then for the first time.
(C) This discussion resolved several important issues.
(D) We will also discuss plans for the magazine spread.

146. (A) be prepared
(B) preparing
(C) in preparation of
(D) having prepared

PART 7

Directions: In this part, you will be asked to read several texts, such as advertisements, articles, instant messages, or examples of business correspondence. Each text is followed by several questions. Select the best answer and mark the corresponding letter (A), (B), (C), or (D) on your answer sheet.

PART 7 권장 풀이 시간 54분

Questions 147-148 refer to the following text message.

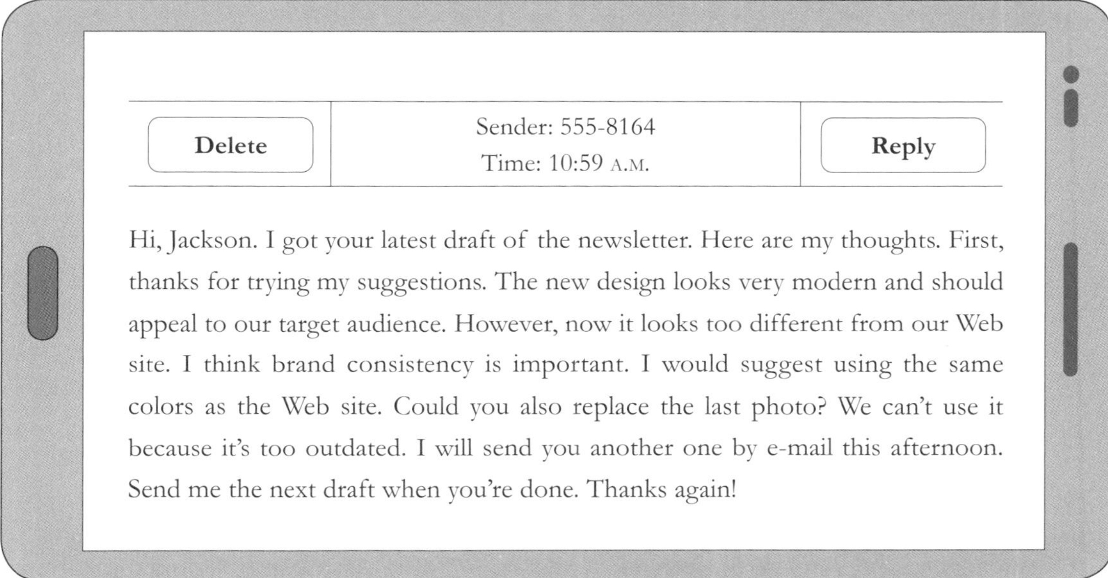

Delete	Sender: 555-8164 Time: 10:59 A.M.	Reply

Hi, Jackson. I got your latest draft of the newsletter. Here are my thoughts. First, thanks for trying my suggestions. The new design looks very modern and should appeal to our target audience. However, now it looks too different from our Web site. I think brand consistency is important. I would suggest using the same colors as the Web site. Could you also replace the last photo? We can't use it because it's too outdated. I will send you another one by e-mail this afternoon. Send me the next draft when you're done. Thanks again!

147. Why was the message sent?

(A) To comment on some changes
(B) To request a copy of a file
(C) To ask for a cost estimate
(D) To explain a company procedure

148. What is indicated about a newsletter?

(A) It is supported by advertisements.
(B) It includes inaccurate information.
(C) It has too many pages.
(D) It requires a new photo.

GO ON TO THE NEXT PAGE

Questions 149-150 refer to the following article.

Sandi Vincent to Throw First Pitch

March 21—Country music star Sandi Vincent will visit Warwick next month to help our baseball team, the Harpoons, start the new season. Mayor Belinda Cutter invited Ms. Vincent to throw the first pitch at the opening game on April 7.

Ms. Vincent gained nationwide fame through the success of her third album, *Prairies and Plains*. More recently, she made her acting debut in the film *Uncle Trevor's Farm*.

Due to her busy touring schedule, Ms. Vincent was unavailable for comment, but her manager stated, "Sandi is looking forward to visiting Warwick for the first time. She's a huge baseball fan, and I'm sure she'll enjoy herself. Let's hope she throws a lucky pitch so that the Harpoons have a successful season."

149. What is the article mainly about?

(A) The admission of a team into a league
(B) A musician's recent performance
(C) The successful premiere of a movie
(D) A celebrity's participation in an event

150. What is suggested about Ms. Vincent?

(A) She hoped to become an athlete.
(B) She has recorded several albums.
(C) She visits Warwick on a regular basis.
(D) She appeared in a television advertisement.

Questions 151-153 refer to the following notice.

Rumfax Shared Garden Opening Soon

The growing season for Rumfax Shared Garden (RSG) is from March 31 to September 15 this year, so now is the time to register for your own garden plot. Returning gardeners from last year will pay $40 for membership, while new gardeners will be charged $55.* Anyone who lives in Rumfax is welcome to apply at www.rumfaxgarden.com. However, be sure to note the following regulations.

- Each gardener is responsible for maintaining his or her plot. This includes doing all the necessary watering, weeding, and harvesting.
- Plots may not be expanded unless RSG coordinators grant special consent. Our personnel must also approve any structures added to plots before they are put in.
- RSG members may only plant in their own plots and must ensure that what they grow does not shade a neighbor's plants.
- Tools are available in the storage shed for all to use, but they must be returned afterward.

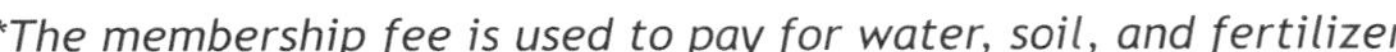

**The membership fee is used to pay for water, soil, and fertilizer.*

151. What is indicated about Rumfax Shared Garden?

(A) It can be used by residents of a certain area.
(B) Its produce is sold at a local market.
(C) It receives part of its funding from a corporation.
(D) It helps other communities introduce similar programs.

152. According to the notice, when can plots be expanded?

(A) When neighboring gardens create shade
(B) When gardeners pay an extra fee
(C) When staff members give permission
(D) When additional structures are completed

153. Why does Rumfax Shared Garden have to charge for membership?

(A) To purchase advertising space
(B) To buy construction materials
(C) To provide wages to employees
(D) To pay for necessary supplies

GO ON TO THE NEXT PAGE

Questions 154-155 refer to the following text-message chain.

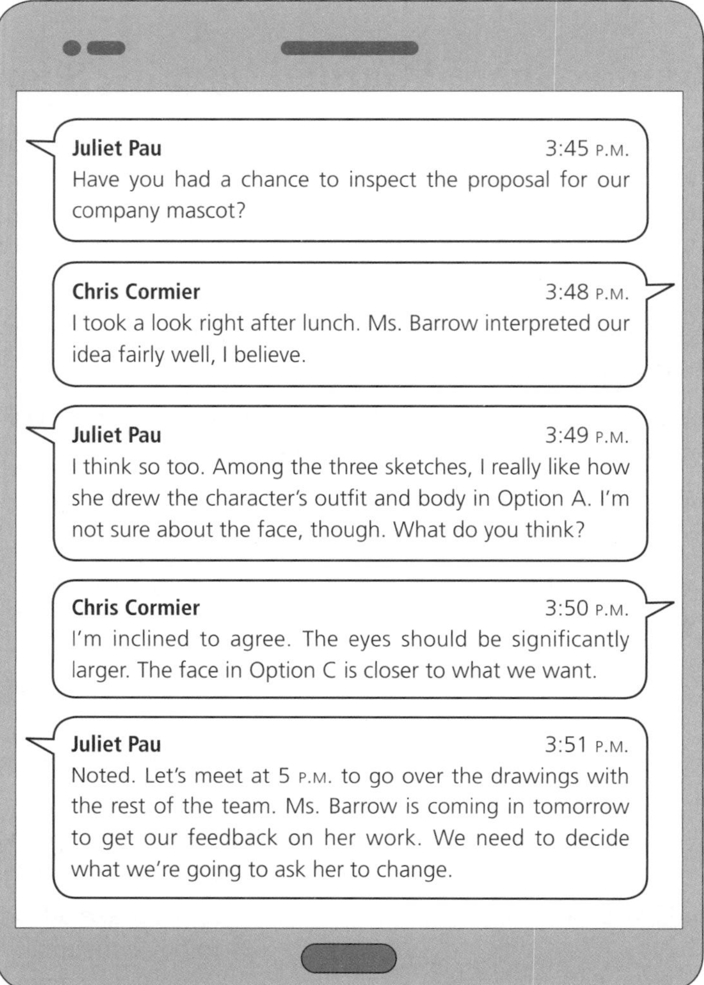

Juliet Pau 3:45 P.M.
Have you had a chance to inspect the proposal for our company mascot?
Chris Cormier 3:48 P.M.
I took a look right after lunch. Ms. Barrow interpreted our idea fairly well, I believe.
Juliet Pau 3:49 P.M.
I think so too. Among the three sketches, I really like how she drew the character's outfit and body in Option A. I'm not sure about the face, though. What do you think?
Chris Cormier 3:50 P.M.
I'm inclined to agree. The eyes should be significantly larger. The face in Option C is closer to what we want.
Juliet Pau 3:51 P.M.
Noted. Let's meet at 5 P.M. to go over the drawings with the rest of the team. Ms. Barrow is coming in tomorrow to get our feedback on her work. We need to decide what we're going to ask her to change.

154. Who most likely is Ms. Barrow?

(A) A fashion designer
(B) A marketing specialist
(C) A contract negotiator
(D) A graphic artist

155. At 3:50 P.M., what does Mr. Cormier most likely mean when he writes, "I'm inclined to agree"?

(A) He has no choice but to follow his supervisor's orders.
(B) He does not like an aspect of a sketch.
(C) He thinks a task needs to be simplified.
(D) He believes it is important to reach a group decision.

Questions 156-158 refer to the following article.

DAR ES SALAAM (April 19)—Touchstone Ventures announced yesterday that it had acquired Tanzania Train Lines (TTL). This deal follows Touchstone's takeover of Umoja Transport in mid-February.

"Our acquisition of TTL will help us move into other East African nations," said company chief Mieke de Graaf. "At this point, Touchstone has to venture out into rapidly developing regions. — [1] —."

TTL is a formerly state-owned railway company that has struggled to remain profitable, and some of its rail lines are in urgent need of repair. "Touchstone will need to invest heavily in upgrading TTL's infrastructure," said Dr. Patrick Maguli, a professor at Arusha Business University.

"According to my research, a growing number of Tanzanians are choosing to drive or take a bus rather than a ride in a train. — [2] —. Touchstone's challenge will be to reverse this tendency," Dr. Maguli added.

Touchstone's plan has four parts. Its first priority will be to repair and upgrade established rail lines. After that, it plans to switch from diesel-powered trains to electric ones. The third phase will be to build new routes in order to take advantage of the growing cargo traffic to and from neighboring countries. — [3] —. Finally, Touchstone Ventures aims to develop TTL's rail network for tourism purposes. For instance, it may begin offering scenic journeys on steam-powered heritage trains. — [4] —.

156. What is NOT true about Touchstone Ventures?

(A) It owns Umoja Transport.
(B) It has organized a project into stages.
(C) It was previously owned by the government.
(D) It aims to deal in cargo transport.

157. What is suggested about Dr. Maguli?

(A) He has traveled to a construction site.
(B) He has studied Tanzanian transportation trends.
(C) He does consulting work for corporations.
(D) He is working to develop a new technology.

158. In which of the positions marked [1], [2], [3], and [4] does the following sentence best belong?

"These are expected to appeal to travelers who want to see the country's landscapes at a leisurely pace."

(A) [1]
(B) [2]
(C) [3]
(D) [4]

GO ON TO THE NEXT PAGE

Questions 159-160 refer to the following advertisement.

Goliath Storage: Secure and Convenient Spaces for Your Extra Belongings!

Has your home or business become uncomfortably full? Well, rather than relocating, check out Goliath Storage, located at 452 East Island Way, just outside of Toronto. We have more than 800 units and offer great prices on monthly or yearly leases. Long-term leases are negotiable. You can rest assured that your belongings will be safe—we have a state-of-the-art camera system and security guards on duty 24 hours a day. For local businesses, we also have ten cold-storage units for lease, perfect for keeping goods requiring refrigeration. For the month of December only, those purchasing insurance for their stored items through our office will receive a 20 percent discount on their policy! To inquire about our unit availability, prices, and regulations, go to www.goliathstorage.on.ca.

159. For whom is the advertisement most likely intended?

(A) Someone who needs to find an apartment
(B) Someone who prefers to use a private workplace
(C) Someone who wants to begin exporting products
(D) Someone who is running out of storage space

160. What is being offered as part of a promotion?

(A) Discounts on monthly fees
(B) Upgrades to larger sizes
(C) Complimentary pickup of belongings
(D) Lower prices for insurance

Questions 161-164 refer to the following e-mail.

To: <Member List>
From: <info@windsorbiz.org>
Subject: Notification
Date: December 2

Dear Members,

We appreciate your continued membership as local businesses in the Windsor Business Association. Please join us for our upcoming free seminar. — [1] —. Following last month's topic on conserving electricity, this month's topic is about reducing water waste. The seminar will take place on December 13 from 10 a.m. to 12 p.m. in Room B of the Windsor Business Centre. — [2] —.

Ecologist and water conservation expert Calvin Randall will explain how local businesses can take steps to reduce costs and help preserve the environment. He will provide simple tips and techniques to follow. He will also offer free one-on-one consultations after the seminar.

Mr. Randall is a highly respected scientist and has appeared on numerous television and radio programs over the years. — [3] —. It will be a good opportunity to learn how you can cut your water expenses and protect our planet at the same time. Local business owners are also encouraged to bring along recent utility statements to learn about the different areas where savings are possible.

To sign up for this month's seminar, please reply to this e-mail. — [4] —. Thank you.

Windsor Business Association

161. What is indicated about the Windsor Business Association?

(A) It recently accepted new members.
(B) It relocated its head office.
(C) It regularly offers seminars.
(D) It partnered with an environmental group.

162. The word "steps" in paragraph 2, line 2, is closest in meaning to

(A) cases
(B) movements
(C) instructions
(D) actions

163. What are interested participants asked to bring?

(A) Photo identification
(B) Proof of registration
(C) Recent water bills
(D) Business cards

164. In which of the positions marked [1], [2], [3], and [4] does the following sentence best belong?

"That's why you shouldn't miss this seminar."

(A) [1]
(B) [2]
(C) [3]
(D) [4]

GO ON TO THE NEXT PAGE

Questions 165-167 refer to the following survey.

Arturo Realty - Customer Satisfaction Survey

Thank you for using Arturo Realty. We want to know how effectively our services met your needs, so please take a few moments to fill out this survey.

I was buying a property ______ I was selling a property __x__

Why did you choose to work with us?

I got in touch with several real estate agencies, but yours responded the most promptly. Also, Mr. Hamlin was able to answer my initial questions thoroughly.

What aspect of our services were you most pleased with?

After I accepted the buyer's offer, Mr. Hamlin kept me informed during every step of the transaction. He called me regularly to let me know what was going on.

What aspect of our services were you most disappointed with?

I would have preferred receiving more advance notice when potential buyers came to look at my house. It would have been convenient to receive at least one hour's notice.

Would you recommend our services to your family or friends?

Yes __x__ No ______

Your name: Rosemary Woodard

165. What did Ms. Woodard do before choosing Arturo Realty?

(A) Compared the prices of various houses
(B) Talked to a previous customer
(C) Visited a company Web site
(D) Contacted several realtors

166. With what statement would Ms. Woodard probably agree?

(A) Mr. Hamlin has an extensive network of contacts.
(B) Arturo Realty complies with local regulations.
(C) Mr. Hamlin provides frequent updates.
(D) Arturo Realty's office is conveniently located.

167. What aspect of Arturo Realty's service was Ms. Woodard unsatisfied with?

(A) An agent was sometimes unavailable to meet in person.
(B) Notifications about visits were not given early enough.
(C) Some negotiations were not conducted efficiently.
(D) Some personal information was not kept confidential.

Questions 168-171 refer to the following online chat discussion.

Maria Sanchez	[12:06 P.M.]	Sales have been disappointing these last few quarters, both online and at our stores. Any ideas how we might turn things around?
William Behar	[12:09 P.M.]	How about working with a celebrity on a collection of furniture and home accessories? We'd need someone that is well-known and has a great sense of style.
Robert Gillibrand	[12:12 P.M.]	Fiona Connolly might work. She's a famous interior decorator.
William Behar	[12:13 P.M.]	That would be a great fit. Her reality television show is popular right now, and I don't think she's worked with another retail store before.
Maria Sanchez	[12:14 P.M.]	Also, she has a large following on social media. Any thoughts, Gabrielle?
Gabrielle Shepard	[12:15 P.M.]	I like the idea. I can collaborate with her on designing new furniture pieces but give her the freedom to choose fabrics.
William Behar	[12:17 P.M.]	Right. Or you could work together on designing a new bed, for example, and she could design related items like bed linens.
Robert Gillibrand	[12:18 P.M.]	OK. I'll reach out to her representative. If this works out, it could develop into a long-lasting partnership.
Maria Sanchez	[12:19 P.M.]	We should also think of other candidates in case she turns us down.

168. Why did Ms. Sanchez send the message?

(A) To solicit some recommendations
(B) To request feedback on a campaign
(C) To propose a change of strategy
(D) To schedule a store inspection

169. At 12:13 P.M., what does Mr. Behar mean when he writes, "That would be a great fit"?

(A) He wants to transfer to another location.
(B) He prefers a specific set of fabrics.
(C) He is interested in custom-made pieces.
(D) He agrees with a choice of design partner.

170. What can be inferred about Ms. Shepard?

(A) She has many followers on social media.
(B) She has worked on a reality television show.
(C) She is responsible for creating designs.
(D) She is not sure about a collaboration.

171. What does Ms. Sanchez want to do?

(A) Release more than one collection
(B) Come up with some alternatives
(C) Establish a long-term partnership
(D) Speak with a manager directly

GO ON TO THE NEXT PAGE

Questions 172-175 refer to the following letter.

TICKET NUMBER: 251077

Corrigan Technology Headquarters
703 Shirlington Boulevard
Arlington, VA 22206

October 20

Dear Sir or Madam,

To thank you for placing regular orders of our goods, we would like to invite you to a private preview of our upcoming product line. These items will be released early next year and have not yet been revealed to the public.

The event will fall on November 9, from 5 to 9 P.M., at the address given at the top of this letter. Corrigan Technology CEO Bill Schriver will deliver an introductory talk, after which design team chief Pete Wellington will present our new line of home appliances. Customers are not permitted to take pictures or record the event. A dinner will be served at 6:30 P.M., and then guests will be given a hands-on demonstration of the new products.

If you plan to attend, please call Louise Geisler at 555-4498 by October 27. If she does not hear from you by that date, we will assume that you will not be attending and remove your ticket number from our guest list.

Ticket numbers will be included in a special draw. The winning numbers will be announced at the end of the evening, so make sure to have this letter with you. Winners will receive vouchers that entitle them to a discount when our new product line is released. The vouchers may be used at stores around the country.

We hope you can join us.

Best wishes,

Matthew Schenk
Public Relations Head

172. What is the purpose of the letter?

(A) To thank an organization for hosting a function
(B) To request feedback on a newly released product
(C) To ask certain clients to attend an event
(D) To provide a quarterly update to stockholders

173. What is suggested about the new line of products?

(A) It has not been advertised.
(B) It is still being designed.
(C) It is completely sold out.
(D) Its launch will be delayed.

174. What is NOT indicated about the preview?

(A) It will take place in November.
(B) It will be held at a branch office.
(C) It will be attended by past customers.
(D) It will include a meal.

175. How can attendees receive a voucher?

(A) By presenting a letter
(B) By buying multiple items
(C) By answering a questionnaire
(D) By being selected in a draw

GO ON TO THE NEXT PAGE

Questions 176-180 refer to the following notice and e-mail.

SPECIAL NOTICE FROM THE LUDLOW NAUTICAL MUSEUM

May 14

We are sorry to announce that the Ludlow Nautical Museum is temporarily closed to the public. This is because the insulation material in our walls needs to be replaced. To protect the objects in our collection during the renovation, we have moved many of them to a third-floor storage room.

Next week, museum director Ken Lin will meet with the board of trustees and decide on the date of our reopening, which will hopefully be at the end of the summer. If you would like to receive updates on the progress of our work, please subscribe to our electronic newsletter at www.ludlownautical.org/emailsubscription.

To apologize for the inconvenience, our members will be sent a discount coupon for Crescent Bay Aquarium, which is also operated by the Ludlow Tourism Organization. Meanwhile, a free key chain from our souvenir store will be mailed to each guest whose advance reservation has been canceled.

Thank you for your understanding.

TO: Andrea Smith <andreasmith@sunshineheights.com>
FROM: Ken Lin <kenlin@ludlownautical.org>
DATE: May 15
SUBJECT: Museum closure
ATTACHMENT: Ludlow notice

Dear Ms. Smith,

My records indicate that you scheduled a visit to Ludlow Nautical Museum next Tuesday for a group of senior citizens from Sunshine Heights. Regrettably, the museum had to close for renovations. I am attaching a notice about the current situation.

We hope that you are able to arrange an outing to a different site on Tuesday. My personal recommendation is Crescent Bay Aquarium.

If you would like to reschedule your visit after we reopen, please contact us at that time.

Yours truly,

Ken Lin
Director, Ludlow Nautical Museum

176. According to the notice, why have some objects been moved to the third floor?

(A) To prepare the building for a special exhibit
(B) To protect them from potential damage
(C) To restore their original colors
(D) To respond to a seasonal drop in tourism

177. What will Mr. Lin discuss with the board of trustees?

(A) What activities will take place at an event
(B) How to improve a newsletter
(C) When operations will resume
(D) Where artifacts should be displayed

178. What is mentioned about Ms. Smith?

(A) She volunteers at a local museum.
(B) She is supervising a renovation project.
(C) She serves on a government committee.
(D) She planned an outing for senior citizens.

179. What does Mr. Lin recommend?

(A) Visiting a site run by the Ludlow Tourism Organization
(B) Canceling a workshop at Sunshine Heights
(C) Changing the date of a personal appointment
(D) Checking the performance schedule of a theater

180. What will Ms. Smith most likely receive?

(A) A refunded deposit
(B) An item from a gift shop
(C) A season's pass
(D) An invoice for repairs

GO ON TO THE NEXT PAGE

Questions 181-185 refer to the following memo and e-mail.

COMPANY MEMO

TO: All team leaders
FROM: Helen Malone, CEO, Daisy Corp.
DATE: April 21
SUBJECT: Upcoming Employee Evaluations

Although many of you are already familiar with this process, I'd like to remind you of a few details concerning our annual evaluations for staff members, which will begin on June 1. Next Monday, human resources staff will be e-mailing you information about each member of your team including their start dates at the company and their past evaluation results. Take some time to review this information before the end of May.

If an employee receives a positive performance evaluation and has not gotten a raise or bonus within the past three months, that staff member is eligible for a 5.5 percent salary increase. For questions or concerns, get in touch with Gail Cullen in the human resources department.

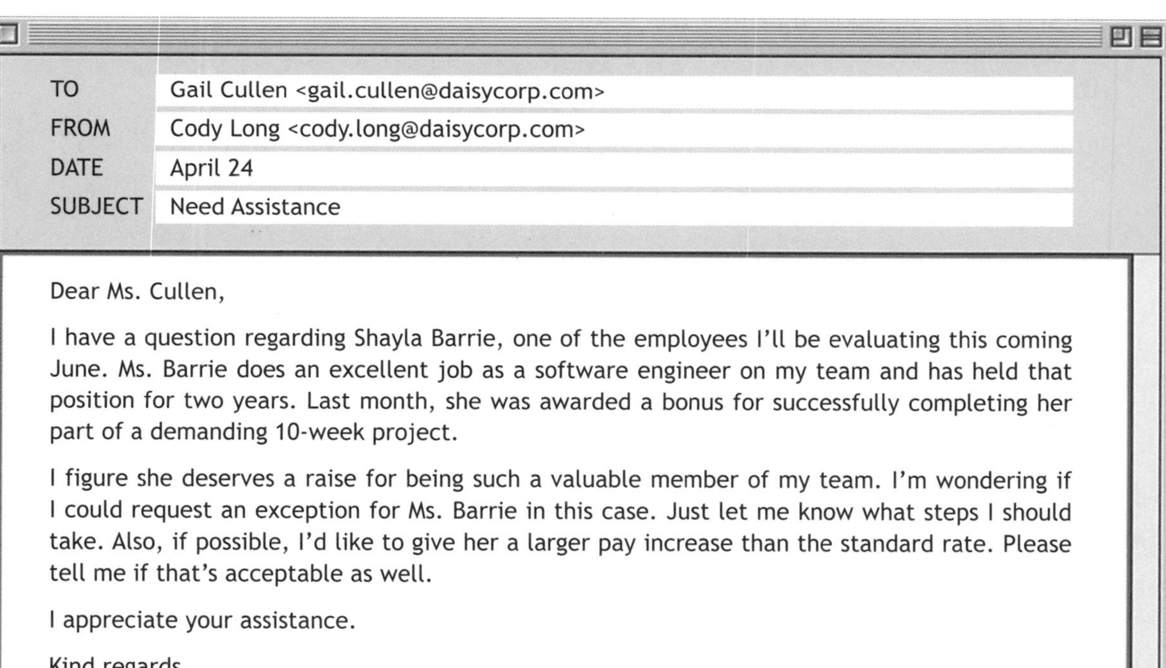

TO	Gail Cullen <gail.cullen@daisycorp.com>
FROM	Cody Long <cody.long@daisycorp.com>
DATE	April 24
SUBJECT	Need Assistance

Dear Ms. Cullen,

I have a question regarding Shayla Barrie, one of the employees I'll be evaluating this coming June. Ms. Barrie does an excellent job as a software engineer on my team and has held that position for two years. Last month, she was awarded a bonus for successfully completing her part of a demanding 10-week project.

I figure she deserves a raise for being such a valuable member of my team. I'm wondering if I could request an exception for Ms. Barrie in this case. Just let me know what steps I should take. Also, if possible, I'd like to give her a larger pay increase than the standard rate. Please tell me if that's acceptable as well.

I appreciate your assistance.

Kind regards,

Cody Long
Software Engineering Team Leader

181. What is the purpose of the memo?

(A) To clarify a policy change
(B) To announce a job opening
(C) To answer some questions
(D) To describe a procedure

182. What is mentioned about human resources staff?

(A) They will send evaluation information.
(B) They will be screening applicants in May.
(C) They began using new payroll software.
(D) They updated a salary database.

183. According to Ms. Malone, what can Ms. Cullen do?

(A) Interview potential candidates
(B) Fix a technical issue
(C) Respond to inquiries from managers
(D) Approve promotions of employees

184. In the e-mail, the word "figure" in paragraph 2, line 1, is closest in meaning to

(A) compute
(B) depict
(C) suppose
(D) represent

185. What factor makes Ms. Barrie ineligible for a raise?

(A) What sort of work arrangements she requires
(B) Who she is in charge of supervising
(C) How long she has held her current position
(D) When she was last given a bonus

GO ON TO THE NEXT PAGE

Questions 186-190 refer to the following letter, registration form, and schedule.

August 28

Mount Llanberis Park Office
122 High Street
Llanberis, Gwynedd LL55 4HB

To Whom It May Concern,

Ever since I was a teenager, I've visited Mount Llanberis Park to participate in some of my favorite activities. While at the park in recent months, I've witnessed some changes that concern me. There used to be a moderate number of people, but the park has begun attracting large crowds during the summer months. With the growing popularity of the area, a number of rules should be introduced.

For instance, I've seen a lot of people leaving the marked trails lately. I recommend that you create a regulation that prohibits people from doing so. Also, at the rock climbing area, I've noticed inexperienced climbers attempting the challenging routes. In order to prevent accidents, learners should be carefully monitored. I also believe that visitors should be required to fill out permission forms in order to engage in adventurous activities.

Thank you for your time.

Regards,
Glenda Ree

Mount Llanberis Park – Adventure Sports Registration Form

Please submit this form to Mount Llanberis Park Ranger Station. You will be allowed to proceed only if your application has been approved by the ranger on duty. First-time visitors will not be allowed to proceed unless accompanied by a certified guide. Please inquire with us if you need to rent any gear.

Name: Branwen Pearse
Group size: 4
Date and time of visit: October 19 / 9:30 A.M.
Expected duration of visit: 6 hours
Is this your first visit? _X_ Yes ____ No

Planned activity and location:

Rock climbing	Hiking	Mountain biking
Giant's Wall ____	Lloyd Peak _X_ Harlech Slope ____	Zipper Descent ____

Rules to keep in mind: (1) Do not litter. (2) The park is open from 6 A.M. to 6 P.M. Visitors must return to the park office by closing time. (3) Always stay on marked trails. (4) Do not feed the wildlife.
∗ ∗ Violators will be subject to a $30 fine. ∗ ∗

For assistance or to report violations of park regulations, call 555-2129.

Mount Llanberis Park

Ranger Station

Visitors Taking Part in Adventure Sports on October 19

Reservation time	Location visited	Name	Notes	Time of return
7:45 A.M.–3:45 P.M.	Giant's Wall	Bryn Hughes	- Group of three people	*3:40 P.M.*
8:00 A.M.–10:15 A.M.	Zipper Descent	Gweneth Edwards	- Mountain bike rented	*11:00 A.M.*
9:30 A.M.–3:30 P.M.	Lloyd Peak	Branwen Pearse	- Accompanied by guide - Group of four people	*2:45 P.M.*
11:15 A.M.–4:00 P.M.	Giant's Wall	Dennis Roberts	- Group of three people	*3:55 P.M.*
12:30 P.M.–5:00 P.M.	Harlech Slope	Owen Price	- Hiking poles rented	*6:10 P.M.*

* Note for staff: Do not forget to record the times when visitors return.

186. Why was the letter written?

(A) To raise concerns about park usage
(B) To request an extension of a hiking trail
(C) To propose a new route to a campsite
(D) To recommend that wildlife be protected

187. Which rule was probably newly adopted by Mount Llanberis Park?

(A) Rule (1)
(B) Rule (2)
(C) Rule (3)
(D) Rule (4)

188. According to the registration form, what is Ms. Pearse required to do?

(A) Hike with a certified guide
(B) Pay a deposit in order to borrow an item
(C) Enroll in some rock climbing classes
(D) Present identification documents at a ranger station

189. According to the schedule, which location was visited by two groups on October 19?

(A) Giant's Wall
(B) Lloyd Peak
(C) Harlech Slope
(D) Zipper Descent

190. What can be inferred about Mr. Price?

(A) He bought hiking poles at a ranger station.
(B) He didn't inform a ranger of a rule violation.
(C) He may have paid a financial penalty.
(D) He encountered some inclement weather.

GO ON TO THE NEXT PAGE

Questions 191-195 refer to the following advertisement, online form, and review.

Viu Athleisure Shop

Athleisure wear is popular for its versatility. We carry 10 brands and are currently offering special promotions until July 31. All discounts apply both online and in our store.

Bemba Team
Bemba Team sells synthetic clothes made with advanced fibers. The material is extremely moisture-absorbent and dries quickly. Enjoy a 20 percent discount on selected products.

Ventra
Ventra specializes in athletic shoes for a variety of sports. Ventra is new in our store and is offering an introductory discount of 30 percent.

Upstar Athletics
Upstar Athletics manufactures its clothing using polyester made from recycled plastic water bottles. It is offering a general discount of 10 percent.

Yogana
Yogana manufactures yoga apparel in many patterns and colors. Yoga shorts are currently on sale for 40 percent.

Enjoy free shipping on all orders over $80. Custom printing on apparel items is available for an added charge. Visit our store at 449 South State Street in Minneapolis or go to our Web site at www.viuathleisure.com.

www.viuathleisure.com/contactus

Contact Form
Please reach out to us if you have any questions regarding our products and services. We promise to respond to your inquiry within 48 hours.

Name: Maria Cortez
E-mail: maria@evanstonbball.com
Date submitted: July 13

Comment:
I am interested in buying 35 sets of matching shirts and shorts for an amateur basketball team that I coach. As the team is composed of individuals from middle school and high school, I will need a range of sizes. Also, I was wondering if we could get a bulk discount in addition to the sales your store is running.

http://www.upstar.com

Review posted on August 4
Author: Maria Cortez

Upstar Athletics is a great company, and their clothes are fantastic. The fabric stretches well and is perfect for sports. Unfortunately, I reached out to a store that carries Upstar Athletics among other brands, and they did not respond to my inquiry. So, I decided to contact Upstar Athletics directly. They sent 35 shirts and shorts in individual sizes with a generous quantity discount and printed our team's name on the clothes for free.

191. Which brand is newly offered at Viu Athleisure?

(A) Bemba Team
(B) Ventra
(C) Upstar Athletics
(D) Yogana

192. What is true about Viu Athleisure's products?

(A) They are only sold online.
(B) They can be shipped overseas.
(C) They sell four brands of clothing.
(D) They can be personalized for a fee.

193. What does Ms. Cortez mention about the basketball team?

(A) It has produced famous athletes.
(B) It won a championship game.
(C) It has players of different ages.
(D) It has been active for many years.

194. What is indicated about Ms. Cortez's purchase?

(A) It was paid with store credit.
(B) It included clothes made of eco-friendly materials.
(C) It qualified for a membership discount.
(D) It can be returned within 30 days.

195. What can be inferred about Viu Athleisure Shop?

(A) It did not follow its own policy.
(B) It is trying to open another location.
(C) It ships all items within 48 hours.
(D) It will modify clothes to fit.

GO ON TO THE NEXT PAGE

Questions 196-200 refer to the following Web page, questionnaire, and online review.

https://www.visionbath.com/serviceinquiry

Vision Bath

Vision Bath is an independent bathroom contractor that aims to provide customers with the best overall home renovation experience. Whether you wish to add a new bathroom to your home or remodel an existing one, we guarantee that our work is high quality. If you want to have the bathroom of your dreams, you'll first need to complete a brief questionnaire to let us know what you're looking for. Within 24 hours, one of our skilled designers will contact you by phone to discuss your preferences further. You'll receive a product catalog and will be able to schedule a face-to-face meeting when you're ready. During this consultation, your designer will present you with a contract, and work will commence shortly thereafter. Click here to begin the process.

https://www.visionbath.com/questionnaire

Vision Bath Questionnaire

Name: Margaret Collins
Phone: 555-9911
E-mail Address: margcollins@wyohi.com

1. Why do you want a new or remodeled bathroom?
My family is too large to continue sharing a single bathroom, so we need another one built.

2. Which term best describes the style of bathroom you want?
☑ Contemporary ☐ Traditional ☐ Luxurious

3. What colors do you want to be used? Blue and White

4. What type of floor material are you interested in?
☐ Tile ☑ Hardwood ☐ Vinyl ☐ Other

5. What type of countertop would you like?
☐ Granite ☑ Porcelain ☐ Glass ☐ Other

6. When would you like this project to begin? Early May

7. What is your budget? Between $10,000 and $15,000

SEND

https://www.businessreviews.com/visionbath

★★★★★ Margaret Collins May 25

I'm extremely impressed with Vision Bath. After submitting my questionnaire, I was contacted by a helpful designer named Sandra Reynolds. She had excellent ideas for everything from sink faucets to cabinet handles and was very patient with me. I spent quite a while studying Vision Bath's catalog and when she visited my home, we went over my selections together. I'm especially glad that she helped me choose the granite countertop. Although it cost more than my original choice, it looks better than I could've imagined.

196. For whom is the Web page most likely intended?

(A) Homeowners
(B) Interior decorators
(C) Hotel managers
(D) Marketing professionals

197. According to the questionnaire, why was Ms. Collins dissatisfied with her home?

(A) It had a faulty plumbing system.
(B) It was not built in a modern style.
(C) It contained only one bathroom.
(D) It was furnished with dark panels.

198. What information is NOT included on the questionnaire?

(A) A maximum cost
(B) A preferred floor material
(C) A completion deadline
(D) A design style

199. What did Ms. Reynolds most likely do when she visited Ms. Collins?

(A) Delivered a catalog
(B) Offered a contract
(C) Took some photographs
(D) Collected a payment

200. What is indicated about the porcelain countertop?

(A) It was featured in a brochure.
(B) It is sold with accompanying items.
(C) It is cheaper than the granite model.
(D) It contains storage compartments.

This is the end of the test. You may review Parts 5, 6, and 7 if you finish the test early.

정답 p.327 / 점수 환산표 p.329 / 해석 p.378 / Part 5&6 무료 해설 바로 보기(정답 및 정답 음성 포함)

* 다음 페이지에 있는 Self 체크 리스트를 통해 자신의 문제 풀이 방식과 태도를 점검해 보세요.

Self 체크 리스트

TEST 07은 무사히 잘 마치셨죠?
이제 다음의 Self 체크 리스트를 통해 자신의 테스트 진행 내용을 점검해 볼까요?

1. 나는 75분 동안 완전히 테스트에 집중하였다.

   □ 예　□ 아니오

   아니오에 답한 경우, 이유는 무엇인가요?

2. 나는 75분 동안 100문제를 모두 풀었다.

   □ 예　□ 아니오

   아니오에 답한 경우, 이유는 무엇인가요?

3. 나는 75분 동안 답안지 표시까지 완료하였다.

   □ 예　□ 아니오

   아니오에 답한 경우, 이유는 무엇인가요?

4. 나는 Part 5와 Part 6를 19분 안에 모두 풀었다.

   □ 예　□ 아니오

   아니오에 답한 경우, 이유는 무엇인가요?

5. Part 7을 풀 때 5분 이상 걸린 지문이 없었다.

   □ 예　□ 아니오

6. 개선해야 할 점 또는 나를 위한 충고를 적어보세요.

* 교재의 첫 장으로 돌아가서 자신이 적은 목표 점수를 확인하면서 목표에 대한 의지를 다지기 바랍니다. 개선해야 할 점은 반드시 다음 테스트에 실천해야 합니다. 그것이 가장 중요하며, 그래야만 발전할 수 있습니다.

TEST 08

PART 5
PART 6
PART 7
Self 체크 리스트

잠깐! 테스트 전 확인사항

1. 휴대 전화의 전원을 끄셨나요? □ 예
2. Answer Sheet, 연필, 지우개를 준비하셨나요? □ 예
3. 시계를 준비하셨나요? □ 예

모든 준비가 완료되었으면 목표 점수를 떠올린 후 테스트를 시작합니다.

문제 풀이를 마치는 시간은 지금부터 75분 후인 ___시 ___분입니다.
테스트 시간은 총 75분이며, 시험 종료 전 2~3분은 정답 검토 및 답안지 마킹을 위해 사용합니다.

READING TEST

In this section, you must demonstrate your ability to read and comprehend English. You will be given a variety of texts and asked to answer questions about these texts. This section is divided into three parts and will take 75 minutes to complete.

Do not mark the answers in your test book. Use the answer sheet that is separately provided.

PART 5

Directions: In each question, you will be asked to review a statement that is missing a word or phrase. Four answer choices will be provided for each statement. Select the best answer and mark the corresponding letter (A), (B), (C), or (D) on the answer sheet.

PART 5 권장 풀이 시간 11분

101. According to the news report, Philby Corporation ------- a new office in Utah at present.

(A) is building
(B) to build
(C) will build
(D) building

102. Ms. Wendt wanted to meet Mr. Andrews in person but had to call ------- instead.

(A) his
(B) himself
(C) him
(D) he

103. Ms. Myers trained all the new staff and ------- offered to mentor anyone needing extra help.

(A) well
(B) both
(C) even
(D) too

104. The contractor asked that payment for his services be ------- by Friday afternoon.

(A) making
(B) made
(C) make
(D) have made

105. The Portland Bearcats have ------- qualified to play in the regional hockey championship.

(A) narrowed
(B) narrowness
(C) narrowly
(D) narrow

106. The city's ------- population growth has resulted in a scarcity of available housing.

(A) rapid
(B) tight
(C) tedious
(D) affluent

107. ------- her many achievements as an opera singer, Gloria Donahue has not yet won any major awards.

(A) Next to
(B) Far from
(C) Because of
(D) In spite of

108. The travel agency's ------- for increasing sales is to post customer testimonials on its Web site.

(A) landmark
(B) portfolio
(C) strategy
(D) approval

109. The ------- of the Rolstein Literary Prize will be selected by a number of literature enthusiasts.

(A) received
(B) receipt
(C) recipient
(D) receiving

110. Mr. McGuire needs only one more issue of a rare comic book series to have a ------- set.

(A) completion
(B) complete
(C) completer
(D) completeness

111. Unable to keep up with rising costs, many airlines have opted to ------- the in-flight meal service on domestic flights.

(A) recover
(B) eliminate
(C) calculate
(D) recognize

112. Conference participants can receive a complimentary lunch by ------- the voucher in their welcome package.

(A) redeem
(B) redeeming
(C) redeemed
(D) redeems

113. Factory robots have made it possible to carry out manufacturing tasks more quickly and -------.

(A) assertively
(B) statistically
(C) accurately
(D) intentionally

114. In the event that the competition results in a tie, the prize money will be divided ------- both contestants.

(A) within
(B) off
(C) along
(D) between

115. Passengers ------- luggage in the airport's arrivals area should note that many bags look alike.

(A) claiming
(B) claim
(C) claims
(D) claimed

116. Mr. Chen has nearly 30 years of advertising experience, making him a ------- professional in his field.

(A) seasons
(B) seasonal
(C) seasoned
(D) seasonally

117. Emperor Fabrics has signed a number of profitable ------- since Ms. Shane took over as a company director.

(A) quotes
(B) deals
(C) petitions
(D) applications

118. The new bridge must be ------- enough to withstand the frequent storms that pass through the area.

(A) severe
(B) separate
(C) genuine
(D) sturdy

119. In ------- with the mall's policies, security guards will be given an access badge once training is complete.

(A) compliance
(B) comply
(C) complied
(D) complies

120. The town of Hamilton has seven parks, all of ------- have hosted outdoor concerts at one time or another.

(A) them
(B) those
(C) which
(D) theirs

GO ON TO THE NEXT PAGE

121. ------- the annual Media Conference in Athens, most downtown hotels are fully booked.

(A) Due to
(B) As soon as
(C) Besides
(D) Such as

122. Mr. Morgan ------- for an electrical installation job at Cuthright Tower by a former employer who was pleased with his work.

(A) recommends
(B) has recommended
(C) was recommended
(D) is recommending

123. Level Field Landscaping has recently been ------- by the city for disposing of yard waste improperly.

(A) commenced
(B) accelerated
(C) measured
(D) fined

124. The assembly plant is on schedule to exceed its quota of tractors, ------- it did last month.

(A) just as
(B) in fact
(C) thus
(D) until

125. In her inspirational talk, Denise Camic argues that the ------- a company is, the greater its success.

(A) more creative
(B) creativity
(C) creative
(D) most creative

126. In order to ensure that information is stored -------, files in the database cannot be accessed without a password.

(A) productively
(B) confidentially
(C) unanimously
(D) voluntarily

127. During his acceptance speech for the Businessperson of the Year Award, Mr. Gordon expressed ------- for his dedicated team members.

(A) commitment
(B) interest
(C) tribute
(D) appreciation

128. Visitors are not allowed in certain sections of the building, ------- are they permitted to wander around without a guide.

(A) so
(B) during
(C) nor
(D) though

129. Rand's Organic Farm was able to increase its customer base ------- a radio advertisement.

(A) in common with
(B) in addition to
(C) on behalf of
(D) by means of

130. Several of the call center employees received outstanding annual evaluations and got a ------- as a result.

(A) proximity
(B) raise
(C) setback
(D) premiere

PART 6

Directions: In this part, you will be asked to read four English texts. Each text is missing a word, phrase, or sentence. Select the answer choice that correctly completes the text and mark the corresponding letter (A), (B), (C), or (D) on the answer sheet.

PART 6 권장 풀이 시간 8분

Questions 131-134 refer to the following memo.

MEMO

To: All staff
From: Warren Harris, Office Manager
Date: August 15
Subject: Electricity use

I would like to bring your attention to the fact that the office utilities bill was ------- **131.** 15 percent higher this month than it was at the same time last year. I feel this is unacceptable, especially as the company ------- **132.** a number of cost-saving measures. These include the installation of energy-efficient lights and windows during our renovation last fall. I would, therefore, like to remind you all to be -------. **133.** With just a bit of rationality and good judgment, I am confident we can take steps to reduce our expenses. -------. **134.** Thank you for your understanding, and if you have any other ideas for saving energy, please let me know.

131. (A) nearest
(B) nearer
(C) nearly
(D) nearby

132. (A) implementing
(B) will implement
(C) will have implemented
(D) has implemented

133. (A) sensible
(B) honest
(C) impartial
(D) tolerant

134. (A) Given the opportunity, I am sure many of you would volunteer.
(B) If in doubt, simply refer to the meeting agenda that's posted online.
(C) To start, we can all make sure to turn off anything that's not in use.
(D) As a result, we will no longer qualify for our current service discount.

GO ON TO THE NEXT PAGE

Questions 135-138 refer to the following press release.

PRESS RELEASE—Basinet Books

Basinet Books to Launch Its Own Podcast

The publishing company Basinet Books will soon begin producing a weekly podcast for fans of historical fiction. The ------- **135.** installment of the series will air on July 15. This first show will discuss the recent popularity of the genre and explore the fascinating relationship between history and fiction. Each subsequent ------- **136.** will focus on a single novel. ------- **137.**. As for who will host it, Basinet Books has hinted that they have hired a prominent actor. Reportedly, this ------- **138.** has starred in several movie adaptations of novels. Each podcast file will be available through the StarLadder mobile application.

135. (A) ultimate
(B) consecutive
(C) controversial
(D) introductory

136. (A) review
(B) workshop
(C) episode
(D) poster

137. (A) Subscribers will have access to already archived shows.
(B) The books that are chosen will all be new releases.
(C) Thus, electronic versions have gained popularity.
(D) Listeners were invited to call in and ask questions.

138. (A) individualistic
(B) individuality
(C) individual
(D) individually

Questions 139-142 refer to the following e-mail.

To: Belinda Wright <bw4637@advertx.com>
From: Jamie Garnett <jg4548@advertx.com>
Subject: Urgent request
Date: February 11

Hello, Belinda.

How is your vacation going? I know that your time off ------- (139.) until Friday, February 14. However, I'm wondering if you can return to work that day. It turns out that Nektar Beverages suddenly wants us to make some changes to the advertisement it commissioned. ------- (140.). Since you were the lead designer, I feel like you'd be the best person to handle the final revisions. The task will probably take five or six hours.

To ------- (141.) you, we would pay you the standard overtime rate on February 14. We would also ------- (142.) an extra vacation day.

Thank you in advance.
Jamie

139. (A) lasted
(B) lasts
(C) has lasted
(D) to last

140. (A) They will do all of the revisions again from the beginning.
(B) Apparently, doing that would be against our corporate regulations.
(C) That is the day when our contractor agreement expires.
(D) This is surprising as they seemed happy with it last week.

141. (A) compensator
(B) compensate
(C) compensating
(D) compensation

142. (A) require
(B) record
(C) provide
(D) prohibit

GO ON TO THE NEXT PAGE

Questions 143-146 refer to the following article.

New Horizons for GEOnet Solutions

BOSTON (October 9)—GEOnet Solutions has announced that it will be extending its reach overseas. -------. (143.) For over 20 years, this Boston-based ------- (144.) in technology development has created innovative ways to use geotechnology and has made countless advances in the field. -------, (145.) the data collection systems and tracking tools used by millions of people every day would not exist without its efforts. In a statement released yesterday, GEOnet Solutions representative Tomas Fuller said that the primary goal of the ------- (146.) is to facilitate cooperation with the London Technology Center. The two believe that their collaboration will be mutually beneficial.

143. (A) Customers will now be able to place orders online.
(B) This increase is a result of growing demand worldwide.
(C) The market is already too crowded to open another branch.
(D) The company will be opening a satellite branch in London.

144. (A) pioneering
(B) pioneer
(C) pioneered
(D) pioneers

145. (A) Notwithstanding
(B) In fact
(C) Meanwhile
(D) Instead

146. (A) experiment
(B) relocation
(C) policy
(D) expansion

PART 7

Directions: In this part, you will be asked to read several texts, such as advertisements, articles, instant messages, or examples of business correspondence. Each text is followed by several questions. Select the best answer and mark the corresponding letter (A), (B), (C), or (D) on your answer sheet.

PART 7 권장 풀이 시간 54분

Questions 147-148 refer to the following memo.

To: All staff
From: Nadori Seiko, CEO
Subject: Monthly sales challenge
Date: December 2

Thank you all for contributing to the monthly sales challenge. We acquired several new clients due to your hard work. The sales challenge started as an individual effort and evolved into a positive team experience. Aaron and Marisol had the highest sales. Thus, they will both get a gift certificate for Spanto Restaurant.

Because I was surprised by the amount of enthusiasm and team spirit this challenge has created, I will offer each of you an additional day off. Furthermore, the executive team has decided to hold this initiative again in the future. Please e-mail me some new prize ideas, which can be for individual staff members or entire teams.

147. What is indicated about the challenge?
(A) It will be repeated.
(B) It was unsuccessful.
(C) Its deadline was extended.
(D) Its participants were anonymous.

148. What does Ms. Seiko want her staff members to do?
(A) Evaluate team members' performances
(B) Recommend some potential rewards
(C) Submit a preferred date for some time off
(D) Send some personal documents by e-mail

GO ON TO THE NEXT PAGE

Questions 149-150 refer to the following information.

Cole Theater Membership Information:

To become a Cole Theater member, apply at www.coletheater.com/join or visit one of our box office booths. Membership cards must be renewed after 12 months.

Membership Benefits:

- Tickets to our exclusive movie premieres, which are attended by famous actors
- $6 entry for morning showings
- 10 percent discount for afternoon, evening, and weekend showings
- Free concession stand items or movie tickets in exchange for reward points

For more information, e-mail extras@coletheater.com.

149. What is NOT mentioned about members of Cole Theater?

(A) They receive a reduced rate at night.
(B) They have to renew a card once a year.
(C) They may redeem points for snacks.
(D) They are required to pay a monthly fee.

150. What is stated about Cole Theater?

(A) It holds a local film festival.
(B) It has installed new ticket machines.
(C) It appeared in a television documentary.
(D) It hosts visits by celebrities.

Questions 151-152 refer to the following text-message chain.

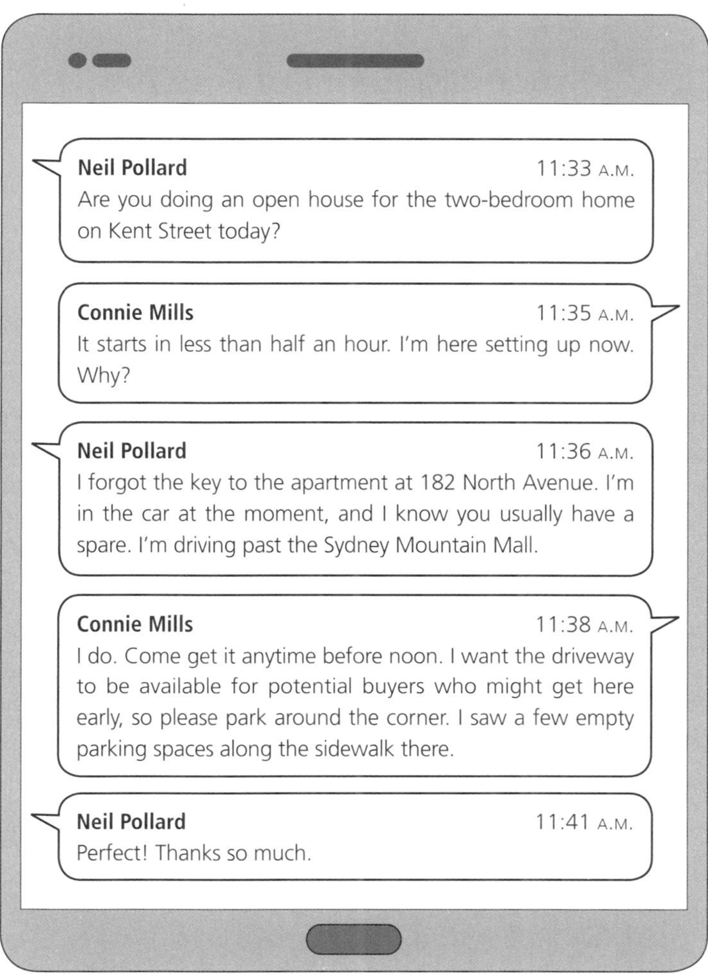

Neil Pollard 11:33 A.M.
Are you doing an open house for the two-bedroom home on Kent Street today?
Connie Mills 11:35 A.M.
It starts in less than half an hour. I'm here setting up now. Why?
Neil Pollard 11:36 A.M.
I forgot the key to the apartment at 182 North Avenue. I'm in the car at the moment, and I know you usually have a spare. I'm driving past the Sydney Mountain Mall.
Connie Mills 11:38 A.M.
I do. Come get it anytime before noon. I want the driveway to be available for potential buyers who might get here early, so please park around the corner. I saw a few empty parking spaces along the sidewalk there.
Neil Pollard 11:41 A.M.
Perfect! Thanks so much.

151. At 11:36 A.M., what does Mr. Pollard mean when he writes, "I know you usually have a spare"?

(A) He needs a key to a property.
(B) He was told about a coworker's routine.
(C) He wants to borrow a car.
(D) He is unable to visit a storage room.

152. What does Ms. Mills ask Mr. Pollard to do?

(A) Sweep a driveway outside a home
(B) Meet with some potential clients
(C) Turn off a security system
(D) Park his vehicle on a street

TEST | 01 | 02 | 03 | 04 | 05 | 06 | 07 | 08 | 09 | 10 | 해커스 토익 실전 1000제 1 Reading

GO ON TO THE NEXT PAGE

Questions 153-154 refer to the following letter.

Brugeri Museum of Fine Art

856 Empire Street
Grants Pass, OR 97527

September 9

Robert Jansen
3111 Helmsview Drive
Arcata, CA 95521

Dear Mr. Jansen,

I am sorry to report that *Descending Cherub*, the statue you so generously lent us from your personal collection this year, was damaged yesterday. Our staff were in the process of moving all the works in the outdoor sculpture garden into the main exhibition hall when the weather changed suddenly. Unfortunately, they did not get to your statue in time. A strong wind caused it to fall from its pedestal, breaking the left hand off. I have enclosed some pictures of the broken area.

Our insurance company will, of course, financially compensate you for the damage. In addition, we will cover the cost of having it expertly repaired. With your consent, we can ask a professional to do this. If you prefer to use someone of your own choosing, simply let us know, and we will ship the item to you right away.

Once again, I apologize for this regrettable accident. I will await your reply.

Mia Hyman
Curator, Brugeri Museum of Fine Art

Enclosure

153. What is mentioned about *Descending Cherub*?

(A) It was exhibited for about a year.
(B) It was dropped while being moved.
(C) It was sculpted by Ms. Hyman.
(D) It was loaned to a museum.

154. What has been included with the letter?

(A) An entrance ticket to a gallery
(B) Photographs of some damage
(C) Insurance claim documents
(D) A reimbursement check

Questions 155-157 refer to the following article excerpt.

Steel Works Inc. has begun operations at its new plant. The mill, built at a cost of $60 million, will contribute to the growth of Malaysia's construction industry. It will be able to produce about 1 million tons of reinforced steel per year.

Established in Kampung Tebing, Steel Works' factory will ship steel bars to various parts of the country, according to company CEO Aiman Musa. "The plant will help Malaysian cities develop their infrastructure," he added.

The plant is Steel Works' second. Its first mill in Rembau now exclusively exports its products to other Asian countries, though it once met almost half of Malaysia's steel demand. The Rembau plant was upgraded last year and is considered one of Asia's most modern steel plants. Steel Works' plants utilize the latest technology to ensure not only that production is efficient but that it has a low environmental impact.

With the establishment of its Kampung Tebing plant, Steel Works' market share in Malaysia is expected to rise to 72 percent. The value of its shares on the local stock exchange increased by 24 percent with the opening of the new plant.

155. What is one purpose of the article?

(A) To report on the state of a region's infrastructure
(B) To provide details about the global steel industry
(C) To give information about a country's exports
(D) To announce the opening of a new factory

156. What does the article suggest about the plant in Rembau?

(A) It no longer produces steel for local use.
(B) It was taken over by a foreign company.
(C) It formerly caused some harm to the environment.
(D) It has begun manufacturing plastic products.

157. What is NOT stated about Steel Works?

(A) It now has multiple steel mills in operation.
(B) Its new facility will aid Malaysia's urban development.
(C) Its market share will double.
(D) It makes use of up-to-date technology.

GO ON TO THE NEXT PAGE

Questions 158-160 refer to the following e-mail.

To: All marketing officers
From: Linda Marks
Subject: Conference transportation
Date: October 14

Dear Colleagues,

Many of you will be attending the social media conference in Wilmington on Friday. — [1] —. If you are planning on taking the company-chartered bus, we will meet in Parking Lot A and leave promptly at 8:30 A.M. The alternatives are to drive or take public transportation. Directions to the Wilmington Conference Center were provided in a previous e-mail. — [2] —.

For those of you who will not be attending, the representatives from Whitaker's Sports Apparel, the client we acquired last week, will be visiting the office around 10 A.M. — [3] —. I have already advised them that the office will be almost empty due to the conference. — [4] —. Robert Buck in the accounting department will be meeting with them and giving them a quick tour. Be sure to introduce yourself if you get the chance.

Thank you.

Linda Marks

158. According to the e-mail, how can employees get directions to a facility?

(A) By calling an event organizer
(B) By listening to an announcement
(C) By checking an e-mail
(D) By looking at a bulletin board

159. What is suggested about Whitaker's Sports Apparel?

(A) It has sent representatives to revise a contract.
(B) It recently made a deal with Ms. Marks's company.
(C) It reimburses its staff for transportation costs.
(D) It is looking for a new accounting manager.

160. In which of the positions marked [1], [2], [3], and [4] does the following sentence best belong?

"However, they would like to stop by since they will be in town for the day."

(A) [1]
(B) [2]
(C) [3]
(D) [4]

Questions 161-164 refer to the following text-message chain.

Ned O'Toole [11:08 A.M.]
I was late yesterday for our beginning-of-November meeting, so I'd like to ask about the changes to our overtime work policy.

Karen Bingham [11:09 A.M.]
Of course. But didn't you get the memo Mr. Ward sent a little while ago? It summarizes the new rules.

Ned O'Toole [11:10 A.M.]
I only glanced at it briefly, but I saw something about a streamlined process. Does that mean we don't have to turn in the request form anymore?

Karen Bingham [11:12 A.M.]
Yes. In the past, a lot of employees worked extra hours to finish projects but only received their regular salary. This happened because they didn't submit the official overtime document. Many found the form to be too complicated.

Gene Shipley [11:13 A.M.]
Now, Ned, anyone who works over 40 hours a week automatically receives extra pay. All we have to do is enter the information into the payroll system.

Karen Bingham [11:13 A.M.]
Right. And it's effective as of 9 A.M., December 1. At the end of every month, your supervisor will review what you inputted. Unless there's a problem that needs to be discussed, it'll be approved at that point.

Ned O'Toole [11:15 A.M.]
That's good to know, especially considering the big project that I'll be working on in the coming weeks. Thanks!

161. At 11:09 A.M., what does Ms. Bingham mean when she writes, "Of course"?
(A) She will send a memo to employees.
(B) She thinks a new policy is fair.
(C) She is willing to update Mr. O'Toole.
(D) She intends to complete some paperwork.

162. What is mentioned about the overtime document?
(A) It can be downloaded from a Web site.
(B) It was difficult for some staff to complete.
(C) It will be modified by department supervisors.
(D) It is in the process of being rewritten.

163. What will happen on December 1?
(A) Some personnel will have to work late.
(B) A company manual will be distributed.
(C) Some conflicts will be discussed.
(D) A policy change will take effect.

164. What is suggested about Mr. O'Toole?
(A) He misunderstood what he heard at a meeting.
(B) He has made some complaints about a procedure.
(C) He expects to work overtime in the near future.
(D) He has not yet been paid for a recently completed project.

GO ON TO THE NEXT PAGE

Questions 165-167 refer to the following article.

DTA Readies for Airport Overhaul

The Denver Transportation Authority (DTA) has announced a $50 million renovation plan for Franklin Airport, on the outskirts of Denver. The announcement comes as a result of the National Airlines Group (NAG) having labeled its runway as dangerous for large aircraft. The NAG sets safety regulations for all US airports.

"When we took over Franklin Airport 11 years ago, we intended to begin rebuilding it right away. Unfortunately, we encountered numerous budget-related delays. However, in light of the NAG's recent judgment, we have managed to secure federal funding and will finally be able to repair our runway and expand our terminals," said DTA chief Elaine Webster.

The DTA has hired several construction companies to carry out the project, which is expected to be completed within 18 months. Work will start on Terminal B only after the expansion of Terminal A is finished, which will leave the airport fully functional the whole time. After the project has concluded, Franklin Airport will begin serving as a point of arrival and departure for international flights.

165. Why will Franklin Airport be renovated?

(A) To address safety concerns
(B) To spend a budget surplus
(C) To create space for retail businesses
(D) To compete with a larger airport

166. What is true about the renovation project?

(A) It has been a goal of the DTA for over a decade.
(B) It is being funded through private donations.
(C) It will be managed by the NAG.
(D) It will take longer than expected.

167. What is implied about Franklin Airport?

(A) It won a customer satisfaction award.
(B) It is connected to a city by a subway line.
(C) It is currently used only by domestic airlines.
(D) It will be completely shut down during renovations.

Questions 168-171 refer to the following e-mail.

To: Joan Stendhal <joan.stendhal@mynextmail.com>
From: Robert Hamilton <r.hamilton@pichaipartners.com>
Date: September 18
Subject: Your application

Dear Ms. Stendhal,

Congratulations! Out of hundreds of applicants, we have selected you to move on to the next stage of the process and participate in an interview at our office. — [1] —.

The interview is scheduled for Friday, September 23, from 1 P.M. to 5 P.M. All applicants will be allowed to take 30-minute breaks between activities. The interview will consist of two parts. During the first part of the interview, you will answer questions from a panel of executives. When you are done, you must stay in the immediate area until you are called for the second part of the interview. For the second part, you will be asked to analyse actual legal cases that our firm has worked on in the past. You will be given an hour to work on one case by yourself. — [2] —. Then, you and the other applicants will form groups of two to work on the second case. This activity will be used to evaluate your communication skills and ability to work with coworkers. Further details will be provided on the day of the interview. — [3] —.

We will supply everything you need to complete the process, including paper, pens, and access to selected law books from our library. — [4] —. We will also provide refreshments.

Please confirm your participation by replying to this e-mail. You can also call me at 555-4883 if you have any questions.

Sincerely,
Robert Hamilton

168. The word "immediate" in paragraph 2, line 4, is closest in meaning to

(A) sudden
(B) nearby
(C) critical
(D) prompt

169. What is an important qualification for the job?

(A) The ability to cooperate with others
(B) Extensive knowledge of international law
(C) A willingness to work long hours
(D) Experience with specific software

170. What are applicants required to do?

(A) Submit additional work references
(B) Send a reply by e-mail
(C) Present a recommendation letter
(D) Create a profile on a firm's Web site

171. In which of the positions marked [1], [2], [3], and [4] does the following sentence best belong?

"You will therefore not need to bring any materials of your own."

(A) [1]
(B) [2]
(C) [3]
(D) [4]

GO ON TO THE NEXT PAGE

Questions 172-175 refer to the following notice.

Run for a Good Cause!

Here at the Highland Employment Center, we need your support for our Tech Training initiative. Many individuals struggle to find work because they lack basic computer skills. Thus, we hope to raise enough funds to hire a computer instructor to run weekly workshops at our center for a full year. Job seekers will be able to attend these sessions for free. By gaining computer proficiency, they will stand a better chance of finding a position and will be able to earn more than they did in the past.

You can help us achieve our goal by participating in a 10-kilometer race in Arthur Park on August 15. The entry fee is $40 throughout July, $45 from August 1-14, and $50 on the day of the race. Those who run in a creative costume will be eligible to win a $100 voucher for Harlan Foods. The costume contest winner will be announced after the race.

Runners will be given packets that include a race bib and storage bag for personal possessions. Those who finish within the two-hour time limit will receive a photograph of themselves crossing the finish line. Go to www.highlandec.com/10k to sign up today!

172. What is one purpose of the notice?

(A) To share some budget calculations
(B) To request participation in a fund-raiser
(C) To announce the fulfillment of a goal
(D) To recruit some volunteers

173. According to the notice, what can race participants do?

(A) Sample some dishes
(B) Wear unusual clothing
(C) Submit route suggestions
(D) Select a preferred running distance

174. What is indicated about the event?

(A) It must be signed up for a month in advance.
(B) Its entry fee varies depending on the registration date.
(C) Its organizer will deliver a speech.
(D) It will be filmed by a television camera crew.

175. What will those who complete the run within two hours receive?

(A) A personalized T-shirt
(B) A certificate of achievement
(C) A gift voucher for groceries
(D) A souvenir photograph

GO ON TO THE NEXT PAGE

Questions 176-180 refer to the following e-mail and magazine contents.

From	Rachel Duval <r.duval@pfmagazine.com>
To	John Hassan <j.hassan@pfmagazine.com>
Date	July 29
Subject	September issue

Hello, John.

Though we have made a lot of progress with the September issue, we still have some decisions to make. First, we have to choose a model for the cover. Since this is typically the most popular issue of the year, we need to get a big celebrity. How about working with Su-min Yoo again? She has a new blockbuster movie coming out in October, and having her on the cover would likely drive up magazine sales. Please contact her agent and try to make an arrangement.

Second, Russo Shampoo abruptly decided not to advertise in the September issue after all. Thus, we urgently need to fill pages 58 and 59. You mentioned that SameSide Cosmetics was interested in running an advertisement in our magazine. This would be for their new line of organic, environmentally friendly skin creams, which will be debuting in October. Could you confirm whether the company wants to take advantage of this opportunity? We could offer them a 20 percent discount.

Lastly, I'd like you to thoroughly check the facts mentioned in our article on the Canadian designer David Burns for the September issue.

Thanks,

Rachel Duval
Editor in Chief
PopFashion Magazine

PopFashion Magazine September Issue

176. Why did Ms. Duval send the e-mail?

(A) To describe some garments
(B) To discuss publication details
(C) To finalize the topic of an article
(D) To assess a set of photographs

177. In the e-mail, the phrase "drive up" in paragraph 1, line 4, is closest in meaning to

(A) operate
(B) motivate
(C) stimulate
(D) travel

178. According to the e-mail, what is SameSide Cosmetics interested in doing?

(A) Developing a new product line
(B) Holding a product demonstration in October
(C) Launching a campaign against chemical ingredients
(D) Buying some advertising space

179. What can be inferred about Ms. Duval?

(A) Her choice for a cover model was unavailable.
(B) She wrote an editorial about a craftsperson.
(C) She is scheduled to attend a clothing fair.
(D) She wants to increase a subscription fee.

180. On which page does the article about Mr. Burns appear?

(A) Page 16
(B) Page 35
(C) Page 52
(D) Page 78

GO ON TO THE NEXT PAGE

Questions 181-185 refer to the following information and schedule of events.

Go Shopping and Make a Difference!

This year, Bristol's Support Your Local Business Day falls on Saturday, April 28. Instead of visiting nationwide chain stores on this day, shop at some of the smaller stores in your neighborhood. By doing so, you'll help the local economy since the revenue earned by such businesses remains in our town. In addition, a group of participating businesses, including the restaurant Birdy Beets, the crafts shop Tinker Time, and the clothing boutique Kara Lee's, have agreed to give 10 percent of their profits from this day to the Bristol Business Association (BBA). The BBA will use these proceeds to continue carrying out charitable projects in the area.

Along with the shopping opportunities, Support Your Local Business Day will feature special programs. Check www.bristolsylbd.com for a list of participating businesses and a schedule of events.

Support Your Local Business Day

April 28 in Bristol

Message for Community Members *9:00 A.M. to 9:30 A.M.*

Location: Anchor Square

Emmanuel Perez, president of the Bristol Business Association (BBA), will give a speech about why local businesses are so important. He will also talk about some of the BBA's upcoming efforts.

Walking Tour *9:40 A.M. to 10:15 A.M.*

Meeting place: Craft Street Antiques

Take a stroll down Dalton Street and learn about the history of its buildings. The last stop is Wayfair House, one of the oldest buildings in Bristol, which will be open to the public for the first time. Admission to Wayfair House is free.

Shop for Your Lunch *10:30 A.M. to 1:00 P.M.*

Location: Downtown Shopping District

If you make a purchase in three different locally owned businesses, you will receive a coupon for a free lunch at a participating restaurant. Present your receipts at the visitors' bureau by 1:30 P.M.

Music on the Green *12:00 P.M. to 4:00 P.M.*

Location: Downtown Green Park

Local bands will play 30-minute concerts on the stage at Green Park. At a tent nearby, plenty of fun arts and crafts workshops for kids will be offered.

181. What is the information mainly about?

(A) A newly opened showroom
(B) A volunteer recruitment session
(C) An event in support of small businesses
(D) A tax incentive for companies

182. What is indicated about the BBA?

(A) It operates a major retail chain.
(B) It has raised its membership fee by 10 percent.
(C) It is opposed to a tax on imported goods.
(D) It contributes to the local community.

183. What information will Mr. Perez include in his speech?

(A) The reasons for a construction
(B) The plans of an organization
(C) The cost of a campaign
(D) The date of a reopening

184. What is NOT one of the activities planned for April 28?

(A) A cooking demonstration by a famous chef
(B) A walk through a historic neighborhood
(C) Some outdoor performances by musicians
(D) Some instructional sessions for children

185. Where most likely can visitors make use of a coupon?

(A) Birdy Beets
(B) Tinker Time
(C) Kara Lee's
(D) Wayfair House

TEST 01 02 03 04 05 06 07 08 09 10 해커스 토익 실전 1000제 1 Reading

GO ON TO THE NEXT PAGE

Questions 186-190 refer to the following article, memo, and e-mail.

February 12—At a press conference on February 10, Mayor David Wilkins announced the planned construction of a new four-lane bridge. The work is scheduled to begin on May 14 and end on December 23. It is expected to relieve traffic congestion in the city, particularly for commuters trying to reach the north side of the city from the downtown area. However, the traffic situation will likely worsen while the new bridge is under construction due to a number of temporary road closures.

Harris Road and Oak Boulevard will be closed from May 14 to August 1. In addition, Center Avenue will be inaccessible to motorists from August 5 to October 10, and Harbor Way will be shut down from October 12 to December 20. Commuters who regularly use these streets should visit the Department of Transportation's Web site for information about alternatives.

To: All Bellwood Sporting Goods Employees
From: Beth Ferrell, Manager
Subject: Response plan
Date: July 10

As I informed everyone in the staff meeting yesterday, the closure of the street in front of our store starting from August 5 will likely have a serious impact on in-store sales. As a result, I have decided to hold two online promotions during that period. Hopefully, we can generate enough sales through our Web site to compensate for having fewer customers coming into the store. All footwear in the shop and online will be marked down by 15 percent. In addition, anyone who places an order online will receive free shipping. Please make sure to tell our customers about these promotions.

To: customerservice@bellwood.com
From: j.adams@ezmail.com
Date: August 12
Subject: Order Number 029384

On August 9, I bought a jacket on your Web site. Unfortunately, I just realized that the size I selected was a large rather than an extra large. I'd like to change this before the order is shipped so that I don't have to return the jacket. Would it be possible for you to just replace the item I mistakenly chose with the correct one? If not, I guess I will have to cancel my original order and place a new one. Please let me know.

Sincerely,

Jeff Adams

186. What did Mayor Wilkins do on February 10?

(A) Presented at a tourism conference
(B) Showed visitors around an office
(C) Spoke about an infrastructure project
(D) Apologized for a traffic accident

187. According to the article, why should some commuters visit a Web site?

(A) To find people to carpool with
(B) To check some route information
(C) To give feedback about a policy
(D) To evaluate public transit

188. Where is Bellwood Sporting Goods probably located?

(A) On Harris Road
(B) On Oak Boulevard
(C) On Center Avenue
(D) On Harbor Way

189. What is suggested about Mr. Adams's order?

(A) It was ineligible for a promotional discount.
(B) Its color was different from the one requested.
(C) It is no longer being manufactured.
(D) It will be shipped to a work address.

190. What will Mr. Adams do if an item cannot be replaced?

(A) Delete a customer account
(B) Visit a manufacturer's Web site
(C) Fill out a complaint form
(D) Start a process over again

GO ON TO THE NEXT PAGE

Questions 191-195 refer to the following e-mail, form, and newsletter.

To: Jade Liu <j.liu@zhongacademy.org>
From: Jason Richards <jasonrich382@goodmail.net>
Date: November 20
Subject: Sunday classes

Dear Ms. Liu,

I'm interested in taking your business Chinese class on Sunday mornings. I've studied Chinese using language training software, so I'm somewhat proficient. However, I'd like to take a test to determine my fluency level before I register. Please let me know the procedure for this as I was unable to find information about it on your Web site.

Also, when checking class times online, I noticed that you have free screenings of popular Chinese movies at your academy. My friend went to the one you held on November 12 and said it was educational. I'd like to go to next month's showing, and I'm wondering if I need to sign up.

Kindest regards,

Jason Richards

ZHONG ACADEMY
Class Registration for December

Name	Jason Richards	Level According to Test	Beginner
Address	51 Rye Street Concord, NH 03302	Preferred Class Time	Sundays 10 A.M. – 11:30 A.M.
Phone	555-7244	Tuition Fee	$200
E-mail	jasonrich382@goodmail.net	Tuition Due Date	November 30
Was our academy recommended to you by someone?			Yes
If so, please provide the name of this individual.			Robin Ghose

○ To change your class time, make a request at our main desk.
○ If you recommend us to someone and that person enrolls, you will receive a 15 percent discount on your next class.

Zhong Academy Monthly Newsletter

December 1

Watching a Chinese movie is one way to improve your language skills. Two Chinese film events are taking place locally this month.

The Bright Lights Film Festival will be held at the Cloudbank Hotel on December 20. It will feature a new release from Xu Yue, the director of the critically acclaimed film *Summer Shore*. Xu's latest work, *Washing Away*, is about a young dancer from Shanghai. Tickets for the festival are $20 and can be purchased by logging on to www.blffest.org.

Additionally, you can attend a free viewing of *Grave Mistakes* by Chinese director Wei Chung. It will be shown on December 28 here at Zhong Academy. Viewings at the academy are held monthly and are strictly for students enrolled in intermediate or advanced classes. As we did last month after our showing of *River Goddess*, we will have a discussion in Chinese after this month's screening.

191. According to the e-mail, what information was Mr. Richards unable to find on a Web site?

(A) A class schedule
(B) A service fee
(C) A facility location
(D) A testing process

192. What is NOT stated about Zhong Academy?

(A) It allows scheduling changes.
(B) It has lessons for beginners.
(C) It only holds weekday classes.
(D) It offers discounts for referrals.

193. Which film did Mr. Richards's friend most likely watch?

(A) *Summer Shore*
(B) *Washing Away*
(C) *Grave Mistakes*
(D) *River Goddess*

194. What is true about Ms. Xu?

(A) Her first movie will be screened at a festival.
(B) She will spend a night at the Cloudbank Hotel.
(C) Her projects are funded by a firm based in Shanghai.
(D) She has received positive reviews from critics.

195. What can be inferred about Mr. Richards?

(A) He used to work at a language school.
(B) He bought tickets for an upcoming festival.
(C) He cannot attend a free screening in December.
(D) He went on a business trip to China.

GO ON TO THE NEXT PAGE

Questions 196-200 refer to the following announcement, e-mail, and article.

Seeking Sources for TV Episode on Emerald Falls

Director Hector Almonte is currently seeking interviewees for a television episode on the town of Emerald Falls. The episode is being produced for *The Good Old Days*, an award-winning documentary series that is hosted by Janet Leslie. For its second season, the series will be expanded from 10 to 12 episodes. It will continue to profile historic towns across Belize through video interviews and on-location footage. Interviewees do not need to reside in Emerald Falls but must have a strong connection with the town. For more information, please call (501) 555-7925.

In addition, Mr. Almonte hopes to gain access to letters, photos, and other items that can provide insights into the town's beginnings. If you have such artifacts and are prepared to loan them out, you are kindly asked to contact his assistant Chloe Benbow at c.benbow@sunrise.bz.

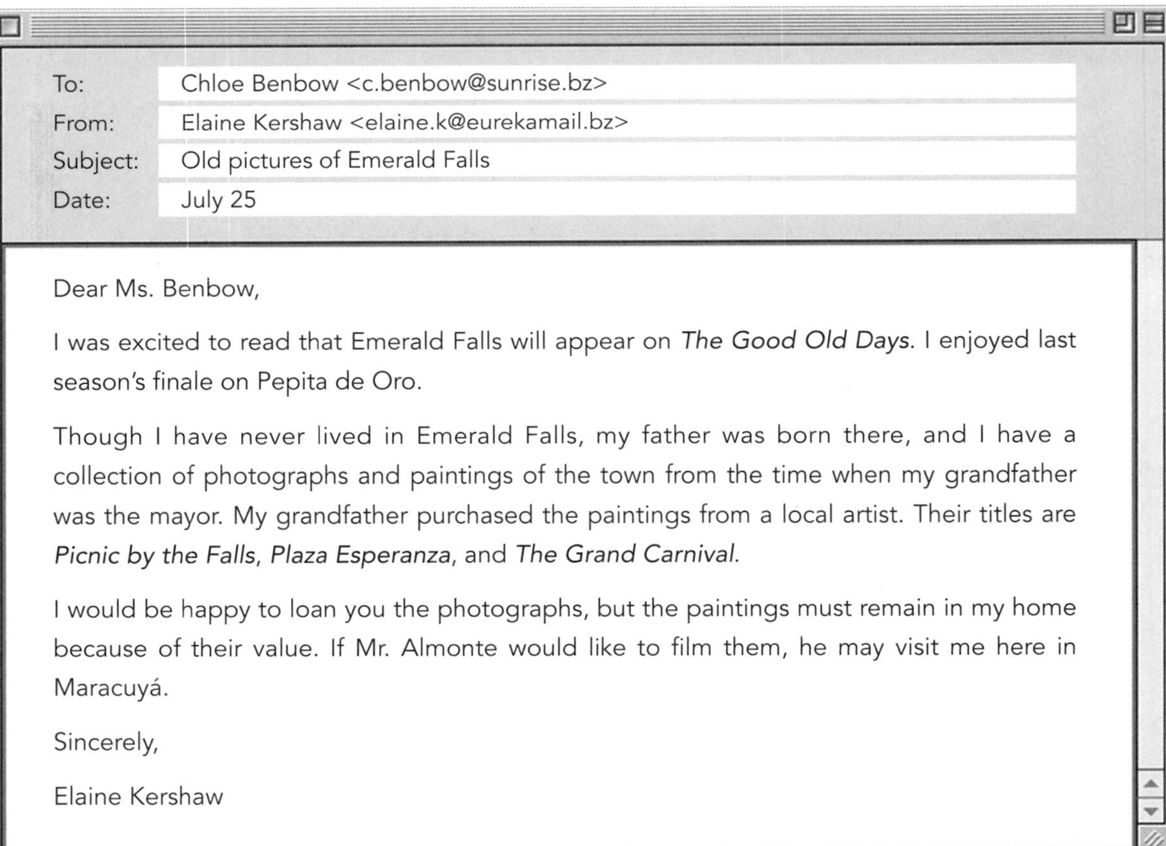

To: Chloe Benbow <c.benbow@sunrise.bz>
From: Elaine Kershaw <elaine.k@eurekamail.bz>
Subject: Old pictures of Emerald Falls
Date: July 25

Dear Ms. Benbow,

I was excited to read that Emerald Falls will appear on *The Good Old Days*. I enjoyed last season's finale on Pepita de Oro.

Though I have never lived in Emerald Falls, my father was born there, and I have a collection of photographs and paintings of the town from the time when my grandfather was the mayor. My grandfather purchased the paintings from a local artist. Their titles are *Picnic by the Falls*, *Plaza Esperanza*, and *The Grand Carnival*.

I would be happy to loan you the photographs, but the paintings must remain in my home because of their value. If Mr. Almonte would like to film them, he may visit me here in Maracuyá.

Sincerely,

Elaine Kershaw

BELIZE CITY (December 15)—Viewer ratings have been rising for *The Good Old Days*, a documentary series on the country's heritage towns. The most recent episode focused on Emerald Falls, a once thriving mining community that has since been depleted of its celebrated mineral deposits. Although the population has dwindled significantly, the town still looks much as it did before. In one scene of the episode, we are shown the Jana Haynes's painting *Plaza Esperanza* that reveals how little Emerald Falls has changed.

Director Hector Almonte commented, "For the second season, we looked for sources with personal links to the towns. The Emerald Falls episode turned out nicely thanks to everyone who shared stories and memorable objects."

Next week, episode 5 will be released. The director says that he wants the location to be a surprise.

196. What is NOT mentioned about *The Good Old Days*?

(A) It includes recorded interviews.
(B) It focuses on old towns.
(C) It features a regular host.
(D) It is sponsored by a travel agency.

197. What is most likely true about Pepita de Oro?

(A) It used to have a large public plaza.
(B) It is celebrating an anniversary this year.
(C) It is a popular destination for foreign tourists.
(D) It was covered in the 10th episode of a show.

198. Who did Ms. Kershaw's grandfather buy some paintings from?

(A) Hector Almonte
(B) Janet Leslie
(C) Chloe Benbow
(D) Jana Haynes

199. What is suggested about Mr. Almonte?

(A) He wrote a book about a journey.
(B) He examined some artwork in Maracuyá.
(C) He held a press conference in October.
(D) He has lent out a collection of artifacts.

200. What was Emerald Falls mainly famous for?

(A) Its educational standards
(B) Its natural scenery
(C) Its mineral resources
(D) Its charity auctions

This is the end of the test. You may review Parts 5, 6, and 7 if you finish the test early.

정답 p.327 / 점수 환산표 p.329 / 해석 p.386 / Part 5&6 무료 해설 바로 보기(정답 및 정답 음성 포함)

* 다음 페이지에 있는 Self 체크 리스트를 통해 자신의 문제 풀이 방식과 태도를 점검해 보세요.

Self 체크 리스트

TEST 08은 무사히 잘 마치셨죠?
이제 다음의 Self 체크 리스트를 통해 자신의 테스트 진행 내용을 점검해 볼까요?

1. 나는 75분 동안 완전히 테스트에 집중하였다.

   □ 예　□ 아니오

   아니오에 답한 경우, 이유는 무엇인가요?

2. 나는 75분 동안 100문제를 모두 풀었다.

   □ 예　□ 아니오

   아니오에 답한 경우, 이유는 무엇인가요?

3. 나는 75분 동안 답안지 표시까지 완료하였다.

   □ 예　□ 아니오

   아니오에 답한 경우, 이유는 무엇인가요?

4. 나는 Part 5와 Part 6를 19분 안에 모두 풀었다.

   □ 예　□ 아니오

   아니오에 답한 경우, 이유는 무엇인가요?

5. Part 7을 풀 때 5분 이상 걸린 지문이 없었다.

   □ 예　□ 아니오

6. 개선해야 할 점 또는 나를 위한 충고를 적어보세요.

* 교재의 첫 장으로 돌아가서 자신이 적은 목표 점수를 확인하면서 목표에 대한 의지를 다지기 바랍니다. 개선해야 할 점은 반드시 다음 테스트에 실천해야 합니다. 그것이 가장 중요하며, 그래야만 발전할 수 있습니다.

TEST 09

PART 5

PART 6

PART 7

Self 체크 리스트

잠깐! 테스트 전 확인사항

1. 휴대 전화의 전원을 끄셨나요? □ 예
2. Answer Sheet, 연필, 지우개를 준비하셨나요? □ 예
3. 시계를 준비하셨나요? □ 예

모든 준비가 완료되었으면 목표 점수를 떠올린 후 테스트를 시작합니다.

문제 풀이를 마치는 시간은 지금부터 75분 후인 ___시 ___분입니다.

테스트 시간은 총 75분이며, 시험 종료 전 2~3분은 정답 검토 및 답안지 마킹을 위해 사용합니다.

READING TEST

In this section, you must demonstrate your ability to read and comprehend English. You will be given a variety of texts and asked to answer questions about these texts. This section is divided into three parts and will take 75 minutes to complete.

Do not mark the answers in your test book. Use the answer sheet that is separately provided.

PART 5

Directions: In each question, you will be asked to review a statement that is missing a word or phrase. Four answer choices will be provided for each statement. Select the best answer and mark the corresponding letter (A), (B), (C), or (D) on the answer sheet.

PART 5 권장 풀이 시간 11분

101. The former tenants will be ------- the property later this afternoon.

(A) vacated
(B) vacancy
(C) vacating
(D) vacate

102. Team members introduced ------- to one another at the start of the first project meeting.

(A) they
(B) them
(C) their
(D) themselves

103. Thanks to a city council budget surplus, it is ------- possible that Davondale Bridge will be replaced this year.

(A) certain
(B) certainty
(C) certainly
(D) certitude

104. Ticket holders were provided with refunds but were not told ------- the concert had been canceled.

(A) why
(B) where
(C) who
(D) which

105. To promote Gaspard Carlock's puppet show, advertisements will be ------- around the city.

(A) packed
(B) posted
(C) priced
(D) practiced

106. Since the two programs have a number of similar elements, viewers have drawn ------- between them.

(A) comparisons
(B) comparing
(C) comparative
(D) comparable

107. Attendees found the computer tutorial offered by Offenburg Community Center to be ------- helpful.

(A) fast
(B) enough
(C) quite
(D) soon

108. To find his printer's model number, Mr. Jansen turned it ------- and checked the bottom.

(A) past
(B) against
(C) in
(D) over

109. Earth Preserve hopes that everyone ------- to a fund-raiser held in the coming week.

(A) contributing
(B) will contribute
(C) contributed
(D) had contributed

110. Several local ski lodges have delayed opening ------- mid-November due to the warm weather.

(A) about
(B) despite
(C) until
(D) across

111. Some employees may have to work overtime during the final ------- of the project.

(A) figure
(B) judgment
(C) phase
(D) piece

112. The vocabulary in *Words in Russian* becomes ------- harder after the first section of the book.

(A) progressive
(B) progressively
(C) progress
(D) progressed

113. The ------- trail Ms. Vigneux had ever hiked was located in Flint Valley National Park.

(A) roughly
(B) rougher
(C) roughest
(D) rough

114. As a result of an exclusivity agreement, the drink Nitro-Sip is available ------- at Duggarti Foods.

(A) densely
(B) fully
(C) solely
(D) fairly

115. Accounting department employees had to work longer hours during the -------, which took nearly a month.

(A) auditor
(B) auditorial
(C) audited
(D) audit

116. Though the ------- findings suggested that the medication was effective, further research proved otherwise.

(A) congested
(B) upcoming
(C) hazardous
(D) original

117. If Mr. Alton ------- for the conference in advance, he will receive a 15 percent discount on the price of admission.

(A) registers
(B) had registered
(C) will register
(D) registered

118. Mr. Isaac manages the store and his ------- include handling staff concerns.

(A) responsive
(B) responsible
(C) responsibility
(D) responsibilities

119. Ahead of his retirement, Director John Bailey ------- his colleague Vanessa Gail as his successor.

(A) consented
(B) estimated
(C) amended
(D) nominated

TEST | 01 | 02 | 03 | 04 | 05 | 06 | 07 | 08 | 09 | 10 | 해커스 토익 실전 1000제 1 Reading

GO ON TO THE NEXT PAGE

120. The company's new workplace safety policy is high ------- the agenda for tomorrow's meeting.

(A) of
(B) to
(C) at
(D) on

121. The head of the National Medical Association also ------- as the director of a private hospital.

(A) accepts
(B) serves
(C) answers
(D) regards

122. Students are ------- arguing for the renovation of Central Library, which is now over 50 years old.

(A) immeasurably
(B) strongly
(C) mutually
(D) inadvertently

123. ------- they are entered into the payroll system, new employees must provide the finance department with some banking information.

(A) As if
(B) During
(C) Before
(D) Instead of

124. ------- you complete this form, bring it to the front desk and leave it with the secretary.

(A) Once
(B) Or
(C) Since
(D) Either

125. Due to the success of his prototypes, the inventor currently has a ------- reputation for innovation.

(A) grown
(B) growing
(C) grower
(D) growth

126. Roscast Communications employees may work from home, but it is ------- for them to have a reliable Internet connection.

(A) definite
(B) necessary
(C) optimistic
(D) absolute

127. The ------- of LRB Pharmaceuticals and Hough Laboratories may result in the elimination of some positions.

(A) merger
(B) potential
(C) dedication
(D) obligation

128. Amberview Beach Resort is a popular summer destination, but it is open for business all ------- the year.

(A) among
(B) without
(C) through
(D) beyond

129. Ms. Ross acquired the ------- number of new customers in May, falling behind all the other sales representatives.

(A) steadiest
(B) brightest
(C) longest
(D) smallest

130. Completing an important project under a time ------- calls for careful scheduling.

(A) constraint
(B) relief
(C) quality
(D) proposal

PART 6

Directions: In this part, you will be asked to read four English texts. Each text is missing a word, phrase, or sentence. Select the answer choice that correctly completes the text and mark the corresponding letter (A), (B), (C), or (D) on the answer sheet.

PART 6 권장 풀이 시간 8분

Questions 131-134 refer to the following e-mail.

To: Paige Lagarde <paigelagarde@peoplemail.com>
From: Brad Jeong <jeongbrad@cucinaaid.com>
Date: March 2
Subject: Re: CucinaAid mixer problem

Dear Ms. Lagarde,

You wrote to let us know that the whisk attachment for your CucinaAid mixer isn't tight enough when you screw it on. You have every reason to be concerned. -------, loose **131.** attachments pose a safety risk, and we are glad that you brought the matter to our attention.

We believe that the defect ------- **132.** during a recent production run, when we may have used the wrong parts by mistake. We are very sorry and would like to offer to ------- **133.** your machine. Just stop by any of our service centers, and one of our technicians will be glad to fix it for you at no charge. To make up for the inconvenience, please also accept the following coupon code for $25 off your next CucinaAid purchase: UW3-G6BQ1. ------- **134.**.

Sincerely,

Brad Jeong
CucinaAid, Customer Service Agent

131. (A) However
(B) Thus
(C) In fact
(D) Otherwise

132. (A) causes
(B) caused
(C) was causing
(D) was caused

133. (A) repair
(B) replace
(C) refund
(D) return

134. (A) Our receptionist can direct you to the billing department.
(B) Your recommendations will be taken into consideration.
(C) Damage that results from user error is not covered by the warranty.
(D) Simply type it into our Web site at checkout when shopping online.

GO ON TO THE NEXT PAGE

Questions 135-138 refer to the following article.

As local shoppers are aware, Diamond Plaza Mall is currently undergoing a major -------. **135.** Now that it has been closed for a month, its management has revealed that the renovation is going smoothly and that House Lab has agreed to lease 7,000 square feet. House Lab, a top appliance retailer, will no doubt attract plenty of people to the mall. -------. **136.** There has already been speculation that it will occupy the space to the left of the main entrance. While this is certainly significant news, ------- **137.** other information about the renovation has been released yet. ------- **138.** the food court will finally undergo a much-needed expansion, for instance, is still unknown. More details are expected to be disclosed at a press conference next month.

135. (A) crisis
(B) reduction
(C) transformation
(D) inspection

136. (A) The mall's final floor plan was released to the press early last week.
(B) Given its profit-making potential, it will likely have a prime location.
(C) Hundreds of customers attended its grand opening ceremony.
(D) Based in Texas, its main store is more than 15,000 square feet.

137. (A) few
(B) much
(C) many
(D) little

138. (A) What
(B) Whether
(C) This
(D) Who

Questions 139-142 refer to the following memo.

To: All staff
From: Robert Valdez, Management Department
Subject: End of the Year
Date: December 1

As the year comes to an end, the managers at Voyager Communications would like to thank everyone for their hard work and perseverance. Because of your efforts, sales were higher than anticipated, allowing us to reward you with larger bonuses. We will be increasing the standard annual bonus to 2 percent of your salary. -------, it was 1 percent. -------.
139. **140.**

Also, in case you are wondering if the well-deserved pay raise many of you received last week will be factored into the bonus amount, the answer is yes. The bonus will be calculated using your new, higher -------.
141.

Please come and see me in my office ------- me know if you have any questions.
142.

139. (A) Formerly
(B) Conversely
(C) Meanwhile
(D) Appropriately

140. (A) This is our highest profit increase in the past decade.
(B) The company will be donating to a charitable organization.
(C) The chosen candidate will sometimes have to work extra hours.
(D) It will be included in your last paycheck of the year.

141. (A) price
(B) position
(C) salary
(D) quality

142. (A) let
(B) will let
(C) to let
(D) lets

GO ON TO THE NEXT PAGE

Questions 143-146 refer to the following advertisement.

The Harlington Improvisation Players (HIP) -------- **143.** to the Ferris Greene Performing Arts Center on July 9. If you like to laugh, don't miss Liza Smythe, Dennis Armstrong, Jackson Parcell, and Charlie Cousins as they take the stage on this Saturday. As always, HIP -------- **144.** performances by using on-the-spot suggestions from the audience as inspiration. -------- **145.**. And they will make you smile for a good cause. -------- **146.** from ticket sales will go to benefit extracurricular art-related activities at Harlington City High School. Visit www.ferrisgreenepac.com/shows to reserve your seats and get more information.

143. (A) would have come
(B) is coming
(C) came
(D) has come

144. (A) delivers
(B) reaches
(C) meets
(D) fulfills

145. (A) They are seeking talented comedians to join their group.
(B) All of the performances have been sold out for months.
(C) This means that every single one of their shows is unique.
(D) A list of their upcoming appearances is available online.

146. (A) Proceeded
(B) Proceeding
(C) Proceed
(D) Proceeds

PART 7

Directions: In this part, you will be asked to read several texts, such as advertisements, articles, instant messages, or examples of business correspondence. Each text is followed by several questions. Select the best answer and mark the corresponding letter (A), (B), (C), or (D) on your answer sheet.

PART 7 권장 풀이 시간 **54분**

Questions 147-148 refer to the following document.

Central Valley Financial Partners

REIMBURSEMENT REQUEST FORM

Number: 382625

Purchases:

Description of Items	**Amount**
8 pizzas ($15 each)	$120
Balloons and decorations	$22
1 decorated cake	$38
1 retirement card	$5
Total amount	**$185**

Notes: Celebration for Richard Dugas on December 9

Submitted by: Elisa Cooper
Signature: *Elisa Cooper*
Date: December 10

Authorized by: Patrick Rhodes
Signature: *Patrick Rhodes*
Date: December 10

Please submit receipts with this request form.

147. What type of event most likely took place at Central Valley Financial Partners?

(A) A retirement celebration
(B) A product release party
(C) An opening ceremony
(D) A welcome reception

148. What did Mr. Rhodes most likely do on December 10?

(A) Told a team member to purchase some party supplies
(B) Authorized the repayment of some money to an employee
(C) Sent a reservation deposit to a catering company
(D) Attended a special event at a banquet hall

GO ON TO THE NEXT PAGE

Questions 149-150 refer to the following job announcement.

Pearson & Lennox

Dorney—Full-time and Part-time Sales Consultants

As a premium brand, we take pride in our reputation for providing exemplary customer service to all of our clients. Currently, we are seeking two full-time and two part-time sales consultants with a passion for customer service to work at our store on Village Road in Dorney.

You must have proven sales experience in the high-end clothing sector as well as enthusiasm, an outgoing personality, and a unique sense of style. Experience in the menswear industry is an advantage.

If you are interested in joining our team, please send your résumé to recruitment@pearsonlennox.com, specifying whether you would like to work half or full days.

149. What kind of business does Pearson & Lennox most likely engage in?

(A) Travel accommodations
(B) Business consulting
(C) Consumer research
(D) Fashion retail

150. What is indicated about applicants for the positions?

(A) They will need to attend an interview in person.
(B) They must have expertise in men's clothing.
(C) They must state their preferred workhours amount.
(D) They will all be eligible for the same salaries.

Questions 151-152 refer to the following text-message chain.

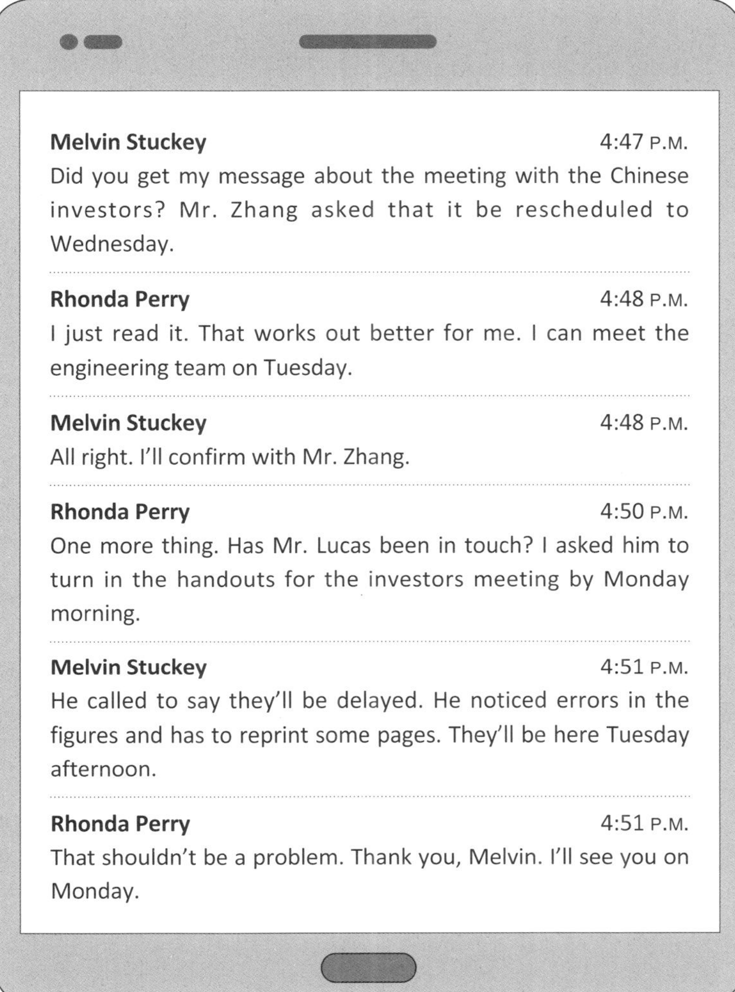

Melvin Stuckey 4:47 P.M.
Did you get my message about the meeting with the Chinese investors? Mr. Zhang asked that it be rescheduled to Wednesday.

Rhonda Perry 4:48 P.M.
I just read it. That works out better for me. I can meet the engineering team on Tuesday.

Melvin Stuckey 4:48 P.M.
All right. I'll confirm with Mr. Zhang.

Rhonda Perry 4:50 P.M.
One more thing. Has Mr. Lucas been in touch? I asked him to turn in the handouts for the investors meeting by Monday morning.

Melvin Stuckey 4:51 P.M.
He called to say they'll be delayed. He noticed errors in the figures and has to reprint some pages. They'll be here Tuesday afternoon.

Rhonda Perry 4:51 P.M.
That shouldn't be a problem. Thank you, Melvin. I'll see you on Monday.

151. At 4:48 P.M., what does Ms. Perry most likely mean when she writes, "That works out better for me"?

(A) She is pleased with the outcome of a meeting.
(B) She intends to see clients at the start of the week.
(C) She has time to take care of another task.
(D) She prefers to be contacted by e-mail.

152. Why does Mr. Lucas need more time to prepare the handouts?

(A) A printer is not working.
(B) An employee is on leave.
(C) Some pages have been misplaced.
(D) Some data needs to be corrected.

GO ON TO THE NEXT PAGE

Questions 153-154 refer to the following notice.

Green City Farmers' Market
Admission Guidelines

Green City Farmers' Market prides itself on being a traditional West Hollywood institution with the highest standards. Any new farms wishing to rent a booth must do the following:

- Receive an organic label from the state-run Organic Certification Services (OCS)
- Undergo a water inspection by the Green City Farmers' Market management
- Pay the vendor fee for the whole season

To inquire about specific rental options, please e-mail the market coordinator, Cathy Keller, at c.keller@greencityfm.org.

153. Why was the notice written?

(A) To announce an additional market location
(B) To inform clients about a price increase
(C) To specify participant requirements
(D) To provide details about booth changes

154. What must a farm do to sell produce at the market?

(A) Obtain a certificate issued by the government
(B) Pay a fee through online banking
(C) Submit a price list for items
(D) Send some samples to the market management

Questions 155-157 refer to the following e-mail.

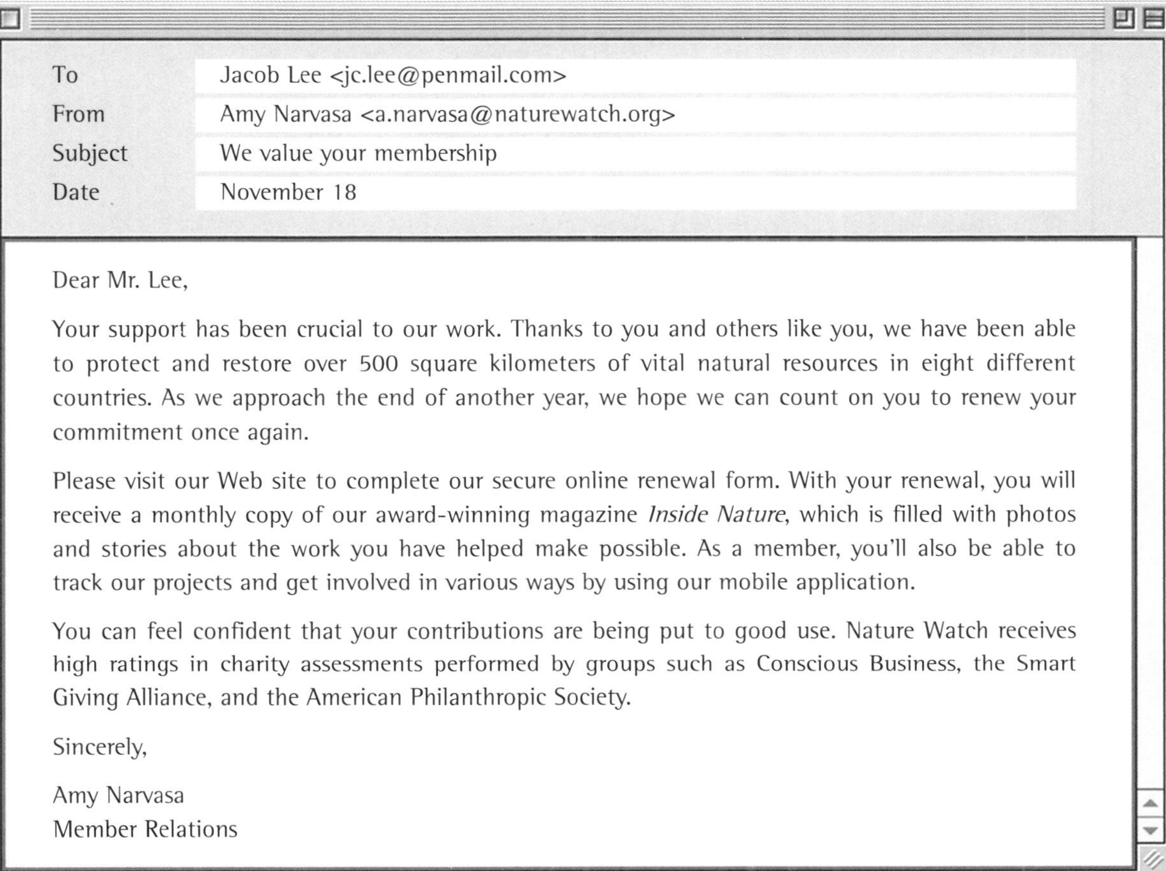

To	Jacob Lee <jc.lee@penmail.com>
From	Amy Narvasa <a.narvasa@naturewatch.org>
Subject	We value your membership
Date	November 18

Dear Mr. Lee,

Your support has been crucial to our work. Thanks to you and others like you, we have been able to protect and restore over 500 square kilometers of vital natural resources in eight different countries. As we approach the end of another year, we hope we can count on you to renew your commitment once again.

Please visit our Web site to complete our secure online renewal form. With your renewal, you will receive a monthly copy of our award-winning magazine *Inside Nature*, which is filled with photos and stories about the work you have helped make possible. As a member, you'll also be able to track our projects and get involved in various ways by using our mobile application.

You can feel confident that your contributions are being put to good use. Nature Watch receives high ratings in charity assessments performed by groups such as Conscious Business, the Smart Giving Alliance, and the American Philanthropic Society.

Sincerely,

Amy Narvasa
Member Relations

155. What is the main purpose of the e-mail?

(A) To offer information about a restoration
(B) To promote an exclusive event
(C) To review the terms of a contract
(D) To ask for continued support

156. What can Mr. Lee receive with a renewed membership?

(A) A photography book
(B) A monthly publication
(C) A ticket for a nature area
(D) A digital device

157. What is stated about Nature Watch?

(A) It is celebrating its first anniversary.
(B) It is opening several new offices.
(C) It has corporate partners in several countries.
(D) It is evaluated by other organizations.

GO ON TO THE NEXT PAGE

Questions 158-160 refer to the following memo.

Sachs Export Furnishings
MEMO

To: All department managers
From: Hilda Marley, IT director
Subject: CRM software
Date: March 20

As you know, I am shopping for customer relationship management (CRM) software to replace our current system, which is not computerized. The need for CRM software has become increasingly apparent as our client list has expanded. It should allow us to better manage customer data, leading to enhanced customer service, streamlined order processing, and improved product development, among other things. — [1] —.

In connection with the above, I would like each of you to select two members from your department to take part in product trials. I have narrowed down our options to three vendors. — [2] —. Each vendor's product will be tested over a 30-day period. At the end of this time, trial participants will provide feedback in a report.

Once we have selected appropriate software, I will also need your help with implementing its use. — [3] —. We want to make sure that all staff are aware of the benefits of the CRM software and how easy it is to use.

Please e-mail me your recommendations by tomorrow. — [4] —. We will meet on Friday and hopefully begin testing by early April.

158. What is indicated about Sachs Export Furnishings?

(A) It currently uses outdated accounting software.
(B) It receives many customer complaints.
(C) It is expanding into new product fields.
(D) Its customer base has grown.

159. What is each department manager asked to do?

(A) Update a list of vendors
(B) Provide training to staff
(C) Choose test participants
(D) Try out some products

160. In which of the positions marked [1], [2], [3], and [4] does the following sentence best belong?

"Some employees are hesitant about learning new technology."

(A) [1]
(B) [2]
(C) [3]
(D) [4]

Questions 161-164 refer to the following online chat discussion.

Oskar Jensen	[9:18 A.M.]	Good morning, team. Just checking in to see if you have any last-minute concerns about the career fair.
Emma Blom	[9:21 A.M.]	None on my part, Oskar. The layout has been finalized and approved by all corporate participants. I'm holding a final meeting with the volunteers in two days to go over various procedures.
Lilly Mattson	[9:24 A.M.]	Same here. People are continuing to register through our Web site and download our mobile application. We're also seeing a lot of activity on social media.
Emma Blom	[9:25 A.M.]	Oh, I actually do have one concern. Any news on my request for Chinese language interpreters?
Oskar Jensen	[9:27 A.M.]	Yes, Emma. I put your request in. I'm still waiting to hear back from Axel. He needs to approve the additional cost.
Lilly Mattson	[9:29 A.M.]	I just saw him walk in. Let me get him to join the discussion.
Axel Lofgren	[9:35 A.M.]	Hi, everyone. I'm happy to report that the request was approved.
Oskar Jensen	[9:36 A.M.]	Thank you, Axel. Emma, please go ahead and make arrangements with Exalan Interpretation Agency.
Emma Blom	[9:39 A.M.]	Already on it. Thanks.

Send

161. What did corporate participants most likely do?

(A) Checked a layout for an event
(B) Sent volunteers to a fair
(C) Had meetings with Mr. Jensen
(D) Made arrangements for translators

162. At 9:24 A.M., what does Ms. Mattson most likely mean when she writes, "Same here"?

(A) She has decided to organize a meeting.
(B) Some preparations are going smoothly.
(C) An important message was not sent.
(D) She is struggling to recruit volunteers.

163. What is suggested about the career fair?

(A) It will require language services.
(B) It is usually held on a university campus.
(C) It is being partially funded by Exalan Interpretation Agency.
(D) It will last for an entire weekend.

164. What is Mr. Lofgren most likely responsible for?

(A) Updating mobile applications
(B) Reviewing expenses
(C) Contacting suppliers
(D) Promoting an event

GO ON TO THE NEXT PAGE

Questions 165-167 refer to the following letter.

City of Columbus

January 23

CEO Julia Peron
Mindmatter
1135 Enos Lane
Bakersfield, CA 93314

Dear Ms. Peron,

I am writing in support of Columbus's bid to become the site of Mindmatter's second corporate headquarters. I strongly believe that our city would be an ideal location.

To begin with, Columbus is business friendly and has a history of fostering companies in industries as diverse as telecommunications, health care, and software development. As a leading online retailer, Mindmatter would no doubt appreciate the various forms of infrastructure that we have in place. For instance, our air, road, and rail links provide convenient access to cities around the world as well as to neighboring regions. In addition, Columbus offers an abundance of cultural attractions, entertainment facilities, and outdoor spaces to help your employees enjoy a healthy work-life balance. And speaking of employees, the population here is well educated, with our world-class universities promising a deep pool of future talent to tap into. Best of all, Columbus provides all of the above without the high property costs typical of other cities.

I am confident that you will recognize the advantages of establishing a headquarters in Columbus, and I would be glad to arrange a meeting to discuss specific sites. Thank you for your consideration.

Sincerely,

Tom Vickers
Tom Vickers
Mayor of Columbus

165. Why did Mr. Vickers write to Ms. Peron?
(A) To state some preferences
(B) To encourage a choice
(C) To share a new development
(D) To evaluate a bid

166. What is stated about Mindmatter?
(A) It has regional offices around the globe.
(B) It is acquiring a firm based in Columbus.
(C) It sells merchandise over the Internet.
(D) It is attempting to register some patents.

167. What is NOT a benefit that Mindmatter could enjoy in Columbus?
(A) Transport connections
(B) An educated workforce
(C) Recreational opportunities
(D) Corporate tax exemptions

Questions 168-171 refer to the following notice.

NOTICE

Following the approval of Springdale City Council, construction of a 10,000-square-meter community center will soon be under way. — [1] —. The center's main facilities will be a children's playground, a library, and a senior center. It will also contain an event space with a catering kitchen. Future plans involve adding a full-size gymnasium for indoor sports.

A groundbreaking ceremony is set for March 20 at the corner of Thompson Street and Huntsville Avenue. — [2] —. The center will open in the fall of next year and the gymnasium the year after that. After the center opens next year, free public access will be granted to all the facilities except for the event space, which will have an hourly rental fee. However, a discount on this will be given to anyone who presents proof of local residency. — [3] —.

More information about this project can be found at www.springdale.gov/communitycenter. — [4] —. Residents are encouraged to visit this site to submit their ideas for the name of the center. The winning name will be announced prior to the center's opening.

168. What is NOT expected to be completed by next year?

(A) The playground
(B) The gymnasium
(C) The event space
(D) The senior center

169. What is mentioned about the event space in the new community center?

(A) It will contain some advanced equipment.
(B) It will be the largest area in the facility.
(C) It will open to the public on March 20.
(D) It will be rented out to residents at a discount.

170. According to the notice, what are Springdale residents advised to do?

(A) Sign up for membership cards
(B) Make a personal donation
(C) Propose a name for a structure
(D) Book seats for a grand opening event

171. In which of the positions marked [1], [2], [3], and [4] does the following sentence best belong?

"It will contain facilities that meet the needs of local citizens."

(A) [1]
(B) [2]
(C) [3]
(D) [4]

GO ON TO THE NEXT PAGE

Questions 172-175 refer to the following article.

Mazzi Milk Makes a Comeback

NAIROBI, October 4—Mazzi is back in the spotlight several decades after it first appeared on store shelves. Sales of the sweetened milk rose 32 percent in September, according to results announced yesterday by Kamba Foods, the company that makes the product.

"Traditionally, we have not invested heavily in Mazzi," said Kamba Foods CEO Roger Biwott. "The product was successful at the start, but sales slowly stopped rising over time."

According to Sophie Oduya, a market analyst with Food Web Africa, Kamba Foods has responded to a regional trend. "More and more people want something quick and easy that they can pick up at a supermarket or convenience store. It's no surprise then that Mazzi has enjoyed strong sales." In its original form, which is still available, consumers must add water to Mazzi powder. The newly fashionable Mazzi comes in bottles, ready-to-drink.

Mr. Biwott credits the new Mazzi with helping to push Kamba Foods' total sales up by 4.1 percent for the year. Although this is slightly lower than last year's figure, stock analysts believe year-end results will be much higher. So far, shares have risen 3.6 percent since the results were announced.

172. What is the article mainly about?

(A) A distribution of free samples
(B) A company's return to profitability
(C) An event for regional manufacturers
(D) A product's renewed popularity

173. What does Ms. Oduya attribute Mazzi's strong sales to?

(A) An expansion of a product line
(B) A successful product launch
(C) A demand for convenient items
(D) A growing number of supermarkets

174. What can be inferred about Kamba Foods?

(A) It pioneered the use of a new packaging material.
(B) It has sold products for decades.
(C) It has merged with another manufacturer.
(D) It set a sales record this year.

175. The word "enjoyed" in paragraph 3, line 3, is closest in meaning to

(A) saved
(B) experienced
(C) liked
(D) appreciated

GO ON TO THE NEXT PAGE

Questions 176-180 refer to the following Web page and form.

www.chersterville.gov/commercialbicycling

City of Chesterville

Commercial Bicycling

Cyclists can deliver food, mail, and other items to locations around the city. To help reduce congestion and to avoid traffic problems, the following legislation for cyclists and the businesses that employ them has been implemented.

Requirements for Businesses

- Businesses must ensure that cyclists have received a commercial biking permit from the Transportation Office at City Hall. This card will feature a three-digit ID number.
- Cyclists must be provided with protective headgear and reflective vests that display the name of the business and the employee's ID number.
- Businesses must keep a list of all their current and former cyclists and update it regularly. Templates for this list can be downloaded here.

Requirements for Cyclists

- While working, commercial cyclists must carry the card featuring their ID number.
- Commercial cyclists are personally responsible for completing Chesterville's Bicycle Safety Course. It can be taken for free here.

Penalties

Failure to comply with any of these requirements will result in a $100 fine. The fine will be doubled to $200 if the same violation is repeated.

Commercial Bicyclist List

Business/Address: East Street Diner, 367 East Street, Chesterville

Name: Tony Esposito	ID Number: 983
Address: 26 Laudner Street, Chesterville	Bicycle Safety Course Completion: Yes
Shift Hours: 8 A.M. – 3 P.M. Monday-Friday	Notes: Weekend hours may be available upon request

Name: Gina Doncaster	ID Number: 979
Address: 745 Cranston Lane, Chesterville	Bicycle Safety Course Completion: Yes
Shift Hours: 3 P.M. – 9 P.M. Monday-Friday 8 A.M. – 3 P.M. Saturday	Notes: Final paycheck issued August 30

Name: Freddy Velasquez	ID Number: 993
Address: 347 Prescott Boulevard, Chesterville	Bicycle Safety Course Completion: No
Shift Hours: 3 P.M. – 9 P.M. Monday-Friday 8 A.M. – 3 P.M. Saturday	Notes: May be available to work extra shifts

176. What is the purpose of the Web page?

(A) To promote cycling as a means of transportation
(B) To provide tips for maintaining a bicycle
(C) To recommend usage of local bike lanes
(D) To disclose rules for business deliveries

177. What is mentioned about the ID numbers of cyclists?

(A) They should be visible on reflective apparel.
(B) They can be requested by completing an online form.
(C) They have to be changed on an annual basis.
(D) They must be stated in a job application.

178. What will happen if any of the regulations are violated more than once?

(A) Cyclists will have to repeat a training course.
(B) Employees will be temporarily suspended from work.
(C) The amount of a fine will be increased.
(D) Delivery service licenses will be revoked.

179. What is indicated about East Street Diner's cyclists?

(A) They usually deliver groceries.
(B) They were hired at the same time.
(C) They are all residents of Chesterville.
(D) They are not available to work on weekends.

180. What can be inferred about Mr. Velasquez?

(A) He will work more hours than usual next week.
(B) He may have to pay a penalty charge.
(C) He will be taking time off next month.
(D) He must update his ID number.

GO ON TO THE NEXT PAGE

Questions 181-185 refer to the following flyer and e-mail.

ADBG's 10th Annual Baseball Game
June 23
Portez Stadium, Atlanta, Georgia

Over the past 10 years, the Atlanta Downtown Business Group (ADBG) baseball game has been an engaging way to provide small business owners with the opportunity to promote and market themselves in the community. The ADBG is pleased to offer the following levels of sponsorship for the fund-raising game:

Sponsorship Level	Price	Benefits
1st Base	$250	- A 24x36 inch company poster put up at the stadium entrance
2nd Base	$500	- The benefit of 1st Base level - A 5x2 foot company display stand set up at the ticket office
3rd Base	$750	- All the benefits of 2nd Base level - A 4x5 foot company banner hung at the baseball field
Home Plate	$1,000	- All the benefits of 3rd Base level - A 10x12 foot billboard next to viewer seats - Company logo printed on one of the team's uniforms

Please contact our office manager, Tessa Reynolds, at treynolds@adbg.org if you are interested in becoming a sponsor.

To: Rajiv Patel <rajiv.patel@nstflorists.com>
From: Tessa Reynolds <treynolds@adbg.org>
Date: April 30
Subject: Thank you

Dear Mr. Patel,

Thank you for registering North Street Florists as a sponsor for our upcoming baseball game. I was pleased to hear that your sponsorship of this event in previous years was beneficial to your business.

I received the design you e-mailed me, and I have already forwarded it to the company that makes the banners. After they're printed, they'll be delivered to the address provided. However, I forgot to ask you one question when we spoke yesterday. The Atlanta Bears and Charleston Raptors are the two teams that have volunteered to play the game.

Do you have a preference regarding which team wears your logo? Please let me know as soon as possible. Thank you!

Sincerely,
Tessa Reynolds

181. What is the purpose of the flyer?
(A) To encourage businesses to raise funds
(B) To sell some tickets to a sports event
(C) To promote a baseball workshop
(D) To offer a marketing opportunity

182. Which level of sponsorship does NOT include the display of a company logo at the ticket office?
(A) 1st-Base-level sponsorship
(B) 2nd-Base-level sponsorship
(C) 3rd-Base-level sponsorship
(D) Home-Plate-level sponsorship

183. What is mentioned about North Street Florists?
(A) It plans to form its own baseball team.
(B) It operates stores throughout Georgia.
(C) It will donate some of its profits to a charity.
(D) It has sponsored the ADBG game before.

184. According to the e-mail, what has Mr. Patel already done?
(A) Distributed promotional materials
(B) Sent a design to Ms. Reynolds
(C) Printed a banner
(D) Provided a billboard advertisement

185. How much did Mr. Patel probably pay the ADBG?
(A) $250
(B) $500
(C) $750
(D) $1,000

GO ON TO THE NEXT PAGE

Questions 186-190 refer to the following e-mails and memo.

To: Catherine Millstone <catherinemillstone@drexco.com>
From: Ron Pruitt <ronpruitt@drexco.com>
Subject: Your internship
Date: August 13

Dear Catherine,

As I'm sure you're aware, your internship with Drexco's advertising department will be ending on September 3. During your time with us, you've worked hard and taken your job seriously. That's why I'd like to offer you the permanent full-time position of junior creative coordinator here. Please take some time to consider this offer carefully. I'll be leaving today to attend a media conference that begins tomorrow, but I'll be back on Friday. I'd appreciate it if you could drop by my office then to let me know your decision.

Best,

Ron Pruitt
Director of Advertising

To: Ginger Rollins <gingerrollins@drexco.com>
From: Harry Shute <harryshute@drexco.com>
Subject: Open advertising department position
Date: August 16

Dear Ms. Rollins,

Ron Pruitt just got back from the Los Angeles conference today, and I spoke to him about the open junior creative coordinator position. It seems that he offered it to one of his interns, but she turned it down because she is returning to school for graduate studies next month.

Mr. Pruitt has indicated that he may offer the job to another of his interns but only after conducting some evaluations on September 3. If Mr. Pruitt decides not to make this offer, you may post some advertisements on employment Web sites. If we go ahead and hire an outside candidate, this person will have to take our aptitude test. Note, though, that this would not apply to an intern who was promoted.

Thanks,

Harry Shute
Director of Human Resources

To: All Drexco advertising department staff
From: Ron Pruitt
Subject: Tomorrow
Date: September 11

I am pleased to announce that Wendy Sommers will be our new junior creative coordinator. Based on her aptitude test score, I believe that she will be a valuable addition to our department. She will start working in our office tomorrow, and I would like to do something to make her feel welcome. I was thinking we could go to a restaurant in the area right after work, so please let me know before 5 P.M. today if you have any preferences.

186. Why was the first e-mail written?

(A) To arrange an interview with a candidate
(B) To make an offer of employment
(C) To advise staff of future plans
(D) To ask for feedback about an internship program

187. What did Mr. Pruitt do on August 16?

(A) Returned from a conference
(B) Conducted some evaluations
(C) Sent an e-mail to office coordinators
(D) Applied for a vacant position

188. What is indicated about Ms. Millstone?

(A) She received job offers from multiple companies.
(B) She served as an intern for three months.
(C) She inspected Drexco's office.
(D) She will be going back to university soon.

189. What is suggested about the junior creative coordinator position?

(A) It has remained vacant for over a month.
(B) It was not filled by an intern.
(C) It will involve monthly business trips.
(D) It does not require commuting to an office.

190. Why does Mr. Pruitt want the advertising staff to contact him?

(A) To confirm their attendance at a party
(B) To suggest local eating establishments
(C) To provide training tips for a new employee
(D) To volunteer to set up an office space

GO ON TO THE NEXT PAGE

Questions 191-195 refer to the following memo, testing schedule, and form.

Fitness Friends

Memo

To: Testing division
From: Ed Burtoft
Date: August 2
Subject: Research for Z-Model

Work has been coming along well on our newest fitness tracker, which we are currently referring to by its temporary name, Z-Model. Chief marketing officer Signe Jepsen has shared a short list of possible final names for the product, including Trail Blazer and Split Second. If the marketing department is unable to make a final decision on the name by August 11, we will ask survey respondents for their opinions.

On Thursday, you will be given a prototype of the Z-Model from the research department for testing. First, though, we need to finalize our list of test subjects. When I went through our testing schedule, I noticed that all of them are in their 20s or 30s. I would like to have at least one or two subjects who are in their 40s or 50s in order to get responses from users who are a bit older.

Testing Schedule for Z-Model

9:30 A.M. Subject: Dorothy Glen Age and gender: 57/female Location: Grand Park Activity: Walking Focus: Testing the heart-rate function	**11:30 A.M.** Subject: Farid Saman Age and gender: 23/female Location: Caribou Lake Activity: Running Focus: Testing the pacing feature
2:30 P.M. Subject: Michael Flint Age and gender: 37/male Location: Parklane Community Swimming Pool Activity: Swimming Focus: Testing the waterproofing	**4:30 P.M.** Subject: Pat Durban Age and gender: 32/female Location: Oak Mountain Activity: Cycling Focus: Testing the ability to withstand shocks

Survey of Test Subject

Name: Michael Flint

Now that you've tested the prototype for our next fitness tracker, we'd like to learn more about your impressions.

To what extent do you agree or disagree with the following statements?

1. The product was comfortable to wear.

Strongly agree / Agree / Neither agree nor disagree / (Disagree) / Strongly disagree

2. The product was easy to use.

(Strongly agree) / Agree / Neither agree nor disagree / Disagree / Strongly disagree

3. What did you like about the product?

It was easy to change the information that was displayed using the buttons on the side. The battery seemed to last a long time—it was at 98 percent at the start of my 60-minute workout and when I finished, it was down to 90 percent.

4. What did you dislike about the product?

Though I tightened the band to the maximum level, it still felt loose around my wrist. Whenever I raised my left arm, the fitness tracker moved around, which was uncomfortable.

5. What do you think the product should be called?

Trail Blazer / Split Second / Mad Dash / (Fast Track)

191. What is the main purpose of the memo?

(A) To offer an incentive
(B) To schedule a test
(C) To provide an update
(D) To request feedback

192. Which subject was probably added to the testing schedule?

(A) Dorothy Glen
(B) Farid Saman
(C) Michael Flint
(D) Pat Durban

193. What aspect of the product was tested at Oak Mountain?

(A) The heart-rate monitor
(B) Product durability
(C) Water resistance
(D) The pacing function

194. What is suggested about the Z-Model device?

(A) It was popular among most of the test subjects.
(B) The marketing team was unable to select a name for it.
(C) It was given to test participants for free.
(D) The researchers suggested changing its launch schedule.

195. What does Mr. Flint indicate about the prototype?

(A) Its strap needs to be improved.
(B) Its battery does not last long.
(C) Its signals are not loud enough.
(D) Its screen is difficult to adjust.

GO ON TO THE NEXT PAGE

Questions 196-200 refer to the following article, e-mail, and memo.

Verta Recalls Vacuums

Appliance manufacturer Verta has requested that 5,000 vacuum cleaners be brought to service centers for inspection. According to Verta, the model in question—the Zurupat A7—contains a faulty part. "This problem could potentially cause the device to overheat," said Verta product designer Bryce Gooding. "Thankfully, none of our customers have reported any incidents yet."

Verta has revealed that this problem occurred because tests of newly manufactured vacuum cleaners were not being carried out comprehensively enough. The company has decided to stop production at all plants on November 3 to address the situation.

To: Kenneth Sheeran <k_sheeran@bgwgroup.com>
From: Deanna Clark <d_clark@bgwgroup.com>
Subject: Vacuum cleaners
Date: October 30
Attachment: Verta_Inspection_Notice

Hi, Kenneth.

I received a notice today stating that all the Zurupat A7 vacuum cleaners we bought for our headquarters need to be brought to a Verta service center. There's a problem with one of the parts, it seems, though no problems have been reported in the six months we've had them.

The attached notice contains the manufacturer's contact information. Please call the service number for the Westland region and find out exactly where the vacuum cleaners need to be taken. I'm not sure there's a Verta service center here in Blythville, so BGW Group staff might have to take them to a different city. In any case, let me know as soon as possible, so I can provide the relevant staff with the necessary information.

Thanks,
Deanna Clark, Office Administrator
BGW Group

To: All staff
From: Ben Aduba, Westland Regional Manager, Verta
Date: October 28
Subject: Update

As you all know, we will be shutting down production for one day. During this time, I will be teaching factory workers new testing processes. Also, I have received a list of locations where people can take their Zurupat A7 vacuum cleaners to be inspected. When answering any inquiries, please be sure to refer to it in order to provide customers with information.

City	Verta Service Center Locations
East Granyard	367 Van Dam Avenue
Bellmeadow	184 Southhaven Circle
Blythville	2956 Marina Boulevard
Woodebourne	5631 Campus Passage

196. What problem is mentioned in the article?

(A) A technical manual contained an error.
(B) A production deadline was difficult to meet.
(C) Assembly line equipment was out of operation.
(D) New products were not sufficiently tested.

197. In the article, the phrase "carried out" in paragraph 2, line 2, is closest in meaning to

(A) transported
(B) influenced
(C) performed
(D) negotiated

198. What will happen on November 3?

(A) Mr. Gooding will plan an inspection of the Westland plant.
(B) Mr. Sheeran will assess the quality of some components.
(C) Ms. Clark will attend a meeting at Verta's headquarters.
(D) Mr. Aduba will conduct some training.

199. What is mentioned about BGW Group?

(A) It is receiving advice from a consultant.
(B) It has owned Verta products for less than a year.
(C) It has had to replace some of its cleaning staff.
(D) It is located in the largest city in the region.

200. Where will Ms. Clark tell employees to take some devices?

(A) To 367 Van Dam Avenue
(B) To 184 Southhaven Circle
(C) To 2956 Marina Boulevard
(D) To 5631 Campus Passage

This is the end of the test. You may review Parts 5, 6, and 7 if you finish the test early.

정답 p.328 / 점수 환산표 p.329 / 해석 p.394 / Part 5&6 무료 해설 바로 보기(정답 및 정답 음성 포함)
* 다음 페이지에 있는 Self 체크 리스트를 통해 자신의 문제 풀이 방식과 태도를 점검해 보세요.

Self 체크 리스트

TEST 09은 무사히 잘 마치셨죠?
이제 다음의 Self 체크 리스트를 통해 자신의 테스트 진행 내용을 점검해 볼까요?

1. 나는 75분 동안 완전히 테스트에 집중하였다.

   □ 예　□ 아니오

   아니오에 답한 경우, 이유는 무엇인가요?

2. 나는 75분 동안 100문제를 모두 풀었다.

   □ 예　□ 아니오

   아니오에 답한 경우, 이유는 무엇인가요?

3. 나는 75분 동안 답안지 표시까지 완료하였다.

   □ 예　□ 아니오

   아니오에 답한 경우, 이유는 무엇인가요?

4. 나는 Part 5와 Part 6를 19분 안에 모두 풀었다.

   □ 예　□ 아니오

   아니오에 답한 경우, 이유는 무엇인가요?

5. Part 7을 풀 때 5분 이상 걸린 지문이 없었다.

   □ 예　□ 아니오

6. 개선해야 할 점 또는 나를 위한 충고를 적어보세요.

* 교재의 첫 장으로 돌아가서 자신이 적은 목표 점수를 확인하면서 목표에 대한 의지를 다지기 바랍니다. 개선해야 할 점은 반드시 다음 테스트에 실천해야 합니다. 그것이 가장 중요하며, 그래야만 발전할 수 있습니다.

TEST 10

PART 5
PART 6
PART 7
Self 체크 리스트

잠깐! 테스트 전 확인사항

1. 휴대 전화의 전원을 끄셨나요? □ 예
2. Answer Sheet, 연필, 지우개를 준비하셨나요? □ 예
3. 시계를 준비하셨나요? □ 예

모든 준비가 완료되었으면 목표 점수를 떠올린 후 테스트를 시작합니다.

문제 풀이를 마치는 시간은 지금부터 75분 후인 ___시 ___분입니다.

테스트 시간은 총 75분이며, 시험 종료 전 2~3분은 정답 검토 및 답안지 마킹을 위해 사용합니다.

READING TEST

In this section, you must demonstrate your ability to read and comprehend English. You will be given a variety of texts and asked to answer questions about these texts. This section is divided into three parts and will take 75 minutes to complete.

Do not mark the answers in your test book. Use the answer sheet that is separately provided.

PART 5

Directions: In each question, you will be asked to review a statement that is missing a word or phrase. Four answer choices will be provided for each statement. Select the best answer and mark the corresponding letter (A), (B), (C), or (D) on the answer sheet.

PART 5 권장 풀이 시간 11분

101. Users of social media sites should reset ------- login passwords every 60 days.

(A) they
(B) them
(C) theirs
(D) their

102. When taking customers' menu orders, please ------- to ask about food allergies.

(A) remembering
(B) remember
(C) will remember
(D) remembered

103. Holdwell Department Store is known for its ------- window displays, particularly around the holidays.

(A) attraction
(B) attractively
(C) attractiveness
(D) attractive

104. The CEO made the ------- prediction that the company would double its profits by the end of the year.

(A) vertical
(B) spacious
(C) applicable
(D) optimistic

105. Wanting to pursue a more ------- fulfilling career, Ms. Conway left her job as an accountant.

(A) creatively
(B) create
(C) creating
(D) creation

106. There is one ------- at Stonebridge Apartments, and the unit is available for viewing.

(A) branch
(B) condition
(C) degree
(D) vacancy

107. The 8:00 A.M. train is usually ------- with people commuting to work.

(A) disliked
(B) crowded
(C) clear
(D) calm

108. Customer inquiries related to the product's quality must be answered as ------- as possible.

(A) long
(B) highly
(C) soon
(D) always

109. The venue for CRG Communications' annual conference ------- later this week.

(A) deciding
(B) will be decided
(C) have decided
(D) can decide

110. Mr. Richards ------- met the deadline for his report since his schedule was very busy with meetings.

(A) carefully
(B) barely
(C) frequently
(D) fairly

111. A large ------- of valuable contemporary art has recently been donated to the Beldonni Museum.

(A) collects
(B) collected
(C) collection
(D) collector

112. Mr. Godwin's flight reservations are -------, but he has yet to choose a hotel.

(A) attended
(B) maintained
(C) founded
(D) confirmed

113. Most companies advertise online as the Internet has a significant ------- on consumer behavior.

(A) direction
(B) influence
(C) atmosphere
(D) obligation

114. ------- becoming an actor and musician, Mr. Austin worked in the construction industry as an electrician.

(A) Prior to
(B) In case of
(C) Provided that
(D) In accordance with

115. In order to register for the class, prospective students have to ------- some paperwork.

(A) check in
(B) fill out
(C) make over
(D) give up

116. The company gives a percentage of its sales revenue to charity, and many consumers have expressed ------- for this policy.

(A) admires
(B) admired
(C) admire
(D) admiration

117. Mr. Harrelson is the ideal candidate for the position as he possesses ------- work experience and the required academic credentials.

(A) either
(B) neither
(C) not only
(D) both

118. Due to low consumer prices and a supply surplus, producing natural gas is no longer ------- for many companies.

(A) profitability
(B) profits
(C) profitable
(D) profit

119. Sewell Packaging originally wanted to open a factory in Ohio, but it chose to open one in Illinois -------.

(A) yet
(B) almost
(C) instead
(D) indeed

GO ON TO THE NEXT PAGE

120. These documents ------- that a restaurant has passed its inspection and meets all the health and safety standards.

(A) certify
(B) protect
(C) devise
(D) qualify

121. There is ------- more important for Soundwave Inc. than regaining the trust of its clients.

(A) other
(B) whatever
(C) anyone
(D) nothing

122. The public's positive attitude ------- environmental protection has resulted in many businesses adopting ecologically friendly practices.

(A) behind
(B) by
(C) toward
(D) like

123. ------- new staff members for the company is a duty of the human resources department.

(A) Recruited
(B) Recruitment
(C) Recruit
(D) Recruiting

124. New businesses should consider participating in industry trade fairs to gain -------.

(A) fluency
(B) closure
(C) exposure
(D) proximity

125. Coming up with ways ------- a business from its competitors can be challenging, especially in a global market.

(A) differentiate
(B) differentiation
(C) to differentiate
(D) differentiates

126. Figure skater Erica Mikahailov earned an ------- high tournament score and is likely to become the new champion.

(A) adversely
(B) impressively
(C) identically
(D) importantly

127. According to various management experts, planning ahead and prioritizing tasks can help raise one's -------.

(A) product
(B) productivity
(C) produced
(D) producer

128. The actress who played singer Sabrina Newton in the movie *Monochrome* won an award ------- her excellent performance.

(A) aside from
(B) contrary to
(C) together with
(D) because of

129. ------- sell her home for less than its market value, Ms. Danvers decided to rent it out temporarily.

(A) Unless
(B) Only if
(C) Rather than
(D) Whether

130. The mobile app allows users to ------- objects up to 20 times their actual size.

(A) assume
(B) magnify
(C) provoke
(D) multiply

PART 6

Directions: In this part, you will be asked to read four English texts. Each text is missing a word, phrase, or sentence. Select the answer choice that correctly completes the text and mark the corresponding letter (A), (B), (C), or (D) on the answer sheet.

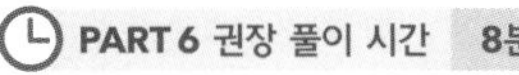

Questions 131-134 refer to the following notice.

Reminder about Guest Parking

Recently, it has been reported that the basement parking area here at Deschamps Apartments is being used inappropriately by guests visiting our renters. Please note that 10 spaces -------**131.** for visitors. They are clearly marked and located to the left of the elevator. In the event that they are all occupied, guests should be able to find spots on Trenton Street. -------**132.**.

Effective immediately, unauthorized vehicles occupying the spaces of -------**133.** will be towed at the discretion of management. -------**134.**, their owners will be issued a $25 ticket. For more information, talk to Building Services Manager Vince Romboni.

131. (A) reserved
(B) are reserved
(C) will be reserved
(D) were being reserved

132. (A) Outstanding tickets can be settled at our main office.
(B) One of these is guaranteed in your rental agreement.
(C) City parking meters can be found on the sidewalk.
(D) Another option is to have security cameras put in.

133. (A) employees
(B) vendors
(C) customers
(D) tenants

134. (A) For instance
(B) However
(C) Nonetheless
(D) Furthermore

GO ON TO THE NEXT PAGE

Questions 135-138 refer to the following article.

Vision Pay

The credit card company Echo ------- (135.) a new mobile application. Named Vision Pay, it simplifies Internet shopping for Echo credit card users. It was ------- (136.) on February 1. Following this release, it was quickly downloaded by nearly 50,000 users.

Because Vision Pay stores card details and shipping information, completing online ------- (137.) is much faster than it used to be. In fact, the payment process on most Web sites now takes under five seconds. ------- (138.). "We've incorporated cutting-edge security features that should give our clients peace of mind when shopping online," says Echo Vice President Wallace Tan.

If you own an Echo credit card and would like to begin using Vision Pay, visit your phone's application store.

135. (A) has developed
(B) is developing
(C) will develop
(D) developing

136. (A) proposed
(B) launched
(C) designed
(D) financed

137. (A) returns
(B) cancellations
(C) purchases
(D) searches

138. (A) To dispute an unauthorized charge, contact the merchant directly.
(B) Applying for a credit card over the Internet is fast and simple.
(C) The back of the card must be signed by the user to be valid.
(D) Using Echo's application also makes electronic transactions safer.

Questions 139-142 refer to the following invitation.

Help Us Celebrate Our Grand Opening!

We are pleased to announce the grand opening of River Reed Mall, Portland's newest shopping -------. Standing at three stories and comprising 1.7 million square feet, River Reed Mall is home to more than 130 shops and restaurants as well as an aquarium and skating rink.
139.

The ribbon-cutting ceremony will be held at 10:30 A.M. on March 15. -------. To attend, simply go to Harper Square on Boswell Street and then ------- the main entrance. Here, a presentation will be given on the development of the mall, questions will be answered, and gift certificates will be distributed. Finally, the doors will officially open, giving attendees a chance to ------- explore the shopping center on their own.
140. **141.** **142.**

139. (A) facilitator
(B) facilitate
(C) facilitation
(D) facility

140. (A) Don't forget to prepare for your speech.
(B) Choose a time that conveniently suits your schedule.
(C) It is open to the public and requires no reservations.
(D) The event was deemed a great success.

141. (A) proceed to
(B) take over
(C) drive by
(D) point out

142. (A) free
(B) freedom
(C) freely
(D) freeness

TEST | 01 | 02 | 03 | 04 | 05 | 06 | 07 | 08 | 09 | 10

해커스 토익 실전 1000제 1 Reading

GO ON TO THE NEXT PAGE

Questions 143-146 refer to the following letter.

August 29
Marcel Vastine
77 Rue du Perche
Paris, France 75003

Dear Mr. Vastine,

I am writing to inform you that your request ------- (143.) pictures inside the London Modern Art Gallery has been approved. Be sure to bring the document enclosed with this letter and present it at the ticket desk when you arrive. -------. (144.) Also, make sure you are prepared to pay the fee of £300.

On your application form, you stated that the ------- (145.) will appear in *Globe Traveler* magazine. Be aware that the gallery name must be mentioned in the article. Moreover, by signing the request form, you have agreed to ------- (146.) send us a copy. We expect to receive it within three business days of publication.

Sincerely,

Jane Rahman
Public Relations Officer
London Modern Art Gallery

143. (A) to take
(B) taken
(C) took
(D) will take

144. (A) This would normally be possible, but we will be closed for renovations.
(B) I have indicated which of the questions you neglected to answer.
(C) In this case, you are allowed to take pictures without any charge.
(D) Otherwise, you will not be able to bring your camera into the exhibits.

145. (A) maps
(B) links
(C) images
(D) reviews

146. (A) promptly
(B) regularly
(C) originally
(D) never

PART 7

Directions: In this part, you will be asked to read several texts, such as advertisements, articles, instant messages, or examples of business correspondence. Each text is followed by several questions. Select the best answer and mark the corresponding letter (A), (B), (C), or (D) on your answer sheet.

PART 7 권장 풀이 시간 54분

Questions 147-148 refer to the following request form.

Shiner Electronics

Service Request Form

Date of request: *August 24* **Time of request:** *1:20 P.M.*

Requested by: *Anita Ellis* **Location:** *Office 702*

Description of problem:

The air conditioner in our marketing research office is leaking again. Normally, this would not be an urgent matter, but it is happening for the second time this month. We would appreciate a response in the next 24 hours, particularly since the weather has been especially warm these past few weeks.

Priority:

__X__ High: Immediate attention required

_____ Medium: Complete within two to three days

_____ Low: Complete within one week

147. Who most likely is Ms. Ellis?

(A) An electrician
(B) A building manager
(C) A marketing employee
(D) A product designer

148. What is suggested about Shiner Electronics?

(A) Its staff moved to a new office last month.
(B) Its air conditioner underwent maintenance last summer.
(C) It recently replaced some office equipment.
(D) Its most service requests will be handled within a week.

GO ON TO THE NEXT PAGE

Questions 149-150 refer to the following advertisement.

Magnificent One-Bedroom Apartment

The last remaining one-bedroom apartment at Cerulean Tower is available for rent. Located on the 28th floor, it has a wide view of downtown Saint Paul below and the Mississippi River beyond. An elegant entrance area leads to spacious living and dining spaces. The kitchen is equipped with sleek appliances, the bedroom has large windows, and the bathroom has a contemporary-style bathtub. The property comes with a sofa, coffee table, bed, nightstands, and plenty of storage space. Cerulean Tower is a modern, full-service luxury building with a theater and fitness center. Rental parking is available in a private garage nearby. Call 555-5784 to arrange a viewing.

149. What is indicated about Cerulean Tower?

(A) It is a famous landmark.
(B) It is newly refurbished.
(C) It is almost fully occupied.
(D) It is near a transit stop.

150. What is NOT included with the advertised apartment?

(A) Free parking area
(B) Kitchen appliances
(C) Pieces of furniture
(D) Recreational facilities

Questions 151-152 refer to the following text-message chain.

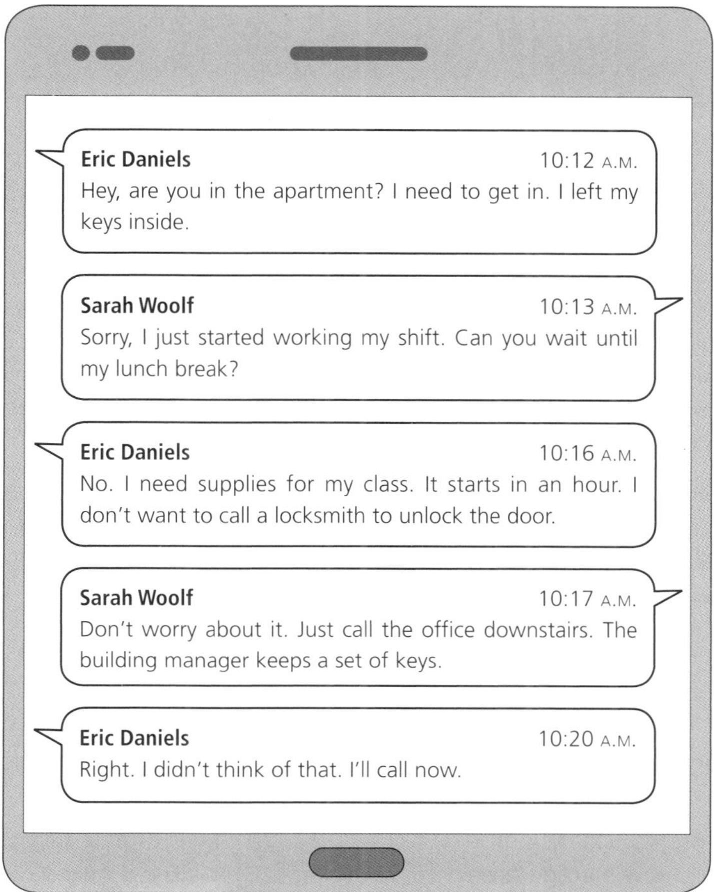

Eric Daniels 10:12 A.M.
Hey, are you in the apartment? I need to get in. I left my keys inside.
Sarah Woolf 10:13 A.M.
Sorry, I just started working my shift. Can you wait until my lunch break?
Eric Daniels 10:16 A.M.
No. I need supplies for my class. It starts in an hour. I don't want to call a locksmith to unlock the door.
Sarah Woolf 10:17 A.M.
Don't worry about it. Just call the office downstairs. The building manager keeps a set of keys.
Eric Daniels 10:20 A.M.
Right. I didn't think of that. I'll call now.

151. What problem does Mr. Daniels mention?

(A) He accidentally broke a lock.
(B) He is late for a work shift.
(C) He cannot access his apartment.
(D) He cannot contact his supervisor.

152. At 10:17 A.M., what does Ms. Woolf mean when she writes, "Don't worry about it"?

(A) She will be at the apartment soon.
(B) Mr. Daniels doesn't have to call a locksmith.
(C) Some school materials are not important.
(D) She will cover Mr. Daniels's shift.

GO ON TO THE NEXT PAGE

Questions 153-154 refer to the following notice.

Notice: for all members

We are sorry to report to Waltrop Leisure Center members that our pool closure will be extended. We have discovered a lot of damaged tiles and have decided to retile the entire pool.

We understand that this closure is disruptive and are working hard to resolve the problem. Currently, the estimated date of completion for the repairs is July 16. In the meantime, the community of Eving has generously offered the free use of its swimming pool to our members. Members who have paid for swimming lessons in advance can obtain reimbursement or credit their payments toward future lessons.

While our pool is being retiled, our gym, basketball court, and dance studio will remain open. As always, these facilities can be accessed from 7 A.M. to 9 P.M. every day of the week. We will post updates about the pool repairs on our Web site. Thank you.

153. What is one purpose of the notice?

(A) To announce a fee increase
(B) To report a project extension
(C) To describe a new storage area
(D) To warn against breaking a rule

154. What is suggested about Waltrop Leisure Center?

(A) It will remain fully closed until July 16.
(B) It is used by the citizens of several towns.
(C) It has added content to its enrollment form.
(D) It normally offers classes at its facility.

Questions 155-158 refer to the following online chat session.

Tanya Huang	10:05 A.M.	Good afternoon, Mr. Benedict. I'm a member of the Analyte support team. I understand you sent a request for assistance yesterday regarding our accounting software.
Rick Benedict	10:06 A.M.	That's correct. I can't figure out how to transfer some data in an Analyte file to Upcell.
Tanya Huang	10:07 A.M.	I see. That's one of our competitors' programs, but it's compatible with Analyte software. You need to click on "File," choose "Export," and select "Upcell" from the list.
Rick Benedict	10:07 A.M.	That's the thing. I tried that but it didn't work.
Tanya Huang	10:08 A.M.	Oh, I'm sorry. Please give me a moment.
Tanya Huang	10:10 A.M.	Mr. Benedict, do you use our $15 a month plan by any chance? Because exporting to other programs, including Upcell, is only possible with plans of $35 and above.
Rick Benedict	10:12 A.M.	I see. Since I really need the access, is there any way you could upgrade me right now?
Tanya Huang	10:13 A.M.	Absolutely. I can connect you to our billing department, but you'll need to have your credit card ready.
Rick Benedict	10:14 A.M.	That's fine. Let's go ahead and do that.

Send

155. What did Mr. Benedict do yesterday?

(A) Went shopping at a computer store
(B) Transferred some funds to a consultant
(C) Printed out some tax documents
(D) Contacted a customer support service

156. What is Mr. Benedict having trouble doing?

(A) Locating a misplaced file
(B) Accessing an online account
(C) Downloading an essential update
(D) Sharing information between programs

157. At 10:07 A.M., what does Mr. Benedict most likely mean when he writes, "That's the thing"?

(A) He is surprised that a new item was released.
(B) He has already attempted a solution.
(C) He would like to redeem some points.
(D) He is willing to make a compromise.

158. What does Ms. Huang ask Mr. Benedict to do?

(A) Select a mailing option from a list
(B) Renew an expired subscription
(C) Prepare to make a payment
(D) Submit a form to another department

GO ON TO THE NEXT PAGE

Questions 159-161 refer to the following e-mail.

To: Alicia Carpenter <alicia@epost.net>
From: Bobby McCord <b.mccord@brancafitness.com>
Subject: Branca Fitness
Date: January 4

Dear Ms. Carpenter,

Thank you for agreeing to participate in Branca Fitness's focus group on exercise equipment. Your session is scheduled for January 15, from 5 P.M. to 8 P.M. — [1] —. The focus group will take place at our head office at 189 Bellflower Road in Seattle.

Upon your arrival in the office, you will be asked to sign a confidentiality agreement. Since the products being tested have yet been released to the public, please don't share any information about them with anyone.

For the first activity, you will be asked to test some exercise equipment. Please make sure to wear comfortable clothing or bring an extra set of clothes. — [2] —. This activity will be followed by a group discussion. During the discussion, you will be presented with different marketing ideas. When asked for your opinion on these ideas, please give honest and detailed answers. — [3] —.

As mentioned in the notice, a payment of $150 will be provided to each participant via bank transfer. — [4] —. If you have any questions, feel free to contact me at any time.

Sincerely,

Bobby McCord

159. What is the e-mail mainly about?

(A) Invitations to an exercise class
(B) Information about a focus group
(C) Preparations for a trade fair
(D) Details regarding a fitness plan

160. What is Ms. Carpenter encouraged to do?

(A) Bring along a guest
(B) Post a product review
(C) Wear an appropriate outfit
(D) Park in front of a building

161. In which of the positions marked [1], [2], [3], and [4] does the following sentence best belong?

"This will take two to three days."

(A) [1]
(B) [2]
(C) [3]
(D) [4]

Questions 162-164 refer to the following Web page.

Home	**About**	Services	Careers	Contact Us

Maksma was founded 15 years ago in Estonia, with the goal of making it easier for people to shop online. When its original office opened, it had just 46 staff members. Since then, Maksma has become one of Europe's largest payment gateways, facilitating online purchases for over 60 million consumers and 70,000 merchants in 22 countries. Maksma differentiates itself by giving customers the option to pay now, later, or in partial amounts over a specified period of time. Whichever option customers choose, they are guaranteed a secure, convenient experience. Merchants also benefit by being able to offer a wider range of payment options.

Maksma is headquartered in Tallinn, with satellite offices in London and New York City. Its more than 1,500 employees are led by an international team of executives. It is valued at over $2.5 billion and handles roughly $10 billion in online sales per year.

162. What information is included in the Web page?

(A) Reasons to buy some investment shares
(B) The names of some business partners
(C) Details about a company's beginnings
(D) A link to an online shopping site

163. According to the Web page, what benefit does Maksma offer customers?

(A) A wide product selection
(B) Specially negotiated discounts
(C) The ability to defer payments
(D) Chances to view used goods

164. What is stated about Maksma?

(A) It employs senior managers from various countries.
(B) It receives monthly payments from vendors.
(C) It made a profit of over $2.5 billion last year.
(D) It will be introducing a mobile application.

GO ON TO THE NEXT PAGE

Questions 165-168 refer to the following brochure.

FILLYAN MASTER

CORPORATE SOLUTIONS INC.'S NEWEST PRODUCT

In today's hypercompetitive world, companies must utilize every advantage available to them. Fillyan Master is a program that allows you to control the electronic equipment in your business environment using a mobile device. — [1] —.

It enables you to use a phone or tablet to monitor and manage audiovisual equipment, lighting, room temperature, and more. — [2] —. Program your electronic window shades in order to maximize their cooling potential at various times of the day.

Moreover, you can collaborate with others by accessing voice and video channels from anywhere that has wireless Internet. Several participants can simultaneously view and collaborate on a presentation using a laptop or smart device. — [3] —.

Fillyan Master also enables you to collect data about room and energy usage. Use this information to guide budget decisions, save your company time and money, and maximize your resources. — [4] —.

Visit www.fillyan.com for more information about this and other products, or call our hotline at 555-5205 to schedule a demonstration.

165. What is mentioned about Fillyan Master?

(A) It requires expert training to learn how to operate.
(B) It will be demonstrated at an industry event.
(C) It must be connected to computer hardware.
(D) It can be used with mobile devices.

166. What function of Fillyan Master is NOT indicated in the brochure?

(A) It enables remote teams to work together.
(B) It gathers information about energy use.
(C) It determines optimal room layouts.
(D) It adjusts the temperature in workspaces.

167. Why will some customers call a hotline number?

(A) To order large quantities of an item
(B) To arrange a product presentation
(C) To schedule an office inspection
(D) To obtain technical assistance

168. In which of the positions marked [1], [2], [3], and [4] does the following sentence best belong?

"This creates new possibilities when it comes to audience involvement."

(A) [1]
(B) [2]
(C) [3]
(D) [4]

Questions 169-171 refer to the following profile.

Lynn Foster's Writing Career

Lynn Foster is a fantasy novelist living and working in Portland, Oregon. Best known for *The Last Rancher*, she has been actively writing since she was 18 years old. Originally from Louisiana, she moved at the age of 11 to Butte, Montana. From its vast, open landscapes she would later draw inspiration for her writing.

Ms. Foster began her career by contributing short stories to magazines across the country. Her short story *Bear in the Creek* won an award from the Montana Arts Council. Two years later, she published her first novel, *Meadowlark*. It was succeeded by a four-volume tale, *The Darkening Brow*, which was made into an animated movie. Her current work in progress, tentatively titled *There and Back*, is set in the town of her birth.

Ms. Foster's books have been translated into over 20 languages.

169. The word "draw" in paragraph 1, line 5, is closest in meaning to

(A) gather
(B) deduce
(C) illustrate
(D) extend

170. What is implied about *There and Back*?

(A) Its story takes place in Louisiana.
(B) It is one of four in a series.
(C) It was written during a journey.
(D) It is Ms. Foster's longest book.

171. What is NOT true about Ms. Foster?

(A) Her stories have appeared in various publications.
(B) Her work is available in foreign languages.
(C) She had some books that were developed into a film.
(D) She won a contest while in university.

GO ON TO THE NEXT PAGE

Questions 172-175 refer to the following e-mail.

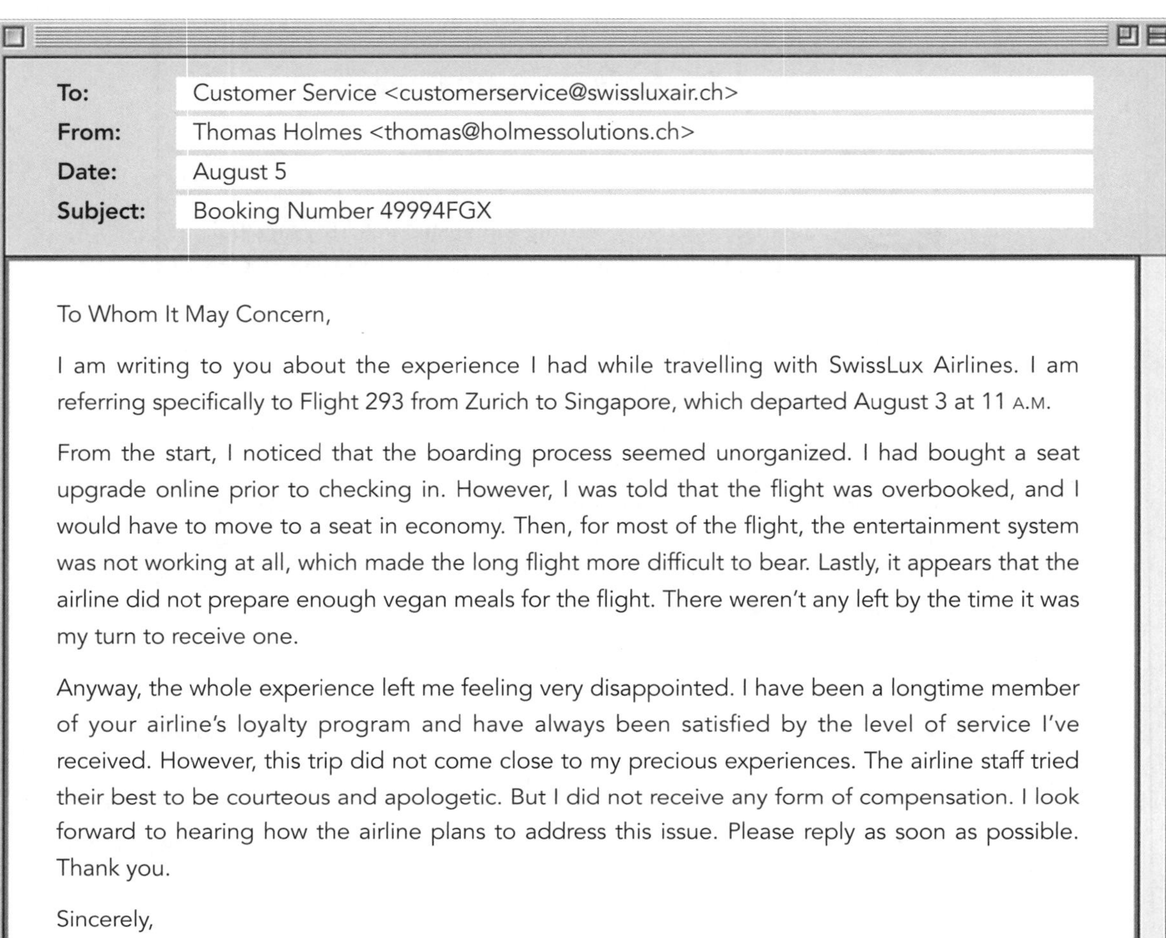

To: Customer Service <customerservice@swissluxair.ch>
From: Thomas Holmes <thomas@holmessolutions.ch>
Date: August 5
Subject: Booking Number 49994FGX

To Whom It May Concern,

I am writing to you about the experience I had while travelling with SwissLux Airlines. I am referring specifically to Flight 293 from Zurich to Singapore, which departed August 3 at 11 A.M.

From the start, I noticed that the boarding process seemed unorganized. I had bought a seat upgrade online prior to checking in. However, I was told that the flight was overbooked, and I would have to move to a seat in economy. Then, for most of the flight, the entertainment system was not working at all, which made the long flight more difficult to bear. Lastly, it appears that the airline did not prepare enough vegan meals for the flight. There weren't any left by the time it was my turn to receive one.

Anyway, the whole experience left me feeling very disappointed. I have been a longtime member of your airline's loyalty program and have always been satisfied by the level of service I've received. However, this trip did not come close to my precious experiences. The airline staff tried their best to be courteous and apologetic. But I did not receive any form of compensation. I look forward to hearing how the airline plans to address this issue. Please reply as soon as possible. Thank you.

Sincerely,

Thomas Holmes

172. Why did Mr. Holmes write the e-mail?

(A) To request changes to a flight
(B) To inquire about loyalty points
(C) To report some lost baggage
(D) To complain about a level of service

173. What can be inferred about SwissLux Airlines?

(A) It recently replaced its entertainment system.
(B) It offers a direct route between Zurich and Singapore.
(C) It does not serve vegan meals to passengers.
(D) It experienced a long delay in Zurich.

174. The word "bear" in paragraph 2, line 4, is closest in meaning to

(A) carry
(B) present
(C) deliver
(D) endure

175. What is suggested about Mr. Holmes?

(A) He booked his airline ticket late.
(B) He received a reimbursement.
(C) He has flown with SwissLux Airlines before.
(D) He often travels to Singapore for business.

GO ON TO THE NEXT PAGE

Questions 176-180 refer to the following job advertisement and letter.

Work for Soleil Cruises

If you're looking for the chance of a lifetime, a job with Soleil Cruises may be for you! Among the many benefits of working for Soleil Cruises is the opportunity to save money. Not only do we provide staff with accommodation and breakfast, lunch, and dinner each day, but we also cover medical insurance and travel expenses. Even the family of crew members benefit; employees at the managerial level may bring their spouse and children on board free of charge, while family members of all other staff are entitled to discounts on package trips.

Positions Available

▶ **Spa specialist**

Provides facials and skincare treatments to passengers. Sells bath and beauty products. Must possess an aesthetician license. Also required to have served on a cruise ship in the past.

▶ **Restaurant manager**

Coordinates restaurant and bar staff. Responsibilities include maintaining service standards and handling passenger concerns. Must have strong organizational skills and have held a similar position on a cruise ship for at least two years.

Call 555-8800 to find out more.

Richard Bates
36 Bayview Road
Pygery, South Australia 5655
Australia

November 1

Dear Mr. Bates,

I enjoyed meeting with you at our office in Sydney last week and would like to offer you the position. As I mentioned, managerial staff schedules are demanding. You'll be working six days a week for a period of nine months, from January to September. Then you will have the next three months off before beginning a new assignment.

You'll have to regularly train new recruits as most of our kitchen and wait staff are students who work for two or three months at a time. Fortunately, your experience working at Luzollo Cruise restaurant has prepared you for such a high turnover rate.

I should also mention that you will have to return to Sydney for two weeks of training starting on December 6. If all goes well, you will likely be assigned to one of our ships by late December, which should give you enough time to get your affairs in order.

I look forward to hearing back from you.

Regards,

Corey Lauzone

176. What is NOT a benefit that Soleil Cruises offers its workers?

(A) Daily meals
(B) Health coverage
(C) Tuition assistance
(D) Free lodging

177. What is a requirement of both job openings?

(A) Willingness to fulfill passengers' special requests
(B) Familiarity with a product line
(C) The acquisition of a license
(D) Experience working on a ship

178. What is one purpose of the letter?

(A) To praise an educational background
(B) To state a period of duty
(C) To propose alternate arrangements
(D) To ask about preferred destinations

179. What is suggested about Mr. Bates?

(A) He is currently unemployed.
(B) His résumé was sent by mail.
(C) He will have to purchase a uniform.
(D) His family will be able to travel for free.

180. What does Mr. Lauzone indicate about kitchen staff?

(A) They do not tend to work for a long period of time.
(B) They come from various countries.
(C) They live in shared accommodation.
(D) They are hired by the restaurant manager.

GO ON TO THE NEXT PAGE

Questions 181-185 refer to the following information and form.

At Polson Electronics, we take great pride in the quality of our merchandise. If you are unhappy with one of our products, you may return it for a refund or exchange it for another item. The following terms and conditions apply to purchases made through our Web site and at any of our 28 stores nationwide:

- Products may be returned within 21 days of purchase as long as the packaging remains sealed.
- Returns of online purchases by mail take 7 to 14 days to process.
- The original receipt must be included with all returns.
- Discounted products cannot be returned.
- Items that have been removed from their packaging can only be returned in exchange for store credit.

Thank you for shopping at Polson Electronics.

Polson Electronics – Product Return Form

Customer: Beth Yang
Phone Number: 555-0393
Address: 35 Elm Street, Chicago, IL 60176
E-Mail: b.yang@dmail.com

Product Name: Digital 350X Printer
Model Number: 7849484XE
Date of Purchase: May 7
Place of Purchase: Harrisburg Branch

Reason for Return:

Despite my best efforts, I cannot get this printer to work with my laptop. After checking a few online forums, I realized that it has compatibility issues with my computer. I even took both devices to a service center on May 11, but the technician was unable to solve the problem. So, I decided to put it back in its box and return it. Rather than immediately purchasing another model, I would like to wait and get the Sonical MDM-0. I have read that it will be released next month. Please let me know by e-mail when exactly you will begin selling it.

Action Requested: ☐ Exchange ■ Refund

181. What is the purpose of the information?

(A) To list some incentives
(B) To state some concerns
(C) To describe some policies
(D) To announce a merger

182. What is NOT indicated about Polson Electronics in the information?

(A) It has branches throughout the country.
(B) It has implemented a recycling program.
(C) It sells products through a Web site.
(D) It prohibits returns of sale items.

183. What is most likely true about Ms. Yang?

(A) She will be visited by a repairperson.
(B) She sent a product by mail.
(C) She will receive store credit.
(D) She bought a gift for a friend.

184. Why is Ms. Yang returning a printer?

(A) It does not fit in her workspace.
(B) It is incompatible with another device.
(C) It has been recalled by the manufacturer.
(D) It was damaged during shipping.

185. What information does Ms. Yang ask for?

(A) The name of a sales assistant
(B) The place where a catalog can be received
(C) The date when a product will be on sale
(D) The reason a specific store was closed

GO ON TO THE NEXT PAGE

Questions 186-190 refer to the following notice, Web page, and receipt.

May 6

The Latin American Journal of Medicine is pleased to announce that Dr. Juan Lima is the winner of this year's Health Service Award. For decades, Dr. Lima has been working as a general surgeon in Domingo Hospital in Bolivia, his home country. We are honoring him because he launched a national health campaign to alert the population about a new strain of flu virus last year. While treating many infants and elderly people—the two groups that were most affected by the outbreak—Dr. Lima advocated for help from the government. Due to his insistence, the Bolivian Health Organization, headed by Mr. Rodrigo Guerrero, ran educational advertisements about preventing and treating the flu.

Join us to honor Dr. Lima on May 27 at 8 P.M. in the Buena Vista Banquet Hall. One of Dr. Lima's colleagues will present him with the award. Last year's winner, Dr. Santiago Castillo will be in attendance. To purchase tickets for this event, visit www.lajm.com/tickets.

www.lajm.com/tickets

The Latin American Journal of Medicine
Awards Ceremony

May 27 at 8 P.M.

Buena Vista Banquet Hall

Thank you for your interest in attending our awards ceremony. Please read through the following information before purchasing your tickets. All sales are final.

☆ All event attendees must have a paper or electronic ticket. This will need to be scanned at the door by one of our event staff.

☆ A ticket includes free parking in either the Buena Vista Parking Lot on the corner of Sunset Street and Orange Avenue or the Belmonte Parking Garage on La Paz Street.

☆ A ticket also includes a buffet dinner, unlimited drinks, and participation in a networking session with the renowned author Dr. Maria Quintero, who will be presenting Dr. Lima's award.

We look forward to seeing you at the ceremony!

Purchase Tickets
Now

Belmonte Parking Garage Receipt

Receipt Date: May 27
Driver: Stephanie Vera
Price: Not applicable–event guest at Buena Vista Banquet Hall

Time In: 7:45 P.M.
Car Model: Volper 900
Car Color: Blue
License Plate Number: SXC 894

**Please place this receipt on the dashboard of your car while it is parked in the garage. A security guard will ask you for it on your way out.*

186. Why will Dr. Lima be receiving an award?
(A) He trained young doctors overseas.
(B) He raised awareness about a medical issue.
(C) He has been praised by his patients.
(D) He helped to operate a hospital.

187. What is stated about the Bolivian Health Organization?
(A) It developed a new treatment.
(B) It received complaints from the public.
(C) It was influenced by Dr. Lima.
(D) It started a program for elderly people.

188. What is indicated about event tickets?
(A) They are nonrefundable.
(B) They come with only one drink.
(C) They must be purchased in person.
(D) They are for a standing section.

189. Who does Dr. Lima most likely work with?
(A) Rodrigo Guerrero
(B) Santiago Castillo
(C) Maria Quintero
(D) Stephanie Vera

190. What is suggested about Ms. Vera?
(A) She bought a ticket on a Web site.
(B) She is driving a rented vehicle.
(C) She will be reimbursed for an admission fee.
(D) She is late for an award ceremony.

GO ON TO THE NEXT PAGE

Questions 191-195 refer to the following letter, memo, and e-mail.

November 9

Elisabeth Baker
Grandville Science Museum
4747 Prairie Street SW
Grandville, MI 49418

Dear Ms. Baker,

I am writing to let you know that I will not be able to lead tours at the museum for all of January. This is because I will be going on a research trip to South America with several of my colleagues at Lakeshore University. During our expedition, we will be digging for the remains of extinct life-forms in the Atacama Desert.

I look forward to guiding museum guests again from February 2 onward. While I have been leading tours on Sundays up to this point, I would like to switch to Saturdays after I return. Also, if you are in need of any speakers for the museum's Real Science lecture series, I would be glad to give a presentation on my findings during the trip.

Sincerely,

James Uttley

TO: All staff
FROM: Michelle Lawrence, museum director
SUBJECT: Changes regarding tours
DATE: November 13

I have several announcements for you about our tour program here at Grandville Science Museum. Firstly, our tours will be taking place on weekdays only, effective December 1. This is because our average number of weekend visitors has risen, and tour groups have become inconvenienced by the congestion. As before, all tours will begin at 10 A.M. and end at noon. The new schedule will be posted on our Web site and on the wall behind our ticket counter. The changes are as follows:

Tour	Day Currently Held		Day to Be Held Starting Dec. 1
Dinosaurs and Fossils	Sunday	→	Monday
The Technology around Us	Monday	→	Tuesday
Life in the Ocean	Thursday	→	Wednesday
Our Place in the Universe	Saturday	→	Friday

Secondly, one of our volunteers, Dr. James Uttley, will not be able to lead his tour in January. Please let me know by e-mail if you would be willing to take over for Dr. Uttley temporarily. All I require is that you have a degree in archaeology.

FROM: Dale Vinson <dalevins@grandvillesm.com>
TO: Michelle Lawrence <michlawr@grandvillesm.com>
DATE: November 19
SUBJECT: Tour Opportunity

Dear Ms. Lawrence,

While I'm enjoying my work coordinating our museum's Energy Sources experience center, I'm keen to lead Dr. Uttley's tour during his absence. I don't think this would interfere with my regular duties because no new interactive exhibits will be added to the experience center that month. As you know, I studied physics in university, which is not directly related to the tour. However, I'm highly familiar with each of our facility's exhibit halls. I also assisted Dr. Uttley when the number of participants in his tour exceeded our 25-person limit due to a registration error. If you'd like, I'd be happy to discuss this further with you at the staff cafeteria during lunch. Let me know if you want to meet.

Best,

Dale Vinson
Junior Curator, Grandville Science Museum

191. Why was the letter written?
(A) To ask for a financial contribution
(B) To confirm attendance at a talk
(C) To clarify some research goals
(D) To temporarily suspend a commitment

192. Which tour has Mr. Uttley been leading?
(A) Dinosaurs and Fossils
(B) The Technology around Us
(C) Life in the Ocean
(D) Our Place in the Universe

193. According to the memo, why will a schedule be changed?
(A) Some volunteers requested greater flexibility.
(B) Season passes have been discontinued.
(C) Some exhibit spaces are being renovated.
(D) Large crowds visit on certain days.

194. What is indicated about Mr. Vinson?
(A) He was unable to attend a team meeting.
(B) He is not qualified to replace Dr. Uttley.
(C) He has been granted access to a laboratory.
(D) He has not yet signed a contract with the Grandville Science Museum.

195. According to the e-mail, what is NOT true about the Grandville Science Museum?
(A) It runs a dining facility for workers.
(B) It limits the size of its tours.
(C) It screens a movie once an hour.
(D) It has an interactive section.

GO ON TO THE NEXT PAGE

Questions 196-200 refer to the following advertisement, memo, and e-mail.

Satisfy Your Thirst for Knowledge at Devon Music Institute

At Devon Music Institute, we know that the desire to learn doesn't stop after graduation from university. That's why, in addition to providing training for aspiring performers and composers, we offer a range of continuing education courses taught by highly qualified instructors. If you'd like to enhance your life through a better understanding of music, consider taking one of our upcoming music history workshops.

Workshop	Instructor	Date	Cost
Early Italian Opera	Denise Murray	May 6	$35
The Madrigal Tradition	Clayton Higgins	May 13	$55
North American Folk Music	Lara Wiseman	May 20	$40
Improvisational Music in the Middle East	Zoe Gomez	May 27	$60

Additional information about these workshops is available at www.devonmusicinstitute.com.

To register, drop by our facility on the corner of Bedford Avenue and Davis Street.

To: Promotion Department Staff, Periform Records
From: Greg Hong, promotions manager, Periform Records
Date: April 15
Subject: Workshops

At our April 10 meeting, I asked you to tell me how you think our workplace can be improved. Several of you indicated that you would like to be given more opportunities to learn about music. I called Devon Music Institute yesterday morning and confirmed that each of its regularly offered one-day workshops will take place next month. Staff members interested in attending any of these workshops should register and pay themselves. Then they should request reimbursement from the accounting department. I would like to add that I took one of the sessions—Early Italian Opera—last month with supervisors from the marketing and distribution departments. We were highly impressed by how much information was covered.

To: Darrel Wilson <d.wilson@periform.com>
From: Mandy Parker <m.parker@periform.com>
Date: July 1
Subject: Reimbursement Request

Dear Mr. Wilson,

I just wanted to follow up on my reimbursement request. It was for a workshop I joined at Devon Music Institute on May 13. Do you have any idea why my request has not been processed yet? In the past, it has never taken more than three weeks. One of my coworkers who participated in a training session at the same institute on May 20 has already received the funds he requested. The workshop I attended was authorized by my manager, Mr. Hong. You may want to call him at extension 457 to confirm this. Thank you.

Sincerely,

Mandy Parker

196. What is suggested about Devon Music Institute?

(A) It has classes on musical composition.
(B) It bought advertising space on Davis Street.
(C) It has received funding from Periform Records.
(D) It specializes in online learning.

197. What aspect of the workshop at Devon Music Institute did Mr. Hong find impressive?

(A) Its affordable fees
(B) Its flexible format
(C) Its supplementary readings
(D) Its amount of educational content

198. How much does Ms. Parker expect to be reimbursed?

(A) $35
(B) $55
(C) $40
(D) $60

199. What is indicated about Ms. Parker?

(A) She attended a seminar with one of her coworkers.
(B) She received the wrong amount of money from the accounting department.
(C) She planned to attend several workshops at an institute.
(D) She submitted a request at least three weeks ago.

200. Which department does Ms. Parker probably work in?

(A) Promotion
(B) Accounting
(C) Marketing
(D) Distribution

This is the end of the test. You may review Parts 5, 6, and 7 if you finish the test early.

정답 p.328 / 점수 환산표 p.329 / 해석 p.402 / Part 5&6 무료 해설 바로 보기(정답 및 정답 음성 포함)

* 다음 페이지에 있는 Self 체크 리스트를 통해 자신의 문제 풀이 방식과 태도를 점검해 보세요.

Self 체크 리스트

TEST 10은 무사히 잘 마치셨죠?
이제 다음의 Self 체크 리스트를 통해 자신의 테스트 진행 내용을 점검해 볼까요?

1. 나는 75분 동안 완전히 테스트에 집중하였다.

   □ 예　□ 아니오

   아니오에 답한 경우, 이유는 무엇인가요?

2. 나는 75분 동안 100문제를 모두 풀었다.

   □ 예　□ 아니오

   아니오에 답한 경우, 이유는 무엇인가요?

3. 나는 75분 동안 답안지 표시까지 완료하였다.

   □ 예　□ 아니오

   아니오에 답한 경우, 이유는 무엇인가요?

4. 나는 Part 5와 Part 6를 19분 안에 모두 풀었다.

   □ 예　□ 아니오

   아니오에 답한 경우, 이유는 무엇인가요?

5. Part 7을 풀 때 5분 이상 걸린 지문이 없었다.

   □ 예　□ 아니오

6. 개선해야 할 점 또는 나를 위한 충고를 적어보세요.

* 교재의 첫 장으로 돌아가서 자신이 적은 목표 점수를 확인하면서 목표에 대한 의지를 다지기 바랍니다. 개선해야 할 점은 반드시 다음 테스트에 실천해야 합니다. 그것이 가장 중요하며, 그래야만 발전할 수 있습니다.

정답
점수 환산표
해석
Answer Sheet

《해커스 토익 실전 1000제 1 Reading》
무료 Part 5&6 해설은 해커스토익(Hackers.co.kr)에서
다운로드 받거나 QR 코드를 스캔하여
모바일로도 확인할 수 있습니다.

정답

TEST 01

101 (D)	102 (A)	103 (B)	104 (D)	105 (C)
106 (C)	107 (D)	108 (B)	109 (A)	110 (C)
111 (D)	112 (D)	113 (C)	114 (B)	115 (A)
116 (C)	117 (C)	118 (B)	119 (A)	120 (B)
121 (C)	122 (B)	123 (C)	124 (A)	125 (D)
126 (A)	127 (A)	128 (D)	129 (C)	130 (B)
131 (B)	132 (C)	133 (C)	134 (D)	135 (C)
136 (A)	137 (D)	138 (B)	139 (D)	140 (C)
141 (A)	142 (D)	143 (A)	144 (C)	145 (A)
146 (B)	147 (B)	148 (D)	149 (C)	150 (C)
151 (B)	152 (D)	153 (A)	154 (D)	155 (B)
156 (D)	157 (A)	158 (D)	159 (C)	160 (A)
161 (A)	162 (C)	163 (B)	164 (B)	165 (D)
166 (B)	167 (A)	168 (B)	169 (C)	170 (C)
171 (A)	172 (D)	173 (D)	174 (C)	175 (D)
176 (C)	177 (B)	178 (A)	179 (C)	180 (B)
181 (B)	182 (D)	183 (C)	184 (A)	185 (D)
186 (C)	187 (C)	188 (C)	189 (D)	190 (B)
191 (C)	192 (A)	193 (D)	194 (A)	195 (D)
196 (B)	197 (A)	198 (D)	199 (B)	200 (D)

TEST 02

101 (C)	102 (B)	103 (D)	104 (A)	105 (B)
106 (A)	107 (D)	108 (A)	109 (C)	110 (D)
111 (B)	112 (A)	113 (C)	114 (D)	115 (C)
116 (B)	117 (D)	118 (A)	119 (A)	120 (C)
121 (A)	122 (D)	123 (C)	124 (C)	125 (B)
126 (B)	127 (D)	128 (C)	129 (B)	130 (A)
131 (A)	132 (B)	133 (D)	134 (C)	135 (D)
136 (C)	137 (D)	138 (C)	139 (C)	140 (C)
141 (A)	142 (C)	143 (B)	144 (D)	145 (B)
146 (C)	147 (D)	148 (C)	149 (D)	150 (D)
151 (B)	152 (A)	153 (D)	154 (D)	155 (C)
156 (B)	157 (D)	158 (A)	159 (D)	160 (D)
161 (B)	162 (C)	163 (A)	164 (C)	165 (D)
166 (C)	167 (D)	168 (A)	169 (B)	170 (D)
171 (C)	172 (B)	173 (D)	174 (B)	175 (C)
176 (C)	177 (B)	178 (C)	179 (B)	180 (D)
181 (C)	182 (A)	183 (C)	184 (B)	185 (B)
186 (A)	187 (B)	188 (C)	189 (C)	190 (D)
191 (A)	192 (C)	193 (D)	194 (A)	195 (B)
196 (C)	197 (D)	198 (B)	199 (D)	200 (B)

TEST 03

101 (C)	102 (D)	103 (A)	104 (B)	105 (B)
106 (D)	107 (A)	108 (C)	109 (B)	110 (C)
111 (C)	112 (B)	113 (B)	114 (B)	115 (A)
116 (D)	117 (B)	118 (A)	119 (C)	120 (D)
121 (B)	122 (C)	123 (D)	124 (A)	125 (B)
126 (B)	127 (D)	128 (A)	129 (D)	130 (D)
131 (B)	132 (A)	133 (C)	134 (D)	135 (C)
136 (D)	137 (A)	138 (C)	139 (C)	140 (D)
141 (A)	142 (B)	143 (C)	144 (B)	145 (C)
146 (B)	147 (D)	148 (A)	149 (C)	150 (B)
151 (B)	152 (C)	153 (A)	154 (C)	155 (B)
156 (C)	157 (D)	158 (C)	159 (C)	160 (B)
161 (C)	162 (A)	163 (D)	164 (B)	165 (C)
166 (B)	167 (B)	168 (B)	169 (B)	170 (A)
171 (C)	172 (D)	173 (A)	174 (B)	175 (D)
176 (D)	177 (C)	178 (B)	179 (A)	180 (C)
181 (B)	182 (D)	183 (A)	184 (D)	185 (B)
186 (B)	187 (B)	188 (D)	189 (B)	190 (A)
191 (B)	192 (B)	193 (C)	194 (A)	195 (D)
196 (A)	197 (B)	198 (A)	199 (D)	200 (C)

TEST 04

101 (B)	102 (B)	103 (D)	104 (C)	105 (C)
106 (D)	107 (B)	108 (D)	109 (C)	110 (C)
111 (D)	112 (C)	113 (A)	114 (D)	115 (B)
116 (C)	117 (A)	118 (A)	119 (C)	120 (C)
121 (B)	122 (D)	123 (C)	124 (C)	125 (C)
126 (B)	127 (C)	128 (B)	129 (D)	130 (B)
131 (A)	132 (A)	133 (C)	134 (B)	135 (C)
136 (A)	137 (C)	138 (B)	139 (C)	140 (D)
141 (C)	142 (C)	143 (C)	144 (A)	145 (D)
146 (B)	147 (B)	148 (D)	149 (C)	150 (A)
151 (B)	152 (A)	153 (D)	154 (A)	155 (D)
156 (A)	157 (B)	158 (D)	159 (C)	160 (B)
161 (D)	162 (B)	163 (B)	164 (C)	165 (C)
166 (C)	167 (B)	168 (B)	169 (B)	170 (C)
171 (C)	172 (C)	173 (B)	174 (C)	175 (D)
176 (C)	177 (C)	178 (D)	179 (B)	180 (B)
181 (C)	182 (A)	183 (D)	184 (C)	185 (B)
186 (C)	187 (D)	188 (B)	189 (C)	190 (A)
191 (C)	192 (B)	193 (B)	194 (D)	195 (A)
196 (C)	197 (A)	198 (D)	199 (B)	200 (C)

TEST 05

101 (B)	102 (B)	103 (C)	104 (A)	105 (B)
106 (C)	107 (C)	108 (A)	109 (B)	110 (C)
111 (A)	112 (A)	113 (D)	114 (C)	115 (A)
116 (A)	117 (B)	118 (B)	119 (D)	120 (B)
121 (B)	122 (D)	123 (D)	124 (B)	125 (B)
126 (C)	127 (A)	128 (C)	129 (D)	130 (D)
131 (D)	132 (C)	133 (D)	134 (D)	135 (B)
136 (C)	137 (C)	138 (A)	139 (D)	140 (B)
141 (A)	142 (D)	143 (C)	144 (A)	145 (C)
146 (D)	147 (C)	148 (C)	149 (B)	150 (A)
151 (C)	152 (C)	153 (A)	154 (D)	155 (D)
156 (C)	157 (C)	158 (B)	159 (D)	160 (B)
161 (B)	162 (D)	163 (C)	164 (B)	165 (D)
166 (C)	167 (B)	168 (A)	169 (A)	170 (D)
171 (D)	172 (B)	173 (D)	174 (A)	175 (B)
176 (C)	177 (D)	178 (C)	179 (A)	180 (A)
181 (A)	182 (C)	183 (B)	184 (B)	185 (D)
186 (C)	187 (C)	188 (D)	189 (C)	190 (A)
191 (A)	192 (C)	193 (B)	194 (C)	195 (D)
196 (B)	197 (C)	198 (D)	199 (B)	200 (A)

TEST 06

101 (D)	102 (B)	103 (A)	104 (B)	105 (B)
106 (D)	107 (A)	108 (A)	109 (B)	110 (C)
111 (C)	112 (A)	113 (C)	114 (D)	115 (C)
116 (A)	117 (B)	118 (C)	119 (B)	120 (D)
121 (B)	122 (D)	123 (D)	124 (A)	125 (A)
126 (D)	127 (C)	128 (B)	129 (D)	130 (B)
131 (B)	132 (D)	133 (A)	134 (B)	135 (B)
136 (C)	137 (A)	138 (B)	139 (C)	140 (D)
141 (A)	142 (C)	143 (D)	144 (C)	145 (D)
146 (A)	147 (B)	148 (C)	149 (C)	150 (D)
151 (D)	152 (C)	153 (A)	154 (B)	155 (D)
156 (C)	157 (C)	158 (D)	159 (B)	160 (B)
161 (A)	162 (A)	163 (C)	164 (C)	165 (A)
166 (B)	167 (C)	168 (A)	169 (B)	170 (D)
171 (B)	172 (A)	173 (C)	174 (A)	175 (D)
176 (D)	177 (C)	178 (A)	179 (C)	180 (D)
181 (B)	182 (C)	183 (B)	184 (C)	185 (D)
186 (D)	187 (B)	188 (D)	189 (C)	190 (B)
191 (B)	192 (A)	193 (D)	194 (A)	195 (B)
196 (C)	197 (C)	198 (A)	199 (B)	200 (D)

TEST 07

101 (D)	102 (D)	103 (B)	104 (A)	105 (A)
106 (A)	107 (C)	108 (C)	109 (B)	110 (A)
111 (B)	112 (B)	113 (C)	114 (D)	115 (D)
116 (B)	117 (D)	118 (C)	119 (C)	120 (C)
121 (D)	122 (B)	123 (D)	124 (A)	125 (A)
126 (B)	127 (C)	128 (B)	129 (D)	130 (B)
131 (D)	132 (A)	133 (B)	134 (D)	135 (D)
136 (C)	137 (C)	138 (D)	139 (B)	140 (D)
141 (A)	142 (C)	143 (C)	144 (A)	145 (D)
146 (A)	147 (A)	148 (D)	149 (D)	150 (B)
151 (A)	152 (C)	153 (D)	154 (D)	155 (B)
156 (C)	157 (B)	158 (D)	159 (D)	160 (D)
161 (C)	162 (D)	163 (C)	164 (C)	165 (D)
166 (C)	167 (B)	168 (A)	169 (D)	170 (C)
171 (B)	172 (C)	173 (A)	174 (B)	175 (D)
176 (B)	177 (C)	178 (D)	179 (A)	180 (B)
181 (D)	182 (A)	183 (C)	184 (C)	185 (D)
186 (A)	187 (C)	188 (A)	189 (A)	190 (C)
191 (B)	192 (D)	193 (C)	194 (B)	195 (A)
196 (A)	197 (C)	198 (C)	199 (B)	200 (C)

TEST 08

101 (A)	102 (C)	103 (C)	104 (B)	105 (C)
106 (A)	107 (D)	108 (C)	109 (C)	110 (B)
111 (B)	112 (B)	113 (C)	114 (D)	115 (A)
116 (C)	117 (B)	118 (D)	119 (A)	120 (C)
121 (A)	122 (C)	123 (D)	124 (A)	125 (A)
126 (B)	127 (D)	128 (C)	129 (D)	130 (B)
131 (C)	132 (D)	133 (A)	134 (C)	135 (D)
136 (C)	137 (B)	138 (C)	139 (B)	140 (D)
141 (B)	142 (C)	143 (D)	144 (B)	145 (B)
146 (D)	147 (A)	148 (B)	149 (D)	150 (D)
151 (A)	152 (D)	153 (D)	154 (B)	155 (D)
156 (A)	157 (C)	158 (C)	159 (B)	160 (D)
161 (C)	162 (B)	163 (D)	164 (C)	165 (A)
166 (A)	167 (C)	168 (B)	169 (A)	170 (B)
171 (D)	172 (B)	173 (B)	174 (B)	175 (D)
176 (B)	177 (C)	178 (D)	179 (A)	180 (C)
181 (C)	182 (D)	183 (B)	184 (A)	185 (A)
186 (C)	187 (B)	188 (C)	189 (A)	190 (D)
191 (D)	192 (C)	193 (D)	194 (D)	195 (C)
196 (D)	197 (D)	198 (D)	199 (B)	200 (C)

TEST 09

101 (C)	102 (D)	103 (C)	104 (A)	105 (B)
106 (A)	107 (C)	108 (D)	109 (B)	110 (C)
111 (C)	112 (B)	113 (C)	114 (C)	115 (D)
116 (D)	117 (A)	118 (D)	119 (D)	120 (D)
121 (B)	122 (B)	123 (C)	124 (A)	125 (B)
126 (B)	127 (A)	128 (C)	129 (D)	130 (A)
131 (C)	132 (D)	133 (A)	134 (D)	135 (C)
136 (B)	137 (D)	138 (B)	139 (A)	140 (D)
141 (C)	142 (C)	143 (B)	144 (A)	145 (C)
146 (D)	147 (A)	148 (B)	149 (D)	150 (C)
151 (C)	152 (D)	153 (C)	154 (A)	155 (D)
156 (B)	157 (D)	158 (D)	159 (C)	160 (C)
161 (A)	162 (B)	163 (A)	164 (B)	165 (B)
166 (C)	167 (D)	168 (B)	169 (D)	170 (C)
171 (A)	172 (D)	173 (C)	174 (B)	175 (B)
176 (D)	177 (A)	178 (C)	179 (C)	180 (B)
181 (D)	182 (A)	183 (D)	184 (B)	185 (D)
186 (B)	187 (A)	188 (D)	189 (B)	190 (B)
191 (C)	192 (A)	193 (B)	194 (B)	195 (A)
196 (D)	197 (C)	198 (D)	199 (B)	200 (C)

TEST 10

101 (D)	102 (B)	103 (D)	104 (D)	105 (A)
106 (D)	107 (B)	108 (C)	109 (B)	110 (B)
111 (C)	112 (D)	113 (B)	114 (A)	115 (B)
116 (D)	117 (D)	118 (C)	119 (C)	120 (A)
121 (D)	122 (C)	123 (D)	124 (C)	125 (C)
126 (B)	127 (B)	128 (D)	129 (C)	130 (B)
131 (B)	132 (C)	133 (D)	134 (D)	135 (A)
136 (B)	137 (C)	138 (D)	139 (D)	140 (C)
141 (A)	142 (C)	143 (A)	144 (D)	145 (C)
146 (A)	147 (C)	148 (D)	149 (C)	150 (A)
151 (C)	152 (B)	153 (B)	154 (D)	155 (D)
156 (D)	157 (B)	158 (C)	159 (B)	160 (C)
161 (D)	162 (C)	163 (C)	164 (A)	165 (D)
166 (C)	167 (B)	168 (C)	169 (A)	170 (A)
171 (D)	172 (D)	173 (B)	174 (D)	175 (C)
176 (C)	177 (D)	178 (B)	179 (D)	180 (A)
181 (C)	182 (B)	183 (C)	184 (B)	185 (C)
186 (B)	187 (C)	188 (A)	189 (C)	190 (A)
191 (D)	192 (A)	193 (D)	194 (B)	195 (C)
196 (A)	197 (D)	198 (B)	199 (D)	200 (A)

점수 환산표

* 아래 점수 환산표로 자신의 토익 리딩 점수를 예상해봅니다.

정답 수	리딩 점수	정답 수	리딩 점수	정답 수	리딩 점수
100	495	66	305	32	125
99	495	65	300	31	120
98	495	64	295	30	115
97	485	63	290	29	110
96	480	62	280	28	105
95	475	61	275	27	100
94	470	60	270	26	95
93	465	59	265	25	90
92	460	58	260	24	85
91	450	57	255	23	80
90	445	56	250	22	75
89	440	55	245	21	70
88	435	54	240	20	70
87	430	53	235	19	65
86	420	52	230	18	60
85	415	51	220	17	60
84	410	50	215	16	55
83	405	49	210	15	50
82	400	48	205	14	45
81	390	47	200	13	40
80	385	46	195	12	35
79	380	45	190	11	30
78	375	44	185	10	30
77	370	43	180	9	25
76	360	42	175	8	20
75	355	41	170	7	20
74	350	40	165	6	15
73	345	39	160	5	15
72	340	38	155	4	10
71	335	37	150	3	5
70	330	36	145	2	5
69	320	35	140	1	5
68	315	34	135	0	5
67	310	33	130		

※ 점수 환산표는 해커스토익 사이트 유저 데이터를 근거로 제작되었으며, 주기적으로 업데이트되고 있습니다. 해커스토익(Hackers.co.kr) 사이트에서 최신 경향을 반영하여 업데이트된 점수환산기를 이용하실 수 있습니다. (토익 > 토익게시판 > 토익점수환산기)

▌TEST 01 해석

* 무료 해설은 해커스토익(Hackers.co.kr)에서 다운로드 받을 수 있습니다.

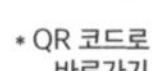

PART 5

101 최고경영자는 베를린으로의 방문 동안 고객들과 짧게 만날 것이다.

102 Lee Valley 소방서는 무엇이 산불을 야기했는지 원인을 밝히기 위해 수사에 착수했다.

103 완료하는 데 약 4시간 정도 걸릴 것이므로 도보 여행을 위해 간식을 조금 챙기세요.

104 Ms. Ewing은 지난달의 설문 조사 결과를 수집할 것이고 그러고 나서 다음 주에 개요를 작성할 것이다.

105 Charles Hayes는 많은 이전 우승자들을 이긴 영국 최고의 체스 선수들 중의 한 사람이다.

106 직원들이 콘서트홀에서 발견하는 것은 무엇이든 분실물 보관소 센터에 일주일 동안만 남아있을 것이다.

107 Mr. Robinson은 그 회사의 조건을 모두 충족시켰고 따라서 정규직에 지원할 자격이 있다.

108 연극 *Middle of Summer*는 관객들을 충격에 빠트린 생각지 않은 예상 밖의 전개가 있는 인상적인 결말을 맺었다.

109 비록 Mactran사가 작년에 종합적인 재활용 프로그램을 수립했지만, 많은 직원들은 지침을 제대로 따르지 않는다.

110 새해 퍼레이드의 경로가 윤곽이 그려졌지만, 주최자들은 여전히 세부 사항을 마무리 짓고 있다.

111 Wilkinsburg 시의회 회의에서, 재산세가 인상되어야 한다는 전반적인 합의가 있었다.

112 고객의 수요를 충족시키기 위해 CX사의 공장들에서는 지금 100만 개의 새로운 비디오 게임기가 제조되고 있다.

113 카메라를 가진 사람은 누구나 시드니 48시간 사진 촬영 대회에 참가할 자격이 있다.

114 일기 예보에 따르면, Wilshire 마을은 내일 최고 8인치의 눈이 올 것을 예상할 수 있다.

115 직원들은 이번 주말의 식품 박람회 무대에서 Harmon사의 최신 주방용품을 보여줄 것이다.

116 그의 폭넓은 경험 때문에, 임원들은 Mr. Peters를 최고경영자 직책에 이상적인 후보자로 생각한다.

117 모든 Florian 대학교 경영학 석사 과정 지원서는 1월 1일까지 마감이다.

118 그 회사는 오래된 사업 모델에서 완전히 디지털 방식의 모델로 급진적으로 바뀌었다.

119 Priyanka Reddy는 지금까지 명성 높은 Clinton 영화상을 받은 최연소 감독이다.

120 공식 기자 신분증을 가지고 있지 않은 기자들은 그 장소에 들어오는 것이 허용되지 않을 것이다.

121 그 종업원은 음식이 제때 제공되지 않아서 매우 미안해했다.

122 제품 품질 보증서가 만료된 것을 고려하면, Jassen 제조사는 그 고객의 제품을 무료로 수리하지 않을 것이다.

123 지난 10년 동안, 줄기세포 연구에서 많은 진전이 있었고, 많은 의학적 발전으로 이어졌다.

124 Johnny Baker는 텔레비전으로 방송되는 *Channel 10 Holiday Show*를 진행해달라는 제안을 여러 차례 거절해왔다.

125 고객 보상 프로그램의 회원들은 그들의 구매에 대해 포인트를 받을 수 있을 뿐만 아니라 할인 혜택을 이용할 수도 있다.

126 그 제품은 대중에 공개될 수 있기 전에 추가 테스트를 받아야 한다.

127 그 팝 가수가 그녀의 최근 월드 투어 중에 방문했던 모든 도시들 중에서, 서울이 그녀가 특히 좋아한 곳이었다.

128 그 요리사는 시청자들에게 그들이 구하기 어려운 품목은 구할 수 있는 어느 재료로든 대체할 수 있다고 자주 상기시킨다.

129 그의 수상 소감에서, Mitchell Cummings는 그의 투자자들에게 그들의 끊임없는 지지에 대해 감사를 표했다.

130 그 리조트는 지난 1년 동안 방문객들을 끌어모으기 위해 객실 요금을 크게 할인해야 했다.

PART 6

131-134는 다음 공고에 관한 문제입니다.

Carmel 타워 주민들을 위한 공고

131 7월 20일에, Carmel 타워는 건물의 복도를 재단장하는 작업을 시작할 것입니다. 그 프로젝트는 완료하는 데 4주가 걸릴 것입니다. 이 기간 동안, 작업자들이 건물에 들어가야 할 것입니다. **132** 따라서, 서비스 엘리베이터의 출입이 일시적으로 제한될 것입니다. **133** 건물 입주자분들께 지장을 드리지 않도록 노력할 것이므로 안심하십시오. 그러나, 약간의 소음과 먼지가 예상될 수 있습니다. **134** 불편을 최소화하기 위해 문을 닫아주십시오. 우려가 있으시면 건물 관리 사무소로 연락해 주십시오.

135-138은 다음 안내문에 관한 문제입니다.

Audipro SL-2 설치

Audipro SL-2 스피커 시스템을 구입하신 것을 축하드립니다. **135** SL-2는 설치하기 쉬운 패키지로 강력한 가정용 오디오를 제공하도록 설계되었습니다.

설치 과정을 시작하시려면, Audipro 앱을 다운로드하시고 당신의 스피커를 등록하십시오. **136** 상자에 있는 제품 번호를 입력하시면 됩니다. 그런 다음, 앱에 계속 있으시면서, 스피커를 당신의 와이파이 네트워크에 연결하십시오. **137** 스피커는 당신의 네트워크에서 호환되는 미디어 플레이어 또는 텔레비전을 자동으로 찾아낼 것입니다. **138** 앱의 지시에 따라 각 장치에 연결하십시오. SL-2는 박스 안에 동봉된 케이블을 사용하여 수동으로 연결될 수도 있습니다.

139-142는 다음 이메일에 관한 문제입니다.

수신: Beth Carlin <bcarlin@eduswiftsystems.org>
발신: John Statler <statler@agpfoundation.org>
날짜: 10월 22일
제목: AGP 비영리 단체 대상

Ms. Carlin께,

139 AGP를 대표하여, EduSwift Systems가 올해의 AGP 비영리 단체 대상 최종 후보 명단에 올랐음을 알려드리게 되어 영광입니다. 연말 시상식 연회에 대한 초대장이 곧 올 것입니다. **140** 귀하의 참석은 대단히 환영받을 것입니다. 그 행사는 비슷한 단체들의 구성원들과 네트워크를 형성할 기회를 제공할 것입니다. **141** 또한, *The National Herald*와 같은 저명한 출판사들이 매년 각 결승전 진출자의 대표들을 인터뷰합니다. 그래서, 그 행사는

언론의 관심을 늘리는 데 좋을 것입니다.

확인하기 위해, 이 이메일에 회신해 주십시오. 142 귀하의 단체의 인원수를 명시해 주십시오. 그 행사에 귀하를 위해 최대 8석까지 예약해 드릴 수 있습니다.

다시 한번 축하드리며,
John Statler 드림
AGP 재단

143-146은 다음 기사에 관한 문제입니다.

(브랜슨)—143 지역 어린이 자선 단체인 Riley's Kids가 1백만 달러의 기부를 받았다. Riley's Kids의 최고경영자인 Amber Thomas는 지난달 초에 이뤄진 기부에 대해 감사를 표했다. 144 듣기로는, 그것은 익명의 한 기부자로부터 왔다. Thomas는 "저희는 이전에 밝혀지지 않은 출처로부터 기부를 받은 적이 있었지만, 이 정도 규모의 것은 한 번도 없었습니다."라고 말했다. Thomas는 그 기부로 Riley's Kids가 시내의 Branson 청소년 센터를 계속해서 확장할 수 있게 할 것이라고 말했다. 145 그것은 곧 새로운 도서관과 농구장을 갖게 될 것이다. 146 그 작업은 예산 부족으로 인해 작년에 중단되었다. 이제 그 센터는 이르면 내년 4월에 문을 열 수도 있다.

PART 7

147-148은 다음 공고에 관한 문제입니다.

통근자분들은 주목해주십시오

현재, Rider Hollow 역에서 선로에 떨어진 나뭇가지들 때문에 지하철의 보라색 노선에 상당한 지연이 있습니다.

저희 직원들은 나뭇가지를 치우는 작업을 하고 있습니다. 그것이 완료될 때까지, 북행과 남행 열차 모두 Rider Hollow 역과 Clint Village 역 사이에서 단일 선로를 공유하게 될 것입니다.

다른 지하철 정보뿐만 아니라 지연에 대한 정기적인 업데이트를 위해, www.shelbyvillesubway.com을 방문하시거나 저희의 열차 추적 애플리케이션인 Shelbyville Ride Tracker를 다운로드하십시오.

147 보라색 노선은 왜 지연을 겪고 있는가?
(A) 폭풍우가 선로에 손상을 입혔다.
(B) 열차 선로에 일부 잔해가 떨어졌다.
(C) 기계 고장이 열차가 움직일 수 없게 했다.
(D) 역에 혼잡이 있었다.

148 보라색 노선에 대해 사실인 것은?
(A) 동쪽에서 서쪽으로 운행한다.
(B) 무료로 이용할 수 있을 것이다.
(C) 그 도시에서 가장 긴 지하철 노선이다.
(D) 어떤 소프트웨어를 사용하여 추적될 수 있다.

149-150은 다음 메시지 대화문에 관한 문제입니다.

Jim Leonard [오전 10시 18분]
안녕하세요, Tricia. 저는 Jim입니다. 아까 당신의 아파트에 있는 오븐이 작동하지 않는다는 문자를 받았어요.

Tricia Madison [오전 10시 21분]
안녕하세요, Jim. 네, 어젯밤에 쿠키를 구우려고 350도까지 올려놨는데, 30분이 지나도 여전히 차가웠어요. 전혀 작동하지 않는 것 같아요.

Jim Leonard [오전 10시 22분]
네. 혹시 점화용 불씨가 나갔는지 아세요?

Tricia Madison [오전 10시 23분]
사실, 확인하지 않았어요. 저는 지금 확인하고 싶지만, 저는 일하는 중이에요.

Jim Leonard [오전 10시 25분]
음, 저는 모든 사람의 가구의 열쇠를 가지고 있어서, 오늘 오후에 점화용 불씨를 확인하기 위해 들를 수 있어요. 만약 문제가 더 심각하면, 수리공을 불러야 할 거예요.

Tricia Madison [오전 10시 28분]
좋아요. 빨리 고쳐지면 좋겠어요. 이 문제를 신속히 처리해 주셔서 정말 감사합니다!

149 오전 10시 23분에, Ms. Madison이 "I'm at work"라고 썼을 때 그녀가 의도한 것은?
(A) 만남을 연기해야 한다.
(B) 문제를 해결하려고 노력하고 있다.
(C) 점검을 행할 수 없다.
(D) 기기를 수리할 수 없다.

150 Mr. Leonard는 누구일 것 같은가?
(A) 아파트 주민
(B) 수리공
(C) 건물 관리인
(D) 예비 세입자

151-152는 다음 설문조사에 관한 문제입니다.

Snappeshop

이름: *Gabe Edwards*

저희 회사를 다른 사람들에게 추천하시겠습니까? 네 / 아니오

아래 질문에 대해, 1부터 5(5가 가장 높음)까지의 선택지를 골라주십시오.

저희 서비스에 얼마나 만족하십니까?
1 ☐ 2 ☐ 3 ☐ 4 ☒ 5 ☐

저희 배달 서비스는 얼마나 효율적입니까?
1 ☐ 2 ☐ 3 ☐ 4 ☐ 5 ☒

저희 고객 서비스를 어떻게 평가하시겠습니까?
1 ☐ 2 ☒ 3 ☐ 4 ☐ 5 ☐

저희 상품 목록에 대해 어떻게 생각하십니까?
다른 온라인 매장들에 비해, 품목이 다양하지 않습니다.

저희 고객 서비스에 대해 어떻게 생각하십니까?
제가 고객 서비스에 전화했을 때, 그들은 저를 계속해서 다른 부서들로 넘겼습니다.

저희 서비스의 어느 측면이 가장 마음에 드십니까?
저렴한 배송료와 배송 속도가 마음에 듭니다.

151 Mr. Edwards에 대해 암시되는 것은?
(A) Snappeshop의 오랜 사용자이다.
(B) 여러 온라인 쇼핑 사이트들을 이용한다.
(C) 이전에 환불을 요청한 적이 있다.
(D) 최근에 그의 주소를 변경했다.

152 Mr. Edwards는 Snappeshop의 어느 측면을 좋아하는가?
(A) 제공되는 품목의 다양성
(B) 연휴 동안의 특가 상품
(C) 빠른 고객 서비스
(D) 저렴한 배송료

153-155는 다음 구인 광고에 관한 문제입니다.

HISTORIC LONDON 여행사: 가이드 모집

당신은 당신 스스로를 지역 역사 전문가라고 생각하십니까? 당신은 매력적

인 연설가입니까? 당신은 도시에 대해 열정적입니까? 만약 그렇다면, Historic London 여행사에서 가이드가 되는 것에 지원하는 것을 고려해보십시오. 저희는 이 도시에서 가장 오래되고 가장 인기 있는 여행사입니다. 저희는 매년 수천 명의 방문객들을 위한 버스, 보트, 그리고 도보 여행을 준비합니다. 현재, 저희가 도보 여행을 안내하는 것을 도와줄 다섯 사람을 찾고 있습니다.

지원자들은 다음을 수행해야 합니다:
- 30분짜리 시험을 쳐서 도시의 역사에 대한 완벽한 지식을 보여줍니다.
- 자신이 선택한 도시의 지역에 대해 10분짜리 발표를 합니다.
- 신원 조사를 통과합니다.

합격자들은 주말을 포함해 주당 25시간에서 30시간 정도 근무할 것이며, 여름 동안 시간 외 근무 시간이 추가될 것입니다. 기본급은 시간당 14파운드이고, 저희는 휴일에 시간당 21파운드를 지급합니다. 완전 고용 혜택이 제공됩니다.

지원하시려면, www.historiclondon.co.uk/jobs에 접속하여 이력서와 당신이 이상적인 지원자가 될 이유를 설명하는 자기소개서를 제출하십시오. 지원서 마감일은 3월 31일입니다.

153 Historic London 여행사에 대해 언급된 것은?
(A) 다양한 종류의 여행을 제공한다.
(B) 다른 도시들로 서비스를 확장하고 있다.
(C) 다른 여행사들보다 더 저렴하다.
(D) 직원들을 몇 달 동안 교육시킨다.

154 구직자들은 무엇을 해야 하는가?
(A) 자격증 사본을 제출한다
(B) 추천서를 제공한다
(C) 여행 일정을 준비한다
(D) 역사 시험을 완료한다

155 가이드 직에 대해 암시되는 것은?
(A) 특별한 유니폼을 필요로 한다.
(B) 여름 동안에 더 바쁘다.
(C) 경력이 있는 사람들에게 더 많은 돈을 준다.
(D) 종종 고위 관리직으로 이어진다.

156-157은 다음 문자 메시지에 관한 문제입니다.

발신: Swift Link (555-4278)
발송됨: 5월 18일, 오후 12시 10분

이것은 귀하의 국제 여행 요금제가 활성화되었다는 알림입니다. 5월 18일에서 5월 25일 사이에, 폴란드 내에서 이동 전화 서비스를 받으실 것입니다. 이 서비스 구역의 비용은 하루에 10달러입니다. 5기가바이트의 데이터를 초과하면 추가 요금이 부과될 것이므로, 많은 데이터를 쓰는 애플리케이션을 끄는 것을 추천합니다. 더 많은 데이터가 있는 요금제로 바꾸시려면, Swift Link 모바일 애플리케이션을 사용하십시오. 감사합니다.

156 문자 메시지는 왜 발송되었는가?
(A) 데이터 한도가 초과되었음을 알리기 위해
(B) 수신자에게 미납 청구서에 대해 상기시키기 위해
(C) 새로운 국제 여행 요금제를 홍보하기 위해
(D) 수신자가 서비스를 받고 있음을 알리기 위해

157 메시지는 수신자에게 무엇을 하라고 추천하는가?
(A) 데이터 소진을 제한한다
(B) 새로운 휴대폰 모델로 업그레이드한다
(C) 사용자 설명서를 다운로드한다
(D) 특정 지역 내에 머무른다

158-160은 다음 기사에 관한 문제입니다.

Paisley Park 식당이 관리자를 바꾸다

수십 년 동안, Paisley Park 식당은 인디애나폴리스에서 가장 상징적인 식당들 중 하나였다. 고전적인 물건들로 가득 찬 화려한 인테리어는 순수한 지나간 시대를 불러일으킨다. *Indianapolis Now*지에 따르면, 그것은 또한 도시에서 가장 친절한 직원들과 최고의 사과파이를 자랑한다.

이제, 설립자이자 오랜 경영자인 Guy Hubert가 사임하기로 결정했다. — [1] —. 72세로, Mr. Hubert는 뒤에서 식당을 경영하는 것에 대한 스트레스를 떨쳐버릴 준비가 되어 있으며 그의 은퇴 생활을 즐기게 되기를 기대한다. 38세인 그의 아들 Gavin이 그의 뒤를 이을 것이다. Mr. Hubert는 "Gavin은 식당에서 15년 넘게 주방장으로 일해왔습니다."라고 말한다. — [2] —. "저는 그가 그곳을 원활하게 운영하기 위해 무엇이 필요한지 알고 있다고 전적으로 확신합니다."

젊은 Hubert는 식당의 핵심적인 측면을 완전히 원래대로 유지할 계획이라고 말한다. — [3] —. 하지만, 그는 전통적인 미국 요리를 넘어 국제적인 요리를 메뉴에 추가하고 싶어 한다. — [4] —. 그는 또한 배달을 이용할 수 있는 엄선된 메뉴 항목을 만드는 것을 목표로 한다.

158 Paisley Park 식당의 매력이 아닌 것은?
(A) 시각적으로 매력적인 인테리어
(B) 친절한 서비스 직원들
(C) 인기 있는 디저트 품목
(D) 특정 요일에 음식 할인

159 Gavin Hubert는 그가 경영자가 되면 무엇을 하고 싶어 하는가?
(A) 인테리어를 리모델링한다
(B) 영업시간을 연장한다
(C) 배달 옵션을 추가한다
(D) 두 번째 지점을 연다

160 [1], [2], [3], [4]로 표시된 위치 중, 다음 문장이 들어갈 곳으로 가장 적절한 것은?
"그의 마지막 날은 2월 28일이 될 것이다."
(A) [1]
(B) [2]
(C) [3]
(D) [4]

161-164는 다음 온라인 채팅 대화문에 관한 문제입니다.

Fumiko Suzuki [오전 10시 51분]
직원 만족에 대한 여러분의 의견을 듣고 싶어요. 직원 설문 조사에서, 몇몇 직원들이 일이 너무 많은 것에 대해 불평했어요. 이것이 야기한 스트레스는 전반적인 생산성에 영향을 미쳤어요. 무엇이 해결책이 될 수 있을까요?

Jintao Bang [오전 10시 52분]
저는 사무실이 문을 닫은 후에 업무와 관련된 이메일을 보내는 것을 중단하는 것이 하나의 좋은 아이디어라고 생각해요.

Hendrick Schulz [오전 10시 54분]
도움이 되겠네요. 게다가, 더 많은 휴식이 장려되어야 해요. 어쩌면 사무실에서 팀워크 활동을 제공해볼 수도 있어요. 동료들과 사회적으로 관계를 맺는 것이 스트레스를 없애거나 줄인다는 것이 입증되었어요.

Fumiko Suzuki [오전 10시 56분]
그것들은 좋은 제안들이에요. 제가 이사회에 그것들을 가져가서 개선을 요구할게요. 다른 사무실들도 비슷한 특전과 편의 시설을 제공하는 것으로 알고 있어요.

Hendrick Schulz [오전 10시 58분]
네, 하지만 그것은 다른 회사들을 따라 하는 것에 대한 게 아니에요. 그러한 것들은 실제로 고도로 숙련된 인재를 유지하고 끌어들이는 데 도움을 줘요. 요즘, 직원들과 고용주들 사이에 서로 유익한 관계를 유지하는 것이 중요해요.

Fumiko Suzuki [오전 10시 59분]
우리는 또한 지난 분기에 예산 잉여금이 있었어요. 저는 우리가 다른 개선에 투자하는 것을 제안해요. 예를 들어, 우리는 구내식당 인테리어를 새롭게 하거나 새로운 메뉴 종류를 추가할 수 있어요.

Jintao Bang [오전 11시 01분]
저는 메뉴를 바꾸는 아이디어가 좋아요. 그것은 모든 사람들로부터 긍정적인 반응을 가져올 거예요. 저는 지인인 Stacy Hill과 상의할 수 있어요. 그녀는 자신의 음식 공급업체를 운영하곤 했어요. 지금, 그녀는 건강에 좋은 요리법에 대한 책을 쓰고 있어요.

Fumiko Suzuki [오전 11시 02분]
우리 모두 이 아이디어들에 대해 좀 더 생각해보고 내일 아침에 만나서 더 논의해요.

161 설문 조사에 대해 언급된 것은?
(A) 직원들 사이의 문제를 드러냈다.
(B) 한동안 연기되었다.
(C) 전반적인 업무 부족을 암시한다.
(D) 직원 평가와 관련이 있다.

162 오전 10시 54분에, Mr. Schulz가 "That would be beneficial"이라고 썼을 때 그가 의도한 것은?
(A) 새로운 기기를 구입하는 것의 가치를 알고 있다.
(B) 계약 연장을 지지한다.
(C) 업무 이메일을 제한하는 것에 동의한다.
(D) 추가 도움을 요청하고 싶어 한다.

163 Ms. Suzuki는 무엇을 제안하는가?
(A) 정부 보조금을 신청하는 것
(B) 사용 가능한 일부 자금을 쓰는 것
(C) 사무실을 다른 건물로 이전하는 것
(D) 마케팅 전문가를 고용하는 것

164 Stacy Hill에 대해 사실인 것은?
(A) 구내식당 메뉴를 개발했다.
(B) 더 이상 사업체를 운영하지 않는다.
(C) 제안서를 제출했다.
(D) 일과 삶의 균형이 있는 사업체를 돕는다.

165-168은 다음 이메일에 관한 문제입니다.

수신: Harry Riley <h.riley@webmail.com>
발신: Brenda O'Connell <b.oconnell@secondcity.com>
제목: 정보
날짜: 6월 18일

Mr. Riley께,

Second City Temp 대행사에 당신의 이력서를 제출해 주셔서 감사합니다. 저는 저희가 당신의 능력에 맞는 일자리를 찾았다고 믿습니다. — [1] —.

Ross and Donahue 법률 사무소는 데이터 입력을 도와줄 보조를 찾고 있습니다. 그들은 일주일 전에 공고를 올렸습니다. 기본적으로, 당신은 그 회사의 고객 데이터베이스를 업데이트할 것입니다. 당신의 이력서에 따르면, 당신은 대학 시절 내내 HX2와 Organizer를 포함하여 다양한 데이터베이스 프로그램들로 작업했습니다. — [2] —. 모든 점들을 고려해 볼 때, 당신은 그 일자리에 적합한 경력을 갖추고 있습니다.

당신의 동의를 받으면, 진행하고 당신의 자료를 Ross and Donahue 법률 사무소에 제출할 것입니다. — [3] —. 그들은 지금 지원자들을 인터뷰하고 있고 6월 28일까지 결정을 내릴 것입니다. 만약 당신이 인터뷰를 제안 받는다면, 저는 회사의 웹사이트에 들어가서 그들의 사명과 그들이 어떤 종류의 법을 전문으로 하는지에 대해 읽으실 것을 강력히 제안합니다. — [4] —. 제가 당신의 지원서를 보내길 원하시면 제게 알려 주십시오.

Brenda O'Connell 드림

165 이메일은 왜 쓰였는가?
(A) 기술 지원을 요청하기 위해
(B) 새로운 법률 사무소를 홍보하기 위해
(C) 데이터 입력에 대한 지침을 제공하기 위해
(D) 가능성이 있는 일자리에 대해 알림을 주기 위해

166 Mr. Riley에 대해 언급된 것은?
(A) 법학 학위를 가지고 있다.
(B) 데이터베이스 소프트웨어에 대해 알고 있다.
(C) 넓은 고객 네트워크를 가지고 있다.
(D) 현재 대학생이다.

167 Ms. O'Connell은 Mr. Riley에게 무엇을 하라고 추천하는가?
(A) 온라인으로 법률 사무소에 대해 읽는다
(B) 프로그램에 대한 그의 지식을 확인한다
(C) 그녀와 구직 면접을 연습한다
(D) 데이터베이스의 일부 정보를 변경한다

168 [1], [2], [3], [4]로 표시된 위치 중, 다음 문장이 들어갈 곳으로 가장 적절한 것은?
"당신은 또한 이전에 Kelson 법률 사무소에서 인턴으로 근무했습니다."
(A) [1]
(B) [2]
(C) [3]
(D) [4]

169-171은 다음 이메일에 관한 문제입니다.

수신: Gelson Cable사 <customerservice@gelsoncable.com>
발신: Candice Novak <c.novak@raymailer.com>
날짜: 2월 13일
제목: 구독

관계자분께,

저는 최근에 당신의 직원들 중 한 명과 제 케이블 구독과 관련된 문제에 대해 통화하기 위해 50분 동안 기다렸습니다. 이런 일이 일어난 것이 이번이 처음이 아니고, 저는 충분히 겪었습니다. 저는 즉시, 제 구독을 취소하고 싶습니다.

몇 년 동안, 저는 정기적으로 저희 건물에서의 신호 품질에 대해 전화했지만, 당신의 직원들은 제 불평을 무시해왔습니다. 게다가, 그들은 제가 가장 좋아하는 케이블 채널들 중 일부가 왜 갑자기 제 구독에서 빠졌는지 설명하지 않았습니다. 제가 이것에 대해 알아보기 위해 전화했을 때, 저는 이제 그것들이 프리미엄 패키지에서만 이용 가능하다는 것을 통지받았습니다.

10년 넘게 단골 고객으로 지내온 후에, 저는 한 달 더 서비스 비용을 지불할 의향이 없습니다. 저는 또한 귀사가 구독자들을 다르게 대하기 시작해야 한다고 강력히 제안 드립니다.

Candice Novak 드림

169 Ms. Novak은 무엇을 하려고 하는가?
(A) 서비스 업그레이드에 대해 문의한다
(B) 수리 일정을 잡는다
(C) 케이블 요금제를 취소한다
(D) 고객 보상 프로그램에 가입한다

170 Gelson 케이블사에 대해 추론될 수 있는 것은?
(A) 잘못된 주소로 고지서를 보냈다.
(B) 장비 수리에 비용을 청구한다.
(C) 케이블 패키지에 변경을 가했다.
(D) 다른 회사에 의해 매입되었다.

171 Ms. Novak은 어떤 조언을 제공하는가?
(A) 고객 서비스를 개선하는 것

(B) 일부 무료 상품을 제공하는 것
(C) 가입비를 적용하지 않는 것
(D) 계약을 연장하는 것

172-175는 다음 보도 자료에 관한 문제입니다.

BookED 최고경영자가 회사의 역사에 새로운 장을 열다

8월 26일—1월에 그 역할을 이어받은 BookED의 최고경영자 Lisa Wang은 인기 있는 온라인 애플리케이션에 중요한 변화를 이미 도입했다. 기존 구독 기반의 모델은 사용자들이 대형 출판사에 의해 후원되지 않는 작가들의 각종 에세이, 책, 기타 출판물을 읽을 수 있도록 한다. 이러한 독립적인 공개물은 BookED의 문학 전문가팀에 의해 엄선되며 고객들에게 맞춤 추천으로 제시된다.

이제, BookED는 자체 독자적인 자료를 출판할 것이다. 이들은 다음 달부터 공개될 콘텐츠를 제작하기 위해 프리랜서로 일하는 언론인들과 소설가들에게 직접적으로 의뢰했다. 이것은 애플리케이션의 포인트 시스템 개시와 동반되었다. BookED는 소셜 미디어 플랫폼에서 회사의 새로운 콘텐츠를 추천함으로써 고객들이 포인트를 얻을 수 있게 하는 시스템을 제작했다. 포인트는 애플리케이션에서 제공되는 모든 다른 콘텐츠를 이용하는 데 사용될 수 있다. BookED는 사용자들이 포인트를 얻을 수 있는 새로운 방법을 지속적으로 개발하겠다고 말했다.

업계 전문가들은 이러한 변화들이 애플리케이션의 고객층을 증가시킬 것이라고 말한다. 그들은 또한 BookED가 내년부터 대중에게 그 회사의 주식을 살 기회를 제공하기 시작할 수도 있다는 의견을 가진다.

172 Ms. Wang은 1월에 무엇을 했는가?
(A) 작가 대리인과 계약했다
(B) 소설을 출판했다
(C) 벤처 사업을 창립했다
(D) 새로운 일을 맡았다

173 1문단 다섯 번째 줄의 단어 "backed"는 의미상 -와 가장 가깝다.
(A) 격려되다
(B) 역전되다
(C) 퇴직하다
(D) 지원받다

174 BookED에 대해 언급된 것은?
(A) 소셜 미디어에 많은 팔로워들이 있다.
(B) 언론사들과 협력했다.
(C) 자체 콘텐츠를 제작한다.
(D) 발표 후에 더 많은 투자자들을 끌어들였다.

175 포인트 시스템에 대해 암시되는 것은?
(A) 사전에 승인된 은행 계좌가 필요하다.
(B) 다음 해에 출시될 것이다.
(C) 포인트가 사용자들 간에 공유될 수 있게 허용한다.
(D) 새로운 사용자들을 만들어내는 데 도움을 줄 수 있다.

176-180은 다음 두 이메일에 관한 문제입니다.

수신: Sally Hartley <sally.hartley@southgeorgiafinancial.com>
발신: Raymond Moran <raymond@trebeldesigns.com>
제목: 주문 번호 7190-1715
날짜: 4월 1일

Ms. Hartley께,

귀사를 위한 맞춤형 마케팅 물품들을 만들기 위해 Trebel Designs사를 선택해주셔서 매우 기쁩니다. 귀사의 주문품인 500개의 펜은 어제 발송되었고, 그것은 영업일 1~2일 이내에 도착할 것입니다. 귀하는 저희 웹사이트에서 송장을 보실 수 있습니다. 언급했듯이, 귀사는 처음 구매하는 고객이기 때문에 10퍼센트 할인을 받으셨습니다.

귀사의 주문과 함께, 저는 저희가 제공하는 모든 제품들의 카탈로그도 포함시켰습니다. 저희의 많은 고객분들이 회사 로고가 새겨진 티셔츠, 모자, 커피 머그잔, 펜, 가방, 또는 다른 물건들을 나눠주는 것이 그들의 사업을 광고하는 효과적인 방법이라는 것을 발견했습니다. Trebel Designs사는 귀사가 저희에게 보내주시는 모든 로고 디자인을 사용할 수 있으며, 아니면 당사의 견본 디자인 중 하나를 사용하여 기꺼이 새로운 로고 디자인을 만들어 드리겠습니다. 저희가 디자인을 만드는 데 일주일이 걸릴 것이라는 점을 알아두시길 바랍니다.

귀사의 거래에 감사드리며, 앞으로 또 귀사와 함께 일하기를 고대합니다.

Raymond Moran 드림

수신: Raymond Moran <raymond@trebeldesigns.com>
발신: Sally Hartley <sally.hartley@southgeorgiafinancial.com>
제목: 회신: 주문 번호 7190-1715
날짜: 4월 2일

Mr. Moran께,

훌륭한 고객 서비스에 감사드리고 싶습니다. 오늘 아침에 주문품을 받았는데, 모든 것이 훌륭해 보입니다. 사실, 다음 달에 일부 신입사원을 채용하기 위해 저희 중 몇몇이 직업 박람회에 참석할 것이어서, 같은 물품으로 300개를 더 주문하고 싶습니다.

신입사원을 대상으로 계획하고 있는 교육 프로그램을 위한 로고도 디자인해 주셨으면 합니다. 이 일을 바로 시작해주실 수 있습니까? 다음 회의 때 그것을 이사회에 공개하고 싶습니다. 자세한 내용은 다른 이메일로 보내드렸습니다.

다시 한번 감사합니다.

Sally Hartley 드림
선임 마케팅 이사
South Georgia Financial사

176 첫 번째 이메일의 하나의 목적은 무엇인가?
(A) 정책 업데이트를 공지하기 위해
(B) 일부 사양을 확인하기 위해
(C) 발송을 확인해 주기 위해
(D) 지급 계획을 설정하기 위해

177 Trebel Designs사에 대해 언급된 것은?
(A) 막 매장을 열었다.
(B) 신규 고객들에게 할인을 제공한다.
(C) 웹사이트를 개설할 계획이다.
(D) 그래픽 아티스트를 고용하려고 하고 있다.

178 South Georgia Financial사는 5월에 무엇을 할 것인가?
(A) 취업 박람회에 참가한다
(B) 일부 직원들을 전근시킨다
(C) 마케팅 학회에 참석한다
(D) 기자회견을 연다

179 Ms. Hartley는 어떤 물품들을 더 주문하고 싶어 하는가?
(A) 모자
(B) 커피 머그잔
(C) 펜
(D) 가방

180 Ms. Hartley의 디자인에 대해 사실인 것은?
(A) 직업 박람회를 위한 것이다.
(B) 완료하는 데 일주일이 걸릴 것이다.
(C) 흑백이어야 한다.
(D) 신입사원들의 아이디어를 포함할 것이다.

181-185는 다음 안내문과 양식에 관한 문제입니다.

Bull Run 스키 리조트 스포츠 상점
장비 대여 정보

여러 제조업체들의 장비를 판매하는 것에 더하여, Bull Run 스키 리조트의 스포츠 상점은 여러분이 스키 슬로프에서 시간을 즐기실 수 있도록 다양한 장비를 대여해 드립니다.

다음이 있습니다:
- 하루당 50달러 또는 주당 150달러부터인 스키, 부츠, 폴을 포함한 스키 패키지
- 하루당 30달러 또는 주당 90달러부터인 스키 재킷과 바지
- 하루당 15달러 또는 주당 45달러인 헬멧*
- 하루당 10달러 또는 주당 30달러인 고글
- 하루당 5달러 또는 주당 15달러인 장갑

저희는 어린이와 성인을 위한 다양한 사이즈를 제공합니다. 키와 몸무게를 기준으로 정확한 사이즈를 정하는 데 도움을 줄 사이즈 표가 카운터에서 제공됩니다. 모든 대여 청구 금액은 즉시 지불되어야 합니다. Bull Run 스키 리조트에 머무르는 손님들에게 15퍼센트 할인이 제공됩니다.

*안전상의 이유로, 모든 스키 타는 사람들은 슬로프에 있을 때 헬멧을 착용해야 합니다.

Bull Run 스키 리조트 스포츠 상점
장비 대여 양식

이름: Marcus Carver
주소: 945번지 Elgin가, 위니펙, 매니토바주 R3E 1B3, 캐나다
전화번호: 555-9708
날짜: 2월 15일
대여 기간: 1일

신용카드 번호: ****-****-****-3533
청구서 발송 주소: 위와 동일

품목	수량	품목당 가격	비용
스키 패키지	2	50달러	100달러
헬멧	2	15달러	30달러
고글	2	10달러	20달러
장갑	2	5달러	10달러
소계			160달러
15% 할인			-24달러
총 요금			136달러

유의하십시오: 하루 대여는 대여된 당일에 이용되어야 합니다. 대여료는 환불되지 않습니다.

181 Bull Run 스키 리조트 스포츠 상점에 대해 언급된 것은?
(A) 모든 최고의 스포츠웨어 브랜드를 제공한다.
(B) 의무적인 안전 장비를 대여해준다.
(C) 1년 중 몇 주 동안 문을 닫는다.
(D) 중고 장비를 저렴한 가격에 판매한다.

182 안내문에 따르면, 사람들은 그들이 필요한 사이즈가 무엇인지 어떻게 알 수 있는가?
(A) 안내원을 부름으로써
(B) 팸플릿을 읽어봄으로써
(C) 웹사이트를 방문함으로써
(D) 표를 봄으로써

183 안내문에서, 3문단 두 번째 줄의 단어 "settled"는 의미상 -와 가장 가깝다.
(A) 놓여지다
(B) 요구되다
(C) 지불되다
(D) 수립되다

184 Mr. Carver의 대여에 대해 암시되는 것은?
(A) 그 장비는 한 명보다 더 많은 사람을 위한 것이다.
(B) 총액은 그에게 회원제 요금의 자격을 준다.
(C) 추가 비용 없이 연장될 수 있다.
(D) 일부 금액이 환불될 수 있다.

185 Mr. Carver에 대해 암시되는 것은?
(A) 초보자로서 수업을 들을 것이다.
(B) 일주일 동안 겨울 스포츠를 연습할 계획이다.
(C) 최근에 스키 재킷을 구입했다.
(D) 리조트에서 객실을 빌렸다.

186-190은 다음 웹페이지, 목록, 이메일에 관한 문제입니다.

ROSENSTEIN 부동산

홈 | 소개 | 중개인 | 연락처

Rosenstein 부동산은 시카고 지역에서 가장 신뢰받고 있는 부동산 중개업소들 중 한 곳입니다. 저희는 도시와 인근 교외의 어느 곳에서나 부동산을 찾도록 도와드릴 수 있지만, 도시의 북부와 북서부 지역에 있는 고급 주택을 찾는 것을 전문으로 하고 있습니다.

여러분이 부동산을 찾기 위해 저희를 이용하실 때, 여러분은 그 부동산을 철저히 둘러볼 수 있을 뿐만 아니라, 최선의 결정을 내리는 데 도움이 되는 광범위한 정보를 얻으실 수도 있습니다. 저희는 부동산의 생활 편의 시설에 대한 완전한 설명과 그곳의 내력에 대한 개요를 제공합니다.

저희가 제시하는 모든 부동산의 목록은 여기에서 이용하실 수 있습니다. 시카고 내 부동산은 부동산 중개인 George Rosenstein과 Mary Kowalski에 의해 제시됩니다. 주변 지역의 부동산은 Karl Mitchell에 의해 제시됩니다.

1월 1일 현재 Rosenstein 부동산에 의해 제시되는 부동산

주소	가격	침실	욕실
980번지 Boston가, 시카고, 일리노이주	380,000달러	3	2
118번지 Michigan가, 시카고, 일리노이주	410,100달러	4	3
1001번지 Lipton가, 에번스턴, 일리노이주	360,500달러	2	2
280번지 Irving가, 시카고, 일리노이주	550,400달러	4	3
190번지 Sherman로, 시카고, 일리노이주	290,900달러	2	1

방문 일정을 잡으시려면 555-3928로 전화주세요. 저희는 평일 오전 9시부터 오후 6시까지 이용하실 수 있습니다.

수신: Rosenstein 부동산 <inquiries@rosenstein.com>
발신: Anne Dahlberg <anned98@mittermail.com>
제목: 아파트
날짜: 1월 3일

관계자분께,

제 남편과 저는 최근에 시카고의 Northbrook 대학교에서 교편을 잡았습니다. 아들과 함께, 저희는 다음 달에 그 도시로 이사할 계획입니다. 저희는 지금 한동안 부동산 목록을 둘러보고 있습니다. 이상적으로는, 저희는 40만 달러 미만의 가격이고, 침실 두 개와 욕실 두 개가 있는 아파트를 원합니다. 그러나, 저희는 이러한 필요 조건에 대해 어느 정도 융통성이 있습니다. 190번지 Sherman로에 있는 아파트가 꽤 매력적입니다. 저희는 그곳이 저희 대학교와 가까워서 좋습니다. 그 아파트가 아직 이용 가능한가요? 그렇다면, 가급적이면 남편과 제가 그 도시에 있을 때인 다가오는 이번 주말에 그곳의 방문을 계획하고 싶습니다. 저에게 알려주세요.

Anne Dahlberg 드림

186 Rosenstein 부동산에 대해 사실인 것은?
(A) 12명이 넘는 부동산 중개인을 고용하고 있다.
(B) 임차인들이 신원 보증을 제공할 것을 요구한다.
(C) 시카고의 특정 지역에 집중한다.
(D) 세 개의 다른 도시에 사무실을 가지고 있다.

187 Rosenstein 부동산은 고객들이 결정하는 것을 돕기 위해 무엇을 하는가?
(A) 온라인에 부동산의 영상을 게시한다.
(B) 주인들과의 만남을 주선한다.
(C) 포괄적인 정보를 제공한다.
(D) 수리에 대한 전문적인 견적을 제공한다.

188 어느 부동산이 Mr. Rosenstein이나 Ms. Kowalski에 의해 제시되지 않는가?
(A) 980번지 Boston가
(B) 118번지 Michigan가
(C) 1001번지 Lipton가
(D) 280번지 Irving가

189 Ms. Dahlberg에 대해 암시되는 것은?
(A) 대학교 과정을 막 마쳤다.
(B) 주말에 이사할 계획이다.
(C) 아파트를 팔기를 원한다.
(D) 현재 시카고 바깥쪽에 살고 있다.

190 Ms. Dahlberg의 방문 요청에 대해 추론될 수 있는 것은?
(A) 그녀는 차량을 빌려야 한다.
(B) 중개인은 만날 수 없을 것이다.
(C) 그녀는 주인 없이 갈 수 없다.
(D) 방문은 가상으로 이루어질 것이다.

191-195는 다음 공고, 편지, 보고서에 관한 문제입니다.

공고

Crystal 아파트는 1월 6일부터 10일까지 모든 세대를 점검할 예정입니다. 시설 관리자가 FailSafe Home Inspections사의 기술자가 건물을 둘러볼 때 동행할 것입니다. 각 점검은 약 60분 정도 소요될 것입니다.

점검은 다음 사항에 대한 확인을 포함할 것입니다:
· 벌레 출몰
· 배관 문제
· 가스 누출

여러분의 점검이 언제 예정되어 있는지를 알려드리기 위해 추가 정보를 우편함으로 받으실 것입니다. 점검 당일에는, 기술자가 언제 여러분의 세대를 들어가고 나가는지를 알리는 문자 메시지 알림도 받을 것입니다.

1호에서 20호의 주민들은 1월 11일에 그들의 점검 보고서를 받을 것입니다. 21호에서 40호의 주민들은 1월 15일에 그들의 점검 보고서를 받을 것입니다.

Ms. Alyssa Matthews
38호

Ms. Matthews께,

귀하의 점검은 1월 10일 오전 10시에 예정되어 있습니다. 시설 관리자가 기술자를 위해 귀하의 세대 문을 열어줄 것이고 기술자가 나갈 때 다시 잠글 것입니다.

기술자가 자유롭게 작업할 수 있도록 점검 중에는 세대에서 나가 계시는 것을 권장합니다. 예정된 시간 동안 집에 계셔야 할 필요가 있다면, 가능한 한 빨리 시설 관리자에게 알려주십시오.

또한 귀하께서 가지고 있을 수 있는 어떠한 문제라도 시설 관리자에게 알려주십시오.

관리사무소 드림

Crystal 아파트 점검 보고서

아래는 최근 귀하의 아파트 세대 점검 결과입니다. 이 보고서를 주의 깊게 검토하십시오.

점검 날짜: 1월 10일
도착 시간: 오전 10시 30분
세대: 38호
기술자: Allen Scott

점검 기호 설명:
A – 발견된 문제 없음
B – 사소한 문제 발견됨
C – 주요한 문제 발견됨

항목	등급	문제	권장 조치
창문	A		
벽/천장	B	식당 천장의 경미한 균열	작업 필요 없음
경보 시스템	A		
연기 탐지기	B	기기 세 대에서 배터리 교체	추가 작업 필요 없음
일산화탄소 검출기	A		
배관	B	주방 싱크 아래 파이프에서 경미한 누출	수리를 계획하기 위해 시설 관리자에게 연락
가스	A		
전기	A		
벌레	B	식당에 있는 개미 몇 마리	해충 구제약을 마련하기 위해 시설 관리자에게 연락

의견: 38호는 대체로 상태가 양호합니다. 다만, 거주자는 시설 관리자에게 연락하여 주방의 누수 배관 수리를 진행해야 합니다. 38호는 또한 추후 곤충 문제를 예방하기 위해 구제 서비스를 받아야 합니다.

191 공고는 누구를 대상으로 하는 것 같은가?
(A) FailSafe 기술자
(B) Crystal 아파트 관리자
(C) Crystal 아파트 주민들
(D) 건물 유지 보수 작업자들

192 편지에서 찾을 수 있는 정보는 무엇인가?
(A) 점검 날짜
(B) 기술자의 이름
(C) 문제에 대한 세부 정보
(D) 사무실의 위치

193 Ms. Matthews는 언제 그녀의 점검 보고서를 받았을 것 같은가?
(A) 1월 6일
(B) 1월 10일
(C) 1월 11일
(D) 1월 15일

194 Mr. Scott에 대해 암시되는 것은?
(A) 약속 시간에 늦었다.
(B) 간단한 배관 수리를 했다.
(C) 오전 11시 전에 아파트를 떠났다.
(D) 몇 가지 문제에 대해 미리 통지를 받았다.

195 보고서에 따르면, 어느 항목이 추가 조치가 필요한가?
(A) 창문
(B) 벽
(C) 경보 시스템
(D) 배관

196-200은 다음 광고지, 일정표, 이메일에 관한 문제입니다.

작가 워크숍
11월 17일
Kilwin 시립 도서관

항상 자신의 소설이나 시집을 출판하는 것을 꿈꿔오셨나요? 여러분이 작가가 되기 위해 필요한 자질을 가지고 있는지 궁금한가요?
이 꿈을 현실로 만들 때입니다!

남부 오하이오 작가 협회의 후원을 받고 있는
저희의 작가 워크숍 시리즈에 참여하세요.

워크숍은 Kilwin 시립 도서관에서 열립니다. Blueberry 베이커리와 카페의 호의인 가벼운 다과가 제공될 것입니다. 남부 오하이오 작가 협회에 의해 진행되는 모든 워크숍은 참가자들에게 무료로 이용 가능합니다. 하지만, 공간이 한정되어 있으니, 오늘 신청하세요!

더 많은 정보가 필요하시면 저희 사서들 중 한 명에게 문의하시거나 남부 오하이오 작가 협회의 Lola Nicholson에게 lnicholson@sowg.org로 연락하세요.

Kilwin 시립 도서관 작가 워크숍 일정표

워크숍 제목	날짜	시간	장소
위대한 미국 소설	12월 1일부터 2월 13일까지	월요일, 오후 6시부터 8시까지	A 회의실
소네트 쉽게 하기	12월 18일부터 2월 13일까지	목요일, 오후 1시부터 2시까지	A 회의실
영시	12월 19일부터 2월 14일까지	금요일, 오후 3시부터 4시까지	주 강당
청소년 에세이 쓰기	12월 20일부터 2월 15일까지	토요일, 오후 3시부터 4시까지	어린이실

작가 워크숍은 정기적인 출석을 필요로 합니다. 사전 통지 없이 워크숍에 2회 넘게 출석하지 않은 참석자들은 명부에서 빠질 수 있습니다.

좀 더 가벼운 분위기에 관심이 있으시다면, 남부 오하이오 작가 협회가 수요일 오후 4시부터 5시까지 Blueberry 카페와 베이커리에서 작가들을 위한 주간 커피 다과회를 주최합니다. 사전 등록은 필요 없으며, 예약 없이 오시는 분들 모두 환영합니다!

수신: Barbara Espinoza <barbespin@capomail.com>
발신: Lola Nicholson <lnicholson@sowg.org>
날짜: 11월 27일
제목: 회신: 워크숍

안녕하세요, Barbara! 귀하께서 요청하신 워크숍에 등록해 드렸습니다. 첫 번째 세션은 12월 18일 오후 1시에 예정되어 있습니다. 하지만, 워크숍 자료를 받으시려면 적어도 10분 일찍 도착해주십시오. 귀하의 워크숍은 Kilwin 시립 도서관에서 지난여름에 참석하셨던 교양 워크숍과 같은 장소에서 개최될 것입니다.

워크숍에는 노트북이 필요하지 않지만, 참가자분들은 그것을 가져오셔도 좋습니다. 당신의 작품이 검토되도록 하실 의향이 있으시다면, 몇 가지 샘플도 가져오시길 권하지만, 몇 가지 간단한 엄선된 것들로 제한해 주십시오.

다른 질문이 있으시면 제게 알려주십시오!

Lola Nicholson 드림
복지 활동 관리자
남부 오하이오 작가 협회

196 일정표에 따르면, 남부 오하이오 작가 협회의 주간 커피 다과회에 대해 암시되는 것은?
(A) 참석을 원하는 개인들은 사전에 좌석을 예약해야 한다.
(B) 작가들은 각 세션에 참석하도록 요구되지 않는다.
(C) 손님들은 이 모임들에 방문하는 것이 허용되지 않는다.
(D) 학생들은 무료 커피나 차를 받을 수 있다.

197 이메일의 목적은 무엇인가?
(A) 등록을 확인해주기 위해
(B) 새로운 비용을 알리기 위해
(C) 일정의 변경을 알리기 위해
(D) 연사를 소개하기 위해

198 Kilwin 시립 도서관에 대해 암시되는 것은?
(A) 노트북 컴퓨터를 대여해 준다.
(B) Ms. Nicholson의 이전 직장이었다.
(C) 지역 작가들의 작품을 소유하고 있다.
(D) 과거에 무료 행사를 열었다.

199 Ms. Espinoza가 등록한 워크숍은 무엇인가?
(A) 위대한 미국 소설
(B) 소네트 쉽게 하기
(C) 영시
(D) 청소년 에세이 쓰기

200 이메일에 따르면, 워크숍 참가자들은 무엇을 하도록 권장되는가?
(A) 별개의 세미나에 참석한다
(B) 일부 정보를 다운로드한다
(C) 상세한 후기를 남긴다
(D) 개인의 작품 견본을 가져온다

TEST 02 해석

* 무료 해설은 해커스토익(Hackers.co.kr)에서 다운로드 받을 수 있습니다.

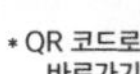

PART 5

101 인턴들은 연구부장의 지휘하에 일할 것이다.

102 Ambrose가에 있는 역사적인 주택은 150년 전에 그것이 지어진 이래로 상당히 바뀌었다.

103 PenTex사의 임원들은 DRW사의 경영진과 만나고 있으며, 그들은 그곳과 합병하는 것에 관해 이야기했었다.

104 임대차 계약을 끝내고 싶은 세입자들은 이사 가기 최소 30일 전에 소유주에게 통지해야 한다.

105 Sylvia Lyman은 그녀의 반에서 1등으로 졸업했고 일류 법률 사무소에 의해 바로 채용되었다.

106 샘플을 비교하는 것은 고객들이 그들의 화장실 벽과 바닥에 적합한 타일을 선택하도록 도울 수 있다.

107 호텔 지배인들은 순조롭게 운영되고 있는지 확실하게 하기 위해 그들의 직원들과 정기적으로 의사소통한다.

108 Arrow 광고사는 18세에서 25세 사이의 시청자들의 흥미를 끌도록 고안된 광고를 제작했다.

109 회사는 새로운 신입사원들에게 교육을 제공할 것이므로, 경력도 학위도 필요하지 않다.

110 Meta 철도사의 승객들은 오직 열차가 취소되거나 지연되는 경우에만 표를 전액 환불받을 권리가 있다.

111 분석가들은 내년에 유가가 약 30퍼센트 오를 것으로 예측했다.

112 직원들은 이제 주간 근무 시간의 절반까지 재택근무할 수 있는 혜택을 제공받을 것이다.

113 Knoll 컨설팅사는 개인적인 가치관이 회사의 것과 맞는 직원들을 고용하려고 한다.

114 기존의 휴대전화와는 달리, Tektone사의 혁신적인 TX-81은 다른 회사에 의해 생산된 부품들로 수리될 수 있다.

115 Colora 주택용 페인트는 시판 중인 비슷한 제품들보다 기상 재해에 50퍼센트만큼 더 잘 견딘다.

116 몇몇 새로운 사무용 가구는 크기가 어색하게 만들어져 계획된 사무실 공간에 맞지 않는다.

117 뉴욕의 주거 비용은 인근 주인 뉴저지의 것보다 훨씬 더 비싸다.

118 Martinsburg 미술관은 고전주의 회화 소장품으로 널리 알려져 있다.

119 설문 조사를 익명으로 하는 것은 소비자들로부터 솔직한 의견을 받는 좋은 방법이다.

120 예약했기 때문에, Mr. Quinn과 그의 동료들은 식당에 도착하자마자 바로 앉았다.

121 한쪽 당사자가 합의 조건을 이행하지 못하는 경우 계약은 합법적으로 해지될 수 있다.

122 편집장으로서의 첫해 동안, Ms. Reed는 *The National Gazette지*의 독자 수를 25만 명 이상으로 확대했다.

123 종이를 아껴 쓰기 위해, Florence 미디어 제작사는 직원들이 하루에 만들 수 있는 복사본의 수에 제한을 두었다.

124 운전할 때 안경을 써야 할 의무가 있는 사람들은 그렇게 하지 않는 것에 대해 처벌받을 수 있다.

125 Laudner Holdings사의 Mr. Duchene에게서 온 이메일은 Ms. Coleman이 기다리고 있던 것이다.

126 주민들은 새로운 시립 도서관을 위해 제안된 건설 사업이 한 달 후에 시작될 것으로 예상한다.

127 Dr. Andrea Griffin은 새로운 남아메리카 나비 종에 대한 발견으로 과학 공로상을 받았다.

128 Ms. Kowalski의 마케팅 직원들은 발표 자료를 준비하기 위해 밤새도록 열심히 일했다.

129 업무 현장에서의 부상에 대한 보상으로, Mr. Galvert는 3개월의 유급 휴가를 받았다.

130 혹독한 겨울이 예보된 후 Forest 양털 재킷의 판매 실적은 향상을 보였다.

PART 6

131-134는 다음 기사에 관한 문제입니다.

Palm Lane 청소년 센터의 개관식이 어젯밤 Jalisco 시내에서 열렸다. **131** 이 센터는 8세에서 18세의 사람들을 위해 계획된 시의 네 개 시설 중 첫 번째 건물이다. 앞으로 몇 년에 걸쳐 세 개가 더 지어질 것이며, 이는 시의 어린이들과 청소년들에게 오락 및 교육의 기회를 제공하겠다는 시장의 선거 공약을 이행할 것이다.

132 전반적으로, 기념식은 상당히 잘 진행되었다. 지역 사회의 주요 구성원들이 그들의 지지를 보여 주기 위해 대거 참가했다. **133** 몇몇 유명 인사들도 참석했다. **134** 시장은 센터에 대한 공헌에 대해 모두에게 감사를 표했으며 리본을 자를 때가 오자 그를 도와줄 한 무리의 지역 어린이들을 무대로 초대했다.

135-138은 다음 편지에 관한 문제입니다.

Vince Johnson
4897번지 Buford가
애틀랜타, 조지아주 30329

Mr. Johnson께,

Skyspan 항공사의 고객 보상 프로그램인 Skyspan Rewards에 가입하신 것을 환영합니다. **135** 회원으로서, 귀하는 저희와 함께 비행할 때마다 포인트를 받으시게 될 것입니다.

5만 포인트 이상을 모으시면, Skyspan 항공사의 무료 왕복 국내선 항공권을 받을 자격이 주어질 것입니다. **136** 10만 포인트 이상을 적립하시면, 플래티넘 등급 멤버십의 독점적인 혜택을 받을 자격을 얻으실 것입니다. 이는 가장 높은 등급의 카드 소지자들만 이용할 수 있는 저희의 호화로운 특별 플래티넘 라운지의 완전한 사용을 포함합니다.

귀하의 멤버십 카드는 온라인 계정에 대한 임시 비밀번호와 함께, 이 편지에 동봉되어 있습니다. **137** 로그인하기 위해 그것을 사용한 다음 비밀번호를 변경하십시오. **138** 포인트를 얻는 것과 그것의 정보를 얻는 방법에 대해 웹사이트에서 더 많이 알아보실 수 있습니다.

Karen Lawson 드림
멤버십 관리자

139-142는 다음 공고에 관한 문제입니다.

Valentine Fragrances는 Verona에 있는 저희 부티크가 3월 2일 오전 10시에 공식적으로 개점한다는 것을 발표하게 되어 매우 기쁩니다. **139** 지난

2년 동안 저희 온라인 매장을 계속 영업할 수 있도록 해주신 것에 대해 단골 손님들께 감사드리고 싶습니다. **140** 여러분의 도움은 저희가 마침내 실제 지점을확보할 수 있게 해주었습니다. **141** 개점 행사는 623번지 Main가에 있는 부티크에서 열릴 것입니다. 모두 마음껏 들르셔서 샘플을 써보고, 향수 제조 과정에 대한 시연을 보고, 창립자인 Ms. Carly Brown도 만나보십시오. 부가적으로, Valentine Fragrances는 다양한 근무 시간에 대한 세 명의 판매 직원이 필요합니다. **142** 지원서는 2월 22일까지 받을 것입니다.

143-146은 다음 웹페이지에 관한 문제입니다.

www.shanemcgovernaccounting.com

정확한 기록을 작성하고 관리하기 위해 고심하는 것은 여러분이 생각할 수 있는 것보다 기업가들 사이에서 더 흔합니다. **143** 하지만, Shane McGovern과 같이 경험이 풍부한 회계사를 고용하는 것은 여러분이 회계의 기본을 이해하도록 도와주고 손실이 큰 실수가 발생하는 것을 막아줄 수 있습니다. **144** Mr. McGovern은 세금 신고서 제출, 기록 관리, 그리고 재정 관리에 있어서 수많은 사업주들을 도와왔습니다. **145** 그는 또한 개개인의 요구에 맞춘 조직 시스템을 제공합니다. 이 서비스는 특히 많은 저명한 경영주들에 의해 인정받아왔습니다. 여기에서 이전 고객들의 의견을 확인해보세요: 추천의 글.

Shane McGovern 회계사무소가 사업과 관련하여 여러분을 도와줄 수 있을지 아직도 확신하지 못하시나요? **146** 무료 상담 일정을 잡기 위해 오늘 전화하세요.

PART 7

147-148은 다음 웹페이지에 관한 문제입니다.

https://www.kileyandjulien.com/alexandria/contactus

KILEY AND JULIEN

아이들을 위한 멋진 옷

홈	제품	특별 할인	연락처

오하이오에 있는 저희 본점은 5250번지 Harville대로, 알렉산드리아, 오하이오주 43002에 있습니다.
방문하시려면, 다음 길 안내를 따르십시오:

자동차로 오시는 경우
- 43번 고속도로를 타고, Maple가로 나가십시오.
- Harville대로에서 우회전하십시오.
- 매장은 우측에 있을 것입니다.

버스로 오시는 경우
- 34번 버스를 타십시오.
- Harville대로 버스 정류장에서 하차하십시오.

저희는 또한 다음 위치에 더 작은 소매점들을 가지고 있습니다:
350번지 Acrewood가, 알렉산드리아 45249 (길 안내)
119번지 Indianwoods로, 알렉산드리아 45249 (길 안내)

모든 소매점의 정상 영업시간은 월요일부터 토요일은 오전 9시부터 오후 8시까지이며, 일요일은 오전 10시부터 오후 7시까지입니다. 모든 공휴일에는 매장이 문을 닫습니다.

문의 사항이나 용무가 있으시면, 다음으로 연락하실 수 있습니다:
전화: 614-555-3010
이메일: jenwoods@kileyandjulien.com

질문에 대한 신속한 답변이 필요하시면 여기에서 채팅을 시작하실 수도 있습니다.

147 Kiley and Julien에 대해 사실이 아닌 것은?
(A) 알렉산드리아에 지점들을 가지고 있다.
(B) 본점은 대중교통으로 갈 수 있다.
(C) 일요일에는 평소보다 일찍 문을 닫는다.
(D) 휴일에는 특별 할인을 한다.

148 고객은 신속한 답변을 받기 위해 무엇을 할 수 있는가?
(A) 이메일을 작성한다
(B) 번호를 입력한다
(C) 온라인 상담을 시작한다
(D) 전화를 한다

149-150은 다음 메시지 대화문에 관한 문제입니다.

Marvin Lee [오후 1시 46분]
안녕하세요 Sandra. 이 회의는 당분간 계속될 것 같아요. 당신이 가셔서 State가 개발에 관한 책자들을 찾아오실 수 있을까요?

Sandra Vasquez [오후 1시 47분]
물론이죠. 길 아래쪽의 Harry's 인쇄소를 고르셨나요?

Marvin Lee [오후 1시 48분]
아니요. 그들은 할 수 없었어요. 저는 Dearborn가에 있는 가게를 선택했어요. Simple 인쇄소라는 곳이에요. 정확한 주소는 기억나지 않지만, 제가 찾아볼 수 있어요.

Sandra Vasquez [오후 1시 50분]
그럴 필요 없어요. 저는 이전에 그들과 함께 일한 적이 있어요. 10분 정도 후에 출발할 수 있어요. 사무실 또는 다른 곳에서 그것들이 필요하신가요?

Marvin Lee [오후 1시 51분]
사무실이 괜찮아요. 정말 감사해요.

149 Mr. Lee는 왜 Ms. Vasquez에게 연락하는가?
(A) 기술적인 문제를 보고하기 위해
(B) 회의에 대한 업데이트를 제공하기 위해
(C) 추천을 받기 위해
(D) 물건을 찾으러 가는 것을 준비하기 위해

150 오후 1시 50분에, Ms. Vasquez가 "There's no need for that"이라고 썼을 때 그녀가 의도한 것은?
(A) 일부 인쇄물은 책상 위에 남겨져도 된다.
(B) Mr. Lee는 그의 다음 회의를 쉽게 연기할 수 있다.
(C) 일부 추가 자료는 수집되지 않아도 된다.
(D) Mr. Lee는 정보를 찾아볼 필요가 없다.

151-152는 다음 기사에 관한 문제입니다.

눈 관광이 급상승하고 있다!
Pete Jenkins 작성

2월 28일—Boulder 관광청에 의해 시행된 조사에 따르면, 지난 50년간의 그 어떤 겨울에보다도 더 많은 사람들이 지난 12월과 1월에 그 도시와 인근 스키 별장을 방문했다. 더 많은 관광객은 그 지역의 경제가 예상치 못한 경기 부양을 겪었다는 것을 의미한다. 물론, 지역 사업주들은 추가 수익에 더할 나위 없이 기뻐했다.

유명한 지역 기상학자인 Laura Nowak은 0도의 날씨 속에서 그 지역에 몇 주간 가벼운 가루 상태의 눈이 내릴 것으로 예측했다. 그녀는 스키 타는 사람들에게 "완벽한 눈 상태"임을 언급했고, 그녀의 예측은 이번 시즌에 기록적인 수로 관광객들을 Boulder 지역으로 끌어들이는 데 도움을 주었다. Nowak은 내년 겨울, 그리고 아마 내후년 겨울에 대해서도 비슷한 날씨를 예상한다. 이는 그 지역 내의 호텔과 스키장에게 희소식이다. 내년에 대한 예약이 이미 꽉 차고 있으며, 대부분의 지역 사업체들은 관광 호황이 계속되기를 기대하고 있다.

151 기사가 지역 사업주들에 대해 언급하는 것은?
(A) 1년 내내 관광객을 끌어들일 방법을 모색하고 있다.
(B) 수익이 증가했다.
(C) Boulder의 경제 계획에 만족한다.
(D) 별장과 스키장을 확충하고 있다.

152 Ms. Nowak에 대해 언급된 것은?
(A) 사람들의 여행 계획에 영향을 주었다.
(B) 여행사 직원으로 일한다.
(C) 동계 스포츠에 종사한다.
(D) 12월에 Boulder로 이사했다.

153-155는 다음 공고에 관한 문제입니다.

Excellent 출판사의 모든 구독자께:

— [1] —. 50년 넘게, 독자들은 세계의 사건에 대한 기사를 보기 위해, 저희의 월간 인쇄 잡지인 *The World Today*지를 구독했습니다. 하지만, 그것은 단종되었고, 대신에, 독자들은 그것의 마지막 인쇄판이 발행된 직후, 저희가 *The Thinker*지라고 명칭을 바꾼 그 잡지의 첫 온라인판을 이용했습니다. — [2] —.

그 변화로부터 1년이 지났고, Excellent 출판사는 오로지 인터넷에서만 이전과 같은 훌륭한 기사들을 구독자들에게 계속해서 제공해왔습니다. — [3] —. 그 새로운 인터넷 뉴스 잡지는 계속해서 인기가 상승하고 있지만, 일부 독자들은 여전히 기존의 인쇄판을 다시 돌려달라고 요구하고 있습니다. 따라서, 저희는 올해부터 *The Thinker*지의 연간 인쇄판을 발행하기로 결정했습니다. 그 인쇄판은 지난 12개월 동안 가장 인기 있었던 기사들을 포함할 것입니다. — [4] —. 그것은 연말에 덤으로 모든 디지털 구독자들의 집에 배달될 것입니다. 연간 인쇄판과 관련한 질문이 있으시면, www.thethinker.com/bonusprint를 방문해주십시오.

153 Excellent 출판사에 대해 언급된 것은?
(A) 최근에 그것의 창립 기념일을 축하했다.
(B) 이전 호를 할인하여 계속 판매할 것이다.
(C) 50년 전에 새로운 소유주에게 매각되었다.
(D) 작년에 새로운 매체로 전환했다.

154 *The Thinker*지의 인쇄판에 대해 암시되는 것은?
(A) 독자들이 기고한 내용을 특집으로 다룰 것이다.
(B) 전국의 신문 가판대에서 판매될 것이다.
(C) 해외 독자들을 위한 번역본을 포함할 것이다.
(D) 온라인에서 발행되었던 기사들을 포함할 것이다.

155 [1], [2], [3], [4]로 표시된 위치 중, 다음 문장이 들어갈 곳으로 가장 적절한 것은?
"이 짧은 기간에, *The Thinker*지의 구독자 수는 두 배 이상이 되었습니다."
(A) [1]
(B) [2]
(C) [3]
(D) [4]

156-157은 다음 이메일에 관한 문제입니다.

수신: 전 직원
발신: Carl Eklund
제목: 회의
날짜: 7월 1일

안녕하세요, 여러분.

저는 여러분 모두에게 올해 8월 7일부터 9일까지 몬트리올에서 열릴 제11회 연례 조류 보존 회의에 대한 최신 정보를 제공하고 싶었습니다. 우리는 보통 그 회의에 참석할 대표 한 명을 무작위로 뽑습니다. 하지만, 올해는 참석하는 사람이 여느 때보다 더 많은 책임을 지게 될 것이기 때문에 지원자를 구하고 있습니다. 저는 그때 남극 대륙에 있는 연구소에 있을 것이므로, 직접 자원할 수 없습니다.

회의의 책임자인 Georgia Proctor가 제게 연락을 취해서 올해 우리 연구소의 누군가가 발표를 할 수 있는지 물어보았습니다. 그녀는 남극 대륙에서의 펭귄의 이동 패턴에 대한 우리의 연구 결과에 특히 관심이 있었습니다. 따라서, 지원자는 이 주제에 대해 발표해야 할 것입니다.

이 기회에 관심이 있으시면, 가능한 한 빨리 제게 알려 주십시오.

Carl Eklund 드림
수석 연구원
야생동물 연구소

156 이메일의 목적은 무엇인가?
(A) 과학자들에게 새로운 발견에 관한 최신 정보를 알려주기 위해
(B) 발표를 위한 지원자를 요청하기 위해
(C) 새로운 부서에 일을 배정하기 위해
(D) 다가오는 자선행사를 알리기 위해

157 야생동물 연구소에 대해 암시되는 것은?
(A) 원래 조류 이동을 연구하기 위해 설립되었다.
(B) 전 직원을 학술 회의에 보낼 것이다.
(C) 남극 대륙에서 프로젝트를 수행하기 위한 승인을 기다리고 있다.
(D) 이전에 조류 보존 회의에 참석한 적이 있다.

158-160은 다음 공고에 관한 문제입니다.

공고

오늘 와주셔서 감사합니다. 저희는 Hannah Levi의 곧 있을 콘서트 투어를 위해 20명의 무용수를 선발하는 오늘의 활동을 준비했습니다. 저희 광고에 대한 압도적인 반응으로 인해 일부 조정이 이루어졌습니다.

저희는 더 이상 각 무용수와 개별 시간을 진행하지 않을 것입니다. 대신, 한 번에 여섯 명의 그룹으로 볼 것입니다. 오디션실에 들어오시면, 여러분의 이력서와 사진을 심사위원의 책상에 놓아주세요. 그러고 나서 여섯 명의 모든 무용수들은 Ms. Levi의 노래들 중 하나에 맞춰 함께 춤을 출 것입니다.

만약 여러분이 다음 라운드로 나아가도록 선발된다면 여러분에게 통보될 것입니다. 만약 선발되었다면, 근처에 머무르십시오. 두 번째 라운드에서, 무용수들은 저희의 수석 안무가와 함께 작업할 것입니다. 이후에, 최종 발표가 나기 전에 남은 후보자들은 저녁에 한 라운드를 더 치를 것입니다. 행운을 빕니다!

158 공고는 주로 무엇에 관한 것인가?
(A) 선발 절차의 과정
(B) 장소 대여에 대한 요구 사항
(C) 순회공연 계약의 세부 사항
(D) 콘서트 연기의 이유

159 3문단의 첫 번째 줄의 단어 "advance"는 의미상 -와 가장 가깝다.
(A) 가져오다
(B) 촉진하다
(C) 소개하다
(D) 나아가다

160 최종 발표에 대해 암시되는 것은?
(A) 단체의 규모에 따라 결정될 것이다.
(B) 웹사이트에 게시될 것이다.
(C) Hannah Levi에 의해 결정될 것이다.
(D) 세 번째 라운드 이후에 이루어질 것이다.

161-164는 다음 광고에 관한 문제입니다.

Reliance 7이 공개됩니다!

오늘날의 세계에서 이동 중의 생산성은 필수적입니다. 저희는 당신이 어디에나 들고 갈 수 있도록 Reliance 7 태블릿을 아주 얇고 가볍게 만들었습니다!

저희의 태블릿은 세련된 디자인과 당신이 즉시 이용할 수 있기 위해 필요한 모든 기능을 가지고 있습니다. 당신은 고해상도 화면의 풍부한 색상과 선명한 이미지를 매우 좋아하게 될 것입니다. 또한, 이 새로운 태블릿에는 독특하게 디자인된 스타일러스가 딸려 있습니다.

경쟁에서 돋보이기 위해, Reliance사는 가방 디자인 업체인 Top Crafter사와 협력했습니다. 이 브랜드는 Reliance 7을 위해 단 30달러에 판매될 멋진 파우치를 만들었습니다. 이것은 한정판 상품으로, 오직 1,000개만 만들어졌고, 각각 일련번호가 찍혀 있습니다.

Reliance 7은 1월 12일부터 소매점에서 구입할 수 있을 것이나, 열성적인 고객들은 저희 웹사이트 www.reliance.com에서 그것들을 선주문할 수 있습니다. 오늘 저희 사이트에서 당신의 것을 예약하세요!

161 Reliance 7에 대해 언급된 것은?
(A) 이전 모델들보다 더 크다.
(B) 높은 수준의 화질을 가지고 있다.
(C) 독특한 모양이다.
(D) 사무 업무에 가장 알맞다.

162 Top Crafter사에 대해 언급된 것은?
(A) 늘어난 경쟁을 겪고 있다.
(B) 제품 가격을 인하했다.
(C) 다른 사업체와 협력했다.
(D) 수제 가방을 판매한다.

163 파우치에 대해 언급되지 않은 것은?
(A) 여러 상점에 갖추어져 있을 것이다.
(B) 첫 세트가 다 떨어진 후에는 구매할 수 없다.
(C) 모바일 장치를 보관하기 위해 특별히 디자인되었다.
(D) 제조 중에 특유의 방법으로 표시되었다.

164 광고에 따르면, 고객들은 웹사이트에서 무엇을 하도록 권장되는가?
(A) 의견을 제공한다
(B) 기기 부대용품을 주문한다
(C) 물품을 예약한다
(D) 애플리케이션을 다운로드한다

165-167은 다음 편지에 관한 문제입니다.

1월 6일

Debonair 출판사
1800번지 Dundee가
토론토, 온타리오주
M6J 1X7

관계자분께:

저는 지금까지 오랫동안 Brian Warburton의 작품의 열렬한 팬이었고, 그의 저서들은 수년간 제게 큰 영감이 되었습니다. 저는 제 소설 집필을 막 끝마쳤으며, 그의 Lost Sanctuary 시리즈의 세 번째이자 마지막 권인 *The Returning*의 두 행을 꼭 인용하고 싶습니다. 이 행들은 항상 제게 깊은 의미가 있었습니다. 그 때문에, 저는 그 인용구가 제목 및 헌정사 페이지 뒤에 있는, 제 소설의 첫머리에 나오기를 원합니다.

저는 인용구를 사용하기 위한 허가를 받는 방법에 대해 확실히는 알지 못합니다. 제가 가진 Mr. Warburton의 책을 확인해보았고, 그것이 인쇄된 해에 귀사가 저작권자였다는 것을 알게 되었습니다. 귀사가 여전히 저작권을 가지고 있다면, 제가 인용구를 사용해도 될지 알려주시겠습니까? 만약 그래도 된다면, 어떻게 진행하면 되는지와 제가 얼마를 낼 것으로 예상하면 될지 알려주십시오. 만약 귀사가 더 이상 저작권을 가지고 있지 않다면, 저작권을 가지고 있는 사람 또는 회사의 이메일 주소나 전화번호를 주실 수 있으십니까?

감사드리며, 답변을 기다리겠습니다.

Chester M. Gleason 드림

165 Mr. Warburton에 대해 암시되는 것은?
(A) 그의 저작권을 가족 구성원에게 양도했다.
(B) 헌정사 페이지에서 감사를 받을 것이다.
(C) 30년 전에 집필을 시작했다.
(D) 세 권이 한 세트인 책을 썼다.

166 Mr. Gleason은 무엇에 대해 잘 모른다고 말하는가?
(A) 초판이 어디에서 인쇄되었는지
(B) 그가 벌금을 내야 할 것인지
(C) 요청에 대한 승인을 어떻게 받는지
(D) 누가 소설을 편집할 것인지

167 Mr. Gleason은 Debonair 출판사에 어떤 정보를 제공해 달라고 요청하는가?
(A) 서점의 위치
(B) 인쇄 견적
(C) 우편 주소
(D) 요금의 액수

168-171은 다음 기사에 관한 문제입니다.

복구 활동을 시작하다

Mary Harding 작성

대략 50년 전, Wester Point시는 초기 주민들 중 한 명인 Lester Muller를 기억하기 위해 공들인 기념 공원을 건설했다. Mr. Muller는 이곳에서 첫 번째 공장을 열었던 부유한 자본가였다. — [1] —. 유명한 시계탑이 있는 이 공원은 연간 2만 명이 넘는 사람들을 유입시키면서, 방문객들에게 인기 있는 행선지가 되었다.

하지만, 몇 년 동안, 그 공원은 유지 보수 문제로 고통받아 왔다. — [2] —. 탑의 시계는 더 이상 작동하지 않고, 건물 내부 페인트가 바랬다. 결과적으로, 그 공원의 운영을 감독하는 위원회는 두 달간의 복구를 위해 그 탑을 폐쇄하기로 결정했다. 위원회는 HC 건설사의 전문가 팀을 고용했다. 그 팀은 Sam Hunt를 포함하는데, 그는 워싱턴 DC의 Rosenberg 기념비와 같은 유사한 복원 프로젝트를 작업한 적이 있다. — [3] —. 다음 두 달 동안, 그가 필요한 수리를 감독할 것이다.

이 기간 동안, 인접한 조각 정원과 공원의 다른 구역들은 대중들에게 계속 자유롭게 이용 가능할 것이다. — [4] —. 개장 시간은 화요일부터 일요일, 오전 8시부터 오후 7시까지이다. 시계탑의 수리는 10월 1일까지 완료되어야 한다.

168 기사에 따르면, Mr. Muller는 무엇을 했는가?
(A) 몇몇 공장을 설립했다
(B) 유명한 시를 썼다
(C) 시장의 역할을 했다
(D) 시계탑을 건설했다

169 Mr. Hunt에 대해 언급된 것은?
(A) 기념 공원의 책임자이다.
(B) 다른 장소들을 보수하는 것을 도왔다.
(C) 새로운 복원 기술을 개척했다.
(D) Rosenberg 기념비의 직원이다.

170 조각 정원에 대해 사실인 것은?
(A) 공원 입구 건너편에 위치해 있다.
(B) 두 달 동안 문을 닫을 것이다.
(C) 일 년 중 일부 동안만 연다.
(D) 모든 방문객들에게 입장을 제공한다.

171 [1], [2], [3], [4]로 표시된 위치 중, 다음 문장이 들어갈 곳으로 가장 적절한 것은?

"그는 이 분야에서 최고의 전문가들 중 한 명이다."

(A) [1]
(B) [2]
(C) [3]
(D) [4]

172-175는 다음 온라인 채팅 대화문에 관한 문제입니다.

Andrew Marks [오후 5시 9분]
자, 회의에 대한 후속 조치를 취하자면, GDE Motors사의 Ms. Foster가 협상을 맺을 준비가 된 것 같네요. 그녀는 다음 주에 계약 조건을 논의하기 위해 Mr. Mueller와 만나고 싶어 해요.

Robert Crane [오후 5시 11분]
Mr. Mueller는 다음 주에 뉴질랜드로 출장 가지 않나요?

Allison West [오후 5시 12분]
맞아요. 그는 다음 주에 여기에 없을 거예요. Ms. Foster와의 약속을 Deanna Lane과 잡는 것은 어때요?

Andrew Marks [오후 5시 13분]
그녀는 이미 업무가 매우 많아요. 약속을 위한 시간이 없을 거예요.

Robert Crane [오후 5시 15분]
Mr. Mueller에게 뉴질랜드에서 화상 회의를 해달라고 요청할 수 있을까요?

Allison West [오후 5시 16분]
가능할 수 있겠네요. 그리고 고객이 그렇게 하는 것을 꺼려할 것 같지 않아요.

Andrew Marks [오후 5시 18분]
지금 바로 가서 Mr. Mueller와 이야기해보고 그가 그렇게 할 의향이 있는지 알아볼게요. Allison, 만약 그렇다면, 당신이 Ms. Foster와 일시를 정할 수 있을 거예요.

Allison West [오후 5시 19분]
문제없어요. 당신에게서 연락이 올 때까지 기다릴게요.

172 Ms. Foster는 무엇을 하고 싶어 하는가?
(A) 임원 회의의 일정을 다시 잡는다
(B) 계약을 마무리 짓는다
(C) 계약을 갱신한다
(D) 출장을 예약한다

173 Ms. West는 무엇을 추천하는가?
(A) Mr. Mueller를 출장 보내는 것
(B) 약속을 위한 시설을 예약하는 것
(C) 새로운 장비를 사는 것
(D) Ms. Lane을 고객과 만나게 하는 것

174 오후 5시 16분에, Ms. West가 "That could work"라고 썼을 때 그녀가 의도한 것은?
(A) 고객이 계약 조건에 동의할 것으로 생각한다.
(B) 화상 회의가 문제를 해결할 수 있을 것으로 생각한다.
(C) Ms. Lane이 휴식을 좀 가져도 된다는 것에 동의한다.
(D) Mr. Mueller가 출장을 연기하기를 원한다.

175 Mr. Marks는 다음에 무엇을 할 것인가?
(A) 회의 안건을 준비한다
(B) 고객에게 이메일을 보낸다
(C) 동료와 이야기한다
(D) 예약을 변경한다

176-180은 다음 제품 후기와 광고에 관한 문제입니다.

www.reviews.com/refrigerators00071

Kitchen-Max사의 ColdPro 2000
1월 5일에 Roger Ling에 의해 평가됨

ColdPro 2000 냉장고는 Kitchen-Max사의 모든 가전제품과 마찬가지로, 최고급입니다. ColdPro의 두 번째 버전에서, 그 회사는 대부분의 주방과 잘 어울리는 현대적인 디자인인 스테인리스를 그대로 유지했습니다. 그것은 편리한 냉수기를 포함하여, 몇 가지 추가 기능을 가지고 있습니다.

하지만, 이 모델의 한 가지 큰 단점은 정수 필터의 배치입니다. 그것은 선반 뒤에 숨겨져 있는데, 이는 교체를 어렵게 만듭니다. 사용자 설명서에 따르면, 필터는 3개월마다 교체되어야 하는데, 이는 소유자들에게 부담이 될 수 있습니다.

전반적으로, 이것은 아주 좋은 냉장고지만, 비교적 비쌉니다. 하지만 Kitchen-Max사는 12월에 있었던 기자 회견에서 다가오는 2월에 냉장고 라인의 다음 모델을 소개할 것이라고 발표했습니다. 그때 ColdPro 2000의 가격이 낮아질 것으로 예상되기 때문에, 저는 그때까지 결정을 보류하는 것을 추천합니다.

가전제품의 미래: Kitchen-Max사의 ColdPro 3000 냉장고!

Kitchen-Max사는 최첨단 기술을 사용한 최신 냉장고 ColdPro 3000을 소개하게 되어 자랑스럽습니다. 이 가전제품은 저희의 이전 모델인 ColdPro 2000의 모든 유용한 기능을 가지고 있으며, 얼음 제조 기능 및 농산물을 위한 온도 조절 보관함도 포함합니다.

www.kitchenmax.com/refrigerators를 방문하셔서 이 혁신적인 가전제품에 대해 더 많은 것을 알아보세요. ColdPro 3000은 2월 25일부터 여러분 근처의 소매점에서 구매할 수 있습니다! 저희 웹사이트에 방문하셔서 Kitchen-Max사 제품이 판매되는 지점 목록을 확인하세요.

176 Kitchen-Max사에 대해 암시되는 것은?
(A) 냉장고만 판매한다.
(B) 다른 제조업체와 합병하는 중이다.
(C) 고품질의 가전제품을 만든다.
(D) 2월에 기자 회견을 열었다.

177 제품 후기에 따르면, ColdPro 2000의 특징은 무엇인가?
(A) 다양한 색상으로 나온다.
(B) 현대적인 외관을 가지고 있다.
(C) 비교적 가볍다.
(D) 사용자화 가능한 설정을 가지고 있다.

178 Mr. Ling은 무엇을 추천하는가?
(A) 판촉 행사에 참석하는 것
(B) 다른 브랜드를 살펴보는 것
(C) 다음 달까지 기다리는 것
(D) 제조업체에 연락하는 것

179 ColdPro 2000과 ColdPro 3000의 공통점은 무엇인가?
(A) 영구적인 정수 필터를 가지고 있다.
(B) 냉수기를 포함한다.
(C) 얼음 제조 기능을 포함한다.
(D) 온도 조절 보관함을 특징으로 한다.

180 2월 25일에는 무슨 일이 일어날 것인가?
(A) 회사가 신규 지점의 위치를 발표할 것이다.
(B) 할인권들이 소매점에 의해 배부될 것이다.
(C) 냉장고 모델에 대한 회수가 공표될 것이다.
(D) 고객들은 새로운 가전제품 모델을 구매할 수 있을 것이다.

181-185는 다음 편지와 회람에 관한 문제입니다.

Allen 부동산
www.allenrealty.com

3월 5일

Michelle Simon
Simon Digital 컨설팅사
5883번지 Dunn로
메이블턴, 조지아주 30126

Ms. Simon께,

축하드립니다! 애틀랜타에서 귀하의 요구를 완벽히 충족시킨 유일한 곳인 North가에 있는 사무실 소유주가 귀하의 제안을 수락했습니다. 이 편지에 동봉되어 있는 제시된 계약서를 검토해주십시오. 그것은 귀하께서 요청하신 신규 조항을 포함하도록 수정되었습니다. 임대료는 4월 1일부터 3년 동안 그 공간을 사용하겠다는 귀하의 합의를 조건으로 하여, 월 220달러로 내려졌습니다. 또한, 그 전에 소유주가 바닥 타일을 확인하고 필요한 모든 것을 설치할 것입니다. 하지만, 에어컨은 귀하께서 스스로 준비하셔야 할 것입니다.

만족하신다면, 제게 서명된 계약서의 사본을 다시 보내주십시오. 만약 그렇지 않으시다면, 저희는 사안에 대해 더 논의할 수 있습니다.

Damien Horowitz 드림
부동산 컨설턴트

동봉물: 계약서

Simon Digital 컨설팅사
회람

수신: 전 직원
발신: Michelle Simon
제목: 이동
날짜: 3월 7일

좋은 소식이 있습니다. 우리의 부동산 중개인인 Mr. Horowitz가 우리의 요건을 모두 충족하는 애틀랜타의 사무실을 임대하도록 도와주었습니다. 우리는 다음 달에 새 사무실로 이동할 것입니다. 앞서 말씀드렸듯이, 이 변화는 우리가 기존 고객에게 더 가까워지고, 새로운 사업 기회를 추구하고, 추가 직원들을 수용하게 해줄 것입니다. 저는 여러분 모두가 만족할 것이라고 확신합니다. 걸어서 단 5분 거리에 기차역이 있으며 여러 식당이 그 지역에 있습니다.

새 사무실에 있는 대부분의 것들은 소유주에 의해 관리되고 있지만, 몇몇 필수 가전제품은 제공되지 않습니다. 그래서, 4월 2일에 영업팀의 비품과 사무용 가구가 새로운 장소로 옮겨지기 전, 4월 1일에 그러한 가전제품들을 설치할 것입니다. 영업 직원들은 4월 3일에 새로운 장소에서 일하기 시작할 것입니다. 경영 및 회계팀들은 4월 15일에 그렇게 하기 시작할 것입니다. 편집 장치는 5월 1일에야 설치될 것이므로 제작팀이 마지막이 될 것입니다. 따라서, 그들의 이동은 5월 2일에 이루어질 것입니다.

181 편지의 주 목적은 무엇인가?
(A) 계약에 대한 변경을 요청하기 위해
(B) 약속 날짜를 확정하기 위해
(C) 수정된 계약서를 제시하기 위해
(D) 새롭게 고용된 임원을 환영하기 위해

182 North가에 있는 사무실에 대해 암시되는 것은?
(A) 정류장 근처에 있다.
(B) 1층에 식당이 있다.
(C) 지난달에 건설되었다.
(D) 소유주에 의해 내부가 완비되었다.

183 회람에서, 1문단 네 번째 줄의 단어 "positive"는 의미상 -와 가장 가깝다.
(A) 기꺼이 ~하는
(B) 힘껏
(C) 확실히
(D) 사이가 좋은

184 회람에 따르면, Ms. Simon의 회사는 이동으로부터 어떻게 이득을 얻을 것인가?
(A) 직원들이 더 많은 휴게실을 가질 것이다.
(B) 고객들에게 더 접근하기 쉬울 것이다.
(C) 납세 의무가 줄어들 것이다.
(D) 더 많은 업계 행사에 참여할 수 있을 것이다.

185 4월 1일에 무엇이 일어날 것 같은가?
(A) 회계팀 직원들이 이동될 것이다.
(B) 냉방 장치가 설치될 것이다.
(C) 영업 직원들이 새로운 사무실에서 일하기 시작할 것이다.
(D) 가구와 비품이 옮겨질 것이다.

186-190은 다음 이메일, 일정표, 공고에 관한 문제입니다.

수신 Elsie McDaniel <emd333@weblively.com>
발신 Wayne Sward <wsward@bluescreen.au>
제목 애들레이드로의 여행
날짜 8월 14일
첨부 Buxton 수업

Elsie께,

지난주에 당신은 9월에 있을 우리의 애들레이드로의 여행 동안 요리 수업을 함께 들으면 좋을 것 같다고 말했죠. 제가 이것에 대해 알아봤는데 반나절의 수업을 제공하는 요리 학원을 찾았어요. Buxton 요리 학원이라는 곳이고, 우리 호텔에서 아주 가까워요.

거기에는 우리가 들을 수 있는 네 개의 수업이 있는데, 일정을 고려해볼 때, 평일 수업을 들어야 할 것 같아요. 당신이 Joel Denton의 요리책을 가지고 있으며 그의 요리법을 매우 좋아한다는 것을 알고 있어요. 그가 수업 중 하나를 가르치므로, 우리는 그를 실제로 직접 만날 수 있을 거예요.

당신을 위해 Buxton 요리 학원의 일정표를 첨부할게요. 확인하고 다시 연락해주세요. 당신에게 다시 연락을 받는 대로 수업을 예약할게요.

Wayne 드림

Buxton 요리 학원 ⇨ 9월 수업 일정표

	오전 8시-오전 11시	오후 1시-오후 4시	오후 4시-오후 7시
화요일		해산물 탐험 (Sheila Ryer)	채소 사용법 (Martin Ames)
수요일	제빵 (Joel Denton)		채소 사용법 (Martin Ames)
목요일		해산물 탐험 (Sheila Ryer)	
금요일			소스 만들기 (Marie Pierre)
토요일	해산물 탐험 (Sheila Ryer)	제빵 (Joel Denton)	소스 만들기 (Marie Pierre)
일요일	채소 사용법 (Martin Ames)		제빵 (Joel Denton)

주의:
□ 월요일에는 수업이 열리지 않습니다.
□ 최소 수업 인원은 5명이며, 최대 수업 인원은 20명입니다.
□ 오전 수업은 Pinkston 식품 시장 방문을 포함하며, 그곳에서 설명이 주어질 것입니다.

Pinkston 식품 시장의 단체 방문객들은 주목해주십시오

Pinkston 식품 시장은 쇼핑객들과 둘러보는 분들을 모두 환영하지만, 최근 몇몇 노점상들은 통로를 막으면서 일반 손님들의 접근을 방해하는 5명 이상의 단체에 대해 불평을 호소했습니다. 따라서, 노점상들은 단체 견학

인솔자들과 요리 수업 강사들에게 그들의 단체를 노점에서 다음 노점으로 계속 이동하게 해달라고 요청했습니다. 단체에게 간단한 설명을 해주길 원하는 지도자들은 부디 저희의 푸드 코트에서 해주시길 요청드립니다. 그곳에는 자리가 많으며 다수의 방문객들을 다룰 수 있도록 설비가 갖춰져 있습니다. 또한, 참가자들은 푸드 코트에서 지역 특산물을 무료로 시식해볼 수 있습니다.

186 Mr. Sward는 왜 Ms. McDaniel에게 연락했는가?
(A) 활동에 대한 최신 정보를 알려주기 위해
(B) 대안이 되는 여행 경로를 제공하기 위해
(C) 요리 경력 수준에 대해 문의하기 위해
(D) 다른 도시로 이사하는 것의 이점을 열거하기 위해

187 Mr. Sward는 언제 Buxton 요리 학원의 수업에 참가할 것 같은가?
(A) 화요일에
(B) 수요일에
(C) 목요일에
(D) 금요일에

188 일정표에 따르면, Buxton 요리 학원에 대해 사실인 것은?
(A) 매달 특별 수업을 연다.
(B) 소스 만들기 수업은 주말에만 제공한다.
(C) 매주 하루는 문을 닫는다.
(D) 채소 관련 수업은 다수의 강사들이 가르친다.

189 공고에 따르면, 몇몇 노점상들이 무엇을 요청했는가?
(A) 시장 통로를 넓히는 것
(B) 식사 공간에 더 많은 좌석이 설치되는 것
(C) 단체들이 한 장소에 너무 오래 머무르지 않는 것
(D) 손님들이 신선한 제품들을 만지지 않는 것

190 Buxton 요리 학원의 오전 수업 수강생들에 대해 암시되는 것은?
(A) 견학 중 5명으로 이루어진 그룹으로 나누어질 것이다.
(B) 무료 식사를 제공받을 것이다.
(C) 개인 재료를 구매해야 할 것이다.
(D) Pinkston 시장에 있는 푸드 코트를 방문할 것이다.

191-195는 다음 기사, 광고, 이메일에 관한 문제입니다.

Westburg가 물 절약 계획을 발표하다
Augustus Brandt 작성

Westburg시 의회는 물 사용을 줄이기 위한 계획을 발표했다. 그 계획은 물 재활용 장치를 설치하는 사업체 및 주택에 보조금을 지급하는 것을 포함한다. "물 소비량을 줄이는 한 가지 주요 방법은 물을 재사용하는 것입니다."라고 시장 Arnell Lee가 말했다. 그녀는 시에서 물 재활용 장치를 설치하는 주택 소유자들에게 지불액 일부의 환급을 제공할 것이지만, 장치가 늦어도 8월까지는 가동되어야 한다고 설명했다.

대단히 낮은 강수량은 지난 10년 동안 도시의 심각한 물 부족으로 이어졌다. 그로 인해, 물 가격은 급등했고, Westburg의 모든 공공 장소를 환경 친화적으로 유지하는 비용은 이 도시로 하여금 지역 재산세를 인상하게 했다. 시는 물 공급 문제를 해결하기 위해 약 890만 달러의 예산을 세웠다.

Home-Vert사 물 재활용 장치로 돈을 절약하세요!

Home-Vert사 물 재활용 장치를 설치하여 고지서 요금을 낮추고, 물을 절약하는 것을 도우세요!

- 가정이나 회사에 장치를 설치해드립니다.
- 수도 요금을 줄이도록 도와드릴 수 있습니다.
- 위치에 따라, 1-3일 이내에 설치를 완료할 수 있습니다.

저희 직원들은 장치 작동 방식 및 관리 방법도 가르쳐드릴 것입니다. 설치를 위한 신청서를 작성하려면 www.home-vert.com을 방문하세요. 작성된 양식을 제출하시는 모든 분들은 저희의 많은 지역 협력업체 중 한 곳으로부터 50달러 상당의 상품권을 받으실 겁니다!

수신: Edward Bircher <edbirch@sspmail.com>
발신: Karl Hutcherson <karlh@home-vert.com>
제목: 회신: 설치 요청
첨부: Badevoucher
날짜: 7월 15일

Mr. Bircher께,

물 재활용 장치를 설치하기 위한 저희의 신청서를 작성해 주셔서 감사합니다. 17번지 Wilmont가, Westburg에 있는 귀하의 댁으로 다음 주 월요일 오전 10시 30분에 직원을 보내드리게 되어 매우 기쁩니다. 저 날짜와 시간이 귀하에게 적합한지 알려주십시오. 신청서를 작성해주신 것에 감사드리기 위해, Bade Hardware사의 50달러 상당의 상품권을 첨부했습니다. 상품권은 12월까지 유효합니다.

Karl Hutcherson 드림

191 기사는 왜 쓰였는가?
(A) 물 관련 도시 계획을 알리기 위해
(B) 물 장치의 업그레이드에 대한 세부 사항을 제공하기 위해
(C) 새로운 재활용 센터를 소개하기 위해
(D) 공공 요금 인상에 관한 정보를 제공하기 위해

192 기사에 따르면, 무엇이 물 가격이 상승하도록 했는가?
(A) 물 재활용 비용
(B) 인구 증가
(C) 낮은 강수량
(D) 시 보조금 삭감

193 Home-Vert사의 직원들은 고객들을 위해 무엇을 할 것인가?
(A) 정기적인 수질 검사 일정을 잡는다
(B) 설치 기술자를 추천한다
(C) 대금 청구서를 인쇄한다
(D) 장치 관리 절차를 설명한다

194 Mr. Bircher에 대해 암시되는 것은?
(A) 장치 설치 비용을 부분적으로 환급받을 것이다.
(B) 시 예산 위원회에서 일한다.
(C) 수도 요금의 납부 기한을 놓쳤다.
(D) Mr. Brandt로부터 Home-Vert사에 대해 알게 되었다.

195 Bade Hardware사에 대해 추론될 수 있는 것은?
(A) 물 정수 장치를 제공한다.
(B) Home-Vert사와 제휴하고 있다.
(C) 12월부터 상품권을 받아줄 것이다.
(D) 그것의 일부 제품을 할인하고 있다.

196-200은 다음 양식, 이메일, 웹페이지 광고에 관한 문제입니다.

www.websitewizards.com/contact_us/

Web Site Wizards사

홈 | 소개 | **서비스** | 포트폴리오 | 자주 묻는 질문 | 일자리

이름	Brady	이메일 주소	brady@ponderosaclothing.com
성	Grayson	전화 번호	555-3786
현재 웹사이트	www.ponderosaclothing.com	주소	31번지 North Pima로, 스코츠데일, 애리조나주

저희가 귀하를 위해 하길 바라는 일을 말씀해주세요.

저는 티셔츠를 전문으로 하는 Ponderosa Clothing이라는 가게를 운영합니다. 웹사이트를 가지고 있긴 하지만, 그것은 업체에 대한 간단한 설명, 가장 많이 팔리는 제품에 대한 몇 가지 정보, 그리고 약도만을 포함하고 있습니다. 저는 고객들이 물건을 주문하는데 그것을 사용할 수 있도록 하기 위해 사이트를 업그레이드 하고 싶습니다.

저희가 어떻게 연락하길 원하시나요?

■ 이메일로　　□ 전화로

다음 서비스 중 무엇을 찾고 계신가요?

■ 사이트 디자인　■ 인터넷 광고　□ 홍보 영상
■ 전자 상거래 구축　□ 로고 디자인　□ 이메일 마케팅
■ 웹사이트 트래픽 분석　□ 웹사이트 보안　□ 모바일 애플리케이션 설계

필요한 서비스를 선택하시면, 견적서를 보내드리겠습니다.

수신: Brady Grayson <brady@ponderosaclothing.com>
발신: Anita Hernandez <customerservice@websitewizards.com>
제목: 견적 요청
날짜: 8월 2일
첨부: 프로젝트 견적서

Mr. Grayson께,

Web Site Wizards사에 연락해주셔서 감사합니다. 저희 디자이너 중 한 명이 귀하의 현재 웹사이트를 검토하여 프로젝트 견적서를 작성했으며, 제가 그것을 첨부해두었습니다. www.ponderosaclothing.com을 디자인하고 전자 상거래 기능을 구축하기 위한 총비용은 1,250달러로 예상됩니다.

견적에 만족하신다면, 귀하가 마음에 드는 웹사이트들의 링크를 저희에게 보내주십시오. 저희는 이것들을 검토하여 유사한 디자인 요소를 귀하의 새로운 버전의 웹사이트에 사용하도록 할 것입니다. 또한, 귀하의 가게의 사진이 웹사이트의 메인 페이지에 나타날 것이므로 그것을 보내주셔야 할 것입니다.

마음을 바꾸셔서 홍보 영상이나 모바일 애플리케이션 개발과 같은 다른 서비스를 추가하시려는 경우, 저희 고객 서비스 부서가 견적을 다시 계산할 수 있도록 그들에게 이메일을 보내주십시오.

Anita Hernandez 드림.

Ponderosa Clothing: 스코츠데일에서의 완벽한 기억!

스코츠데일에서의 시간을 기억하기 위해 진정하고 특별한 기념품을 찾고 계신가요? 그렇다면 Ponderosa Clothing의 판매 상품들 중 몇 가지를 살펴보는 것은 어떠신가요? 많은 품목들이 미국 남서부에서 발견되는 예술적인 무늬를 특징으로 하며, 모든 옷에는 식물성 염료만이 사용됩니다. 저희는 수세기 전부터 내려오는 지역 전통을 보존하기 위해 이렇게 하는 것입니다.

Ponderosa Clothing의 제품은 스코츠데일에 있는 매장, 새로 디자인된 웹사이트, 그리고 다운로드할 수 있는 모바일 애플리케이션을 통해 구입하실 수 있습니다! www. ponderosaclothing.com을 방문하셔서 홍보 영상을 보시고, 가장 인기 있는 제품들을 둘러보시고, 구매하기 위해 새로운 쇼핑 카트 기능을 이용해보세요. 국내 배송은 모든 온라인 주문에 대해 무료이지만, 해외 구매에 대해서는 수수료가 있습니다.

196 양식에서, Ponderosa Clothing에 대해 추론될 수 있는 것은?
(A) 남서부에 몇몇 지점을 가지고 있다.
(B) 이전에 로고를 만들기 위해 Web Site Wizards사를 고용했다.
(C) 원래의 웹사이트는 물품 판매가 가능하지 않았다.
(D) 대부분의 주문을 해외 고객들에게 발송한다.

197 이메일의 하나의 목적은 무엇인가?
(A) 매출 증대를 위한 전략을 제안하기 위해
(B) 구매 가능한 제품의 카탈로그를 제공하기 위해
(C) 제품 가격에 대해 문의하기 위해
(D) 웹페이지를 다시 디자인하는 것을 논의하기 위해

198 Ponderosa Clothing의 새로운 웹사이트에 무엇이 나타날 것 같은가?
(A) 염료 제작 과정을 보여주는 도표
(B) North Pima로에 있는 가게의 사진
(C) 팔린 셔츠의 총 개수를 보여주는 계측기
(D) Mr. Grayson의 사진

199 Mr. Grayson은 무엇을 한 것 같은가?
(A) 프로젝트 견적을 거절했다
(B) 그의 가게에 많은 신상품을 추가했다
(C) 그의 웹사이트에서 지도를 삭제했다
(D) 고객 서비스 부서에 연락했다

200 Ponderosa Clothing의 제품에 대해 언급된 것은?
(A) 관광객을 위한 책자에 특집으로 실렸다.
(B) 전통적인 방법으로 만들어진다.
(C) 대량으로 구매되면 무료로 배송될 수 있다.
(D) 지역 예술가 단체에 의해 디자인되었다.

TEST 03 해석

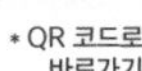

* 무료 해설은 해커스토익(Hackers.co.kr)에서 다운로드 받을 수 있습니다.

* QR 코드로 바로가기

PART 5

101 Ms. Ortega는 그녀의 투자 포트폴리오에 대한 도움을 구하기 위해 재정 자문가와 상담했다.

102 미성년자는 콘서트에 참석할 수 있지만 부모나 보호자를 동반해야 한다.

103 Ms. Conner는 동료의 판매 실적이 그녀의 것보다 더 좋았기 때문에 올해의 직원 상을 받지 못했다.

104 어제 세미나에 있던 모든 사람들은 그들의 전자기기를 무음 상태로 두라고 요청받았다.

105 Ruby Cakes의 직원은 개점을 기념하여 제과 제품의 무료 샘플을 나누어 주었다.

106 그것이 훌륭한 배움의 기회가 될 것이라고 생각했기 때문에, Ms. Koenig는 1년 동안 노르웨이로 전근 가는 것에 동의했다.

107 베스트셀러 소설 *Vaunted*를 각색한 영화의 대본은 책에서 직접 가져왔다.

108 *The Awakening*이라는 제목의 사진 전시회가 현재 Pulsen 미술관의 중앙 홀에서 선보여지고 있다.

109 지방 정부는 시내 교통량을 줄이기 위한 조치를 취할 것을 약속했다.

110 탄산음료 제조업체인 Fizz Life사는 작년에 Ricochet 콜라의 제조법을 변경한 후 고객들의 반발에 직면했다.

111 지점장으로서, Mr. Finley는 그의 직무 중에서 직원들의 갈등을 해결하는 것이 가장 어렵다고 생각한다.

112 Tessio사에 의해 제조된 정찬용 접시와 식기는 어떤 상황에서든 적합하다.

113 요즘 Villier 리조트는 방문객을 끌어들이기 위해 애쓰고 있지만, 그곳은 한때 매우 인기 있는 휴양지였다.

114 은행의 대출 담당 직원은 Ms. Demers가 그녀의 새 주택을 위해 얼마나 많은 돈을 빌릴 자격이 있을지 산정했다.

115 직원들의 약점을 해결하기 위해, 관리자는 그들에게 추가 교육을 제공하기로 결정했다.

116 회의 중 토론에서 의견을 말하는 것은 진취성을 보여주는 좋은 방법이다.

117 시내 사업주들은 오후 7시 이후로 가게를 열어두고 있는 것을 달가워하지 않아 왔다.

118 Ms. Diaz는 기차가 제때 도착하는 한 회의에 참석할 수 있을 것이다.

119 Mr. Miller는 학회 장소로 가는 명확한 길 안내를 받았음에도 불구하고, 그것을 그냥 지나쳐 갔다.

120 수영 대회의 참가자들은 네 개의 서로 다른 연령 부문으로 나눠질 것이다.

121 신입 사원들은 관련 경력을 가지고 있더라도 교육 과정에 참여하도록 요구된다.

122 내일 따로 비행기를 탈 Ms. Bateman을 제외한 모든 팀원들은 함께 이동할 것이다.

123 제안된 예산이 투자자들에게 받아들여질 수 있다면 사무실 확장이 승인될 것이다.

124 재택근무를 채택하는 회사는 직원들이 장소에 상관없이 일하도록 허용한다.

125 식당 주방장은 메뉴 기획을 포함하여, 여러 가지 업무에 대한 책임이 있다.

126 Ms. Turner는 기능을 시험해볼 수 있도록 프로그램의 무료 체험판을 다운로드했다.

127 편집자의 직무는 철자 및 문법 오류를 살피는 것과 정보가 사실에 비춰 정확한지 확인하는 것으로 이루어진다.

128 다음 그룹 과제에서, 학생들은 자유롭게 그들이 원하는 누구든지 함께 조를 짤 수 있다.

129 정치인들이 그들의 공약을 이행하지 않으면, 신용을 잃고 평판이 나빠진다.

130 직장에서 자주 불평하는 것은 전문가답지 못하며, 동료들도 불편하게 만든다.

PART 6

131-134는 다음 편지에 관한 문제입니다.

12월 8일

Ms. Ambrosio께,

여기 Dane County 리조트에서는 손님들께 제공하는 제품들에 대해 아주 선별적입니다. 그런데, 저희는 귀하께서 보내주신 치약 샘플에 놀랐습니다. **131** 그것은 상쾌한 향을 가지고 있는 것에 더하여, 저희가 시험해본 여러 다른 브랜드의 것들보다 잇몸에 더 순했습니다. **132** 따라서, 저희는 귀하의 치약을 저희 호텔의 새로운 세면용품 패키지에 포함하기로 결정했습니다. 이 결정은 그것이 저희의 모든 손님들께 매일 제공될 것임을 의미합니다. **133** 먼저, 1월에 쓸 500개를 보내주시면 좋겠습니다. **134** 이 수량에 대한 견적을 최대한 빨리 보내주십시오. 저희는 앞으로 이 주문을 반복할 생각이므로, 할인이 적용될 수 있는지도 알고 싶습니다.

Teddy Lawrence 드림
총지배인
Dane County 리조트

135-138은 다음 안내문에 관한 문제입니다.

Swansea Ferries사
승객분들을 위한 권고

135 Swansea 터미널에 도착하시면, 차량 수속 부스로 향하는 표지판을 따라가십시오. 이곳에서, 관리자가 여러분의 예약 번호를 확인할 것이며, 여러분은 여객선 내에서 주차할 구역이 표시된 탑승 카드를 받으실 것입니다. **136** 국제 목적지로 여행 중이시라면, 이때 여권도 제시하셔야 할 것입니다. 하지만, 국내로 여행 중이시라면, 그 대신 운전 면허증을 보여달라고 요청받으실 것입니다. 탑승 시간 전에, 알림이 있을 것입니다. **137** 이는 출발 30분 전쯤에 일어날 것입니다. **138** 여러분은 탑승 통로로 이동하셔야 하며, 그곳에서 직원들이 여러분의 차량을 여객선 위로 인도하는 것을 도와드릴 것입니다.

139-142는 다음 기사에 관한 문제입니다.

젊은 아프리카 디자이너가 찬사를 받다

Futuristic Furniture지

Rhonda Thiessen 작성

올해의 Basel 실내 장식 박람회를 앞둔 몇 주 동안, 경험이 풍부한 디자이너들이 대부분의 언론의 주목을 받았다. **139** 그러나 행사가 시작되자, 거의 알려지지 않은 디자이너인 Harry Mashaba에게로 갑자기 주목이 옮겨졌다. 그는 중앙 홀에 있는 공간에서 그의 작품들을 전시하고 있었다. **140** 참석한 평론가들은 그것들이 전시되어 있는 다른 그 어떤 것들과도 다르다는 데 동의했다.

"Mr. Mashaba의 작품은 매우 독특합니다. 그는 전통적인 남아프리카 가구가 요즘 사람들에게 매력적이고 편리하도록 현대화해냈습니다."라고 박람회

주최자인 Lara Dahn이 말했다. **141** "그의 작품들은 현대적인 거실에 완벽하게 들어맞습니다."

142 박람회에서의 성공 덕분에, Mr. Mashaba는 스위스 가구 제조업체인 Rulesten사에서 식탁 세트를 디자인하도록 고용되었다. 그것은 올가을에 유럽에서 출시될 것이다.

143-146은 다음 광고에 관한 문제입니다.

Avenuu를 소개하며, 이는 세상에서 최고의 스트리밍 서비스입니다. 수백 개의 인기 있는 TV 시리즈, 영화, 어린이 쇼, 그리고 라이브 콘서트를 보세요. **143** 스마트폰, 태블릿, 그리고 컴퓨터를 포함한 모든 장치에서 고품질로 그것들을 스트림 해보세요. **144** Avenuu는 또한 당신의 내역을 바탕으로 추천을 제공합니다. 당신이 그것을 더 많이 사용할수록, 저희는 당신이 좋아하는 것을 더 많이 알게 됩니다. **145** 그러므로, 메뉴를 스크롤하는 것과 당신의 시간을 낭비하는 것을 멈추세요. 오늘 가입하시고 고품질의 콘텐츠를 시청해보세요.

146 당신은 당신이 어떻게 구독하기를 원하는지 선택할 수도 있습니다. 한 달에 5.99달러로 광고가 있는 서비스를 써보거나, 한 달에 10.99달러로 광고가 없는 것을 시도해 보세요. 오늘 www.avenuu.com을 방문하세요!

PART 7

147-148은 다음 공고에 관한 문제입니다.

Wilson 쇼핑몰의 직원 출입구가 지난주 태풍에 의해 파손되었으며 8월 2일에 수리될 것입니다. 쇼핑몰 직원들은 건물 남쪽에 있는 비상구를 이용하여 들어올 수 있습니다. 여러분의 신분 확인 명찰은 이 출입구에 대한 접근 권한을 부여하기 위해 자동적으로 보안 시스템에서 업데이트될 것입니다. 평소에 하듯이 이 출입구에 명찰을 대십시오. 하지만, 8월 2일 이후에는 이곳에서 쇼핑몰로 출입할 수 없을 것임을 유의하십시오.

147 공고의 이유는 무엇인가?
(A) 건설 프로젝트의 상황을 알리기 위해
(B) 직원들에게 연장된 휴일 영업 시간에 대해 상기시키기 위해
(C) 비상사태에 대한 지침을 제공하기 위해
(D) 직원들을 대상으로 한 일시적인 변경을 알리기 위해

148 Wilson 쇼핑몰에 대해 암시되는 것은?
(A) 보통 통제되는 출구가 있다.
(B) 직원들이 항상 명찰을 착용하도록 요구한다.
(C) 경비원을 더 고용하고 있다.
(D) 보수를 위해 문을 닫을 것이다.

149-150은 다음 이메일에 관한 문제입니다.

수신: 전 직원
발신: Eun-jung Cho
날짜: 11월 3일
제목: Cornerstone Solutions사 거래

동료들께,

우리는 올해의 목표 중 하나를 달성하는 중입니다. 다음 주에 Cornerstone Solutions사의 고위 관리들이 세부 사항에 대해 논의하고, 바라건대, 계약을 맺기 위해 방문할 것입니다. 그들이 우리와 계약하면, 우리는 수백만 달러의 거래를 보유하게 될 것입니다. 이는 더 많은 책무와 함께 증가된 수익을 의미할 것입니다. 우리는 추가 임시 직원을 고용하거나 현재 직원들의 업무를 확장해야 할 것입니다. 추가 세부 사항들은 내일 예정된 회의에서 논의될 것입니다. 이 새로운 거래를 다루는 데 관심이 있다면, 그 직무가 포함할 것에 대한 예비 개요를 보내드릴 수 있도록 제게 이메일을 보내주십시오. 그렇게 하면, 여러분은 내일 회의 전까지 그 정보를 훑어보실 수 있을 겁니다.

감사합니다.
Eun-jung Cho 드림
관리자, Cho & Associates사

149 Cornerstone Solutions사에 대해 언급된 것은?
(A) 몇몇 협상에서 손을 뗄 것으로 예상된다.
(B) 여분의 자금을 어떻게 쓸지 정하려고 하는 중이다.
(C) Cho & Associates사의 서비스를 확보하는 데 동의할지도 모른다.
(D) 다른 회사를 매입하는 것을 제안했다.

150 Ms. Cho는 그녀의 직원들에게 무엇을 해달라고 요청하는가?
(A) 계약서에 몇 가지 조항을 추가한다
(B) 직무의 세부 사항을 얻기 위해 그녀에게 연락한다
(C) 동료를 평가한다
(D) 회의를 위한 공간을 준비한다

151-152는 다음 메시지 대화문에 관한 문제입니다.

Farrah Keller [오전 10시 43분]
오늘 밤 행사에 관해 Janice Catering과 방금 통화했어요. 그들은 다른 고객 때문에 늦어지고 있어요. 그들은 오후 6시 30분이 되어서야 음식을 배달할 수 있어요.

Teddy Park [오전 10시 45분]
아, 하지만 우리는 오후 6시에 에피타이저를 제공하기 시작하기로 되어 있어요.

Farrah Keller [오전 10시 46분]
우리가 직접 음식을 가지러 가는 건 어떤가요?

Teddy Park [오전 10시 47분]
현명하네요! 그것이 가능한지 그들에게 물어봐 줄 수 있나요?

Farrah Keller [오전 10시 49분]
제가 그것을 바로 할게요. 저는 또한 우리의 계약서에 따라 가격 인하를 요청할 수 있어요.

Teddy Park [오전 10시 51분]
좋아요. 그들이 뭐라고 하는지 저에게 알려주세요. 그동안에, 저는 회사의 트럭을 준비할게요.

151 오전 10시 47분에, Mr. Park가 "Smart"라고 썼을 때 그가 의도한 것 같은 것은?
(A) 고객에게 알리는 것이 현명할 것이라고 생각한다.
(B) 그의 동료의 아이디어에 감명을 받았다.
(C) 음식 제공업체가 문제를 해결할 수 있다고 믿는다.
(D) 그녀가 직원을 고용한 것이 기쁘다.

152 Janice Catering에 대해 암시된 것은?
(A) 다양한 지역 음식을 전문으로 한다.
(B) 이전에 Mr. Park에 의해 고용된 적이 있다.
(C) 계약서에서 할인에 대해 언급한다.
(D) 한 대의 음식 배달 트럭만 운영한다.

153-154는 다음 공고에 관한 문제입니다.

Athens 대학 행사 목록

Artist Spotlight

지난 몇 번의 Artist Spotlight 행사는 뛰어난 화가들을 출연시켰지만, 이번 달의 초대 손님은 Grant Marek이라는 독학한 만화 영화 제작자가 될 것입니다. 그는 그의 최신 영화인 *Coloratura*를 보여줄 것이며, 이것은 세계 만화 영화 축제에서 상영되었습니다. *Georgia Sentinel*지는 Mr. Marek의 최신 영화를 "정신이 고양되며 훌륭한 장면과 음향의 상호 작용"이라고

묘사했습니다. 영화 상영은 실황 내레이터와 음향 효과, 그리고 Wallace Herbert교수가 이끄는 4인조 음악가들을 포함할 것입니다. 상영 후, 관객들은 Mr. Marek에게 그의 영화에 관해 질문할 기회를 가질 것입니다. 그는 상영 하루 뒤인 2월 12일 금요일 오후 7시에 Watkins 강당에서의 공개 토론회에도 참여할 것입니다.

입장료: 무료이며 일반인에게 개방됨
일시: 2월 11일 목요일, 오후 6시 30분
장소: Charles 극장

153 Athens 대학의 Artist Spotlight에 대해 암시되는 것은?
(A) 반복되어 발생하는 행사이다.
(B) 미술 전시회를 포함한다.
(C) 오직 음악가들만을 출연시킨다.
(D) 텔레비전 방송을 위해 녹화될 것이다.

154 Mr. Marek에 대해 언급되지 않은 것은?
(A) Athens 대학에서 하나 이상의 활동에 참여할 것이다.
(B) 만화 영화에 대한 정식 교육을 받지 않았다.
(C) Charles 극장에서 리허설할 것이다.
(D) 그의 작품이 국제 영화 축제에서 상영되었다.

155-157은 다음 광고에 관한 문제입니다.

Palm Creek 관광

캘리포니아의 어떤 방문도 12개의 국립공원들 중 하나를 방문하지 않고는 완성되지 않습니다. 매년, 전 세계의 수백만 명의 방문객들이 이 주의 놀라운 자연 풍경과 광범위한 야외 활동을 즐기기 위해 옵니다. — [1] —.

Palm Creek 관광은 캘리포니아 국립공원의 완벽하게 맞춤형인 관광을 계획하는 것을 전문으로 합니다. 저희는 1일 패키지부터 한 곳 이상의 장소로의 며칠 간의 여행까지 모든 것을 제공합니다. — [2] —. 당신은 텐트, 별 다섯 개짜리 리조트, 또는 그 사이에 있는 무엇에서든 잠을 잘 수 있습니다. 만약 당신이 어떤 활동에 대한 가이드가 필요하다면, 저희는 추가 비용으로 당신을 위해 그것을 준비할 수 있습니다. 저희의 다국어를 하는 가이드들은 당신과 당신의 동반자들이 편안함을 느끼도록 도울 수 있고 당신의 여행이 원활하게 진행되도록 보장할 수 있습니다. — [3] —.

관광 패키지는 식사와 교통수단을 포함한 1일 여행에 1인당 150달러부터 시작합니다. 모든 패키지는 최소 네 명이 필요합니다. — [4] —. 오늘 555-8012로 Palm Creek 관광에 전화하거나, www.palmcreektours.com을 방문하세요.

155 관광 패키지에 대해 암시되는 것은?
(A) 제한된 시간 동안 제공되고 있다.
(B) 관광 가이드들을 포함하지 않는다.
(C) 몇 달 전에 예약되어야 한다.
(D) 여섯 명보다 적게 예약될 수 없다.

156 Palm Creek 관광에 대해 사실인 것은?
(A) 뛰어난 서비스로 인정받았다.
(B) 오로지 외국인 방문객들만 응대한다.
(C) 여러 언어로 서비스를 제공한다.
(D) 캘리포니아 전역에 리조트를 운영한다.

157 [1], [2], [3], [4]로 표시된 위치 중, 다음 문장이 들어갈 곳으로 가장 적절한 것은?

"저희는 이 규정에 어떠한 예외도 만들 수 없습니다."

(A) [1]
(B) [2]
(C) [3]
(D) [4]

158-160은 다음 브로슈어에 관한 문제입니다.

Biz-Equip 수리 서비스

고장 나거나 제대로 기능하지 못하는 사무 장비를 교체하는 비용은 비쌀 수 있습니다! 새로운 프린터, 복사기, 영사기, 컴퓨터, 또는 다른 사무기기를 사러 뛰어나가기 전에, Biz-Equip 수리 서비스에 연락하세요!

장비 수리

저희에게는 귀하의 기계를 점검하기 위해 방문할 수 있는 숙련된 전문가 집단이 있습니다. 만약 귀하의 물품을 현장에서 수리하는 것이 가능하다면, 그렇게 할 것입니다. 주요한 수리가 필요하다면, 귀하의 장비는 저희 서비스 센터로 가져와져서, 정상적으로 잘 작동하는 상태로 귀하께 돌려보내질 것입니다. 대다수 종류의 수리는 48시간 이내로 완료됩니다!

장비 유지보수

Biz-Equip은 회사 및 기타 기관에 정기적인 유지보수 서비스도 제공합니다. 저희 기술자들은 모든 것이 제대로 작동하고 있는지 확실히 하기 위해 귀하의 장비에 대해 주 1회의 점검을 실시할 수 있습니다.

장비 카트리지 제공

게다가, Biz-Equip은 대부분의 사무용 프린터와 복사기에 맞는 엄선된 잉크 및 토너 카트리지를 보유하고 있습니다. 가격은 브랜드와 종류에 따라 다릅니다. 세부 사항을 위해서는, www.bizequiprepairservices.com/products를 방문하십시오.

기술자와 예약을 잡으시려면, 저희의 수신자 부담 번호인 1-800-555-9288로 전화하십시오. 귀하의 사무실이나 사업소의 주소를 알려주시면, 최대한 빨리 사람을 보내드리겠습니다.

158 Biz-Equip에 대해 언급되지 않은 것은?
(A) 고객들에게 정기적인 서비스를 제공한다.
(B) 현장 장비 점검을 제공한다.
(C) 사무기기 라인을 판매한다.
(D) 수리를 위한 센터를 운영한다.

159 브로슈어에 따르면, 고객들은 Biz-Equip의 웹사이트에서 무엇을 할 수 있는가?
(A) 대금 청구서를 인쇄한다
(B) 프린터 카트리지 비용을 지불한다
(C) 상품에 대한 가격 정보를 찾는다
(D) 장비 업그레이드를 요청한다

160 Biz-Equip은 기술자의 방문을 주선하기 위해 어떤 정보를 요구하는가?
(A) 고객 계정번호
(B) 사무실 위치
(C) 구매 증명서
(D) 품질 보증서 카드에 적힌 날짜

161-164는 다음 기사에 관한 문제입니다.

벽화가 시내 중심부에 활기와 색채를 가져오다

Charlotte시, 10월 19일—지난 6월에 Charlotte시가 시내 중심부에서 벽화 프로그램을 시작했을 때, 그 발상은 지역을 재활성화하고 활기를 주기 위한 것이었다. 예술적인 대형 그림들이 건물 벽에 직접 그려지고 있으며 완성에 가까워지고 있다. — [1] —. 계획은 모든 벽화가 두 달 이내에 완성될 것을 요한다. 이 프로젝트는 도심을 야외 미술관으로 탈바꿈시켰으며, 그 모든 예술품을 보존하는 것이 중요해질 것이다. Axon 예술단이 이 프로젝트를 맡고 있으며, 또한 벽화를 관리하도록 다음 5년 동안 계약되어 있을 것이다. — [2] —.

Axon 예술단은 지난 20년 동안 지역 학교 및 시민 문화회관에서 미술 워크숍을 진행해왔기 때문에 이 프로젝트를 수행하도록 선정되었다. — [3] —. 지난봄 Charlotte시의 기획 위원회에 의해 처음 제안 받았을 때, 그 단체는 그것을 몹시 받아들이고 싶어 했다. "많은 지역 예술가들이 이 프로젝트에 들떠 있습니다."라고 Axon 예술단의 공동 창립자 Matthew Stewart는 말했다. "이것은 그들 중 다수에게 평생 단 한 번뿐인 기회입니다." 초기 자금은 지역 사회 기획 재단에 의해 제공된 5만 달러의 보조금이었다. — [4] —. 그 후 얼마 되지 않아서 Charlotte시 관광청이 그 기부금에 필적했다. "이제 사람들이 우리 도시를 방문하러 오면, 그들은 이곳이 긍정과 영감으로 가득 차 있는 것을 볼 것이고, 다시 방문하고 싶어 할 것입니다."라고 관광청장 Jill Myers는 말했다.

161 Charlotte시는 왜 벽화 프로그램을 시행했는가?
(A) 지역 예술가들을 장려하기 위해
(B) 시내 쇼핑객들을 더 많이 끌어들이기 위해
(C) 도시의 일부를 재활성화하기 위해
(D) 학생들에게 회화를 가르치기 위해

162 Axon 예술단에 대해 암시되는 것은?
(A) 도시를 위해 5년 동안 일할 것이다.
(B) 지역 미술관을 운영한다.
(C) 대중에게 벽화에 대한 의견을 요청했다.
(D) 시민 문화회관에 사무실이 있다.

163 Charlotte시 관광청에 대해 추론될 수 있는 것은?
(A) 공공 기금 모금 행사를 개최하고 있다.
(B) 예술에 관한 정보 캠페인을 시작했다.
(C) 지역 사회 기획 재단으로부터 자금을 요청했다.
(D) 프로젝트를 위해 약 5만 달러를 제공했다.

164 [1], [2], [3], [4]로 표시된 위치 중, 다음 문장이 들어갈 곳으로 가장 적절한 것은?
"이는 필요에 따라 그것들을 청소하는 것과 손보는 것을 포함할 것이다."
(A) [1]
(B) [2]
(C) [3]
(D) [4]

165-167은 다음 이메일에 관한 문제입니다.

수신 전 직원 <staff@portlandvalleyjournal.com>
발신 Isaac Dyer <isdyer@portlandvalleyjournal.com>
제목 1월호
날짜 12월 2일

안녕하세요, 여러분.

우리의 1월호는 그해의 나머지 잡지에 대한 성격을 정해주기 때문에 언제나 특별합니다. 저는 이미 기사 및 특집의 레이아웃을 작업하기 시작했습니다. 선임 기자들과 저는 내년에 우리 직원들과 독자들 간에 더 많은 소통이 있으면 좋을 것 같다는 데 동의했습니다. 그래서, 1월호 표지는 독자들과 직원들 모두가 참여할 수 있는 사진 대회를 통해 결정될 것입니다. 저는 그것과 관련하여 이미 지역 신문사에 보도 자료를 보냈습니다. 오늘까지 우리 웹사이트에 대회 규정 및 지침도 게시할 것입니다.

말했듯이, 대회는 직원들에게 열려 있습니다. 유감스럽게도, 우리 사진작가들은 불공평한 이점을 가지게 될 것이므로 그들에게는 이것이 해당되지 않습니다. 하지만, 저는 수석 사진작가인 Brianna Griffin과 이야기했으며, 우리는 그들이 대회의 심사위원으로 기여할 수 있다고 결정했습니다. 우승한 사진이 표지에 게재되는 것 외에 다른 상품은 없습니다.

가능하다면 모두가 참여하기를 바랍니다. 12월 10일까지 여러분의 제출물을 제게 이메일로 보내주십시오. 우승자는 12월 20일에 발표될 것입니다.

행운을 빕니다!
Isaac Dyer, 편집장
*Portland Valley Journal*지

165 Mr. Dyer는 왜 이메일을 보냈는가?
(A) 새로운 출판 지침을 알리기 위해
(B) 팀원에게 보도 자료를 작성해달라고 요청하기 위해
(C) 직원들에게 사진을 보내라고 장려하기 위해
(D) 몇몇 표지 작품에 대한 의견을 요청하기 위해

166 이메일에 따르면, Mr. Dyer가 아직 하지 않은 것은?
(A) 신문사에 연락했다
(B) 온라인에 규칙을 게시했다
(C) 기자들과 상의했다
(D) 레이아웃을 작업했다

167 Ms. Griffin에 대해 암시되는 것은?
(A) 최근에 승진했다.
(B) 대회를 심사하는 것을 도울 것이다.
(C) Mr. Dyer의 사무실 근처에 앉는다.
(D) 여러 잡지사에서 일한다.

168-171은 다음 온라인 채팅 대화문에 관한 문제입니다.

Lenny Vogler 오전 11시 57분
안녕하세요, 여러분. 우리의 온라인 마케팅이 효과가 없는 것이 걱정스럽네요. 우리가 온라인에서의 지명도를 향상할 방법이 있을까요?

Dorothy Hughes 오전 11시 57분
소셜 미디어 페이지를 확장하는 게 어때요?

Lenny Vogler 오전 11시 58분
우리의 소셜 미디어 페이지는 그곳에 고객들이 볼 수 있는 상품 사진들을 그다지 잘 마련해두지 못했어요. 사진들은 우리 제품 라인을 홍보하는 데 큰 도움이 돼요.

Burl Seaver 오전 11시 58분
어쩌면 Momento-Pic 계정을 개설해야 하겠네요. 그건 사람들이 사진을 공유하고 그것에 대한 의견을 말하기 위해 사용하는 사진 공유 애플리케이션이에요. 그건 우리의 소셜 미디어 페이지로 가는 링크도 게시하게 해줄 거예요.

Anya Pearson 오전 11시 59분
그것을 들어본 적이 있어요. 하지만 사업체들은 요금을 내야 해요.

Lenny Vogler 오전 11시 59분
한 달 요금이 적정하다면, 우리의 마케팅 예산을 넘지 않을 거예요. 진행하고 계정을 만들까요?

Burl Seaver 오후 12시
그러기 전에 다른 유명한 사진 공유 애플리케이션도 조사해보는 게 좋을 것 같아요.

Dorothy Hughes 오후 12시 1분
동의해요. Momento-Pic보다 훨씬 더 많은 이용자를 보유하고 있는 다른 사진 공유 프로그램들도 있어요.

Lenny Vogler 오후 12시 2분
알겠어요. 음, 가입하는 것이 이득이 될 수 있는 애플리케이션 목록을 여러분 중 한 명이 제시해줄 수 있나요? 그것들의 요금과 기능도 알아봐 주세요.

Anya Pearson 오후 12시 3분
제가 지금 바로 그걸 처리할 수 있어요. 오늘 오후에 그 정보를 이메일로 보내드릴게요.

168 Mr. Vogler는 무엇에 대해 걱정하는가?
(A) 잠재 고객들을 상품 진열실로 끌어들이는 것
(B) 인터넷에서 상품에 대한 대중의 인식을 높이는 것
(C) 컴퓨터 프로그램의 효율성을 개선하는 것
(D) 사진 공유 애플리케이션을 출시하는 것

169 Momento-Pic에 대해 암시되는 것은?
(A) 체험 기간 동안 무료로 사용될 수 있다.
(B) 사업체가 가입하는 것에 요금을 청구한다.
(C) 경쟁업체보다 더 많은 이용자를 보유하고 있다.
(D) 사용자들이 그들의 사진을 편집할 수 있게 한다.

170 사람들은 어느 부서에서 일하는 것 같은가?
(A) 마케팅
(B) 제품 개발
(C) 고객 지원
(D) 정보 기술

171 오후 12시 1분에, Ms. Hughes가 "I agree"라고 썼을 때 그녀가 의도한 것은?
(A) 현재의 이용자들에게 연락하고 싶어 한다.
(B) 소셜 네트워크 페이지를 확장하기를 바란다.
(C) 팀이 다른 프로그램들을 알아봐야 한다고 생각한다.
(D) Momento-Pic에서 계정을 개설하기를 바란다.

172-175는 다음 안내문에 관한 문제입니다.

새로운 기술을 배우거나 새로운 취미를 시작하는 것을 생각하고 계신가요? 5월 11일에 시작되는 주부터 Anderson 시민 문화회관에 무슨 일이 일어나는지 확인해보세요!

화려한 제빵 행사
월요일마다, 오후 6-8시, 수업당 35달러
이 도시의 파티시에 중 한 명으로부터 간단한 제과 제품을 만드는 방법에 대해 알아보세요. 매주, 서로 다른 초대 선생님과 함께 새로운 요리법을 배웁니다. 모든 재료가 제공됩니다.

성인들을 위한 피아노
화요일마다, 오후 5-6시, 수업당 15달러
클래식 피아니스트 Susan Dickinson에게서 피아노 연주에 대한 기초를 배우세요. 어떠한 경험도 필수적이지 않습니다. 어떠한 도구도 필요하지 않습니다.

단편 소설 쓰기
수요일마다, 오후 7-9시, 수업당 25달러
책을 출간한 작가 William Davis와 여러분의 작문 실력을 개발하세요. 이 매력 있는 주간 세미나는 초보 작가들을 위해 의도되었습니다. 펜과 종이, 또는 노트북 컴퓨터를 가져오세요.

뜨개질 입문
목요일마다, 오후 5시 30분-7시, 수업당 30달러
Paula Booker가 가르치는 이 수공예 수업에서 장갑, 목도리, 양말, 그리고 다른 많은 물건을 만들어보세요. 실과 장비는 제공됩니다. 하지만, 특정 색깔의 실로 뜨개질하고 싶으시다면, 자유롭게 여러분의 것을 가져오세요.

172 안내문의 목적은 무엇인가?
(A) 시설의 새로운 영업시간을 알리기 위해
(B) 수제 제품들에 대해 설명하기 위해
(C) 조기 등록 할인을 제공하기 위해
(D) 새로운 수업들에 대한 정보를 제공하기 위해

173 어느 수업에 여러 명의 강사가 있을 것인가?
(A) 화려한 제빵 행사
(B) 성인들을 위한 피아노
(C) 단편 소설 쓰기
(D) 뜨개질 입문

174 Mr. Davis에 대해 언급된 것은?
(A) 출판하는 것에 대해 조언을 제공할 것이다.
(B) 경험이 부족한 작가들을 가르칠 것이다.
(C) 목요일마다 수업을 열 것이다.
(D) 필기도구를 제공할 것이다.

175 Anderson 시민 문화회관에 대해 언급된 것은?
(A) 수공예품을 판매해 자금을 마련한다.
(B) 강사들은 자원봉사로 일한다.
(C) 각 수업은 2시간 동안 지속된다.
(D) 모든 수업은 매주 한 번 열린다.

176-180은 다음 기사와 회람에 관한 문제입니다.

Colfer사의 과일 주스 매출이 줄어들다

음료 제조업체 Colfer사는 올해 7월과 9월 사이에 과일 주스 매출에서의 12퍼센트 감소를 겪었다. 그 회사의 대변인인 Fred Hines에 따르면, 다양한 요인들이 제품 매출 감소의 원인이 되었는데, 이 제품들은 일반적으로 회사의 연간 수익 중 50만 달러 이상을 차지한다. "여름이 평소만큼 덥지 않았기 때문에, 더 적은 사람들이 열을 식히기 위해 저희 주스를 구매했습니다."라고 그는 말했다. "또한, 재료비 상승으로 인해 Colfer사의 주스 음료 중 일부의 가격이 올랐습니다. 예를 들어, 포도의 가격이 올라서, 포도 맛 음료의 제조비도 올랐습니다."라고 Mr. Hines는 설명했다.

경쟁의 심화 또한 Colfer사의 매출에 영향을 미쳤다. Colfer사와 다른 대기업들은 더 건강한 대체물을 제공하는 소규모 브랜드들에게 입지를 뺏기고 있다. 실제로, 조사 자료는 당이 첨가되지 않은 천연 주스의 인기가 계속해서 상승하고 있는 것을 보여주었다. 변화하는 소비자 선호에 대처하기 위해, Colfer사는 건강한 식음료를 생산하는 다수의 급성장하는 기업들과 제휴를 맺기 시작했다. 또한 오랫동안 그것의 과일 주스가 포장되어 온 파란색 병을 새롭게 디자인된 빨간색 병으로 교체했다. 회사는 이것이 브랜드 이미지를 바꾸는 데 도움이 될 것이라고 생각한다.

수신: Colfer사 이사회
발신: Carl Bryant, 회장, Colfer사
제목: 변화
날짜: 11월 30일

지난 몇 달이 힘겨웠다는 것을 알고 있습니다만, 저는 우리가 정상으로 돌아올 것이라고 확신합니다. Friendly Farm 식품사 및 Natgreen Cereals사와의 제휴는 이런 점에서 도움을 주었지만, 저는 Colfer사가 근본적으로는 시대에 맞춰 변화해야 할 것이라고 생각합니다. 그러므로, 이번 주 회의에서, 저는 새로운 맛을 개발하는 것과 우리 제품의 가격폭을 확장하는 것에 대해 논의하고 싶습니다. 또한, 새로운 색상과 디자인이 소비자들에게 인기가 없었기 때문에 원래의 주스 병을 다시 도입해야 한다고 생각합니다. 독창적인 고급 제품을 제공하는 데 주력합시다. 그것이 우리가 내년의 목표를 달성할 방법입니다.

176 기사의 주 목적은 무엇인가?
(A) 소비자 선호가 변하고 있는 이유를 설명하기 위해
(B) 새로운 제조업체를 소개하기 위해
(C) 새로운 제품 라인의 출시를 알리기 위해
(D) 제품 매출의 감소를 알리기 위해

177 기사에서 무슨 문제가 언급되는가?
(A) 필수 재료의 부족
(B) 유통비의 상승
(C) 평소보다 더 시원한 여름
(D) 경쟁사의 물건 가격 하락

178 Colfer사에 대해 언급된 것은?
(A) 대부분의 제품을 포도로 만든다.
(B) 건강식품 업체들과 제휴했다.
(C) 전 세계에 공장을 운영한다.
(D) 몇 년간 계속해서 손해를 봤다.

179 Mr. Bryant는 Colfer사가 무엇을 해야 한다고 생각하는가?
(A) 몇몇 제품에 파란색 용기를 사용한다
(B) 덜 비싼 지역 공급업체를 찾는다
(C) 품질 관리 과정을 도입한다
(D) 다른 회사들과 더 많이 협력한다

180 회람에서, 1문단 아홉 번째 줄의 단어 "meet"은 의미상 -와 가장 가깝다.
(A) 소개하다
(B) 마주치다
(C) 달성하다
(D) 조정하다

181-185는 다음 이메일과 양식에 관한 문제입니다.

수신: George Billings <g.billings@southernbakedgoods.com>
발신: Lane Emerson <l.emerson@gourmetdessert.com>
제목: 회신: 고급 디저트 박람회
날짜: 10월 27일

Mr. Billings께,

동종 행사 중에서 가장 크고 성공적이라는 명성을 얻은 제16회 고급 디저트 박람회에서 케이크를 판매하는 것에 보여주신 관심에 감사드립니다. 질문에 답변드리자면, 만약 귀하께서 캐나다 특별 식품 협회(CSFA)의 회원이 아니시라면 공간 대여비는 크기에 상관없이 55달러입니다. 회원들에게는 45달러입니다. 또한, 모든 판매자는 무료 컴퓨터 사용 및 판매업체들을 잠재 고객들에게 소개하는 저희의 특별 판매업체 프로그램에 대한 이용을 누리실 수 있습니다.

위 가격은 우선 예약에 대한 것이며 11월 30일까지 접수되는 지원 및 납부에만 적용된다는 것을 유념해주십시오. 12월에, 부스 비용은 회원들에게는 65달러로, 비회원들에게는 75달러로 오릅니다.

Lane Emerson 드림
행사 책임자

제16회 고급 디저트 박람회
1월 4일부터 8일 | 밴쿠버, 캐나다

등록 세부 사항
사업체: Southern 제과점
대표자 성명: George Billings
전화번호: 555-5497
이메일: g.billings@southernbakedgoods.com

☒ CSFA 회원이라면 여기에 표시하십시오

부스 선호 사항
☐ 스탠다드 ☐ 더블 ☒ 코너
- 우선 예약하신 분들에 한해서만 부스 선호 사항이 보장된다는 것을 유념하십시오. 모든 부스는 테이블, 의자, 그리고 표지판을 포함합니다.

선택 포함 사항:
☐ 출품업체 점심식사 (1월 8일)
☒ 특별 판매업체 프로그램

동봉된 지불금: 45.00달러
등록일: 11월 16일
- 모든 수표는 고급 디저트 박람회를 수취인으로 해야 합니다.

181 Ms. Emerson은 왜 이메일을 썼는가?
(A) 동료를 행사에 초대하기 위해
(B) 판매업체의 문의에 답변하기 위해
(C) 주문 절차를 설명하기 위해
(D) 서비스 비용 납부를 요청하기 위해

182 이메일에서, 1문단 두 번째 줄의 단어 "distinction"은 의미상 -와 가장 가깝다.
(A) 차이
(B) 분할
(C) 만족
(D) 명성

183 이메일에 따르면, 부스 비용에 대해 사실인 것은?
(A) 공간의 크기에 영향을 받지 않는다.
(B) 협회 가입비를 포함한다.
(C) 참가자 수에 따라 달라진다.
(D) 작년부터 인상되었다.

184 Southern 제과점은 행사에서 무엇을 할 수 있는가?
(A) 추가 테이블과 의자를 요청한다
(B) 제품 시연을 연다
(C) 공급업체에서 상품을 구매한다
(D) 잠재 고객들을 만난다

185 Mr. Billings에 대해 암시되는 것은?
(A) CSFA 회원권을 갱신하고 싶어 한다.
(B) 그가 선택한 부스를 보장받을 것이다.
(C) 신용카드로 예약금을 지불했다.
(D) 하루 일찍 행사 장소에 있을 것이다.

186-190은 다음 두 이메일과 기사에 관한 문제입니다.

수신: Fiona Bezark <fiona.bezark@wallacerealty.com>
발신: Ronald Hasbun <rhasbun@myemail.com>
제목: 임대 부동산
날짜: 10월 12일

Ms. Bezark께,

어제 저와 전화로 이야기하는 시간을 내주셔서 감사드립니다. 말씀드렸듯이, 저는 12월 1일부터 임대차 계약이 시작되는 Lakeview 지역의 아파트를 찾고 있습니다. 현재 제 아파트는 약 1,200제곱피트입니다. 저는 최소한 침실 2개에 화장실 2개가 있는 더 큰 곳이 필요합니다. 또한 1층이나 2층에 위치하며 할당된 주차 공간을 가지고 있는 아파트를 선호합니다.

저는 11월 내내 출장으로 인해 도시를 떠나 있을 것이므로, 이번 달에 몇몇 아파트를 보고 싶습니다. 저는 프리랜서 기자로 재택근무를 하기 때문에 일정이 꽤 탄력적입니다. 어떤 시간과 날짜가 당신에게 가장 좋으실 것 같은지 알려주십시오.

Ronald Hasbun 드림

수신: Ronald Hasbun <rhasbun@myemail.com>
발신: Fiona Bezark <fiona.bezark@wallacerealty.com>
제목: 회신: 임대 부동산
날짜: 10월 15일

Mr. Hasbun께,

구할 수 있는 아파트와 관련한 귀하의 최근 문의에 감사드립니다. 저는 귀하께 적합할 것 같은 네 개의 부동산을 염두에 두고 있습니다. 각각에 대한 기본 정보 목록이 아래에 있습니다. 하나는 귀하의 모든 요건을 충족하지만, 다른 것들은 귀하께서 요구하신 측면 중 몇 가지만을 가지고 있습니다. 하나를 제외하고는 전부 귀하께서 희망했던 지역에 있습니다. 그것이 최근에 전면 개조를 진행한 유일한 부동산이기 때문에 목록에 포함하였습니다. 그것은 Edgewater 지역에 있는 아름답고 오래된 건물입니다.

이 아파트 중 한 군데 이상을 둘러보는 데 관심이 있으시다면, 다음 주 중에 제가 그것들을 보여드릴 수 있습니다.

장소	침실/화장실	층	크기 (제곱피트)	세부 사항
Georgian 아파트	침실 3개 화장실 2개	1층	1,400	- 주차 공간 포함
Peterson 주택	침실 3개 화장실 1개	15층	1,600	- 가구 내 세탁기 및 건조기 - 요금제 주차
Lawrence 타워	침실 2개 화장실 2개	2층	1,300	- 도로 주차만 가능 (시 발급 스티커 필요)
Sunnyside 아파트	침실 2개 화장실 2개	2층	1,700	- 새로운 가전 제품 - 주차 공간 포함

Fiona Bezark 드림
Wallace 부동산

Sunnyside 아파트가 새롭게 단장하다
Leslie Reed 작성

시카고(10월10일)—123번지 Wilson대로에 위치한 Sunnyside 아파트의 개조가 지난주에 드디어 완료되었다. 그 건물은 1년 넘게 개량 공사를 진행했다. 지난 20년 동안 그 아파트 단지를 운영해온 Mr. Robert Kern은, 세입자 중 아무도 내보내지 않고 건물을 완전히 수리하고 싶어 했다. 밝혀진 바에 의하면, 사실 그들 중 일부는 Mr. Kern이 페인트칠, 배관 설비, 그리고 보수를 포함한 개조 작업을 하는 것을 돕기 위해 자진하여 시간을 냈다. 그 건물은 완전히 바뀌었으며, 이제 몇몇 가구는 임대가 가능하다. 관심 있는 사람들은 Wallace 부동산의 Ms. Fiona Bezark에게 555-9888로 연락할 수 있다.

186 Mr. Hasbun에 대해 언급된 것은?
(A) 현재 룸메이트와 함께 살고 있다.
(B) 11월에 부재 중일 것이다.
(C) Ms. Bezark와 그녀의 사무실에서 만났다.
(D) 최근에 기자로 고용되었다.

187 Lawrence 타워의 어느 요소가 Mr. Hasbun의 요건을 충족하지 못하는가?
(A) 층수
(B) 주차 조건
(C) 침실 개수
(D) 제곱피트

188 어느 건물이 Lakeview에 위치하지 않는가?
(A) Georgian 아파트
(B) Peterson 주택
(C) Lawrence 타워
(D) Sunnyside 아파트

189 Mr. Kern의 몇몇 세입자들은 무엇을 했는가?
(A) 임대차 계약을 연장해달라고 요청했다
(B) 건물을 개조하는 것을 도왔다
(C) 신문 기자에게 이야기했다
(D) 시민 문화회관에서 자원봉사를 했다

190 Sunnyside 아파트에 대해 암시되는 것은?
(A) 일부 가구는 현재 비어 있다.
(B) 수십 년 동안 임대료를 인상하지 않았다.
(C) 기업에 의해 관리된다.
(D) 일부 임대 아파트는 가구가 완비되어 있다.

191-195는 다음 온라인 광고, 웹페이지, 온라인 후기에 관한 문제입니다.

Winwright 미술관 재개관식에 오세요!

3월 1일 토요일 오후 5시부터 자정까지로 예정되어 있는 Winwright 미술관의 개관 기념 행사를 놓치지 마세요. 건물 밖에 있는 광장에서 라이브 음악이 연주될 것이며, 미술관에 자금을 기부한 분들은 누구나 견학에 참여하도록 초대될 것입니다.

Winwright 미술관은 지난 7월에 개조를 위해 폐쇄한 이후 처음으로 사람들을 맞이할 것입니다. 전시 공간 및 IT 시설에 대한 상당한 개선에 더하여, Winwright 미술관은 새로운 부속 건물을 추가했습니다. 그 부속 건물은 신흥 예술가들의 작품을 전시하는 데 쓰이는 동시에, 미술관의 유일한 식당인 Column이 위치하는 곳도 될 것입니다.

행사 및 미술관의 다가오는 전시에 대한 더 많은 정보를 얻기 위해서는, www.winwrightgallery.com을 방문하십시오.

www.winwrightgallery.com/membership

연간 회원제

Winwright 미술관의 회원들은 독점적인 혜택을 받습니다. 아래의 옵션 중 하나를 고르고 "선택"을 클릭하십시오.

종류	가격	혜택
▭ 개인	100달러	- 모든 전시 공간으로의 무료 입장 - 강연에 대한 20퍼센트 할인
▭ 가족	200달러	- 본인과 한 명의 손님에 대한 모든 전시 공간으로의 무료 입장 - 어린이들을 위한 수업 및 강연에 대한 20퍼센트 할인
▭ 애호가	600달러	- 본인과 두 명의 손님에 대한 모든 전시 공간으로의 무료 입장 - 강연 및 미술관 상점 상품에 대한 20퍼센트 할인 - 행사에 대한 티켓 우선권 및 특별 전시 시사회 초대
▭ 전문가	1,000달러	- Winwright 미술관의 연례 휴일 오찬 초대 - 본인과 최대 네 명의 손님에 대한 모든 전시 공간으로의 무료 입장 - 강연, 미술관 상점 상품 및 식당 음식에 대한 20퍼센트 할인 - 북아메리카 내 30개 이상의 제휴 미술관으로의 무료 입장

선택

www.triptips.com/attractions/reviews/winwrightgallery

Tania Swanson 4월 9일에 평가됨

★★★★☆ 멋진 저녁

오늘 친구가 Winwright 미술관에 함께 방문하자고 권했을 때 매우 들떴었습니다. 발표를 보고 추상 미술품의 제작 기법들을 보는 것은 대단히 흥미로웠습니다. 그렇게 붐비지만 않았으면 좋았겠다고 생각했습니다. 우리는 2시간쯤 돌아다니고 나서 미술관의 새로운 부속 건물에 있는 식당에서 식사했습니다. 우리는 그 아래에 있는 조각 공원이 보이는 테라스에 앉았습니다. 음식은 훌륭했고, 제 친구가 회원이기 때문에, 청구된 금액에서 할인도 받았습니다. 예약이 가능하지만 필수는 아닙니다.

191 Winwright 미술관에 대해 사실이 아닌 것은?
(A) 신흥 예술가들의 작품을 전시하기 위한 구역을 추가했다.
(B) 모든 방문객에게 무료 견학을 제공하고 있다.
(C) 공사를 진행했다.
(D) 광장에 인접해 있다.

192 웹페이지가 애호가 회원권에 대해 언급한 것은?
(A) 신흥 예술가들에게 추천된다.
(B) 전시회의 사전 관람에 대한 입장을 허용한다.
(C) 제휴 미술관에서의 할인을 포함한다.
(D) 월 단위로 요금이 지불되어야 한다.

193 Column에 대해 언급된 것은?
(A) 예약이 필요하다.
(B) 이탈리아 음식을 전문으로 한다.
(C) 정원이 내려다보인다.
(D) 연례 오찬을 주최한다.

194 Ms. Swanson은 4월 9일에 Winwright 미술관에서 무엇을 했는가?
(A) 시연을 봤다
(B) 미술품을 만들었다
(C) 상품권을 상품으로 교환했다
(D) 유명한 디자이너를 만났다

195 Ms. Swanson의 친구는 미술관 회원권에 얼마를 지불했는가?
(A) 100달러
(B) 200달러
(C) 600달러
(D) 1,000달러

196-200은 다음 웹페이지, 이메일, 의견에 관한 문제입니다.

www.nilsoncandy.com

여러분의 사업체를 계속 달콤하게 하세요

Nilson Candy사는 호텔, 운송 회사, 비즈니스 컨벤션 등을 위해 대량의 사탕을 제공합니다. 여러분이 가장 좋아하는 사탕을 오늘 구매하세요!

수백 가지의 인기 있는 간식 중에 선택해주세요, 다음을 포함합니다:
민트
캐러멜
초콜릿
막대 사탕

전체 주문에 250달러 넘게 쓰시고, 추가 비용 없이 포장에 여러분의 회사 이름과 로고를 붙여 구매품을 맞춤 제작하실 수 있습니다! 선물 바구니와 사탕 꽃다발도 이용하실 수 있습니다. 여러분의 고객들과 소비자들이 잊지 못할 달콤한 별미를 제공하세요!

저희 자동 주문 상담 전화 555-9635로 전화하시거나 저희 온라인 채팅을 이용하여 Nilson Candy사 직원과 이야기하십시오. 특별 상품 이용을 위해 저희 연휴 카탈로그 한 부를 요청하는 것과 추가 할인에 대해 알아보시기 위해 저희의 뉴스레터에 가입하시는 것을 잊지 마시기 바랍니다!

초콜릿 제품은 특허받은 GOOD-SEAL 팩으로 배송될 것이라는 점을 알아두십시오. 이것들은 최대 4일까지 녹는 것을 막을 수 있습니다. 배송을 받는 데 문제가 있을 것으로 예상하시면, 배송 날짜를 조정할 수 있도록 저희에게 알려주시기를 바랍니다.

수신: Lisa Choi <lisachoi@starsoftware.com>
발신: Nilson Candy <orders@nilsoncandy.com>
날짜: 6월 16일
제목: 귀하의 주문이 접수되었습니다

Nilson Candy사에 주문해주셔서 감사합니다! 아래의 주문 세부 사항을 검토해주십시오.

주문 번호: 34V8K **배송지:** Star Software사
연락처: Lisa Choi **전화:** 555-3202

품목	수량	가격
페퍼민트	10킬로그램 - 대량	99달러
초콜릿	5킬로그램 - 대량	79달러
캐러멜	5킬로그램 - 대량	89달러
작은 사탕 꽃다발	50개	225달러
	배송료	50달러
	총비용	542달러

모든 주문에 대한 저희의 일반 배송 기간은 2일입니다. 하지만, 맞춤 제작 라벨을 요청하셨다면, 배송은 7일까지 걸릴 수 있습니다.

---

www.nilsoncandy.com

온라인 의견 양식

제 이름은 Lisa Choi입니다. 전반적으로, 저는 제 주문에 만족했습니다. 배송은 제때 이루어졌고 물건들은 완전했습니다. 그러나, 대부분의 사탕이 온전하게 도착하긴 했지만, 몇몇 캐러멜은 배송 중에 부서졌습니다. 그래도, 거의 두 시간 동안 그것을 밖에 놓아두었음에도 불구하고 포장이 물건을 잘 보존해 준 것 같습니다. 그리고 저희 고객들은 모든 사탕을 매우 맛있게 먹었습니다! 저는 시간 부족으로 인해 맞춤 제작 옵션을 시도할 수 없었지만, 추후에는 반드시 그것을 시도해 보고 싶습니다.

196 웹페이지에 따르면, Nilson Candy사의 고객들은 무엇을 하도록 권장되는가?
(A) 연휴 카탈로그를 요청한다
(B) 매장 지점을 방문한다
(C) 온라인 후기들을 읽는다
(D) 몇몇 샘플들을 맛본다

197 GOOD-SEAL이 제공하는 기능은 무엇인가?
(A) 제품이 진품임을 인증한다.
(B) 상품의 상태를 유지한다.
(C) 고객들이 배송을 추적할 수 있게 해준다.
(D) 회사가 높은 기준을 충족시킨다는 것을 증명한다.

198 주문 번호 34V8K에 대해 암시되는 것은?
(A) 무료 맞춤 제작 대상으로 적합하다.
(B) 할인을 받을 자격이 있다.
(C) 본인이 직접 가져갈 것이다.
(D) 해외로부터의 상품을 포함한다.

199 Ms. Choi가 그녀의 주문에서 경험했던 문제점은 무엇인가?
(A) 사탕 하나가 맛이 없었다.
(B) 초콜릿이 더위에 녹았다.
(C) 제품들이 분실되었다.
(D) 상품들이 손상되었다.

200 Ms. Choi의 주문에 대해 사실인 것은?
(A) 거주지로 보내졌다.
(B) 전년도에도 주문되었다.
(C) 이틀 안에 배달되었다.
(D) 부정확하게 라벨이 붙었다.

TEST 04 해석

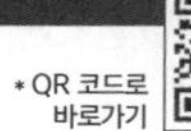

* 무료 해설은 해커스토익(Hackers.co.kr)에서 다운로드 받을 수 있습니다.

* QR 코드로 바로가기

PART 5

101 인터뷰에서, Billy Zuckerman은 기타 치는 법을 혼자서 배웠다고 말했다.

102 설치 설명서는 사용자들이 무엇을 해야 하는지 명확하게 기술한다.

103 최고 재무 책임자는 새로운 복리 후생 정책에 관해 부서장들과 대화를 나눴다.

104 Baron사는 해외 운영에 대해 이미 잘 알고 있는 내부 지원자를 승진시키는 것을 선호한다.

105 그 건물의 엘리베이터들은 하나를 제외하고 모두 상태가 좋은데, 그것은 교체되어야 할 수도 있다.

106 시장은 62번 고속도로를 따라 다인승 차량 차선을 만듦으로써 교통 혼잡을 줄이는 것을 계획하고 있다.

107 Medland사 인사부장은 이력서와 함께 작문 샘플을 제출하도록 요구했다.

108 Wilsonville 도심지를 상업 중심지로 재개발하기로 동의한 시 공무원들에 의해 계획 제안서가 승인될 것이다.

109 Palace Golf의 신규 고객들은 매장의 방대한 선택 가능한 것들 중에서 무료 골프공 한 세트를 선택할 수 있다.

110 전 세계에 걸친 밀 가격의 상승은 밀가루 생산비를 현저하게 상승시킬 수 있다.

111 Mr. Carver는 부동산 중개인으로서 출세하기 위해 도시로 이사했다.

112 그녀의 식당을 열기 전에, 요리사 Andrea Michaels는 상을 받은 여러 주방에서 연마했다.

113 그 회사는 웹사이트의 첫 번째 페이지에 야유회 사진을 게시했다.

114 동봉된 책자는 귀하가 가질 수 있는 어떠한 질문에도 답변해줄 것입니다.

115 지난주 기상 상태는 제21회 Emerald만 요트 대회에 적합했다.

116 심각한 건축 법규 위반이 발견될 경우, 시 의회는 타워의 건설을 중단시킬 권한이 있다.

117 소매점을 운영해본 경험이 없어서, Ms. Philips는 동업자의 조언에 의존했다.

118 근속 연수에 관계없이, 각 직원들은 연간 15일의 유급 휴가를 받을 수 있다.

119 Mr. Alden은 일본에서 방문하는 고객들이 건물 로비에 도착하자마자 통보해달라고 요청했다.

120 직원들이 어떻게 옷을 입는지는 회사를 반영하므로, 주중 근무 시간에는 전문적인 복장을 갖춰 주십시오.

121 연례 독립 기념일 불꽃놀이 쇼는 Stapleton 공원 뒤에서 오후 8시에 시작할 것이다.

122 만약 협상이 결렬되지 않았다면 Jenkins Hospitality사가 Starlite 호텔을 매입했을 것이다.

123 Ms. Sutter는 신청서를 작성하는 데 필요한 모든 정보를 알고 있지는 않았기 때문에 일부를 비워두었다.

124 Dearden사는 명확하게 눈에 보이는 비상구 표지판을 모든 층에 설치함으로써 안전 규정을 준수해야 한다.

125 휴스턴을 강타할 것으로 예상되는 폭풍 때문에 내일 있을 야구 경기가 취소되었다.

126 대부분의 운동 전문가들은 체중을 줄이길 원하는 사람들에게 저칼로리의 고섬유질 식단을 추천한다.

127 Ms. Simpson은 이사회와 회의 중이며 긴급 상황이 있는 것이 아니라면 방해받지 않아야 한다.

128 Ray's Sandwiches는 10년 전에 문을 열었으며 그 이후로 Weyburn의 회사원들에게 인기 있는 점심 식사 장소가 되었다.

129 쉽게 수정될 수 있는 몇몇 오타를 제외하고, 이 보고서는 제출될 준비가 된 것 같다.

130 천체물리학자 Dr. Bryan Healy와 항공우주 공학자 Dr. Marie Duns는 그들 각자의 분야에서 전문가들이다.

PART 6

131-134는 다음 설명서에 관한 문제입니다.

프린터 카트리지를 교체하려면, 프린터의 뚜껑을 여는 것으로 시작하십시오. 이는 잉크 카트리지가 인쇄 구역의 중앙으로 이동한 다음 멈추게 할 것입니다. **131** 교체하고 싶은 카트리지를 선택하고 본인 쪽으로 당기십시오. 그것은 쉽게 미끄러져 나올 것입니다. **132** 새로운 카트리지가 준비되면, 잉크가 사방으로 움직이도록 그것을 흔드십시오. **133** 이는 색의 고른 분포를 보장해 줄 것입니다. 다음으로, 바닥을 밀봉하고 있는 보호용 테이프 한 장을 찾으십시오. 이것은 사용 전에 벗겨져야 합니다. **134** 그렇지 않으면, 잉크가 나오지 않을 것입니다. 마지막으로, 프린터 뚜껑을 닫고 색상이 모니터에 나타나는 것과 일치하는지 확인하기 위해 몇 장의 시험 페이지를 인쇄하십시오.

135-138은 다음 웹페이지에 관한 문제입니다.

http://www.weissert.com

홈 | **소개** | 계정 | 도움 | 연락

Weissert 항바이러스 소프트웨어는 컴퓨터와 네트워크를 보호합니다. 5년 전에 출시된 이래로, 그것은 바이러스와 악성 소프트웨어에 대비하여 선두적인 보호 형태 중 하나가 되었습니다. **135** 오늘 무료 시험 버전을 다운로드하십시오. 당신은 90일 동안 어떠한 하나의 장치에서 저희 서비스에 완전한 접근을 갖게 될 것입니다. **136** 이 기간이 끝날 때, 당신은 쉽게 서비스를 연장할 수 있습니다. 간단하게 구독 요금제를 선택하고, 당신의 결제 정보를 입력하십시오. **137** 저희는 모든 주요 신용카드를 받으며 직접 인출도 가능합니다. 그것이 전부입니다. **138** 90일 미만은, 저희가 당신에게 요금을 전혀 청구하지 않을 것입니다. 설치를 시작하시려면, 여기를 클릭하십시오.

139-142는 다음 이메일에 관한 문제입니다.

수신: Cynthia Ryerson <cynry@terratiles.com>
발신: Alex Jones <jones@jonesinteriors.com>
날짜: 11월 18일
제목: 구매 주문

Ms. Ryerson께,

139 요청했던 대로 타일 견본을 보내주셔서 감사합니다. 실제 제품은 당신의 웹사이트에서 보이는 것보다 더 좋아 보입니다. 저는 제 고객을 방문하여 그것들을 보여주었습니다. **140** 그녀는 석조와 도자기 타일에 좋은 인상을 받기는 했지만, 그 선택지들 중 어느 것도 가격이 알맞지 않다고 생각했습니다. 반면에, 테라코타 타일들은 정확히 그녀가 찾고 있는 것입니다. **141** 그것들은 그녀의 지중해풍 식당을 완벽하게 보완해줄 것입니다.

귀하께 치수를 전달드렸으니, 재료 및 설치의 총비용이 얼마일지 알려 주시겠습니까? **142** 얼마나 빨리 그 작업을 시행하실 수 있는지도 알고 싶습니다. 제 고객은 2주 후에 그녀의 가구와 가전제품들이 도착할 것으로 예상하고 있는 것 같으니, 그 전에 설치하는 것이 가장 좋겠습니다.

다시 한번 감사드리며, 곧 연락 주시기 바랍니다.

Alex Jones
Jones 인테리어사

143-146은 다음 기사에 관한 문제입니다.

Jackson시가 현저한 경기 회복의 조짐을 보이면서, 주민들과 사업체 모두의 상당한 유입을 불러일으키고 있다. **143** 이러한 성장은 34번 고속도로를 지나며 이전에는 Sibbet 제조사에 공간을 제공했던 370만 제곱피트의 토지를 매각한 것에 기인한다. 그 회사는 운영한지 3년 후에 파산하여 10년도 더 전에 문을 닫았으며, 그 부지에 있는 기본 시설을 사용되지 않은 채로 남겨두었다. **144** 새로운 소유주는 모든 것을 철거하고 새로운 사무실 건물을 건설할 계획이다. 이 개발이 성공적이면, 그것은 향후 몇 년 간 5만 개 이상의 일자리를 제공할 것이다. **145** 결과적으로 인근 지역의 사람들도 Jackson시로 이사해오고 있다. 주택에 대한 수요는 이미 상승 추세에 있다. **146** 마찬가지로, 궁극적으로 장래 주민들의 요구를 채워줄 상업 용지들도 전례 없는 속도로 임대되고 있다.

PART 7

147-148은 다음 정책 성명서에 관한 문제입니다.

Whitmore강 야영지 예약 취소 정책

예약을 취소해야 할 경우, 도착 예정 최소 48시간 전에 555-7722로 공원 사무소에 전화하는 경우에만 보증금 전액을 환급해드릴 것입니다. 공원 사무소는 매일 오후 5시까지만 열려 있다는 점과, 문자 메시지 및 이메일로 발송된 예약 취소 통지는 인정되지 않는다는 점을 유의해 주시기 바랍니다. 촉박하게 취소하거나 도착하지 못하는 경우, 보증금을 받지 못하실 것이며, 저희는 그 텐트 자리에 다른 손님을 숙박시킬 권리가 있을 것입니다.

147 정책 성명서에 언급되지 않은 정보는?
(A) 예약 취소 기한
(B) 규정이 변경된 이유
(C) 사무실 연락처
(D) 시설 폐장 시간

148 Whitmore강 야영지는 고객이 나타나지 않는 경우에 무엇을 할 수 있는가?
(A) 그 사람이 다시 예약하는 것을 제한한다
(B) 취소 수수료에 대한 청구서를 보낸다
(C) 대여료 전액을 청구한다
(D) 예약된 공간을 다른 사람에게 준다

149-150은 다음 안내서에 관한 문제입니다.

자원봉사자 지원

Coral Rock 수족관에서 자원봉사를 하는 것에 대한 여러분의 관심에 감사드립니다. 해당 분기가 현재 진행 중이기 때문에 가을 자원봉사자 자리에 대한 지원을 더 이상 받지 않고 있습니다. 다른 분기에 지원하고 싶으시면, 아래의 표에서 관련 날짜를 확인해 주십시오.

분기	자원봉사 참가 날짜	신청서 접수 날짜
봄	3월 1일부터 5월 31일	12월 15일부터 2월 15일
여름	6월 1일부터 8월 31일	3월 15일부터 5월 15일
가을	9월 1일부터 11월 30일	6월 15일부터 8월 15일
겨울	12월 1일부터 2월 28일	9월 15일부터 11월 15일

지원 절차의 첫 부분은 신청서 제출 및 자원봉사자 관리자와의 면접을 포함합니다. 저희의 요건을 충족하시면, 3시간짜리 오리엔테이션에 참여하셔야 하며, Coral Rock 수족관은 2월 24일, 5월 23일, 8월 22일, 그리고 11월 22일에 이를 진행합니다.

149 Coral Rock 수족관의 현재 자원봉사 기간은 언제 종료될 것인가?
(A) 5월 31일에
(B) 8월 15일에
(C) 11월 30일에
(D) 12월 1일에

150 자원봉사자의 요건이 아닌 것은?
(A) 전문가의 추천서 목록을 제출한다
(B) 면접에 참가한다
(C) 작성한 서류를 제출한다
(D) 정보를 제공하는 모임에 참석한다

151-152는 다음 메시지 대화문에 관한 문제입니다.

Charlene Timmerson [7월 11일, 오후 3시]
안녕하세요. 죄송하지만, 오늘 오후 3시 30분 약속에 전기 기술자를 만나기 위해 시간에 맞춰 집에 갈 수 없을 것 같아요. 일이 생겨서, 결국 일찍 퇴근할 수가 없게 되었어요. 하지만, 오후 5시까지는 갈 수 있어요. 그것을 뒤로 옮길 수 있을까요?

McGovern 전기 수리점 [7월 11일, 오후 3시 8분]
안녕하세요. 안타깝게도, 저희 기술자들이 매우 바빠서, 오늘은 남아있는 시간대가 없습니다. 다음 빈 시간은 7월 15일 오후 1시입니다. 아니면, 7월 18일이나 19일 정오에 시간을 내어 귀하를 만날 수 있을 것 같습니다.

Charlene Timmerson [7월 11일, 오후 3시 15분]
알겠습니다. 방금 제 상사와 이야기했는데, 그녀는 제가 7월 19일에 일을 쉬고 집에 있어도 된다고 말했어요.

151 오후 3시에, Ms. Timmerson이 "Can it be moved back"이라고 썼을 때 그녀가 의도한 것은?
(A) 갑자기 늘어난 작업량에 대해 화가 났다.
(B) 약속 일정을 변경하고 싶어 한다.
(C) 가구가 재배치될 수 있기를 바란다.
(D) 이사 날짜를 바꾸고 싶어 한다.

152 Ms. Timmerson은 언제 전기 기술자를 만날 것인가?
(A) 오후 12시에
(B) 오후 1시에
(C) 오후 3시 30분에
(D) 오후 5시에

153-154는 다음 광고에 관한 문제입니다.

저희 책을 구매하는 것이 이토록 쉬웠던 적은 없습니다!

Bell Tower 출판사에서, 저희는 다양하게 구비된 과학 교과서, 합리적인 가격, 그리고 최고의 고객 서비스로 오랫동안 알려져 왔습니다. 최근까지, 저희의 상품은 웹사이트에서만 주문할 수 있었습니다. 하지만 이제 쇼핑할 수 있는 더 빠르고 간편한 방법이 있는데, 바로 휴대전화 및 태블릿용 애플리케이션인 Bell Tower Helper입니다.

앱스토어에서 Bell Tower Helper를 다운로드하시고 사용자 프로필을 생성하기만 하시면 됩니다. 그리고 로그인하셔서, 서적을 고르시고, "주문" 버튼을 누르세요. 프로필을 가지고 있는 것은 여러분의 결제 세부 정보를 저장하고 주문 처리 상태를 확인할 수 있게 해줍니다. 책에 따라 다르긴 하지만, 항상 그랬듯이, 대량 주문에 대해서는 할인이 제공됩니다. 물론, 원하신다면 여전히 www.belltowerpublishing.com에서 주문하실 수 있습니다.

153 Bell Tower 출판사에 대해 사실인 것은?
(A) 소설 및 소설 이외의 책을 모두 판매한다.
(B) 학교 교내에서 판촉 행사를 연다.

(C) 이제 막 대량 주문에 대한 가격 할인을 제공하기 시작했다.
(D) 이전에는 웹사이트에서만 상품을 판매했다.

154 Bell Tower 출판사의 고객들은 사용자 프로필을 가지고 있는 경우 무엇을 할 수 있을 것 같은가?
(A) 구매한 것이 발송되었는지 알아낸다
(B) 고객 서비스 직원과 이야기한다
(C) 책의 처음 몇 페이지를 미리 본다
(D) 후기를 써서 포인트를 받는다

155-157은 다음 안내문에 관한 문제입니다.

South Loop 야드 세일

South Loop 지역 센터에 의해 개최되는 두 번째 연례 이웃 야드 세일에 참여하십시오. 작년의 행사는 모든 기대를 능가했고 연례 전통을 만드는 데 영감을 주었습니다. 그 행사는 9월 2일 토요일에 열릴 것입니다. 오셔서 할인 상품을 구매하시고, 지역 음악을 들으시고, 맛있는 음식을 맛보십시오.

올해, 저희는 Dearborn 센터로 옮겨갔습니다. 그것은 작년의 장소보다 참가자들을 위한 더 많은 공간을 제공합니다. 부스 공간은 아직 판매자들에게 이용 가능합니다. 참여하시려면, www.southloop.org/yardsale에서 자리를 신청하시기만 하면 됩니다.

작년과 달리, 저희는 50달러의 참가비를 요구할 것입니다. 이것은 이번 크리스마스에 단체의 선물 기부 활동에 자금을 제공하는 데 바로 쓰일 것입니다. 만약 기부하는 데 관심이 있으시다면, www.southloop.org/donate를 방문하십시오.

155 1문단 두 번째 줄의 단어 "topped"는 의미상 -와 가장 가깝다.
(A) 경쟁했다
(B) 순위를 차지했다
(C) 패배시켰다
(D) 능가했다

156 행사에 대해 언급된 것은?
(A) 이전보다 더 많은 방문객들을 수용할 것이다.
(B) 지역 신문에 광고되고 있다.
(C) 어린이들을 위한 오락거리를 특별히 포함할 것이다.
(D) 동네에서 처음 있는 행사이다.

157 요금에 대해 사실인 것은?
(A) 신용카드로 결제될 수 없다.
(B) 작년에는 요구되지 않았다.
(C) 방문객들에게 무료 선물을 받을 자격을 준다.
(D) 사람의 나이에 따라 다르다.

158-160은 다음 보도 자료에 관한 문제입니다.

Newberry사가 계속해서 시장 점유율을 차지하다

3월 1일—Newberry사는 전자책 단말기 시장에서 경쟁사들에 빠르게 가까워지고 있다. 그것의 최신 제품은 전면 색상 디스플레이, 여러 개의 사전, 그리고 글을 소리 내어 읽을 수 있는 다양한 종류의 컴퓨터 음성과 같은 특징들로 강력한 추종자들을 끌어모았다. 다른 어떤 기기와도 달리, Newberry사의 제품은 스피커 시스템에도 무선으로 연결할 수 있다. 이것은 사용자들이 더 높은 음성 선명도로 책을 소리 내어 읽는 것을 들을 수 있게 한다.

이런 기능과 더 많은 것들 때문에, Newberry 전자책 단말기는 시장 점유율의 꾸준한 증가를 경험해왔다. 그 제품이 2년 전에 출시된 이후 매달, 그 회사는 점점 더 많은 새로운 사용자들이 추가되었다. 이는 훨씬 오래되고 큰 회사인 Vandaread사와 Spectlight Reader사에 이어 3위를 차지하게 하며, 현재 전자책 판매량의 대략 22퍼센트를 차지하고 있다. 분석가들은 Newberry의 점유율이 더 늘어날 가능성이 높다고 보고 있다.

Newberry사의 최고경영자인 Ross Franklin은 그 회사가 인기 판타지 작가 Larry Hamlin과 곧 있을 광고 캠페인에서 Newberry 전자책 단말기를 홍보하는 계약을 체결했다고 최근에 발표했다. 그 캠페인은 텔레비전 광고와 전국의 가장 큰 서점들의 선정된 지점에서의 연설 약속을 포함할 것이다. 그 회사는 또한 늘어난 메모리 용량을 포함하는 새로운 버전의 제품을 내년에 출시할 계획이다.

158 Newberry 전자책 단말기는 무엇이 독특한가?
(A) 오래 지속되는 배터리를 가지고 있다.
(B) 경쟁 제품들보다 더 저렴하다.
(C) 다양한 색상으로 나온다.
(D) 오디오 시스템과 무선으로 연결한다.

159 2문단 두 번째 줄의 단어 "consistent"는 의미상 -와 가장 가깝다.
(A) 균형이 잡힌
(B) 예상되는
(C) 꾸준한
(D) 내구성이 있는

160 Newberry 전자책 단말기 광고에 대해 언급된 것은?
(A) 인쇄된 형태로 출시될 것이다.
(B) 유명한 작가를 쓸 것이다.
(C) 젊은 독자들의 관심을 끌 것이다.
(D) 유명한 감독에 의해 제작될 것이다.

161-164는 다음 편지에 관한 문제입니다.

Gloria Schaeffer
1763번지 Stanton로
챈들러, 애리조나주 85226

2월 11일

Ms. Schaeffer께,

제 이름은 Maury Dekalb이며, 20년 넘게 챈들러 지역에서 부동산 중개인으로 일해왔습니다. — [1] —. 저는 귀하께서 지역 부동산 안내서에 귀하의 집을 내놓음으로써 그것을 독자적으로 판매하려고 하고 계신다는 것을 알게 되었습니다. 저는 제가 귀하의 집의 구매자를 찾아 드릴 수 있다고 생각합니다. — [2] —.

많은 부동산들이 도시 곳곳에서 판매를 위해 내놓아져 있지만, 현재는 구매자가 많지 않습니다. 이러한 상황이 귀하의 집을 판매하는 것을 힘들게 만들 것이라는 데에는 의심의 여지가 없는 것 같습니다. — [3] —. 저를 고용하시면, 더 이상 그렇게 걱정하실 필요가 없을 것이라고 보장합니다. 저는 잠재적 구매자들 사이에서 귀하의 부동산에 대한 관심을 유발하고, 그들과 약속을 잡아 귀하의 집을 볼 수 있게 하며, 협상 중에 중재인 역할을 할 것입니다. — [4] —.

언제든 저와 만나고 싶으시다면, 알려주십시오. 협동하여, 저희는 귀하의 요구를 충족하는 판매 전략을 생각해 낼 수 있습니다. 저는 낮이든 밤이든 555-7411로 연락 가능합니다.

Maury Dekalb 드림
Dekalb 부동산

161 Ms. Schaeffer에 대해 암시되는 것은?
(A) 챈들러 신문을 구독한다.
(B) 전략을 논의하기 위해 Mr. Dekalb와 만난 적이 있다.
(C) 올해 부동산 면허를 취득했다.
(D) 현재 부동산업자와 일하고 있지 않다.

162 Ms. Schaeffer는 어떤 문제에 직면하고 있는 것 같은가?
(A) 건설 사업이 예정보다 늦어지고 있다.
(B) 주택 시장이 침체기에 있다.
(C) 은행 대출을 확보할 수 없다.
(D) 그녀의 부동산이 대중교통 정류장에서 멀다.

163 Mr. Dekalb가 Ms. Schaeffer를 위해 하겠다고 약속하지 않은 것은?
(A) 구매자들의 관심을 얻는다

(B) 그녀의 주택의 가격을 높인다
(C) 둘러보는 시간을 주선한다
(D) 합의를 이끌어 내도록 돕는다

164 [1], [2], [3], [4]로 표시된 위치 중, 다음 문장이 들어갈 곳으로 가장 적절한 것은?

"하지만, 귀하께서 적절한 종류의 도움을 받으신다면, 구매자를 찾는 것이 꼭 불가능한 것은 아닙니다."

(A) [1]
(B) [2]
(C) [3]
(D) [4]

165-167은 다음 구인 광고에 관한 문제입니다.

Tulsa 대학에서 연구 조교를 찾습니다

Tulsa 대학 경제학과는 소득 데이터를 수집하고 분석하는 것을 돕는 지식 있는 연구 조교를 찾고 있습니다. 그 조교는 적어도 일주일에 40시간을 업무에 기꺼이 전념해야 합니다. 정상 근무 시간은 월요일부터 금요일까지, 오전 8시부터 오후 5시까지입니다. 업무는 6개월 동안 지속될 것이고 시간당 18달러를 지급합니다.

직무에는 포함합니다:
- 발표된 연구 결과에서 소득 데이터를 수집하는 것
- 데이터 기반으로 스프레드시트와 인포그래픽을 만드는 것
- 진행 중인 여러 프로젝트의 진행 상황에 대한 보고서를 작성하는 것

모든 지원자들은 수행해야 합니다:
- 적어도 경제학 학사 학위 소지
- 대학 기간 동안 최소 평점 3.5 획득
- 면접 동안 해당 분야에 대한 지식 입증

관심이 있으시다면, 이력서와 자기소개서를 Tulsa 대학의 경제학과 학과장인 Dr. William Ling에게 w.ling@tulsacollege.edu로 제출해 주십시오. 합격자들은 면접 날짜를 정하기 위해 이메일로 연락될 것입니다. 모든 면접은 고용 위원회 구성원들과 함께 현장에서 이루어질 것입니다.

165 1문단 두 번째 줄의 단어 "dedicate"는 의미상 -와 가장 가깝다.
(A) 연설하다
(B) 약속하다
(C) 전념하다
(D) 임명하다

166 연구 조교직에 대해 언급된 것은?
(A) 일주일에 6일 일하는 것을 요구할 것이다.
(B) 참가자들에게 대학 학점을 줄 것이다.
(C) 단지 임시직일 것이다.
(D) 초과 근무에 더 많은 돈을 지급할 것이다.

167 업무 지원자들에 대한 요구 조건은 무엇인가?
(A) Tulsa 대학의 졸업자인 것
(B) 심사원단 면접에 참석하는 것
(C) 이전 작업의 샘플을 제공하는 것
(D) 관련 회사에서 경력이 있는 것

168-171은 다음 공고에 관한 문제입니다.

North Portal가 주민들에게 알림

Renwah 제작사가 North Portal가에서 QCC의 TV 시리즈 *Farther Gone*의 다가오는 에피소드를 위한 몇 장면을 촬영할 것입니다. — [1] —. 촬영은 5월 8일부터 5월 12일까지 다음 장소 및 시간에 실시될 예정입니다:

1. 5월 8일 월요일 & 5월 9일 화요일: Charbonneau 카페, 1542번지 North Portal가, 오전 8시 30분부터 오후 7시까지
2. 5월 10일 수요일 & 5월 11일 목요일: Azalea 아파트 바깥쪽, 1294번지 North Portal가, 오전 5시부터 오후 3시까지
3. 5월 12일 금요일: Get-and-Grab 편의점, 1628번지 North Portal가, 오전 10시부터 오후 9시까지

제작진의 차량 및 장비를 수용하기 위해, 관련 일시에 촬영장 근처에 "주차 금지" 표지판이 설치될 것입니다. — [2] —.

Renwah 제작사는 교통 혼란을 최소화할 것을 약속했습니다. — [3] —. 촬영이 진행 중인 동안 첫 번째와 세 번째 촬영 장소는 대중에게 개방되지 않을 것이라는 점을 유의해 주십시오. 두 번째 장소에 대한 접근은 뒤쪽 입구를 통해서만 허용될 것입니다. — [4] —.

여러분의 이해와 협조에 감사드립니다.

168 공고의 목적은 무엇인가?
(A) 아파트 주민들에게 승인되지 않은 방문자를 신고하도록 요청하기 위해
(B) 촬영 일정에 관한 세부 사항을 제공하기 위해
(C) 지역 사업체를 추천하기 위해
(D) 공연 참석의 요건을 명시하기 위해

169 Charbonneau 카페에 대해 암시되는 것은?
(A) 오전에만 촬영지로 사용될 것이다.
(B) 5월 9일에는 평소보다 인근 주차 공간이 적을 것이다.
(C) 이전의 *Farther Gone* 에피소드를 촬영하는 데 사용되었다.
(D) 특정 기간에는 테이크아웃 주문만 제공할 것이다.

170 Azalea 아파트의 주민들에 대해 사실인 것은?
(A) 다음 주에 상기시켜 주는 메모를 받을 것이다.
(B) 보안 검사를 통과해야 할 것이다.
(C) 촬영이 진행되는 동안 뒷문을 이용할 수 있다.
(D) 일주일 동안 Portal가에서 운전하는 것이 허용되지 않는다.

171 [1], [2], [3], [4]로 표시된 위치 중 다음 문장이 들어갈 곳으로 가장 적절한 것은?

"하지만, 몇몇 학교 버스의 노선은 약간 조정될 수 있습니다."

(A) [1]
(B) [2]
(C) [3]
(D) [4]

172-175는 다음 메시지 대화문에 관한 문제입니다.

Jeff Hervey [오전 10시 35분]
Rosanne, 지금 사무실에 있나요? 부탁이 있어요.

Rosanne Rutherford [오전 10시 37분]
안녕하세요. 당신은 Vermont가에 있는 주택에서 지붕 타일을 교체하기로 되어 있는 것 아닌가요?

Jeff Hervey [오전 10시 39분]
그게 문제예요. 저는 지금 여기에 있는데, 예상했던 것보다 할 일이 많아요. 제가 지난번 측정에 실수했음이 틀림없어요. 저는 와서 저를 도와줄 몇 사람들이 필요해요.

Rosanne Rutherford [오전 10시 43분]
제가 지금 사무실에 없지만, 당신을 도와줄 수 있어요. Todd도 가능할 거예요. 그가 Grant가에서 하기로 예정되어 있던 울타리를 치는 작업이 취소되었어요.

Jeff Hervey [오전 10시 45분]
다행이네요. 고마워요!

Jeff Hervey [오전 10시 46분]
Todd, 62번지 Vermont가의 지붕을 덮는 작업을 도와줄 시간이 있나요? 당신이 여분의 도구를 가져와야 할 것 같아요.

Todd Billings [오전 10시 48분]
안녕하세요, Jeff. 네, 저는 시간이 있어요.

Jeff Hervey [오전 10시 49분]
고마워요, Todd! 당신이 여기에 얼마나 일찍 올 수 있는지 저에게 알려주세요.

Rosanne Rutherford [오전 10시 52분]
Jeff, 제가 Ms. Richards에게 알렸고, 그녀는 저희가 거기로 가는 걸 승인했어요. 저는 곧 출발할 거예요.

Todd Billings [오전 10시 53분]
알았어요, Jeff. 저는 약 45분 후에 그곳에 있을 수 있어요.

172 필자들은 어느 업계에서 일할 것 같은가?
(A) 소매
(B) 제조
(C) 건설 공사
(D) 조경

173 오전 10시 45분에, Mr. Hervey가 "That's a relief"라고 썼을 때 그가 의도한 것은?
(A) 최종 기한이 연장된 것에 감사한다.
(B) 그가 도움을 받을 것임을 알게 되어 기쁘다.
(C) 동료가 회의에 참석할 것에 감사한다.
(D) 그의 업무들 중 하나가 취소되어 기쁘다.

174 Vermont가에서 얼마나 많은 사람들이 일하게 될 것인가?
(A) 1
(B) 2
(C) 3
(D) 4

175 Ms. Richards는 누구일 것 같은가?
(A) 새로운 고객
(B) 영업 사원
(C) 회사 운전기사
(D) 작업 감독관

176-180은 다음 이메일과 광고에 관한 문제입니다.

수신: Jake Boyne <jake_boyne@renswoodinc.com>
발신: Betty Herzfeld <betty_herzfeld@renswoodinc.com>
제목: 고장 난 프로젝터
날짜: 8월 5일

안녕하세요, Jake,

제가 어제 당신에게 말했듯이, 2층 회의실에 있는 프로젝터가 제대로 작동하지 않습니다. 보증 기간은 작년에 만료되었기 때문에 그것을 수리하기보다는 새로운 장비를 마련하고 싶습니다. 보기에는, 지금의 것에 4,000시간 지속되는 전구가 있는 것 같습니다. 저는 이 점에서 더 나은 장비를 마련하고 싶습니다. 가능하다면, 더 높은 해상도의 프로젝터로 바꾸는 것도 좋겠습니다.

저는 지금의 프로젝터에 그다지 만족해오지 않았으니, 이번에는 GelwayCo사의 장비를 구입합시다. 어쨌든, 다른 인턴들과 함께 조사를 좀 해 보고 적절한 장비를 찾으면 알려 주세요. 우리가 이 품목에 사용할 수 있는 최대 금액은 600달러입니다.

감사합니다,

Betty Herzfeld 드림
구매부

회의를 개선하고 싶으십니까?

GelwayCo사의 프로젝터가 귀하의 사무실이 필요로 하는 바로 그것일 수도 있습니다!

모델	가격	광도	해상도	전등 수명
DR-7 업무용으로 맞춰진 대표적인 프로젝터	550달러	2,000루멘	1024 x 768	5,000
DR-8 무선 옵션	650달러	3,000루멘	1280 x 800	5,000
BR-103X 얇고, 가벼운 모델	1,200달러	3,000루멘	1280 x 800	4,000
F6-UR 비좁은 공간에서 이미지를 보여주기 위한 모델	850달러	2,700루멘	1024 x 768	5,000

저희는 고객들이 소프트웨어 업데이트, 설명서, 그리고 FAQ 페이지에 쉽게 접근할 수 있도록 함으로써 그들의 장비를 최대한 활용하도록 돕는 데 전념합니다. 온라인에서, 전국의 어느 매장에서든지 직접, 그리고 1-800-555-9222에서 전화로 도움을 받을 수 있습니다.

176 이메일의 목적은 무엇인가?
(A) 몇몇 장비에 대한 조언을 제공하기 위해
(B) 문의에 답변하기 위해
(C) 조사 업무를 맡기기 위해
(D) 회의 결과를 공유하기 위해

177 지금의 프로젝터에 대해 사실이 아닌 것은?
(A) 더 이상 보증 기간에 포함되지 않는다.
(B) Ms. Herzfeld를 만족시키지 못했다.
(C) GelwayCo사에 의해 만들어졌다.
(D) 회의실에서 사용된다.

178 Ms. Herzfeld에 대해 추론될 수 있는 것은?
(A) 사무용품에 대한 예산안을 승인할 것이다.
(B) 어제 발표를 할 수 없었다.
(C) 문제를 해결하기 위해 기술자와 만났다.
(D) 인턴으로부터 선택할 수 있는 것에 대해 들을 것이다.

179 구매부는 왜 DR-8을 구매하지 않을 것인가?
(A) 최대 광도가 불충분하다.
(B) 가격이 사용 가능한 예산을 초과한다.
(C) 화질이 충분히 좋지 않다.
(D) 전구가 너무 자주 교체되어야 한다.

180 GelwayCo사에 대해 언급된 것은?
(A) 각종 사무용품을 판매한다.
(B) 전국에 지점이 있다.
(C) 지원 상담 전화가 하루 24시간 이용 가능하다.
(D) 가정과 사무실 모두를 위한 장비를 만든다.

181-185는 다음 도시 소식지의 기사와 이메일에 관한 문제입니다.

콩코드 소식지, 9월 30일 호

계절 음료가 콩코드 내 카페 매출에 활기를 불어넣다

지역 카페들이 계절을 테마로 한 커피 음료를 제공함으로써 더 많은 손님을 끌어들이고 매출을 증대시키고 있다. 9월 23일에 열린 콩코드 식음료 컨벤션에서, 카페 소유주 단체는 그들의 메뉴에 더 많은 계절 음료를 추가하고 다양한 판촉 행사를 진행하겠다는 계획을 발표했다. 그렇게 함으로써, 그들은 콩코드를 인근 지역에 있는 커피 애호가들의 목적지로 바꿔 놓을 수 있다고 생각한다. 그들의 최종 목표는 이 도시를 미국의 가향 커피 중심지로 만드는 것이다.

이미, 콩코드에서는 커피를 기반으로 한 독특한 음료들을 1년 내내 볼 수 있다. Bean Brewers의 소유주인 Olivia Lang은 Pumpkin Spice가 가을에 그녀의 카페에서 가장 인기 있는 맛이라고 말한다. Creative Cups에서는, 직원들이 독특한 이름을 가진 맛을 개발함으로써 겨울 매출을 증가시키려고 한다. 작년에, 그들은 겨울을 테마로 한 커피 음료인 Xmas Espresso와 Christmas Tree Cappuccino를 제공했다. 올해, 그들은 Santa Latte를 선보일 계획이다.

한편, Chill 커피숍은 지난 3월에 처음으로 선보여 6월까지 제공되었던 상쾌한 Coconut Java를 다시 제공할 것이며, 4th Street Coffee는 인기 있는 Cherry Cappuccino를 여름에 다시 이용할 수 있게 할 예정이다.

수신: 콩코드 소식지 광고부 <advertising@connews.com>
발신: Kiana Lee <kianalee@entrepreneur.com>
날짜: 10월 5일
제목: 광고
첨부: 광고_초안

광고부 담당자께,

저는 제 커피숍인 Creative Cups가 귀사의 9월 30일 호 기사에 언급된 것을 보고 들떴습니다. 이번 주에, 이미 몇몇 손님들이 새로운 맛을 언제 판매하기 시작할 것인지 물었습니다. 홍보에 감사드리며 잇따라서 귀사의 소식지에 광고를 내고 싶습니다.

제가 관심 있는 크기는 한 페이지의 8분의 1입니다. 광고의 초안을 첨부하였습니다. 필요하다면 귀사의 직원들이 변경 사항을 제안해 주셔도 됩니다. 귀사의 웹사이트에서 가격정책을 살펴보았고 출판물의 식음료란에 광고를 내는 것이 한 달에 200달러라는 것을 확인했습니다. 이것이 맞는 금액인지 확인해 주시면, 바로 비용을 지불하겠습니다.

연락을 기다리고 있겠습니다.

감사합니다,
Kiana Lee 드림

181 9월 23일에 무슨 일이 일어났는가?
(A) 기사를 위한 인터뷰가 진행되었다.
(B) 광고가 출판물에 인쇄되었다.
(C) 업계 행사가 개최되었다.
(D) 몇몇 투자자들이 환영받았다.

182 기사에 따르면, 콩코드의 커피숍들은 왜 더 많은 계절 음료를 선보이고 있는가?
(A) 다른 지역의 고객들을 끌어들이기 위해
(B) 축제에 참가하기 위해
(C) 지역 내에서 생산되는 재료를 이용하기 위해
(D) 전국적인 유행을 기회로 활용하기 위해

183 Chill의 Coconut Java에 대해 언급된 것은?
(A) 테이크아웃 창구에서만 구매할 수 있다.
(B) 다양한 크기로 구매할 수 있다.
(C) 식품과 함께 주문하면 더 저렴하다.
(D) 올해 한정된 기간 동안 제공되었다.

184 이번 주에 몇몇 손님들이 Ms. Lee에게 어느 음료에 대해 물었을 것 같은가?
(A) Pumpkin Spice
(B) Xmas Espresso
(C) Santa Latte
(D) Cherry Cappuccino

185 Ms. Lee는 광고부에 무엇을 해달라고 요청하는가?
(A) 구독자 목록을 보낸다
(B) 광고 요금을 확인한다
(C) 음료 이름을 제안한다
(D) 사진을 컬러로 인쇄한다

186-190은 다음 공고, 목록, 이메일에 관한 문제입니다.

Hyde Park 채용 박람회
날짜: 10월 13일
장소: Hyde Park 문화 회관, 본관

당신은 학사 또는 석사 학위를 받은 최근 졸업생입니까? Hyde Park 채용 박람회에 오셔서 보건부터 소프트웨어 개발 등 다양한 분야의 일자리에 바로 지원하세요. 박람회는 탬파시가 행사를 위한 자금을 제공했기 때문에 신청자들에게 무료입니다.

참여 기업들은 숙련된 지원자들을 위한 시급한 빈자리가 있는 국내와 국제 기업들을 포함합니다. 이것들은 시간제 근무직, 정규직, 그리고 유급 인턴직을 포함합니다. 저희는 참가자들에게 참여 기업들에 대한 사전 조사를 하고 여러 장의 이력서 사본을 가져올 것을 조언합니다. Hyde Park 문화 회관은 또한 그것을 필요로 하는 학생들을 위해 이력서에 대한 전문적인 조언을 제공할 것입니다.

Hyde Park 문화 회관
참가하는 기업 목록

기업명	산업	세부 사항	회사 대표자
Brentura Diagnostics사	과학	화학 또는 생물학 석사 학위를 가진 실험실 컨설턴트 모집 *지역 대학교 졸업생 선호	Sandra Parker
Gerber사	공학	건설업 프로젝트를 위한 공학 전공자 모집	Carter Lewis
Heston사	통신	다양한 공석을 채울 마케팅 졸업생 모집	Eun-jung Bae
Jones사	소프트웨어 개발	프로젝트 기반 업무를 위한 정통한 프로그래머 모집	Mario Lopez
Spitexx사	보건	의료 영업직을 위한 인턴 모집	Angela Mitchell
Verity Care사	서비스	어린이와 함께 일하는 데 적격인 사람 모집	Belinda Hough

채용 공고가 확정되었다면 더 많은 회사들이 이 목록에 추가될 것입니다. 계속되는 업데이트에 대해 다시 확인하십시오.

수신: Alex Conner <aconner@hydeparkcenter.org>
발신: Eun-jung Bae <e.bae@heston.us>
제목: 박람회 참석
날짜: 10월 9일

Mr. Conner께,

곧 있을 채용 박람회에서 저희의 부스 예약을 확정해 주셔서 감사합니다. 저희는 많은 자격을 갖춘 지원자들을 만나기를 고대하고 있고 일류 학교 졸업생들이 참석할 것이라고 들었습니다.

저희의 계획은 가능한 한 빨리 여러 사람을 고용하는 것입니다. 그러므로, 저희는 그 행사에서 지원자들을 심사할 것입니다. 저는 또한 같은 날 면접을 하고 싶습니다. 저는 싱가포르와 일본에 있는 동료들이 가상으로 그 과정에 참여하면 좋겠습니다. 이런 목적을 위해 와이파이가 있는 작은 회의실을 빌리는 것이 가능할까요? 한 시간이면 충분할 것입니다. 저에게 알려주세요.

Eun-jung Bae 드림
인사 담당자
Heston사

186 공고는 누구를 대상으로 하는 것 같은가?
(A) 문화 회관 직원들
(B) 교직원들
(C) 최근 졸업생들
(D) 회사 임원들

187 목록에 따르면, Verity Care사에서 일하기 위한 자격은 무엇인가?
(A) 소프트웨어 프로그램에 대한 이해

(B) 영업에서의 경력
(C) 컴퓨터에 대한 세부적인 지식
(D) 어린이와 상호 작용하는 능력

188 Brentura Diagnostics사에 대해 언급된 것은?
(A) 회사의 최고경영자에 의해 대표될 것이다.
(B) 탬파 지역 출신의 고급 학위를 가진 사람을 찾고 있다.
(C) 사전 업무 경험이 있는 사람들을 필요로 한다.
(D) 과학 학위를 가진 모든 지원자를 고려할 것이다.

189 Ms. Bae에 대한 암시되는 것은?
(A) 그녀의 부서를 위한 사람들을 모집하고 있다.
(B) 출장을 위해 일찍 떠나야 한다.
(C) 현장에서 마케팅 졸업생들을 면접할 것이다.
(D) 작년에 채용 박람회에 참가했다.

190 Ms. Bae의 회사에 대해 암시되는 것은?
(A) 다수의 해외 사무소를 가지고 있다.
(B) 무급 교육생들을 찾고 있다.
(C) 여러 개의 회의실을 빌리고 싶어 한다.
(D) 부스에서의 인터넷 연결을 필요로 한다.

191-195는 다음 기사, 회람, 이메일에 관한 문제입니다.

Dorwing 항공사가 계속해서 조정하다
Aaron Sheffield 작성

어느 특정 항공편이든, 예약한 일부 승객들이 나타나지 않을 것이라는 점은 거의 확실하다. 놀랄 것도 없이, 대부분의 항공사는 초과 예약을 받음으로써 빈 좌석을 채우려고 한다. 하지만, 이 방법은 간혹 좌석보다 승객이 더 많아지는 것을 초래하여 일부 티켓 구매자들이 대체 이동 계획을 세워야 하도록 만들기 때문에 논란이 없는 것은 아니다.

항공편에 타지 못하도록 강요되는 승객들이 직면하는 스트레스를 덜어 주기 위해, 국제 항공사인 Dorwing 항공사는 최근 초과 예약 정책을 변경했다. 피해를 입은 몇몇 이코노미석 승객들은 다음 항공편에서 비즈니스 좌석을 제공받을 것이다. 다른 모든 방법이 안 되면, Dorwing 항공사는 일부 티켓 소지자들에게 보상으로 1,000달러까지도 제공할 것이다. Dorwing 항공사의 최고 경영자 Valery Suarez는 "이러한 조치가 저희의 고객 만족도를 향상하도록 도울 것이라고 확신합니다."라고 말했다.

수신: Dorwing 항공사 여객 서비스 전 직원
발신: Dorwing 항공사 경영진
제목: 초과 예약 정책 주의서
날짜: 11월 5일

지금쯤 여러분 모두가 새로운 정책에 대해 들었을 것이라고 확신하지만, 만일에 대비해 몇 가지 상기시켜 드리고 싶은 것이 있습니다:

1. 항공편이 초과 예약되었다면, 다음 항공편을 타겠다고 자원하는 승객들에게 SkySaver 쿠폰을 제시하십시오. 그들은 추후 Dorwing 항공사 항공편을 예약할 때 요금을 할인받기 위해 이것들을 사용할 수 있습니다.
2. 출발 시간 30분 이내까지 항공편이 여전히 초과 예약되어 있다면, 승객들에게 다음으로 이용 가능한 항공편의 비즈니스 좌석 및 기다리는 동안 VIP 라운지를 이용할 수 있는 기회를 제공하십시오.
3. 승객들이 곧 탑승을 시작할 때까지도 사안이 해결되지 않으면, 해당 항공편에 대해 가능한 최대 보상 금액을 제시할 수 있습니다.

수신: Joan Kreeger <joan_kreeger@wentleco.com>
발신: Lewis Hopps <lew_hopps@wentleco.com>
제목: Mr. Hunt의 항공편
날짜: 11월 10일
첨부: 가격_견적

안녕하세요, Joan,

저는 방금 Mr. Hunt로부터 메시지를 받았습니다. 그는 어제 있었던 Vorin 건설사 대표와의 회의가 잘 진행되었다고 말했습니다. 그는 지금 Roystonville에 있는 공항에 있으며 한 시간 정도 늦게 도착할 것이라고 말했습니다.

그의 오후 1시 10분 항공편이 초과 예약되었지만, Dorwing 항공사가 그에게 오후 2시 5분에 출발하는 항공편의 비즈니스 좌석을 확보해주었습니다. 그것은 당신에게 공항으로 가는 시간을 더 줄 것입니다. 그를 데리러 가기 위해 오후 5시쯤 사무실에서 출발하면 될 겁니다. 그때까지, 제가 보내드리는 파일이 정확한지 확인해 주십시오.

Lewis 드림

191 기사는 왜 쓰였는가?
(A) 기술적인 해결책을 제시하기 위해
(B) 상황 처리를 비판하기 위해
(C) 정책 변경 사항을 설명하기 위해
(D) 임원 채용을 발표하기 위해

192 항공편이 초과 예약되면 Dorwing 항공사 여객 서비스 직원들은 무엇을 할 수 있는가?
(A) 호텔 시설을 제공한다
(B) 할인 상품권을 제시한다
(C) 제휴 항공사에 연락한다
(D) 확인되지 않은 예약을 취소한다

193 탑승 직전에 좌석을 포기한 티켓 소지자들은 무엇을 받을 권리가 있는가?
(A) 좌석 업그레이드
(B) 최고 1,000달러의 금액
(C) 프리미엄 대기 공간에 입장할 수 있는 권리
(D) 추가 마일리지 포인트

194 Mr. Hunt에 대해 암시되는 것은?
(A) 공항에서 바로 사무실로 갈 것이다.
(B) 신규 고객과 합의에 도달할 수 있었다.
(C) 며칠 동안 Roystonville에 있었다.
(D) 전용 대기실을 이용할 수 있는 기회가 주어졌다.

195 Mr. Hopps는 Ms. Kreeger에게 무엇을 해달라고 요청하는가?
(A) 파일이 정확한지 확인한다
(B) 제휴 업체의 대표자들을 만난다
(C) 비행 일정표를 보낸다
(D) 국제 항공편을 예약한다

196-200은 다음 이메일, 공고, 양식에 관한 문제입니다.

수신: Bennet Fraser <b.fraser@invercargill.com>
발신: Clara Walker <c.walker@pos.co.nz>
제목: 제5회 연례 POS 회의
날짜: 12월 8일

Dr. Fraser께,

이곳 태평양 치과 교정 협회(POS)에서는, 4월 23일부터 24일까지 열릴 내년 회의를 위한 준비를 시작했습니다. 특별 강연 및 학술 토론회와 함께, 저희는 패널 토론을 열고자 합니다. 귀하는 직장에서 획기적인 연구를 주도하셨으므로, 회의의 둘째 날에 연단에서 Dr. Ellie Williams와 Dr. Hannah Brown과 함께 귀하의 연구에 관해 이야기하시도록 초청하고 싶습니다.

각 연사는 보상으로 2,000달러를 받습니다. 또한, 여행 경비는 변제되고 여러 가지 활동에 대한 손님용 자유 입장권이 제공되며, 이는 회의 장소의 연회장에서 열리는 비공개 파티를 포함합니다. 연사들을 위해 지역 호텔의 객실이 예약되었으며, 이곳에는 다양한 시설이 잘 갖추어져 있습니다. 저는 귀하께서 그 호텔의 체육관을 높이 평가하실 것이라고 확신하며, 모든 손님들은 그곳을 무료로 이용할 수 있습니다. 또한 스파도 있으며, 이는 적정한 입장료를 받습니다.

귀하의 답변을 기다리고 있겠습니다.

Clara Walker 드림, 회의 조직위원

4월 23일 & 24일로 예정된
제5회 연례 POS 회의에 대한 공고

올해 태평양 치과 교정 협회(POS) 회의는 오클랜드에서 열릴 것입니다. 남태평양 지역 최고의 전문가들이 치아 교정의 최신 기법 및 기술에 대해 발표할 것입니다. 다음 행사들은 이미 확정되었습니다:

특별 강연	치아 교정기의 최신 발전	Dr. James Reid
학술 토론회	새로운 종류의 치아 임플란트	Dr. Serena Singh
학술 토론회	저렴한 치아 정렬 키트	Dr. Hazel Collins
패널 토론	스캐닝 기술	Dr. Hannah Brown Dr. Bennet Fraser Dr. Ellie Williams

입장료는 POS 회원들에게는 540달러이며 비회원에게는 600달러이고, 결제 마감일은 3월 30일입니다. 지불금은 www.pos.co.nz/congress5에서 신용카드로 납부될 수 있습니다.

POS 여행 보상 양식

POS에 기여해 주셔서 감사합니다. 귀하께서 제대로 보상받을 수 있도록 하기 위해, 이 양식을 작성해서 이것의 스캔본과 모든 영수증을 bh.accounting@pos.co.nz로 Blake Henry에게 보내주십시오. Eden Lake 호텔에서의 귀하의 숙박은 POS에 의해 이미 지불되었습니다.

참가자 성명: Hannah Brown

참석 행사: 제5회 연례 POS 회의

행사 장소: Centennial 호텔, 오클랜드

지출

날짜	설명	비용	총계
4월 22일	Te Anau 항공사, 이코노미석	547달러	556달러
	문구용품	9달러	
4월 24일	노트북 연결 코드	90.75달러	90.75달러
4월 25일	Ether 항공사, 비즈니스석	612달러	635달러
	새벽 공항행 택시	23달러	
총계			1,281.75달러

196 Ms. Walker는 왜 Dr. Fraser에게 연락했는가?
(A) 그가 협회의 회원이 되도록 권하기 위해
(B) 대학에서의 학술 토론회 일정을 잡기 위해
(C) 그의 회의 참가를 요청하기 위해
(D) 새로 개발된 시스템을 분석하기 위해

197 스캐닝 기술에 관한 패널 토론에 대해 암시되는 것은?
(A) 4월 24일에 열렸다.
(B) 뜻밖의 손님을 특별히 포함했다.
(C) 많은 청중들이 참석했다.
(D) 기술적인 시연을 포함했다.

198 공고에 따르면, 몇몇 사람들은 왜 웹사이트에 방문해야 하는가?
(A) 의견을 제공하기 위해
(B) 사진을 업로드하기 위해
(C) 좌석 배치도를 보기 위해
(D) 거래를 완료하기 위해

199 Dr. Brown은 Eden Lake 호텔에서 무엇을 무료로 받았을 것 같은가?
(A) 컴퓨터 부대 용품
(B) 헬스장 이용 권한
(C) 무제한 인터넷 사용
(D) 스파에서의 관리

200 Dr. Brown에 대해 언급된 것은?
(A) 동료들과 함께 여행했다.
(B) 오클랜드에서의 체류 동안 임대 자동차를 운전했다.
(C) 두 개의 서로 다른 항공사의 항공편을 예약했다.
(D) Centennial 호텔에 도착하기 위해 23달러를 썼다.

TEST 05 해석

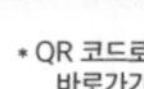

* 무료 해설은 해커스토익(Hackers.co.kr)에서 다운로드 받을 수 있습니다.

* QR 코드로 바로가기

PART 5

101 소비자 조사는 사람들이 기꺼이 새로운 컴퓨터에 최대 1,200달러까지 쓸 것임을 보여준다.

102 잘 정리된 이력서는 당신의 면접을 볼 수 있는 가능성을 증가시킨다.

103 Alicia Doone의 삽화는 도시 곳곳의 잡지에 게재되었다.

104 자선 가게의 24시간 투입함은 사람들이 언제든 그들이 편할 때 중고 의류를 기부할 수 있도록 한다.

105 Chemie's 아이스크림은 계절마다 바뀌는 여러 가지의 상품들을 제공한다.

106 여행자들은 새로운 Perspectiva Plus 신용카드로 그 어느 때보다 더 빠르게 보상 포인트를 받을 수 있다.

107 손님들로부터 수집된 의견에 따르면, 대부분의 고객들은 식당의 새로운 메뉴에 만족한다.

108 Sally's 과자점은 Grant가에 있는 중앙 광장으로부터 세 번째 건물이다.

109 사진 대회의 우승자는 다섯 명의 유명한 심사위원단에 의해 결정될 것이다.

110 Emblem Motor사의 신차 라인업은 내년 초에 연례 시카고 자동차 전시회에서 발표될 것이다.

111 부장은 Ms. Springs가 휴가에서 돌아오면 그녀에게 새로운 프로젝트를 배정할 것이다.

112 회사가 다른 무엇보다도 고객의 요구를 우선시할 때, 재구매가 발생하는 경향이 있다.

113 기술자들은 기존의 태양 전지판에 약간의 수정을 가하는 것이 그것들을 더 효과적이게 만들 것이라고 주장했다.

114 Waterford 아파트에 거주하는 세입자들은 매달 1일에 집세를 내야 한다.

115 충분한 공적 자금이 없다면, Scott 재단은 민간 공급자로부터 더 많은 자금을 조달해야 할 것이다.

116 Mr. Black은 2년의 경력밖에 없었는데도 불구하고, TVD사의 지역 영업부장으로 임명되었다.

117 손님에게 실수로 요금이 두 번 청구되어서, 그녀의 신용카드로 환불금이 지급되었다.

118 Manuel사의 근로자들은 이제부터 고용 혜택 중 하나로 생명 보험 보장을 받을 것이다.

119 Ms. Jung은 한 번도 이동을 요청한 적이 없었으므로, 휴스턴 지사로 전근 가게 되었다는 것을 알게 되어 기분이 상했다.

120 이번 주말의 Phoenix 마라톤 경주는 우천 예보에도 불구하고 예정대로 열릴 것이다.

121 Shiller 어린이 박물관의 방문객들은 전시된 물품들과 매우 자유롭게 상호 작용할 수 있다.

122 Paulson 전자회사는 일반 우편 또는 추가 요금을 수반하는 속달 배송을 통해 제품을 배달할 수 있다.

123 텔레비전 광고가 방송된 후, Seaborn Cruises사는 잠재적인 승객들로부터 대량의 문의를 받았다.

124 무대가 설치되고 있었을 때 음악가들은 무대 뒤에서 연습했다.

125 배터리를 폐기하기보다는 재활용함으로써, 쓰레기 매립지에 들어가는 유독성 물질의 양을 줄이는 것이 가능하다.

126 Folza Bar and Grill의 종업원들은 2주마다 시간당 9달러의 급료를 받는다.

127 실제 사건에 기초한 소설들은 보통 모든 연령대의 독자들에 매우 인기가 있다.

128 가능한 한 포괄적으로 설계된 교육 과정 동안, 직무의 모든 측면이 다뤄질 것이다.

129 대통령은 공급 부족에 대해 가능한 해결책을 논의하기 위해 국내 최고의 몇몇 제조업체들을 만났다.

130 납세 신고서를 제대로 제출하지 않는 것은 국세청으로부터의 시정 요청으로 이어질 수 있다.

PART 6

131-134는 다음 회람에 관한 문제입니다.

수신: 부서장들
발신: Ronaldo Reyes
제목: 내년 예산
날짜: 5월 15일

월례 부서장 회의가 5월 30일 수요일 오후 7시에 열릴 것입니다. 언제나처럼, 그것은 16층에 있는 회의실에서일 것입니다.

회의의 주요 논제는 내년의 부서별 예산이 될 것입니다. 이것은 대단히 중요한 주제입니다. **131** 따라서, 회사의 최고 경영자가 저희와 함께할 것입니다. **132** 회의에 대비하여, 여러분이 각자 본인 부서의 연간 경비를 요약하고 예산에서 만들어져야 할 수도 있는 변화를 강조하는 보고서를 준비해 주시기 바랍니다. **133** 특히, 없앨 수 있는 불필요한 지출을 찾아봐 주시는데, 이것이 회사 공금을 전반적으로 절약할 것이기 때문입니다.

134 이 회람을 수신했다는 사실을 알려 주십시오. 이를 위해서는 그저 제 비서인 Ms. Hertz에게 여러분의 참석을 확정해 주시면 됩니다. 감사합니다.

135-138은 다음 후기에 관한 문제입니다.

135 제가 True Colors 페인트용품점에 첫 번째로 방문했을 때에는, 훌륭한 고객 서비스를 받았었습니다. 안타깝게도, 그곳에 대한 제 두 번째 경험은 이전보다 결코 좋지 않았습니다. 어제 제가 들어갔을 때, 가게의 프런트에 직원이 아무도 없었습니다. 10분 동안 색상 견본을 본 후에, 마침내 한 직원이 제게 다가왔습니다. 하지만, 그녀는 전화를 받으러 가기 위해 거의 바로 자리를 비웠습니다. **136** 솔직히, 저는 그렇게 전문가답지 못한 행동을 목격하여 충격을 받았습니다. 그뿐만 아니라, 제가 마침내 도움을 받았을 때 또 다른 사람이 제 주문에서 실수를 저질렀습니다. **137** 저는 Candy Apple Red를 요청했는데 그 대신 Scarlet Red를 받았습니다. **138** 다음에는, 손님들에게 더 주의를 기울이는 다른 가게에서 쇼핑할 것입니다.

139-142는 다음 이메일에 관한 문제입니다.

수신: Julie Evans <julie@juliepaints.com>
발신: David Whetzel <director@artunlimited.com>
제목: 미술 수업
날짜: 2월 12일

Ms. Evans께,

저는 최근 Wave 미술관에서 당신의 작품을 보았으며 당신의 독특한 기법에 매우 감명받았다고 말씀드리고 싶습니다. **139** 저는 당신의 것과 비슷한 그림을 본 적이 없습니다. **140** 저는 일주일에 여러 번 회화 수업을 여는 작은 미술 스튜디오를 운영하고 있어 오늘 이메일을 쓰게 되었습니다. 저희는 가끔 학생들에게 기본적인 유화나 아크릴화 기법 외에 다른 무언가를 가르쳐 줄 수 있는 미술가들을 초대하는데, 저는 당신이 다음 초청 강사가 되는 것에 관심이 있을지 궁금해하고 있었습니다. **141** 당신은 강의를 계획하는 것에 있어 많은 융통성을 가질 것입니다. 선생님으로서, 당신은 사용할 재료와 가르칠 개념을 단독으로 결정하게 될 것입니다.

당신의 연락을 기다리고 있겠습니다. **142** 만약 관심이 있을 경우 이 이메일 주소가 제게 연락할 가장 좋은 방법입니다.

David Whetzel 드림
Art Unlimited 책임자

143-146은 다음 공고에 관한 문제입니다.

직원들은 주목해주십시오:

143 Sebastian Hill 호텔이 6월 내내 문을 닫을 예정입니다. 그 건물은 손님들이 이곳에 있는 동안에는 완료될 수 없는 몇 가지 보수를 필요로 합니다.

6월은 가장 바쁜 시기가 시작될 때이므로, 협력 지점들에 모두에게 충분한 임시 일자리가 있습니다. **144** 따라서, 모든 Sebastian Hill 직원들이 이곳에서의 마지막 날인, 5월 31일 이후에 Daytona 호텔 또는 New Orleans 리조트에서 일을 시작할 것입니다.

일하고 싶은 호텔에 대한 선호가 있다면, 이번 주말 전까지 지점장인 Jim Stevens에게 이야기하십시오. **145** 그는 어떤 요청도 충족시켜줄 것을 약속할 수는 없지만 그것들을 신중히 고려할 것입니다. **146** 5월 20일까지 임시 근무지에 관한 모든 결정이 내려질 것입니다.

PART 7

147-148은 다음 온라인 양식에 관한 문제입니다.

*Global Engineering Monthly*지 (GEM)

30년이 넘도록, 저희는 공학 분야의 전문가들을 위해 선택된 간행물이었습니다. *Global Engineering Monthly*지의 각 호는 장비 평가, 최신 동향에 대한 기사, 그리고 성공적인 공학자들의 인물 소개를 포함합니다.

구독 패키지

6개월 구독	□ 36달러 (6달러/1부)
1년 구독	■ 66달러 (5.50달러/1부)
2년 구독	□ 96달러 (4달러/1부)

편리하게 이메일로 발송되는 GEM의 주간 소식지를 구독하고 싶으신가요?
예 □ 아니오 ■

귀하의 정보

성명	Lorenza Cassar
주소	17번지 Triq Annetto Caruana
도시	콰아라
국가	몰타
우편번호	SPB 1215
이메일 주소	lorenza@rcengineering.com

*1년 구독을 신청하는 고객들은 무료 소형 공구 키트를 받습니다!
*2년 구독을 신청하는 고객들은 5월 9일에 뉴욕시에서 열리는 초국적 공학 학회의 무료 입장권을 받습니다!

계산서 작성란으로 가기

147 *Global Engineering Monthly*지에 대해 언급된 것은?
(A) 개별 호를 할인가에 판매한다.
(B) 공학 학회를 후원한다.
(C) 독자층은 그들 분야의 전문가들을 포함한다.
(D) 출판사에서 다른 잡지 서적들도 발행한다.

148 Ms. Cassar는 그녀의 구독으로 무엇을 받을 것인가?
(A) 주간 소식지
(B) 학회 입장권
(C) 소형 공구 키트
(D) 특별판

149-151은 다음 공고에 관한 문제입니다.

주목:

만약 여러분이 자주 불면증으로 고통받거나 수면 장애를 가지고 있다고 의심한다면, 여러분은 Carson 의료 기관에서 진행되고 있는 새로운 연구에 참가할 자격이 있을 것입니다. 저희는 현재 사람들이 불면증을 없애는 데 도움을 줄 수 있는 약을 개발하고 있습니다. 연구 동안에, 여러분이 해야 하는 모든 것은 2주 동안 매일 밤의 일정한 시간에 그것을 복용하기만 하면 됩니다. 그런 다음, 여러분은 모든 부작용뿐만 아니라 수면에 미치는 영향에 대한 보고서를 작성하도록 요청받을 것입니다.

만약 당신이 18세에서 50세 사이의 연령이라면, 당신은 이 연구에 참가할 자격이 있습니다. 등록하려면, sleepstudy@cmi.org로 연락주세요. 이메일에는, 약물에 방해가 될 수 있는 당신이 가지고 있는 의학적 문제를 명시해주세요. 업무 일정과 기타 의무 사항도 기재해주세요. 등록 마감일은 12월 1일입니다. 모든 참가자들은 그들의 시간에 대해 200달러를 지급받을 것입니다.

149 Carson 의료 기관은 무엇을 할 계획인가?
(A) 연구소를 개설한다
(B) 약을 시험한다
(C) 신규 직원들을 채용한다
(D) 광고를 시작한다

150 1문단 네 번째 줄의 단어 "regular"는 의미상 -와 가장 가깝다.
(A) 일정한
(B) 질서 있는
(C) 곧은
(D) 보통의

151 사람들은 이메일에 무엇을 명시해야 하는가?
(A) 약에 대한 익숙함
(B) 선호되는 치료 방법
(C) 시간상의 의무
(D) 이전 연구에 대한 참여

152-153은 다음 메시지 대화문에 관한 문제입니다.

Kathleen Massee [오후 6시 18분]
안녕하세요, Evan. 다음 주 일정이 이미 게시된 것을 방금 알았는데, 제가 월요일 오전에 일하기로 되어 있는 것 같아서, 이것이 이상하네요. 저는 보통 오전 교대 근무를 받지 않아요.

Evan Rosenblatt [오후 6시 19분]
제 생각에 Ms. Ross는 Ms. Kovac이 휴가 간 동안 그녀를 대체할 누군가가 필요한 것 같아요.

Kathleen Massee [오후 6시 20분]
그렇군요. 음, 어쨌든, 제가 그날 치과 예약을 해 둬서 당신이 저 대신 그 근무를 맡아줄 수 있는지 궁금해하고 있었어요.

Evan Rosenblatt [오후 6시 22분]
전혀 문제 없어요. 어차피 그때 다른 할 일도 없어요. 이 변경 사항이 분명 Ms. Ross에게도 괜찮겠지만, 그녀가 일정을 수정할 수 있도록 오늘 중으로 알려주셔야 해요.

Kathleen Massee [오후 6시 23분]
정말 고마워요. 신세를 졌네요.

152 Ms. Kovac에 대해 암시되는 것은?
(A) 휴가 시간을 요청할 것이다.
(B) 그녀의 관리자에게 연락하기를 원치 않는다.
(C) 보통 오전 근무를 맡는다.
(D) 다른 지사로 전근가게 될 것이다.

153 오후 6시 22분에, Mr. Rosenblatt가 "Not a problem at all"이라고 썼을 때 그가 의도한 것은?
(A) 동료의 근무를 맡을 의향이 있다.
(B) 비용이 이미 Ms. Ross에 의해 충당되었다.
(C) 치과 치료 과정은 오래 걸리지 않을 것이다.
(D) 최근의 일정 충돌에 대해 듣지 못했다.

154-155는 다음 광고에 관한 문제입니다.

공예는 아이들만을 위한 것이 아닙니다!

이번 여름에, 지역 용품점 Arts and Scraps가 성인 학습자들을 위해 매주 화요일과 목요일 오후 6시 30분부터 오후 8시 30분까지 소규모의 영업 후 수업을 열 것입니다. 수업은 유리화, 리놀륨 판화, 그리고 혼합 매체 콜라주 제작을 포함하여, 다양한 기법에 대한 교육을 제공할 것입니다. 이는 삽화가 Maude Cumby가 가르칠 것인데, 그녀는 뉴욕에서 10년 동안 화가로 일했고 Pulford 디자인 학교의 졸업생입니다.

수업 시작 한 달 전인 5월 2일 이전에 자리를 예약한다면 12번의 수업 과정에 대한 비용은 100달러입니다. 그 날 이후로는, 130달러의 정규 요금이 적용됩니다. 모든 재료는 제공됩니다. 등록하시기 위해서는 www.artsandscraps.com/classes를 방문하시거나, 정상 영업시간인 오전 10시부터 오후 6시 중에 저희 가게에 들르셔서 등록하세요.

154 Arts and Scraps에 대해 언급된 것은?
(A) 뉴욕에 위치해 있다.
(B) Ms. Cumby가 소유하고 있다.
(C) 오후 6시 30분에 문을 닫는다.
(D) 매주 두 번의 수업 과정이 있을 것이다.

155 다가오는 수업에 대해 언급된 것은?
(A) 최근 디자인 학교 졸업생이 가르칠 것이다.
(B) 수업료는 수업 재료를 포함하지 않는다.
(C) 5월에 열릴 것이다.
(D) 등록 날짜에 따라 요금이 다르다.

156-158은 다음 안내문에 관한 문제입니다.

Corogo사 직원 이동 정책

Corogo사는 직원들의 전문성 개발을 지원하며 몇몇 직원들이 사내에서 승진 기회를 추구하고 싶어 할 수도 있다는 점을 인지하고 있습니다. Corogo사의 직원들은 다음의 경우 회사 웹사이트에 게시된 공석에 내부적으로 지원할 수 있습니다:

- 현재 직책에서 최소 12개월 동안 일해 왔다면*
- 구인 공고 중 하나에 열거된 최소한의 자격 또는 요건을 갖추고 있다면
- 지난 6개월 이내에 최소 "만족스러움" 수준의 인사 고과를 받았다면
- 지난 12개월 이내에 서면 경고 또는 주의를 받은 적이 없다면

다른 직책에 지원하는 데 관심이 있는 직원들은 가능한 한 빨리 현재 관리자에게 통지하도록 권고됩니다. 풀타임 정직원들은 지원서를 제출하기 최소 2주 전에는 관리자에게 통보하도록 요구됩니다.

만약 직원이 다른 부서의 직책에 합격한다면, 이전에 승인된 휴일 계획은 변경의 대상이 될 것입니다.

*위 요건을 충족하지 않는 직원들은 드문 경우에만 이동이 고려될 것입니다. 이러한 경우에는, Corogo사 인사 직원이 이동이 적절한지 결정하기 위해 해당 직원의 현재 관리자와 만날 것입니다.

156 Corogo사에 대해 언급된 것은?
(A) 직원들에게 전문성 개발 수업을 제공한다.
(B) 내부에서 관리자를 고용하는 것을 고려해 보고 있다.
(C) 지원 가능한 직책을 웹사이트에 올린다.
(D) 1년에 한 번 직원들을 평가한다.

157 이동된 직원들에 대해 무엇이 바뀔 것 같은가?
(A) 주차 공간
(B) 월급
(C) 휴일
(D) 근무 시간

158 안내문에 따르면, 어떤 경우에 관리자와 인사 직원이 만날 것 같은가?
(A) 징계통보서가 무효화되었을 때
(B) 지원자가 현재 직책을 1년 이하로 유지했을 때
(C) 인사 고과가 부정확할 때
(D) 교육 기간이 끝나갈 때

159-160은 다음 안내문에 관한 문제입니다.

http://www.contestcraze.com/advertise

홈	일일 특집 대회	**홍보**	연락	양식

Contest Craze에서 홍보하기:
당신의 기업 또는 단체를 위한 대회, 추첨, 또는 증정을 홍보하고 계신가요? 입소문을 내는 데 도움이 필요하시다면, 알맞은 곳에 오셨습니다. 사람들이 알아야 한다고 생각하시는 대회가 있다면, 저희에게 설명을 보내주시고, 저희가 하루 동안 무료로 저희 홈페이지에 그것을 게시할 것입니다. 더욱 많은 노출을 원하신다면, 당신의 게시물을 특집 대회로 만들기 위해 아래의 저희 홍보 옵션 중 하나를 선택하십시오. 이는 그것이 저희 홈페이지 상단에 유지될 것이며 저희 회원들에게 발송되는 일일 이메일 소식지에 포함될 것을 의미합니다.

특집 대회의 가격:

1일	35달러
2일	65달러
3일	90달러
1주일	200달러

참가비를 요구하는 대회에 대한 정보는 게시하지 않는다는 점을 유의해 주십시오.

159 안내문의 목적은 무엇인가?
(A) 기업을 위해 제품을 홍보하기 위해
(B) 온라인 당첨 팁을 공유하기 위해
(C) 홈페이지 관리에 대한 조언을 제공하기 위해
(D) 홍보 서비스에 대한 세부 정보를 제공하기 위해

160 특집 대회에 대해 사실인 것은?
(A) 일주일 동안 광고되어야 한다.
(B) 단체 이메일에 서술된다.
(C) 다양한 웹사이트에 홍보된다.
(D) 참가자로부터 참가비를 요구한다.

161-164는 다음 기사에 관한 문제입니다.

환경 인식의 날 증정품

기자 Brenda Galway 작성

5월 1일에 환경 인식의 날을 기념하기 위해서, Winstonville은 지역 사회 구성원들에게 선착순으로 2,000그루의 무료 나무 모종을 나누어 줄 것이다. 이 계획은 도시의 지속 가능성을 향상하기 위해 10,000그루의 나무를 심기로 한 시 행정부 공약의 일부이다. 도시 계획 관리자 Jane Stein에 따르면, 오전 8시부터 오전 11시 30분까지 Fennel가의 Mulligan's 유치원과 중앙 시민

문화 회관에서 나무들을 얻을 수 있다. 오전에 올 수 없는 사람들을 위해 Clifton가의 Home and Garden 가게에서 오후 4시 30분부터 오후 8시까지도 많은 나무들을 구할 수 있다.

"그저 가져가신 각각의 나무를 심고 돌보기 위해 시 웹사이트에 게시된 안내를 따르는 것을 기억해 주세요."라고 Ms. Stein은 말했다. "저희는 나무의 발육 경과를 추적하고 있습니다. 공식 목록에 따르면, 저희가 지금까지 이미 800그루의 새로운 나무를 도시에 심었다는 것을 말씀드리게 되어 기쁩니다." 본인 소유의 토지는 없지만 그래도 계획에 참여하고 싶은 주민들은 지역 비영리 기구 Planet Plant가 여는 특별 원예 행사에 참여할 수 있다. 더 많은 세부 사항을 위해서는 www.winstonvillegov.org/parksandrecdept를 방문하면 된다.

161 기사의 목적은 무엇인가?
(A) 도시에 있는 나무들의 이로움을 설명하기 위해
(B) 시의 프로젝트를 설명하기 위해
(C) 캠페인 공약을 발표하기 위해
(D) 최근에 열린 행사를 평가하기 위해

162 무료 나무에 대해 언급된 것은?
(A) 오전에만 배포될 것이다.
(B) 비영리 기구에 의해 제공되었다.
(C) 교육 책자가 딸려 있을 것이다.
(D) 주민들이 한정된 수량으로 구할 수 있다.

163 Ms. Stein은 사람들에게 무엇을 하라고 상기시키는가?
(A) 정원에 나무를 위한 공간을 마련한다
(B) 지역에서 자원봉사 활동을 하는 것을 신청한다
(C) 설명을 찾기 위해 웹사이트를 방문한다
(D) 나무를 심기 위해 시의 허가를 받는다

164 2문단 두 번째 줄의 단어 "tracking"은 의미상 -와 가장 가깝다.
(A) 찾다
(B) 지켜보다
(C) 유지하다
(D) 뒤쫓다

165-168은 다음 웹페이지에 관한 문제입니다.

www.dpqtransport.com/aboutus

소개:
DPQ 운송사는 일주일 내내, 하루 24시간 전국적으로 서비스를 제공하는 전세버스 대여 회사입니다. 관광을 가든 기업 휴양지를 가든 단체를 태워야 한다면, 저희와 함께 이동하는 것이 올바른 선택이라는 것을 보장합니다.

안전은 저희의 첫 번째 우선순위입니다. 따라서, 저희 기사들은 수년의 운전 경력을 가진 고도로 훈련된 사람들입니다. — [1] —. 게다가, 저희 차량은 출발 시 항상 제대로 기능하는 것을 보장하도록 정기적으로 정비됩니다.

저희는 안락함과 편리함에서도 자부심을 가지고 있습니다. — [2] —. 다리를 뻗을 수 있는 충분한 공간이 있는 것과 더불어, 차량 내 각각의 등받이가 넘어가는 좌석은 조절 가능한 에어컨 통풍구뿐만 아니라 기기들을 위한 전기 콘센트도 갖추고 있습니다. 무료 무선 인터넷 또한 이용 가능합니다. 또한 당신은 가벼운 식사나 간식을 가지고 오거나 유명한 식당에서의 정차 계획을 세울 수도 있습니다. — [3] —.

마지막으로, 저희 버스들은 56명까지 수용할 수 있으며, 이는 저희 서비스를 이용하는 것이 단체로 이동하는 데 있어 비용 효율이 높은 방법이라는 의미입니다. — [4] —.

DPQ 운송사가 당신을 위한 올바른 선택이라면, 여행의 세부 정보를 queries@dpqtransport.com으로 보내 주십시오. 저희가 경쟁력 있는 견적과 여행 일정 제안을 포함하여 24시간 이내로 답변할 것입니다.

165 DPQ 운송사에 대해 사실인 것은?
(A) 국제적인 교통수단을 제공한다.
(B) 관광 단체만 독점적으로 상대한다.
(C) 급행 서비스를 개시했다.
(D) 하루 종일 운영한다.

166 DPQ 운송사 차량 좌석에 대해 언급되지 않은 것은?
(A) 공간이 넓다.
(B) 기기를 위한 콘센트가 있다.
(C) 붙박이 화면이 있다.
(D) 온도 조절 기능이 있다.

167 웹페이지에 따르면, 사람들은 이메일을 통해 무엇을 할 수 있는가?
(A) 특정 기사를 선택한다
(B) 가격 견적을 받는다
(C) 여행자 수를 조정한다
(D) 차내 식사를 특별 주문한다

168 [1], [2], [3], [4]로 표시된 위치 중, 다음 문장이 들어갈 곳으로 가장 적절한 것은?

"그들은 고용된 직후 철저히 심사되며 연간 평가를 통과해야 합니다."

(A) [1]
(B) [2]
(C) [3]
(D) [4]

169-171은 다음 기사에 관한 문제입니다.

이동전화 기지국 건설이 곧 시작된다

일부 지역 주민들에게는 매우 실망스럽게도, 해변 마을 Farview에서 새로운 이동전화 기지국 건설이 곧 시작할 예정이다. — [1] —. 3년 전 처음 제안되었지만, 그 프로젝트는 사람들이 해변 주차장의 제안된 장소에 대한 우려를 제기하기 시작하며 지연되었다. 많은 사람들이 기지국이 그 지역의 자연미를 망칠 것이라고 말했다. 다른 사람들은 그것의 존재가 부동산 가치를 하락시키는 것은 말할 것도 없으며, 그 장소 가까이에 사는 사람들에게 여러 가지 건강 및 안전 문제를 야기할 수 있다는 두려움을 표했다. — [2] —.

이러한 점에서, 시 공무원들은 기지국이 안전할 뿐만 아니라 그것의 공간을 임대하는 각 무선 통신사로부터 매년 약 2만 달러 금액의 상당한 임대 수익을 발생시킬 것이라고 대중을 안심시켰다. — [3] —. 게다가, 여름마다 Farview로 오는 관광객들의 유입은 기지국이 실용적인 이유로 점점 더 필요해지고 있다는 것을 의미한다. "방문객들이 더 많을수록, 더 많은 전화기들이 있습니다."라고 시 위원 Fred White가 말했다. — [4] —. 건물의 외관에 대한 우려에 관해서는, 기지국이 자연환경과 충분히 조화를 이룰 수 있도록 지역 화가인 Katherine Tatum이 그것의 설계를 도왔다.

169 기지국에 대한 우려로 언급되지 않은 것은?
(A) 지역의 야생 생물에 피해를 줄 수 있다.
(B) 여러 가지 건강 문제를 야기할 수 있다.
(C) 부동산 가치에 부정적으로 영향을 미칠 수 있다.
(D) 지역을 보기 안 좋게 만들 수 있다.

170 Farview에 대해 암시되는 것은?
(A) 아직 이동전화 기지국이 없다.
(B) 관광업을 위해 해변 지역을 개발할 계획이다.
(C) 토지 사용에 대해 임대료를 낸다.
(D) 새로운 구조물을 통해 돈을 벌 것이다.

171 [1], [2], [3], [4]로 표시된 위치 중, 다음 문장이 들어갈 곳으로 가장 적절한 것은?

"그리고 그것은 이동전화 서비스에 대한 더 큰 수요가 있다는 것을 의미한다."

(A) [1]
(B) [2]
(C) [3]
(D) [4]

172-175는 다음 온라인 채팅 대화문에 관한 문제입니다.

Bryce Turner [오후 2시 30분]
우리 회사의 주주들이 우리가 폐기물을 줄이길 바란다는 것을 들었나요? 그들의 바람을 존중해주는 것이 중요한 것 같아서, 여기 Meerson사에서 우리가 사용하는 재활용이 불가능한 포장재의 양을 줄일 방법들을 좀 찾아보고 싶어요.

Sophie Moore [오후 2시 31분]
우리는 최근에 상자 안에 넣는 플라스틱 폼의 양을 40퍼센트 줄였어요. 그밖에 우리가 할 수 있는 다른 방법이 있을까요?

Bryce Turner [오후 2시 34분]
폼을 완전히 없애고 그 대신 잘게 조각난 신문을 사용하기 시작할 수 있을까요?

Randy Poehler [오후 2시 35분]
그리고 깨지기 쉬운 물품들에만 추가 충전재가 필요해요. 예를 들어, 우리의 세제는 플라스틱 병에 담겨 들어와서, 어떤 특별한 보호물도 필요하지 않죠.

Randy Poehler [오후 2시 36분]
배송 재료에만 초점을 맞추는 것 대신에, 일부 제품의 용기도 변경하면 어떨까요?

Bryce Turner [오후 2시 38분]
용기에 어떤 다른 종류의 재료를 사용하자고 제안하는 건가요? 저는 그것이 어떻게 조금이라도 더 나을지 잘 모르겠어요.

Randy Poehler [오후 2시 39분]
아뇨. 단지 플라스틱을 더 효율적으로 사용할 수 있다고 말하는 거예요. 우리의 일부 경쟁업체들은 빈 용기를 리필하기 위해 사용될 수 있는 파우치에 세제를 넣어서 판매해요. 그들은 플라스틱을 사용하고 있지만, 훨씬 더 적게 사용해요. 우리도 똑같이 할 수 있을 거예요.

Bryce Turner [오후 2시 41분]
그건 사실 우리의 비용도 절약시켜 주겠네요.

Sophie Moore [오후 2시 42분]
그렇게 변경할 수 있을지 알아볼게요.

172 Mr. Turner는 무엇을 줄이고 싶어 하는가?
(A) 유통망의 규모
(B) 재활용이 불가능한 재료의 사용
(C) 병에 담긴 세정제의 양
(D) 판매하는 깨지기 쉬운 물품의 개수

173 Meerson사에 대해 암시되는 것은?
(A) 주주들로부터 의견을 구할 계획이다.
(B) 일부 병은 재활용된 플라스틱으로 만들어진다.
(C) 상품 보관 부서 직원들을 감축하고 있다.
(D) 일부 제품은 충전재가 필요하지 않다.

174 파우치에 대해 암시되는 것은?
(A) 플라스틱으로 만들어졌다.
(B) 병에 비해 생산이 더 오래 걸린다.
(C) 다양한 크기로 들어온다.
(D) Meerson사에 의해 특허가 났다.

175 오후 2시 39분에, Mr. Poehler가 "We could do the same"이라고 썼을 때 그가 의도한 것은?
(A) 모든 플라스틱 포장을 없앨 방안이 있다.
(B) 다른 종류의 용기를 사용하기를 바란다.
(C) 일부 세제가 개선되어야 한다고 제안한다.
(D) 경쟁업체들과 협력을 시작하기를 원한다.

176-180은 다음 공고와 광고에 관한 문제입니다.

Bentota Beach 호텔이 능력 있는 지도자를 얻었습니다

인도의 가장 신뢰받는 숙박 시설 체인 중 하나인 Gold Frond 리조트는 가장 최근에 지어진 건물인 Bentota Beach 호텔의 방문객 서비스 관리자로 Gareth Sunderland를 선출했습니다. Mr. Sunderland는 리조트가 영업을 개시하기 3주 전인, 6월 14일에 새로운 직무를 맡을 것입니다. 그는 20년 이상의 접대 경력을 가지고 있으며, 그의 경력 중 지난 10년은 Gold Frond 리조트에서 보냈습니다. 가장 최근에, 그는 저희의 섬 지점에서 프런트 지배인으로 근무했습니다. 그곳에서의 성과에 기인하여, 그는 방문객 서비스 관리자라는 더 높은 직책을 탁월하게 해낼 것으로 기대됩니다.

Bentota Beach 호텔에서, Mr. Sunderland는 고객들을 직접 상대하는 모든 직원들을 관리할 것입니다. 그는 저희의 예약 및 체크인 시스템을 담당할 것입니다. 또한, 그는 저희가 양질의 서비스를 유지하도록 돕기 위해 직원 교육을 책임질 것입니다. 마지막으로 그러나 역시 주요한 것으로, 그는 수상 스포츠에서부터 문화 여행에 이르기까지, 투숙객들을 위한 다양한 오락 활동을 편성하는 것을 도울 것입니다.

Gold Frond 리조트에는 모두를 위한 무언가가 있습니다!

호화로운 Bentota Beach 지점의 개업과 함께, 저희는 이제 인도 전역에서 선택할 수 있는 총 5개의 리조트를 갖고 있습니다. 당신의 예산이 얼마이든, 즐거움이나 휴식 중 무엇을 찾고 있으시든, 저희는 당신에게 가장 알맞은 경험을 제공해 드릴 수 있습니다.

리조트:

Komari Cove	최초의 건물이며, 최근 다른 어떤 지점보다도 많은 315개의 객실로 확장했음
Matara Oceanside	가장 저렴한 선택지이며, 본토의 유명한 공공 해수욕장에서 걸어서 금방 갈 수 있음
Tangalle Retreat	*Leisurist*지로부터 최고의 리조트로 지명되었으며, 본토 해변에 있는 40개의 전용 별장으로 구성되어 있음
Vergual Paradise	Pondicherry 공항에서 배를 타고 20분 걸리며, 섬 전체를 차지하고 있음
Bentota Beach	활동적인 휴가를 보내고자 하시는 분들께 가장 적합하며, 본토의 유명한 서핑 해변에 위치함

각 리조트에서 할 수 있는 활동에 대한 정보는 www.goldfrondresorts.com에서 찾으실 수 있으며, 편리하게 온라인으로 예약하실 수도 있습니다.

176 공고의 주요 주제는 무엇인가?
(A) 건물의 개장 지연
(B) 회사 행사 개최
(C) 승진하는 직원
(D) 새로운 직원 교육 프로그램

177 공고에 따르면, 방문객 서비스 관리자의 책임이 아닌 것은?
(A) 예약 시스템 관리
(B) 여가 활동 편성
(C) 직원들에게 서비스 교육 제공
(D) 시설에 대한 불만 처리

178 Mr. Sunderland에 대해 암시되는 것은?
(A) Gold Frond 리조트에서 직장 생활을 시작했다.
(B) 사업 확장 계획을 개발했다.
(C) Vergual Paradise에서 고용되었다.
(D) 관광업 학위를 받았다.

179 Gold Frond 리조트에 대해 사실인 것은?
(A) 첫 번째 지점이 최근에 수용 인원을 늘렸다.
(B) 쇼핑을 하고자 하는 방문객들이 선호한다.
(C) 저렴한 리조트를 세울 계획이다.
(D) 모든 리조트들이 전용 해변을 가지고 있다.

180 사람들은 리조트 활동에 대한 정보를 어떻게 얻을 수 있는가?
(A) 웹사이트를 확인함으로써
(B) 연락처로 전화함으로써
(C) 여행사에 연락함으로써

(D) 문자 메시지를 보냄으로써

181-185는 다음 두 이메일에 관한 문제입니다.

수신 고객 서비스 부서 <cservice@framecaster.com>
발신 Erik Mercado <erikmerc@coolmail.com>
제목 구매
날짜 4월 28일

관계자분께,

저는 최근 귀하의 웹사이트에서 직접 귀사의 Spin Genie 400을 샀으며 조립을 위해 그것을 지역 자전거 가게로 가져갔습니다. 하지만, 자전거를 조립하던 도중, 정비공이 두 세트의 브레이크 모두에 결함이 있다는 것을 알아차렸습니다.

저는 이 사안과 관련하여 귀하의 고객 서비스 부서에 연락했으며, 직원인 Nora Santos가 제게 두 가지 선택권이 있다고 알려주었습니다. 그녀는 무료로 브레이크를 교체하기 위해 제가 FrameCaster 제품의 지역 소매점에 가거나, 또는 배송 비용을 내야 한다는 의미이기는 하지만, 그 교환 부품을 제 주소로 보낼 수 있다고 말했습니다.

저는 지금 샌프란시스코로 이사하기 위해 짐을 싸느라 바빠서 부품을 찾아볼 시간이 없습니다. 이사한 후에 브레이크를 배송받고 싶지만, 제품에 결함이 있었는데 제가 왜 배송 비용을 내야 하는지 이해할 수 없습니다. 다른 어떤 선택권이 있는지 그리고 이를 어떻게 진행하고 싶으신지 알려주십시오.

Erik Mercado 드림

수신 Erik Mercado <erikmerc@coolmail.com>
발신 Jade Estrada <jadee@framecaster.com>
제목 회신: 구매
날짜 4월 29일
첨부 FrameCaster.v45-b

Mr. Mercado께,

귀하께서 최근 구매하신 Spin Genie 400의 문제를 듣게 되어 유감스럽습니다. 저는 그 사안을 살펴보았고 저희 직원이 귀하께 잘못된 정보를 드렸다는 것을 발견했습니다. 저희는 제품 결함으로 인해 교환 부품을 배송하는 것에 대해 고객들께 요금을 청구하지 않습니다. 작년에는 그러한 요금이 있었으나, 그 이후로 저희 정책이 변경되었으므로, 부품은 귀하께 무료로 보내드릴 수 있습니다. 저희 직원에게 오해에 대해 알렸으며, 그녀는 이러한 종류의 상황이 다시 발생하지 않도록 추가 교육을 받을 것입니다.

귀하의 새로운 주소를 제공해 주시면, 그 물품을 바로 보내드리겠습니다. 추가적으로, 어떤 불편이라도 보상해드리기 위해, 추후 FrameCaster의 어떤 부대용품 구매에서든 사용하실 수 있는 20달러짜리 상품권을 첨부하였습니다.

귀하의 인내심에 감사드립니다.

Jade Estrada 드림
고객 서비스 부장
FrameCaster Cycles

181 Spin Genie 400에 대해 암시되는 것은?
(A) 조립되지 않은 상태로 구매할 수 있다.
(B) 샌프란시스코에 있는 시설에서 제조된다.
(C) 가벼운 재료로 구성된다.
(D) 특가품에 포함되어 있었다.

182 Mr. Mercado에 대해 언급된 것은?
(A) 지역 상점에서 자전거를 구매했다.
(B) 신속 배송을 위해 추가 요금을 지불했다.
(C) 두 가지의 교환 선택권이 있다.
(D) 제품을 무료로 조립했다.

183 두 번째 이메일은 왜 쓰였는가?
(A) 오류의 원인을 조사하기 위해
(B) 상황을 해결하려고 시도하기 위해
(C) 규칙의 타당성에 대해 이의를 제기하기 위해
(D) 불이익을 적용하는 것을 제안하기 위해

184 Nora Santos는 무엇을 할 것인가?
(A) 고객에게 사과문을 쓴다
(B) 추가 교육을 받는다
(C) 갱신된 주소로 물품을 보낸다
(D) 판매원과 이야기한다

185 두 번째 이메일에 따르면, Mr. Mercado에게 무엇이 제공되었는가?
(A) 부분적인 환불
(B) 가게 안내 책자
(C) 자전거 부대 용품
(D) 제품 상품권

186-190은 다음 회람, 이메일, 기사에 관한 문제입니다.

발신: Dillon Zhou
수신: 전 직원
제목: 사무실 방문
날짜: 2월 20일

*The Sydney Sun*지의 기자가 3월 1일에 우리의 새로운 사무실을 방문할 예정입니다. 그녀는 우리의 사무실 디자인과 직원 혜택에 대한 짧은 기사를 쓰고 있습니다. 기사를 위한 사진 몇 장을 이미 보냈기 때문에 사진 촬영은 없을 것입니다. 기자가 복도를 가로질러 안내되는 동안, 여러분의 재량에 따라 자유롭게 그녀와 교류하십시오. 고위 간부 중 한 명이 그녀에게 최신 소프트웨어 개발 계획을 간단히 소개할 것입니다. 그 기자는 모든 레저 및 오락 시설을 자유로이 이용할 수 있습니다.

발신: Sela Singh <s.singh@thesydneysun.au>
수신: Dillon Zhou <d.zhou@zazoosoftware.com>
제목: 기사
날짜: 2월 27일

Mr. Zhou께,

촉박한 통보에 대해 사과드립니다만, 여행 중 긴급 상황으로 인해 제가 3월 1일에 시드니로 돌아오지 못할 것입니다. 만약 제가 다른 날짜에 방문할 수 있다면, 제 비서인 Dennis Worley에게 d.worley@thesydneysun.au로 연락해주시면, 그가 모든 세부 사항을 처리할 것입니다. 그럴 수 없다면, 이 이메일의 답신으로 새로운 시설의 기본적인 설명을 보내 주십시오.

또한, 당신이 보내 주셨던 사진 중 일부가 그다지 선명하지 않습니다. 각각의 더 큰 사본을 보내 주시겠습니까? 그것이 매우 도움이 될 것입니다.

감사합니다.

Sela Singh 드림
*The Sydney Sun*지

Zazoo사에서의 사무실 스트레스 완화
3월 8일
Sela Singh 작성

거대 컴퓨터 기업인 Zazoo 소프트웨어사가 최근 시드니에 최신 사무실을 열었으며 그것이 직원들에게 제공하는 혜택에 대한 많은 추측을 불러일으켰다. 보살핌이 있는 근무 환경을 제공하는 것으로 알려진 Zazoo 소프트웨어사는 새로운 사무실 건물에 휴식을 취할 수 있는 많은 공간을 가지고 있다. 필자는 그 시설들을 견학하게 되었던 3월 4일에 이것들을 직접 볼 수 있었다. 모든 구내식당에서 직원들을 위한 무료 음식이 이용 가능하며, 건강한 선택권들이 많다.

운동 시설에 관해서는, 농구 코트, 수영장, 그리고 체육관이 있다. 게다가, 연말까지 요가 및 명상 스튜디오가 추가될 계획이다. 이 모든 시설은 직원들이 높은 수준의 효율로 업무를 수행하도록 돕고, 사무실에 있던 시간 동안 이것이 사실이었다는 것을 확인할 수 있었다.

"저희는 현재 새로운 소프트웨어 프로그램을 설계하는 마지막 단계에 있습니다."라고 Cathy Sanchez가 프로젝트에 대한 계획을 보여주며 말했다. "모두가 엄청난 압박 하에 일하고 있지만, 저희의 환경이 그런 스트레스를 완화하고 일을 더 재미있게 만드는 데 도움을 줄 것입니다."

186 회람이 방문객에 대해 언급하는 것은?
(A) 직원들과 이야기하지 않을 것이다.
(B) 레저 시설에서 그녀의 방문을 시작할 것이다.
(C) 어떠한 사진도 찍지 않을 것이다.
(D) 몇 가지 영업 전략에 대해 글을 쓸 것이다.

187 Mr. Zhou에 대해 암시되는 것은?
(A) 기자에게 사진을 찍혔다.
(B) 협의를 하기 위해 Ms. Singh과 만났다.
(C) 일정에 관해 Mr. Worley에게 이메일을 보냈다.
(D) Zazoo 소프트웨어 본사에 기반을 두고 있지 않다.

188 Ms. Sanchez는 누구일 것 같은가?
(A) 지역 신문 기자
(B) 새 사무실 건물의 건축가
(C) 건물 관리자
(D) 소프트웨어 회사의 간부

189 기사에 따르면, Zazoo 소프트웨어사의 작업 환경의 이점은 무엇인가?
(A) 팀 구성원들 간의 협력을 장려한다.
(B) 작업장 부상을 줄이기 위해 고안되었다.
(C) 직원들의 업무 수행 능력을 향상시킨다.
(D) 고객들과의 만남을 위한 넓은 공간을 제공한다.

190 Zazoo 소프트웨어사의 최신 사무실에서 아직 문을 열지 않은 시설은?
(A) 요가 스튜디오
(B) 직원 식당
(C) 사무실 체육관
(D) 수영장

191-195는 다음 메모, 양식, 청구서에 관한 문제입니다.

Rosa Mengistu로부터

안녕하세요, Mr. Fekade. 당신이 오늘 기획 회의에 참석하지 못해 유감입니다. 우리가 결정한 한 가지는 Dire Dawa 중앙 공원의 사진이 필요하다는 것이었습니다. 그 사진은 낮 동안에 분수 주변에서 휴식을 취하고 있는 사람들을 보여줘야 합니다. 그러한 사진을 찾는 일은 당신에게 달렸으며, 그것이 고해상도여야 한다는 것을 명심하십시오. 우리가 이 설명을 충족시키는 것을 이미 가지고 있을 수도 있으므로, 우리의 사진 저장소를 확인해 주십시오. 만약 그렇지 않으면, 당신은 Flash Photos나 Baumgard Pics와 같은 사진 업체의 모음집을 찾아볼 수 있습니다. 다른 방법이 전부 안 된다면, 프리랜서 사진사를 고용하는 선택지가 있습니다.

Baumgard Pics ★ 전 세계로부터의 사진 자료

고객:	사진 세부 사항:	가격은 사진 크기에 따라 책정됩니다:
Dawit Fekade	사진명: 음악 공연을 보고 있는 사람들 범주: 야외 활동 장소: Dire Dawa 중앙 공원 분수 사진 코드: HEWZYXP 파일 크기: 20메가바이트 출처: Delores Ashburn	□ 스몰 3.99달러 (500x449) □ 미디엄 4.99달러 (1000x899) □ 라지 5.99달러 (2000x1798) □ 엑스트라 라지 6.99달러 (3172x2851)

지금 사진을 구입하세요!

Baumgard Pics를 선택해 주셔서 감사합니다!

770번지 Hickory가
오마하, 네브래스카주 미국 68124
(402) 555-2882
http://baumgardpics.org

사진 코드	청구서 발송 주소	지불 금액	
HEWZYXP	Dawit Fekade Aksum Services사 4번지 Adwa가 아디스 아바바 에티오피아	사진 가격	5.99달러
		세금	0.59달러
		총	6.58달러

귀하의 청구서를 다운로드하려면, Baumgard Pics의 웹사이트에 로그인해 '구매 내역' 탭을 클릭하십시오. 저장하고자 하는 청구서를 선택한 다음, 다운로드 버튼을 클릭하십시오.

귀하의 현재 주문은 6월 25일부터 사용할 수 있습니다. 사진을 사용할 수 있는 권한은 5년 후 만료된다는 것을 알아두십시오. 사용 기간을 연장하고 싶다면, 저희 웹사이트에서 그것을 할 수 있습니다.

191 메모는 왜 쓰였는가?
(A) 업무를 맡기기 위해
(B) 실망을 표하기 위해
(C) 기기를 추천하기 위해
(D) 조언을 구하기 위해

192 양식에 포함되지 않은 정보는?
(A) 사진 제목
(B) 사진이 찍힌 장소
(C) 고객 연락처
(D) 사진사 이름

193 Mr. Fekade에 대해 추론될 수 있는 것은?
(A) 업체와 계약을 협상할 수 있도록 허가를 받았다.
(B) 직장에서 알맞은 사진을 찾지 못했다.
(C) 아직 최근 고용된 직원들을 위한 교육을 받고 있다.
(D) 잘못된 장소에서 찍힌 사진 몇 장을 제출했다.

194 Mr. Fekade는 어떤 크기의 사진을 구매했는가?
(A) 스몰
(B) 미디엄
(C) 라지
(D) 엑스트라 라지

195 청구서에 따르면, 5년이 지난 후에 무슨 일이 일어날 것인가?
(A) 사진 공급업체가 사용자 계약을 갱신할 것이다.
(B) 회사가 사진 공급처를 교체할 것이다.
(C) 웹사이트 회원권이 만료될 것이다.
(D) 고객이 더 이상 사진을 사용할 권리가 없을 것이다.

196-200은 다음 공고와 두 이메일에 관한 문제입니다.

Blue Ravine 의과 대학(BRMS)
공지: *전 학생 및 교수진*

Kowloon 동양 의과 대학(KUEM)의 Dr. Janice Shen이 9월 4일에 강연을 할 것이라는 점에 주목해 주시기 바랍니다. Dr. Shen은 척추 질환의 성공적인 치료법을 설명할 것입니다. 그녀는 침술과 한약의 전문가이며, 주로 요통과 척추 질환을 치료합니다. 지난 12년 동안, 그녀는 KUEM에서 일해 왔고, 그곳에서 여러 가지의 많은 연구 프로젝트를 이끌고 있습니다.

그녀의 강연은 오후 3시에 BRMS 교정의 Fasthead 강당에서 열릴 것입니다. 좌석이 한정되어 있으므로, 교내 행사 사무실을 방문하거나, 내선 번호 #364로 전화하거나, 또는 jaynemarche@brms.edu로 행사 사무실의 Jayne Marche에게 이메일을 보내서 예약하시기 바랍니다. 강연은 BRMS의 모든 교수진과 학생들에게 무료이지만, 손님들은 16달러를 내야 합니다.

수신: Jayne Marche <jaynemarche@brms.edu>
발신: Grayden Higgins <graydenhiggins@brms.edu>
제목: 요청
날짜: 8월 19일

안녕하세요, Jayne.

저는 여기 BRMS에서 대체 의학의 고급 과정을 가르치고 있고, 현재 9명의 학생이 등록되어 있습니다. 곧 있을 Dr. Shen의 강연에 저희 10명이 모두 참석할 수 있도록 예약하고 싶습니다. 모든 학생들의 이름이 필요하신지 아니면 제 이름으로 자리를 예약할 수 있을지 알려주십시오.

또한, 저는 누군가가 그 강연을 녹화할 것인지 궁금해하고 있었습니다. 저는 될 수 있는 한 그녀의 강연을 향후의 학생들과 공유하고 싶습니다. 유감스럽게도, 아무도 그녀의 이전 방문을 녹화할 생각을 하지 않았었는데, 이번에는 그렇지 않기를 바랍니다.

감사드리며, 곧 답변을 듣기를 바랍니다.

Dr. Grayden Higgins 드림
BRMS, 골격 및 근육 질환 학부

수신: Angelo Conti <angeloconti@brms.edu>
발신: Jayne Marche <jaynemarche@brms.edu>
제목: 강연 행사 업무
날짜: 8월 20일

안녕하세요, Angelo.

BRMS의 강사가 9월 4일에 열리는 강연을 녹화해 달라고 요청했습니다.

이 촬영 업무를 당신의 일정에 추가해 주세요. Dr. Shen의 이전 발표에 근거해, 제 생각에는 강연이 약 1시간 반 정도 계속되고, 30분 정도의 질의응답 시간이 이어질 것 같습니다. 후자 역시 촬영해야 할 것 같으므로, 영상의 전체 시간은 약 두 시간 정도가 될 것입니다.

사흘 안에 자료 영상의 편집을 완료하도록 노력해 주시고 영상 파일을 제게 보내주세요. 제가 그것을 BRMS 웹사이트에 게시하고, 우리 멀티미디어 도서관의 모음집에 추가하고, 그것을 요청했던 강사에게 전달할 것입니다. 당신이 준비할 시간이 있도록 한 시간 전에 강당이 열려 있는 것을 확인하겠습니다.

감사합니다!
Jayne 드림

196 Dr. Shen은 현재 어떤 종류의 일을 하는가?
(A) 기업을 위해 약제를 개발한다.
(B) 대학에서 프로젝트를 지휘한다.
(C) 물리치료 병원을 운영한다.
(D) 보건 교과서를 집필한다.

197 공고에 따르면, 곧 있을 강연을 위한 예약 방법이 아닌 것은?
(A) 사무실 방문하기
(B) 전화 걸기
(C) 온라인 양식 작성하기
(D) 이메일 발송하기

198 Dr. Higgins의 학생들에 대해 암시되는 것은?
(A) 의학 과정의 마지막 학년에 있다.
(B) 타 대학에서 온 교환 학생이다.
(C) 강연 후에 보고서를 제출할 것이다.
(D) 무료로 강연에 참석할 것이다.

199 Dr. Shen의 강연 마지막에 무슨 일이 일어날 것인가?
(A) 영상이 상영될 것이다.
(B) 질문이 답변될 것이다.
(C) 과제가 주어질 것이다.
(D) 수료증이 수여될 것이다.

200 Ms. Marche는 9월 4일 이후에 무엇을 할 것 같은가?
(A) Dr. Higgins에게 녹화 영상을 공유한다
(B) KUEM에서의 특별 의학 세미나에 참석한다
(C) Dr. Shen에게 또 다른 초대장을 보낸다
(D) BRMS의 학과장을 만난다

TEST 06 해석

* 무료 해설은 해커스토익(Hackers.co.kr)에서 다운로드 받을 수 있습니다.

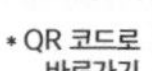

PART 5

101 연금 제도에 투자함으로써 은퇴를 대비해 스스로를 준비하는 것은 현명하다.

102 Carver Financial사의 일자리 지원자는 3년의 관련 경력이 없으면 고려되지 않을 것이다.

103 바르셀로나로 가는 LT 항공사 항공편의 승객들은 지정된 장소에서 기다리라는 요청을 받았다.

104 신제품 출시를 준비하는 것은 부서들 간 협조가 필요하다.

105 허리케인의 피해자들을 돕는 것에 초점을 맞추는 동안 그 재단의 평소 자선 활동들은 일시적으로 중단되었다.

106 Median 은행은 고객들의 개인 정보 보호를 위해 엄격한 지침을 따른다.

107 16개 회사 중에서, 올랜도시는 새로운 스포츠 경기장을 짓도록 Flaremont 건설사를 선정했다.

108 12월 14일의 일기예보가 한파를 예보하므로, 사람들은 그에 맞춰 옷을 입어야 한다.

109 무역 박람회 직원은 참석을 확인하기 위해 행사 한 달 전에 각 참가자에게 전화했다.

110 최근의 보고서에 따르면, Keller Auto사는 호주의 선두적인 자동차 타이어 제조사들 중 한 곳이다.

111 미술사학자는 그 그림이 원본인 것을 증명하려고 하는 동안 많은 연구를 했다.

112 스트리밍 서비스의 가격을 낮춤으로써, Jolio사는 기존 시장의 범위를 넘어서 고객들에게 닿는 것을 목표로 한다.

113 체조 선수 Anna Stamos는 Knobel 아침 식사 시리얼의 현재의 브랜드 홍보대사를 대신할 것이다.

114 몇 시간의 연습 덕분에, 영업팀은 고객에게 자신 있게 제안서를 제시할 수 있었다.

115 Buyer's 클럽 회원들에게 미국 내 배송은 무료이지만, 국제 배송은 추가 요금을 지불하는 것을 필요로 할 것이다.

116 전기차 충전기가 전국의 주유소에 설치될 것이다.

117 Davidson역의 에스컬레이터는 제대로 작동하는지 확실하게 하기 위해 정기적인 점검의 대상이다.

118 일 년에 25,000달러 미만을 버는 어느 West Bay 주민이라도 주거 지원을 신청할 자격이 있다.

119 새로운 난로를 위한 광고는 외관과 사용 편의성에 중점을 둔다.

120 Farrco사와 Slansea사의 제휴는 그들을 더 경쟁력 있게 만듦으로써 회사들에 전략적으로 이익을 줄 것이다.

121 Mill Creek 지역 문화 센터는 도시 주변의 쓰레기를 치우기 위한 대청소 계획을 시작했다.

122 악화되고 있는 경제 상황 때문에, 그 회사는 직원들을 고용하는 것을 중단하기로 결정할 수도 있다.

123 Six Stars 호텔의 주차 담당 안내원은 어느 차가 Mr. Carlton의 것인지 확신하지 못했다.

124 Mr. Grady는 신입 사원들에게 요구가 많은 고객들을 침착한 태도로 다루는 방법을 교육하고 있다.

125 Joseph Baker는 오직 그가 요구한 20퍼센트의 임금 인상을 받는 경우에만 승진을 수락할 것이다.

126 매년, Corehouse Technics사의 모든 직원은 성과 평가를 받는다.

127 운송비를 최소화하기 위해, 그 회사는 항구 가까이 사무실을 옮겼다.

128 Rob Marshall의 *Smart Investor's Guide*는 주식 시장을 이해하는 데 많은 도움이 되는 통찰력을 제공한다.

129 10월에 있을 회의의 참석자들은 연사들에 대한 좀 더 구체적인 정보를 사전에 받을 것이다.

130 저장 시설은 실내 공기 온도의 작은 변화를 감지할 수 있는 시스템을 사용한다.

PART 6

131-134는 다음 광고에 관한 문제입니다.

유행에 맞춰 타십시오

만약 당신이 자전거 타기의 열광적인 팬이라면, Bango와 함께 탑승할 때입니다. 131 저희 헬멧은 유행을 따를 뿐만 아니라, 당신을 안전하게도 해드립니다. 헬멧은 충격 흡수 작용이 뛰어난 튼튼하고 견고한 소재 세 겹으로 만들어집니다. 그것들은 국가안전위원회 자격 요건을 충족합니다. 132 그것들은 일반 라이더들을 위한 편리함도 제공합니다. 133 예를 들어, 그것들은 손쉬운 보관을 위해 작은 크기로 깔끔하게 접게 되어 있습니다. 오늘 Bango 헬멧을 써보지 않을 변명의 여지가 전혀 없습니다. 134 지금 바로 그것을 구입하시고 특별 판촉 행사를 이용하십시오. 만약 정가로 사신다면, 50퍼센트 할인된 가격으로 두 번째 헬멧을 받으실 것입니다. www.bangohelmets.com을 확인하시고, Bango와 함께 다음 자전거 여행을 시작하십시오.

135-138은 다음 이메일에 관한 문제입니다.

발신: Hampton 교육원 <accountmanage@hamptoninstitute.org>
수신: Kate Whitman <k.whitman@braxton.ca>
제목: 결제 방식
날짜: 5월 25일

Ms. Whitman께,

135 이 메시지는 6월 30일부터 8월 31일까지 Hampton 교육원의 코딩 세미나에 귀하의 등록을 확인하기 위한 것입니다. 할부로 등록하셨기 때문에, 귀하께서는 월 단위로 청구 받으실 것입니다. 136 첫 번째 청구서는 7월 1일에 이메일로 발송될 것입니다. 137 언제든지, 귀하께서는 결제 방식을 변경하시면 됩니다. 그렇게 하시려면, 귀하의 계정에 간단히 로그인하시고 "방식 변경"을 선택하세요. 여기에서도 하실 수 있습니다. 저희가 제공하는 가장 긴 할부가 18개월 동안임을 알아두시기 바랍니다. 138 어려움이 있으시면 바로 제게 이메일을 보내주십시오. 항상 기쁘게 도와드리겠습니다.

Hampton 교육원 계정 관리팀 드림

139-142는 다음 공고에 관한 문제입니다.

Lake 자치주 동물 협회가 모금 행사를 개최하다

Lake 자치주 동물 협회는 지난 몇 년 동안 이뤄진 공헌에 감사드립니다. 139 그것들은 단체가 수백 마리의 동물들에게 먹이와 보호소를 제공하는 것을 할 수 있게 해주었습니다.

12월 11일에 Morrissey Civic 센터에서 열리는 모금 행사에 함께해 주십시오오. 좋은 목적을 위한 즐거운 밤이 될 것입니다. 140 참석자들은 저녁 식사와 라이브 공연을 대접받으실 것입니다. 입장권은 장당 100달러만 내면 이용 가능하실 것입니다. 141 건물의 지붕이 교체되어야 해서 수익금은 단체의 Willoughby 시설을 수리하는 데 주로 사용될 것입니다. 142 그러나, 일부는 또한 사람들이 저희 보호소에서 자원봉사를 하도록 장려하는 프로그램을 확장하는 데 쓰일 것입니다. 이러한 캠페인은 저희 사업에 대한 지역 사회의 관심을 유지하는 데 필수적입니다.

143-146은 다음 공고에 관한 문제입니다.

Jefferson 스포츠 센터 공고

143 4월 8일부터 시행되어, 실내 수영장이 일주일간 폐쇄될 것입니다. 수영장은 청소되고, 수리되고, 살균되기 전에 완전히 배수되어야 합니다. 이것은 모든 사람들에게 안전하고 위생적인 환경을 제공하기 위해 필요한 연간 절차입니다. 144 그동안에, 다른 실내 시설들은 계속 이용할 수 있을 것입니다. 145 이것들은 사우나, 체육관, 그리고 건강 관리 구역을 포함합니다. 야외 수영장 또한 사용될 수 있을 것입니다. 이 일이 야기할 수 있는 모든 불편에 대해 사과드립니다. 146 그것이 완료되면 정상 운영이 재개될 것입니다. 더 많은 소식과 업데이트를 원하시면, 소셜 미디어에서 저희를 팔로우 해 주십시오.

PART 7

147-148은 다음 광고에 관한 문제입니다.

대부분의 화장품이 당신에게 발진을 생기게 하거나 당신의 피부를 가렵게 하나요? Betteskin Cosmetics사는 민감한 피부를 가진 사람들을 위해 특별히 고안된 새로운 제품군을 테스트해볼 사람들을 찾고 있습니다.

참여하려면, www.betteskin.com을 방문하십시오. 저희가 당신의 피부 문제를 확인하는 것을 돕도록 6월 30일 전에 간단한 온라인 설문조사에 응답하십시오. 저희가 상세한 설명서와 함께 제품 샘플을 집으로 보내드릴 것입니다. 각 제품은 일주일 동안 테스트 되어야 합니다. 그 대신, 참여자들은 저희 웹사이트의 25달러 쿠폰을 받게 될 것입니다.

147 사람들은 어떻게 테스트에 참여할 수 있는가?
(A) 인터넷에서 제품군을 홍보함으로써
(B) 마감 일자 전에 설문조사를 완료함으로써
(C) 요청서를 제출함으로써
(D) 인터뷰에 직접 참여함으로써

148 참여자들은 무엇을 받을 것인가?
(A) 무료 식사
(B) 회원 카드
(C) 온라인 상품권
(D) 행사 초대장

149-151은 다음 안내문에 관한 문제입니다.

모든 Charlotte 식료품 잡화점 쇼핑객들에게 알림

Charlotte 식료품 잡화점이 매장에서 Hero Coco Water의 판매를 중단했습니다. 전 세계의 제품 회수로 인해 현재 이 제품은 구할 수 없지만, 회수 명령이 해제되자마자 재고가 다시 채워질 것입니다.

현재로는, 저희는 Cocolait와 Biba 코코넛 워터 브랜드를 시도해보는 것을 추천합니다. 저희는 전국 매장에서 두 브랜드를 취급합니다. 저희 매장에서 판매되는 모든 제품들과 마찬가지로, 유기농 인증 기관에서 인증을 받고 식품 안전에 대한 모든 규제 요건을 충족합니다.

불편을 드려 죄송합니다. 이 문제에 관한 우려 사항에 대해서는, 가장 가까운 매장의 고객 서비스 데스크를 방문하십시오. 그리고 판촉 할인을 포함한 주간 소식지를 받기 위해 www.charlottegrocer.com에 여러분의 이메일 주소를 등록하실 것을 기억해 주십시오.

149 Charlotte 식료품 잡화점이 겪고 있는 문제는 무엇인가?
(A) 식품 공급업자가 폐업했다.
(B) 금전 등록기 시스템이 작동하지 않는다.
(C) 제품이 획득될 수 없다.
(D) 매장이 일찍 문을 닫아야 할 것이다.

150 Charlotte 식료품 잡화점에 대해 추론될 수 있는 것은?
(A) 경쟁업체와 합병했다.
(B) 자체 브랜드의 물을 출시했다.
(C) 전 세계적으로 지점을 관리한다.
(D) 특정 제품 기준을 따른다.

151 고객들은 왜 웹사이트에 등록해야 하는가?
(A) 제품 의견을 제공하기 위해
(B) 특별 행사에 참여하기 위해
(C) 가정배달 계획을 짜기 위해
(D) 이메일로 소식지를 받기 위해

152-153은 다음 메시지 대화문에 관한 문제입니다.

Christina Sanchez [오후 12시 23분]
Kenichi, 제 오후 회의를 연기해 주시겠어요? 저는 Ms. Kim과 점심 식사를 하고 있는데, 그녀는 Lakewood 주택에 값을 제의할 준비가 된 것 같아요. 따라서, 저는 곧 그녀를 그 주택으로 태워다 줄 것이고, 바라건대 저희가 계약서에 서명할 거예요.

Kenichi Yamamoto [오후 12시 24분]
좋은 소식이네요. 네, Mr. Zhou를 내일 아침으로 옮길 수 있어요. 오전 9시에 빈자리가 있습니다.

Christina Sanchez [오후 12시 26분]
저는 좋아요. 이건 마지막 순간의 변경이니 그에게 이메일을 보내기보다 Mr. Zhou에게 즉시 전화해주세요.

Kenichi Yamamoto [오후 12시 27분]
그렇게 할게요. 저는 제 앞에 그의 전화번호가 있어요.

Christina Sanchez [오후 12시 29분]
정말 감사해요. 급한 일이 없는 한, 전화를 건 다른 분들에게 제가 내일 사무실에 돌아올 거라고 알려주세요.

152 Ms. Sanchez는 왜 Mr. Yamamoto에게 연락했는가?
(A) 그를 점심 회의에 초대하기 위해
(B) 계약서 사본을 요청하기 위해
(C) 약속을 옮기기 위해
(D) 주택 방문 일정을 잡기 위해

153 오후 12시 27분에, Mr. Yamamoto가 "Will do"라고 썼을 때 그가 의도한 것 같은 것은?
(A) 고객에게 전화로 연락할 것이다.
(B) 계약을 더 알아볼 것이다.
(C) 제안된 약속을 수락한다.
(D) 회의에서 Ms. Sanchez의 역할을 대신할 수 있다.

154-155는 다음 이메일에 관한 문제입니다.

수신: Dennis Gunther <d.gunther@bauerhofffarms.com>
발신: Karina Schneider <k.schneider@bauerhofffarms.com>
제목: 최근 농작물
날짜: 8월 19일

Dennis께,

이번 철에 우리는 평소와 달리 많은 수확량의 토마토가 있는 것으로 보입니다. 그 수량은 철이 시작되기 전에 우리의 고정 거래처들이 구매하기로 약속한 것을 훨씬 초과합니다. 그래서, 우리는 초과분을 팔 방법을 생각해내야 합니다. 현재, 저는 촉박한 통보에도 우리의 잉여 생산물을 가져갈 수 있을 수 있는 식당들, 호텔들, 그리고 소규모 식료품점들의 목록을 작성하고 있습니다. 동시에, 저는 당신이 우리 지역 농산물 직판장에서 평소보다 더 많은 수량을 판매해주었으면 합니다. 만약 더 많은 토마토를 파는 데 도움이 될 것이라고 생각한다면 자유롭게 가격을 낮추세요. 만약 우리가 주말까지 여전히 너무 많이 가지고 있다면, 우리는 남은 것들을 시민회관 또는 자선단체에 기부할 수 있습니다. 다른 아이디어가 있으면 알려주세요. 저는 우리가 이익을 극대화할 수 있기를 바랍니다.

Karina 드림

154 Bauerhoff 농장의 토마토에 대해 언급된 것은?
(A) 수확될 준비가 되어 있지 않다.
(B) 그들 중 일부는 새로운 고객들에게 판매되어야 한다.
(C) 지난 철의 것보다 더 낮은 품질이다.
(D) 그들 중 일부는 고정 거래처들에 의해 거절당했다.

155 Mr. Gunther는 무엇을 해달라고 요청받는가?
(A) 직원들에게 지시사항 전달한다
(B) 일부 식당 주인들에게 연락한다
(C) 자선단체와 합의를 한다
(D) 지역 시장에서 매출을 증가시킨다

156-157은 다음 기사에 관한 문제입니다.

공유경제가 끝나가고 있는가?

4월 23일—뭄바이는 소위 공유 경제라고 불리는 회사들과의 문제를 다루기 위한 조치를 취하고 있다. 어제, 뭄바이는 아파트 공유 애플리케이션 Househunt와 교통 서비스 CallAuto와 같은 기업을 대상으로 한 새로운 규제를 발표했다. 두 회사 모두, 그리고 그들과 같은 다른 곳들은 이제 시에서 운영하기 위해 더 엄격한 요구 조건을 충족해야 한다. 예를 들어, Househunt는 시의 호텔과 동일한 위생 및 안전 기준을 충족해야 할 것이며 특정 지역으로 제한될 수 있다. CallAuto에 대해서는, 운전기사들을 정규직으로 대우해야 할 것이고 그들에게 유급휴가와 건강보험을 제공해야 할 것이다. 영향을 받은 기업들은 이러한 조치들이 수익성을 해칠 것이라고 주장해왔다. 하지만, 공무원들은 그것들이 대중의 안전과 복지를 향상시키기 위해 필요하다고 반박한다.

156 기사는 주로 무엇에 대한 것인가?
(A) 직원들의 더 나은 처우에 대한 요구
(B) 사고의 수를 줄이기 위한 캠페인
(C) 특정 유형의 회사들을 규제하려는 시의 노력
(D) 선정된 사업체들에 대한 세금 인상 계획

157 CallAuto에 대해 암시되는 것은?
(A) 업계에서 경쟁업체가 없다.
(B) 뭄바이시를 떠날 계획을 가지고 있다.
(C) 운전자들에게 고용 혜택을 주어야 할 것이다.
(D) 서비스 품질을 개선하기 위한 조치를 취했다.

158-161은 다음 광고에 관한 문제입니다.

Peacelid를 소개합니다

Peacelid는 재사용할 수 있는 컵, 빨대, 그리고 식기를 판매하는 친환경 회사입니다. 저희 제품들은 100퍼센트 대나무로 만들어집니다. Peacelid의 제품들은 또한 생분해성이어서, 그것들은 폐기된 후에 안전하고 자연적으로 분해됩니다.

게다가, Peacelid는 환경친화적인 소비 관행을 옹호하며 삼림 파괴를 방지하는 것과 관련된 단체들에 모든 구매의 3퍼센트를 기부합니다.

저희의 카탈로그를 보시려면 www.peacelid.com을 확인하십시오. 신규 고객들은 체크아웃 페이지에서 "PEACE20" 코드를 입력하시면 첫 주문에 20퍼센트 할인을 받으실 수 있습니다. 게다가, 200달러 이상의 모든 주문은 재사용할 수 있는 무료 빨대를 포함할 것입니다.

158 Peacelid에 대해 사실이 아닌 것은?
(A) 먹고 마시는 것을 위한 제품들을 만든다.
(B) 다른 단체들을 후원한다.
(C) 천연 재료를 사용한다.
(D) 체인점을 운영한다.

159 Peacelid 제품들의 장점은 무엇인가?
(A) 내구성
(B) 안전한 처분
(C) 적당한 가격
(D) 광범한 이용 가능성

160 쿠폰 코드에 대해 언급된 것은?
(A) 여러 번 사용될 수 있다.
(B) 일부 고객들에게만 적용된다.
(C) 이메일로 요청되어야 한다.
(D) 한 달 후에 만료된다.

161 고객들은 어떻게 재사용할 수 있는 빨대를 받을 수 있는가?
(A) 200달러가 넘는 상당의 상품들을 구매함으로써
(B) 환경 기금에 기부함으로써
(C) 몇몇 플라스틱 제품들을 교환함으로써
(D) 청소 활동에 지원함으로써

162-164는 다음 공고에 관한 문제입니다.

Gymspan 고객들은 주목해주십시오

8월부터, Gymspan 앱에 구독권을 가진 사용자들은 더 이상 제휴된 헬스클럽 체인에서 무제한 운동을 이용할 수 없을 것입니다. 이 변화에 대해 사과드리지만, 이것은 필요한 비용 절감 조치입니다.

현재 무제한 회원 요금제에 가입되어 있는 고객들은 그들의 현재 대금 청구 주기가 끝날 때까지 혜택을 계속 사용할 수 있습니다. 그 후에, 그들은 자동으로 다른 요금제로 바뀔 것입니다. — [1] —. 이 변화를 보상하기 위해, Gymspan은 고객 포인트 500점을 드릴 것인데, 이것은 다른 제품과 서비스 구매에 사용될 수 있습니다. — [2] —.

게다가, Gymspan은 그 앱에 몇 가지 개선점을 도입했습니다. 매달, 고객들은 한 요금제에서 다른 요금제로 쉽게 전환할 수 있는 선택권을 갖습니다. 여러분은 해외에 나가 있을 때도 일시적으로 결제를 정지할 수 있습니다. — [3] —. 마지막으로, 여러분은 포인트를 빨리 적립하는 더 많은 방법을 즐길 수 있습니다. 이러한 개선 사항은 Gymspan 회원 자격을 진정으로 융통성 있고 여러분의 요구에 즉각 대응할 수 있도록 만들기 위한 것입니다. — [4] —. 추가 정보를 원하시면, www.gymspan.com을 방문하시거나 오늘 앱을 다운로드하십시오.

162 Gymspan에 대해 언급된 것은?
(A) 사용 요금제를 없앨 것이다.
(B) 일부 계열사들과 관계를 끊었다.
(C) 신규 회원들을 위한 포인트를 제공하고 있다.
(D) 다른 회사와 합병했다.

163 공고에 따르면, 고객들은 무엇을 할 수 있는가?
(A) 무료 체험 회원권을 신청한다
(B) 애플리케이션에서 헬스 스튜디오를 평가한다
(C) 월 단위로 요금제를 조정한다
(D) 프랜차이즈 기회에 대해 문의한다

164 [1], [2], [3], [4]로 표시된 위치 중, 다음 문장이 들어갈 곳으로 가장 적절한 것은?

"이제 계정은 1년에 최대 두 달 동안 정지될 수 있습니다."

(A) [1]
(B) [2]
(C) [3]
(D) [4]

165-167은 다음 편지에 관한 문제입니다.

11월 20일

Bernard Davidson
180번지 Whitfield로
에드먼턴, 앨버타주 T5A 0A2

Mr. Davidson께,

축하합니다! 귀하의 지원 자료를 검토한 후, 저희는 당신에게 공대생들을 위한 Clark Newman 장학금을 수여하기로 결정했습니다. 이것은 당신의 등록금을 전액 지급하여 당신이 앨버타 공과 대학에서 기계 공학 학위를 계속하게 할 것입니다.

아시다시피, 이 장학금은 1년에 5명의 지원자들에게만 수여됩니다. 지원자들은 뛰어난 학업 성적과 공학에 대한 열정을 바탕으로 선발되었습니다. 모든 수상자들은 1,000명이 넘는 지원자 그룹에서 선발되었습니다.

앨버타 공과 대학에서의 첫해 동안, 당신은 다른 공대 학생들과 함께 Kensing House라는 작은 기숙사에서 살게 될 것입니다. 이곳은 공학 건물 본관인 Mitchell 홀에서 단지 몇 걸음 떨어진 곳에 위치해 있습니다. 다음 주에, 저희가 당신의 주거 환경에 대한 더 많은 정보뿐만 아니라 학생증을 보내드릴 것입니다. 다시 한번, 축하드립니다!

Donald Neilson 드림
학장, 공학 대학
앨버타 공과 대학

165 편지의 주된 목적은 무엇인가?
(A) Mr. Davidson에게 장학금에 대해 알리기 위해
(B) 새 프로그램에 대한 세부 정보를 제공하기 위해
(C) Mr. Davidson을 대학에 채용하기 위해
(D) 추가 지원 자료를 요청하기 위해

166 Mr. Davidson에 대해 암시되는 것은?
(A) 대학 전공을 바꾸고 싶어 한다.
(B) 매우 경쟁적인 과정에 참가했다.
(C) 이미 첫 등록금을 냈다.
(D) 앨버타 공과 대학 근처에 산다.

167 다음 주에 Mr. Davidson에게 무엇이 보내질 것인가?
(A) 행사 책자
(B) 주택 신청서
(C) 신분증
(D) 재정 지원서

168-171은 다음 기사에 관한 문제입니다.

산타 모니카(3월 30일)—지난 몇 달 동안, 맞춤형 향수를 제공하는 새로운 콘셉트의 상점이 많은 관심을 끌고 있다. 그곳은 3번가를 따라 관광객들로 붐비는 장소를 차지하고 있다. 고객들은 자신만의 향수를 만들거나, 독특한 향기의 조합으로 미리 만들어진 수십 개의 향수 중 하나를 살 수 있다. 모든 향수는 천연 오일을 사용한다.

지난 4년 동안, 주인인 Sarah McKellen은 향수에 관한 그녀의 영상으로 소셜 미디어에서 팬을 형성했다. — [1] —. 작년에, 그녀는 그녀의 창작품을 온라인에서 팔기 시작했다. 그 모험적 사업의 성공은 그녀가 1월에 첫 번째 Freesha 상점을 열도록 설득했다. 놀랍게도, 그녀는 일주일 안에 모든 재고를 다 팔았다. — [2] —.

Ms. McKellen에 따르면, 대부분의 고객들은 향수를 만든다는 아이디어를 즐긴다. — [3] —. 그것이 그녀가 한 번에 최대 네 명의 방문객들이 향수가 어떻게 만들어지는지 볼 수 있는 작은 방을 추가한 이유이다. 머지않아, Ms. McKellen은 더 큰 단체를 위한 직접 해보는 워크숍 공간을 제공하기 위해 방을 확장할 계획이다. — [4] —.

168 기사는 주로 무엇에 관한 것인가?
(A) 최근에 인정받는 사업체
(B) 회사의 천연 재료로의 전환
(C) 성장하는 지역의 번화한 거리
(D) 새롭게 다시 문을 연 관광 명소

169 1문단 두 번째 줄의 단어 "spot"은 의미상 -와 가장 가깝다.
(A) 일자리
(B) 장소
(C) 얼룩
(D) 상황

170 Freesha에 대해 암시되는 것은?
(A) 계획했던 것보다 일주일 늦게 문을 열었다.
(B) 곧 두 번째 장소를 갖게 될 것이다.
(C) 새로운 재료 공급 회사를 찾고 있다.
(D) 다섯 명 이상의 사람들을 위한 워크숍을 열 것이다.

171 [1], [2], [3], [4]로 표시된 위치 중, 다음 문장이 들어갈 곳으로 가장 적절한 것은?

"Ms. McKellen은 예상 밖의 수요를 충족시키도록 그녀를 도울 더 많은 직원을 고용해야 했다."

(A) [1]
(B) [2]
(C) [3]
(D) [4]

172-175는 다음 메시지 대화문에 관한 문제입니다.

Dwayne Jackson 오전 9시 22분
아시다시피, 내일 저희의 식물원을 위한 대규모 모금 행사가 있습니다. 가능하다면, 저는 두 분이 오후 6시까지 오면 좋겠어요.

Sarah Chen 오전 9시 24분
물론이죠. 저는 사실 그곳에 일찍 가려고 했어요.

Frank Daniels 오전 9시 27분
제가 오후 6시 30분까지 Fry Factory에서 일해야 해서 저는 시작 시간 가까이 되어서야 나타날 수 있을 거예요.

Dwayne Jackson 오전 9시 28분
네, 알려줘서 고마워요, Frank. Sarah, 당신이 일찍 올 거니까, 제가 탁자와 의자를 설치하는 것을 도와줄 수 있을지 궁금해요.

Sarah Chen 오전 9시 30분
기꺼이 하죠. 배치는 정해졌나요?

Dwayne Jackson 오전 9시 31분
네. 방이 어떻게 보여야 하는지에 대한 사진을 당신에게 이메일로 보내줄게요. Frank, 당신은 시작 시간쯤에 여기 올 거니까, 입구에서 차례표 좀 나눠 주겠어요?

Frank Daniels 오전 9시 32분
네, 물론이죠.

Dwayne Jackson 오전 9시 34분
참가자들에게 인사하고 그들이 행사나 기부하는 방법에 관해 가지고 있는 질문들에 대해 돕도록 준비해주세요.

Frank Daniels 오전 9시 35분
알겠습니다. 저는 행사 시작 15분 전인 오후 6시 45분까지 그곳에 가겠습니다.

172 Mr. Daniels는 왜 일찍 올 수 없는가?
(A) 다른 직장에서 근무를 해야 한다.
(B) 진료 예약에 가야 한다.
(C) 수업에 참석할 것이다.
(D) 회의에 참석해야 한다.

173 Mr. Jackson은 Ms. Chen에게 무엇을 요청하는가?
(A) 그에게 배치를 보낸다
(B) 몇몇 참석자들을 맞이한다
(C) 가구를 배치한다
(D) 행사 후에 정리를 한다

174 오전 9시 35분에, Mr. Daniels가 "Got it"이라고 썼을 때 그가 의도한 것은?
(A) 도움을 줄 것이다.
(B) 물건을 받았다.
(C) 배치를 이해한다.
(D) 회의 시간을 적어 둘 것이다.

175 모금 행사는 공식적으로 언제 시작될 것인가?
(A) 오후 6시에
(B) 오후 6시 30분에
(C) 오후 6시 45분에
(D) 오후 7시에

176-180은 다음 두 이메일에 관한 문제입니다.

수신: Olivia Brunelli <olivia@nathalieresort.fr>
발신: Roger Keller <roger.keller@lowefinances.com>
날짜: 3월 21일
제목: 문의

Ms. Brunelli께,

작년 휴가 동안, 저는 로슈모어에 있는 귀하의 아름다운 휴양지를 우연히 발견했습니다. 저는 마사지를 예약할 수 있었고 저의 경험을 충분히 즐길 수 있었습니다. 저는 이번 5월에 저희 회사의 여행 준비를 담당하고 있고, 귀하와 예약하고 싶습니다. 저희는 해외에서 온 몇몇 투자자들을 맞이하고 단체로 그곳에서 편안한 시간을 보내고 싶습니다.

저희는 5월 3일부터 7일까지 리조트에 머무를 것입니다. 저희는 5월 3일 저녁 늦게 도착해서 5월 7일에 일찍 떠날 것입니다. 5월 4일 오후에 저희 투자자들을 위해 스파 관리를 예약해 주실 수 있나요? 모두 여덟 명입니다. 저녁 식사가 뒤이어 있을 것입니다. 날씨가 허락한다면, 저희는 야외이고 조용한 곳에 앉고 싶습니다.

저희는 여행 기간 동안 12개의 1인용 객실이 필요할 것입니다. 저희는 또한 와인 시음과 라벤더 농장 방문에 관심이 있습니다.

이 모든 것이 가능한지 이 이메일에 답장을 보내 저에게 알려 주십시오. 저는 귀하와 함께 예약을 좀 더 검토하기를 기대합니다.

Roger Keller 드림
Lowe Finances사

수신: Roger Keller <roger.keller@lowefinances.com>
발신: Olivia Brunelli <olivia@nathalieresort.fr>
날짜: 3월 25일
제목: 귀하의 문의

Mr. Keller께,

귀하의 멋진 메시지에 감사드립니다. 이전 방문 동안 즐거운 시간을 보내셨다니 기쁩니다. 저희는 귀하의 단체를 수용할 수 있음을 알려드리게 되어 기쁩니다. 저희는 저녁 식사를 위한 야외 공간 전체를 예약할 수 있습니다. 하지만, 만약 마음대로 바꾸실 수 있으시다면, 그것은 다음 날 밤으로 옮겨져야 할 것입니다. 제안해주신 날짜는 이미 예약되어 있습니다. 물론, 저희는 실내에도 식당이 있습니다. 게다가, 저희는 동시에 여섯 개의 스파 예약에 대해서만 공간을 제공할 수 있습니다. 다른 활동들에 대해서는, 일단 귀하께서 이곳에 오시면 예약될 수 있습니다.

어떻게 진행하고 싶으신지 저희에게 알려 주십시오.

Olivia Brunelli 드림
리조트 관리자
Nathalie 리조트 & 스파

176 Mr. Keller는 왜 이메일을 썼는가?
(A) 일부 변경의 이유를 설명하기 위해
(B) 사업 협력에 대해 문의하기 위해
(C) 동료의 환대에 감사하기 위해
(D) 여행 준비를 하기 위해

177 Mr. Keller는 무엇을 필요한 것으로 언급하는가?
(A) 대규모 회의실을 임대하는 것
(B) 특별 식사를 준비하는 것
(C) 1인실을 예약하는 것
(D) 전망 좋은 방에 묵는 것

178 첫 번째 이메일에서, 4문단 첫 번째 줄의 표현 "going over"는 의미상 -와 가장 가깝다.
(A) 검토하다
(B) 건너다
(C) 획득하다
(D) 응답하다

179 Ms. Brunelli가 야외 공간에 대해 언급하는 것은?
(A) 이국적인 식물들로 장식되어 있다.
(B) 스파 가까이에 있다.
(C) 5월 4일에 이미 예약되어 있다.
(D) 1년 중 일부 동안 문을 닫는다.

180 투자자들에 대해 추론될 수 있는 것은?
(A) 리조트에서 하룻밤 동안 묵지 않을 것이다.
(B) 처음부터 Lowe Finances사를 후원했다.
(C) 프랑스에서 여러 개의 사업체를 열고 싶어 한다.
(D) 스파 관리를 같은 시간대에 받지 않을 것이다.

181-185는 다음 양식과 이메일에 관한 문제입니다.

양식

도착하는 모든 승객들은 다음 양식을 작성해야 합니다. 가족 구성원들과 함께 여행하는 경우, 단체를 위해 하나의 양식을 작성하세요. 도착하실 때, 이 양식을 여권과 함께 세관 공무원에게 제시해 주십시오.

성	Larson
이름	Harry
가운데 이름	Hughes
동반하는 가족 구성원들의 수	3
주소	88번지 Pingree로, 스탬퍼드, 코네티컷 06831
여권 발행 국가	미국
이번 여행에서 방문한 국가들	스페인, 포르투갈

이번 여행의 주된 목적은 ☐ 사업 ☐ 휴가 ☑ 기타 이다

만약 기타라면, 명시해 주세요: 제 가족과 저는 아버지가 새집으로 이사하는 것을 돕기 위해 스페인에 비행기를 타고 갔습니다. 그러고 나서 저희는 포르투갈에서 짧은 관광 여행을 했습니다.

과일, 고기, 동물을 반입하시나요? ☐ 네 ☑ 아니오

만약 그렇다면, 해당 항목을 여기에 나열하십시오:
해당 없음

서명: *Harry Larson*

수신: Harry Larson <harrylarson@worldmail.com>
발신: 고객 서비스 <service@internationalairlines.com>
제목: 회신: 요청 사항
날짜: 7월 28일

Mr. Larson께,

당신의 잃어버린 더플 백에 대해 저희에게 이메일을 써주셔서 감사합니다. 광범위한 수색 끝에, 저희는 마침내 그것을 찾았고, 저희는 그것을 당신의 집 주소로 배송해드릴 것입니다. 불편에 대해 사과드립니다.

분실된 가방에 대해 보상하기 위해, 고객님의 계정에 8,000점의 비행기 승객 포인트를 추가해드릴 것입니다. 저희 기록에 따르면, 귀하는 이제 한 번의 국내 왕복 항공 여행을 받을 자격이 있으시다는 것을 의미합니다. 귀하께서는 언제든지 이 기회를 이용하실 수 있습니다. 이것을 사용하시려면, 당사 웹사이트를 방문하셔서 결제 과정 중에 "비행기 승객 포인트 상환"을 클릭하십시오.

국제 항공사 고객 서비스 드림

181 Mr. Larson은 왜 양식을 작성했는가?
(A) 물품을 운반할 승인을 얻기 위해
(B) 도착 요건을 준수하기 위해
(C) 공항에서 문제를 보고하기 위해
(D) 여행 문서에 대한 도움을 받기 위해

182 양식에서 제공되는 정보가 아닌 것은?
(A) Mr. Larson의 단체에 있는 사람들의 수
(B) Mr. Larson이 방문했던 국가들
(C) Mr. Larson이 타고 간 항공사
(D) Mr. Larson이 그의 여권을 받은 나라

183 Mr. Larson은 왜 여행을 갔는가?
(A) 사업을 하기 위해
(B) 가족 구성원을 돕기 위해
(C) 식에 참석하기 위해
(D) 몇몇 수업을 가르치기 위해

184 국제 항공사는 무엇을 하기로 약속하는가?
(A) 항공편 세부 정보를 살펴본다
(B) 누락된 패키지를 검색한다
(C) 스탬퍼드로 물품을 발송한다
(D) 몇몇 계정 정보를 수정한다

185 Mr. Larson은 어떻게 무료 국내 항공편을 이용할 수 있는가?
(A) 항공사 직원에게 이메일을 보냄으로써
(B) 특정 여행사에 전화함으로써
(C) 모바일 앱을 다운로드함으로써
(D) 웹사이트에서 예약함으로써

186-190은 다음 브로슈어, 신청서, 회람에 관한 문제입니다.

Mario's
지중해 요리 출장 연회 서비스

Mario's는 30년 넘게 영업을 해오고 있습니다. 이곳은 여전히 설립자 Mario Robledo에 의해 소유되어 있지만 현재 그의 남동생 Sandro에 의해 운영됩니다. 출장 연회 회사는 매우 다양한 요리를 제공합니다. 게다가, 7738번지 Market가에 실내와 야외 좌석을 모두 갖춘 행사 공간을 소유하고 있습니다. 야외 테라스는 5월 1일부터 9월 30일까지 개방됩니다.

Mario's는 또한 모든 식이 요법 필요 조건과 식품 민감성을 수용할 수 있습니다.

다음 메뉴 옵션들을 이용할 수 있습니다:

메뉴	요리 종류	1인당 가격
메뉴 A	애피타이저 2개, 메인 요리 2개, 디저트 1개	30달러
메뉴 B	메뉴 A + 애피타이저 1개	35달러
메뉴 C	메뉴 B + 메인 요리 1개	40달러
메뉴 D	메뉴 C + 디저트 1개 * 40인 이상 단체에는 20퍼센트 할인이 적용됩니다.	45달러

달리 명시되지 않는 한, 모든 메뉴는 채식주의자 옵션을 포함합니다. 특별한 요청이 있으시거나 예약을 완료하시려면, www.marios.com을 방문하십시오.

Mario's 출장 연회 신청서

연락처 이름: Marissa Thomas
단체: Madison 개인 은행
이메일: m.thomas@madisonprivatebank.com
행사 날짜: 8월 28일
행사 시간: 오후 7시
손님 수: 45

시설: ___ Mario's   X 다른 곳
다른 곳을 선택하셨다면, 여기에 명시해 주십시오: Madison 개인 은행

선호 메뉴:
___ 메뉴 A
___ 메뉴 B
___ 메뉴 C
X 메뉴 D

의견:
작년의 행사에서 어떤 요리를 먹었는지 기억나지는 않지만, 굉장히 맛있었습니다. 올해의 고객 감사 만찬에서는 조금 다른 게 있어도 좋겠지만, 어느 것이든 괜찮습니다. 적어도 한 개의 완전 채식주의자 애피타이저와 메인 요리를 꼭 포함해주십시오.

수신: 팀
발신: Marissa Thomas
날짜: 8월 25일
제목: 곧 있을 저녁 식사

저희의 연례 고객 감사 만찬이 9월 3일 수요일에 열린다는 것을 상기시켜 드리고 싶습니다. 날짜가 변경되었음을 참고해주십시오. 저희는 이번에 대부분 새로운 고객분들이 오시기를 기대하고 있고, 저는 그들이 제공되는 것을 좋아할 것이라고 확신합니다. 한 고객인 Ms. Kim이 완전 채식주의자이므로, 저는 그녀가 먹을 수 있는 메인 요리와 애피타이저 요리가 하나씩 있는지 확인했습니다. 게다가, 일반적인 디저트 외에, 저는 여러분 모두가 즐길 거라고 생각하는 과일 모듬 요리도 추가했습니다. 이것은 비즈니스 업무로 여겨지므로 꼭 정장을 착용하십시오. 그곳에서 여러분을 뵙기를 기대합니다.

186 Mario's에 대해 언급된 것은?
(A) 요리로 상을 받았다.
(B) 새로운 메뉴를 시험해 보고 있다.
(C) 행사 공간을 추가할 계획이다.
(D) 소유주의 남동생에 의해 운영된다.

187 Ms. Thomas에 대해 사실인 것은?
(A) 고객으로부터 Mario's에 대해 들었다.
(B) 전에 Mario's의 서비스를 이용한 적이 있다.
(C) 엄격한 식이 요법 필요 조건이 있다.
(D) Mario's의 야외 공간을 요청했다.

188 Madison 개인 은행에 대해 암시되는 것은?
(A) Mario's와 같은 거리에 위치해 있다.
(B) 최근에 직원 규모를 늘렸다.
(C) 1인당 40달러의 예산이 있다.

(D) 20퍼센트 할인을 받을 자격이 있다.

189 고객 감사 만찬에 대해 추론될 수 있는 것은?
(A) 온라인 시스템에 등록되지 않았다.
(B) 주로 완전 채식주의자 요리를 포함한다.
(C) 다음 달로 연기되었다.
(D) 9월 이전에 지불되어야 한다.

190 Ms. Thomas는 그녀의 동료들에게 무엇을 하라고 지시하는가?
(A) 식당에 일찍 온다
(B) 복장 규정을 따른다
(C) 행사에 합승해서 간다
(D) 고객 몇 명을 태우러 간다

191-195는 다음 이메일, 온라인 양식, 웹페이지에 관한 문제입니다.

수신: 전 직원 <staff@craftmagazine.com>
발신: Alicia Mendez <a.mendez@craftmagazine.com>
제목: 이사
날짜: 4월 23일

직원분들께,

오랜 조사 후에, 저희는 마침내 저희 잡지사의 새 사무실 공간을 결정했습니다. 올스턴에 있는 82번지 Grant가 5층 사무실입니다. 저희의 현재 장소보다 훨씬 넓어서, 저희가 지난 몇 주 동안 고용한 새로운 작가들과 광고 직원들을 수용할 수 있습니다. 게다가, 그것은 버스 정류장 근처에 있고, 아래층에 피자집이 있고, 아름다운 찰스강을 내려다보는 창문이 있습니다.

임대차 계약이 시작되는 5월 1일에 새로운 사무실로 이사하기 시작할 것입니다. 그 토요일에 한가하고 도와줄 수 있으시면, 저에게 알려주십시오. 저는 트럭 두 대를 빌리려고 했는데, 저희가 사용할 수 있는 대형 밴 또는 소형 오픈 트럭을 누군가가 갖고 계신다면, 한 대만 빌릴 필요가 있을 것입니다. 이용할 수 있는 것이 있으시다면 저에게 바로 알려주십시오.

Alicia Mendez 드림
편집장, Craft 잡지사

---

www.bostontruckhire.com

보스턴 트럭 임대

이름	Alicia Mendez
전화번호	555-9182
운전면허 번호	013403412
대여 날짜(들)	5월 1일, 2일
차량 수	1
예상 주행 거리	10마일
픽업 장소	32번지 Cooper가, 보스턴
반환 장소	918번지 West Harding가, 보스턴
의견	지금으로서는, 48시간 동안 차량이 필요합니다. 만약 제가 그것을 더 오래 사용하기로 결정하게 되면 직원분께 알려드리겠습니다.

---

www.salepages.com

보스턴 > 광고란 > 판매

Craft 잡지사가 새로운 장비와 함께 새로운 장소로 이사를 할 것이라서, 저희가 판매할 몇몇 물품들이 있을 것입니다. 이것들은 DX 컬러 프린터, XRM6 팩스기, 5년 된 Vista Plus 노트북, 20인치 컴퓨터 모니터, 5개의 키보드를 포함합니다. 만약 당신이 이 물건들 중 어떤 것에 관심이 있으시다면, Alicia Mendez에게 a.mendez@craftmagazine.com으로 연락주세요. 가격은 협의할 수 있습니다. 저희는 몇몇 물품들은 심지어 기꺼이 무료로 나누어 드리려고 합니다. 이 물품들은 이사 사흘째이자 마지막 날인 5월 3일이 되어서야 수거하실 수 있을 것임을 알아두시기 바랍니다. 그날이 저희가 이삿짐 트럭에 마지막 물건들을 싣고 이전 사무실을 완전히 닫을 때입니다.

191 Craft 잡지사는 최근에 무엇을 했는가?
(A) 창간호를 발행했다
(B) 새로운 직원들을 고용했다
(C) 웹사이트를 만들었다
(D) 캠페인을 시작했다

192 새로운 사무실의 특징은 무엇인가?
(A) 경치가 좋은 전망
(B) 회의실
(C) 지하철에 대한 접근성
(D) 건물 내의 체육관

193 Ms. Mendez의 직원들 중 한 명은 무엇을 했을 것 같은가?
(A) 물품을 포장하기 위해 아침에 일찍 도착했다
(B) 이사 날짜를 바꿔 달라고 요청했다
(C) 몇 가지 불만 사항을 접수했다
(D) 사용할 차량을 빌려줬다

194 Craft 잡지사에 대해 추론될 수 있는 것은?
(A) 장비 일부를 교체하고 있다.
(B) 중고 가구를 사는 것에 관심이 있다.
(C) 서비스 비용을 지불하기 위해 돈을 모으려고 하고 있다.
(D) 고객들과 더 가까이 있기 위해 이사하고 있다.

195 Craft 잡지사의 이사에 대해 암시되는 것은?
(A) 할인 후에 금액이 더 저렴해질 것이다.
(B) 처음에 계획했던 것보다 더 오래 걸릴 것이다.
(C) 예상했던 것보다 더 먼 거리를 이동해야 할 것이다.
(D) 궂은 날씨 때문에 연기될 것이다.

196-200은 다음 웹페이지, 회람, 일정표에 관한 문제입니다.

http://www.rolandoesteban.com

Rolando Esteban 소개

Rolando Esteban은 깔끔한 붓선, 역동적인 구성, 그리고 선명한 색상으로 찬사를 받아온 시각 예술가입니다.

마닐라에서 자라, Mr. Esteban은 다양한 형태의 미국 대중문화에 노출되었고 유명한 만화책 삽화가 Chad Grohl로부터 영감을 받게 되었습니다. Mr. Esteban은 그림 그리는 법을 독학했고, 정규 교육의 부족에도 불구하고, 많은 상징적인 영화와 여행 포스터를 제작했습니다. 그는 마드리드에서 그림 장학금을 추구하기 위해 30대에 마닐라를 떠났고, 그곳에서 그는 마침내 그의 독특한 그림 스타일을 발전시켰습니다.

이제, 마드리드의 Vivi 미술관은 Mr. Esteban의 후기 작품을 다루는 전시회를 열 것입니다. *Brush and Line*이라는 제목의 전시회는 8월 21일에 예정되어 있는 환영 연회와 더불어, 8월 22일에 공개적으로 열립니다.

Vivi 시각 예술 미술관
회람

수신: Leon Aguilar
발신: Esther Hernandez
제목: *Brush and Line*
날짜: 7월 20일

전시장이 빠른 보수를 진행해야 하기 때문에 *Brush and Line*을 옮겨야 합니다. 이 작업을 시작하기 위해 우리가 일정을 잡을 수 있는 유일한 시간은 환영 연회 당일입니다. 제가 그 예술가와 이야기를 나눴는데 그는 새로운 공개 날짜인 8월 30일에 동의했습니다. 이것은 우리가 환영 연회 일정을 8월 28일로 다시 잡아야 할 것임을 의미합니다. 그다음에 예정된 전시회도 옮겨져야 할 것이라서, 저는 어떤 새로운 날짜가 괜찮은지 알아보기 위해 당신이 그 예술가와 소통해 보시면 좋겠습니다.

Vivi 시각 예술 미술관
전시회 일정

미술관 시간은 화요일부터 토요일, 오전 10시부터 오후 6시까지입니다.
환영 연회는 월요일마다 오후 6시에서 오후 8시까지 열립니다.

7월 12일에서 7월 29일
- Delia Romano: *Of One Mind*
- 환영 연회는 7월 10일

8월 2일에서 8월 19일
- Tom Moskowitz: *Ba Bi Bo Bu*
- 환영 연회는 7월 31일

8월 30일에서 9월 20일
- Rolando Esteban: *Brush and Line*
- 환영 연회는 8월 28일

9월 27일에서 10월 14일
- Remy Artaud: *Up is Down*
- 환영 연회는 9월 25일

196 Mr. Esteban에게 초기에 영향을 끼친 사람은 누구였는가?
(A) 예술 교수
(B) 직장 동료
(C) 유명한 삽화가
(D) 영화감독

197 Mr. Esteban에 대해 사실이 아닌 것은?
(A) 마닐라의 도시에서 자랐다.
(B) 영화 포스터를 제작했다.
(C) 마닐라에서 예술 학교를 다녔다.
(D) 선명한 색상을 사용하는 것으로 알려져 있다.

198 미술관은 언제 보수 공사를 위해 문을 닫을 것인가?
(A) 8월 21일
(B) 8월 22일
(C) 8월 28일
(D) 8월 30일

199 일정표에 따르면, Vivi 미술관에 대해 암시되는 것은?
(A) 주말마다 문을 닫는다.
(B) 개회 전에 환영 연회를 연다.
(C) 지역 예술가들의 작품만을 특별히 포함한다.
(D) 어떠한 전시된 작품도 팔지 않는다.

200 Mr. Aguilar는 누구에게 연락했을 것 같은가?
(A) Delia Romano
(B) Tom Moskowitz
(C) Rolando Esteban
(D) Remy Artaud

TEST 07 해석

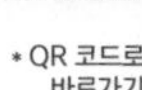

* 무료 해설은 해커스토익(Hackers.co.kr)에서 다운로드 받을 수 있습니다.

* QR 코드로 바로가기

PART 5

101 Ms. Ament는 회의에 늦을 것이라고 우리에게 알리기 위해 전화했다.

102 모든 분들은 Camellia 카페의 개업식에 정중히 초대되며, 이곳은 지하철 시청역 옆에 위치해 있습니다.

103 개인 비서는 Ms. Petrovsky의 약속 목록을 검토한 후 그녀의 하루 일정표를 매일 아침 업데이트한다.

104 그 리조트의 수상 스포츠 장비는 한 번에 최대 두 시간까지만 대여될 수 있다.

105 Ms. McCabe는 직접적인 감독 없이도 일할 수 있는 유능한 직원이다.

106 Mr. Coulter는 일찍 일어나는 것이 익숙해서, 밤 교대 근무 대신에 아침 교대 근무를 맡고 싶어 한다.

107 안전한 금융 상품에 투자하는 것은 퇴직자들이 상당한 손실을 경험하는 것으로부터 보호할 수 있다.

108 Bell Lake사는 최근에 150명의 추가 직원을 고용했을 때 지역에서 가장 큰 회사가 되었다.

109 승무원은 착륙 전에 모든 헤드폰이 반납될 것을 요청했다.

110 Solomo 제조사는 주 공장에서 새로운 품질관리 공정을 시행할 것이다.

111 정비 직원들은 전원이 여전히 켜져 있는 동안에는 기계를 안전하게 고칠 수 없다.

112 주민들은 다음 시장 선거 동안에 누구를 지지할 것인지에 있어 첨예하게 분열되어 있다.

113 연구는 갈등 해결에 대해 훈련받은 관리자들이 더 강하고 효과적인 팀을 만든다는 것을 보여준다.

114 Hislop사의 신입 사원들은 그들의 취업 후 한 달 이내에 의무 교육 과정을 완료해야 한다.

115 Veraville에서 유일한 다른 이탈리안 식당이 폐점했으므로 Gamberetti는 매우 바쁘다.

116 수백 대의 차량이 정부의 배기가스 기준을 충족시키지 못해 회수되어야 했다.

117 Ventera사는 베이징 출장에 임원들과 동행할 수 있는 중국어 통역사를 찾고 있다.

118 Victory Holdings사의 최고 경영자는 유럽으로의 확장 이후 회사의 미래를 위한 그의 비전에 대해 자신 있게 말했다.

119 고객은 그녀가 10월 13일에 주문한 것에 관해 문의했다.

120 시내의 식당 Chez Jacques의 식사는 아주 뛰어나서, 기다릴 만한 가치가 있다.

121 Blossom Kitchen의 물품을 대량 주문하는 고객은 할인을 위해 협상할 수 있다.

122 Mr. McIntyre는 발표 중에 긴장했지만, 그의 불안은 참석한 그 누구에게도 눈에 띄지 않았다.

123 개선이 필요한 가능한 모든 부분을 확인하기 위해 제품 견본이 철저히 분석되었다.

124 어젯밤 공연은 힘들이지 않는 동작을 보여주는 우아한 무용수들을 출연시켰다.

125 10층에 있는 회의실은 거의 사용되지 않아서, 더 실용적인 용도로 쓰이도록 개조될 수도 있다.

126 운영 관리자는 수족관에 최첨단 여과 장치를 갖추는 것을 목표로 한다.

127 구매 후 30일 이상이 지난 제품의 반품을 받는 것은 상점 정책에 반대된다.

128 검사관은 제과점이 개장할 수 있기 전에 여전히 충족되어야 하는 몇 가지 요건들을 기재했다.

129 Mr. Jackson은 적당한 가격의 점심을 먹고 싶을 때마다, Central Market에 있는 푸드코트로 간다.

130 주민들의 요구를 충족시키기 위해 새로운 아파트 단지 근처에 식당들이 점점 더 비일비재하게 개업하고 있다.

PART 6

131-134는 다음 공고에 관한 문제입니다.

여행자들에게 알림

131 10월 5일부터, Barings 공항은 국제선을 수용하기 위한 새로운 터미널 건설을 시작할 것입니다. **132** 도합해서, 터미널의 추가는 저희의 수용 능력을 40퍼센트만큼 증가시킬 것입니다. 5터미널이라고 불리는 새로운 터미널은 현재 운영하는 네 개의 건물과는 별도의 건물에 위치할 것입니다. 결과적으로, 그것은 경전철이나 셔틀버스를 통해서만 접근할 수 있을 것입니다. **133** 두 선택지 모두 다른 네 개의 터미널에서 이용할 수 있을 것입니다. **134** 4터미널의 일부를 포함하여, 공항의 일부 구역도 일시적인 폐쇄를 겪을 수 있습니다. 하지만, 모든 터미널은 내년쯤에는 완전히 개방될 것입니다.

135-138은 다음 공고에 관한 문제입니다.

135 Duluth Grand 영화관은 10월 22일 목요일 오후 7시에 Elwood Barker의 다큐멘터리 *Gideon's Revenge*를 개봉한다는 것을 발표하게 되어 자랑스럽습니다. 영화는 115분 동안 상영되며, 행사는 총 3시간 동안 계속될 것입니다. 그러고 나서 Mr. Barker가 남은 시간 동안 관객들의 질문에 답변할 것입니다. **136** 이는 팬들에게 그의 창작 과정에 대한 이해를 제공할 것입니다.

137 *Gideon's Revenge*는 4년 동안 시리아, 레바논, 그리고 이라크를 지나온 Mr. Barker의 폭넓은 여행을 바탕으로 합니다. **138** 이 중동에서의 삶을 직접 경험한 이야기를 보는 것에 관심이 있으시다면, 빨리 행동하십시오. 표는 한정된 수량만 있습니다.

139-142는 다음 편지에 관한 문제입니다.

3월 17일

Clara Rodriguez
644번지 Lockley가
골트 시티, 온타리오주 N1R 3Y8

Ms. Rodriguez께,

139 귀하의 지난 인터넷 서비스 납입금 지불 불이행에 관하여 편지를 씁니다. 저희는 전화로 귀하와 연락하기 위해 여러 번 시도했지만 성공하지 못했습니다. **140** 귀하의 Loft Net에서의 잔금, 총액 63.97달러가 3월 15일에 지불 기일이었다는 점을 유의해 주십시오. 최종 기한 이후 일주일 동안은 추가 요금의 적용 없이 납입금을 받는 것이 저희의 방침입니다. **141** 그 후에, 저희는 이자를 청구해야만 합니다. 저희는 귀하의 거래를 존중하므로, 이 일에 대한 즉각적인 조치를 해 주시면 감사하겠습니다. **142** 청구서를 정산하시기 위해서는, 555-7843으로 연락하시고, 신용 카드를 가까이에 두십시오.

Albert Sanders 드림
Loft Net 고객 서비스부

143-146은 다음 회람에 관한 문제입니다.

발신: Mila Larson, 마케팅 커뮤니케이션 부장
수신: 전 직원
제목: Liang사 캠페인
날짜: 7월 25일

직원분들께,

Liang사 홍보 캠페인 제안서에 기여해 주신 것에 대해 모든 분들께 감사드리고 싶습니다. **143** Liang사의 임원들은 우리의 디자인에 대해 매우 감명을 받았으며 우리를 고용하기로 결정했습니다. **144** 텔레비전 광고를 위해, 우리 모두가 참여해야 할 것입니다. 다음 몇 주 동안 할 일이 많을 것이므로, 여러분의 협력이 필수적입니다. 상세한 일정을 파악할 수 있도록 우리 모두가 7월 27일에 Liang사의 최고 경영자를 만나는 자리를 마련해 두었습니다. **145** 우리는 또한 잡지 배포에 대한 계획도 논의할 것입니다.

146 어떤 의견이나 추가적인 아이디어가 있다면, 회의 중에 발표할 수 있도록 준비해 주십시오.

감사합니다.
Mila Larson 드림

PART 7

147-148은 다음 문자 메시지에 관한 문제입니다.

삭제	발신자: 555-8164 시간: 오전 10시 59분	답장

안녕하세요, Jackson. 소식지에 대한 당신의 최신 초안을 받았습니다. 제 생각은 다음과 같습니다. 먼저, 제 제안을 시도해 주셔서 감사합니다. 그 새로운 디자인은 매우 현대적으로 보이고 저희 목표 독자의 관심을 끌 것입니다. 하지만, 이제 그것이 저희의 웹사이트와 너무 다르게 보입니다. 저는 브랜드의 일관성이 중요하다고 생각합니다. 저는 웹사이트와 같은 색상을 사용하는 것을 제안하고자 합니다. 마지막 사진도 바꿔주실 수 있나요? 그것이 너무 구식이어서 저희는 그것을 사용할 수 없습니다. 오늘 오후에 이메일로 다른 것을 보내드리겠습니다. 다음 초안이 완료되면 제게 보내주세요. 다시 한번 감사합니다!

147 메시지는 왜 보내졌는가?
(A) 일부 변경 사항에 대한 의견을 말하기 위해
(B) 파일 사본을 요청하기 위해
(C) 견적서를 요청하기 위해
(D) 회사 절차를 설명하기 위해

148 소식지에 대해 언급된 것은?
(A) 광고로부터 지원을 받는다.
(B) 부정확한 정보를 포함한다.
(C) 페이지가 너무 많다.
(D) 새로운 사진이 필요하다.

149-150은 다음 기사에 관한 문제입니다.

시구하는 Sandi Vincent

3월 21일—컨트리 음악의 인기 가수인 Sandi Vincent가 야구팀 Harpoons가 새로운 시즌을 시작하는 데 도움을 주기 위해 다음 달 Warwick를 방문한다. Belinda Cutter 시장은 4월 7일의 개막전에서 Ms. Vincent가 시구하도록 초청했다.

Ms. Vincent는 그녀의 세 번째 앨범, *Prairies and Plains*의 성공을 통해 전국적인 명성을 얻었다. 보다 최근에는, 영화 *Uncle Trevor's Farm*에서 연기 데뷔를 했다.

바쁜 투어 일정으로 인해, Ms. Vincent는 이야기를 해 줄 수 없었지만, 그녀의 매니저는 "Sandi는 처음으로 Warwick를 방문하는 것을 기대하고 있습니다. 그녀는 굉장한 야구팬이고, 저는 그녀가 즐거운 시간을 보낼 것이라고 확신합니다. Harpoons가 성공적인 시즌을 보낼 수 있도록 그녀가 행운의 시구를 하기를 바랍시다."라고 말했다.

149 기사는 주로 무엇에 대한 것인가?
(A) 팀의 리그 진입
(B) 음악가의 최근 공연
(C) 영화의 성공적인 개봉
(D) 유명 인사의 행사 참여

150 Ms. Vincent에 대해 암시되는 것은?
(A) 운동선수가 되고 싶어 했었다.
(B) 여러 앨범을 녹음했다.
(C) 정기적으로 Warwick를 방문한다.
(D) 텔레비전 광고에 출연했다.

151-153은 다음 공고에 관한 문제입니다.

곧 개장하는 Rumfax 공유 정원

올해 Rumfax 공유 정원(RSG)의 재배 시기는 3월 31일부터 9월 15일까지이므로, 지금이 여러분 소유의 정원 부지를 등록할 시기입니다. 돌아오는 작년의 정원사들은 회원권을 위해 40달러를 낼 것이나, 새로운 정원사들에게는 55달러가 청구될 것입니다.* Rumfax에 거주하는 사람은 누구든지 자유롭게 www.rumfaxgarden.com에서 신청할 수 있습니다. 하지만, 다음 규정들을 반드시 주의해 주십시오.

- 각 정원사는 그들의 부지를 관리할 책임이 있습니다. 이는 모든 필수적인 급수, 제초, 그리고 수확 작업을 포함합니다.
- 부지는 RSG 책임자들이 특별 허가를 승인하지 않는 한 확장될 수 없습니다. 저희 직원들은 또한 부지에 추가되는 어떤 구조물이든 그것이 설치되기 전에 승인해야 합니다.
- RSG 회원들은 그들 소유의 부지에만 작물을 심을 수 있으며 반드시 그들이 재배하는 것이 이웃의 식물을 가리지 않도록 해야 합니다.
- 연장은 창고 작업장에서 모두가 이용할 수 있지만, 그 후에는 반환되어야 합니다.

**회비는 물, 흙, 그리고 비료의 비용을 지불하는 데 사용됩니다.*

151 Rumfax 공유 정원에 대해 암시되는 것은?
(A) 특정 지역 주민들이 이용할 수 있다.
(B) 농작물은 지역 시장에서 판매된다.
(C) 기업으로부터 일부 자금을 받는다.
(D) 다른 지역 사회에서 비슷한 프로그램을 도입하도록 돕는다.

152 공고에 따르면, 부지는 언제 확장될 수 있는가?
(A) 인근 정원들이 그늘을 만들 때
(B) 정원사들이 추가 요금을 낼 때
(C) 직원들이 허가할 때
(D) 추가 구조물들이 완성될 때

153 Rumfax 공유 정원은 왜 회비를 청구해야 하는가?
(A) 광고 지면을 구매하기 위해
(B) 건축 자재를 사기 위해
(C) 직원들에게 임금을 주기 위해
(D) 필요한 용품의 비용을 지불하기 위해

154-155는 다음 메시지 대화문에 관한 문제입니다.

Juliet Pau [오후 3시 45분]
우리 회사 마스코트의 시안을 살펴볼 기회가 있었나요?

Chris Cormier [오후 3시 48분]
점심 식사 후에 바로 봤어요. 제 생각에는, Ms. Barrow가 우리의 의도를 상당히 잘 해석한 것 같아요.

Juliet Pau [오후 3시 49분]
저도 그렇게 생각해요. 세 가지 초안 중에서, 그녀가 A안에서 캐릭터의 복장과 몸을 그린 방식이 정말 마음에 들어요. 하지만, 얼굴에 대해서는 확신이 가지 않네요. 어떻게 생각하나요?

Chris Cormier [오후 3시 50분]
저도 동의하고 싶어요. 눈이 훨씬 더 커야 해요. C안에 있는 얼굴이 우리가 원하는 것에 더 가깝네요.

Juliet Pau [오후 3시 51분]
알겠어요. 나머지 팀원들과 그림에 대해 검토하기 위해 오후 5시에 만나기로 해요. Ms. Barrow는 내일 그녀의 작업에 대한 피드백을 받으러 올 거예요. 우리는 그녀에게 무엇을 바꿔 달라고 요청할지 결정해야 해요.

154 Ms. Barrow는 누구일 것 같은가?
(A) 패션 디자이너
(B) 마케팅 전문가
(C) 계약 협상가
(D) 그래픽 아티스트

155 오후 3시 50분에, Mr. Cormier가 "I'm inclined to agree"라고 썼을 때 그가 의도한 것 같은 것은?
(A) 관리자의 지시에 따를 수밖에 없다.
(B) 초안에서 한 가지 측면이 마음에 들지 않는다.
(C) 업무가 간단해져야 한다고 생각한다.
(D) 집단적 결정에 도달하는 것이 중요하다고 생각한다.

156-158은 다음 기사에 관한 문제입니다.

다르에스살람 (4월 19일)—Touchstone Ventures사는 어제 탄자니아 철도(TTL)를 인수했음을 공표했다. 이 계약은 2월 중순에 있었던 Touchstone사의 Umoja Transport사 인수에 뒤따른 것이다.

"TTL 인수는 저희가 다른 동아프리카 국가들에 진입할 수 있도록 도울 것입니다."라고 Mieke de Graaf 사장은 말했다. "이 시점에서, Touchstone사는 급속하게 발전하고 있는 지역들로 대담하게 나아가야 합니다. — [1] —."

TTL은 과거 국영 철도 회사로 계속 이윤을 내기 위해 분투했으며, 이곳의 몇몇 철로는 시급한 수리가 필요하다. "Touchstone사는 TTL의 기반 시설을 개선하는 데 상당히 투자해야 할 것입니다."라고 Arusha 경영 대학교의 교수, Dr. Patrick Maguli가 말했다.

"제 연구에 따르면, 점점 더 많은 탄자니아 사람들이 기차를 타는 것보다 운전하거나 버스를 타는 것을 선택하고 있습니다. — [2] —. Touchstone사의 과제는 이러한 추세를 역전시키는 것이 될 것입니다."라고 Dr. Maguli는 덧붙였다.

Touchstone사의 계획은 네 단계이다. 그것의 최우선 사항은 설치된 철로들을 수리하고 개선하는 일이 될 것이다. 그 후, 디젤 엔진을 사용하는 기차들을 전기 기차로 전환할 계획이다. 세 번째 단계는 점점 늘어나고 있는 인근 국가들로의 왕복 화물 교통량을 활용하기 위해 새로운 경로를 건설하는 일이 될 것이다. — [3] —. 마지막으로, Touchstone Ventures사는 TTL의 철도망을 관광 목적으로 개발하는 것을 목표로 한다. 예를 들어, 그것은 증기 엔진을 사용하는 전통 열차에서의 풍경 여행을 제공하기 시작할 수도 있다. — [4] —.

156 Touchstone Ventures사에 대해 사실이 아닌 것은?
(A) Umoja Transport사를 소유한다.
(B) 사업을 단계별로 구성했다.
(C) 이전에 정부 소유였다.
(D) 화물 수송을 취급하는 것을 목표로 한다.

157 Dr. Maguli에 대해 암시되는 것은?
(A) 건설 현장으로 출장을 갔다.
(B) 탄자니아의 운송 동향을 연구했다.
(C) 기업들을 위한 자문 업무를 한다.
(D) 새로운 기술을 개발하기 위해 작업하고 있다.

158 [1], [2], [3], [4]로 표시된 위치 중, 다음 문장이 들어갈 곳으로 가장 적절한 것은?
"이것들은 여유로운 속도로 이 나라의 풍경을 보고 싶어 하는 여행자들의 관심을 끌 것으로 예상된다."
(A) [1]
(B) [2]
(C) [3]
(D) [4]

159-160은 다음 광고에 관한 문제입니다.

Goliath 보관소: 여분의 소지품을 위한 안전하고 편리한 공간!

귀하의 집이나 회사가 불편할 정도로 가득 찼습니까? 그렇다면, 이전하는 대신, 토론토 바로 외곽의 452번지 East Island로에 위치해 있는 Goliath 보관소를 확인해 보십시오. 저희는 800개 이상의 유닛을 가지고 있으며 월간 또는 연간 임대 계약에서 훌륭한 가격을 제공합니다. 장기 임대 계약은 협상 가능합니다. 귀하의 소지품은 안전할 것이라고 확신하실 수 있는데, 이는 저희에게 최신식 카메라 시스템과 하루 24시간 내내 근무하는 보안 요원들이 있기 때문입니다. 지역 사업체들을 위해, 임대할 수 있는 10개의 냉장실 또한 있으며, 이는 냉장이 필요한 상품들을 보관하는 데 최적입니다. 그리고 12월 한 달 동안만, 저희 회사를 통해 보관품을 위한 보험을 구매하시는 분들은 보험 증서에서 20퍼센트 할인을 받으실 것입니다! 유닛의 이용 가능성, 가격, 그리고 규정에 관해 문의하시기 위해서는, www.goliathstorage.on.ca를 방문하십시오.

159 광고는 누구를 대상으로 하는 것 같은가?
(A) 아파트를 찾아야 하는 사람
(B) 개인 작업장 이용을 선호하는 사람
(C) 상품 수출을 시작하고 싶은 사람
(D) 보관 공간이 부족해지고 있는 사람

160 판촉 행사의 일부로 무엇이 제공되고 있는가?
(A) 월별 요금에 대한 할인
(B) 더 큰 크기로의 업그레이드
(C) 무료 소지품 집배
(D) 더 저렴한 보험 가격

161-164는 다음 이메일에 관한 문제입니다.

수신: <회원 목록>
발신: <info@windsorbiz.org>
제목: 알림
날짜: 12월 2일

회원 여러분께,

저희는 Windsor 사업 협회에서 지역 사업체로의 지속적인 회원 신분에 감사드립니다. 곧 있을 무료 세미나에 저희와 함께해주시기를 바랍니다. — [1] —. 전기 절약에 관한 지난달의 주제에 이어, 이번 달의 주제는 물 낭비를 줄이는 것에 관한 것입니다. 세미나는 12월 13일 오전 10시부터 오후 12시까지 Windsor 비즈니스 센터 B실에서 열립니다. — [2] —.

생태학자이자 물 보존 전문가인 Calvin Randall은 지역 사업체들이 비용을 절감하고 환경을 보존하는 데 도움이 되는 조치를 취할 수 있는 방법을 설명할 것입니다. 그는 따를 수 있는 간단한 팁과 기술을 제공할 것입니다. 그는 또한 세미나가 끝난 후 무료 일대일 상담도 제공할 것입니다.

Mr. Randall은 매우 존경받는 과학자이고 수년 동안 수많은 텔레비전과 라디오 프로그램에 출연했습니다. — [3] —. 여러분의 수도 비용을 줄일 수 있고 동시에 지구를 보호할 수 있는 방법을 배울 좋은 기회가 될 것입니다. 지역 사업주들은 또한 절약이 가능한 다양한 분야에 대해 배우기 위해 최근의 공공요금 명세서를 가지고 오도록 권장됩니다.

이번 달의 세미나에 참가하시려면, 이 이메일에 회신해 주세요. — [4] —. 감사합니다.

Windsor 사업 협회

161 Windsor 사업 협회에 대해 암시되는 것은?
(A) 최근에 신규 회원들을 받았다.
(B) 본사를 이전했다.
(C) 정기적으로 세미나를 제공한다.
(D) 환경 보호 단체와 협력했다.

162 2문단 두 번째 줄의 단어 "steps"는 의미상 -와 가장 가깝다.
(A) 사례
(B) 운동
(C) 지시
(D) 조치

163 관심 있는 참가자들은 무엇을 가지고 오도록 요구되는가?
(A) 사진이 부착된 신분증
(B) 등록 증명서
(C) 최근 수도 고지서
(D) 명함

164 [1], [2], [3], [4]로 표시된 위치 중, 다음 문장이 들어갈 곳으로 가장 적절한 것은?
"그것이 이 세미나를 놓치면 안 되는 이유입니다."
(A) [1]
(B) [2]
(C) [3]
(D) [4]

165-167은 다음 설문조사에 관한 문제입니다.

Arturo 부동산 - 고객 만족 설문조사

Arturo 부동산을 이용해 주셔서 감사합니다. 저희의 서비스가 귀하의 요구를 얼마나 효과적으로 충족시켰는지 알고자 하니, 잠시 시간을 내어 이 설문조사를 작성해 주십시오.

부동산을 구매하는 중이었다 __ 부동산을 판매하는 중이었다 X

왜 저희와 함께 일하기로 결정하셨습니까?
저는 여러 부동산 중개소에 연락했는데, 당신의 중개소가 가장 신속하게 응답했습니다. 또한, Mr. Hamlin이 저의 초반 질문들에 완벽하게 대답해 줄 수 있었습니다.

저희 서비스의 어떤 측면이 가장 마음에 드셨습니까?
제가 구매자의 제안을 받아들인 후, Mr. Hamlin이 거래 도중의 모든 단계마다 정보를 제공해 주었습니다. 그는 정기적으로 제게 전화해서 무엇이 진행되고 있는지 알려주었습니다.

저희 서비스의 어떤 측면이 가장 실망스러우셨습니까?
잠재적인 구매자가 저희 집을 보러 방문했을 때 좀 더 사전에 공지를 받았다면 좋았을 것입니다. 최소 한 시간 전에 공지를 받았다면 편리했을 것입니다.

귀하의 가족이나 친구에게 저희 서비스를 추천하시겠습니까?
네 X 아니오 __

성명: *Rosemary Woodard*

165 Ms. Woodard는 Arturo 부동산을 선택하기 전에 무엇을 했는가?
(A) 다양한 집의 가격을 비교했다
(B) 이전 고객과 이야기했다
(C) 회사 웹사이트를 방문했다
(D) 여러 부동산 중개인들과 연락했다

166 Ms. Woodard는 어떤 진술에 동의할 것 같은가?
(A) Mr. Hamlin은 광범위한 연락망을 가지고 있다.
(B) Arturo 부동산은 지역 규정을 준수한다.
(C) Mr. Hamlin은 최신 정보를 자주 제공한다.
(D) Arturo 부동산의 사무실은 편리하게 위치해 있다.

167 Ms. Woodard는 Arturo 부동산의 서비스 중 어떤 측면이 불만족스러웠는가?
(A) 때때로 중개인을 직접 만날 수 없었다.
(B) 방문 알림이 충분히 일찍 주어지지 않았다.
(C) 몇몇 협상이 효율적으로 수행되지 않았다.
(D) 몇몇 개인 정보가 기밀로 유지되지 않았다.

168-171은 다음 온라인 채팅 대화문에 관한 문제입니다.

Maria Sanchez [오후 12시 06분]
온라인과 저희 매장 모두에서 지난 몇 분기 동안 매출이 실망스러웠습니다. 상황을 호전시킬 방법이 있을까요?

William Behar [오후 12시 09분]
유명인과 함께 가구와 실내 장식용 소품 컬렉션을 작업해 보는 것은 어떨까요? 우리는 유명하고 스타일 감각이 뛰어난 사람이 필요할 거예요.

Robert Gillibrand [오후 12시 12분]
Fiona Connolly가 적합할지도 몰라요. 그녀는 유명한 실내 장식가예요.

William Behar [오후 12시 13분]
정말 잘 맞을 것 같아요. 그녀의 리얼리티 텔레비전 쇼는 지금 인기가 있고, 저는 그녀가 이전에 다른 소매점과 일한 적이 없다고 생각해요.

Maria Sanchez [오후 12시 14분]
또한, 그녀는 소셜 미디어에서 많은 팬을 보유하고 있어요. 다른 의견이 있나요, Gabrielle?

Gabrielle Shepard [오후 12시 15분]
저는 그 아이디어가 좋아요. 저는 그녀와 새로운 가구들을 디자인하는 것에 협업할 수 있으나 그녀에게 직물을 선택할 자유를 줄 수 있어요.

William Behar [오후 12시 17분]
맞아요. 아니면, 예를 들어, 당신은 새로운 침대를 디자인하는 것을 함께 작업할 수 있고, 그녀가 침대 시트나 베갯잇과 같은 관련 물품들을 디자인할 수 있어요.

Robert Gillibrand [오후 12시 18분]
네. 제가 그녀의 대리인에게 연락할게요. 만약 이것이 잘 진행된다면, 오래 지속되는 동업자로 발전할 수 있을 거예요.

Maria Sanchez [오후 12시 19분]
우리는 그녀가 우리를 거절할 경우에 대비해서 다른 후보자들도 생각해야 해요.

168 Ms. Sanchez는 왜 메시지를 보냈는가?
(A) 몇몇 권장 사항을 요청하기 위해
(B) 캠페인에 대한 피드백을 요청하기 위해
(C) 전략 변경을 제안하기 위해
(D) 가게 점검 일정을 잡기 위해

169 오후 12시 13분에, Mr. Behar가 "That would be a great fit"이라고 썼을 때 그가 의도한 것은?
(A) 다른 곳으로 옮기고 싶어 한다.
(B) 특정한 직물들을 선호한다.
(C) 주문 제작 작품에 관심이 있다.
(D) 디자인 파트너의 선정에 동의한다.

170 Ms. Shepard에 대해 추론될 수 있는 것은?
(A) 소셜 미디어에서 많은 팬들을 보유하고 있다.
(B) 리얼리티 텔레비전 쇼를 작업했다.
(C) 디자인 만드는 것을 담당하고 있다.

(D) 협업에 대해 확신하지 못한다.

171 Ms. Sanchez는 무엇을 하고 싶어 하는가?
(A) 한 개보다 많은 컬렉션을 출시한다
(B) 몇 가지 대안을 생각한다
(C) 장기적인 동업자 관계를 확립한다
(D) 관리자와 직접 대화한다

172-175는 다음 편지에 관한 문제입니다.

티켓 번호: 251077

Corrigan Technology사 본사
703번지 Shirlington대로
알링턴, 버지니아주 22206

10월 20일

관계자분께,

저희 상품을 정기적으로 주문해 주시는 데 감사를 표하기 위해, 귀하를 곧 공개될 제품 라인의 비공개 시사회에 초대하고자 합니다. 이 품목들은 내년 초에 발표될 것이며 아직 대중에게 공개되지 않았습니다.

이 행사는 11월 9일 오후 5시부터 9시까지, 이 편지의 맨 위에 있는 주소에서 있을 것입니다. Corrigan Technology사 최고경영자인 Bill Schriver가 소개 연설을 할 것이고, 그 후 디자인 팀장인 Pete Wellington이 저희의 새로운 가전제품 라인을 발표할 것입니다. 고객들은 사진을 찍거나 행사를 녹화하는 것이 허용되지 않습니다. 저녁 식사는 오후 6시 30분에 제공될 것이며, 그러고 나서 손님들이 신제품을 직접 사용해 보는 시연이 있을 것입니다.

만약 참석할 계획이시라면, 10월 27일까지 555-4498로 Louise Geisler에게 전화해 주십시오. 만약 그 날짜까지 그녀가 귀하로부터 연락을 받지 못하면, 저희는 귀하께서 참석하지 않을 것이라고 가정하고 손님 명단에서 귀하의 티켓 번호를 삭제할 것입니다.

티켓 번호는 특별 추첨에 포함될 것입니다. 당첨 숫자들은 그날 저녁이 끝날 무렵에 발표될 것이므로, 반드시 이 편지를 지참하십시오. 당첨자들은 저희의 새로운 제품 라인이 공개되면 할인을 받을 자격을 주는 상품권을 받을 것입니다. 상품권은 전국의 상점에서 사용될 수 있습니다.

귀하께서 함께하실 수 있기를 바랍니다.

Matthew Schenk 드림
홍보부장

172 편지의 목적은 무엇인가?
(A) 행사를 주최한 것에 대해 단체에 감사를 표하기 위해
(B) 새롭게 공개된 제품에 대한 의견을 요청하기 위해
(C) 특정 고객들에게 행사에 참석하도록 요청하기 위해
(D) 주주들에게 분기별 최신 정보를 제공하기 위해

173 새로운 제품 라인에 대해 암시되는 것은?
(A) 광고된 적이 없다.
(B) 아직 디자인되고 있다.
(C) 완전히 품절되었다.
(D) 출시가 지연될 것이다.

174 시사회에 대해 언급되지 않은 것은?
(A) 11월에 열릴 것이다.
(B) 지사에서 열릴 것이다.
(C) 이전 고객들이 참석할 것이다.
(D) 식사를 포함할 것이다.

175 참석자들은 어떻게 상품권을 받을 수 있는가?
(A) 편지를 제시함으로써
(B) 여러 물품을 구매함으로써
(C) 설문지에 답변함으로써
(D) 추첨에서 뽑힘으로써

176-180은 다음 공고와 이메일에 관한 문제입니다.

Ludlow 해상 박물관 특별 공고
5월 14일

Ludlow 해상 박물관이 일시적으로 대중들에게 문을 닫는다는 것을 알려드리게 되어 유감입니다. 이는 벽의 단열재가 교체되어야 하기 때문입니다. 보수 공사를 하는 동안 소장 물품들을 보호하기 위해, 저희는 그것들 대부분을 3층 보관실로 옮겼습니다.

다음 주에, 박물관장 Ken Lin이 이사회를 만나 재개장 날짜를 결정할 것이며, 바라건대 이는 올여름의 끝 무렵이 될 것입니다. 만약 저희 작업의 진전 사항에 대한 최신 정보를 받고 싶으시다면, www.ludlownautical.org/emailsubscription에서 저희의 온라인 소식지를 구독해 주십시오.

불편에 대해 사과드리기 위해, 저희 회원들은 Crescent Bay 수족관의 할인 쿠폰을 받으실 것이고, 이곳 또한 Ludlow 관광 협회에서 운영합니다. 한편, 사전 예약이 취소된 각 손님께는 저희 기념품 가게의 열쇠고리가 무료로 배송될 것입니다.

이해해 주셔서 감사합니다.

수신: Andrea Smith <andreasmith@sunshineheights.com>
발신: Ken Lin <kenlin@ludlownautical.org>
날짜: 5월 15일
제목: 박물관 폐장
첨부: Ludlow 공고

Ms. Smith께,

제 기록으로는 귀하께서 다음 주 화요일에 Sunshine Heights의 노인분들 그룹을 위해 Ludlow 해상 박물관을 방문하는 일정을 잡으신 것으로 보입니다. 유감스럽게도, 박물관은 보수 공사를 위해 문을 닫아야 했습니다. 현재 상황에 대한 공고를 첨부합니다.

귀하께서 화요일에 다른 장소로 견학을 계획하실 수 있길 바랍니다. 개인적으로는 Crescent Bay 수족관을 추천합니다.

만약 저희가 재개장한 이후 방문 일정을 다시 잡고 싶으시다면, 그때 연락해 주시기 바랍니다.

Ken Lin 드림
관장, Ludlow 해상 박물관

176 공고에 따르면, 일부 물품들은 왜 3층으로 옮겨졌는가?
(A) 건물에 특별 전시를 준비하기 위해
(B) 잠재적인 손상으로부터 보호하기 위해
(C) 본래 색을 복원하기 위해
(D) 계절에 따른 관광 감소에 대응하기 위해

177 Mr. Lin은 이사회와 무엇을 논의할 것인가?
(A) 행사에 어떤 활동들이 있을지
(B) 소식지를 어떻게 개선할지
(C) 운영이 언제 재개될지
(D) 유물이 어디에 전시되어야 할지

178 Ms. Smith에 대해 언급된 것은?
(A) 지역 박물관에서 자원봉사 활동을 한다.
(B) 보수 공사 사업을 감독하고 있다.
(C) 정부 위원회에서 근무한다.
(D) 노인을 위한 견학을 계획했다.

179 Mr. Lin은 무엇을 추천하는가?
(A) Ludlow 관광 협회가 운영하는 장소를 방문하는 것
(B) Sunshine Heights에서의 워크숍을 취소하는 것
(C) 개인적인 약속 날짜를 변경하는 것
(D) 극장의 공연 일정을 확인하는 것

180 Ms. Smith는 무엇을 받을 것 같은가?
(A) 보증금 환불
(B) 기념품점의 물품
(C) 시즌 패스
(D) 수리 청구서

181-185는 다음 회람과 이메일에 관한 문제입니다.

사내 회람

수신: 팀장 전체
발신: Helen Malone, 최고경영자, Daisy사
날짜: 4월 21일
제목: 다가오는 직원 평가

여러분 중 많은 분께서 이미 이 과정에 익숙하시겠지만, 6월 1일에 시작할 연례 직원 평가와 관련된 몇 가지 세부 사항을 상기시켜 드리고 싶습니다. 다음 주 월요일에, 인사부 직원들이 입사 일자와 지난 평가 결과를 포함해 여러분의 각 팀원에 대한 정보를 이메일로 보낼 것입니다. 5월 말 전까지 이 정보를 검토하는 시간을 좀 가지시기 바랍니다.

만약 어떤 직원이 긍정적인 실적 평가를 받았으며 지난 3개월 이내에 임금 인상이나 상여금을 받지 않았다면, 그 직원은 5.5퍼센트의 임금 인상을 받을 자격이 있습니다. 질문이나 문제가 있으시다면, 인사부의 Gail Cullen에게 연락해 주십시오.

수신: Gail Cullen <gail.cullen@daisycorp.com>
발신: Cody Long <cody.long@daisycorp.com>
날짜: 4월 24일
제목: 도움 요청

Ms. Cullen께,

다가오는 이번 6월에 제가 평가하게 될 직원 중 한 명인 Shayla Barrie에 대한 질문이 있습니다. Ms. Barrie는 저희 팀에서 소프트웨어 기술자로 훌륭하게 일하고 있으며 2년간 그 직책에 있었습니다. 지난달에, 그녀는 10주간의 힘든 프로젝트에서 그녀의 몫을 성공적으로 완수한 것에 대해 상여금을 받았습니다.

저는 그녀가 저희 팀에 매우 귀중한 팀원으로서 임금 인상을 받을 자격이 있다고 생각합니다. 이 경우에 제가 Ms. Barrie를 위한 예외를 요청할 수 있는지 궁금합니다. 그저 제가 어떤 조치를 취해야 하는지만 알려주십시오. 또한, 가능하다면, 저는 그녀에게 표준 비율보다 높은 임금 인상분을 제공하고 싶습니다. 그것이 허용되는지도 알려 주십시오.

도움에 감사드립니다.

Cody Long 드림
소프트웨어 기술팀장

181 회람의 목적은 무엇인가?
(A) 정책 변경 사항을 명확하게 하기 위해
(B) 채용 공고를 알리기 위해
(C) 몇 가지 질문에 답변하기 위해
(D) 절차를 설명하기 위해

182 인사부 직원에 대해 언급된 것은?
(A) 평가 정보를 보낼 것이다.
(B) 5월에 지원자들을 심사할 것이다.
(C) 새로운 임금 대장 소프트웨어를 사용하기 시작했다.
(D) 임금 데이터베이스를 갱신했다.

183 Ms. Malone에 따르면, Ms. Cullen은 무엇을 할 수 있는가?
(A) 가능성 있는 후보들의 면접을 본다
(B) 기술적인 문제를 고친다
(C) 관리자들의 문의에 응답한다
(D) 직원들의 진급을 승인한다

184 이메일에서, 2문단 첫 번째 줄의 단어 "figure"는 의미상 -와 가장 가깝다.
(A) 계산하다
(B) 묘사하다
(C) 생각하다
(D) 대표하다

185 어떤 요소가 Ms. Barrie가 임금 인상에 자격이 되지 않도록 하는가?
(A) 그녀가 어떤 종류의 업무 방식을 요구하는지
(B) 그녀가 누구의 관리 담당인지
(C) 그녀가 얼마나 오래 현재 직책을 유지했는지
(D) 그녀가 언제 마지막으로 상여금을 받았는지

186-190은 다음 편지, 등록 양식, 일정표에 관한 문제입니다.

8월 28일

란베리스산 자연 공원 사무실
122번지 High가
란베리스, 귀네드 LL55 4HB

관계자분께,

10대였을 때부터, 저는 제가 좋아하는 몇몇 활동에 참여하기 위해 란베리스산 자연 공원을 방문해왔습니다. 최근 몇 달간 공원에 있으면서, 저는 걱정스러운 몇 가지 변화를 목격했습니다. 예전에는 적당한 숫자의 사람들이 있었는데, 여름 몇 달 동안 공원이 많은 사람들을 끌어들이기 시작했습니다. 이곳의 더해가는 인기와 더불어, 여러 규칙이 도입되어야 합니다.

예를 들어, 저는 최근 많은 사람들이 표시된 길을 벗어나는 것을 보았습니다. 사람들이 그렇게 하는 것을 금지하는 규정을 만드시길 권합니다. 또한, 암벽 등반 구역에서, 저는 미숙한 등반가들이 어려운 경로를 시도하는 것을 인지했습니다. 사고를 예방하기 위해, 초심자들은 주의 깊게 관리되어야 합니다. 저는 또한 방문자들이 위험한 활동에 참여하기 위해서는 허가 양식을 작성하도록 요구되어야 한다고 생각합니다.

귀하의 시간에 감사드립니다.

Glenda Ree 드림

란베리스산 자연 공원 - 어드벤처 스포츠 등록 양식

이 양식을 란베리스산 자연 공원 관리소에 제출해 주십시오. 귀하의 신청서가 근무 중인 공원 관리원에 의해 승인된 경우에만 진행이 허용될 것입니다. 최초 방문객들은 공인된 가이드와 동행하는 경우가 아닌 이상 진행이 허용되지 않을 것입니다. 어떤 장비를 대여하셔야 한다면 저희에게 문의해 주십시오.

성명: Branwen Pearse
단체 인원: 4
방문 일시: 10월 19일 / 오전 9시 30분
예상 방문 시간: 6시간
이번이 최초 방문입니까? X 예 __ 아니오
예정 활동 및 장소:

암벽 등반	하이킹	산악자전거
Giant's Wall __	Lloyd Peak X Harlech Slope __	Zipper Descent __

유의하셔야 하는 규칙: (1) 쓰레기를 버리지 마십시오. (2) 공원은 오전 6시부터 오후 6시까지 개장합니다. 방문객들은 폐장 시간까지 공원 사무소로 돌아오셔야 합니다. (3) 항상 표시된 길에 머무르십시오. (4) 야생동물에게 먹이를 주지 마십시오.

* * 위반자는 30달러 벌금의 대상이 될 것입니다. * *

도움을 원하시거나 공원 규정 위반을 신고하시려면, 555-2129로 전화해 주십시오.

란베리스산 자연 공원
관리소

TEST 01 02 03 04 05 06 07 08 09 10
해커스 토익 실전 1000제 1 Reading

10월 19일 에 어드벤처 스포츠에 참여하는 방문객들

예약 시간	방문 장소	성명	비고	복귀 시각
오전 7시 45분-오후 3시 45분	Giant's Wall	Bryn Hughes	- 3인 단체	*오후 3시 40분*
오전 8시-오전 10시 15분	Zipper Descent	Gweneth Edwards	- 산악자전거 대여	*오전 11시*
오전 9시 30분-오후 3시 30분	Lloyd Peak	Branwen Pearse	- 가이드 동행 - 4인 단체	*오후 2시 45분*
오전 11시 15분-오후 4시	Giant's Wall	Dennis Roberts	- 3인 단체	*오후 3시 55분*
오후 12시 30분-오후 5시	Harlech Slope	Owen Price	- 등산용 지팡이 대여	*오후 6시 10분*

*직원 주의사항: 방문객들이 복귀한 시각을 기록하는 것을 잊지 마십시오.

186 편지는 왜 쓰였는가?
(A) 공원 이용에 대한 우려를 제기하기 위해
(B) 등산로 연장을 요청하기 위해
(C) 캠프장으로의 새로운 경로를 제안하기 위해
(D) 야생 동물이 보호되도록 권고하기 위해

187 어느 규칙이 란베리스산 자연 공원에 의해 새롭게 채택되었을 것 같은가?
(A) 규칙 (1)
(B) 규칙 (2)
(C) 규칙 (3)
(D) 규칙 (4)

188 등록 양식에 따르면, Ms. Pearse는 무엇을 하도록 요구되는가?
(A) 공인된 가이드와 함께 하이킹한다
(B) 물품을 빌리기 위해 보증금을 지불한다
(C) 몇몇 암벽 등반 수업에 등록한다
(D) 관리소에 신분 증명 서류를 제시한다

189 일정표에 따르면, 10월 19일에 어느 장소가 두 단체의 방문을 받았는가?
(A) Giant's Wall
(B) Lloyd Peak
(C) Harlech Slope
(D) Zipper Descent

190 Mr. Price에 대해 추론될 수 있는 것은?
(A) 관리소에서 등산용 지팡이를 샀다.
(B) 공원 관리원에게 규칙 위반에 대해 알리지 않았다.
(C) 벌금을 냈을 수도 있다.
(D) 궂은 날씨에 맞닥뜨렸다.

191-195는 다음 광고, 온라인 양식, 후기에 관한 문제입니다.

Viu 애슬레저 상점

애슬레저 운동복은 다목적성으로 인기가 있습니다. 저희는 10개의 브랜드를 취급하고 있고 현재 7월 31일까지 특별 판촉행사를 진행하고 있습니다. 모든 할인은 온라인과 저희 매장에서 모두 적용됩니다.

Bemba Team
Bemba Team은 고급 섬유로 만든 합성 물질의 옷을 판매합니다. 이 직물은 흡습성이 매우 뛰어나며 빨리 마릅니다. 엄선된 제품들에 대해 20퍼센트 할인을 누리세요.

Ventra
Ventra는 다양한 스포츠를 위한 운동화를 전문으로 합니다. Ventra는 저희 매장에 새로 입점하여 30퍼센트의 소개용 할인을 해드리고 있습니다.

Upstar Athletics
Upstar Athletics는 재활용된 플라스틱 물병으로부터 만들어진 폴리에스테르를 사용하여 옷을 생산합니다. 10퍼센트의 일반 할인을 해드리고 있습니다.

Yogana
Yogana는 여러 패턴과 색깔의 요가 의류를 생산합니다. 요가 반바지는 현재 40퍼센트 할인으로 판매되고 있습니다.

80달러가 넘는 모든 주문에 무료 배송을 누리세요. 의류 품목에 대한 맞춤 인쇄는 추가 요금으로 가능합니다. 449번지 South State가 미니애폴리스에 있는 저희 매장을 방문하거나 저희 웹사이트 www.viuathleisure.com을 방문하세요.

---

www.viuathleisure.com/contactus

연락 양식
저희 제품과 서비스에 대해 궁금한 점이 있으시면 연락 주십시오. 저희는 48시간 이내에 당신의 문의에 답변드릴 것을 약속합니다.

이름: Maria Cortez
이메일: maria@evanstonbball.com
제출된 날짜: 7월 13일

의견:
저는 제가 지도하는 아마추어 농구팀을 위한 조화를 이루는 셔츠와 반바지 35세트를 구매하는 것에 관심이 있습니다. 그 팀은 중학교와 고등학교의 학생들로 구성되어 있기 때문에, 저는 다양한 사이즈가 필요할 것입니다. 또한, 저는 당신의 상점이 진행하고 있는 할인에 추가로 대량 할인을 받을 수 있는지 궁금합니다.

---

http://www.upstar.com

8월 4일에 게시된 후기
작성자: Maria Cortez

Upstar Athletics는 훌륭한 회사이고, 그들의 옷은 환상적입니다. 원단이 잘 늘어나고 운동하기에 적합합니다. 안타깝게도, 다른 브랜드들 중의 하나로 Upstar Athletics를 취급하는 매장에 연락했는데, 그들이 제 문의에 답변하지 않았습니다. 그래서, 저는 Upstar Athletics에 직접 연락하기로 결정했습니다. 그들은 후한 수량 할인을 한 셔츠와 반바지 35벌을 개별 사이즈로 보냈고 옷에 저희 팀 이름을 무료로 인쇄해주었습니다.

191 Viu 애슬레저에서 어느 브랜드가 새롭게 제공되는가?
(A) Bemba Team
(B) Ventra
(C) Upstar Athletics
(D) Yogana

192 Viu 애슬레저의 제품들에 대해 사실인 것은?
(A) 온라인에서만 판매된다.
(B) 해외로 배송될 수 있다.
(C) 네 가지 브랜드의 옷을 판매한다.
(D) 요금을 내면 맞춤 제작될 수 있다.

193 Ms. Cortez가 농구팀에 대해 언급한 것은?
(A) 유명한 운동선수들을 배출했다.
(B) 챔피언 결정전에서 우승했다.
(C) 다양한 연령대의 선수들이 있다.
(D) 수년간 활동해 왔다.

194 Ms. Cortez의 구매에 대해 언급된 것은?
(A) 상점 포인트로 지불되었다.
(B) 친환경 소재로 만들어진 옷을 포함했다.
(C) 회원 할인에 대한 자격이 있었다.
(D) 30일 이내에 반품될 수 있다.

195 Viu 애슬레저 상점에 대해 추론될 수 있는 것은?
(A) 자체 정책을 따르지 않았다.
(B) 다른 지점을 열려고 하는 중이다.
(C) 모든 상품을 48시간 이내에 배송한다.
(D) 옷이 잘 맞도록 변형할 것이다.

196-200은 다음 웹페이지, 설문지, 온라인 후기에 관한 문제입니다.

www.visionbath.com/serviceinquiry

Vision Bath

Vision Bath는 고객들에게 최고의 주택 전반 개조 경험을 제공하는 것을 목표로 하는 독자적인 욕실 도급업체입니다. 당신이 집에 새로운 욕실을 추가하기를 원하시든 혹은 기존의 것을 개조하기를 원하시든, 저희의 작업은 고품질임을 보장합니다. 꿈의 욕실을 갖고 싶으시다면, 당신이 찾고 있는 것이 무엇인지 저희가 알 수 있도록 먼저 간단한 설문지를 작성해 주셔야 할 것입니다. 24시간 이내에, 저희의 숙련된 디자이너 중 한 명이 당신의 선호도에 대해 더 상의하기 위해 전화로 연락할 것입니다. 당신은 제품 안내 책자를 받으실 것이며, 준비가 되시면 대면 회의 일정을 잡으실 수 있을 것입니다. 이 상담 동안, 당신의 디자이너가 계약서를 제시할 것이고, 그 후에 곧 작업이 시작될 것입니다. 이 과정을 시작하시려면 여기를 클릭하세요.

---

www.visionbath.com/questionnaire

Vision Bath 설문지

이름: Margaret Collins
전화: 555-9911
이메일 주소: margcollins@wyohi.com

1. 왜 새로운, 또는 개조된 욕실을 원하십니까?
   욕실 하나를 계속 함께 쓰기에는 저희 가족의 인원이 너무 많아서, 하나를 더 지어야 합니다.
2. 당신이 원하는 욕실의 스타일을 가장 잘 표현하는 용어는 무엇입니까?
   ☑ 현대적인 ☐ 전통적인 ☐ 호화로운
3. 어떤 색이 사용되길 원하십니까? 파란색과 흰색
4. 어떤 종류의 바닥재에 관심이 있으십니까?
   ☐ 타일 ☑ 견목 ☐ 비닐 ☐ 기타
5. 어떤 종류의 세면대를 원하십니까?
   ☐ 화강암 ☑ 자기 ☐ 유리 ☐ 기타
6. 이 프로젝트를 언제 시작하고 싶으십니까? 5월 초
7. 예산은 얼마입니까? 10,000달러에서 15,000달러 사이

보내기

---

www.businessreviews.com/visionbath

★★★★★ Margaret Collins 5월 25일

저는 Vision Bath에 굉장히 깊은 감명을 받았습니다. 설문지를 제출한 후, 저는 Sandra Reynolds라는 이름의 도움이 되는 디자이너로부터 연락을 받았습니다. 그녀는 개수대 수도꼭지부터 수납장 손잡이에 이르기까지 모든 것에 대해 탁월한 방안을 가지고 있었으며 매우 인내심을 가지고 저를 대했습니다. 저는 Vision Bath의 안내 책자를 살펴보는 데 꽤 오랜 시간을 보냈으며 그녀가 저희 집을 방문했을 때, 우리는 선택한 사항들에 대해 함께 검토했습니다. 제가 화강암 세면대를 선택하도록 그녀가 도와준 것이 특히 고맙습니다. 원래 선택한 것보다 비용이 더 많이 들었지만, 제가 상상할 수 있었던 것보다도 더 좋아 보입니다.

196 웹페이지는 누구를 대상으로 하는 것 같은가?
(A) 주택 소유주
(B) 실내 장식가
(C) 호텔 지배인
(D) 마케팅 전문가

197 설문지에 따르면, Ms. Collins는 왜 그녀의 집에 만족하지 않았는가?
(A) 배관 설비에 결함이 있었다.
(B) 현대적인 스타일로 지어지지 않았다.
(C) 욕실이 하나밖에 없다.
(D) 어두운색의 패널이 설치되었다.

198 설문지에 포함되지 않은 정보는?
(A) 최대 비용
(B) 선호하는 바닥재
(C) 완공 기한
(D) 디자인 스타일

199 Ms. Reynolds는 Ms. Collins를 방문했을 때 무엇을 했을 것 같은가?
(A) 안내 책자를 전달했다
(B) 계약서를 제시했다
(C) 사진을 몇 장 찍었다
(D) 대금을 회수했다

200 자기 세면대에 대해 언급된 것은?
(A) 브로슈어에 특별히 포함되었다.
(B) 동반 품목과 함께 판매된다.
(C) 화강암 모델보다 저렴하다.
(D) 보관용 칸을 포함한다.

TEST 08 해석

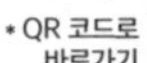

* 무료 해설은 해커스토익(Hackers.co.kr)에서 다운로드 받을 수 있습니다.

• QR 코드로 바로가기

PART 5

101 신문 기사에 따르면, Philby사는 현재 유타주에 새로운 사무실을 짓고 있다.

102 Ms. Wendt는 Mr. Andrews를 직접 만나고 싶어 했지만 그 대신 그에게 전화를 해야 했다.

103 Ms. Myers는 모든 신입 사원을 교육했으며 심지어 추가 도움이 필요한 누구에게든 조언해 주겠다고 제안했다.

104 도급업자는 금요일 오후까지 서비스에 대한 대금이 지불될 것을 요청했다.

105 Portland Bearcats는 가까스로 지역 하키 선수권 대회에 출전할 자격을 얻었다.

106 그 도시의 급속한 인구 증가는 구할 수 있는 주택의 부족을 야기했다.

107 오페라 가수로서의 많은 업적에도 불구하고, Gloria Donahue는 아직 어떤 주요한 상도 받지 못했다.

108 매출을 늘리기 위한 여행사의 전략은 고객의 추천 글을 웹사이트에 게시하는 것이다.

109 Rolstein 문학상의 수상자는 다수의 문학 애호가들에 의해 선정될 것이다.

110 Mr. McGuire가 완전한 세트를 갖기 위해서는 희귀한 만화책 시리즈에서 단 한 권이 더 필요하다.

111 증가하는 비용을 따라갈 수가 없어서, 많은 항공사들은 국내선에서 기내식 서비스를 없애는 것을 택했다.

112 회의 참가자들은 환영 패키지 안에 있는 쿠폰과 교환하여 무료 점심을 받을 수 있다.

113 공장의 로봇들은 제조 작업을 더 빠르고 정확하게 수행하는 것을 가능하게 했다.

114 만약 시합이 무승부로 끝나는 경우에, 상금은 두 명의 참가자들 사이에서 분배될 것이다.

115 공항의 도착 구역에서 수하물을 찾는 승객들은 많은 가방들이 비슷하게 보인다는 점에 주의해야 한다.

116 Mr. Chen은 거의 30년의 광고 경력이 있는데, 이는 그를 그의 분야에서 노련한 전문가로 만들었다.

117 Emperor Fabrics사는 Ms. Shane이 대표이사직을 인계받고 난 이래로 다수의 수익성 있는 계약을 맺어왔다.

118 새로운 다리는 그 지역을 관통하는 잦은 폭풍을 견뎌내도록 충분히 견고해야 한다.

119 백화점의 정책에 따라, 경비원들은 교육이 완료되면 출입 배지를 받을 것이다.

120 Hamilton 마을에는 7개의 공원이 있는데, 이것들은 모두 한 번쯤은 야외 콘서트를 개최했다.

121 아테네에서 열리는 연례 미디어 회의 때문에, 대부분의 시내 호텔들은 예약이 꽉 찼다.

122 Mr. Morgan은 그의 작업에 만족한 이전 고용주에 의해서 Cuthright 타워의 전기설비 일자리에 추천되었다.

123 Level Field Landscaping사는 최근에 정원 쓰레기를 부적절하게 처리한 것에 대해 시로부터 벌금을 부과받았다.

124 조립 공장은 지난달에 그랬던 것처럼, 예정대로 트랙터의 할당량을 초과한다.

125 영감을 주는 연설에서, Denise Camic은 회사가 더 창의적일수록, 성공은 더 클 것이라고 주장한다.

126 정보가 반드시 기밀로 보관되게 하기 위해, 데이터베이스의 파일은 암호 없이 접근될 수 없다.

127 올해의 사업가 상의 수상 소감 중에, Mr. Gordon은 그의 헌신적인 팀원들에 대한 감사를 표했다.

128 방문객들은 건물의 특정 구역에 들어갈 수 없고, 안내자 없이 돌아다니는 것도 허용되지 않는다.

129 Rand's 유기농 농장은 라디오 광고의 도움으로 고객층을 늘릴 수 있었다.

130 콜 센터 직원 중 여러 명이 뛰어난 연례 평가를 받았으며 그 결과로 급여 인상을 받았다.

PART 6

131-134는 다음 회람에 관한 문제입니다.

회람

수신: 전 직원
발신: Warren Harris, 사무실 관리자
날짜: 8월 15일
제목: 전력 사용

131 저는 이번 달에 사무실 공공요금이 작년 이맘때보다 거의 15퍼센트 더 높았다는 사실에 여러분의 주의를 모으고 싶습니다. 132 저는 이를 받아들이기 어렵다고 생각하는데, 특히 회사에서 많은 경비 절감책을 시행해 왔기 때문입니다. 이것들은 지난가을의 보수 공사 동안 에너지 효율이 좋은 조명과 창문을 설치한 것을 포함합니다. 133 그러므로, 여러분 모두 합리적이어야 함을 상기시켜 드리고 싶습니다. 그저 약간의 합리성과 적절한 판단만으로도, 저는 우리가 비용을 줄이기 위한 조치를 취할 수 있다고 확신합니다. 134 우선, 우리 모두는 무엇이든 사용 중이 아닌 것을 반드시 끄도록 할 수 있습니다. 여러분의 이해에 감사드리며, 에너지 절약을 위한 다른 방안을 가지고 계신다면, 제게 알려주시기 바랍니다.

135-138은 다음 보도 자료에 관한 문제입니다.

보도 자료—Basinet Books

독자적인 팟캐스트를 출시할 예정인 Basinet Books

Basinet Books 출판사는 곧 역사 소설 팬들을 위한 주간 팟캐스트의 제작을 시작할 것이다. 135 그 시리즈의 소개 회차는 7월 15일에 방송될 것이다. 이 첫 번째 쇼는 그 장르의 최근 인기에 대해 이야기하고 역사와 소설 간의 흥미진진한 관계를 탐구할 것이다. 136 각각의 차후 에피소드는 개개의 소설에 초점을 맞출 것이다. 137 선정되는 책들은 모두 신간일 것이다. 누가 진행할 것인지에 대해 말하자면, Basinet Books는 그들이 유명 배우를 고용했다는 암시를 주었다. 138 소문에 의하면, 이 사람은 소설을 각색한 여러 영화들에서 주연을 맡았었다고 한다. 각 팟캐스트 파일은 StarLadder 모바일 애플리케이션을 통해 이용할 수 있을 것이다.

139-142는 다음 이메일에 관한 문제입니다.

수신: Belinda Wright <bw4637@advertx.com>
발신: Jamie Garnett <jg4548@advertx.com>
제목: 긴급 요청
날짜: 2월 11일

안녕하세요, Belinda.

휴가는 어떠신가요? 139 당신의 휴가가 2월 14일 금요일까지 지속된다고 알고 있습니다. 하지만, 저는 당신이 그날 회사에 복귀할 수 있을지 알고 싶습니다. Nektar Beverages사가 그곳이 의뢰했던 광고에서 갑작스럽게 몇 가지를 변경해 주길 원한다는 것이 드러났습니다. 140 지난주에는 그들이 그것에 대해 만족해하는 것처럼 보였기 때문에 이것은 의외입니다. 당신이 책임 디자이너였기 때문에, 저는 당신이 이 최종 수정을 처리할 적임자일 것이라고 생각합니다. 해당 업무에는 아마 대여섯 시간이 소요될 것입니다.

141 당신에게 보상해 드리기 위해, 저희는 2월 14일에 대한 기본 초과근무 수당을 지급할 것입니다. 142 저희는 또한 하루의 추가 휴일을 제공하겠습니다.

미리 감사드립니다.
Jamie 드림

143-146은 다음 기사에 관한 문제입니다.

GEOnet Solutions사의 새 지평

보스턴(10월 9일)—GEOnet Solutions사는 회사의 범위를 해외로 확장할 것이라고 발표했다. 143 그 회사는 런던에 부속 지점을 열 것이다. 144 20년이 넘도록, 보스턴에 근거지를 둔 이 기술 개발의 선구자는 지질 공학을 이용하는 획기적인 방안을 만들어왔고 그 분야에서 셀 수 없이 많은 발전을 이룩해왔다. 145 사실, 그것의 노력이 없었다면 수백만의 사람들에 의해 매일 사용되는 자료 수집 시스템과 추적 도구들은 존재하지 않았을 것이다. 146 어제 발표된 성명에서, GEOnet Solutions사의 대표 Tomas Fuller는 이 확장의 주된 목적은 런던 기술 센터와의 협력을 촉진하기 위한 것이라고 말했다. 그 둘은 그들의 공동 연구가 서로에게 유익할 것이라고 생각한다.

PART 7

147-148은 다음 회람에 관한 문제입니다.

수신: 전 직원
발신: Nadori Seiko, 최고 경영자
제목: 월간 판매 과제
날짜: 12월 2일

월간 판매 과제에 기여해 주셔서 여러분 모두에게 감사드립니다. 여러분의 노고 덕분에 우리는 여러 신규 고객들을 얻었습니다. 판매 과제는 개인 활동으로 시작하여 긍정적인 단체 경험으로 발전했습니다. Aaron과 Marisol이 가장 높은 매출을 올렸습니다. 따라서, 그 둘 모두 Spanto 레스토랑의 상품권을 받게 될 것입니다.

이 과제가 만들어낸 열정과 연대 의식의 수준에 놀랐기 때문에, 저는 여러분 각자에게 하루의 추가 휴가를 제공할 것입니다. 그뿐만 아니라, 임원진은 향후 이 기획을 다시 주최하기로 결정했습니다. 직원 개개인 혹은 팀 전체를 위한 몇 가지 새로운 상품 아이디어들을 제게 이메일로 보내주십시오.

147 과제에 대해 언급된 것은?
(A) 반복될 것이다.
(B) 성공적이지 못했다.
(C) 마감일이 연장되었다.
(D) 참가자들이 익명이었다.

148 Ms. Seiko는 직원들이 무엇을 하기를 원하는가?
(A) 팀원들의 성과를 평가한다
(B) 가능한 몇 가지 보상을 추천한다
(C) 휴가에 대해 선호하는 날짜를 제출한다
(D) 이메일로 몇몇 개인 서류를 보낸다

149-150은 다음 안내문에 관한 문제입니다.

Cole 극장 회원권 안내:

Cole 극장의 회원이 되기 위해서는, www.coletheater.com/join에서 신청하시거나 저희 매표소 부스 중 한 곳을 방문하십시오. 회원권 카드는 12개월 이후 갱신되어야 합니다.

회원권 혜택:

- 유명 배우들이 참석하는 독점적인 영화 시사회 표
- 오전 상영은 6달러에 입장
- 오후, 저녁, 그리고 주말 상영에서 10퍼센트 할인
- 보상 포인트와 교환되는 무료 매점 품목 또는 영화표

더 많은 정보를 위해서는, extras@coletheater.com으로 이메일을 보내주십시오.

149 Cole 극장의 회원에 대해 언급되지 않은 것은?
(A) 밤에는 할인된 요금을 받는다.
(B) 1년에 한 번 카드를 갱신해야 한다.
(C) 포인트를 간식으로 교환할 수 있다.
(D) 월별 요금을 내야 한다.

150 Cole 극장에 대해 언급된 것은?
(A) 지역 영화 축제를 개최한다.
(B) 새로운 매표기를 설치했다.
(C) 텔레비전 다큐멘터리에 나왔다.
(D) 유명 연예인들의 방문을 주최한다.

151-152는 다음 메시지 대화문에 관한 문제입니다.

Neil Pollard 오전 11시 33분
오늘 Kent가에 있는 방 2개짜리 집의 공개 행사를 진행하나요?

Connie Mills 오전 11시 35분
30분 이내에 시작해요. 저는 지금 여기서 준비 중이에요. 왜요?

Neil Pollard 오전 11시 36분
182번지 North가의 아파트 열쇠를 깜빡했어요. 저는 지금 차에 있는데, 당신이 보통 여분을 가지고 있는 걸로 알고 있어요. 저는 Sydney Mountain 쇼핑몰을 지나서 운전하고 있어요.

Connie Mills 오전 11시 38분
맞아요. 정오 전에 언제든지 와서 가져가세요. 이곳에 일찍 도착할 수도 있는 잠재적 구매자들이 진입로를 이용할 수 있게 하고 싶으니, 길모퉁이 주위에 주차해 주세요. 그곳의 길가를 따라 몇몇 비어 있는 주차 공간을 봤어요.

Neil Pollard 오전 11시 41분
완벽해요! 정말 고마워요.

151 오전 11시 36분에, Mr. Pollard가 "I know you usually have a spare"라고 썼을 때 그가 의도한 것은?
(A) 건물의 열쇠가 필요하다.
(B) 직장 동료의 일과에 대해 들었다.
(C) 차를 빌리고 싶어 한다.
(D) 창고에 방문할 수 없다.

152 Ms. Mills는 Mr. Pollard에게 무엇을 해달라고 요청하는가?
(A) 집 바깥의 차도를 청소한다
(B) 잠재적 고객들과 만난다
(C) 보안 장치를 끈다
(D) 그의 차량을 거리에 주차한다

153-154는 다음 편지에 관한 문제입니다.

Brugeri 미술관
856번지 Empire가
그랜츠패스, 오리건주 97527

9월 9일

Robert Jansen
3111번지 Helmsview로
아르카타, 캘리포니아주 95521

Mr. Jansen께,

귀하께서 올해 귀하의 개인 소장품으로부터 매우 관대하게도 저희에게 대여해 주신 조각상 *Descending Cherub*이 어제 파손되었다는 것을 알려 드리게 되어 유감입니다. 날씨가 갑작스럽게 바뀌었을 때 저희 직원들은 야외 조각공원에 있는 모든 작품을 주 전시회장 안으로 옮기는 중이었습니다. 안타깝게도, 그들은 제때 귀하의 조각상에 도착하지 못했습니다. 강한 바람이 그것을 받침대에서 떨어지게 했고, 왼쪽 손을 부러뜨렸습니다. 부서진 부분의 사진 몇 장을 동봉하였습니다.

물론, 저희의 보험 회사가 파손에 대해 귀하께 금전적으로 보상해 드릴 것입니다. 또한, 저희는 그것을 전문적으로 수리하는 비용을 부담할 것입니다. 귀하의 동의가 있으면, 저희가 전문가에게 이를 하도록 요청할 수 있습니다. 만약 귀하께서 스스로 선정하신 분을 쓰고 싶으시다면, 그저 저희에게 알려주시고, 그러면 저희가 바로 물품을 보내 드리겠습니다.

다시 한번, 이 유감스러운 사고에 대해 사과드립니다. 귀하의 답변을 기다리겠습니다.

Mia Hyman 드림
큐레이터, Brugeri 미술관

동봉물

153 *Descending Cherub*에 대해 언급된 것은?
(A) 약 1년 동안 전시되었다.
(B) 이동 중에 떨어졌다.
(C) Ms. Hyman에 의해 조각되었다.
(D) 박물관에 대여되었다.

154 편지와 함께 무엇이 포함되었는가?
(A) 미술관의 입장권
(B) 파손에 대한 사진
(C) 보험금 청구 서류
(D) 상환 수표

155-157은 다음 기사 발췌에 관한 문제입니다.

Steel Works사가 새로운 공장의 운영을 시작했다. 6천만 달러의 비용을 들여 지어진 이 공장은, 말레이시아의 건설업 성장에 기여할 것이다. 그것은 1년에 백만 톤의 보강철을 생산할 수 있을 것이다.

회사의 최고경영자 Aiman Musa에 따르면, Kampung Tebing에 설립된 Steel Works사의 공장은 철근을 나라의 다양한 지역으로 수송할 것이다. "공장은 말레이시아 도시들이 사회 기반 시설을 개발하는 데 도움을 줄 것입니다."라고 그는 덧붙였다.

이 공장은 Steel Works사의 두 번째 공장이다. Rembau에 있는 첫 번째 공장은 이제 생산품을 오로지 다른 아시아 국가들로만 수출하지만, 한때 그것은 말레이시아 철강 수요의 거의 절반을 충족시켰다. Rembau 공장은 작년에 개선되었고 아시아의 가장 현대적인 철강 공장들 중 하나로 여겨진다. Steel Works사의 공장들은 생산이 효율적일 뿐만 아니라 환경에 적은 영향을 미치는 것을 보장하기 위해 최신 기술을 사용한다.

Kampung Tebing 공장의 설립에 따라, Steel Works사의 말레이시아에서의 시장 점유율은 72퍼센트까지 증가할 것으로 예상된다. 현지 증권 거래소에서의 주식 가치는 새로운 공장의 개시와 함께 24퍼센트 증가했다.

155 기사의 하나의 목적은 무엇인가?
(A) 지역의 사회 기반 시설의 상태를 알리기 위해
(B) 세계 철강 산업에 대한 세부 사항을 제공하기 위해
(C) 국가의 수출에 대한 정보를 주기 위해
(D) 새로운 공장의 개시를 발표하기 위해

156 기사가 Rembau에 있는 공장에 대해 암시하는 것은?
(A) 더 이상 현지 사용을 위한 철강을 생산하지 않는다.
(B) 외국 기업에 의해 인수되었다.
(C) 이전에 환경에 다소 해를 끼쳤다.
(D) 플라스틱 제품을 제조하기 시작했다.

157 Steel Works사에 대해 언급되지 않은 것은?
(A) 현재 운영 중인 여러 강철 공장이 있다.
(B) 새로운 시설은 말레이시아의 도시 개발을 도울 것이다.
(C) 시장 점유율이 두 배가 될 것이다.
(D) 최신 기술을 활용한다.

158-160은 다음 이메일에 관한 문제입니다.

수신: 모든 마케팅 담당자
발신: Linda Marks
제목: 회의 교통수단
날짜: 10월 14일

동료분들께,

여러분 중 많은 분들이 금요일에 Wilmington에서의 소셜 미디어 회의에 참석할 것입니다. — [1] —. 만약 회사에서 대절한 버스를 타고 갈 예정이라면, 우리는 A 주차장에서 만나서 오전 8시 30분에 시간을 엄수하여 출발할 것입니다. 다른 방법으로는 운전하거나 대중교통을 타는 것이 있습니다. Wilmington 회의 센터로 찾아가는 길 안내는 이전 이메일에서 제공되었습니다. — [2] —.

참석하지 않는 분들에게는, 지난주에 저희가 얻은 고객인 Whitaker's 스포츠 의류회사의 대표들이 오전 10시쯤 사무실을 방문할 것입니다. — [3] —. 회의로 인해서 사무실이 거의 비어 있을 것이라고 이미 그들에게 알렸습니다. — [4] —. 회계부서의 Robert Buck이 그들과 만나서 짧게 견학을 시켜줄 것입니다. 기회가 된다면 꼭 자기소개를 하세요.

감사합니다.

Linda Marks 드림

158 이메일에 따르면, 직원들은 시설로 찾아가는 길을 어떻게 알 수 있는가?
(A) 행사 주최자에게 전화함으로써
(B) 공고를 들음으로써
(C) 이메일을 확인함으로써
(D) 게시판을 봄으로써

159 Whitaker's 스포츠 의류회사에 대해 암시되는 것은?
(A) 계약서를 수정하기 위해 대표들을 보냈다.
(B) 최근에 Ms. Marks의 회사와 거래했다.
(C) 직원들에게 교통비를 상환해준다.
(D) 새로운 경리부장을 찾고 있다.

160 [1], [2], [3], [4]로 표시된 위치 중, 다음 문장이 들어갈 곳으로 가장 적절한 것은?

"하지만, 그들이 그날 이 지역에 있을 예정이어서 잠시 들르고 싶어 합니다."

(A) [1]
(B) [2]
(C) [3]
(D) [4]

161-164는 다음 메시지 대화문에 관한 문제입니다.

Ned O'Toole [오전 11시 8분]
제가 어제 11월 초 회의에 늦어서, 초과 근무 정책의 변경 사항에 대해서 물어보고 싶어요.

Karen Bingham [오전 11시 9분]
물론이죠. 그런데 Mr. Ward가 조금 전에 보낸 회람을 못 받았나요? 그게 새로운 규정들을 요약하고 있어요.

Ned O'Toole [오전 11시 10분]
간단히 훑어보기만 했는데, 간소화된 절차에 관한 무언가를 봤어요. 이는 우리가 더 이상 신청서를 제출하지 않아도 된다는 의미인가요?

Karen Bingham [오전 11시 12분]
네. 이전에는, 많은 직원들이 프로젝트를 끝내기 위해서 초과 근무를 했지만 정규 급여만을 받았어요. 이는 그들이 공식적인 초과 근무 서류를 제출하지 않았기 때문에 발생했죠. 많은 사람들이 그 양식을 너무 복잡하다고 여겼어요.

Gene Shipley [오전 11시 13분]
이제, Ned, 한 주에 40시간 이상 일하는 사람은 누구나 자동적으로 추가 수당을 받아요. 우리는 그저 급여 대장 시스템에 정보를 입력하기만 하면 돼요.

Karen Bingham [오전 11시 13분]
맞아요. 그리고 이건 12월 1일 오전 9시부터 시행돼요. 매달 말에, 당신의 관리자가 당신이 입력한 것을 검토할 거예요. 논의가 필요한 문제가 있지 않은 한, 그 시점에 승인될 거예요.

Ned O'Toole [오전 11시 15분]
특히 제가 다음 몇 주 동안 작업하게 될 큰 프로젝트를 생각해봤을 때, 그건 정말 좋은 일이네요. 고마워요!

161 오전 11시 9분에, Ms. Bingham이 "Of course"라고 썼을 때 그녀가 의도한 것은?
(A) 직원들에게 회람을 보낼 것이다.
(B) 새로운 정책이 타당하다고 생각한다.
(C) Mr. O'Toole에게 최신 정보를 알려줄 의향이 있다.
(D) 서류 작업을 완료하려고 한다.

162 초과 근무 서류에 대해 언급된 것은?
(A) 웹사이트에서 다운로드 받을 수 있다.
(B) 일부 직원들에게는 작성하기 어려웠다.
(C) 부서 관리자들이 수정할 것이다.
(D) 다시 쓰이고 있는 중이다.

163 12월 1일에 무슨 일이 일어날 것인가?
(A) 몇몇 직원들이 늦게까지 일해야 할 것이다.
(B) 회사 지침이 배부될 것이다.
(C) 몇몇 갈등이 논의될 것이다.
(D) 정책 변경이 시행될 것이다.

164 Mr. O'Toole에 대해 암시되는 것은?
(A) 회의에서 들은 것을 오해했다.
(B) 절차에 대해 조금 불평했다.
(C) 가까운 미래에 초과 근무를 할 것으로 예상한다.
(D) 최근에 완료된 프로젝트에 대한 보수를 아직 받지 못했다.

165-167은 다음 기사에 관한 문제입니다.

DTA가 공항 정비를 준비하다

덴버 교통 공단(DTA)은 덴버 교외에 있는 Franklin 공항에 대한 5천만 달러 규모의 보수 계획을 발표했다. 이 발표는 국제 항공사 단체(NAG)에서 그곳의 활주로가 대형 항공기에 위험하다고 명시한 결과이다. NAG는 모든 미국 공항에 대한 안전 규정을 세운다.

"저희가 11년 전에 Franklin 공항을 인수했을 때, 저희는 그것을 바로 재건하기 시작하려고 했습니다. 유감스럽게도, 저희는 예산과 관련된 수많은 유예에 맞닥뜨렸습니다. 하지만, NAG의 최근 판단을 고려하여, 저희는 연방 자금 지원을 확보해냈으며 마침내 활주로를 수리하고 터미널을 확장할 수 있게 될 것입니다."라고 DTA 이사장 Elaine Webster가 말했다.

DTA는 18개월 이내에 완료될 것으로 예상되는 이 프로젝트를 수행하기 위해 여러 건설회사를 고용했다. B 터미널의 작업은 A 터미널의 확장이 끝나고 나서야 시작될 것이며, 이는 공항이 전체 기간 내내 완전히 정상 가동될 수 있게 할 것이다. 프로젝트가 끝나고 난 후에, Franklin 공항은 국제 항공편들의 입출국 지점으로 쓰이기 시작할 것이다.

165 Franklin 공항은 왜 보수될 것인가?
(A) 안전 문제를 해결하기 위해
(B) 예산 흑자를 지출하기 위해
(C) 소매업자들을 위한 공간을 만들기 위해
(D) 더 큰 공항과 경쟁하기 위해

166 보수 프로젝트에 대해 사실인 것은?
(A) 10년 넘게 DTA의 목표였다.
(B) 민간 기부금을 통해 자금을 제공받고 있다.
(C) NAG에 의해 관리될 것이다.
(D) 예상보다 더 오래 걸릴 것이다.

167 Franklin 공항에 대해 암시되는 것은?
(A) 고객 만족 상을 받았다.
(B) 지하철 노선으로 도시와 연결되어 있다.
(C) 현재 국내 항공편에 의해서만 이용되고 있다.
(D) 보수 동안 완전히 폐쇄될 것이다.

168-171은 다음 이메일에 관한 문제입니다.

수신: Joan Stendhal <joan.stendhal@mynextmail.com>
발신: Robert Hamilton <r.hamilton@pichaipartners.com>
날짜: 9월 18일
제목: 귀하의 지원서

Ms. Stendhal께,

축하합니다! 수백 명의 지원자 중에서, 저희는 과정의 다음 단계로 넘어가서 저희 사무실에서 있을 인터뷰에 참여하도록 귀하를 선발했습니다. ─ [1] ─.

인터뷰는 9월 23일 금요일 오후 1시부터 5시까지로 예정되어 있습니다. 모든 지원자들은 활동 사이에 30분간의 휴식을 취하도록 허용될 것입니다. 인터뷰는 두 부분으로 구성될 것입니다. 인터뷰의 첫 번째 부분 동안, 귀하는 임원 심사원단의 질문에 답할 것입니다. 귀하가 마치면, 귀하는 인터뷰의 두 번째 부분을 위해 불릴 때까지 인접한 구역에 남아 있어야 합니다. 두 번째 부분에서, 귀하는 저희 회사가 과거에 작업했던 실제 법률 사건을 분석하도록 요청될 것입니다. 귀하는 한 개의 사건을 혼자서 처리하도록 한 시간이 주어질 것입니다. ─ [2] ─. 그런 다음, 귀하와 다른 지원자들은 두 번째 사건을 작업하기 위해 두 명의 그룹을 구성할 것입니다. 이 활동은 귀하의 의사소통 능력과 동료들과 함께 일하는 능력을 평가하는 데 사용될 것입니다. 자세한 내용은 인터뷰 당일에 제공될 것입니다. ─ [3] ─.

저희는 종이, 펜, 그리고 저희 도서관의 엄선된 법률 서적에 대한 접근을 포함하여, 과정을 완료하는 데 필요한 모든 것을 제공할 것입니다. ─ [4] ─. 저희는 다과도 제공할 것입니다.

이 이메일에 회신하셔서 참석 여부를 확인해주세요. 문의 사항이 있으시면 555-4883으로 전화하실 수도 있습니다.

Robert Hamilton 드림

168 2문단 네 번째 줄의 단어 "immediate"는 의미상 -와 가장 가깝다.
(A) 갑작스러운
(B) 인접한
(C) 중요한
(D) 즉각적인

169 일자리에 중요한 자질은 무엇인가?
(A) 타인과 협력하는 능력
(B) 국제법에 대한 광범위한 지식
(C) 장시간 노동을 기꺼이 하는 마음
(D) 특정 소프트웨어에 대한 경험

170 지원자들은 무엇을 하도록 요구되는가?
(A) 추가적인 업무 참고 자료를 제출한다
(B) 이메일로 답장을 보낸다
(C) 추천서를 제출한다
(D) 회사 웹사이트에 프로필을 만든다

171 [1], [2], [3], [4]로 표시된 위치 중, 다음 문장이 들어갈 곳으로 가장 적절한 것은?
"그러므로 귀하는 자신의 어떠한 자료도 가져올 필요가 없을 것입니다."
(A) [1]
(B) [2]
(C) [3]
(D) [4]

172-175는 다음 공고에 관한 문제입니다.

좋은 목적을 위해 달리세요!

이곳 Highland 고용 센터에서, 저희는 Tech Training 계획을 위한 여러분의 지원이 필요합니다. 많은 사람들이 기본적인 컴퓨터 기술이 부족하기 때문에 일자리를 찾는 데 어려움을 겪습니다. 따라서, 저희는 센터에서 1년 내내 주간 워크숍을 진행해 줄 컴퓨터 강사를 고용할 수 있을 만큼 충분한 기금을 모으기를 희망합니다. 구직자들은 이 수업에 무료로 참석할 수 있을 것입니다. 컴퓨터 능력을 얻음으로써, 그들에게는 일자리를 얻을 수 있는 더 나은 기회가 있을 것이고 이전보다 더 많은 돈을 벌 수 있을 것입니다.

여러분은 8월 15일에 Arthur 공원에서 10킬로미터 경주에 참여함으로써 저희가 목표를 달성하는 것을 도울 수 있습니다. 참가비는 7월 내내 40달러, 8월 1일부터 14일까지는 45달러, 그리고 경주 당일에는 50달러입니다. 창의적인 의상을 입고 달리는 사람들은 Harlan Foods의 100달러 상품권을 탈 수 있는 자격이 주어집니다. 의상 대회의 승자는 경주 후에 발표될 것입니다.

경주자들은 경주 번호판과 개인물품을 위한 수납 가방을 포함한 패킷을 받을 것입니다. 2시간의 시간 제한 이내로 마치는 사람들은 자신들이 결승선을 통과하는 모습을 담은 사진을 받을 것입니다. www.highlandec.com/10k로 가셔서 오늘 신청하세요!

172 공고의 하나의 목적은 무엇인가?
(A) 예산 산정을 공유하기 위해
(B) 모금 행사의 참여를 요청하기 위해
(C) 목표 달성을 알리기 위해
(D) 자원봉사자들을 모집하기 위해

173 공고에 따르면, 경주 참가자들은 무엇을 할 수 있는가?
(A) 몇 가지 요리를 시식한다
(B) 독특한 옷을 입는다
(C) 경로 제안을 제출한다
(D) 선호하는 달리기 거리를 선택한다

174 행사에 대해 언급된 것은?
(A) 한 달 앞서 신청되어야 한다.
(B) 참가비가 접수 일자에 따라 다르다.
(C) 주최자가 연설할 것이다.
(D) 텔레비전 촬영진에 의해 촬영될 것이다.

175 2시간 이내로 경주를 마치는 사람들은 무엇을 받을 것인가?
(A) 맞춤 티셔츠
(B) 성취 증명서
(C) 식료품 상품권
(D) 기념 사진

176-180은 다음 이메일과 잡지 목차에 관한 문제입니다.

발신: Rachel Duval <r.duval@pfmagazine.com>
수신: John Hassan <j.hassan@pfmagazine.com>
날짜: 7월 29일
제목: 9월호

안녕하세요, John.

비록 우리가 9월호와 관련해 많은 진전을 이루었지만, 여전히 몇 가지 결정을 내려야 합니다. 첫째로, 표지 모델을 선정해야 합니다. 이것은 보통 1년 중 가장 인기 있는 호이므로, 인기 있는 유명인을 구해야 합니다. 다시 Su-min Yoo와 함께 작업하는 것은 어떤가요? 그녀는 10월에 새로운 블록버스터 영화 개봉을 앞두고 있어서, 그녀가 표지에 나오는 것은 잡지 판매를 끌어올릴 가능성이 높습니다. 그녀의 에이전트에 연락해서 계획을 잡도록 해 주세요.

둘째로, 결국 Russo Shampoo가 갑작스럽게 9월호에 광고를 하지 않기로 결정했습니다. 따라서, 급히 58쪽과 59쪽을 채워야 합니다. 당신은 SameSide Cosmetics사가 우리 잡지에 광고를 내는 것에 관심이 있다고 언급했었습니다. 이건 그들이 10월에 선보일 유기농이면서 환경 친화적인 새로운 피부용 크림 라인에 대한 것이 될 겁니다. 그 회사가 이 기회를 활용하길 원하는지 확인해 줄 수 있나요? 우리는 그들에게 20퍼센트를 할인해 줄 수 있습니다.

마지막으로, 캐나다 디자이너 David Burns에 대해 9월호의 기사에 언급된 사실들을 철저히 확인해 주면 좋겠어요.

고맙습니다.

Rachel Duval 드림
편집장
PopFashion 잡지사

PopFashion지 9월호

미리 보기

패션 산업

정보

특별 기사

176 Ms. Duval은 왜 이메일을 보냈는가?
(A) 몇몇 의류를 묘사하기 위해
(B) 출판 세부 사항을 논의하기 위해
(C) 기사의 주제를 마무리 짓기 위해
(D) 일련의 사진을 평가하기 위해

177 이메일에서, 1문단 네 번째 줄의 표현 "drive up"은 의미상 -와 가장 가깝다.
(A) 작동하다
(B) 자극하다
(C) 촉진시키다
(D) 여행하다

178 이메일에 따르면, SameSide Cosmetics사는 무엇을 하는 데 관심이 있는가?
(A) 새로운 제품 라인을 개발하는 것
(B) 10월에 제품 시연을 여는 것
(C) 화학 성분에 반대하는 캠페인을 시작하는 것
(D) 광고 지면을 사는 것

179 Ms. Duval에 대해 추론될 수 있는 것은?
(A) 그녀가 선택한 표지 모델을 쓸 수 없었다.
(B) 장인에 대한 사설을 썼다.
(C) 의류 박람회에 참석할 예정이다.
(D) 구독료를 올리고 싶어 한다.

180 Mr. Burns에 대한 기사는 어느 페이지에 나오는가?
(A) 16쪽
(B) 35쪽
(C) 52쪽
(D) 78쪽

181-185는 다음 안내문과 행사 일정표에 관한 문제입니다.

쇼핑을 해서 변화를 만드세요!

올해, 브리스톨의 지역 사업체 지원의 날이 4월 28일 토요일에 있습니다. 이 날에는 전국적인 체인점을 방문하는 대신, 여러분의 동네에 있는 더 작은 규모의 가게들에서 쇼핑해 보세요. 그렇게 함으로써, 그러한 가게들이 버는 수익이 우리 도시에 남기 때문에 여러분은 지역 경제를 돕게 될 것입니다. 게다가, Birdy Beets 레스토랑, Tinker Time 공예품 가게, 그리고 Kara Lee's 의류 부티크를 포함해 일단의 참가 사업체들이 이날 수익의 10퍼센트를 브리스톨 사업체 협회(BBA)에 기부하는 데 동의했습니다. BBA는 지역의 자선 프로젝트를 계속해서 수행하는 데 이 수익금을 사용할 것입니다.

쇼핑 기회와 더불어, 지역 사업체 지원의 날은 특별 프로그램들을 포함할 것입니다. www.bristolsylbd.com에서 참가 사업체들의 목록과 행사 일정표를 확인하세요.

지역 사업체 지원의 날
4월 28일 브리스톨에서

지역 주민들을 위한 메시지 *오전 9시부터 오전 9시 30분*
장소: Anchor 광장
브리스톨 사업체 협회(BBA)의 회장, Emmanuel Perez가 왜 지역 사업체들이 그토록 중요한지에 대한 연설을 할 것입니다. 그는 또한 곧 있을 BBA의 몇 가지 활동들에 대해서도 이야기할 것입니다.

도보 투어 *오전 9시 40분부터 오전 10시 15분*
만나는 장소: Craft Street Antiques
Dalton가를 따라 산책하면서 그곳의 건물들의 역사에 대해 배워 보세요. 마지막 장소는 브리스톨에서 가장 오래된 건물 중 하나인 Wayfair House인데, 이곳은 처음으로 대중에게 개방될 것입니다. Wayfair House의 입장은 무료입니다.

점심 식사를 위해 쇼핑하세요 *오전 10시 30분부터 오후 1시*
장소: 시내 쇼핑 지구
서로 다른 세 개의 지역 소유 사업체에서 구매하면, 여러분은 참가 레스토랑에서의 무료 점심 쿠폰을 받을 것입니다. 오후 1시 30분까지 방문객 접수처에 영수증을 제시하세요.

잔디 위의 음악 *오후 12시부터 오후 4시*
장소: 시내 Green 공원
지역 밴드가 Green 공원의 무대에서 30분 동안 공연을 할 것입니다. 근처의 천막에서는, 아이들을 위한 여러 재미있는 공예 워크숍이 제공될 것입니다.

181 안내문은 주로 무엇에 대한 것인가?
(A) 새로 연 전시실
(B) 자원봉사자 모집 기간
(C) 소기업을 지지하는 행사
(D) 회사를 위한 세금 혜택

182 BBA에 대해 암시되는 것은?
(A) 대규모의 소매점 체인을 운영한다.
(B) 회비를 10퍼센트 올렸다.
(C) 수입품에 대한 세금에 반대한다.
(D) 지역 사회에 기여한다.

183 Mr. Perez는 어떤 정보를 연설에 포함할 것인가?
(A) 공사의 이유
(B) 단체의 계획
(C) 캠페인의 비용
(D) 재개장 날짜

184 4월 28일에 계획되어 있는 활동 중 하나가 아닌 것은?
(A) 유명 요리사의 요리 시연
(B) 역사적인 지역에서의 산책
(C) 음악가들의 야외 공연
(D) 아이들을 위한 교육 시간

185 방문객들은 어디에서 쿠폰을 사용할 수 있을 것 같은가?
(A) Birdy Beets
(B) Tinker Time
(C) Kara Lee's
(D) Wayfair House

186-190은 다음 기사, 회람, 이메일에 관한 문제입니다.

2월 12일—2월 10일의 기자회견에서, David Wilkins 시장은 새로운 4차선 다리의 건설 계획을 발표했다. 이 작업은 5월 14일에 시작해서 12월 23일에 끝날 예정이다. 이것은 특히 도심지에서 도시의 북쪽으로 가려고 하는 통근자들을 위해, 도시의 교통체증을 완화해 줄 것으로 기대된다. 하지만, 새로운 다리가 건설되는 동안에는 다수의 일시적인 도로 폐쇄로 인해 교통 상황이 아마 악화될 것이다.

Harris로와 Oak대로는 5월 14일부터 8월 1일까지 폐쇄될 것이다. 덧붙여, Center가에는 8월 5일부터 10월 10일까지 운전자들이 접근할 수 없을 것이고, Harbor로는 10월 12일부터 12월 20일까지 폐쇄될 것이다. 이 도로들을 정기적으로 이용하는 통근자들은 다른 방도에 대한 정보를 위해 교통국의 웹사이트를 방문해야 한다.

수신: Bellwood 스포츠용품점 전 직원
발신: Beth Ferrell, 관리자
제목: 대응 계획
날짜: 7월 10일

어제 직원회의에서 모두에게 알려드렸듯이, 8월 5일부터 시작되는 우리 가게 앞 도로의 폐쇄가 매장 내의 매출에 심각한 영향을 미칠 수 있습니다. 결론적으로, 저는 그 기간 동안 두 가지의 온라인 판촉 행사를 열기로 결정했습니다. 바라건대, 매장에 더 적은 손님들이 오는 것을 상쇄하도록 우리의 웹사이트를 통해 충분한 매출을 만들어낼 수 있기를 바랍니다. 매장과 온라인에서 모든 신발의 가격은 15퍼센트 인하될 것입니다. 또한, 누구든 온라인으로 주문하는 사람들은 무료 배송을 받을 것입니다. 우리 고객들에게 이러한 판촉 행사에 대해 반드시 전해주세요.

수신: customerservice@bellwood.com
발신: j.adams@ezmail.com
날짜: 8월 12일
제목: 주문 번호 029384

8월 9일에, 저는 귀하의 웹사이트에서 재킷을 구입했습니다. 안타깝게도, 제가 선택한 사이즈가 특대가 아니라 대라는 것을 방금 알아차렸습니다. 제가 재킷을 환불할 필요가 없도록 주문 상품이 배송되기 전에 이것을 변경하고 싶습니다. 제가 잘못 선택한 상품을 올바른 것으로 그저 교체해 주시는 것이 가능할까요? 만약 안 된다면, 원래 주문을 취소하고 새로 주문해야 할 것 같습니다. 제게 알려주세요.

Jeff Adams 드림

186 Wilkins 시장은 2월 10일에 무엇을 했는가?
(A) 관광업 학회에서 발표했다
(B) 방문객들에게 사무실을 둘러보도록 안내했다
(C) 사회 기반 시설 사업에 대해 말했다
(D) 교통사고에 대해 사과했다

187 기사에 따르면, 일부 통근자들은 왜 웹사이트를 방문해야 하는가?
(A) 합승할 사람을 찾기 위해
(B) 경로 정보를 확인하기 위해
(C) 정책에 대한 피드백을 주기 위해
(D) 대중교통을 평가하기 위해

188 Bellwood 스포츠용품점은 어디에 위치해 있을 것 같은가?
(A) Harris로에
(B) Oak대로에
(C) Center가에
(D) Harbor로에

189 Mr. Adams의 주문에 대해 암시되는 것은?
(A) 판촉 할인을 받을 자격이 되지 않았다.
(B) 색깔이 요청한 것과 달랐다.
(C) 더 이상 생산되지 않는다.
(D) 회사 주소로 배송될 것이다.

190 Mr. Adams는 상품이 교체될 수 없다면 무엇을 할 것인가?
(A) 고객 계정을 삭제한다
(B) 제조사의 웹사이트를 방문한다
(C) 불만 신고 양식을 작성한다
(D) 절차를 다시 시작한다

191-195는 다음 이메일, 양식, 소식지에 관한 문제입니다.

수신: Jade Liu <j.liu@zhongacademy.org>
발신: Jason Richards <jasonrich382@goodmail.net>
날짜: 11월 20일
제목: 일요일 수업

Ms. Liu께,

저는 일요일 아침에 당신의 비즈니스 중국어 수업을 듣는 데 관심이 있습니다. 저는 언어 교육 소프트웨어를 사용해 중국어를 공부해 왔으므로, 어느 정도 능숙합니다. 하지만, 등록하기 전에 저의 유창성 수준을 알 수 있는 시험을 보고 싶습니다. 이에 관한 정보를 웹사이트에서 찾을 수 없었으니 이를 위한 절차를 알려주십시오.

또한, 온라인으로 수업 시간을 확인했을 때, 저는 당신의 학원에서 인기 있는 중국 영화의 무료 상영을 한다는 것을 알았습니다. 제 친구가 11월 12일에 당신이 주최했던 것에 갔었고 그것이 교육적이었다고 이야기했습니다. 저는 다음 달의 상영에 가고 싶은데, 제가 신청을 해야 하는지 궁금합니다.

Jason Richards 드림

ZHONG 학원
12월 수업 등록

이름	Jason Richards	시험에 따른 수준	초보자
주소	51번지 Rye가 콩코드, 뉴햄프셔주 03302	선호 수업 시간	일요일 오전 10시 - 오전 11시 30분
전화 번호	555-7244	수업료	200달러
이메일	jasonrich382@goodmail.net	수업료 납부 기한	11월 30일
누군가 저희 학원을 귀하께 추천했나요?			네
만약 그렇다면, 이 사람의 이름을 제공해 주십시오.			Robin Ghose

○ 수업 시간을 변경하기 위해서는, 메인 데스크에서 요청해 주십시오.
○ 만약 저희를 다른 누군가에게 추천하시고 그 사람이 등록하면, 귀하께서는 다음 수업에서 15퍼센트 할인을 받으실 것입니다.

Zhong 학원 월별 소식지

12월 1일

중국 영화를 보는 것은 당신의 언어 실력을 향상시킬 수 있는 하나의 방법입니다. 이번 달에 두 차례의 중국 영화 행사가 근처에서 열릴 예정입니다.

Bright Lights 영화 축제는 Cloudbank 호텔에서 12월 20일에 개최될 것입니다. 비평가들의 극찬을 받은 영화 *Summer Shore*의 감독인 Xu Yue의 신작을 특별히 포함할 것입니다. Xu의 최신 작품, *Washing Away*는 상해에서 온 젊은 무용수에 대한 내용입니다. 축제 티켓은 20달러이고 www.blffest.org에 로그인해서 구입할 수 있습니다.

추가적으로, 중국 감독 Wei Chung의 *Grave Mistakes*의 무료 상영에 참석할 수 있습니다. 이는 12월 28일에 여기 Zhong 학원에서 상영될 것입니다. 학원에서의 상영은 월별로 개최되며 오로지 중급 또는 고급 수업에 등록된 학생들을 위한 것입니다. 지난달 *River Goddess* 상영 후에 그랬던 것처럼, 이번 달의 상영 후에도 중국어 토론이 있을 것입니다.

191 이메일에 따르면, Mr. Richards가 웹사이트에서 찾을 수 없었던 정보는 무엇인가?
(A) 수업 일정
(B) 서비스 요금
(C) 시설의 위치
(D) 시험 절차

192 Zhong 학원에 대해 언급되지 않은 것은?
(A) 일정 변경을 허용한다.
(B) 초보자를 위한 수업이 있다.
(C) 평일 수업만 연다.
(D) 소개에 대한 할인을 제공한다.

193 Mr. Richards의 친구는 어떤 영화를 봤을 것 같은가?
(A) *Summer Shore*
(B) *Washing Away*
(C) *Grave Mistakes*
(D) *River Goddess*

194 Ms. Xu에 대해 사실인 것은?
(A) 그녀의 첫 영화가 축제에서 상영될 것이다.
(B) Cloudbank 호텔에서 하룻밤을 지낼 것이다.
(C) 그녀의 프로젝트는 상해에 근거지를 둔 기업에서 자금을 받는다.
(D) 비평가들로부터 긍정적인 평가를 받았다.

195 Mr. Richards에 대해 추론될 수 있는 것은?
(A) 어학원에서 일했었다.
(B) 다가오는 축제의 티켓을 샀다.
(C) 12월의 무료 상영에 참석할 수 없다.
(D) 중국으로 출장을 갔다.

196-200은 다음 공고, 이메일, 기사에 관한 문제입니다.

Emerald Falls에 대한 TV 에피소드를 위한 정보원 구함

Hector Almonte 감독이 현재 Emerald Falls 마을에 대한 텔레비전 에피소드를 위해 인터뷰 대상자를 찾고 있습니다. 이 에피소드는 Janet Leslie에 의해 진행되는, 상을 받은 다큐멘터리 시리즈 *The Good Old Days*를 위해 제작되고 있습니다. 두 번째 시즌에서, 이 시리즈는 10화에서 12화로 확장될 것입니다. 그것은 비디오 인터뷰와 현지 촬영 화면을 통해 벨리즈 전역에 있는 유서 깊은 마을들을 계속해서 소개할 것입니다. 인터뷰 대상자들은 Emerald Falls에 거주할 필요는 없지만 그 마을과 강한 연관성을 가지고 있어야 합니다. 더 많은 정보를 위해서는, (501) 555-7925로 전화해 주십시오.

덧붙여, Mr. Almonte는 편지, 사진, 그리고 마을의 초기에 대한 통찰을 제공할 수 있는 다른 물건들에 접근할 기회를 얻기를 바랍니다. 만약 그러한 문화 유물들을 가지고 있으며 그것들을 빌려주실 준비가 되어 있으시다면, 그의 조수 Chloe Benbow에게 c.benbow@sunrise.bz로 연락해 주시길 진심으로 요청합니다.

수신: Chloe Benbow <c.benbow@sunrise.bz>
발신: Elaine Kershaw <elaine.k@eurekamail.bz>
제목: Emerald Falls의 옛 사진들
날짜: 7월 25일

Ms. Benbow께,

저는 Emerald Falls가 *The Good Old Days*에 나오게 될 것을 읽고 매우 들떴습니다. 저는 Pepita de Oro에 대한 지난 시즌의 마지막 회를 재미있게 보았습니다.

비록 한 번도 Emerald Falls에 살아본 적은 없지만, 저희 아버지께서 그곳에서 태어나셨으며, 저는 할아버지께서 시장이셨던 시기부터의 마을 사진과 그림 모음집을 가지고 있습니다. 저희 할아버지께서 그 지역 화가로부터 그림들을 구매하셨습니다. 그것들의 제목은 *Picnic by the Falls*, *Plaza Esperanza*, 그리고 *The Grand Carnival*입니다.

저는 기꺼이 사진들을 빌려드리고자 하지만, 그림들은 가치 때문에 저희 집에 있어야 합니다. 만약 Mr. Almonte가 그것들을 촬영하고 싶어 한다면, 이곳 Maracuyá를 방문하셔도 됩니다.

Elaine Kershaw 드림

벨리즈 시티 (12월 15일)—전국의 전통 마을에 관한 다큐멘터리 시리즈인 *The Good Old Days*의 시청률이 증가해 오고 있다. 가장 최신 에피소드는 한때 번성한 광산촌이었지만 이후 그곳의 유명한 광물 매장층이 고갈된 Emerald Falls에 초점을 맞췄다. 비록 인구는 상당히 감소했지만, 마을은 여전히 이전의 모습과 흡사하다. 이 에피소드의 한 장면에서는, Emerald Falls가 얼마나 변한 것이 거의 없는지를 밝혀주는 Jana Haynes의 그림 *Plaza Esperanza*가 보여진다.

Hector Almonte 감독은 "두 번째 시즌을 위해, 저희는 마을과 개인적인 관련이 있는 정보원들을 찾았습니다. Emerald Falls 에피소드는 이야기와 기억할 만한 물건들을 공유해 주신 모든 분들 덕분에 결과가 잘 나왔습니다."라고 언급했다.

다음 주에, 5번째 에피소드가 공개될 것이다. 감독은 그 장소가 놀랍기를 바란다고 말한다.

196 *The Good Old Days*에 대해 언급되지 않은 것은?
(A) 녹화된 인터뷰를 포함한다.
(B) 오래된 마을에 초점을 맞춘다.
(C) 고정 진행자가 출연한다.
(D) 여행사에 의해 후원된다.

197 Pepita de Oro에 대해 사실일 것 같은 것은?
(A) 한때 큰 공공 광장이 있었다.
(B) 올해 기념일을 축하하고 있다.
(C) 외국인 관광객들에게 인기 있는 목적지이다.
(D) 쇼의 10번째 에피소드에서 다뤄졌다.

198 Ms. Kershaw의 할아버지는 누구로부터 그림을 샀는가?
(A) Hector Almonte
(B) Janet Leslie
(C) Chloe Benbow
(D) Jana Haynes

199 Mr. Almonte에 대해 암시되는 것은?
(A) 여행에 관한 책을 썼다.
(B) Maracuyá에서 미술품을 살펴보았다.
(C) 10월에 기자 회견을 열었다.
(D) 문화 유물 모음을 빌려줬다.

200 Emerald Falls는 주로 무엇으로 유명했는가?
(A) 교육 수준
(B) 자연 풍경
(C) 광물 자원
(D) 자선 경매

TEST 09 해석

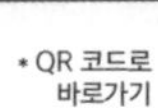

* 무료 해설은 해커스토익(Hackers.co.kr)에서 다운로드 받을 수 있습니다.

• QR 코드로 바로가기

PART 5

101 이전 세입자들은 오늘 오후 늦게 건물을 비울 것이다.

102 팀원들은 첫 프로젝트 회의를 시작할 때 서로에게 자기소개를 했다.

103 시 의회의 예산 흑자 덕분에, 올해 Davondale 다리가 교체되는 것은 확실히 가능하다.

104 티켓 소지자들은 환불을 받았지만 콘서트가 왜 취소되었는지는 듣지 못했다.

105 Gaspard Carlock의 인형극을 홍보하기 위해, 도시 곳곳에 광고가 게시될 것이다.

106 두 개의 프로그램에 비슷한 요소가 많아서, 시청자들은 그것들을 비교했다.

107 참가자들은 Offenburg 시민 문화회관에 의해 제공되는 컴퓨터 개별 지도 시간이 상당히 도움이 된다고 생각했다.

108 프린터의 모델 번호를 찾기 위해, Mr. Jansen은 그것을 뒤집어서 바닥을 확인했다.

109 Earth Preserve사는 다음 주에 개최되는 모금 행사에 모두가 기부하기를 바란다.

110 따뜻한 날씨로 인해 지역 내 여러 스키 별장들이 11월 중순까지 개장을 연기했다.

111 몇몇 직원들은 프로젝트의 마지막 단계 동안 초과 근무를 해야 할 수도 있다.

112 *Words in Russian*에 있는 어휘는 그 책의 첫 번째 섹션 이후로 점차 어려워진다.

113 Ms. Vigneux가 지금까지 하이킹해본 곳 중 가장 거친 길은 Flint Valley 국립 공원에 있다.

114 독점 계약의 결과로, 음료 Nitro-Sip은 오직 Duggarti Foods에서만 살 수 있다.

115 회계부 직원들은 회계 감사 동안 더 오래 일해야 했는데, 이는 거의 한 달이 걸렸다.

116 초기의 연구 결과는 그 약이 효과적이라고 시사했지만, 추가 연구는 다르게 입증했다.

117 회의에 미리 등록하면, Mr. Alton은 입장료에 대해 15퍼센트 할인을 받을 것이다.

118 Mr. Issac은 가게를 운영하고 그의 책무는 직원들의 문제를 다루는 것을 포함한다.

119 은퇴 전에, 이사 John Bailey는 그의 동료인 Vanessa Gail을 후임자로 지명했다.

120 회사의 새로운 산업 안전 규정은 내일 회의의 중요한 안건이다.

121 전국 의료 조합장은 개인 병원 원장의 역할도 한다.

122 학생들은 현재 50년이 넘은 중앙 도서관의 수리에 강력하게 찬성 의견을 말하고 있다.

123 신입사원들은 급여 대상자 명단 시스템에 등록되기 전에, 재무부에 몇 가지 금융 정보를 제공해야 한다.

124 양식을 작성하는 대로, 안내 데스크로 가져오셔서 비서에게 맡기십시오.

125 시제품의 성공으로 인해, 현재 그 발명가는 기술 혁신에 대해 증가하는 명성을 가지고 있다.

126 Roscast Communications사의 직원들은 재택근무를 할 수도 있지만, 확실한 인터넷 연결을 보유하는 것이 필수적이다.

127 LRB 제약회사와 Hough 연구소의 합병은 몇몇 일자리가 배제되도록 할 수도 있다.

128 Amberview Beach 리조트는 유명한 여름철 여행 목적지이지만, 그곳은 1년 내내 영업한다.

129 Ms. Ross는 5월에 가장 적은 수의 신규 고객을 얻어서, 다른 모든 판매원들보다 뒤쳐졌다.

130 중요한 프로젝트를 시간 제한 내에 완료하는 것은 철저한 일정 관리를 필요로 한다.

PART 6

131-134는 다음 이메일에 관한 문제입니다.

수신: Paige Lagarde <paigelagarde@peoplemail.com>
발신: Brad Jeong <jeongbrad@cucinaaid.com>
날짜: 3월 2일
제목: 회신: CucinaAid사 믹서기 문제

Ms. Lagarde께,

귀하께서는 CucinaAid 믹서기의 거품기 부속품을 고정시킬 때 그것이 단단히 고정되지 않는다고 알려주시기 위해 저희에게 이메일을 보내주셨습니다. 충분히 걱정하실 만합니다. **131** 실제로, 헐거운 부속품은 안전상의 위험을 제기하며, 귀하께서 저희가 이 문제에 주목하게 해주셔서 다행입니다.

132 저희는 최근 생산이 진행되는 중에 결함이 야기된 것으로 생각하는데, 이때 실수로 잘못된 부품을 쓴 것 같습니다. **133** 굉장히 죄송하게 생각하며 귀하의 기계를 수리해드리는 것을 제안하고자 합니다. 저희 서비스 센터 중 아무 데나 들르시면, 기술자 중 한 명이 흔쾌히 그것을 무상으로 고쳐드릴 것입니다. 이 불편을 보상해드리기 위해, 다음 번의 CucinaAid사 구입품에 25달러 할인을 받을 수 있는 다음 쿠폰 번호도 받아주시기 바랍니다: UW3-G6BQ1. **134** 온라인 쇼핑 시 계산 단계에서 이것을 저희 웹사이트에 입력하시기만 하면 됩니다.

Brad Jeong 드림
CucinaAid사, 고객 서비스 직원

135-138은 다음 기사에 관한 문제입니다.

135 지역 내 쇼핑객들이 알고 있다시피, Diamond Plaza 쇼핑몰은 현재 큰 변화를 겪고 있다. 그곳은 이제 한 달째 문을 닫았는데, 운영진은 개조 작업이 원만하게 진행되고 있으며 House Lab이 7천 제곱피트를 임차하기로 결정했다고 밝혔다. 최고의 가전제품 소매업체인 House Lab은 틀림없이 많은 사람들을 쇼핑몰로 끌어들일 것이다. **136** 이익 창출 가능성을 고려했을 때, 그것은 가장 좋은 위치를 차지할 것으로 예상된다. 이미 그것이 정문 왼쪽의 공간을 차지할 것이라는 추측이 있어 왔다. **137** 이것은 분명 중요한 소식이지만, 아직 개조와 관련하여 발표된 다른 정보는 거의 없다. **138** 예를 들면, 푸드 코트가 꼭 필요로 했던 확장을 마침내 진행할 것인지는 아직 알려지지 않았다. 더 많은 세부 사항들은 다음 달 기자회견에서 밝혀질 것으로 예상된다.

139-142는 다음 회람에 관한 문제입니다.

수신: 전 직원
발신: Robert Valdez, 경영부

주제: 연말
날짜: 12월 1일

올해가 끝나감에 따라, Voyager Communications사의 경영진은 모두의 노고와 인내에 감사드리고 싶습니다. 여러분의 노력 덕분에, 매출이 예상보다 높았고, 이는 저희가 여러분께 더 많은 상여금으로 보상할 수 있게 해주었습니다. 저희는 표준 연간 상여금을 여러분의 연봉의 2퍼센트로 늘릴 것입니다. **139** 이전에, 이것은 1퍼센트였습니다. **140** 이것은 여러분의 올해 마지막 급여에 포함될 것입니다.

또한, 지난주에 여러분 다수가 받은 충분한 자격이 있는 임금 인상분이 상여금 액수에 고려될 것인지 궁금해하고 계시다면, 대답은 그렇습니다. **141** 상여금은 여러분의 새롭고, 더 높은 급여를 사용하여 계산될 것입니다.

142 질문이 있다면 제게 알리기 위해 사무실로 찾아오셔서 저를 만나십시오.

143-146은 다음 광고에 관한 문제입니다.

143 Harlington 즉흥극단(HIP)이 7월 9일에 Ferris Greene 공연 예술 센터에 올 것입니다. 웃고 싶으시다면, Liza Smythe, Dennis Armstrong, Jackson Parcell, 그리고 Charlie Cousins가 이번주 토요일에 무대에 오를 때 그들을 놓치지 마세요. **144** 언제나처럼, HIP는 관객의 현장 의견을 영감으로 삼아 공연합니다. **145** 이는 그들의 공연 하나하나가 유일무이하다는 것을 의미합니다. 그리고 그들은 훌륭한 목적으로 인해 당신을 미소 짓게 할 것입니다. **146** 티켓 판매로부터 얻은 수익금은 Harlington 시립 고등학교의 방과 후 예술 관련 활동에 도움을 주는 데 쓰일 것입니다. 자리를 예약하고 더 많은 정보를 얻기 위해 www.ferrisgreenepac.com/shows를 방문하세요.

PART 7

147-148은 다음 문서에 관한 문제입니다.

Central Valley Financial Partners사
환급 신청서

번호: 382625

구입품:

상품 설명	금액
피자 8판 (각 15달러)	120달러
풍선 및 장식품	22달러
장식 케이크 1판	38달러
은퇴 축하 카드 1장	5달러
총액	185달러

참고: 12월 9일에 있었던 Richard Dugas를 위한 축하 행사

제출: Elisa Cooper　　승인: Patrick Rhodes
서명: *Elisa Cooper*　　서명: *Patrick Rhodes*
날짜: 12월 10일　　날짜: 12월 10일

이 신청서와 함께 영수증을 제출해 주십시오.

147 Central Valley Financial Partners사에서 어떤 종류의 행사가 열렸을 것 같은가?
(A) 은퇴 축하 행사
(B) 제품 출시 파티
(C) 개회식
(D) 환영회

148 Mr. Rhodes는 12월 10일에 무엇을 했을 것 같은가?
(A) 팀원들에게 파티용품을 구매하라고 지시했다
(B) 직원에게 비용의 상환을 승인했다
(C) 출장 음식 공급 업체에 예약 보증금을 보냈다
(D) 연회장에서의 특별 행사에 참석했다

149-150은 다음 취업 공고에 관한 문제입니다.

Pearson & Lennox사

Dorney—전임제 및 시간제 판매 컨설턴트

고급 브랜드로서, 저희는 모든 고객에게 훌륭한 고객 서비스를 제공한다는 평판에 자부심을 가지고 있습니다. 현재, 저희는 Dorney의 Village로에 있는 저희 매장에서 고객 서비스에 대한 열정을 가지고 근무할 2명의 전임제 및 2명의 시간제 판매 컨설턴트를 구하고 있습니다.

당신은 열정, 외향적인 성격, 그리고 독특한 스타일 감각뿐만 아니라 고급 의류 분야에서의 입증된 판매 경험을 가지고 있어야 합니다. 남성복 업계에서의 경험은 이점이 됩니다.

저희 팀에 합류하는 데 관심이 있으시다면, 반일 근무를 하고 싶은지 아니면 전일 근무를 하고 싶은지를 명시하여, 당신의 이력서를 recruitment@pearsonlennox.com으로 보내주십시오.

149 Pearson & Lennox사는 어떤 종류의 산업에 종사하는 것 같은가?
(A) 여행 숙박 시설
(B) 경영 컨설팅
(C) 소비자 조사
(D) 패션 소매

150 일자리 지원자들에 대해 언급된 것은?
(A) 인터뷰에 직접 참석해야 할 것이다.
(B) 남성 의류에 대한 전문 지식을 가지고 있어야 한다.
(C) 그들이 선호하는 근무시간의 양을 명시해야 한다.
(D) 모두 같은 급여를 받을 자격이 있을 것이다.

151-152는 다음 메시지 대화문에 관한 문제입니다.

Melvin Stuckey　오후 4시 47분
중국 투자자들과의 회의와 관련한 제 메시지를 받았나요? Mr. Zhang이 그것의 일정을 수요일로 변경해달라고 요청했어요.

Rhonda Perry　오후 4시 48분
방금 읽었어요. 제게는 그 편이 더 좋아요. 저는 화요일에 기술팀을 만날 수 있을 거예요.

Melvin Stuckey　오후 4시 48분
알겠어요. Mr. Zhang과 확정할게요.

Rhonda Perry　오후 4시 50분
한 가지 더요. Mr. Lucas가 연락했나요? 그에게 월요일 오전까지 투자자 회의를 위한 유인물을 제출해달라고 요청했거든요.

Melvin Stuckey　오후 4시 51분
그는 그것들이 늦춰질 거라고 말하기 위해 연락했었어요. 그는 수치에서 오류를 발견했고 몇 페이지를 다시 인쇄해야 해요. 그것들은 화요일 오후에 올 거예요.

Rhonda Perry　오후 4시 51분
그게 문제가 되진 않을 거예요. 고마워요, Melvin. 월요일에 봐요.

151 오후 4시 48분에, Ms. Perry가 "That works out better for me"라고 썼을 때 그녀가 의도한 것 같은 것은?
(A) 회의 결과에 만족한다.
(B) 주 초에 고객들을 만날 생각이다.
(C) 다른 일을 처리할 시간이 있다.
(D) 이메일로 연락받는 것을 선호한다.

152 Mr. Lucas는 유인물을 준비하는 데 왜 더 많은 시간이 필요한가?
(A) 프린터가 작동하지 않는다.
(B) 직원이 휴가 중이다.

(C) 몇 페이지가 잘못 배치되었다.
(D) 몇몇 정보가 수정되어야 한다.

153-154는 다음 공고에 관한 문제입니다.

Green City 농산물 직판장
가입 지침

Green City 농산물 직판장은 최고 수준의 전통적인 West Hollywood 단체라는 것에 자부심을 느낍니다. 점포를 임차하고자 하는 모든 신규 농장들은 다음을 이행해야 합니다:

- 국영 유기농 인증 서비스(OCS)로부터 유기농 라벨을 받아야 합니다
- Green City 농산물 직판장 경영진으로부터 수질 검사를 받아야 합니다
- 전 시즌에 대한 판매자 가입비를 납부해야 합니다

구체적인 대여 옵션에 대해 문의하시려면, 직판장 책임자인 Cathy Keller에게 c.keller@greencityfarmersmarket.org로 이메일을 보내주십시오.

153 공고는 왜 쓰였는가?
(A) 추가 직판장 지점을 발표하기 위해
(B) 고객들에게 가격 인상에 대해 알리기 위해
(C) 참가자 요건을 명시하기 위해
(D) 점포 변경에 대한 세부 사항을 제공하기 위해

154 농장은 직판장에서 농산물을 팔기 위해 무엇을 해야 하는가?
(A) 정부가 발급한 인증서를 보유한다
(B) 온라인 뱅킹으로 가입비를 지불한다
(C) 품목에 대한 가격표를 제출한다
(D) 직판장 경영진에게 샘플을 보낸다

155-157은 다음 이메일에 관한 문제입니다.

수신: Jacob Lee <jc.lee@penmail.com>
발신: Amy Narvasa <a.narvasa@naturewatch.org>
제목: 저희는 귀하의 회원권을 소중하게 생각합니다
날짜: 11월 18일

Mr. Lee께,

귀하의 지원은 저희의 일에 매우 중요합니다. 귀하 및 귀하와 같은 다른 분들 덕분에, 저희는 8개의 서로 다른 나라에서 500제곱킬로미터가 넘게 분포한 중요 천연 자원들을 보호하고 복구할 수 있었습니다. 또 다른 한 해의 끝에 다가감에 따라, 저희는 귀하께서 한 번 더 다시 참여하시리라고 기대할 수 있기를 바랍니다.

안전한 온라인 갱신 양식을 작성하기 위해 저희 웹사이트를 방문해주십시오. 갱신과 함께, 귀하께서는 수상 경력이 있는 저희의 월간 잡지 *Inside Nature* 한 부를 수령하실 것인데, 이것은 귀하께서 가능할 수 있게 도와주셨던 일과 관련된 사진 및 이야기들로 채워져 있습니다. 회원으로서, 귀하께서는 또한 저희 프로젝트의 진행 상황을 추적하실 수 있으며 저희의 모바일 애플리케이션을 이용하여 다양한 방법으로 관여하실 수 있습니다.

귀하께서는 귀하의 기부금이 잘 활용되고 있다고 확신하셔도 됩니다. Natural Watch는 Conscious Business, Smart Giving Alliance, 그리고 American Philanthropic Society와 같은 단체들에 의해 시행되는 자선단체 평가에서 높은 평가를 받습니다.

Amy Narvasa 드림
회원 관리부

155 이메일의 주 목적은 무엇인가?
(A) 복구에 대한 정보를 제공하기 위해
(B) 독점 행사를 홍보하기 위해
(C) 계약 조건을 검토하기 위해
(D) 지속적인 지원을 요청하기 위해

156 Mr. Lee는 갱신된 회원권으로 무엇을 받을 수 있는가?
(A) 사진 촬영 기법 서적
(B) 월간 간행물
(C) 야생 구역 입장권
(D) 디지털 기기

157 Nature Watch에 대해 언급된 것은?
(A) 1주년을 기념하고 있다.
(B) 몇몇 새로운 사무실을 열고 있다.
(C) 여러 나라에 제휴업체를 가지고 있다.
(D) 다른 단체들에 의해 평가된다.

158-160은 다음 회람에 관한 문제입니다.

Sachs Export 가구사
회람

수신: 전 부서장
발신: Hilda Marley, IT부장
제목: CRM 소프트웨어
날짜: 3월 20일

아시다시피, 저는 전산화되지 않은 우리의 현재 시스템을 대체할 고객관계관리(CRM) 소프트웨어를 물색하고 있습니다. CRM 소프트웨어에 대한 필요성은 우리의 고객 명단이 확대됨에 따라 점점 더 명백해지고 있습니다. 그것은 우리가 고객 정보를 더 잘 관리하도록 해 줄 것이며, 무엇보다도, 이는 향상된 고객 서비스, 간소화된 주문 처리, 그리고 개선된 제품 개발로 이어질 것입니다. — [1] —.

위 사항과 관련하여, 여러분 모두 자신의 부서에서 제품 시험에 참여할 두 명의 부서원을 뽑아주시기 바랍니다. 저는 선택권을 3개의 공급업체로 좁혔습니다. — [2] —. 각 공급업체의 제품은 30일의 기간 동안 테스트될 것입니다. 이 기간이 끝날 때, 시험 참가자들은 보고서로 의견을 제공할 것입니다.

적합한 소프트웨어를 선정하면, 그것의 사용을 시행하는 데에도 여러분의 도움이 필요할 것입니다. — [3] —. 우리는 모든 직원이 CRM 소프트웨어의 장점 및 그것이 얼마나 사용하기 쉬운지를 확실히 인지하기를 바랍니다.

여러분의 추천을 내일까지 이메일로 보내주세요. — [4] —. 저희는 금요일에 만날 것이며 바라건대 4월 초에는 테스트를 시작할 것입니다.

158 Sachs Export 가구사에 대해 언급된 것은?
(A) 현재 구식 회계 소프트웨어를 사용한다.
(B) 많은 고객 불만 사항을 받는다.
(C) 새로운 제품 분야로 확대하고 있다.
(D) 고객층이 증가했다.

159 각 부서장은 무엇을 해달라고 요청받는가?
(A) 공급업체 명단을 업데이트한다
(B) 직원들에게 교육을 제공한다
(C) 테스트 참가자들을 선정한다
(D) 제품을 시험해 본다

160 [1], [2], [3], [4]로 표시된 위치 중, 다음 문장이 들어갈 곳으로 가장 적절한 것은?
"일부 직원들은 새로운 기술을 배우기를 주저합니다."
(A) [1]
(B) [2]
(C) [3]
(D) [4]

161-164는 다음 온라인 채팅 대화문에 관한 문제입니다.

Oskar Jensen 오전 9시 18분
안녕하세요, 팀원들. 취업 박람회와 관련해서 막바지 우려 사항이 있는지 확인하려고 해요.

Emma Blom 오전 9시 21분
제 담당에서는 없어요, Oskar. 배치는 마무리되었고 모든 기업 참가자들에게 승인을 받았어요. 다양한 방법을 검토하기 위해 이틀 후에 지원자들과 마지막 회의를 열 거예요.

Lilly Mattson 오전 9시 24분
저도 마찬가지예요. 사람들이 우리 웹사이트를 통해 계속해서 등록하고 있고, 우리의 모바일 애플리케이션을 다운로드하고 있어요. 우리는 소셜 미디어에서의 다양한 활동도 살피고 있어요.

Emma Blom 오전 9시 25분
음, 사실 저는 한 가지 우려 사항이 있어요. 중국어 통역사에 대한 제 요청과 관련해서 소식이 좀 있나요?

Oskar Jensen 오전 9시 27분
네, Emma. 제가 당신의 요청서를 제출했어요. 아직 Axel에게서 연락을 기다리는 중이에요. 그가 추가 비용을 승인해줘야 해요.

Lilly Mattson 오전 9시 29분
저는 방금 그가 걸어 들어오는 것을 봤어요. 그가 이 논의에 참여하게 할게요.

Axel Lofgren 오전 9시 35분
안녕하세요, 여러분. 요청이 승인된 것을 알려드리게 되어 기쁘네요.

Oskar Jensen 오전 9시 36분
고마워요, Axel. Emma, 어서 Exalan 통역 대행사와 협의해주세요.

Emma Blom 오전 9시 39분
벌써 하고 있는 중이에요. 고마워요.

161 기업 참가자들은 무엇을 했을 것 같은가?
(A) 행사에 대한 배치를 점검했다
(B) 지원자들을 박람회에 보냈다
(C) Mr. Jensen과 회의했다
(D) 통역사들을 준비했다

162 오전 9시 24분에, Ms. Mattson이 "Same here"라고 썼을 때 그녀가 의도한 것 같은 것은?
(A) 회의를 준비하기로 결정했다.
(B) 준비가 순조롭게 진행되고 있다.
(C) 중요한 메시지가 전송되지 않았다.
(D) 자원봉사자를 모집하느라 애쓰고 있다.

163 취업 박람회에 대해 암시되는 것은?
(A) 언어 서비스가 필요할 것이다.
(B) 보통 대학 캠퍼스에서 개최된다.
(C) Exalan 통역 대행사에 의해서 일부 자금을 제공 받고 있다.
(D) 주말 내내 계속될 것이다.

164 Mr. Lofgren은 무엇을 담당하는 것 같은가?
(A) 모바일 애플리케이션을 업데이트하는 것
(B) 비용을 검토하는 것
(C) 공급업체에 연락하는 것
(D) 행사를 홍보하는 것

165-167은 다음 편지에 관한 문제입니다.

콜럼버스시

1월 23일
최고경영자 Julia Peron
Mindmatter사
1135번지 Enos로
베이커스필드, 캘리포니아주 93314

Ms. Peron께,

저는 Mindmatter사의 두 번째 회사 본사의 부지가 되기 위한 콜럼버스시의 입찰을 지지하여 편지를 씁니다. 저는 저희 도시가 이상적인 장소가 될 것이라고 굳게 믿습니다.

우선, 콜럼버스시는 기업 친화적이며 통신, 의료 서비스, 그리고 소프트웨어 개발과 같은 다양한 산업의 기업들을 육성한 전력이 있습니다. 선두적인 온라인 소매업체로서, Mindmatter사는 틀림없이 이곳에 있는 다양한 형태의 사회 기반 시설들의 장점을 인식하고 있을 것입니다. 예를 들어, 항공, 도로, 그리고 철도 연결은 인근 지역뿐만 아니라 전 세계의 도시에도 편리한 접근을 제공합니다. 게다가, 콜럼버스시는 귀사의 직원들이 일과 삶의 건강한 균형을 누릴 수 있도록 도와줄 풍부한 문화적 명소, 오락 시설, 그리고 야외 공간을 제공합니다. 그리고 직원들에 관해 말하자면, 이곳의 사람들은 고등 교육을 받았으며, 세계적인 수준의 대학들은 활용할 수 있는 미래의 인재에 대한 깊은 인력 풀을 약속합니다. 무엇보다도, 콜럼버스시는 다른 도시들에서는 일반적인 높은 부동산 가격 없이, 위 모든 것을 제공합니다.

저는 귀사가 콜럼버스시에 본사를 설립하는 것의 이점을 인지할 것이라고 확신하며, 구체적인 부지를 논의하기 위해 회의를 마련하게 된다면 기쁠 것입니다. 귀사의 고려에 감사드립니다.

Tom Vickers
Tom Vickers 드림
콜럼버스 시장

165 Mr. Vickers는 왜 Ms. Peron에게 편지를 썼는가?
(A) 선호하는 것을 명시하기 위해
(B) 선택을 장려하기 위해
(C) 새로운 개발에 대해 공유하기 위해
(D) 입찰을 평가하기 위해

166 Mindmatter사에 대해 언급된 것은?
(A) 전 세계에 지사를 가지고 있다.
(B) 콜럼버스시에 기반을 둔 회사를 매입하고 있다.
(C) 인터넷으로 물품을 판매한다.
(D) 특허권을 등록하려고 시도하고 있다.

167 Mindmatter사가 콜럼버스시에서 누릴 수 있는 혜택이 아닌 것은?
(A) 교통수단 연결
(B) 교육받은 인력
(C) 휴양 기회
(D) 법인세 면제

168-171은 다음 공고에 관한 문제입니다.

공고

Springdale시 의회의 승인에 따라, 만 제곱미터의 시민 문화회관의 건설이 곧 진행될 것입니다. —[1]—. 회관의 주요 시설은 아이들의 놀이터, 도서관, 그리고 노인정이 될 것입니다. 그것은 음식을 제공하는 주방이 딸려 있는 행사 공간도 포함할 것입니다. 추후 계획에는 실내 운동을 위한 대형 체육관을 추가하는 것이 포함됩니다.

기공식은 3월 20일에 Thompson가와 Huntsville가의 모퉁이에서 열릴 예정입니다. —[2]—. 회관은 내년 가을에, 그리고 체육관은 그로부터 1년 후에 문을 열 것입니다. 회관이 내년에 문을 열고 나면, 시간제 이용료가 있을 행사 공간을 제외한 모든 시설에 대해, 일반인 무료 이용 권한이 주어질 것입니다. 하지만, 지역 거주 증명서를 제시하는 누구에게든 이에 대한 할인이 제공될 것입니다. —[3]—.

이 사업에 대한 더 많은 정보는 www.springdale.gov/communitycenter에서 찾을 수 있습니다. —[4]—. 주민들은 회관의 명칭에 대한 의견을 제출하기 위해 이 사이트를 방문하도록 권장됩니다. 당선된 명칭은 회관의 개막식 이전에 발표될 것입니다.

168 내년까지 완료될 것으로 예상되는 것이 아닌 것은?
(A) 놀이터
(B) 체육관
(C) 행사 공간
(D) 노인정

169 새로운 시민 문화회관 내의 행사 공간에 대해 언급된 것은?
(A) 첨단 장비를 포함할 것이다.
(B) 시설 내에서 가장 넓은 장소일 것이다.
(C) 3월 20일에 대중에게 공개될 것이다.
(D) 주민들에게 할인하여 대여될 것이다.

170 공고에 따르면, Springdale시의 주민들은 무엇을 하라고 권고되는가?
(A) 회원 카드를 신청한다
(B) 개인 기부를 한다
(C) 건축물의 명칭을 제안한다
(D) 개장 행사의 자리를 예약한다

171 [1], [2], [3], [4]로 표시된 위치 중, 다음 문장이 들어갈 곳으로 가장 적절한 것은?
"그것은 지역 시민들의 요구를 충족하는 시설을 포함할 것입니다."
(A) [1]
(B) [2]
(C) [3]
(D) [4]

172-175는 다음 기사에 관한 문제입니다.

Mazzi 우유가 다시 인기를 얻다

나이로비, 10월 4일—Mazzi가 가게 진열대에 처음 등장한지 수십 년 만에 다시 각광을 받고 있다. 이 제품을 만드는 기업인 Kamba 식품사가 어제 발표한 결과에 따르면, 이 달콤한 우유의 매출은 9월에 32퍼센트 증가했다.

"기존에, 저희는 Mazzi에 크게 투자하지 않았습니다."라고 Kamba 식품사의 최고경영자인 Roger Biwott가 말했다. "이 제품은 처음에는 성공적이었지만, 시간이 지나면서 매출이 서서히 증가하지 않았습니다."

Food Web Africa사의 시장 분석가인 Sophie Oduya에 따르면, Kamba 식품사는 지역적인 추세에 대응했다. "점점 더 많은 사람들이 슈퍼마켓이나 편의점에서 살 수 있는 빠르고 간편한 것을 원합니다. 따라서 Mazzi가 현저한 매출을 경험한 것은 놀라운 일이 아닙니다." 아직도 구입할 수 있는 그것의 원래 형태에서는, 소비자가 Mazzi 가루에 물을 첨가해야 한다. 최근에 유행하는 Mazzi는 병에 담아져 나와서, 바로 마실 수 있다.

Mr. Biwott는 Kamba 식품사의 올해 총 매출을 4.1퍼센트 올리는 데 도움을 준 것이 새로 나온 Mazzi의 공이라고 말한다. 이것은 작년의 수치보다는 약간 낮지만, 주식 분석가들은 연말 실적은 훨씬 더 높을 것으로 보고 있다. 지금까지, 그 결과가 발표된 이후 주가는 3.6퍼센트 상승했다.

172 기사는 주로 무엇에 대한 것인가?
(A) 무료 샘플의 배포
(B) 기업의 수익성 회복
(C) 지역 제조업체들을 위한 행사
(D) 제품의 회복된 인기

173 Ms. Oduya는 Mazzi의 현저한 매출을 무엇의 결과로 보는가?
(A) 제품 라인의 확대
(B) 성공적인 제품 출시
(C) 편리한 물품에 대한 수요
(D) 증가하는 슈퍼마켓의 수

174 Kamba 식품사에 대해 추론될 수 있는 것은?
(A) 새로운 포장 재료의 사용을 선도했다.
(B) 수십 년 동안 제품을 판매했다.
(C) 다른 제조업체와 합병했다.
(D) 올해 매출 기록을 세웠다.

175 3문단 세 번째 줄의 단어 "enjoyed"는 의미상 -와 가장 가깝다.
(A) 구했다
(B) 경험했다
(C) 좋아했다
(D) 가치를 인정했다

176-180은 다음 웹페이지와 양식에 관한 문제입니다.

www.chersterville.gov/commercialbicycling
Chesterville시
상업용 자전거 이용

자전거 사용자들은 음식, 우편, 그리고 다른 물품들을 도시 전역의 장소로 배달할 수 있습니다. 교통 체증을 줄이는 것을 돕고 통행 문제를 막기 위해, 자전거 사용자들 및 그들을 고용하는 업체들에 대해 다음의 법률이 시행되었습니다.

업체에 대한 요구 사항
- 업체들은 자전거 사용자들이 시청의 교통국에서 상업용 자전거 이용 허가증을 받았는지 확인해야 합니다. 이 카드는 3자리의 ID 번호를 포함할 것입니다.
- 자전거 사용자들에게는 업체명 및 직원의 ID 번호를 표시하는 보호용 헬멧과 빛 반사 조끼가 제공되어야 합니다.
- 업체들은 현재와 이전의 모든 자전거 사용자들의 목록을 보관하고 그것을 정기적으로 업데이트해야 합니다. 이 목록의 서식은 여기에서 다운로드할 수 있습니다.

자전거 사용자에 대한 요구 사항
- 근무 중에, 상업용 자전거 사용자들은 그들의 ID 번호가 포함된 카드를 소지해야 합니다.
- 상업용 자전거 사용자들은 Chesterville시의 자전거 안전 수업을 개인적으로 수료할 책임이 있습니다. 그것은 여기에서 무료로 수강할 수 있습니다.

벌금
이러한 요구 사항을 준수하지 않을 경우 100달러의 벌금이 부과될 것입니다. 같은 위반 사항이 반복되면 벌금은 200달러로 두 배가 될 것입니다.

상업용 자전거 사용자 목록
업체/주소: East Street 식당, 367번지 East가, Chesterville시

이름: Tony Esposito	ID 번호: 983
주소: 26번지 Laudner가, Chesterville시	자전거 안전 수업 수료: 완료
근무 시간: 월요일-금요일 오전 8시-오후 3시	참고: 요청 시 주말 근무 가능할 수 있음

이름: Gina Doncaster	ID 번호: 979
주소: 745번지 Cranston로, Chesterville시	자전거 안전 수업 수료: 완료
근무 시간: 월요일-금요일 오후 3시-오후 9시 토요일 오전 8시 - 오후 3시	참고: 마지막 급여가 8월 30일에 지급되었음

이름: Freddy Velasquez	ID 번호: 993
주소: 347 번지 Prescott대로, Chesterville시	자전거 안전 수업 수료: 미완료
근무 시간: 월요일-금요일 오후 3시-오후 9시 토요일 오전 8시-오후 3시	참고: 초과 근무 가능할 수 있음

176 웹페이지의 목적은 무엇인가?
(A) 교통수단으로서 자전거 타는 것을 장려하기 위해
(B) 자전거 관리에 대한 조언을 주기 위해
(C) 지역 자전거 전용 도로의 이용을 권장하기 위해
(D) 영업상의 배달에 대한 규정을 발표하기 위해

177 자전거 사용자들의 ID 번호에 대해 언급된 것은?
(A) 빛 반사 옷 위로 보여야 한다.

(B) 온라인 양식을 작성하여 신청될 수 있다.
(C) 1년 단위로 변경되어야 한다.
(D) 입사 지원서에 명시되어야 한다.

178 어떤 규정이든 한 번 이상 위반되면 무슨 일이 일어날 것인가?
(A) 자전거 사용자들은 교육 과정을 반복해야 할 것이다.
(B) 직원들은 직장에서 일시적으로 정직될 것이다.
(C) 벌금의 액수가 증가될 것이다.
(D) 배달 서비스 면허가 취소될 것이다.

179 East Street 식당의 자전거 사용자들에 대해 암시되는 것은?
(A) 일반적으로 식료품을 배달한다.
(B) 같은 시기에 고용되었다.
(C) 모두 Chesterville시의 주민이다.
(D) 주말에 일할 수 없다.

180 Mr. Velasquez에 대해 추론될 수 있는 것은?
(A) 다음 주에 평소보다 더 많은 시간을 일할 것이다.
(B) 벌금을 내야 할 수도 있다.
(C) 다음 달에 휴가를 낼 것이다.
(D) ID 번호를 갱신해야 한다.

181-185는 다음 광고지와 이메일에 관한 문제입니다.

ADBG의 제10회 연례 야구 경기
6월 23일
Portez 경기장, 애틀랜타, 조지아주

지난 10년 동안, 애틀랜타 상업 지구 사업체 집단(ADBG) 야구 경기는 소규모 자영업자들이 지역 사회에서 그들을 홍보하고 마케팅할 수 있는 기회를 제공하는 매력적인 방법이었습니다. ADBG는 기금 모금 경기에 대해 다음 단계의 협찬을 제공하게 되어 기쁩니다:

협찬 단계	가격	혜택
1루	250달러	- 경기장 입구에 걸리는 24x36인치 회사 포스터
2루	500달러	- 1루 단계의 혜택 - 매표소에 설치되는 5x2 피트 회사 광고판
3루	750달러	- 2루 단계의 모든 혜택 - 야구장에 걸리는 4x5 피트 회사 현수막
홈베이스	1,000달러	- 3루 단계의 모든 혜택 - 관람석 옆 10x12 피트 광고판 - 한 팀의 유니폼에 인쇄되는 회사 로고

후원자가 되는 데 관심이 있으시다면 사무장인 Tessa Reynolds에게 treynolds@adbg.org로 연락해주십시오.

수신: Rajiv Patel <rajiv.patel@nstflorists.com>
발신: Tessa Reynolds <treynolds@adbg.org>
날짜: 4월 30일
제목: 감사합니다

Mr. Patel께,

North Street 꽃집을 다가오는 야구 경기의 후원자로 등록해주셔서 감사합니다. 지난 몇 년간의 이 행사에 대한 후원이 귀하의 사업체에 유익했다는 것을 듣게 되어 기뻤습니다.

귀하께서 이메일로 보내주신 디자인을 받았으며, 현수막을 제작하는 업체에 이미 그것을 전달했습니다. 인쇄되고 나면, 그것들은 제공해 주신 주소로 배달될 것입니다. 그런데, 어제 우리가 이야기를 나누었을 때 저는 귀하께 한 가지를 질문하는 것을 깜빡했습니다. Atlanta Bears와 Charleston Raptors가 경기를 하겠다고 자원한 두 팀입니다.

어느 팀이 귀하의 로고를 착용하는지에 대해 선호가 있으십니까? 가능한 한 빨리 알려주십시오. 감사합니다!

Tessa Reynolds 드림

181 광고지의 목적은 무엇인가?
(A) 기업들에게 기금을 모금하도록 장려하기 위해
(B) 스포츠 행사의 티켓을 판매하기 위해
(C) 야구 워크숍을 홍보하기 위해
(D) 마케팅 기회를 제공하기 위해

182 어느 단계의 협찬이 매표소에서의 회사 로고 전시를 포함하지 않는가?
(A) 1루 단계 협찬
(B) 2루 단계 협찬
(C) 3루 단계 협찬
(D) 홈베이스 단계 협찬

183 North Street 꽃집에 대해 언급된 것은?
(A) 독자적인 야구팀을 만들 계획이다.
(B) 조지아주 전역에서 매장을 운영한다.
(C) 수익의 일부를 자선 단체에 기부할 것이다.
(D) 이전에 ADBG 경기를 후원한 적이 있다.

184 이메일에 따르면, Mr. Patel은 이미 무엇을 했는가?
(A) 홍보 자료를 배포했다
(B) Ms. Reynolds에게 디자인을 보냈다
(C) 현수막을 인쇄했다
(D) 게시판 광고를 제공했다

185 Mr. Patel은 ADBG에 얼마를 지불했을 것 같은가?
(A) 250달러
(B) 500달러
(C) 750달러
(D) 1,000달러

186-190은 다음 두 이메일과 회람에 관한 문제입니다.

수신: Catherine Millstone <catherinemillstone@drexco.com>
발신: Ron Pruitt <ronpruitt@drexco.com>
제목: 당신의 인턴십
날짜: 8월 13일

Catherine께,

당신이 알고 있다고 제가 확신하는 대로, Drexco사 광고부에서의 당신의 인턴십은 9월 3일에 끝날 예정입니다. 저희와 함께하는 동안, 당신은 열심히 근무했고 당신의 업무에 진지하게 임했습니다. 그것이 제가 당신에게 이곳의 정규직인 전임 보조 광고 제작자를 제안하고 싶은 이유입니다. 이 제안을 신중하게 고려해볼 시간을 좀 가지시기 바랍니다. 저는 내일 시작하는 미디어 회의에 참석하기 위해 오늘 떠날 것이지만, 금요일에 돌아올 예정입니다. 그때 제 사무실에 잠깐 들러서 당신의 결정을 알려주면 고맙겠습니다.

Ron Pruitt 드림
광고부장

수신: Ginger Rollins <gingerrollins@drexco.com>
발신: Harry Shute <harryshute@drexco.com>
제목: 공석인 광고부 자리
날짜: 8월 16일

Ms. Rollins께,

Ron Pruitt가 오늘 로스앤젤레스 회의에서 돌아왔고, 저는 그에게 공석인 보조 광고 제작자 자리에 관해 이야기했습니다. 그가 그것을 인턴 중 한 명에게 제안했지만, 그녀는 다음 달에 대학원 과정을 위해 학교로 돌아갈 것이기 때문에 거절한 것 같습니다.

Mr. Pruitt는 9월 3일에 몇 가지 평가를 실시한 후에만 그 직무를 다른 인턴들에게 제안할 수 있다고 말했습니다. Mr. Pruitt가 이 제안을 하지 않기로 결정하면, 당신은 채용 웹사이트에 공고를 게시할 수 있습니다. 우리가 추진해서 외부 지원자를 고용한다면, 그 사람은 적성 검사를 받아야 할 것입니다.

하지만, 이것은 승진한 인턴에게는 적용되지 않을 것임을 유의해주시기 바랍니다.

감사합니다,

Harry Shute 드림
인사부장

수신: Drexco사 광고부 전 직원
발신: Ron Pruitt
제목: 내일
날짜: 9월 11일

Wendy Sommers가 우리의 새로운 보조 광고 제작자가 될 것임을 발표하게 되어 기쁩니다. 그녀의 적성 검사 점수를 바탕으로, 저는 그녀가 우리 부서에 귀중한 증원 인력이 될 것이라고 믿습니다. 그녀가 내일부터 사무실에서 일하기 시작할 텐데, 그녀가 환영받는다고 느끼게 해줄 무언가를 하고 싶습니다. 퇴근 직후에 지역 내 식당에 갈 수 있을 것 같다고 생각 중이니, 선호하는 것이 있으면 오늘 오후 5시 전까지 알려주세요.

186 첫 번째 이메일은 왜 쓰였는가?
(A) 지원자와의 면접을 마련하기 위해
(B) 채용 제의를 하기 위해
(C) 직원들에게 향후 계획을 알리기 위해
(D) 인턴십 프로그램에 대한 의견을 요청하기 위해

187 Mr. Pruitt는 8월 16일에 무엇을 했는가?
(A) 회의에서 돌아왔다
(B) 평가를 실시했다
(C) 사무실 책임자에게 이메일을 보냈다
(D) 공석인 자리에 지원했다

188 Ms. Millstone에 대해 암시되는 것은?
(A) 여러 회사로부터 일자리 제의를 받았다.
(B) 3개월 동안 인턴으로 일했다.
(C) Drexco사의 사무실을 점검했다.
(D) 곧 대학교로 돌아갈 것이다.

189 보조 광고 제작자 자리에 대해 암시되는 것은?
(A) 한 달 넘게 공석이었다.
(B) 인턴에 의해 채워지지 않았다.
(C) 매월 출장을 포함할 것이다.
(D) 사무실로의 통근이 필요하지 않다.

190 Mr. Pruitt는 왜 광고부 직원들이 그에게 연락하기를 바라는가?
(A) 그들의 파티 참석을 확정하기 위해
(B) 지역 내 식당을 제안하기 위해
(C) 신입사원에 대한 교육 관련 조언을 제공하기 위해
(D) 사무실 공간을 설치하는 데 지원하기 위해

191-195는 다음 회람, 테스트 일정표, 양식에 관한 문제입니다.

Fitness Friends사
회람

수신: 테스트부
발신: Ed Burtoft
날짜: 8월 2일
제목: Z-Model에 대한 조사

우리가 현재 임시 명칭인 Z-Model이라고 지칭하고 있는 최신 건강 추적기에 대한 업무는 순조롭게 잘 진행되고 있습니다. 마케팅 책임자인 Signe Jepsen은 Trail Blazer 및 Split Second를 포함하여, 가능한 제품명의 최종 후보 명단을 공유했습니다. 마케팅부가 8월 11일까지 명칭에 대한 최종 결정을 내리지 못하면, 설문조사 응답자들에게 그들의 의견을 물어볼 것입니다. 목요일에, 여러분은 테스트를 위해 연구부로부터 Z-Model의 시제품을 받을 것입니다. 하지만, 먼저, 우리는 피실험자 명단을 완성해야 합니다. 테스트 일정표를 살펴봤을 때, 저는 그들 모두가 20대 혹은 30대라는 것을 발견했습니다. 조금 더 나이 든 사용자들로부터 응답을 받기 위해 40대나 50대인 피실험자를 최소한 한두 명 포함하고 싶습니다.

Z-Model 테스트 일정

오전 9시 30분	오전 11시 30분
피실험자: Dorothy Glen 연령 및 성별: 57세/여성 위치: Grand 공원 활동: 걷기 주안점: 심장 박동 기능 테스트	피실험자: Farid Saman 연령 및 성별: 23세/여성 위치: Caribou 호수 활동: 달리기 주안점: 거리 측정 기능 테스트
오후 2시 30분	**오후 4시 30분**
피실험자: Michael Flint 연령 및 성별: 37세/남성 위치: Parklane 지역 수영장 활동: 수영 주안점: 방수 테스트	피실험자: Pat Durban 연령 및 성별: 32세/여성 위치: Oak산 활동: 자전거 타기 주안점: 충격 저항 능력 테스트

피실험자 대상 설문조사

이름: Michael Flint

귀하께서 저희의 차기 건강 추적기 시제품을 테스트해보셨으므로, 귀하의 생각에 대해 더 알고 싶습니다.

다음의 진술에 대해 얼마나 동의하거나 동의하지 않으십니까?

1. 제품은 착용하기 편했다.
전적으로 동의한다 / 동의한다 / 동의하지도 반대하지도 않는다 / 동의하지 않는다 / 전적으로 동의하지 않는다

2. 제품은 사용하기 쉬웠다.
전적으로 동의한다 / 동의한다 / 동의하지도 반대하지도 않는다 / 동의하지 않는다 / 전적으로 동의하지 않는다

3. 제품에 대해 무엇이 마음에 드셨습니까?
측면에 있는 버튼을 사용하여, 표시되는 정보를 변경하기 쉬웠습니다. 배터리는 오래 지속되는 것 같았고, 60분짜리 운동을 시작할 때 98퍼센트였다가 운동을 마치자, 90퍼센트로 떨어졌습니다.

4. 제품에 대해 무엇이 마음에 들지 않으셨습니까?
밴드를 최대치로 조였는데도 불구하고, 여전히 손목 주변이 헐거운 것을 느꼈습니다. 왼팔을 들 때마다, 건강 추적기가 움직였고, 이것이 불편했습니다.

5. 제품이 무엇으로 불려야 한다고 생각하십니까?
Trail Blazer / Split Second / Mad Dash / Fast Track

191 회람의 주 목적은 무엇인가?
(A) 장려금을 제공하기 위해
(B) 테스트 일정을 잡기 위해
(C) 최신 정보를 알려주기 위해
(D) 의견을 요청하기 위해

192 테스트 일정표에 어느 피실험자가 추가된 것 같은가?
(A) Dorothy Glen
(B) Farid Saman
(C) Michael Flint
(D) Pat Durban

193 Oak산에서 제품의 어떤 측면이 테스트되었는가?
(A) 심장 박동 감시 장치
(B) 제품 내구성
(C) 내수성
(D) 거리 측정 기능

194 Z-Model 장치에 대해 암시되는 것은?
(A) 대부분의 피실험자들로부터 평판이 좋았다.
(B) 마케팅팀이 그것의 명칭을 선정하지 못했다.
(C) 테스트 참여자들에게 무료로 제공되었다.
(D) 연구원들이 그것의 출시 일정을 바꾸자고 제안했다.

195 Mr. Flint가 시제품에 대해 암시하는 것은?
(A) 끈이 개선되어야 한다.
(B) 배터리가 오래 지속되지 않는다.
(C) 신호가 충분히 크지 않다.
(D) 화면이 조정하기 어렵다.

196-200은 다음 기사, 이메일, 회람에 관한 문제입니다.

Verta사가 진공청소기를 회수하다

가전제품 제조업체인 Verta사는 검사를 위해 5,000대의 진공청소기를 서비스 센터로 가져와달라고 요청했다. Verta사에 따르면, 문제의 모델인 Zurupat A7에는 결함이 있는 부품이 포함되어 있다. "이 문제는 어쩌면 기기가 과열되도록 할 수도 있습니다."라고 Verta사의 제품 설계자인 Bryce Gooding이 말했다. "다행스럽게도, 아직 저희 고객들 중 아무도 어떠한 사고도 신고하지 않았습니다."

Verta사는 이 문제가 새롭게 생산된 진공청소기들에 대한 검사가 충분히 철저하게 수행되지 않았기 때문에 발생했다고 밝혔다. 회사는 이 사태를 해결하기 위해 11월 3일에 모든 공장의 생산을 중단하기로 결정했다.

수신: Kenneth Sheeran <k_sheeran@bgwgroup.com>
발신: Deanna Clark <d_clark@bgwgroup.com>
제목: 진공청소기
날짜: 10월 30일
첨부: Verta사_검사_공고

안녕하세요, Kenneth.

우리가 본사를 위해 구매한 모든 Zurupat A7 진공 청소기들을 Verta사 서비스 센터로 가져가야 한다고 명시하는 공고를 오늘 받았습니다. 부품 중 하나에 문제가 있는 것 같습니다만, 우리가 그것들을 소유했던 6개월 동안에는 아무런 문제도 보고되지 않았습니다.

첨부된 공고에는 제조업체의 연락처가 포함되어 있습니다. Westland 지역의 서비스 번호로 전화해서 진공청소기를 정확히 어디로 가져가야 하는지 알아봐주십시오. 여기 Blythville에 Verta사 서비스 센터가 있는지 확신할 수 없으므로, BGW Group사 직원들은 그것들을 다른 도시로 가져가야 할지도 모릅니다. 어떤 경우든, 제가 관련 직원들에게 필요한 정보를 제공할 수 있도록, 가능한 한 빨리 알려 주십시오.

감사합니다,
Deanna Clark, 사무 관리자 드림
BGW Group사

수신: 전 직원
발신: Ben Aduba, Westland 지역 담당자, Verta사
날짜: 10월 28일
제목: 업데이트

여러분 모두 아시다시피, 우리는 하루 동안 생산을 중단할 예정입니다. 이 기간 동안, 저는 공장 직원들에게 새로운 검사 절차를 알려줄 것입니다. 또한, 저는 사람들이 그들의 Zurupat A7 진공청소기를 검사받게 하도록 가져갈 수 있는 지점 목록을 받았습니다. 문의에 답변할 때, 고객들에게 정보를 제공하기 위해 반드시 그것을 참고하시기 바랍니다.

도시	Verta사 서비스 센터 지점
East Granyard	367번지 Van Dam가
Bellmeadow	184번지 Southhaven 로터리
Blythville	2956번지 Marina대로
Woodebourne	5631번지 Campus로

196 기사에 어떤 문제점이 언급되어 있는가?
(A) 기술 설명서에 오류가 포함되어 있었다.
(B) 생산 마감기한을 맞추기 어려웠다.
(C) 조립 라인 장비가 작동되지 않았다.
(D) 신제품들이 충분히 검사되지 않았다.

197 기사에서, 2문단 두 번째 줄의 표현 "carried out"은 의미상 -와 가장 가깝다.
(A) 운반되다
(B) 영향을 받다
(C) 수행되다
(D) 협상되다

198 11월 3일에 무엇이 일어날 것인가?
(A) Mr. Gooding이 Westland 공장의 검사를 계획할 것이다.
(B) Mr. Sheeran이 부품의 품질을 평가할 것이다.
(C) Ms. Clark가 Verta사 본사에서의 회의에 참석할 것이다.
(D) Mr. Aduba가 교육을 진행할 것이다.

199 BGW Group사에 대해 언급된 것은?
(A) 컨설턴트로부터 지문을 받고 있다.
(B) Verta사의 제품을 1년이 안 되게 소유했다.
(C) 몇몇 청소부원들을 교체해야 했다.
(D) 지역 내에서 가장 큰 도시에 있다.

200 Ms. Clark는 직원들에게 장비를 어디로 가져가라고 말할 것인가?
(A) 367번지 Van Dam가에
(B) 184번지 Southhaven 로터리에
(C) 2956번지 Marina대로에
(D) 5631번지 Campus로에

TEST 10 해석

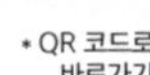

* 무료 해설은 해커스토익(Hackers.co.kr)에서 다운로드 받을 수 있습니다.

• QR 코드로 바로가기

PART 5

101 소셜 미디어 사이트의 이용자들은 그들의 로그인 비밀번호를 60일마다 재설정해야 한다.

102 손님들의 메뉴 주문을 받을 때, 음식 알레르기에 대해 물어보는 것을 기억해 주십시오.

103 Holdwell 백화점은 특히 공휴일 무렵의 멋진 쇼윈도 상품 진열로 알려져 있다.

104 최고경영자는 회사가 연말까지 이윤을 두 배로 늘릴 것이라는 낙관적인 예측을 했다.

105 더욱 창의적으로 만족스러운 직업을 추구하기를 원했으므로, Ms. Conway는 회계사로서의 일을 그만두었다.

106 Stonebridge 아파트에 공실이 하나 있으며, 그 방은 둘러보는 것이 가능하다.

107 오전 8시 기차는 보통 직장으로 통근하는 사람들로 붐빈다.

108 제품의 품질과 관련된 고객 문의는 가능한 한 빨리 답변되어야 한다.

109 CRG Communications사의 연례 회의를 위한 장소는 이번 주 후반에 결정될 것이다.

110 회의로 일정이 매우 바빴기 때문에 Mr. Richards는 보고서의 마감 기한을 가까스로 맞췄다.

111 귀중한 현대 미술품 중 많은 수집품이 최근 Beldonni 박물관에 기증되었다.

112 Mr. Godwin의 항공편 예약은 확정되었지만, 그는 아직 호텔을 정하지 않았다.

113 인터넷이 소비자 행동에 상당한 영향을 미치기 때문에 대부분의 회사들은 온라인으로 광고한다.

114 배우이자 음악가가 되기 이전에, Mr. Austin은 건설 업계에서 전기 기사로 일했다.

115 수업에 등록하기 위해, 예비 학생들은 몇 가지 서류를 작성해야 한다.

116 그 회사는 판매 수익의 일부를 자선 단체에 기부하며, 많은 소비자가 이 정책에 대해 감탄해왔다.

117 Mr. Harrelson은 근무 경력과 필수 학위 둘 다를 보유하고 있으므로 그 직책에 가장 알맞은 지원자이다.

118 낮은 소비자 가격과 공급 과잉으로 인해, 천연가스 생산은 많은 회사들에게 더 이상 이익이 되지 않는다.

119 Sewell Packaging은 원래 오하이오에 공장을 열고 싶어 했지만, 대신에 일리노이에 공장을 열기로 결정했다.

120 이 문서들은 그 식당이 검사를 통과했으며 모든 보건 및 안전 기준을 충족한다는 것을 증명한다.

121 Soundwave사에게 있어 고객의 신뢰를 되찾는 것보다 더 중요한 것은 없다.

122 환경 보호를 향한 대중의 긍정적인 견해는 많은 기업들이 생태 친화적인 관행을 채택하는 결과를 낳았다.

123 회사의 신입 사원들을 뽑는 것은 인사부의 직무이다.

124 신생 기업은 노출될 수 있도록 업계 무역 박람회에 참가하는 것을 고려해봐야 한다.

125 세계 시장에서는 특히, 사업을 경쟁 업체와 차별화시키는 방법을 생각해내는 것은 힘들 수 있다.

126 피겨 스케이팅 선수 Erica Mikahailov는 놀라울 정도로 높은 토너먼트 성적을 받아서 새로운 우승자가 될 것 같다.

127 여러 경영 전문가에 따르면, 사전에 계획하고 업무 우선순위를 매기는 것은 사람들의 생산성을 높일 수 있다.

128 영화 *Monochrome*에서 가수 Sabrina Newton을 연기한 여배우는 그녀의 훌륭한 연기로 인해 상을 받았다.

129 Ms. Danvers는 그녀의 집을 시세보다 낮게 팔기보다는, 그것을 일시적으로 임대하기로 결정했다.

130 그 모바일 앱은 사용자들이 물체들을 실제 크기의 20배까지 확대할 수 있게 한다.

PART 6

131-134는 다음 공고에 관한 문제입니다.

손님 주차에 관한 알림

최근에, 이곳 Deschamps 아파트의 지하 주차 공간이 저희 세입자들을 방문하는 손님들에 의해 부적절하게 이용되고 있다는 보고가 있었습니다. **131** 10개의 공간이 방문객을 위해 지정되어 있다는 점을 유의해 주십시오. 그것들은 명확히 표시되어 있고 엘리베이터 왼쪽에 위치하고 있습니다. 만약 그것들이 모두 사용되고 있는 경우에, 손님들은 Trenton가에서 자리를 찾을 수 있을 것입니다. **132** 주차권 판매기는 인도 위에서 찾을 수 있습니다.

133 즉시 발효되어, 세입자의 공간을 사용하는 미승인 자동차는 운영진의 재량으로 견인될 것입니다. **134** 그뿐만 아니라, 이 차주들에게는 25달러의 딱지가 발부될 것입니다. 더 많은 정보를 위해서는, 건물 서비스 관리자 Vince Romboni에게 이야기하십시오.

135-138은 다음 기사에 관한 문제입니다.

Vision Pay

135 신용카드 회사 Echo사는 새로운 모바일 애플리케이션을 개발해 왔다. Vision Pay로 이름 지어진 이것은 Echo사의 신용카드 사용자들을 위해 인터넷 쇼핑을 간단하게 해 준다. **136** 그것은 2월 1일에 출시되었다. 공개 이후에, 그것은 거의 5만 명의 사용자에 의해 빠르게 다운로드 되었다.

137 Vision Pay는 카드 세부 사항과 배송 정보를 저장하기 때문에, 온라인 구매를 완료하는 것은 예전보다 훨씬 더 빠르다. 실제로, 이제 대부분의 웹사이트에서 지불 과정에 5초 이하가 걸린다. **138** Echo사의 애플리케이션을 사용하는 것은 또한 전자 거래를 더 안전하게 하기도 한다. "저희는 온라인 쇼핑을 할 때 고객들에게 마음의 평안을 줄 최첨단의 보안 기능을 포함시켰습니다."라고 Echo사 부사장 Wallace Tan은 말한다.

만약 당신이 Echo사의 신용카드를 소유하고 있으며 Vision Pay를 이용하기 시작하고 싶다면, 핸드폰의 애플리케이션 스토어를 방문하면 된다.

139-142는 다음 초대장에 관한 문제입니다.

저희의 개장을 기념하는 것을 도와주세요!

139 포틀랜드의 최신 쇼핑 시설인 River Reed 백화점의 개장을 발표하게 되어 기쁩니다. 3층짜리 건물로 170만 제곱피트를 차지하고 있는 River Reed 백화점은 아쿠아리움과 스케이트장뿐만 아니라 130개가 넘는 상점과 레스토랑의 근거지입니다.

개관식은 3월 15일 오전 10시 30분에 열릴 것입니다. **140** 이는 대중에게 개방되어 있으며 예약이 필요하지 않습니다. **141** 참석하시려면, 간단히 Boswell가의 Harper 광장으로 가신 다음 정문으로 이동하세요. 이곳에서, 백화점의 개발에 대한 발표를 하고, 질의응답을 하고, 상품권이 나누어질 것입니다. **142** 마지막으로, 참석자들이 쇼핑 센터를 자유롭게 스스로 살펴볼 수 있는 기회를 주기 위해, 공식적으로 문이 열릴 것입니다.

143-146은 다음 편지에 관한 문제입니다.

8월 29일

Marcel Vastine
77번지 Rue du Perche
파리, 프랑스 75003

Mr. Vastine께,

143 런던 현대 미술관 내부에서 사진을 찍기 위한 귀하의 요청이 승인되었음을 알려드리고자 글을 씁니다. 이 편지에 동봉된 문서를 반드시 가져오도록 하시고 도착하시면 발권 데스크에 그것을 제시하십시오. **144** 그렇지 않으면, 귀하의 카메라를 전시장에 가지고 들어가실 수 없을 것입니다. 또한, 반드시 300파운드의 요금을 지불하실 준비가 되어 있도록 하십시오.

145 신청서에서, 귀하는 이 사진들이 *Globe Traveler*지에 나올 것이라고 명시하였습니다. 미술관의 이름이 기사에 언급되어야 한다는 것을 알고 계셔 주십시오. **146** 더욱이, 요청 양식에 서명함으로써, 귀하는 저희에게 한 부를 즉시 보내주시는 것에 동의하였습니다. 발행 이후 3영업일 이내에 그것을 받을 것으로 예상합니다.

Jane Rahman 드림
홍보 담당자
런던 현대 미술관

PART 7

147-148은 다음 요청 양식에 관한 문제입니다.

Shiner 전자제품사
서비스 요청 양식

요청 날짜: *8월 24일* **요청 시간:** *오후 1시 20분*
요청자: *Anita Ellis* **장소:** *702 사무실*

문제 설명:
저희 마케팅 조사 부서의 에어컨에서 또 물이 새고 있습니다. 보통, 이것은 긴급한 사안이 아니겠지만, 이번 달에 두 번째로 일어나고 있습니다. 특히 지난 몇 주간 날씨가 유난히 더웠으므로, 24시간 안으로 응답을 주시면 감사하겠습니다.

우선 순위:
_X_ 높음: 즉각적인 수리 필요
___ 중간: 2일에서 3일 이내로 완료
___ 낮음: 일주일 이내로 완료

147 Ms. Ellis는 누구일 것 같은가?
(A) 전기 기술자
(B) 건물 관리인
(C) 마케팅 직원
(D) 제품 디자이너

148 Shiner 전자제품사에 대해 암시되는 것은?
(A) 직원들이 지난달에 새로운 사무실로 이사했다.
(B) 지난여름에 에어컨이 정비를 받았다.
(C) 최근에 일부 사무실 비품을 교체했다.
(D) 대부분의 서비스 요청은 일주일 이내로 처리될 것이다.

149-150은 다음 광고에 관한 문제입니다.

훌륭한 침실 한 개짜리 아파트

Cerulean 타워에 마지막으로 남아 있는 침실 한 개짜리 아파트가 임대 가능합니다. 이는 28층에 위치하여, 아래로 세인트폴 시내와 그 너머 미시시피강의 넓은 전경을 가지고 있습니다. 우아한 현관은 넓은 거실과 식당 공간으로 이어집니다. 부엌에는 세련된 전자제품들이 갖추어져 있고, 침실에는 큰 창문들이 있으며, 화장실에는 현대적 스타일의 욕조가 있습니다. 아파트에는 소파, 탁자, 침대, 침실용 탁자, 그리고 충분한 수납 공간이 딸려 있습니다. Cerulean 타워는 극장과 운동 센터가 있는 현대적이며 부대 서비스가 완비된 호화로운 건물입니다. 근처 전용 차고에서 임대 주차를 이용할 수 있습니다. 둘러보는 일정을 잡으시려면 555-5784로 전화하세요.

149 Cerulean 타워에 대해 암시되는 것은?
(A) 유명한 랜드마크이다.
(B) 새로 재단장되었다.
(C) 건물이 거의 다 찼다.
(D) 환승 정류장 가까이에 있다.

150 광고된 아파트에 포함되지 않은 것은?
(A) 무료 주차 구역
(B) 주방용품
(C) 가구 몇 점
(D) 여가 시설

151-152는 다음 메시지 대화문에 관한 문제입니다.

Eric Daniels 오전 10시 12분
안녕하세요, 아파트에 있나요? 저는 들어가야 해요. 제 열쇠를 안에 두고 왔어요.

Sarah Woolf 오전 10시 13분
죄송해요, 저는 방금 근무를 시작했어요. 제 점심시간까지 기다려줄 수 있나요?

Eric Daniels 오전 10시 16분
아니요. 저는 수업을 위한 용품이 필요해요. 그것은 한 시간 후에 시작해요. 저는 문을 열기 위해 자물쇠 수리공을 부르고 싶지 않아요.

Sarah Woolf 오전 10시 17분
그것에 대해 걱정하지 말아요. 아래층에 있는 사무실에 전화만 하면 돼요. 건물 관리자가 열쇠 꾸러미를 가지고 있어요.

Eric Daniels 오전 10시 20분
맞네요. 그건 미처 생각 못했어요. 지금 전화할게요.

151 Mr. Daniels가 어떤 문제를 언급하는가?
(A) 잘못하여 자물쇠를 부러뜨렸다.
(B) 근무 교대에 늦었다.
(C) 그의 아파트에 들어갈 수 없다.
(D) 그의 관리자에게 연락할 수 없다.

152 오전 10시 17분에, Ms. Woolf가 "Don't worry about it"이라고 썼을 때 그녀가 의도한 것은?
(A) 곧 아파트에 있을 것이다.
(B) Mr. Daniels는 자물쇠 수리공을 부르지 않아도 된다.
(C) 일부 수업 자료는 중요하지 않다.
(D) Mr. Daniels의 근무를 대신할 것이다.

153-154는 다음 공고에 관한 문제입니다.

공고: 모든 회원들께

Waltrop 레저 센터 회원들께 저희의 수영장 폐쇄가 연장될 것이라는 점을 알려드리게 되어 유감입니다. 저희는 손상된 타일을 여럿 발견했고 수영장 전체의 타일을 다시 깔기로 결정했습니다.

이러한 폐쇄가 방해된다는 점을 이해하며 저희는 이 문제를 해결하기 위해 열심히 작업하고 있습니다. 현재, 예상되는 수리 완료 날짜는 7월 16일입니다. 그동안에, Eving 지역 사회에서 관대하게도 저희 회원들에게 수영장 무료 이용을 제안했습니다. 사전에 수영 강습에 요금을 지불했던 회원들은 환급을 받거나 장래의 강습을 위해 납부금을 달아 둘 수 있습니다.

수영장에 타일이 다시 깔리는 동안, 저희의 체육관, 농구장, 그리고 댄스 교습소는 계속 열려 있을 것입니다. 언제나처럼, 이 시설들은 일주일 내내 오전 7시부터 오후 9시까지 이용할 수 있습니다. 저희는 웹사이트에 수영장 수리에 대한 최신 정보를 게시할 것입니다. 감사합니다.

153 공고의 하나의 목적은 무엇인가?
(A) 요금 인상을 발표하기 위해
(B) 프로젝트 연장을 알리기 위해
(C) 새로운 창고 구역을 설명하기 위해
(D) 규칙을 어기지 말라고 경고하기 위해

154 Waltrop 레저 센터에 대해 암시되는 것은?
(A) 7월 16일까지 완전히 폐쇄되어 있을 것이다.
(B) 여러 마을의 주민들이 이용한다.
(C) 등록 양식에 내용을 추가했다.
(D) 보통 그곳의 시설에서 수업을 제공한다.

155-158은 다음 온라인 채팅 대화문에 관한 문제입니다.

Tanya Huang 오전 10시 5분
좋은 오후입니다, Mr. Benedict. 저는 Analyte 지원팀의 일원입니다. 귀하께서 어제 저희 회계 소프트웨어와 관련하여 지원 요청을 보내셨다고 알고 있어요.

Rick Benedict 오전 10시 6분
맞아요. Analyte 파일에 있는 일부 데이터를 Upcell로 전환하는 방법을 알아낼 수가 없어요.

Tanya Huang 오전 10시 7분
그렇군요. 그것은 저희 경쟁업체의 프로그램 중 하나이지만, Analyte 소프트웨어와 호환돼요. "파일"을 클릭하셔서, "내보내기"를 선택하시고, 목록에서 "Upcell"을 고르시면 됩니다.

Rick Benedict 오전 10시 7분
그게 문제예요. 그걸 시도해 보았는데 효과가 없었어요.

Tanya Huang 오전 10시 8분
오, 죄송해요. 잠시만요.

Tanya Huang 오전 10시 10분
Mr. Benedict, 혹시 한 달에 15달러 요금제를 쓰고 계신가요? 왜냐하면 Upcell을 포함해서, 다른 프로그램으로 내보내기는 오직 35달러와 그 이상의 요금제에서만 가능해서요.

Rick Benedict 오전 10시 12분
그렇군요. 접근권이 정말 필요해서, 지금 즉시 업그레이드해 줄 수 있는 어떤 방법이 있나요?

Tanya Huang 오전 10시 13분
물론이죠. 저희 경리부로 연결해 드릴 수 있는데, 신용카드를 준비하셔야 할 거예요.

Rick Benedict 오전 10시 14분
괜찮아요. 그렇게 하기로 해요.

155 Mr. Benedict는 어제 무엇을 했는가?
(A) 컴퓨터 상점에 쇼핑을 하러 갔다
(B) 일부 자금을 자문 위원에게 전달했다
(C) 몇몇 세금 문서들을 인쇄했다
(D) 고객 지원 서비스에 연락했다

156 Mr. Benedict는 무엇을 하는 데 어려움을 겪고 있는가?
(A) 잃어버린 파일을 찾아내는 것
(B) 온라인 계정에 접근하는 것
(C) 필수 업데이트를 다운로드하는 것
(D) 프로그램 간의 데이터를 공유하는 것

157 오전 10시 7분에, Mr. Benedict가 "That's the thing"이라고 썼을 때 그가 의도한 것 같은 것은?
(A) 새로운 제품이 출시되어 놀랐다.
(B) 해결책을 이미 시도해 보았다.
(C) 포인트를 상품으로 바꾸고 싶어 한다.
(D) 타협할 의향이 있다.

158 Ms. Huang은 Mr. Benedict에게 무엇을 하도록 요청하는가?
(A) 목록에서 우편 발송 옵션을 선택한다
(B) 만료된 구독을 갱신한다
(C) 지불할 준비를 한다
(D) 다른 부서에 양식을 제출한다

159-161은 다음 이메일에 관한 문제입니다.

수신: Alicia Carpenter <alicia@epost.net>
발신: Bobby McCord <b.mccord@brancafitness.com>
제목: Branca Fitness
날짜: 1월 4일

Ms. Carpenter께,

Branca Fitness의 운동 기구 포커스 그룹에 참가하는 것에 동의해 주셔서 감사합니다. 귀하의 세션은 1월 15일 오후 5시부터 오후 8시까지로 예정되어 있습니다. — [1] —. 포커스 그룹은 189번지 Bellflower로 시애틀에 있는 저희 본사에서 열릴 것입니다.

사무실에 도착하시면, 귀하께서는 기밀유지 계약에 서명하라는 요청을 받으실 것입니다. 테스트 되는 제품들은 아직 대중에게 공개되지 않았으므로, 아무에게도 그것들에 대한 정보를 공유하지 마십시오.

첫 번째 활동에서, 귀하께서는 몇몇 운동 기구를 시험해 보라는 요청을 받으실 것입니다. 반드시 편안한 옷을 착용하시거나 여벌 옷을 가져오세요. — [2] —. 그룹 토론이 이 활동 뒤에 이어질 것입니다. 토론하는 동안, 귀하는 여러 마케팅 아이디어를 제시받을 것입니다. 이러한 아이디어에 대한 귀하의 의견을 질문받는다면, 솔직하고 상세한 답변을 주시기 바랍니다. — [3] —.

공지사항에서 언급했듯이, 각 참가자에게 150달러의 대금이 은행 송금을 통해 지급될 것입니다. — [4] —. 궁금한 점이 있으시면, 언제든지 주저 말고 제게 연락 주세요.

Bobby McCord 드림

159 이메일은 주로 무엇에 대한 것인가?
(A) 운동 수업 초대
(B) 포커스 그룹에 대한 정보
(C) 무역 박람회 준비
(D) 신체 단련 계획에 대한 세부 정보

160 Ms. Carpenter는 무엇을 하도록 권장되는가?
(A) 손님을 데리고 온다
(B) 제품 후기를 게시한다
(C) 적절한 옷을 입는다
(D) 건물 앞에 주차한다

161 [1], [2], [3], [4]로 표시된 위치 중, 다음 문장이 들어갈 곳으로 가장 적절한 것은?

"이것은 2일에서 3일 정도 걸릴 것입니다."

(A) [1]
(B) [2]
(C) [3]
(D) [4]

162-164는 다음 웹페이지에 관한 문제입니다.

홈 | 소개 | 서비스 | 활동 | 연락

Maksma사는 사람들이 온라인 쇼핑을 더 쉽게 할 수 있도록 한다는 목표를 가지고, 15년 전 에스토니아에 설립되었습니다. 최초의 사무실을 열었을 때, 그곳에는 단 46명의 직원들만이 있었습니다. 그 이후로, Maksma사는 유럽의 가장 큰 결제 대행 사업자 중 하나가 되었고, 22개국에서 6천만 명이 넘는 소비자와 7만 명의 소매 상인들에게 온라인 구매를 용이하게 했습니다. Maksma사는 지불을 당장, 나중에, 또는 지정된 기간 동안 일부 금액씩 할 수 있는 선택권을 고객에게 줌으로써 스스로를 차별화합니다. 고객이 어떤 선택권을 고르든 간에, 안전하고 편리한 경험이 보장됩니다. 소매 상인들 또한 더 넓은 범위의 지불 선택권을 제공할 수 있음으로써 이익을 얻습니다.

Maksma사는 탈린에 본사를 두고 있으며, 런던과 뉴욕시에 지사가 있습니다. 1,500명이 넘는 직원들은 국제 경영진에 의해 지휘됩니다. 그것은 25억 달러 이상의 가치가 있다고 평가되며 대략 연간 100억 달러의 온라인 판매를 다룹니다.

162 웹페이지에 어떤 정보가 포함되어 있는가?
(A) 투자 주식을 사야 하는 이유
(B) 몇몇 동업자의 이름
(C) 회사의 초기에 대한 세부 사항
(D) 온라인 쇼핑 사이트 링크

163 웹페이지에 따르면, Maksma사는 고객들에게 어떤 혜택을 제공하는가?
(A) 다양한 상품 선택권
(B) 특별히 협의된 할인
(C) 지불 연기 권한
(D) 중고 상품을 볼 기회

164 Maksma사에 대해 언급된 것은?
(A) 다양한 국적의 고위 간부들을 고용한다.
(B) 판매자로부터 월별 납부금을 받는다.
(C) 작년에 25억 달러가 넘는 수익을 냈다.
(D) 모바일 애플리케이션을 도입할 것이다.

165-168은 다음 브로슈어에 관한 문제입니다.

FILLYAN MASTER
CORPORATE SOLUTIONS사의 신제품

오늘날의 극도로 경쟁적인 세상에서, 기업들은 그들이 이용할 수 있는 모든 이점을 활용해야 합니다. Fillyan Master는 당신의 기업 환경에서 모바일 기기를 이용하여 전자 장비를 조절하게 해주는 프로그램입니다. — [1] —.

그것은 전화 또는 태블릿을 이용해 시청각 장비, 조명, 실내 온도, 그리고 더 많은 것들을 감독하고 관리할 수 있게 해 드립니다. — [2] —. 하루 중 다양한 시간대에 냉방전력을 최대화하도록 전자 블라인드를 설정하세요.

게다가, 무선 인터넷이 있는 어느 곳에서든 음성 및 비디오 채널에 접근함으로써 다른 사람들과 협업할 수 있습니다. 여러 참여자들이 노트북 또는 스마트 기기를 이용해 동시에 발표를 보고 협업할 수 있습니다. — [3] —.

Fillyan Master는 또한 공간 및 에너지 사용에 대한 데이터를 수집할 수 있게 해 드립니다. 예산 책정을 관리하고, 회사의 시간과 돈을 절약하고, 자원을 최대화하도록 이 정보를 이용하세요. — [4] —.

이것과 다른 제품들에 대한 더 많은 정보를 위해서 www.fillyan.com을 방문하시거나, 시범 설명 일정을 잡기 위해 555-5205로 상담 전화를 주세요.

165 Fillyan Master에 대해 언급된 것은?
(A) 작동 방법을 배우기 위해 전문가 교육이 필요하다.
(B) 업계 행사에서 시연될 것이다.
(C) 컴퓨터 하드웨어에 연결되어야 한다.
(D) 휴대용 기기와 함께 사용될 수 있다.

166 브로슈어에서 언급되지 않은 Fillyan Master의 기능은?
(A) 멀리 떨어진 팀들이 함께 일할 수 있게 한다.
(B) 에너지 사용에 대한 정보를 수집한다.
(C) 최적의 실내 배치를 결정한다.
(D) 업무 공간의 온도를 조절한다.

167 몇몇 고객들은 왜 상담 전화번호로 전화할 것인가?
(A) 상품을 대량 주문하기 위해
(B) 제품 설명을 계획하기 위해
(C) 사무실 점검 일정을 잡기 위해
(D) 기술적 도움을 받기 위해

168 [1], [2], [3], [4]로 표시된 위치 중, 다음 문장이 들어갈 곳으로 가장 적절한 것은?
"이는 청중 참여에 관한 새로운 가능성을 창출합니다."
(A) [1]
(B) [2]
(C) [3]
(D) [4]

169-171은 다음 인물 소개에 관한 문제입니다.

Lynn Foster의 집필 경력

Lynn Foster는 오리건주 포틀랜드에 거주하면서 일하는 판타지 소설가입니다. *The Last Rancher*로 가장 잘 알려진 그녀는 18세였을 때부터 활발하게 글을 써 왔습니다. 본래 루이지애나주 출신으로, 그녀는 11세의 나이에 몬태나주 뷰트로 이사했습니다. 그녀는 훗날 그곳의 광활하고, 탁 트인 풍경으로부터 집필에 대한 영감을 얻곤 했습니다.

Ms. Foster는 전국의 잡지들에 단편 소설을 기고함으로써 경력을 시작했습니다. 그녀의 단편 소설 *Bear in the Creek*은 몬태나 예술원으로부터 상을 받았습니다. 2년 후, 그녀는 첫 장편 소설, *Meadowlark*를 출간했습니다. 애니메이션 영화로 만들어진 4권짜리 소설, *The Darkening Brow*가 그 뒤를 이었습니다. 현재 진행 중인, 잠정적으로 *There and Back*이라고 제목이 붙여진 작품은 그녀가 태어난 마을을 배경으로 합니다.

Ms. Foster의 저서들은 20개가 넘는 언어들로 번역되었습니다.

169 1문단 다섯 번째 줄의 단어 "draw"는 의미상 -와 가장 가깝다.
(A) 얻다
(B) 추론하다
(C) 설명하다
(D) 연장하다

170 *There and Back*에 대해 암시되는 것은?
(A) 이야기가 루이지애나주에서 진행된다.
(B) 시리즈의 4권 중 하나이다.
(C) 여행 도중에 쓰였다.
(D) Ms. Foster의 가장 긴 책이다.

171 Ms. Foster에 대해 사실이 아닌 것은?
(A) 그녀의 단편 소설은 다양한 출판물에서 등장했다.
(B) 그녀의 작품은 외국어로 구할 수 있다.
(C) 영화로 각색된 몇몇 책이 있다.
(D) 대학에 다니는 동안 대회에서 우승했다.

172-175는 다음 이메일에 관한 문제입니다.

수신: 고객 서비스 <customerservice@swissluxair.ch>
발신: Thomas Holmes <thomas@holmessolutions.ch>
날짜: 8월 5일
제목: 예약번호 49994FGX

관계자분께,

저는 SwissLux 항공사와 함께 여행하면서 겪었던 경험에 대해 이메일을 씁니다. 저는 구체적으로 취리히에서 싱가포르로 가는 293 항공편에 대해 언급하고 있으며, 그것은 8월 3일 오전 11시에 출발했습니다.

처음부터, 저는 탑승 절차가 체계적이지 않은 것 같다는 것을 알아차렸습니다. 저는 체크인 이전에 온라인으로 좌석 업그레이드를 구매했습니다. 하지만, 비행기 예약이 초과되었고, 제가 이코노미 좌석으로 이동해야 할 거라고 들었습니다. 그 후, 대부분의 여행 동안, 오락 시스템이 전혀 작동하지 않았고, 그것은 긴 비행을 더 견디기 어렵게 만들었습니다. 마지막으로, 항공사가 비행을 위해 완전 채식주의자 식사를 충분히 준비하지 않았던 것으로 보입니다. 제가 그것을 받을 차례가 되었을 때쯤에는 하나도 남아 있지 않았습니다.

어쨌든, 그 모든 경험은 저에게 매우 실망한 감정을 느끼게 했습니다. 저는 귀하 항공사의 로열티 프로그램의 오랜 회원이며 항상 제가 받은 서비스 수준에 만족해 왔습니다. 하지만, 이 여행은 저의 소중한 경험들에 버금가지 않았습니다. 항공사 직원들은 그들의 최선을 다해 정중했고 미안해했습니다. 그러나 저는 어떠한 형태의 보상도 받지 못했습니다. 저는 항공사가 이 문제를 어떻게 처리할 계획인지 듣기를 기대합니다. 가능한 한 빨리 회신해 주세요. 감사합니다.

Thomas Holmes 드림

172 Mr. Holmes는 왜 이메일을 썼는가?
(A) 항공편의 변경을 요청하기 위해
(B) 로열티 포인트에 대해 문의하기 위해
(C) 분실된 수하물을 신고하기 위해
(D) 서비스 수준에 대해 불평하기 위해

173 SwissLux 항공사에 대해 추론될 수 있는 것은?
(A) 최근에 오락 시스템을 교체했다.
(B) 취리히와 싱가포르 간의 직항을 제공한다.
(C) 승객들에게 완전 채식주의자 식사를 제공하지 않는다.
(D) 취리히에서 긴 지연을 겪었다.

174 2문단 네 번째 줄의 단어 "bear"는 의미상 -와 가장 가깝다.
(A) 운반하다
(B) 주다
(C) 배달하다
(D) 견디다

175 Mr. Holmes에 대해 암시되는 것은?
(A) 비행기 표를 늦게 예약했다.
(B) 배상을 받았다.
(C) 이전에 SwissLux 항공사를 이용한 적이 있었다.
(D) 사업차 자주 싱가포르에 간다.

176-180은 다음 구인 광고와 편지에 관한 문제입니다.

Soleil 크루즈에서 일하세요

만약 당신이 일생에 다시없는 기회를 찾고 있다면, Soleil 크루즈의 일자리가 당신을 위한 것일 수도 있습니다! Soleil 크루즈에서 일하는 것의 많은 혜택 중에는 돈을 절약할 기회가 있습니다. 저희는 직원들에게 숙소와 매일 아침, 점심, 저녁을 제공할 뿐만 아니라, 의료 보험과 출장 경비 또한 보장해 드립니다. 심지어 승무원의 가족들도 혜택을 받는데, 관리직급의 직원들은 그들의 배우자와 아이들을 무료로 탑승시킬 수 있는 한편, 다른 모든 직원의 가족 구성원들은 패키지 여행에서 할인을 받을 자격이 있습니다.

가능한 일자리

▶ 스파 전문가
승객들에게 얼굴 마사지와 피부 관리를 제공합니다. 목욕 및 미용 제품을 판매합니다. 미용사 자격증을 보유하고 있어야 합니다. 또한 이전에 크루즈 선박에서 일해 보았어야 합니다.

▶ 식당 관리인
식당과 바 직원들을 관리합니다. 서비스 수준을 유지하고 승객 관련 용무를 다루는 책무를 포함합니다. 강한 조직 기술을 가져야 하며 최소 2년 동안 크루즈 선박에서 비슷한 직책을 맡았어야 합니다.

더 많은 사항을 알기 위해서는 555-8800으로 전화해 주세요.

Richard Bates
36번지 Bayview가
파이거리, 사우스오스트레일리아주 5655
호주

11월 1일

Mr. Bates께,

지난주 저희 시드니 사무실에서의 만남은 즐거웠으며 저는 당신에게 그 직책을 제안하고 싶습니다. 제가 언급했듯이, 관리직 직원들의 일정은 부담이 큽니다. 당신은 1월부터 9월까지, 9개월의 기간 동안 주 6일 근무를 할 것입니다. 그러고 나서 새로운 업무를 시작하기 전인 그다음 3개월을 쉴 것입니다.

대부분의 저희 주방 직원들과 종업원들은 한 번에 2개월 또는 3개월 동안 일하는 학생들이기 때문에 당신은 신입 사원들을 정기적으로 교육해야 할 것입니다. 다행히, Luzollo 크루즈 식당에서 일했던 경력은 당신을 그렇게 높은 교체율에 대비하게 했을 것입니다.

또한 12월 6일에 시작하는 2주간의 교육을 위해 시드니로 돌아오셔야 할 것임을 말씀드려야겠습니다. 모든 것이 잘 된다면, 당신은 아마 12월 말에 저희 선박 중 하나에 배정될 것이고, 이는 당신이 일을 정리할 수 있는 충분한 시간을 줄 것입니다.

답변을 기다리고 있겠습니다.

Corey Lauzone 드림

176 Soleil 크루즈가 직원들에게 제공하는 혜택이 아닌 것은?
(A) 일일 식사
(B) 건강 보험
(C) 등록금 지원
(D) 무료 숙소

177 두 일자리 모두의 요구 조건은 무엇인가?
(A) 승객들의 특별 요청을 충족시킬 의향
(B) 제품 라인에 대한 숙지
(C) 자격증 취득
(D) 선상 근무 경력

178 편지의 하나의 목적은 무엇인가?
(A) 학력을 칭찬하기 위해
(B) 직무 기간을 명시하기 위해
(C) 대안적인 해결책을 제안하기 위해
(D) 선호하는 목적지에 대해 묻기 위해

179 Mr. Bates에 대해 암시되는 것은?
(A) 현재 무직 상태이다.
(B) 이력서가 우편으로 발송되었다.
(C) 유니폼을 구입해야 할 것이다.
(D) 가족이 무료로 여행할 수 있을 것이다.

180 Mr. Lauzone이 주방 직원들에 대해 언급한 것은?
(A) 장기적으로 일하지 않는 경향이 있다.
(B) 다양한 국가 출신이다.
(C) 공동 숙소에 거주한다.
(D) 식당 관리자에 의해 고용된다.

181-185는 다음 안내문과 양식에 관한 문제입니다.

Polson 전자제품사는 저희 상품의 품질에 있어 굉장한 자부심을 가지고 있습니다. 만약 저희 제품 중 하나가 마음에 들지 않으시다면, 환불을 위해 반품하시거나 다른 물품으로 교환하실 수 있습니다. 다음 약관들은 저희 웹사이

트를 통해서나 전국 28개의 매장 중 어디서든 구매된 상품들에 적용됩니다:
- 포장이 밀봉되어 있는 한 제품은 구매한 지 21일 이내에 반품될 수 있습니다.
- 온라인 구매품을 우편을 통해 반품하는 것은 처리하는 데 7일에서 14일이 걸립니다.
- 모든 반품에는 영수증 원본이 포함되어 있어야 합니다.
- 할인받은 제품은 반품될 수 없습니다.
- 포장이 제거되었던 물품들은 상점 포인트로만 교환될 수 있습니다.

Polson 전자제품사에서 쇼핑해주셔서 감사합니다.

Polson 전자제품사 – 제품 반품 양식

고객: Beth Yang　　**전화번호:** 555-0393
주소: 35번지 Elm가, 시카고, 일리노이주 60176　　**이메일:** b.yang@dmail.com

제품명: Digital 350X 프린터　　**모델 번호:** 7849484XE
구매 날짜: 5월 7일　　**구매 장소:** Harrisburg 지점

반품 사유:
최선을 다했음에도 불구하고, 저는 이 프린터를 제 노트북과 함께 작동시킬 수가 없습니다. 몇몇 온라인 포럼을 확인해 보고 나서, 저는 이것이 제 컴퓨터와 호환성 문제가 있다는 것을 알게 되었습니다. 심지어 5월 11일에 두 기기 모두 서비스 센터에 가져갔지만, 기술자가 그 문제를 해결할 수 없었습니다. 그래서, 저는 이것을 다시 상자에 담아 반품하기로 결정했습니다. 즉시 다른 모델을 구매하기보다는, 기다려서 Sonical MDM-0을 사고 싶습니다. 그것이 다음 달에 출시될 것이라는 것을 읽었습니다. 정확히 언제 그것을 판매하기 시작하실 것인지 이메일을 통해 제게 알려주십시오.

요청 조치: □ 교환　■ 반품

181 안내문의 목적은 무엇인가?
(A) 몇몇 우대 조치를 열거하기 위해
(B) 몇몇 우려 사항을 명시하기 위해
(C) 몇몇 정책을 설명하기 위해
(D) 합병을 발표하기 위해

182 안내문에서 Polson 전자제품사에 대해 언급되지 않은 것은?
(A) 전국 곳곳에 지점이 있다.
(B) 재활용 프로그램을 시행해왔다.
(C) 웹사이트를 통해 제품을 판매한다.
(D) 할인 품목의 반품을 금지한다.

183 Ms. Yang에 대해 사실일 것 같은 것은?
(A) 수리공이 방문할 것이다.
(B) 우편을 통해 제품을 보냈다.
(C) 상점 포인트를 받을 것이다.
(D) 친구를 위해 선물을 샀다.

184 Ms. Yang은 왜 프린터를 반품하고 있는가?
(A) 사무실에 어울리지 않는다.
(B) 다른 기기와 호환성이 없다.
(C) 제조사에 의해 회수되었다.
(D) 배송 도중에 파손되었다.

185 Ms. Yang은 어떤 정보를 요청하는가?
(A) 판매원의 이름
(B) 카탈로그를 받을 수 있는 장소
(C) 제품이 판매될 날짜
(D) 특정 가게가 문을 닫은 이유

186-190은 다음 공고, 웹페이지, 영수증에 관한 문제입니다.

5월 6일

*라틴 아메리카 의학 학술지*는 Dr. Juan Lima가 올해의 의료 서비스상 수상자임을 발표하게 되어 기쁩니다. 수십 년 동안, Dr. Lima는 그의 고국인 볼리비아에 있는 Domingo 병원에서 일반 외과의로 일해 왔습니다. 저희는 그가 작년에 사람들에게 새로운 종류의 독감 바이러스에 대해 알리는 전국적인 건강 캠페인을 시작했기 때문에 그에게 영예를 수여합니다. 발병에 가장 영향을 받았던 두 집단인, 많은 유아와 노인을 치료하는 동안, Dr. Lima는 정부로부터의 도움을 주장했습니다. 그의 주장 덕분에, Mr. Rodrigo Guerrero에 의해 이끌어지는 볼리비아 보건 기구에서 독감 예방 및 치료에 대한 교육 광고를 냈습니다.

5월 27일 오후 8시에 Buena Vista 연회장에서 Dr. Lima에게 영예를 수여하는 데 함께해 주십시오. Dr. Lima의 동료 중 한 명이 그에게 시상할 것입니다. 작년 수상자 Dr. Santiago Castillo가 참석할 것입니다. 이 행사의 티켓을 구매하기 위해서는, www.lajm.com/tickets를 방문하십시오.

www.lajm.com/tickets

라틴 아메리카 의학 학술지
시상식
5월 27일 오후 8시
Buena Vista 연회장

저희 시상식에 참석하는 데 관심을 가져 주셔서 감사합니다. 티켓을 구매하시기 전에 다음 안내문을 꼼꼼히 읽어보시길 바랍니다. 모든 구매는 변경될 수 없습니다.

☆ 모든 행사 참석자들은 종이 또는 전자 티켓을 가지고 있어야 합니다. 이는 저희 행사 직원 중 한 명에 의해 입구에서 스캔되어야 할 것입니다.

☆ 티켓은 Sunset가와 Orange가 모퉁이의 Buena Vista 주차장 또는 La Paz가의 Belmonte 실내 주차장의 무료 주차를 포함합니다.

☆ 티켓은 또한 뷔페 저녁 식사, 무제한 음료, 그리고 Dr. Lima의 상을 시상할 유명한 저술가 Dr. Maria Quintero와의 네트워킹 세션 참여를 포함합니다.

행사에서 뵙기를 고대하겠습니다!

지금 티켓 구매하기

Belmonte 실내 주차장 영수증

영수증 날짜: 5월 27일　　**입장 시간:** 오후 7시 45분
운전자: Stephanie Vera　　**차종:** Volper 900
가격: 적용 불가—Buena Vista 연회장 행사 손님　　**차량 색상:** 파란색
차량 등록 번호: SXC 894

**차고에 주차되어 있는 동안 귀하의 차량 계기판에 이 영수증을 놓아 주십시오. 나가시는 길에 경비원이 이것을 요청할 것입니다.*

186 Dr. Lima는 왜 상을 받을 것인가?
(A) 해외에서 젊은 의사들을 교육했다.
(B) 의학적 문제에 대한 인식을 높였다.
(C) 그의 환자들에 의해 칭찬받았다.
(D) 병원 운영을 도왔다.

187 볼리비아 보건 기구에 대해 언급된 것은?
(A) 새로운 치료법을 개발했다.
(B) 대중으로부터 항의를 받았다.
(C) Dr. Lima에 의해 영향을 받았다.
(D) 노인들을 위한 프로그램을 시작했다.

188 행사 티켓에 대해 언급된 것은?
(A) 환불이 되지 않는다.
(B) 음료 한 잔만 딸려 있다.

(C) 직접 구매해야만 한다.
(D) 스탠딩 구역을 위한 것이다.

189 Dr. Lima는 누구와 일할 것 같은가?
(A) Rodrigo Guerrero
(B) Santiago Castillo
(C) Maria Quintero
(D) Stephanie Vera

190 Ms. Vera에 대해 암시되는 것은?
(A) 웹사이트에서 티켓을 샀다.
(B) 임대 차량을 운전하고 있다.
(C) 입장료를 환급받을 것이다.
(D) 시상식에 늦었다.

191-195는 다음 편지, 회람, 이메일에 관한 문제입니다.

11월 9일

Elisabeth Baker
그랜드빌 과학박물관
4747번지 Prairie가 SW
그랜드빌, 미시건주 49418

Ms. Baker께,

제가 1월 내내 박물관에서 투어를 인솔할 수 없을 것임을 알려드리기 위해 편지를 씁니다. 이는 제가 Lakeshore 대학의 여러 동료들과 함께 남아메리카로 연구 출장을 갈 것이기 때문입니다. 원정 동안, 저희는 아타카마 사막에서 멸종된 생명체의 유해를 찾기 위해 발굴을 할 것입니다.

저는 2월 2일부터 다시 박물관 손님들을 안내할 것을 기대하고 있습니다. 저는 이때까지 일요일에 투어를 인솔해 왔지만, 돌아오고 나서는 토요일로 바꾸고 싶습니다. 또한, 박물관의 현실 과학 강연 시리즈에서 누구든 발표자가 필요하시다면, 기꺼이 출장 동안의 연구 결과를 발표하겠습니다.

James Uttley 드림

수신: 전 직원
발신: Michelle Lawrence, 박물관장
제목: 투어에 관한 변경 사항
날짜: 11월 13일

이곳 그랜드빌 과학박물관의 투어 프로그램에 대해 여러분께 몇 가지 발표할 사항이 있습니다. 첫째로, 저희 투어는 평일에만 진행될 것이고, 이는 12월 1일부터 시행될 것입니다. 이는 주말 방문객들의 평균 숫자가 증가하여, 투어 단체들이 혼잡으로 인한 불편을 겪게 되었기 때문입니다. 이전과 마찬가지로, 모든 투어는 오전 10시에 시작해 정오에 끝날 것입니다. 새로운 일정표는 우리 웹사이트와 매표소 뒤편 벽에 게시될 것입니다. 변경 사항은 다음과 같습니다:

투어	현재 진행 요일		12월 1일부터 진행될 요일
공룡과 화석	일요일	→	월요일
우리 주변의 기술	월요일	→	화요일
대양의 생명	목요일	→	수요일
우주에서의 우리의 자리	토요일	→	금요일

둘째로, 우리의 자원봉사자 중 한 명인 Dr. James Uttley가 1월에 그의 투어를 인솔할 수 없을 것입니다. 임시로 Dr. Uttley를 대신하고 싶다면 이메일로 제게 알려주십시오. 제가 요구하는 것은 고고학 학위를 소지해야 한다는 것뿐입니다.

발신: Dale Vinson <dalevins@grandvillesm.com>
수신: Michelle Lawrence <michlawr@grandvillesm.com>
날짜: 11월 19일
제목: 투어 기회

Ms. Lawrence께,

저는 저희 박물관의 에너지원 체험 센터를 관리하는 제 업무를 즐겁게 하고 있지만, Dr. Uttley의 부재 동안 그의 투어를 인솔하고 싶습니다. 그 달에는 체험 센터에 추가되는 새로운 체험형 전시가 없을 것이므로 이것이 제 정규 업무에 지장을 주지 않을 것입니다. 아시다시피, 저는 대학에서 물리학을 공부했고, 그것이 투어와 직접적으로 연관되어 있지는 않습니다. 하지만, 저는 저희 시설의 각 전시실에 매우 익숙합니다. 저는 또한 등록 오류로 인해 Dr. Uttley의 투어에 참가자 수가 25명의 제한을 초과했을 때 그를 보조했습니다. 괜찮으시다면, 점심 시간 동안 직원 식당에서 이에 대해 더 상의하고 싶습니다. 만나기를 원하신다면 제게 알려주십시오.

Dale Vinson 드림
주니어 큐레이터, 그랜드빌 과학박물관

191 편지는 왜 쓰였는가?
(A) 재정적 기부를 요청하기 위해
(B) 강연의 참석을 확정하기 위해
(C) 연구 목표를 명확하게 하기 위해
(D) 일시적으로 책임을 중단하기 위해

192 Mr. Uttley는 어떤 투어를 인솔해 왔는가?
(A) 공룡과 화석
(B) 우리 주변의 기술
(C) 대양의 생명
(D) 우주에서의 우리의 자리

193 회람에 따르면, 일정표는 왜 변경될 것인가?
(A) 일부 자원봉사자들이 더 많은 융통성을 요구했다.
(B) 시즌권이 중단되었다.
(C) 일부 전시 공간이 개조되고 있다.
(D) 특정 요일들에 많은 사람이 방문한다.

194 Mr. Vinson에 대해 암시되는 것은?
(A) 팀 회의에 참석할 수 없었다.
(B) Dr. Uttley를 대체할 자격이 되지 않는다.
(C) 실험실 출입을 허가받았다.
(D) 아직 그랜드빌 과학박물관과 계약하지 않았다.

195 이메일에 따르면, 그랜드빌 과학박물관에 대해 사실이 아닌 것은?
(A) 직원들을 위한 식당 시설을 운영한다.
(B) 투어의 규모를 제한한다.
(C) 한 시간에 한 번 영화를 상영한다.
(D) 체험 구역이 있다.

196-200은 다음 광고, 회람, 이메일에 관한 문제입니다.

Devon 음악 교육원에서 지식에 대한 갈증을 충족시키세요

Devon 음악 교육원은 대학 졸업 이후에도 배움에 대한 갈망이 멈추지 않는다는 것을 압니다. 그것이, 저희가 연주자와 작곡가가 되려는 사람들을 위한 교육을 제공하는 것에 더해, 매우 능력 있는 강사들이 가르치는 다양한 평생 교육 강좌를 제공하는 이유입니다. 음악에 대한 더 나은 이해를 통해 당신의 삶을 향상시키고 싶다면, 다가오는 저희의 음악사 워크숍을 듣는 것을 고려해 보세요.

워크숍	강사	날짜	가격
초기 이탈리아 오페라	Denise Murray	5월 6일	35달러
마드리갈 전통	Clayton Higgins	5월 13일	55달러
북아메리카 민요	Lara Wiseman	5월 20일	40달러
중동의 즉흥 음악	Zoe Gomez	5월 27일	60달러

이 워크숍에 대한 추가 정보는
www.devonmusicinstitute.com에서 이용 가능합니다.

등록하기 위해서는, Bedford가와 Davis가의 모퉁이에
있는 저희 시설에 들르세요.

수신: 홍보 부서 직원, Periform Records사
발신: Greg Hong, 홍보 관리자, Periform Records사
날짜: 4월 15일
제목: 워크숍

4월 10일 회의에서, 저는 여러분에게 우리의 직장이 어떻게 개선될 수 있을지 이야기해 달라고 요청했습니다. 여러분들 중 많은 분들이 음악을 배울 수 있는 더 많은 기회가 주어졌으면 좋겠다고 언급했습니다. 저는 어제 아침에 Devon 음악 교육원에 전화해 각각의 정기적으로 제공되는 일일 워크숍이 다음 달에 열릴 것임을 확인했습니다. 이 워크숍 중 어느 것이라도 참석하는 데 관심이 있는 직원들은 등록한 다음 요금을 직접 지불해야 합니다. 그러고 나서 그들은 회계 부서로부터 환급을 요청해야 합니다. 제가 지난달에 마케팅 및 유통 부서의 관리자들과 함께 그 세션들 중 하나인 초기 이탈리아 오페라 세션을 들었다는 점을 덧붙이고 싶습니다. 우리는 다뤄진 정보의 양에 매우 감명을 받았습니다.

수신: Darrel Wilson <d.wilson@periform.com>
발신: Mandy Parker <m.parker@periform.com>
날짜: 7월 1일
제목: 환급 요청

Mr. Wilson께,

저는 그저 제 환급 요청에 대해 후속 조치를 취하고자 했습니다. 그것은 제가 5월 13일에 Devon 음악 교육원에서 참가했던 워크숍에 대한 것이었습니다. 제 요청이 왜 아직까지 처리되지 않았는지 혹시 알고 계신가요? 예전에는, 이것이 3주 이상 걸렸던 적이 없었습니다. 5월 20일에 같은 기관에서 교육 세션에 참가한 제 동료 중 한 명은 이미 그가 요청했던 금액을 받았습니다. 제가 참석했던 워크숍은 제 관리자인 Mr. Hong에 의해 승인되었습니다. 이를 확인하시려면 내선 번호 457로 그에게 전화하실 수 있습니다. 감사합니다.

Mandy Parker 드림

196 Devon 음악 교육원에 대해 암시되는 것은?
(A) 작곡에 대한 수업이 있다.
(B) Davis가에 광고 자리를 구입했다.
(C) Periform Records사에서 자금을 받았다.
(D) 온라인 교육을 전문으로 한다.

197 Mr. Hong은 Devon 음악 교육원의 워크숍에서 어떤 점이 인상 깊다고 생각했는가?
(A) 적당한 수업료
(B) 유연한 구성 방식
(C) 추가적인 읽을거리
(D) 교육 내용의 분량

198 Ms. Parker는 얼마를 환급 받을 것으로 예상하는가?
(A) 35달러
(B) 55달러
(C) 40달러
(D) 60달러

199 Ms. Parker에 대해 암시되는 것은?
(A) 동료 중 한 명과 함께 세미나에 참석했다.
(B) 회계 부서로부터 잘못된 금액을 받았다.
(C) 교육 기관에서 열리는 여러 워크숍에 참석할 계획이었다.
(D) 요청을 최소 3주 전에 제출했다.

200 Ms. Parker는 어느 부서에서 일할 것 같은가?
(A) 홍보
(B) 회계
(C) 마케팅
(D) 유통

자르는 선

Answer Sheet

TEST **01**

READING (Part V~VII)									
101	A B C D	121	A B C D	141	A B C D	161	A B C D	181	A B C D
102	A B C D	122	A B C D	142	A B C D	162	A B C D	182	A B C D
103	A B C D	123	A B C D	143	A B C D	163	A B C D	183	A B C D
104	A B C D	124	A B C D	144	A B C D	164	A B C D	184	A B C D
105	A B C D	125	A B C D	145	A B C D	165	A B C D	185	A B C D
106	A B C D	126	A B C D	146	A B C D	166	A B C D	186	A B C D
107	A B C D	127	A B C D	147	A B C D	167	A B C D	187	A B C D
108	A B C D	128	A B C D	148	A B C D	168	A B C D	188	A B C D
109	A B C D	129	A B C D	149	A B C D	169	A B C D	189	A B C D
110	A B C D	130	A B C D	150	A B C D	170	A B C D	190	A B C D
111	A B C D	131	A B C D	151	A B C D	171	A B C D	191	A B C D
112	A B C D	132	A B C D	152	A B C D	172	A B C D	192	A B C D
113	A B C D	133	A B C D	153	A B C D	173	A B C D	193	A B C D
114	A B C D	134	A B C D	154	A B C D	174	A B C D	194	A B C D
115	A B C D	135	A B C D	155	A B C D	175	A B C D	195	A B C D
116	A B C D	136	A B C D	156	A B C D	176	A B C D	196	A B C D
117	A B C D	137	A B C D	157	A B C D	177	A B C D	197	A B C D
118	A B C D	138	A B C D	158	A B C D	178	A B C D	198	A B C D
119	A B C D	139	A B C D	159	A B C D	179	A B C D	199	A B C D
120	A B C D	140	A B C D	160	A B C D	180	A B C D	200	A B C D

TEST 01의 점수를 환산한 후 목표 달성기에 TEST 01의 점수를 표시합니다.
점수 환산표는 문제집 329페이지, 목표 달성기는 교재의 첫 장에 있습니다.

맞은 문제 개수: ___ / 100

자르는 선

Answer Sheet

TEST **02**

READING (Part V~VII)									
101	A B C D	121	A B C D	141	A B C D	161	A B C D	181	A B C D
102	A B C D	122	A B C D	142	A B C D	162	A B C D	182	A B C D
103	A B C D	123	A B C D	143	A B C D	163	A B C D	183	A B C D
104	A B C D	124	A B C D	144	A B C D	164	A B C D	184	A B C D
105	A B C D	125	A B C D	145	A B C D	165	A B C D	185	A B C D
106	A B C D	126	A B C D	146	A B C D	166	A B C D	186	A B C D
107	A B C D	127	A B C D	147	A B C D	167	A B C D	187	A B C D
108	A B C D	128	A B C D	148	A B C D	168	A B C D	188	A B C D
109	A B C D	129	A B C D	149	A B C D	169	A B C D	189	A B C D
110	A B C D	130	A B C D	150	A B C D	170	A B C D	190	A B C D
111	A B C D	131	A B C D	151	A B C D	171	A B C D	191	A B C D
112	A B C D	132	A B C D	152	A B C D	172	A B C D	192	A B C D
113	A B C D	133	A B C D	153	A B C D	173	A B C D	193	A B C D
114	A B C D	134	A B C D	154	A B C D	174	A B C D	194	A B C D
115	A B C D	135	A B C D	155	A B C D	175	A B C D	195	A B C D
116	A B C D	136	A B C D	156	A B C D	176	A B C D	196	A B C D
117	A B C D	137	A B C D	157	A B C D	177	A B C D	197	A B C D
118	A B C D	138	A B C D	158	A B C D	178	A B C D	198	A B C D
119	A B C D	139	A B C D	159	A B C D	179	A B C D	199	A B C D
120	A B C D	140	A B C D	160	A B C D	180	A B C D	200	A B C D

TEST 02의 점수를 환산한 후 목표 달성기에 TEST 02의 점수를 표시합니다.
점수 환산표는 문제집 329페이지, 목표 달성기는 교재의 첫 장에 있습니다.

맞은 문제 개수: ___ / 100

자르는 선

Answer Sheet

TEST 03

READING (Part V~VII)																								
101	A	B	C	D	121	A	B	C	D	141	A	B	C	D	161	A	B	C	D	181	A	B	C	D
102	A	B	C	D	122	A	B	C	D	142	A	B	C	D	162	A	B	C	D	182	A	B	C	D
103	A	B	C	D	123	A	B	C	D	143	A	B	C	D	163	A	B	C	D	183	A	B	C	D
104	A	B	C	D	124	A	B	C	D	144	A	B	C	D	164	A	B	C	D	184	A	B	C	D
105	A	B	C	D	125	A	B	C	D	145	A	B	C	D	165	A	B	C	D	185	A	B	C	D
106	A	B	C	D	126	A	B	C	D	146	A	B	C	D	166	A	B	C	D	186	A	B	C	D
107	A	B	C	D	127	A	B	C	D	147	A	B	C	D	167	A	B	C	D	187	A	B	C	D
108	A	B	C	D	128	A	B	C	D	148	A	B	C	D	168	A	B	C	D	188	A	B	C	D
109	A	B	C	D	129	A	B	C	D	149	A	B	C	D	169	A	B	C	D	189	A	B	C	D
110	A	B	C	D	130	A	B	C	D	150	A	B	C	D	170	A	B	C	D	190	A	B	C	D
111	A	B	C	D	131	A	B	C	D	151	A	B	C	D	171	A	B	C	D	191	A	B	C	D
112	A	B	C	D	132	A	B	C	D	152	A	B	C	D	172	A	B	C	D	192	A	B	C	D
113	A	B	C	D	133	A	B	C	D	153	A	B	C	D	173	A	B	C	D	193	A	B	C	D
114	A	B	C	D	134	A	B	C	D	154	A	B	C	D	174	A	B	C	D	194	A	B	C	D
115	A	B	C	D	135	A	B	C	D	155	A	B	C	D	175	A	B	C	D	195	A	B	C	D
116	A	B	C	D	136	A	B	C	D	156	A	B	C	D	176	A	B	C	D	196	A	B	C	D
117	A	B	C	D	137	A	B	C	D	157	A	B	C	D	177	A	B	C	D	197	A	B	C	D
118	A	B	C	D	138	A	B	C	D	158	A	B	C	D	178	A	B	C	D	198	A	B	C	D
119	A	B	C	D	139	A	B	C	D	159	A	B	C	D	179	A	B	C	D	199	A	B	C	D
120	A	B	C	D	140	A	B	C	D	160	A	B	C	D	180	A	B	C	D	200	A	B	C	D

TEST 03의 점수를 환산한 후 목표 달성기에 TEST 03의 점수를 표시합니다.
점수 환산표는 문제집 329페이지, 목표 달성기는 교재의 첫 장에 있습니다.

맞은 문제 개수: ___ / 100

자르는 선

Answer Sheet

TEST 04

READING (Part V~VII)																								
101	A	B	C	D	121	A	B	C	D	141	A	B	C	D	161	A	B	C	D	181	A	B	C	D
102	A	B	C	D	122	A	B	C	D	142	A	B	C	D	162	A	B	C	D	182	A	B	C	D
103	A	B	C	D	123	A	B	C	D	143	A	B	C	D	163	A	B	C	D	183	A	B	C	D
104	A	B	C	D	124	A	B	C	D	144	A	B	C	D	164	A	B	C	D	184	A	B	C	D
105	A	B	C	D	125	A	B	C	D	145	A	B	C	D	165	A	B	C	D	185	A	B	C	D
106	A	B	C	D	126	A	B	C	D	146	A	B	C	D	166	A	B	C	D	186	A	B	C	D
107	A	B	C	D	127	A	B	C	D	147	A	B	C	D	167	A	B	C	D	187	A	B	C	D
108	A	B	C	D	128	A	B	C	D	148	A	B	C	D	168	A	B	C	D	188	A	B	C	D
109	A	B	C	D	129	A	B	C	D	149	A	B	C	D	169	A	B	C	D	189	A	B	C	D
110	A	B	C	D	130	A	B	C	D	150	A	B	C	D	170	A	B	C	D	190	A	B	C	D
111	A	B	C	D	131	A	B	C	D	151	A	B	C	D	171	A	B	C	D	191	A	B	C	D
112	A	B	C	D	132	A	B	C	D	152	A	B	C	D	172	A	B	C	D	192	A	B	C	D
113	A	B	C	D	133	A	B	C	D	153	A	B	C	D	173	A	B	C	D	193	A	B	C	D
114	A	B	C	D	134	A	B	C	D	154	A	B	C	D	174	A	B	C	D	194	A	B	C	D
115	A	B	C	D	135	A	B	C	D	155	A	B	C	D	175	A	B	C	D	195	A	B	C	D
116	A	B	C	D	136	A	B	C	D	156	A	B	C	D	176	A	B	C	D	196	A	B	C	D
117	A	B	C	D	137	A	B	C	D	157	A	B	C	D	177	A	B	C	D	197	A	B	C	D
118	A	B	C	D	138	A	B	C	D	158	A	B	C	D	178	A	B	C	D	198	A	B	C	D
119	A	B	C	D	139	A	B	C	D	159	A	B	C	D	179	A	B	C	D	199	A	B	C	D
120	A	B	C	D	140	A	B	C	D	160	A	B	C	D	180	A	B	C	D	200	A	B	C	D

TEST 04의 점수를 환산한 후 목표 달성기에 TEST 04의 점수를 표시합니다.
점수 환산표는 문제집 329페이지, 목표 달성기는 교재의 첫 장에 있습니다.

맞은 문제 개수: ___ / 100

자르는 선

Answer Sheet

TEST 05

READING (Part V~VII)									
101	Ⓐ Ⓑ Ⓒ Ⓓ	121	Ⓐ Ⓑ Ⓒ Ⓓ	141	Ⓐ Ⓑ Ⓒ Ⓓ	161	Ⓐ Ⓑ Ⓒ Ⓓ	181	Ⓐ Ⓑ Ⓒ Ⓓ
102	Ⓐ Ⓑ Ⓒ Ⓓ	122	Ⓐ Ⓑ Ⓒ Ⓓ	142	Ⓐ Ⓑ Ⓒ Ⓓ	162	Ⓐ Ⓑ Ⓒ Ⓓ	182	Ⓐ Ⓑ Ⓒ Ⓓ
103	Ⓐ Ⓑ Ⓒ Ⓓ	123	Ⓐ Ⓑ Ⓒ Ⓓ	143	Ⓐ Ⓑ Ⓒ Ⓓ	163	Ⓐ Ⓑ Ⓒ Ⓓ	183	Ⓐ Ⓑ Ⓒ Ⓓ
104	Ⓐ Ⓑ Ⓒ Ⓓ	124	Ⓐ Ⓑ Ⓒ Ⓓ	144	Ⓐ Ⓑ Ⓒ Ⓓ	164	Ⓐ Ⓑ Ⓒ Ⓓ	184	Ⓐ Ⓑ Ⓒ Ⓓ
105	Ⓐ Ⓑ Ⓒ Ⓓ	125	Ⓐ Ⓑ Ⓒ Ⓓ	145	Ⓐ Ⓑ Ⓒ Ⓓ	165	Ⓐ Ⓑ Ⓒ Ⓓ	185	Ⓐ Ⓑ Ⓒ Ⓓ
106	Ⓐ Ⓑ Ⓒ Ⓓ	126	Ⓐ Ⓑ Ⓒ Ⓓ	146	Ⓐ Ⓑ Ⓒ Ⓓ	166	Ⓐ Ⓑ Ⓒ Ⓓ	186	Ⓐ Ⓑ Ⓒ Ⓓ
107	Ⓐ Ⓑ Ⓒ Ⓓ	127	Ⓐ Ⓑ Ⓒ Ⓓ	147	Ⓐ Ⓑ Ⓒ Ⓓ	167	Ⓐ Ⓑ Ⓒ Ⓓ	187	Ⓐ Ⓑ Ⓒ Ⓓ
108	Ⓐ Ⓑ Ⓒ Ⓓ	128	Ⓐ Ⓑ Ⓒ Ⓓ	148	Ⓐ Ⓑ Ⓒ Ⓓ	168	Ⓐ Ⓑ Ⓒ Ⓓ	188	Ⓐ Ⓑ Ⓒ Ⓓ
109	Ⓐ Ⓑ Ⓒ Ⓓ	129	Ⓐ Ⓑ Ⓒ Ⓓ	149	Ⓐ Ⓑ Ⓒ Ⓓ	169	Ⓐ Ⓑ Ⓒ Ⓓ	189	Ⓐ Ⓑ Ⓒ Ⓓ
110	Ⓐ Ⓑ Ⓒ Ⓓ	130	Ⓐ Ⓑ Ⓒ Ⓓ	150	Ⓐ Ⓑ Ⓒ Ⓓ	170	Ⓐ Ⓑ Ⓒ Ⓓ	190	Ⓐ Ⓑ Ⓒ Ⓓ
111	Ⓐ Ⓑ Ⓒ Ⓓ	131	Ⓐ Ⓑ Ⓒ Ⓓ	151	Ⓐ Ⓑ Ⓒ Ⓓ	171	Ⓐ Ⓑ Ⓒ Ⓓ	191	Ⓐ Ⓑ Ⓒ Ⓓ
112	Ⓐ Ⓑ Ⓒ Ⓓ	132	Ⓐ Ⓑ Ⓒ Ⓓ	152	Ⓐ Ⓑ Ⓒ Ⓓ	172	Ⓐ Ⓑ Ⓒ Ⓓ	192	Ⓐ Ⓑ Ⓒ Ⓓ
113	Ⓐ Ⓑ Ⓒ Ⓓ	133	Ⓐ Ⓑ Ⓒ Ⓓ	153	Ⓐ Ⓑ Ⓒ Ⓓ	173	Ⓐ Ⓑ Ⓒ Ⓓ	193	Ⓐ Ⓑ Ⓒ Ⓓ
114	Ⓐ Ⓑ Ⓒ Ⓓ	134	Ⓐ Ⓑ Ⓒ Ⓓ	154	Ⓐ Ⓑ Ⓒ Ⓓ	174	Ⓐ Ⓑ Ⓒ Ⓓ	194	Ⓐ Ⓑ Ⓒ Ⓓ
115	Ⓐ Ⓑ Ⓒ Ⓓ	135	Ⓐ Ⓑ Ⓒ Ⓓ	155	Ⓐ Ⓑ Ⓒ Ⓓ	175	Ⓐ Ⓑ Ⓒ Ⓓ	195	Ⓐ Ⓑ Ⓒ Ⓓ
116	Ⓐ Ⓑ Ⓒ Ⓓ	136	Ⓐ Ⓑ Ⓒ Ⓓ	156	Ⓐ Ⓑ Ⓒ Ⓓ	176	Ⓐ Ⓑ Ⓒ Ⓓ	196	Ⓐ Ⓑ Ⓒ Ⓓ
117	Ⓐ Ⓑ Ⓒ Ⓓ	137	Ⓐ Ⓑ Ⓒ Ⓓ	157	Ⓐ Ⓑ Ⓒ Ⓓ	177	Ⓐ Ⓑ Ⓒ Ⓓ	197	Ⓐ Ⓑ Ⓒ Ⓓ
118	Ⓐ Ⓑ Ⓒ Ⓓ	138	Ⓐ Ⓑ Ⓒ Ⓓ	158	Ⓐ Ⓑ Ⓒ Ⓓ	178	Ⓐ Ⓑ Ⓒ Ⓓ	198	Ⓐ Ⓑ Ⓒ Ⓓ
119	Ⓐ Ⓑ Ⓒ Ⓓ	139	Ⓐ Ⓑ Ⓒ Ⓓ	159	Ⓐ Ⓑ Ⓒ Ⓓ	179	Ⓐ Ⓑ Ⓒ Ⓓ	199	Ⓐ Ⓑ Ⓒ Ⓓ
120	Ⓐ Ⓑ Ⓒ Ⓓ	140	Ⓐ Ⓑ Ⓒ Ⓓ	160	Ⓐ Ⓑ Ⓒ Ⓓ	180	Ⓐ Ⓑ Ⓒ Ⓓ	200	Ⓐ Ⓑ Ⓒ Ⓓ

TEST 05의 점수를 환산한 후 목표 달성기에 TEST 05의 점수를 표시합니다.
점수 환산표는 문제집 329페이지, 목표 달성기는 교재의 첫 장에 있습니다.

맞은 문제 개수: ___ / 100

자르는 선

Answer Sheet

TEST 06

READING (Part V~VII)									
101	Ⓐ Ⓑ Ⓒ Ⓓ	121	Ⓐ Ⓑ Ⓒ Ⓓ	141	Ⓐ Ⓑ Ⓒ Ⓓ	161	Ⓐ Ⓑ Ⓒ Ⓓ	181	Ⓐ Ⓑ Ⓒ Ⓓ
102	Ⓐ Ⓑ Ⓒ Ⓓ	122	Ⓐ Ⓑ Ⓒ Ⓓ	142	Ⓐ Ⓑ Ⓒ Ⓓ	162	Ⓐ Ⓑ Ⓒ Ⓓ	182	Ⓐ Ⓑ Ⓒ Ⓓ
103	Ⓐ Ⓑ Ⓒ Ⓓ	123	Ⓐ Ⓑ Ⓒ Ⓓ	143	Ⓐ Ⓑ Ⓒ Ⓓ	163	Ⓐ Ⓑ Ⓒ Ⓓ	183	Ⓐ Ⓑ Ⓒ Ⓓ
104	Ⓐ Ⓑ Ⓒ Ⓓ	124	Ⓐ Ⓑ Ⓒ Ⓓ	144	Ⓐ Ⓑ Ⓒ Ⓓ	164	Ⓐ Ⓑ Ⓒ Ⓓ	184	Ⓐ Ⓑ Ⓒ Ⓓ
105	Ⓐ Ⓑ Ⓒ Ⓓ	125	Ⓐ Ⓑ Ⓒ Ⓓ	145	Ⓐ Ⓑ Ⓒ Ⓓ	165	Ⓐ Ⓑ Ⓒ Ⓓ	185	Ⓐ Ⓑ Ⓒ Ⓓ
106	Ⓐ Ⓑ Ⓒ Ⓓ	126	Ⓐ Ⓑ Ⓒ Ⓓ	146	Ⓐ Ⓑ Ⓒ Ⓓ	166	Ⓐ Ⓑ Ⓒ Ⓓ	186	Ⓐ Ⓑ Ⓒ Ⓓ
107	Ⓐ Ⓑ Ⓒ Ⓓ	127	Ⓐ Ⓑ Ⓒ Ⓓ	147	Ⓐ Ⓑ Ⓒ Ⓓ	167	Ⓐ Ⓑ Ⓒ Ⓓ	187	Ⓐ Ⓑ Ⓒ Ⓓ
108	Ⓐ Ⓑ Ⓒ Ⓓ	128	Ⓐ Ⓑ Ⓒ Ⓓ	148	Ⓐ Ⓑ Ⓒ Ⓓ	168	Ⓐ Ⓑ Ⓒ Ⓓ	188	Ⓐ Ⓑ Ⓒ Ⓓ
109	Ⓐ Ⓑ Ⓒ Ⓓ	129	Ⓐ Ⓑ Ⓒ Ⓓ	149	Ⓐ Ⓑ Ⓒ Ⓓ	169	Ⓐ Ⓑ Ⓒ Ⓓ	189	Ⓐ Ⓑ Ⓒ Ⓓ
110	Ⓐ Ⓑ Ⓒ Ⓓ	130	Ⓐ Ⓑ Ⓒ Ⓓ	150	Ⓐ Ⓑ Ⓒ Ⓓ	170	Ⓐ Ⓑ Ⓒ Ⓓ	190	Ⓐ Ⓑ Ⓒ Ⓓ
111	Ⓐ Ⓑ Ⓒ Ⓓ	131	Ⓐ Ⓑ Ⓒ Ⓓ	151	Ⓐ Ⓑ Ⓒ Ⓓ	171	Ⓐ Ⓑ Ⓒ Ⓓ	191	Ⓐ Ⓑ Ⓒ Ⓓ
112	Ⓐ Ⓑ Ⓒ Ⓓ	132	Ⓐ Ⓑ Ⓒ Ⓓ	152	Ⓐ Ⓑ Ⓒ Ⓓ	172	Ⓐ Ⓑ Ⓒ Ⓓ	192	Ⓐ Ⓑ Ⓒ Ⓓ
113	Ⓐ Ⓑ Ⓒ Ⓓ	133	Ⓐ Ⓑ Ⓒ Ⓓ	153	Ⓐ Ⓑ Ⓒ Ⓓ	173	Ⓐ Ⓑ Ⓒ Ⓓ	193	Ⓐ Ⓑ Ⓒ Ⓓ
114	Ⓐ Ⓑ Ⓒ Ⓓ	134	Ⓐ Ⓑ Ⓒ Ⓓ	154	Ⓐ Ⓑ Ⓒ Ⓓ	174	Ⓐ Ⓑ Ⓒ Ⓓ	194	Ⓐ Ⓑ Ⓒ Ⓓ
115	Ⓐ Ⓑ Ⓒ Ⓓ	135	Ⓐ Ⓑ Ⓒ Ⓓ	155	Ⓐ Ⓑ Ⓒ Ⓓ	175	Ⓐ Ⓑ Ⓒ Ⓓ	195	Ⓐ Ⓑ Ⓒ Ⓓ
116	Ⓐ Ⓑ Ⓒ Ⓓ	136	Ⓐ Ⓑ Ⓒ Ⓓ	156	Ⓐ Ⓑ Ⓒ Ⓓ	176	Ⓐ Ⓑ Ⓒ Ⓓ	196	Ⓐ Ⓑ Ⓒ Ⓓ
117	Ⓐ Ⓑ Ⓒ Ⓓ	137	Ⓐ Ⓑ Ⓒ Ⓓ	157	Ⓐ Ⓑ Ⓒ Ⓓ	177	Ⓐ Ⓑ Ⓒ Ⓓ	197	Ⓐ Ⓑ Ⓒ Ⓓ
118	Ⓐ Ⓑ Ⓒ Ⓓ	138	Ⓐ Ⓑ Ⓒ Ⓓ	158	Ⓐ Ⓑ Ⓒ Ⓓ	178	Ⓐ Ⓑ Ⓒ Ⓓ	198	Ⓐ Ⓑ Ⓒ Ⓓ
119	Ⓐ Ⓑ Ⓒ Ⓓ	139	Ⓐ Ⓑ Ⓒ Ⓓ	159	Ⓐ Ⓑ Ⓒ Ⓓ	179	Ⓐ Ⓑ Ⓒ Ⓓ	199	Ⓐ Ⓑ Ⓒ Ⓓ
120	Ⓐ Ⓑ Ⓒ Ⓓ	140	Ⓐ Ⓑ Ⓒ Ⓓ	160	Ⓐ Ⓑ Ⓒ Ⓓ	180	Ⓐ Ⓑ Ⓒ Ⓓ	200	Ⓐ Ⓑ Ⓒ Ⓓ

TEST 06의 점수를 환산한 후 목표 달성기에 TEST 06의 점수를 표시합니다.
점수 환산표는 문제집 329페이지, 목표 달성기는 교재의 첫 장에 있습니다.

맞은 문제 개수: ___ / 100

자르는 선

Answer Sheet

TEST 07

READING (Part V~VII)																								
101	A	B	C	D	121	A	B	C	D	141	A	B	C	D	161	A	B	C	D	181	A	B	C	D
102	A	B	C	D	122	A	B	C	D	142	A	B	C	D	162	A	B	C	D	182	A	B	C	D
103	A	B	C	D	123	A	B	C	D	143	A	B	C	D	163	A	B	C	D	183	A	B	C	D
104	A	B	C	D	124	A	B	C	D	144	A	B	C	D	164	A	B	C	D	184	A	B	C	D
105	A	B	C	D	125	A	B	C	D	145	A	B	C	D	165	A	B	C	D	185	A	B	C	D
106	A	B	C	D	126	A	B	C	D	146	A	B	C	D	166	A	B	C	D	186	A	B	C	D
107	A	B	C	D	127	A	B	C	D	147	A	B	C	D	167	A	B	C	D	187	A	B	C	D
108	A	B	C	D	128	A	B	C	D	148	A	B	C	D	168	A	B	C	D	188	A	B	C	D
109	A	B	C	D	129	A	B	C	D	149	A	B	C	D	169	A	B	C	D	189	A	B	C	D
110	A	B	C	D	130	A	B	C	D	150	A	B	C	D	170	A	B	C	D	190	A	B	C	D
111	A	B	C	D	131	A	B	C	D	151	A	B	C	D	171	A	B	C	D	191	A	B	C	D
112	A	B	C	D	132	A	B	C	D	152	A	B	C	D	172	A	B	C	D	192	A	B	C	D
113	A	B	C	D	133	A	B	C	D	153	A	B	C	D	173	A	B	C	D	193	A	B	C	D
114	A	B	C	D	134	A	B	C	D	154	A	B	C	D	174	A	B	C	D	194	A	B	C	D
115	A	B	C	D	135	A	B	C	D	155	A	B	C	D	175	A	B	C	D	195	A	B	C	D
116	A	B	C	D	136	A	B	C	D	156	A	B	C	D	176	A	B	C	D	196	A	B	C	D
117	A	B	C	D	137	A	B	C	D	157	A	B	C	D	177	A	B	C	D	197	A	B	C	D
118	A	B	C	D	138	A	B	C	D	158	A	B	C	D	178	A	B	C	D	198	A	B	C	D
119	A	B	C	D	139	A	B	C	D	159	A	B	C	D	179	A	B	C	D	199	A	B	C	D
120	A	B	C	D	140	A	B	C	D	160	A	B	C	D	180	A	B	C	D	200	A	B	C	D

TEST 07의 점수를 환산한 후 목표 달성기에 TEST 07의 점수를 표시합니다.
점수 환산표는 문제집 329페이지, 목표 달성기는 교재의 첫 장에 있습니다.

맞은 문제 개수: ___ / 100

자르는 선

Answer Sheet

TEST 08

READING (Part V~VII)																								
101	A	B	C	D	121	A	B	C	D	141	A	B	C	D	161	A	B	C	D	181	A	B	C	D
102	A	B	C	D	122	A	B	C	D	142	A	B	C	D	162	A	B	C	D	182	A	B	C	D
103	A	B	C	D	123	A	B	C	D	143	A	B	C	D	163	A	B	C	D	183	A	B	C	D
104	A	B	C	D	124	A	B	C	D	144	A	B	C	D	164	A	B	C	D	184	A	B	C	D
105	A	B	C	D	125	A	B	C	D	145	A	B	C	D	165	A	B	C	D	185	A	B	C	D
106	A	B	C	D	126	A	B	C	D	146	A	B	C	D	166	A	B	C	D	186	A	B	C	D
107	A	B	C	D	127	A	B	C	D	147	A	B	C	D	167	A	B	C	D	187	A	B	C	D
108	A	B	C	D	128	A	B	C	D	148	A	B	C	D	168	A	B	C	D	188	A	B	C	D
109	A	B	C	D	129	A	B	C	D	149	A	B	C	D	169	A	B	C	D	189	A	B	C	D
110	A	B	C	D	130	A	B	C	D	150	A	B	C	D	170	A	B	C	D	190	A	B	C	D
111	A	B	C	D	131	A	B	C	D	151	A	B	C	D	171	A	B	C	D	191	A	B	C	D
112	A	B	C	D	132	A	B	C	D	152	A	B	C	D	172	A	B	C	D	192	A	B	C	D
113	A	B	C	D	133	A	B	C	D	153	A	B	C	D	173	A	B	C	D	193	A	B	C	D
114	A	B	C	D	134	A	B	C	D	154	A	B	C	D	174	A	B	C	D	194	A	B	C	D
115	A	B	C	D	135	A	B	C	D	155	A	B	C	D	175	A	B	C	D	195	A	B	C	D
116	A	B	C	D	136	A	B	C	D	156	A	B	C	D	176	A	B	C	D	196	A	B	C	D
117	A	B	C	D	137	A	B	C	D	157	A	B	C	D	177	A	B	C	D	197	A	B	C	D
118	A	B	C	D	138	A	B	C	D	158	A	B	C	D	178	A	B	C	D	198	A	B	C	D
119	A	B	C	D	139	A	B	C	D	159	A	B	C	D	179	A	B	C	D	199	A	B	C	D
120	A	B	C	D	140	A	B	C	D	160	A	B	C	D	180	A	B	C	D	200	A	B	C	D

TEST 08의 점수를 환산한 후 목표 달성기에 TEST 08의 점수를 표시합니다.
점수 환산표는 문제집 329페이지, 목표 달성기는 교재의 첫 장에 있습니다.

맞은 문제 개수: ___ / 100

자르는 선

Answer Sheet

TEST 09

READING (Part V~VII)									
101	A B C D	121	A B C D	141	A B C D	161	A B C D	181	A B C D
102	A B C D	122	A B C D	142	A B C D	162	A B C D	182	A B C D
103	A B C D	123	A B C D	143	A B C D	163	A B C D	183	A B C D
104	A B C D	124	A B C D	144	A B C D	164	A B C D	184	A B C D
105	A B C D	125	A B C D	145	A B C D	165	A B C D	185	A B C D
106	A B C D	126	A B C D	146	A B C D	166	A B C D	186	A B C D
107	A B C D	127	A B C D	147	A B C D	167	A B C D	187	A B C D
108	A B C D	128	A B C D	148	A B C D	168	A B C D	188	A B C D
109	A B C D	129	A B C D	149	A B C D	169	A B C D	189	A B C D
110	A B C D	130	A B C D	150	A B C D	170	A B C D	190	A B C D
111	A B C D	131	A B C D	151	A B C D	171	A B C D	191	A B C D
112	A B C D	132	A B C D	152	A B C D	172	A B C D	192	A B C D
113	A B C D	133	A B C D	153	A B C D	173	A B C D	193	A B C D
114	A B C D	134	A B C D	154	A B C D	174	A B C D	194	A B C D
115	A B C D	135	A B C D	155	A B C D	175	A B C D	195	A B C D
116	A B C D	136	A B C D	156	A B C D	176	A B C D	196	A B C D
117	A B C D	137	A B C D	157	A B C D	177	A B C D	197	A B C D
118	A B C D	138	A B C D	158	A B C D	178	A B C D	198	A B C D
119	A B C D	139	A B C D	159	A B C D	179	A B C D	199	A B C D
120	A B C D	140	A B C D	160	A B C D	180	A B C D	200	A B C D

TEST 09의 점수를 환산한 후 목표 달성기에 TEST 09의 점수를 표시합니다.
점수 환산표는 문제집 329페이지, 목표 달성기는 교재의 첫 장에 있습니다.

맞은 문제 개수: ___ / 100

자르는 선

Answer Sheet

TEST 10

READING (Part V~VII)									
101	A B C D	121	A B C D	141	A B C D	161	A B C D	181	A B C D
102	A B C D	122	A B C D	142	A B C D	162	A B C D	182	A B C D
103	A B C D	123	A B C D	143	A B C D	163	A B C D	183	A B C D
104	A B C D	124	A B C D	144	A B C D	164	A B C D	184	A B C D
105	A B C D	125	A B C D	145	A B C D	165	A B C D	185	A B C D
106	A B C D	126	A B C D	146	A B C D	166	A B C D	186	A B C D
107	A B C D	127	A B C D	147	A B C D	167	A B C D	187	A B C D
108	A B C D	128	A B C D	148	A B C D	168	A B C D	188	A B C D
109	A B C D	129	A B C D	149	A B C D	169	A B C D	189	A B C D
110	A B C D	130	A B C D	150	A B C D	170	A B C D	190	A B C D
111	A B C D	131	A B C D	151	A B C D	171	A B C D	191	A B C D
112	A B C D	132	A B C D	152	A B C D	172	A B C D	192	A B C D
113	A B C D	133	A B C D	153	A B C D	173	A B C D	193	A B C D
114	A B C D	134	A B C D	154	A B C D	174	A B C D	194	A B C D
115	A B C D	135	A B C D	155	A B C D	175	A B C D	195	A B C D
116	A B C D	136	A B C D	156	A B C D	176	A B C D	196	A B C D
117	A B C D	137	A B C D	157	A B C D	177	A B C D	197	A B C D
118	A B C D	138	A B C D	158	A B C D	178	A B C D	198	A B C D
119	A B C D	139	A B C D	159	A B C D	179	A B C D	199	A B C D
120	A B C D	140	A B C D	160	A B C D	180	A B C D	200	A B C D

TEST 10의 점수를 환산한 후 목표 달성기에 TEST 10의 점수를 표시합니다.
점수 환산표는 문제집 329페이지, 목표 달성기는 교재의 첫 장에 있습니다.

맞은 문제 개수: ___ / 100

최신 기출유형으로 실전 완벽 마무리

해커스 토익 RC 실전 1000제 READING 1 문제집

개정 5판 5쇄 발행 2024년 8월 12일

개정 5판 1쇄 발행 2023년 1월 2일

지은이	해커스 어학연구소
펴낸곳	㈜해커스 어학연구소
펴낸이	해커스 어학연구소 출판팀
주소	서울특별시 서초구 강남대로61길 23 ㈜해커스 어학연구소
고객센터	02-537-5000
교재 관련 문의	publishing@hackers.com
동영상강의	HackersIngang.com
ISBN	978-89-6542-505-2 (13740)
Serial Number	05-05-01